Business Essentials

Finance

AF814358

BPP LEARNING MEDIA

Viva Books

New Delhi | Mumbai | Chennai | Kolkata | Bangalore | Hyderabad | Kochi

Copyright © BPP Learning Media Ltd.

First Indian Edition 2009

VIVA BOOKS PRIVATE LIMITED

- 4737/23 Ansari Road, Daryaganj, New Delhi 110 002
  E-mail: vivadelhi@vivagroupindia.net, Tel. 42242200
- 76, Service Industries, Shirvane, Sector 1, Nerul, Navi Mumbai 400 706
  E-mail: vivamumbai@vivagroupindia.net, Tel. 27721273, 27721274
- Jamals Fazal Chambers, 26 Greams Road, Chennai 600 006
  E-mail: vivachennai@vivagroupindia.net, Tel. 28290304, 28294241
- B-103, Jindal Towers, 21/1A/3 Darga Road, Kolkata 700 017
  E-mail: vivakolkata@vivagroupindia.net, Tel. 22836381, 22816713
- 7, Sovereign Park Apartments, 56-58, K. R. Road, Basavanagudi, Bangalore 560 004
  E-mail: vivabangalore@vivagroupindia.net, Tel. 26607409, 26607410
- 101-102 Mughal Marc Apartments, 3-4-637 to 641, Narayanguda, Hyderabad 500 029
  E-mail: vivahyderabad@vivagroupindia.net, Tel. 27564481, 27564482
- Beevi Towers, First Floor, SRM Road, Kaloor, Kochi 682 018, Kerala
  E-mail: vivakochi@vivagroupindia.net, Tel: 0484-2403055, 2403056

www.vivagroupindia.com

Published by arrangement with

BPP Learning Media
1st Floor, BPP House, Aldine Place
142-144, Uxbridge Road
London, W12 8AA

All rights reserved. No part of this book may be reproduced or transmitted in any form or by any means now known or to be invented, electronic or mechanical, including photocopying, recording or by any information storage or retrieval system without written permission of BPP Learning Media Ltd.

This edition is for sale in India, Sri Lanka and Bangladesh only. Not for export elsewhere.

ISBN-10: 81-309-1089-6
ISBN-13: 978-81-309-1089-5

Published by Vinod Vasishtha for Viva Books Private Limited, 4737/23, Ansari Road, Daryaganj, New Delhi-110 002. Printed and bound by Anand Sons, Delhi - 110 092.

CONTENTS

Introduction

This is the first edition of BPP Learning Media's dynamic new Business Essentials range. It is the ideal learning solution for all students studying for business-related qualifications and degrees, and the range provides concise and comprehensive coverage of the key areas that are essential to the business student.

Qualifications in Business are traditionally very demanding. Students therefore need learning resources which get straight to the core of the topics involved, and which build upon students' pre-existing knowledge and experience. The BPP Learning Media Business Essentials range has been designed to meet exactly that need.

Features include:

- In depth coverage of essential topics within business-related subjects
- Plenty of activities, quizzes and topics for class discussion to help retain the interest of students and ensure progress
- Up to date practical illustrations and case studies that really bring the material to life
- A full index

Each chapter contains:

- An introduction and a list of specific study objectives
- Summary diagrams and signposts to guide you through the chapter
- A chapter roundup, quick quiz with answers and answers to activities.

Each book in the series can be used on courses in business at various institutions, as generic texts on a wide range of business-related subjects, and as background reading and reference material for learners and lecturers alike.

BPP Learning Media
2007

Other titles in this series:

Business Essentials

- Accounts
- Advanced Marketing and Sales
- Business Decision Making
- Business Environment
- Business Maths
- Business Strategy
- Economics
- Finance
- Human Resource Management
- Management
- Managing Financial Resources and Decisions
- Marketing
- Organisations and Behaviour
- Research Project

STUDY GUIDE

This Course Book includes features designed specifically to make learning effective and efficient.

(a) Each chapter begins with an introduction, which sets the chapter in context. This is followed by learning objectives, which show you what you will learn as you work through the chapter.

(b) Throughout the book, there are special aids to learning. These are indicated by the following symbols.

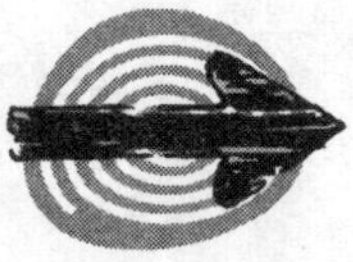

Signposts guide you through the text, showing how each section connects with the next.

Definitions give the meanings of key terms.

Activities help you to test how much you have learnt. An indication of the time you should take on each is given. Answers are given at the end of each chapter.

Topics for discussion are for use in seminars. They give you a chance to share your views with your fellow students. They allow you to highlight holes in your knowledge and to see how others understand concepts. If you have time, try 'teaching' someone the concepts you have learnt in a session. This helps you to remember key points and answering their questions will consolidate your knowledge.

Examples relate what you have learnt to the outside world. Try to think up your own examples as you work through the text.

Chapter roundups present the key information from the chapter in a concise format. Useful for revision.

(c) The wide **margin** on each page is for your notes. You will get the best out of this book if you interact with it. Write down your thoughts and ideas. Record examples, question theories, add references to other pages in the text and rephrase key points in your own words.

(d) At the end of each chapter, there is a **chapter roundup**, and a **quick quiz** with answers. Use these to revise and consolidate your knowledge. The chapter roundup summarises the chapter. The quick quiz tests what you have learnt (the answers refer you back to the chapter so you can look over subjects again).

(e) At the end of the book, there is an index.

PART A

MANAGEMENT ACCOUNTING

Chapter 1 :

COST ACCOUNTING, COST CLASSIFICATION AND COST BEHAVIOUR

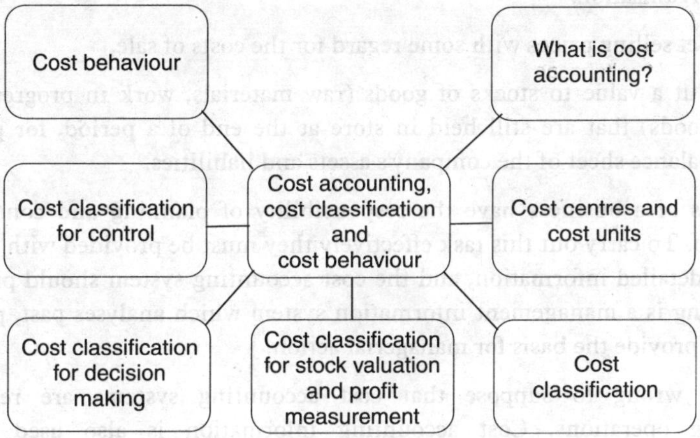

Introduction

Involvement with costs is fundamental to the role of management accountants. Any business, whether it manufactures goods or provides a service, needs to know how much its products or services cost and how these costs might change in response to decisions made. They will use this information to manage the business effectively, for example, in setting prices and determining which products are most profitable, in planning and budgeting for future periods and for monitoring and controlling costs.

Your objectives

In this chapter you will learn about the following.

(a) Cost centres and cost units

(b) Cost classification

(c) Cost behaviour

1 WHAT IS COST ACCOUNTING?

Who can provide the answers to the following questions?

- What was the cost of goods produced or services provided last period?
- What was the cost of operating a department last month?
- What revenues were earned last week?

Yes, you've guessed it, the cost accountant.

Knowing about costs incurred or revenues earned enables management to do the following.

(a) Assess the profitability of a product, a service, a department, or the whole organisation.

(b) Set selling prices with some regard for the costs of sale.

(c) Put a value to stocks of goods (raw materials, work in progress, finished goods) that are still held in store at the end of a period, for preparing a balance sheet of the company's assets and liabilities.

The managers of a business have the responsibility of planning and controlling the resources used. To carry out this task effectively they must be provided with sufficiently accurate and detailed information, and the cost accounting system should provide this. Cost accounting is a management information system which analyses past, present and future data to provide the basis for managerial action.

It would be wrong to suppose that cost accounting systems are restricted to manufacturing operations. Cost accounting information is also used in service industries, government departments and welfare organisations. Within a manufacturing organisation, the cost accounting system should be applied not only to manufacturing operations but also to administration, selling and distribution, research and development and so on.

So, cost accounting is concerned with providing information to assist the following.

- Establishing stock valuations, profits and balance sheet items
- Planning
- Control
- Decision making

2 THE ORGANISATION, COST CENTRES AND COST UNITS

An organisation, whether it is a manufacturing company, a provider of services (such as a bank or a hotel) or a public sector organisation (such as a hospital), may be divided into a number of different **functions** within which there are a number of **departments**. A manufacturing organisation might be structured as follows.

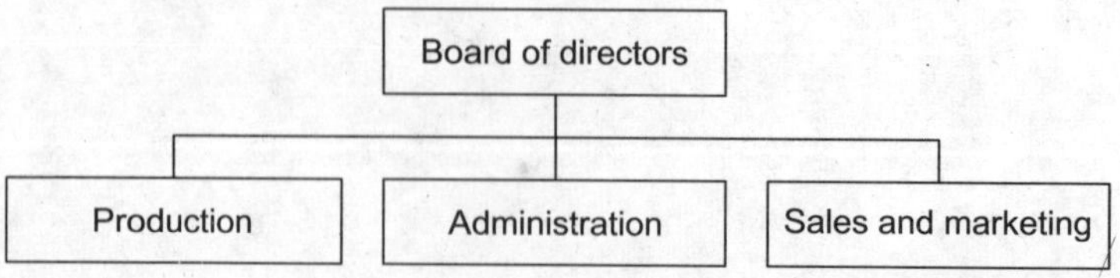

Figure 1.1: Structure of manufacturing organisation

Suppose an organisation produces chocolate cakes for a number of supermarket chains. The production function is involved with the making of the cakes, the administration department with the preparation of accounts and the employment of staff and the marketing department with the selling and distribution of the cakes.

Within the production function there are three departments, two of which are production departments (the mixing department and the baking department) which are actively involved in the production of the cakes and one of which is a service department (stores department) which provides a service or back-up to the production departments.

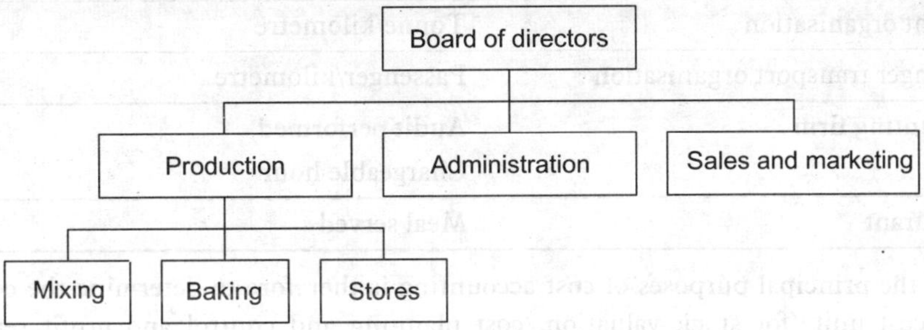

Figure 1.2: Detailed structure of manufacturing organisation

2.1 Cost centres

In general, for cost accounting purposes, departments are termed **cost centres** and the product produced by an organisation is termed the **cost unit**. In our example, the cost centres of the production function could be the mixing department, the baking department and the stores department and the organisation's cost unit could be one chocolate cake.

When costs are incurred, they are generally allocated to a **cost centre**. A cost centre acts as a **collecting place** for certain costs before they are analysed further. Cost centres may include the following.

- A department (as in our example above);
- A machine, or group of machines;
- A project (eg the installation of a new computer system);
- A new product (to enable the costs of development and production to be identified).

2.2 Cost units

Once costs have been traced to cost centres, they can be further analysed in order to establish a cost per cost unit. Alternatively, some items of costs may be charged directly to a cost unit, for example direct materials and direct labour costs, which you will meet later in this Course Book.

Definition

A **cost unit** is a unit of product or service to which costs can be related. The cost unit is the basic control unit for costing purposes.

NOTES

Different organisations use different cost units. Here are some suggestions.

Organisation	Possible cost unit
Steelworks	Tonne of steel produced Tonne of coke used
Hospital	Patient/day Operation Out-patient visit
Freight organisation	Tonne/kilometre
Passenger transport organisation	Passenger/kilometre
Accounting firm	Audit performed Chargeable hour
Restaurant	Meal served

One of the principal purposes of cost accounting is therefore to determine the cost of a single cost unit (for stock valuation, cost planning and control and profit reporting purposes).

3 COST CLASSIFICATION

Before any attempt is made to establish stock valuations and measure profits, to plan, make decisions or exercise control (in other words, do any cost accounting), costs must be classified. Classification involves arranging costs into groupings of similar items in order to make stock valuation, profit measurement, planning, decision making and control easier.

4 COST CLASSIFICATION FOR STOCK VALUATION AND PROFIT MEASUREMENT

For the purposes of stock valuation and profit measurement, the cost accountant must calculate the cost of one unit. The total cost of a cost unit is made up of the following three elements of cost.

- Materials
- Labour
- Other expenses (such as rent and rates, interest charges and so on)

Cost elements can be classified as direct costs or indirect costs.

4.1 Direct cost

Definition

A **direct cost** is a cost that can be traced in full to the product, service, or department that is being costed.

BPP LEARNING MEDIA

(a) **Direct materials costs** are the costs of materials that are known to have been used in making and selling a product (or providing a service).

(b) **Direct labour costs** are the specific costs of the workforce used to make a product or provide a service. Direct labour costs are established by measuring the time taken for a job, or the time taken in 'direct production work'.

(c) **Other direct expenses** are those expenses that have been incurred in full as a direct consequence of making a product, or providing a service, or running a department.

Each of these will be reviewed in more detail later.

4.2 Indirect cost/overhead

Definition

> An **indirect cost** or overhead is a cost that is incurred in the course of making a product, providing a service or running a department, but which cannot be traced directly and in full to the product, service or department. Examples might be the cost of supervisors' wages, cleaning materials and buildings insurance.

Total expenditure may therefore be analysed as follows.

Materials cost	=	Direct materials cost	+	Indirect materials cost
+		+		+
Labour cost	=	Direct labour cost	+	Indirect labour cost
+		+		+
Expenses	=	Direct expenses		Indirect expenses
Total cost	=	Direct cost	+	Overhead cost

Total direct cost is often referred to as **prime cost**. Some authorities restrict the term **prime cost** to direct materials and direct labour, but you will often find that examination questions and assessments also include direct expenses in prime cost.

You should be able to specify whether an item of expenditure is classed as a direct materials cost, a direct labour cost, a production overhead and so on. Further information on such cost items is given below.

4.3 Direct material

Definition

> **Direct material** is all material becoming part of the product (unless used in negligible amounts and/or having negligible cost).

Direct material costs are charged to the product as part of the prime cost. Examples of direct material are as follows.

- **Component parts** or other materials specially purchased for a particular job, order or process.
- **Part-finished work** which is transferred from department 1 to department 2 becomes finished work of department 1 and a direct material cost in department 2.
- **Primary packing materials** like cartons and boxes.

Materials used in negligible amounts and/or having negligible cost can be grouped under indirect materials as part of overhead.

4.4 Direct wages

Definition

> **Direct wages** are all wages paid for labour (either as basic hours or as overtime) expended on work on the product itself.

Direct wages costs are charged to the product as part of the **prime cost**.

Examples of groups of labour receiving payment as direct wages are as follows.

(a) Workers engaged in **altering** the condition, conformation or composition of the product.

(b) Inspectors, analysts and testers **specifically required** for such production.

> **Activity 1** **(15 minutes)**
>
> Classify the following labour costs as either direct or indirect.
>
> (a) The basic pay of direct workers (cash paid, tax and other deductions)
> (b) The basic pay of indirect workers
> (c) Overtime premium, ie the premium above basic pay, for working overtime
> (d) Bonus payments under a group bonus scheme
> (e) Employer's National Insurance contributions
> (f) Idle time of direct workers, paid while waiting for work
> (g) Work on installation of equipment

4.5 Direct expenses

Definition

> **Direct expenses** are any expenses which are incurred on a specific product other than direct material cost and direct wages.

Direct expenses are charged to the product as part of the **prime** cost. Examples of direct expenses are as follows.

- The cost of **special** designs, drawings or layouts
- The **hire of tools** or equipment for a particular job
- **Maintenance costs** of tools, jigs, fixtures and so on

Direct expenses are also referred to as **chargeable expenses.**

4.6 Overheads

Definition

> **Overheads** include all indirect material cost, indirect wages and indirect expenses incurred by a business.

Overheads associated with the **production** process itself include the following.

(a) **Indirect materials** which cannot be traced in the finished product.

(i) Consumable stores, eg material used in negligible amounts

(b) **Indirect wages,** meaning all wages not charged directly to a product.

(i) Salaries and wages of non-productive personnel in the production department, eg production supervisors

(c) **Indirect expenses** (other than material and labour) not charged directly to production.

(i) Rent, rates and insurance of a factory

(ii) Depreciation, fuel, power, repairs and maintenance of plant, machinery and factory buildings

Overheads associated with the **administration** of the business include the following examples.

- **Depreciation** of office equipment
- **Office salaries,** including salaries of secretaries and accountants
- Rent, rates, insurance, lighting, cleaning and heating of general offices, telephone and postal charges, bank charges, legal charges, audit fees

Overheads may also be incurred in the **selling and distribution** of the goods produced. Some examples are as follows.

- **Printing and stationery,** such as catalogues and price lists
- Cost of packing cases
- **Salaries and commission** of sales representatives and sales department staff and wages of packers, drivers and despatch clerks
- **Advertising and sales promotion,** market research

- **Rent, rates** and **insurance** of sales offices and showrooms, bad debts and collection charges, cash discounts allowed, after-sales service
- **Freight and insurance charges**, rent, rates, insurance and depreciation of warehouses, depreciation and running expenses of delivery vehicles

Activity 2 **(10 minutes)**

A direct labour employee's wage in week 5 consists of the following.

		£
(a)	Basic pay for normal hours worked, 36 hours at £4 per hour =	144
(b)	Pay at the basic rate for overtime, 6 hours at £4 per hour =	24
(c)	Overtime shift premium, with overtime paid at time-and-a-quarter $\frac{1}{4} \times 6$ hours $\times$ £4 per hour =	6
(d)	A bonus payment under a group bonus (or 'incentive') scheme – bonus for the month =	30
	Total gross wages in week 5 for 42 hours of work	204

What is the direct labour cost for this employee in week 5?

4.7 Product costs and period costs

Definitions

- **Product costs** are costs identified with a finished product. Such costs are initially identified as part of the value of stock. They become expenses (in the form of cost of goods sold) only when the stock is sold.
- **Period costs** are costs that are deducted as expenses during the current period without ever being included in the value of stock held.

Consider a retailer who acquires goods for resale without changing their basic form. The only product cost is therefore the purchase cost of the goods. Any unsold goods are held as stock, valued at the lower of purchase cost and net realisable value, and included as an asset in the balance sheet. As the goods are sold, their cost becomes an expense in the form of 'cost of goods sold'. A retailer will also incur a variety of selling and administration expenses. Such costs are period costs because they are deducted from revenue without ever being regarded as part of the value of stock.

Now consider a manufacturing firm in which direct materials are transformed into saleable goods with the help of direct labour and factory overheads. All these costs are product costs because they are allocated to the value of stock until the goods are sold. As with the retailer, selling and administration expenses are regarded as period costs.

5 COST CLASSIFICATION FOR DECISION MAKING

Decision making is concerned with future events and hence management require information on expected future costs and revenues. Although cost accounting systems are designed to accumulate **past** costs and revenues this historical information may provide a starting point for forecasting future events.

5.1 Fixed costs and variable costs

A knowledge of how costs will vary at different levels of activity (or volume) is essential for decision making.

Definitions

- A **fixed cost** is a cost which is incurred for a particular period of time and which, within certain activity levels, is unaffected by changes in the level of activity.
- A **variable cost** is a cost which varies with the level of activity.

EXAMPLES

Some examples are as follows.

(a) Direct material costs are **variable costs** because they rise as more units of a product are manufactured.

(b) Sales commission is often a fixed percentage of sales turnover, and so is a **variable cost** that varies with the level of sales.

(c) Telephone call charges are likely to increase if the volume of business expands, and so they are a **variable overhead cost**.

(d) The rental cost of business premises is a constant amount, at least within a stated time period, and so it is a **fixed cost**.

Note that costs can be classified as direct costs or indirect costs/overheads, or as fixed costs or variable costs. These alternative classifications are not, however, mutually exclusive, but are complementary to each other, so that we can find some direct costs that are fixed costs (although they are commonly variable costs) and some overhead costs that are fixed and some overhead costs that are variable.

6 COST CLASSIFICATION FOR CONTROL

6.1 Controllable and uncontrollable costs

One of the purposes of cost accounting is to provide control information to management who wish to know whether or not a particular cost item can be controlled by management action.

Definitions

- A **controllable cost** is a cost which can be influenced by management decisions and actions.
- An **uncontrollable cost** is any cost that cannot be affected by management within a given time span.

7 COST BEHAVIOUR AND LEVELS OF ACTIVITY

Definition

Cost behaviour is 'The variability of input costs with activity undertaken'.

The level of activity refers to the amount of work done, or the number of events that have occurred. Depending on circumstances, the level of activity may refer to measures such as the following.

- The volume of production in a period.
- The number of items sold.
- The value of items sold.
- The number of invoices issued
- The number of units of electricity consumed.

7.1 Basic principles of cost behaviour

The basic principle of cost behaviour is that as the level of activity rises, costs will usually rise. It will probably cost more to produce 2,000 units of output than it will cost to produce 1,000 units; it will usually cost more to make five telephone calls than to make one call and so on. The problem for the accountant is to determine, for each item of cost, the way in which costs rise and by how much as the level of activity increases.

For our purposes in this chapter, the level of activity will generally be taken to be the volume of production/output.

8 COST BEHAVIOUR PATTERNS

8.1 Fixed costs

We discussed fixed costs briefly in Section 5. A **fixed cost** is a cost which tends to be unaffected by increases or decreases in the volume of output. Fixed costs are a **period charge**, in that they relate to a span of time; as the time span increases, so too will the fixed costs. A sketch graph of a fixed cost would look like this.

NOTES

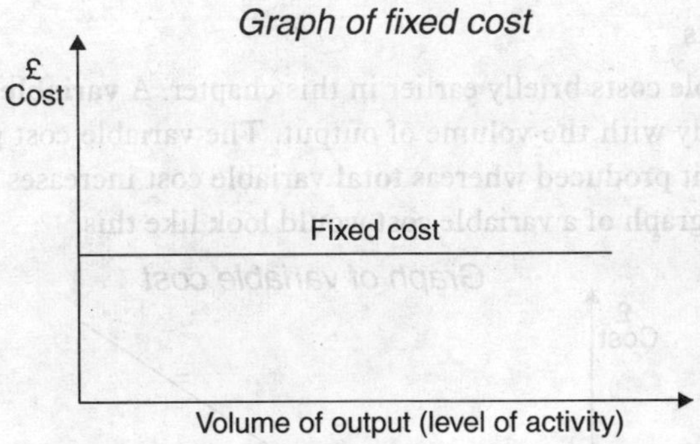

Figure 1.3: Graph of fixed cost

Examples of a fixed cost would be as follows.

- The salary of the managing director (per month or per annum)
- The rent of a single factory building (per month or per annum)
- Straight line depreciation of a single machine (per month or per annum)

8.2 Step costs

Definition

> A **step cost** is a cost which is fixed in nature but only within certain levels of activity.

Consider the depreciation of a machine which may be fixed if production remains below 1,000 units per month. If production exceeds 1,000 units, a second machine may be required, and the cost of depreciation (on two machines) would go up a step. A sketch graph of a step cost could look like this.

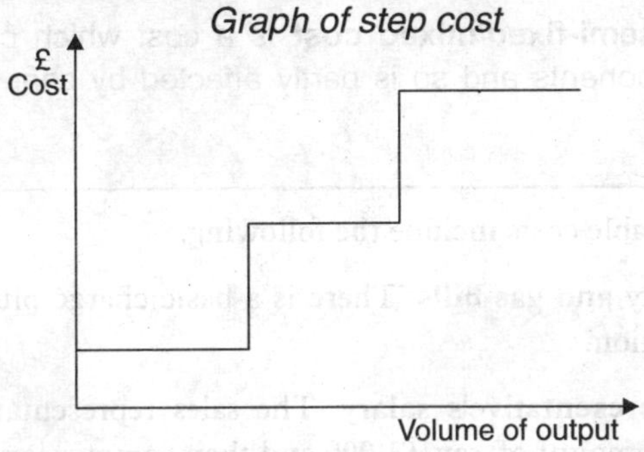

Figure 1.4: Graph of step cost

Other examples of step costs are as follows.

- Rent is a step cost in situations where accommodation requirements increase as output levels get higher.
- Basic pay of employees is nowadays usually fixed, but as output rises, more employees (direct workers, supervisors, managers and so on) are required.

BPP LEARNING MEDIA

NOTES

8.3 Variable costs

We discussed variable costs briefly earlier in this chapter. A **variable cost** is a cost which tends to vary directly with the volume of output. The variable cost **per unit** is the same amount for each unit produced whereas **total** variable cost increases as volume of output increases. A sketch graph of a variable cost would look like this.

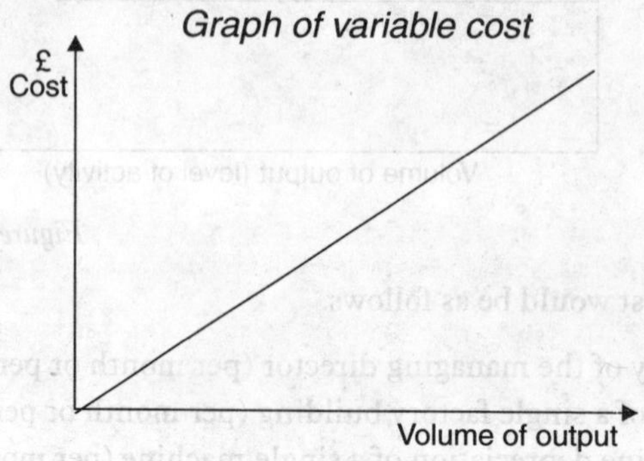

Figure 1.5: Graph of variable cost

Examples of variable costs are as follows.

- The cost of raw materials (where there is no discount for bulk purchasing since bulk purchase discounts reduce the unit cost of purchases).
- Direct labour costs are, for very important reasons which you will study later, usually classed as a variable cost even though basic wages are often fixed.
- Sales commission is variable in relation to the volume or value of sales.

8.4 Semi-variable costs (or semi-fixed costs or mixed costs)

Definition

> A **semi-variable/semi-fixed/mixed cost** is a cost which contains both fixed and variable components and so is partly affected by changes in the level of activity.

Examples of semi-variable costs include the following.

- **Electricity and gas bills.** There is a basic charge plus a charge per unit of consumption.
- **Sales representative's salary**. The sales representative may earn a basic monthly amount of, say, £1,000 and then commission of 10% of the value of sales made.

The behaviour of a semi-variable cost can be presented graphically as follows.

BPP LEARNING MEDIA

NOTES

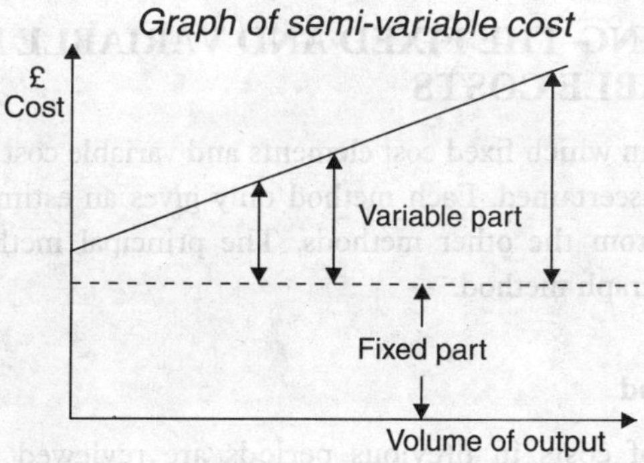

Figure 1.6: Graph of semi-variable cost

8.5 Cost behaviour and total and unit costs

If the variable cost of producing a unit is £5 per unit then it will remain at that cost per unit no matter how many units are produced. However if the business's fixed costs are £5,000 then the fixed cost *per unit* will decrease the more units are produced: one unit will have fixed costs of £5,000 per unit; if 2,500 are produced the fixed cost per unit will be £2; if 5,000 are produced the fixed cost per unit will be only £1. Thus as the level of activity increases the total costs *per unit* (fixed cost plus variable cost) will decrease.

In sketch graph form this may be illustrated as follows.

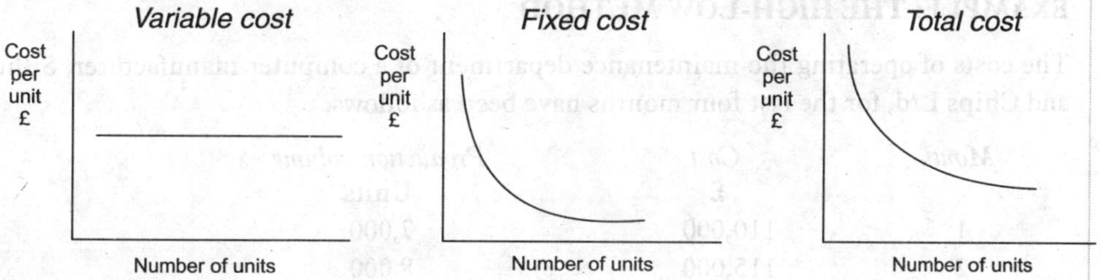

Figure 1.7: Cost behaviour

Activity 3 **(5 minutes)**

Are the following likely to be fixed, variable or mixed costs?

(a) Telephone bill

(b) Annual salary of the chief accountant

(c) The management accountant's annual membership fee to his professional body (paid by the company)

(d) Cost of materials used to pack 20 units of product X into a box

8.6 Assumptions about cost behaviour

It is often possible to assume that, within the normal or relevant range of output, costs are either fixed, variable or semi-variable.

BPP LEARNING MEDIA

9 DETERMINING THE FIXED AND VARIABLE ELEMENTS OF SEMI-VARIABLE COSTS

There are several ways in which fixed cost elements and variable cost elements within semi-variable costs may be ascertained. Each method only gives an estimate, and can therefore give differing results from the other methods. The principal methods are the high-low method and the scattergraph method.

9.1 High-low method

(a) Records of costs in previous periods are reviewed and the costs of the following two periods are selected.

   (i) The period with the highest volume of activity
   (ii) The period with the lowest volume of activity

(b) The difference between the total cost of these two periods will be the variable cost of the difference in activity levels (since the same fixed cost is included in each total cost).

(c) The variable cost per unit may be calculated from this (difference in total costs ÷ difference in activity levels), and the fixed cost may then be determined by substitution.

EXAMPLE: THE HIGH-LOW METHOD

The costs of operating the maintenance department of a computer manufacturer, Sillick and Chips Ltd, for the last four months have been as follows.

Month	*Cost*	*Production volume*
	£	Units
1	110,000	7,000
2	115,000	8,000
3	111,000	7,700
4	97,000	6,000

Calculate the costs that should be expected in month five when output is expected to be 7,500 units. Ignore inflation.

ANSWER

(a)

	Units		£
High output or volume	8,000	Total cost	115,000
Low output or volume	6,000	Total cost	97,000
	2,000	Variable cost of	18,000
Variable cost per unit	£18,000/2,000 =		£9

(b) Substituting in either the high or low volume cost:

		High		*Low*
		£		£
Total cost		115,000		97,000
Variable costs	(8,000 × £9)	72,000	(6,000 × £9)	54,000
Fixed costs		43,000		43,000

(c) Estimated maintenance costs when output is 7,500 units:

	£
Fixed costs	43,000
Variable costs (7,500 × £9)	67,500
Total costs	110,500

Activity 4 **(15 minutes)**

The Valuation Department of a large firm of surveyors wishes to develop a method of predicting its total costs in a period. The following past costs have been recorded at two activity levels.

	Number of valuations (V)	*Total cost (£) (TC)*
Period 1	420	82,200
Period 2	515	90,275

The total cost model for a period could be represented as follows.

A TC = £46,500 + 85V
B TC = £42,000 + 95V
C TC = £46,500 – 85V
D TC = £51,500 – 95V

9.2 Scattergraph method

A scattergraph of costs in previous periods can be prepared (with cost on the vertical axis and volume of output on the horizontal axis). A **line of best fit**, which is a line drawn **by judgement** to pass through the middle of the points, thereby having as many points above the line as below it, can then be drawn and the fixed and variable costs determined.

A scattergraph of the cost and volume data in the high-low method example on the previous page is shown below.

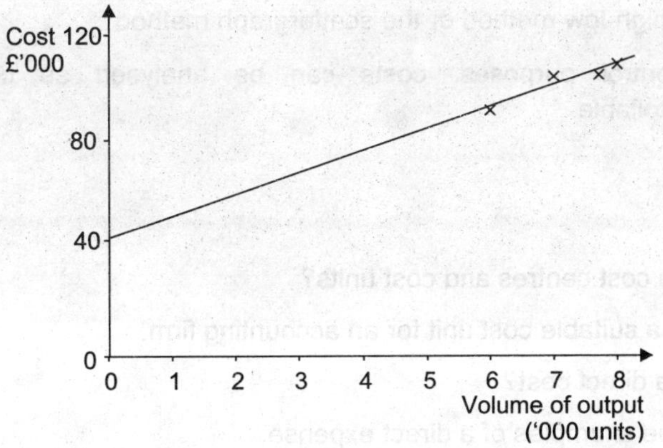

Figure 1.8: Scattergraph

The point where the line cuts the vertical axis (approximately £40,000) is the fixed cost (the cost if there is no output). If we take the value of one of the plotted points which lies close to the line and deduct the fixed cost from the total cost, we can calculate the variable cost per unit.

Total cost for 8,000 units	= £115,000
Variable cost for 8,000 units	= £(115,000 – 40,000) = £75,000
Variable cost per unit	= £75,000/8,000 = £9.375

Chapter roundup

- Cost accounting is a method of establishing stock valuations, profits and balance sheet items as well as a system for planning, control and decision making.
- Cost centres are collecting places for costs before they are further analysed. Cost units are the basic control units for costing purposes.
- A direct cost is a cost that can be traced in full to the product, service or department being costed. An indirect cost (or overhead) is a cost that is incurred in the course of making a product, providing a service or running a department, but which cannot be traced directly and in full to the product, service or department.
- For the preparation of financial statements, costs are often classified as either product costs or period costs. Product costs are costs identified with goods produced or purchased for resale. Period costs are costs deducted as expenses during the current period.
- Costs which are not affected by the level of activity are fixed costs or period costs.
- Step costs are fixed within a certain range of activity.
- Variable costs increase or decrease with the level of activity.
- Semi-fixed, semi-variable or mixed costs are costs which are part fixed and part variable.
- The fixed and variable elements of semi-variable costs can be determined by the high-low method or the scattergraph method.
- For control purposes, costs can be analysed as controllable or uncontrollable.

Quick quiz

1 What are cost centres and cost units?

2 Suggest a suitable cost unit for an accounting firm.

3 What is a direct cost?

4 Give three examples of a direct expense.

5 Give three examples of overheads.

6 What are product costs and period costs?

7 Give an example of a fixed cost and a step cost.

8 Describe the high-low method.

Answers to quick quiz

1 Cost centres are collecting places for costs before they are further analysed (see para 2.1). Cost units are units of product or service to which costs can be related. (see para 2.2)

2 Audit performed or chargeable hour. (para 2.2)

3 A direct cost is a cost that can be traced in full to the product, service, or department that is being costed. (para 4.1)

4 The cost of special designs, the hire of equipment, or the maintenance of tools, all incurred for a specific job. (para 4.5)

5 Any three of the following:

Production overheads: consumable stores, foreman's salary, factory rent, rates and insurance, depreciation and maintenance of plant, fuel and power.

Administration overheads: depreciation of office equipment, office salaries, and other office expenses such as rent, electricity and postage.

Selling overheads: printing of catalogues, sales department salaries, advertising, and other sales department expenses such as bad debts, rent and settlement discounts allowed.

Distribution overheads: packing cases, wages of packers, clerks and van drivers, and other distribution expenses such as depreciation of vans and warehouses, and freight charges. (para 4.6)

6 Product costs are costs identified with a finished product, and are included in the value of stock. Period costs are deducted as expenses in the current period and are not included in the value of stock. (para 4.7)

7 Fixed costs: rent, managing director's salary, straight line depreciation of a single fixed asset. (para 8.1)

Step cost: rent and supervisor's salary, when output increases such that additional resources are acquired (another factory or supervisor). (para 8.2)

8 The high-low method of finding the fixed and variable components of a semi-variable cost involves three steps.

(i) Find the variable cost per unit using the data for the highest and lowest **output** levels.

Variable cost per unit =

$$\frac{\text{(Total cost at highest output level – total cost at lowest output level)}}{\text{(Highest output in units – lowest output in units)}}$$

(ii) Calculate the variable cost at the highest or lowest output (either will do).

Variable cost at highest output = Variable cost per unit x highest output (units)

(iii) Find the fixed costs using the total costs and variable costs at the output level used in (ii).

	£
Total costs at highest output level	x
Less: variable costs at highest output level	(x)
Fixed costs	x

The variable cost per unit and the total fixed costs can now be used to estimate the total costs at any output levels within the range covered by the original observed data (ie between the highest and lowest output levels referred to).(para 9.2)

Answers to activities

1 (a) Direct

(b) Indirect, however, if a customer asks for an order to be carried out which involves the dedicated use of indirect workers' time, the cost of this time would be a direct labour cost of the order as it is a cost which is traceable to a specific order.

(c) Overtime **premium** paid to both direct and indirect workers is usually an indirect cost because it is 'unfair' that an item made in overtime should be more costly just because, by chance, it was made after the employee normally clocks off for the day.

There are two particular circumstances in which the overtime premium might be a direct cost.

(i) Overtime worked at the specific request of a customer to get his order completed.

(ii) Overtime worked regularly by a production department in the normal course of operations.

(d) Generally indirect

(e) Employer's national insurance contributions (which are added to employees' total pay as a wages cost) are normally treated as an indirect labour cost.

(f) Indirect

(g) The cost of work on capital equipment is incorporated into the capital cost of the equipment and is therefore neither a direct nor an indirect production cost

2

		Direct cost	*Indirect cost*
		£	£
(a)	Basic pay	144	
(b)	Basic rate on overtime	24	
(c)	Overtime shift premium		6
(d)	Bonus payment		30
		168	36

Note the basic rate for overtime is a part of direct wages cost. It is only the overtime **premium** that is usually regarded as an overhead or indirect cost.

3 (a) Mixed
(b) Fixed
(c) Fixed
(d) Variable

4 Apply the high-low method.

	Valuations	*Total cost*
	V	£
Period 2 – high	515	90,275
Period 1 – low	420	82,200
Change due to variable cost	95	8,075

∴ Variable cost valuation = £8,075/95 = £85.

Period 2: fixed cost = £90,275 – (515 × £85)
= £46,500

Therefore TC = 46,500 + 85V, option A.

Chapter 2 :

MATERIALS AND LABOUR COSTS

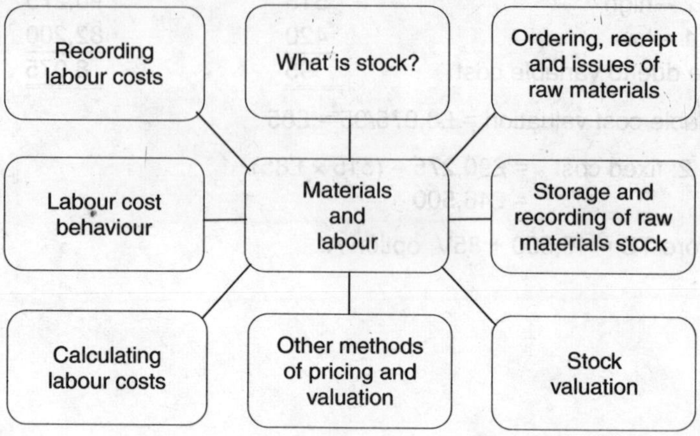

Introduction

The investment in stock is a very important one for most businesses, both in terms of monetary value and relationships with customers (no stock, no sale, loss of customer goodwill). It is therefore vital that management establish and maintain an **effective stock control system** and that they are aware of the major costing problem relating to materials, that of pricing materials issues and valuing stock at the end of each period.

You should note that this chapter does not include detailed material on stock control levels and re-ordering. This topic is covered in Unit 6 (and previously in Unit 5) of the HNC/HND qualification, and you should refer back to the work you did for those units.

Your objectives

In this chapter you will learn about the following.

(a) The nature of stock
(b) The ordering, receipt and issue of raw materials
(c) The storage and recording of raw materials
(d) Stock valuation
(e) FIFO (first in, first out)
(f) LIFO (last in, first out)
(g) Cumulative weighted average pricing
(h) Other methods of pricing and valuation
(i) Stock valuation and profitability
(j) Calculating labour costs
(k) Labour cost behaviour
(l) Recording labour costs

1 WHAT IS STOCK?

The stocks held in any organisation can generally be classified under four main headings.

- Raw materials
- Work in progress
- Finished goods
- Spare parts/consumables

Not all organisations will have stock of all four general categories.

This chapter will concentrate on raw materials, but similar problems and considerations apply to all forms of stock.

2 THE ORDERING, RECEIPT AND ISSUE OF RAW MATERIALS

2.1 Ordering and receiving materials

Proper records must be kept of the physical procedures for ordering and receiving a consignment of materials to ensure the following.

- That enough stock is held
- That there is no duplication of ordering
- That quality is maintained
- That there is adequate record keeping for accounts purposes

EXAMPLE

A typical series of procedures might be as follows.

(a) Current stocks run down to the level where a reorder is required. The stores department issues a **purchase requisition** which is sent to the purchasing department, authorising the department to order further stock. An example of a purchase requisition is shown below.

PURCHASE REQUISITION Req. No.

Department/job number: Date
Suggested Supplier:

Requested by:
Latest date required:

Quantity	Code number	Description	Estimated Cost	
			Unit	£

Authorised signature:

(b) The purchasing department draws a **purchase order** which is sent to the supplier. (The supplier may be asked to return an acknowledgement copy as confirmation of his acceptance of the order.) Copies of the purchase order must be sent to the accounts department and the storekeeper (or receiving department).

Purchase Order/Confirmation

Our Order Ref: Date

To

(Address)

Please deliver to the above address

Ordered by:

Passed and checked by:

Total Order Value £

			Subtotal		
			VAT (@ 17.5%)		
			Total		

(c) The purchasing department may have to obtain a number of quotations if either a new stock line is required, the existing supplier's costs are too high or the existing supplier no longer stocks the goods needed. Trade discounts (reduction in the price per unit given to some customers) should be negotiated where possible.

(d) The supplier delivers the consignment of materials, and the storekeeper signs a **delivery note** for the carrier. The packages must then be checked against the copy of the purchase order, to ensure that the supplier has delivered the types and quantities of materials which were ordered. (Discrepancies would be referred to the purchasing department.)

(e) If the delivery is acceptable, the storekeeper prepares a **goods received note (GRN)**, an example of which is shown below.

GOODS RECEIVED NOTE		WAREHOUSE COPY NO 5565
DATE:	TIME:	
OUR ORDER NO:		WAREHOUSE A
SUPPLIER AND SUPPLIER'S ADVICE NOTE NO:		
QUANTITY	CAT NO	DESCRIPTION
RECEIVED IN GOOD CONDITION:		(INITIALS)

(f) A copy of the **GRN** is sent to the accounts department, where it is matched with the copy of the purchase order. The supplier's invoice is checked against the purchase order and GRN, and the necessary steps are taken to pay the supplier. The invoice may contain details relating to discounts such as trade discounts, quantity discounts (order in excess of a specified amount) and settlement discounts (payment received within a specified number of days).

Activity 1 **(10 minutes)**

What are the possible consequences of a failure of control over ordering and receipt of materials?

2.2 Issue of materials

Materials can only be issued to production against a **materials/stores requisition**. This document must record not only the quantity of goods issued, but also the cost centre or the job number for which the requisition is being made. The materials requisition note may also have a column, to be filled in by the cost department, for recording the cost or value of the materials issued to the cost centre or job.

Materials requisition note			
Date required _ _ _ _ _ _ _ _		Cost centre No/ Job No _ _ _ _ _ _ _ _ _ _	
Quantity	*Item code*	*Description*	£
Signature of requisitioning Manager/ Foreman _ _ _ _ _ _ _ _ _ _ _ _ _ _ _ _ _ _			Date _ _ _ _ _

2.3 Materials transfers and returns

Where materials, having been issued to one job or cost centre, are later transferred to a different job or cost centre, without first being returned to stores, a **materials transfer note** should be raised. Such a note must show not only the job receiving the transfer, but also the job from which it is transferred. This enables the appropriate charges to be made to jobs or cost centres.

Material returns must also be documented on a **materials returned note**. This document is the 'reverse' of a requisition note, and must contain similar information. In fact it will often be almost identical to a requisition note. It will simply have a different title and perhaps be a distinctive colour, such as red, to highlight the fact that materials are being returned.

2.4 Impact of computerisation

Many stock control systems these days are computerised. Computerised stock control systems vary greatly, but most will have the features outlined below.

(a) **Data must be input into the system.** For example, details of goods received may simply be written on to a GRN for later entry into the computer system. Alternatively, this information may be keyed in directly to the computer: a GRN will be printed and then signed as evidence of the transaction, so that both the warehouse and the supplier can have a hard copy record in case of dispute. Some systems may incorporate the use of devices such as bar code readers.

Other types of transaction which will need to be recorded include the following.

(i) **Transfers** between different categories of stock (for example from work in progress to finished goods)

(ii) **Despatch**, resulting from a sale of items of finished goods to customers

(iii) **Adjustments** to stock records if the amount of stock revealed in a physical stock count differs from the amount appearing on the stock records

(b) **A stock master file is maintained.** This file will contain details for every category of stock and will be updated for new stock lines. A database file may be maintained.

Activity 2	**(5 minutes)**
What type of information do you think should be held on a stock master file?	

The file may also hold details of stock movements over a period, but this will depend on the type of system in operation. In a **batch system**, transactions will be grouped and input in one operation and details of the movements may be held in a separate transactions file, the master file updated in total only. In an **on-line system**, transactions may be input directly to the master file, where the record of movements is thus likely to be found. Such a system will mean that the stock records are constantly up to date, which will help in monitoring and controlling stock.

The system may generate orders automatically once the amount in stock has fallen to the reorder level.

(c) **The system will generate outputs**. These may include, depending on the type of system, any of the following.

(i) **Hard copy** records, for example a printed GRN, of transactions entered into the system.

(ii) Output on a **VDU** screen in response to an enquiry (for example the current level of a particular line of stock, or details of a particular transaction).

(iii) Various **printed reports**, devised to fit in with the needs of the organisation. These may include stock movement reports, detailing over a period the movements on all stock lines, listings of GRNs, despatch notes and so forth.

A computerised stock control system is usually able to give more up to date information and more flexible reporting than a manual system but remember that both manual and computer based stock control systems need the same types of data to function properly.

3 THE STORAGE AND RECORDING OF RAW MATERIALS STOCK

Storekeeping involves storing materials to achieve the following objectives.

- Speedy **issue** and **receipt** of materials
- Full **identification** of all materials at all times
- Correct **location** of all materials at all times
- **Protection** of materials from damage and deterioration
- Provision of **secure stores** to avoid pilferage, theft and fire
- **Efficient** use of storage space
- **Maintenance** of correct stock levels
- Keeping correct and up-to-date **records** of receipts, issues and stock levels

3.1 Recording stock levels

One of the objectives of storekeeping is to maintain accurate records of current stock levels. This involves the accurate recording of stock movements (issues from and receipts into stores). The most frequently encountered system for recording stock movements is the use of bin cards and stores ledger accounts.

3.2 Bin cards

A **bin card** shows the level of stock of an item at a particular stores location. It is kept with the actual stock and is updated by the storekeeper as stocks are received and issued. A typical bin card is shown below.

Bin card

Part code no____________			Location ____________			
Bin number ____________			Stores ledger no ____________			
Receipts			*Issues*			Stock balance
Date	Quantity	G.R.N. No.	Date	Quantity	Req. No.	

The use of bin cards is decreasing, partly due to the difficulty in keeping them updated and partly due to the merging of stock recording and control procedures, frequently using computers.

3.3 Stores ledger accounts

A typical stores ledger account is shown below. Note that it shows the value of stock.

Stores ledger account

Material ____________									Maximum Quantity ____________		
Code ____________									Minimum Quantity ____________		
Date	Receipts				Issues				Stock		
	G.R.N. No.	Quantity	Unit Price £	Amount £	Stores Req. No.	Quantity	Unit Price £	Amount £	Quantity	Unit Price £	Amount £

The above illustration shows a card for a manual system, but even when the stock records are computerised, the same type of information is normally included in the computer file. The running balance on the stores ledger account allows stock levels and valuation to be monitored.

3.4 Free stock

Managers need to know the **free stock balance** in order to obtain a full picture of the current stock position of an item. Free stock represents what is really **available for future use** and is calculated as follows.

	Materials in stock	X
+	Materials on order from suppliers	X
–	Materials requisitioned, not yet issued	(X)
	Free stock balance	X

Knowledge of the level of physical stock assists stock issuing, stocktaking and controlling maximum and minimum stock levels: knowledge of the level of free stock assists ordering.

NOTES

Activity 3 **(10 minutes)**

A wholesaler has 8,450 units outstanding for Part X100 on existing customers' orders; there are 3,925 units in stock and the calculated free stock is 5,525 units.

How many units does the wholesaler have on order with his supplier?

3.5 Identification of materials: stock codes (materials codes)

Materials held in stores are **coded** and **classified**. Advantages of using code numbers to identify materials are as follows.

- Ambiguity is avoided.
- Time is saved. Descriptions can be lengthy and time-consuming.
- Production efficiency is improved. The correct material can be accurately identified from a code number.
- Computerised processing is made easier.
- Numbered code systems can be designed to be flexible, and can be expanded to include more stock items as necessary.

The digits in a code can stand for the type of stock, supplier, department and so forth.

3.6 Stocktaking

Stocktaking involves counting the physical stock on hand at a certain date, and then checking this against the balance shown in the stock records. There are two methods of carrying out this process, **periodic stocktaking** and **continuous stocktaking**.

Periodic stocktaking is a process whereby all stock items are physically counted and then valued. This is usually carried out **annually** and the objective is to count all items of stock on a specific date.

Continuous stocktaking is the process of counting and valuing selected items at different times on a rotating basis. This involves a specialist team counting and checking a number of stock items each day, so that each item is checked at least once a year. Valuable items or items with a high turnover could be checked more frequently. The advantages of this system compared to periodic stocktaking are as follows.

(a) The annual stocktaking is unnecessary and the disruption it causes is avoided.

(b) Regular skilled stocktakers can be employed, reducing likely errors.

(c) More time is available, reducing errors and allowing investigation.

(d) Deficiencies and losses are revealed sooner than they would be if stocktaking were limited to an annual check.

(e) Production hold-ups are eliminated because the stores staff are at no time so busy as to be unable to deal with material issues to production departments.

(f) Staff morale is improved and standards raised.

(g) Control over stock levels is improved, and there is less likelihood of overstocking or running out of stock.

3.7 Stock discrepancies

There will be occasions when stock checks disclose discrepancies between the physical amount of an item in stock and the amount shown in the stock records. When this occurs, the cause of the discrepancy should be investigated, and appropriate action taken to ensure that it does not happen again.

3.8 Perpetual inventory

A perpetual inventory system involves recording every receipt and issue of stock as it occurs on bin cards and stores ledger accounts. This means that there is a continuous record of the balance of each item of stock. The balance on the stores ledger account therefore represents the stock on hand and this balance is used in the calculation of closing stock in monthly and annual accounts. In practice, physical stocks may not agree with recorded stocks and therefore continuous stocktaking is necessary to ensure that the perpetual inventory system is functioning correctly and that minor stock discrepancies are corrected.

3.9 Obsolete, deteriorating and slow-moving stocks and wastage

Obsolete stocks are those items which have become out-of-date and are no longer required. Obsolete items are written off to the profit and loss account and disposed of.

Stock items may be wasted because, for example, they get broken. All **wastage** should be noted on the stock records immediately so that physical stock equals the stock balance on records and the cost of the wastage written off to the profit and loss account.

Slow-moving stocks are stock items which are likely to take a long time to be used up. For example, 5,000 units are in stock, and only 20 are being used each year. This is often caused by overstocking. Managers should investigate such stock items and, if it is felt that the usage rate is unlikely to increase, excess stock should be written off as for obsolete stock, leaving perhaps four or five years' supply in stock.

4 STOCK VALUATION

For financial accounting purposes, stocks are valued at the **lower of cost and net realisable value** (ie the lower of what they cost the business and what the business is likely to receive selling them). In practice, stocks will usually be valued at cost in the stores records throughout the course of an accounting period. Only when the period ends will the value of the stock in hand be reconsidered so that items with a net realisable value below their original cost will be revalued downwards, and the stock records altered accordingly.

4.1 Charging units of stock to cost of production or cost of sales

It is important to be able to distinguish between the way in which the physical items in stock are actually issued. In practice a storekeeper may issue goods in the following way.

- The oldest goods first
- The latest goods received first

- Randomly
- Those which are easiest to reach

By comparison the cost of the goods issued must be determined on a **consistently applied basis**, and must ignore the likelihood that the materials issued will be costed at a price different to the amount paid for them.

This may seem a little confusing at first, and it may be helpful to explain the point further. Suppose that there are three units of a particular material in stock.

Units	*Date received*	*Purchase cost*
A	June 20X1	£100
B	July 20X1	£106
C	August 20X1	£109

In September, one unit is issued to production. As it happened, the physical unit actually issued was B. The accounting department must put a value or cost on the material issued, but the value would not necessarily be the cost of B, £106. The principles used to value the materials issued are not concerned with the actual unit issued, A, B, or C. Nevertheless, the accountant may choose to make one of the following assumptions.

(a) The unit issued is valued as though it were the earliest unit in stock, ie at the purchase cost of A, £100. This valuation principle is called FIFO, or first in, first out.

(b) The unit issued is valued as though it were the most recent unit received into stock, ie at the purchase cost of C, £109. This method of valuation is LIFO, or last in, first out.

(c) The unit issued is valued at an average price of A, B and C, ie £105.

In the following sections we will consider each of the pricing methods detailed above (and a few more), using the following transactions to illustrate the principles in each case.

EXAMPLE

TRANSACTIONS DURING MAY 20X3

	Quantity Units	*Unit cost* £	*Total cost* £	*Market value per unit on date of transaction* £
Opening balance, 1 May (the opening stock, or o/s)	100	2.00	200	
Receipts, 3 May	400	2.10	840	2.11
Issues, 4 May	200			2.11
Receipts, 9 May	300	2.12	636	2.15
Issues, 11 May	400			2.20
Receipts, 18 May	100	2.40	240	2.35
Issues, 20 May	100			2.35
Closing balance, 31 May	200			2.38
			1,916	

5 FIFO (FIRST IN, FIRST OUT)

FIFO assumes that materials are issued out of stock in the order in which they were delivered into stock: issues are priced at the cost of the earliest delivery remaining in stock. (Remember this has nothing to do with how the physical stock is issued – we are dealing with stock valuation.)

Using **FIFO**, the cost of issues and the closing stock value in the example would be as follows.

Date of issue	*Quantity issued*	*Value*		
	Units		£	£
4 May	200	100 o/s at £2	200	
		100 at £2.10	210	
				410
11 May	400	300 at £2.10	630	
		100 at £2.12	212	
				842
20 May	100	100 at £2.12		212
Cost of issues				1,464
Closing stock value	200	100 at £2.12	212	
		100 at £2.40	240	
				452
				1,916

Notes

(a) The cost of materials issued plus the value of closing stock equals the cost of purchases plus the value of opening stock (£1,916).

(b) The market price of purchased materials is rising dramatically. In a period of inflation, there is a tendency with FIFO for materials to be issued at a cost lower than the current market value, although closing stocks tend to be valued at a cost approximating to current market value.

5.1 The advantages and disadvantages of the FIFO method

(a) **Advantages**

(i) It is a logical pricing method which probably represents what is physically happening: in practice the oldest stock is likely to be used first.

(ii) It is easy to understand and explain to managers.

(iii) The stock valuation can be near to a valuation based on replacement cost.

(b) **Disadvantages**

(i) FIFO can be cumbersome to operate because of the need to identify each batch of material separately.

(ii) Managers may find it difficult to compare costs and make decisions when they are charged with varying prices for the same materials.

(iii) In a period of high inflation, stock issue prices will lag behind current market value.

NOTES

Activity 4 **(30 minutes)**

Draw up an extract from a stores ledger account using the columns shown below. Complete the columns in as much details as possible using the information in the example on the previous page.

STORES LEDGER ACCOUNT

	Receipts				Issues				Stock		
Date	GRN No.	Quantity	Unit price £	Amount £	Stores Req. No.	Quantity	Unit price £	Amount £	Quantity	Unit price £	Amount £

6 LIFO (LAST IN, FIRST OUT)

LIFO assumes that materials are issued out of stock in the reverse order to which they were delivered: the most recent deliveries are issued before earlier ones, and are priced accordingly.

Using **LIFO**, the cost of issues and the closing stock value in the example above would be as follows.

Date of issue	*Quantity issued* Units	*Valuation*	£	£
4 May	200	200 at £2.10		420
11 May	400	300 at £2.12	636	
		100 at £2.10	210	
				846
20 May	100	100 at £2.40		240
Cost of issues				1,506
Closing stock value	200	100 at £2.10	210	
		100 at £2.00	200	
				410
				1,916

Notes

(a) The cost of materials issued plus the value of closing stock equals the cost of purchases plus the value of opening stock (£1,916).

(b) In a period of inflation there is a tendency with **LIFO** for the following to occur.

   (i) Materials are issued at a price which approximates to current market value.

   (ii) Closing stocks become undervalued when compared to market value.

BPP LEARNING MEDIA

6.1 The advantages and disadvantages of the LIFO method

(a) *Advantages*

(i) Stocks are issued at a price which is close to current market value.

(ii) Managers are continually aware of recent costs when making decisions, because the costs being charged to their department or products will be current costs.

(b) *Disadvantages*

(i) The method can be cumbersome to operate because it sometimes results in several batches being only part-used in the stock records before another batch is received.

(ii) LIFO is often the opposite to what is physically happening and can therefore be difficult to explain to managers.

(iii) As with FIFO, decision making can be difficult because of the variations in prices.

7 CUMULATIVE WEIGHTED AVERAGE PRICING

The **cumulative weighted average pricing method, AVCO,** calculates a weighted average price for all units in stock. Issues are priced at this average cost, and the balance of stock remaining would have the same unit valuation. The average price is determined by dividing the total cost by the total number of units.

A new weighted average price is calculated whenever a new delivery of materials into store is received. This is the key feature of cumulative weighted average pricing.

EXAMPLE

In our example, issue costs and closing stock values would be as follows.

Date	*Received*	*Issued*	*Balance*	*Total stock value*	*Unit cost*	
	Units	Units	Units	£	£	£
Opening stock			100	200	2.00	
3 May	400			840	2.10	
			* 500	1,040	2.08	
4 May		200		(416)	2.08	416
			300	624	2.08	
9 May	300			636	2.12	
			* 600	1,260	2.10	
11 May		400		(840)	2.10	840
			200	420	2.10	
18 May	100			240	2.40	
			* 300	660	2.20	
20 May		100		(220)	2.20	220
						1,476
Closing stock value			200	440	2.20	440
						1,916

* A new stock value per unit is calculated whenever a new receipt of materials occurs.

Notes

(a) The cost of materials issued plus the value of closing stock equals the cost of purchases plus the value of opening stock (£1,916).

(b) In a period of inflation, using the cumulative weighted average pricing system, the value of material issues will rise gradually, but will tend to lag a little behind the current market value at the date of issue. Closing stock values will also be a little below current market value.

7.1 The advantages and disadvantages of cumulative weighted average pricing

(a) *Advantages*

(i) Fluctuations in prices are smoothed out, making it easier to use the data for decision making.

(ii) It is easier to administer than FIFO and LIFO, because there is no need to identify each batch separately.

(b) *Disadvantages*

(i) The resulting issue price is rarely an actual price that has been paid, and can run to several decimal places.

(ii) Prices tend to lag a little behind current market values when there is gradual inflation.

Activity 5 **(30 minutes)**

An organisation has recorded the following details on an item of stock for the month of June.

	Units	*Cost per unit*
Opening stock	300	£5
4 June – issue	50	
7 June – receipt	100	£5.56
10 June – issue	75	
11 June – issue	100	
15 June – receipt	100	£5.27
20 June – issue	200	

What would be the cost of issues and valuation of the closing stock if:

(a) LIFO is used to value stocks?

(b) AVCO is used to value stocks?

8 OTHER METHODS OF PRICING AND VALUATION

8.1 Standard cost pricing

Under the standard cost pricing method, all issues are at predetermined standard price. Such a method is used with a system of standard costing, which will be covered later in this Course Book.

8.2 Replacement cost pricing

Arguments for **replacement cost pricing** include the following.

(a) When materials are issued out of stores, they will be replaced with a new delivery; issues should therefore be priced at the current cost to the business of replacing them in stores.

(b) Closing stocks should be valued at current replacement cost in the balance sheet to show the true value of the assets of the business.

The advantages and disadvantages of **replacement costing** are as follows.

(a) *Advantages*

- (i) Issues are at up-to-date costs so that managers can take recent trends into account when making decisions based on their knowledge of the costs being incurred.
- (ii) It is recommended as a method of accounting for inflation.
- (iii) It is easy to operate once the replacement cost has been determined.

(b) *Disadvantages*

- (i) The price may not be an actual price paid, and a difference will then arise on issues.
- (ii) It can be difficult to determine the replacement cost.
- (iii) The method is not acceptable to the HM Revenue and Customs or for SSAP 9, although this should not be a major consideration in internal cost accounts.

Activity 6 **(5 minutes)**

Which pricing method can be used as a practical alternative to replacement cost pricing?

8.3 Specific price

This method values issues at their individual price and the stock balance is made up of individual items valued at individual prices. It is only really suitable for expensive stock lines where stock holdings and usage rates are low.

9 STOCK VALUATION AND PROFITABILITY

In the previous descriptions of FIFO, LIFO, average costing and so on, the example used raw materials as an illustration. Each method produced different figures for both the value of closing stocks and also the cost of material issues. Since raw materials costs affect the cost of production, and the cost of production works through eventually into the cost of sales, it follows that different methods of stock valuation will provide different profit figures.

NOTES

10 CALCULATING LABOUR COSTS

Labour remuneration methods need to be considered very carefully as they will affect the following.

- The cost of finished products or services.
- The morale and efficiency of employees

There are three basic groups of remuneration method.

- Time work
- Piecework schemes
- Bonus/incentive schemes

We will discuss each of these in the next few paragraphs.

10.1 Time work

Formula to learn

The most common form of **time work** is a **day-rate system** in which wages are calculated by the following formula.

Wages = Hours worked × Rate of pay per hour

If an employee works for more hours than the basic daily requirement he may be entitled to an **overtime payment**. Hours of overtime are usually paid at a premium rate. For instance, if the basic day-rate is £4 per hour and overtime is paid at time-and-a-quarter, eight hours of overtime would be paid the following amount.

	£
Basic pay (8 × £4)	32
Overtime premium (8 × £1)	8
Total (8 × £5)	40

The **overtime premium** is the extra rate per hour which is paid, not the whole of the payment for the overtime hours. Overtime can be at any agreed rate; common examples are time-and-a-half or double time.

If employees work unsocial hours, for instance overnight, they may be entitled to a **shift premium**. This is similar to an overtime premium and means that the employee is paid an increased hourly rate. The extra amount paid per hour, above the basic hourly rate, is the shift premium.

Day-rate systems are most appropriate when the quality of output is more important than the quantity, or where there is no basis for payment by performance because there is no incentive for employees who are paid on this basis to improve their performance.

10.2 Piecework schemes

Formula to learn

> In a **piecework scheme**, wages are calculated by the following formula.
>
> Wages = Units produced × Rate of pay per unit

Suppose for example, an employee is paid £1 for each unit produced and works a 40 hour week. Production overhead is added at the rate of £2 per direct labour hour.

Weekly production	*Pay (40 hours)*	*Overhead*	*Conversion cost*	*Conversion cost per unit*
Units	£	£	£	£
40	40	80	120	3.00
50	50	80	130	2.60
60	60	80	140	2.33
70	70	80	150	2.14

As his output increases, his wage increases and at the same time unit costs of output are reduced.

It is normal for pieceworkers to be offered a **guaranteed minimum wage,** so that they do not suffer loss of earnings when production is low through no fault of their own.

If an employee makes several different types of product, it may not be possible to add up the units for payment purposes. Instead, a **standard time allowance** is given for each unit to arrive at a total of piecework hours for payment.

WORKED EXAMPLE: PIECEWORK

An employee is paid £3 per piecework hour produced. In a 40 hour week he produces the following output.

	Piecework time allowed per unit
15 units of product X	0.5 hours
20 units of product Y	2.0 hours

Calculate the employee's pay for the week.

ANSWER

Piecework hours produced are as follows.

Product X	15 × 0.5 hours	7.5 hours
Product Y	20 × 2.0 hours	40.0 hours
Total piecework hours		47.5 hours

Therefore employee's pay = 47.5 × £3 = £142.50 for the week.

10.3 Differential piecework schemes

These offer an incentive to employees to increase their output by paying higher rates for increased levels of production. An example is shown below.

Rates

up to and including 80 units, rate of pay per unit in this band	=	£1.00
81 to 90 units, rate of pay per unit in this band	=	£1.20
above 90 units, rate of pay per unit in this band	=	£1.30

An employee producing 97 units would therefore receive (80 × £1.00) + (10 × £1.20) + (7 × £1.30) = £101.10.

Employers should obviously be careful to make it clear whether they intend to pay the increased rate on all units produced, or on the extra output only.

10.4 Summary

Piecework schemes may be summarised as follows.

(a) They enjoy fluctuating popularity.

(b) They are occasionally used by employers as a means of increasing pay levels.

(c) They are frequently condemned as a means of driving employees to work too hard to earn a satisfactory wage.

(d) Careful inspection of output is necessary to ensure that quality is maintained as production increases.

10.5 Bonus/incentive schemes

In general, bonus schemes were introduced to compensate workers paid under a time-based system for their inability to increase earnings by working more efficiently. Various types of incentive and bonus schemes have been devised which encourage greater productivity. The characteristics of such schemes are as follows.

(a) A target is set and actual performance is compared with target.

(b) Employees are paid more for their efficiency.

(c) In spite of the extra labour cost, the unit cost of output is reduced and the profit earned per unit of sale is increased; in other words the profits arising from productivity improvements are shared between employer and employee.

(d) Morale of employees should be expected to improve since they are seen to receive extra reward for extra effort.

There are many possible types of incentive schemes.

(a) A **high day-rate system** is an incentive scheme where employees are paid a high hourly wage rate in the expectation that they will work more efficiently than similar employees on a lower hourly rate in a different company.

(b) Under an **individual bonus scheme**, individual employees qualify for a bonus on top of their basic wage, with each person's bonus being calculated separately.

(c) Where individual effort cannot be measured, and employees work as a team, an individual incentive scheme is impractical but a **group bonus scheme** is feasible.

(d) In a **profit sharing scheme**, employees receive a certain proportion of their company's year-end profits (the size of their bonus being related to their position in the company and the length of their employment to date).

(e) Companies operating **incentive schemes involving shares** use their shares, or the right to acquire them, as a form of incentive.

Note that an employer may provide other bonuses and benefits (company cars, non-contributory pension schemes, subsidised canteen). Such benefits do not always improve production so much as reduce labour turnover.

10.6 Labour turnover

Labour turnover is a measure of the rate at which employees are leaving an organisation. It is usually calculated as follows.

$$\text{Labour turnover for the period} = \frac{\text{number of employees leaving and replaced}}{\text{average workforce}} \times 100$$

A high turnover can be costly for an organisation. For example new employees must be recruited and trained, they may work at a slower rate and there may be a loss of output due to a delay in the new labour becoming available.

The level of labour turnover should obviously be minimised and well-designed remuneration and incentive schemes can contribute towards this.

WORKED EXAMPLE: INCENTIVE SCHEMES

Swetton Tyres Ltd manufactures a single product. Its work force consists of 10 employees, who work a 36-hour week exclusive of lunch and tea breaks. The standard time required to make one unit of the product is two hours, but the current efficiency (or productivity) ratio being achieved is 80%. No overtime is worked, and the work force is paid £4 per attendance hour.

Because of agreements with the work force about work procedures, there is some unavoidable idle time due to bottlenecks in production, and about four hours per week per person are lost in this way.

The company can sell all the output it manufactures, and makes a 'cash profit' of £20 per unit sold, deducting currently achievable costs of production but *before* deducting labour costs.

An incentive scheme is proposed whereby the work force would be paid £5 per hour in exchange for agreeing to new work procedures that would reduce idle time per employee per week to two hours and also raise the efficiency ratio to 90%. Evaluate the incentive scheme from the point of view of profitability.

ANSWER

The current situation

Hours paid for: 10 employees × 36 hours per week = 360 hours
Hours working 10 employees × 32 hours working = 320 hours

Note: there are four hours per week of idle time per employee hence 36 – 4 = 32 hours working.

At 80% efficiency:

Expected units produced = 320 hours worked ÷ 2 hours per unit
= 160 expected units

Note: each unit takes two hours to produce

At 80% efficiency: $160 \times \frac{80}{100}$ = 128 units actually produced

	£
Cash profits before deducting labour costs (128 × £20)	2,560
Less labour costs (£4 × 360 hours paid for)	1,440
Net profit	1,120

The incentive scheme

Hours working: 10 employees × 34 hours = 340 hours

Note: idle time has now been reduced to 2 hours per week per employee so 36 – 2 = 34 hours.

Units produced, at 90% efficiency $\frac{340}{2} \times \frac{90}{100}$ = 153 units

	£
Cash profits before deducting labour costs (153 × £20)	3,060
Less labour costs (£5 × 360)	1,800
Net profit	1,260

In spite of a 25% increase in labour costs, profits would rise by £140 per week. The company and the workforce would both benefit provided, of course, that management can hold the work force to their promise of work reorganisation and improved productivity.

Activity 7 **(10 minutes)**

The following data relate to work at a certain factory.

Normal working day	8 hours
Basic rate of pay per hour	£6
Standard time allowed to produce 1 unit	2 minutes
Premium bonus	75% of time saved at basic rate

What will be the labour cost in a day when 340 units are made?

BPP LEARNING MEDIA

NOTES

11 LABOUR COST BEHAVIOUR

(a) When employees are paid on a piecework basis their pay is a variable cost.

(b) When employees are paid a basic day-rate wage, their pay per week is fixed, regardless of the volume of output. The high cost of redundancy payments and the scarcity of skilled labour will usually persuade a company to retain its employees at a basic wage even when output is low.

(c) Because of productivity bonuses, overtime premium, commission and so on, labour costs are often mixed semi-variable costs.

Labour costs tend to behave in a step cost fashion.

(a) Where the steps are short (that is where extra labour is needed for small increases in output volumes), the labour costs tend to approximate a variable cost.

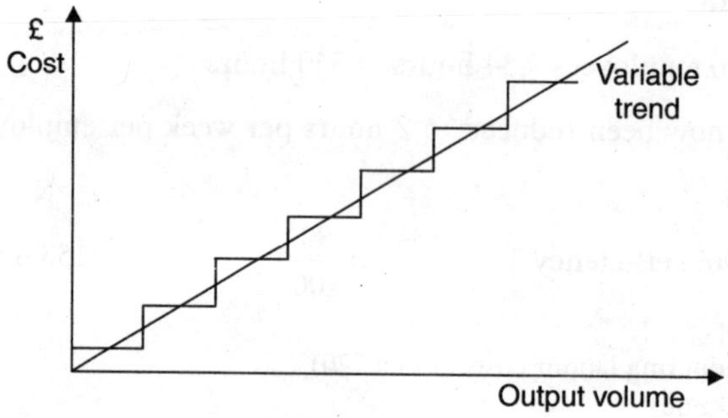

In this graph, the short steps approximate closely to a variable cost line, and for most purposes, it will be sufficiently accurate to treat labour as a purely variable cost.

(b) If, on the other hand, the labour force is static for wide ranges of output, the cost tends to be fixed in nature.

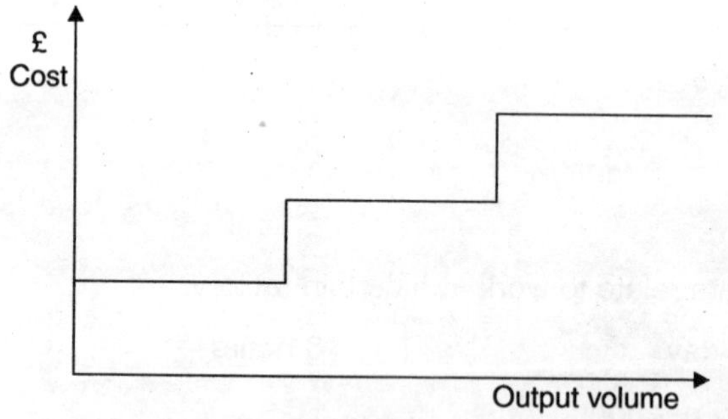

Figure 2.1: Volume cost graphs

The cost accountant has to treat labour costs as fixed or variable.

(a) Direct labour is usually regarded as being a variable cost in labour-intensive work. In highly automated industries it may be regarded as a fixed cost.

(b) For control purposes, direct labour is regarded as a variable cost so that measures of efficiency or productivity can be obtained.

12 RECORDING LABOUR COSTS

12.1 Organisation for controlling and measuring labour costs

Several departments and management groups are involved in the collection, recording and costing of labour. These include the following.

- Personnel
- Production planning
- Timekeeping
- Wages
- Cost accounting

From a cost accounting point of view, the **timekeeping department** provides the most important information to facilitate the recording of labour cost. The timekeeping department is responsible for accurately recording the time spent in the factory by each worker and time spent by each worker on each job or operation: attendance time and job time respectively. Such timekeeping provides basic data for statutory records, payroll preparation, labour costs of an operation or overhead absorption (where based on wages or labour hours) and statistical analysis of labour records for determining productivity and control of labour costs.

12.2 Attendance time

The bare minimum record of employees' time is a simple **attendance record** showing days absent because of holiday, sickness or other reason.

It is also necessary to have a record of the following.

- Time of arrival
- Time of breaks
- Time of departure

These may be recorded as follows.

- In a signing-in book
- By using a time recording clock which stamps the time on a clock card
- By using swipe cards (which make a computer record)

An example of a clock card is shown below.

No Name				Ending	
	HOURS	RATE	AMOUNT	DEDUCTIONS	
Basic O/T Others				Income Tax NI Other Total deduction	
Total Less deductions Net due					
Time		Day		Basic time	Overtime
1230 0803 T 1700 M 1305 M 1234 M 0750 M					
Signature - - - - - - - - - - - - - - -					

12.3 Job time

The next step is to analyse the hours spent at work according to what was done during those hours. The method adopted depends upon the size of the organisation, the nature of the work and the type of incentive scheme in operation.

Continuous production. Where **routine, repetitive** work is carried out it might not be practical to record the precise details. For example if a worker stands at a conveyor belt for seven hours his work can be measured by keeping a note of the number of units that pass through his part of the process during that time.

Job costing. When the work is not of a repetitive nature the records required might be one or several of the following.

(a) **Daily or weekly time sheets.** A time sheet is filled in by the employee as a record of how their time has been spent. The total time on the time sheet should correspond with time shown on the attendance record.

Time Sheet No. ....

Employee Name .... Clock Code .... Dept ....

Date .... Week No. ....

Job No.	Start Time	Finish Time	Qty	Checker	Hrs	Rate	Extension

The time sheet will be filled in by the employee, for hours worked on each job (job code) or area of work (cost code). The cost of the hours worked will be entered at a later stage in the accounting department.

(b) **Job cards.** Cards are prepared for each job or batch, unlike time sheets which are made out for each employee and which may contain bookings relating to numerous jobs. When employees work on a job they record on the job card the time spent on that job and so job cards are likely to contain entries relating to numerous employees. On completion of the job it will contain a full record of the times involved in the job or batch. The problem of job cards, however, is that the reconciliation of job time and attendance time can be a difficult task, especially for jobs which stretch over several weeks. It is therefore difficult to incorporate them directly into wage calculation procedures. They do, however, reduce the amount of writing to be done by the employee and therefore the possibility of error. A typical job card is shown below.

JOB CARD			
Department ______		Job no ______	
Date ______		Operation no ______	
Time allowance ______		Time started ______ Time finished ______ Hours on the job ______	
Description of job	Hours	Rate	Cost
Employee no ______ Signature ______		Certified by ______	

12.4 Piecework

The wages of pieceworkers and the labour cost of work done by them is determined from what is known as a **piecework ticket** or an **operation card**. The card records the total number of items (or 'pieces') produced and the number of rejects. Payment is only made for 'good' production. A typical operation card is shown below.

OPERATION CARD				
Operator's Name ______			Total Batch Quantity ______	
Clock No ______			Start Time ______	
Pay week No ______	Date ______		Stop Time ______	
Part No ______			Works Order No ______	
Operation ______			Special Instructions ______	
Quantity Produced	No Rejected	Good Production	Rate	£
Inspector ______			Operative ______	
Foreman ______			Date ______	
PRODUCTION CANNOT BE CLAIMED WITHOUT A PROPERLY SIGNED CARD				

Note that the attendance record of a pieceworker is still required for calculations of holidays, sick pay and so on.

12.5 Salaried labour

Even though salaried staff are paid a flat rate monthly, they may be required to complete timesheets. The reasons are as follows.

(a) Timesheets provide management with information (eg product costs).

(b) Timesheet information may provide a basis for billing for services provided, for example, a firm of solicitors or accountants may bill clients based on the number of hours work done.

(c) Timesheets are used to record hours spent and so support claims for overtime payments by salaried staff.

12.6 Idle time

In many jobs there are times when, through no fault of their own, employees cannot get on with their work. They may be waiting for another department to finish its contribution to a job, or a machine may break down or there may simply be a temporary shortage of work.

Idle time has a cost because employees will still be paid their basic wage or salary for these unproductive hours and so there should be a record of idle time. This may simply comprise an entry on time sheets coded to 'idle time' generally, or separate idle time cards may be prepared. A supervisor might enter the time of a stoppage, its cause, its duration and the employees made idle on an idle time record card. Each stoppage should have a separate reference number which can be entered on time sheets or job cards as appropriate.

12.7 Cost accounting department

The cost accounting department has the following responsibilities.

(a) The accumulation and classification of all cost data (which includes labour costs).

(b) Preparation of cost data reports for management.

(c) Analysing information on time cards and payroll to obtain details of direct and indirect labour, overtime and so on.

In order to establish the labour cost involved in products, operations, jobs and cost centres, the following documents are used.

- Clock cards
- Job cards
- Idle time cards
- Payroll

Analyses of labour costs are used for the following.

(a) Charging wages directly attributable to production to the appropriate job or operation.

(b) Charging wages which are not directly attributable to production as follows.

  (i) Idle time of production workers is charged to indirect costs as part of the overheads.

(ii) Wages costs of supervisors, or store assistants are charged to the overhead costs of the relevant department.

(c) Producing idle time reports which show a summary of the hours lost through idle time, and the cause of the idle time. Idle time may be analysed as follows.

(i) Controllable eg lack of materials.
(ii) Uncontrollable eg power failure.

Formula to learn

$$\textbf{Idle time ratio} = \frac{\text{Idle hours}}{\text{Total hours}} \times 100\%$$

The idle time ratio is useful because it shows the proportion of available hours which were lost as a result of idle time.

NOTES

Chapter roundup

- Every movement of material in a business should be documented using the following as appropriate: purchase requisition, purchase order, GRN, materials requisition note, materials transfer note and materials returned note.
- Perpetual inventory refers to a stock recording system whereby the records (bin cards and stores ledger accounts) are updated for each receipt and issue of stock as it occurs.
- Stocktaking can be carried out on a continuous or periodic basis.
- Free stock balance calculations take account of stock on order from suppliers, and of stock which has been requisitioned but not yet delivered.
- The valuation of stock is of the utmost importance because it has a direct effect on the calculation of profit.
- FIFO assumes that materials are issued out of stock in the order in which they were delivered into stock: issues are priced at the cost of the earliest delivery remaining in stock.
- LIFO assumes that materials are issued out of stock in the reverse order to which they were delivered: the most recent deliveries are issued before earlier ones and issues are priced accordingly.
- Cumulative weighted average, AVCO, requires a calculation of the average cost of all units of stock after each new receipt.
- There are three basic groups of remuneration method for labour – time work, piecework schemes and bonus/incentive schemes.
- Although labour costs tend to behave in a step cost fashion, cost accountants usually treat labour costs as fixed or variable.
- Labour turnover is the rate at which employees leave a company and this rate should be kept as low as possible.
- Labour attendance time is recorded on, for example, an attendance record or clock card. Job time may be recorded on daily time sheets, weekly time sheets or job cards.
- The labour cost of pieceworkers is recorded on a piecework ticket/operation card.
- Idle time has a cost and must therefore be recorded.

BPP LEARNING MEDIA

NOTES

Quick quiz

1 List five steps in the ordering and receipt of raw materials.

2 Name two key items of information that must be shown on a materials requisition.

3 What is the purpose of a materials transfer note?

4 What is free stock?

5 What are the advantages and disadvantages of using LIFO in materials issues pricing?

6 How would you calculate a cumulative weighted average price?

7 What is a differential piecework scheme?

8 What types of document are used in recording job time?

9 What is idle time?

10 What is the idle time ratio?

Answers to quick quiz

1 (i) Purchase requisition sent from stores to purchasing.

(ii) Purchase order sent from purchasing to supplier.

(iii) Goods received and checked against supplier's delivery note.

(iv) Goods received note (GRN) sent by storekeeper to accounts department.

(v) Supplier's invoice matched with purchase order and GRN in accounts department. (see para 2.1)

2 Any two of the following.

Description of goods required
Quantity of goods required
Date goods required by
Department or job requiring the goods
Signature and date of authorisation (para 2.2)

3 A materials transfer note provides details of goods transferred from one job or cost centre to another so that the costs incurred can be correctly allocated to those jobs or cost centres. (para 2.3)

4 Free stock is the stock available for future use and is calculated as follows.

Materials in stock	X	
Add: materials on order from suppliers	X	
Less: materials requisitioned, not yet issued	(X)	
Free stock balance	X	(para 3.4)

5 Advantages of LIFO: Stocks are issued at a price which is close to current market value and managers are made aware of recent costs when making decisions because their department will be charged with these 'current' costs.

Disadvantages of LIFO: stock records will be 'untidy' as they may include part-used batches; it rarely reflects the actual usage of stock; and decision-making can be difficult because of fluctuating prices. (para 6.1)

BPP LEARNING MEDIA

6 After each receipt calculate: $\frac{\text{Total cost of units in stock}}{\text{Total number of units in stock}}$ (para 7)

7 A differential piecework scheme offers incentives to employees by paying higher rates for increased levels of production. For example, the rate of pay could increase as follows.

Up to 2000 units	50p per unit in this band
2000 to 2200 units	54p per unit in this band
2200 to 2400 units	56p per unit in this band (para 10.3)

8 Daily time sheets
Weekly time sheets
Job cards (para 12.3)

9 Idle time is time when employees are not able to get on with their work through no fault of their own. (para 12.6)

10 Idle time ratio = $\frac{\text{Idle hours}}{\text{Total hours}} \times 100\%$ (para 12.7)

Answers to activities

1
(a) Incorrect materials being delivered, disrupting operations
(b) Incorrect prices being paid
(c) Deliveries other than at the specified time (causing disruption)
(d) Insufficient control over quality
(e) Invoiced amounts differing from quantities of goods actually received or prices agreed

You may, of course, have thought of equally valid consequences.

2 Here are some examples.

(a) Stock code number, for reference
(b) Brief description of stock item
(c) Reorder level
(d) Reorder quantity
(e) Cost per unit
(f) Selling price per unit (if finished goods)
(g) Amount in stock
(h) Frequency of usage

3 Since this is a wholesaler, materials requisitioned are the same as customer orders – they are movements of stock out of stores, so:

Free stock balance = units in stock + units on order – units requisitioned, but not yet issued or in this case customer orders.

5,525 = 3,925 + units on order – 8,450

5,525 – 3,925 + 8,450 = units on order, therefore:

Units on order = 10,050

4

STORES LEDGER ACCOUNT (extract)

		Receipts			Issues				Stock		
Date	GRN No.	Quantity	Unit price £	Amount £	Stores Req. No.	Quantity	Unit price £	Amount £	Quantity	Unit price £	Amount £
1.5.X3									100	2.00	200.00
3.5.X3		400	2.10	840.00					100 400 500	2.00 2.10	200.00 840.00 1,040.00
4.5.X3						100 100	2.00 2.10	200.00 210.00	300	2.10	630.00
9.5.X3		300	2.12	636.00					300 300 600	2.10 2.12	630.00 636.00 1,266.00
11.5.X3						300 100	2.10 2.12	630.00 212.00	200	2.12	424.00
18.5.X3		100	2.40	240.00					200 100 300	2.12 2.40	424.00 240.00 664.00
20.5.X3						100	2.12	212.00	100 100	2.12 2.40	212.00 240.00
31.5.X3									200		452.00

Note: The opening balance on 1 May of 100 units is not a receipt for the period as it would have been received in a previous period. It is just brought forward in the stock column.

5 (a)

	Receipts			Issues			Stock		
Date	Quantity	Unit price £	Amount £	Quantity	Unit price £	Amount £	Quantity	Unit price £	Amount £
Opening stock							300	5.00	1,500
4 June				50	5.00	250	250	5.00	1,250
7 June	100	5.56	556				250 100 350	5.00 5.56	1,250 566 1,806
10 June				75	5.56	417	250 25 275	5.00 5.56	1,250 139 1,389
11 June				25 75 100	5.56 5.00	139 375 514	175	5.00	875
15 June	100	5.27	527				175 100 275	5.00 5.27	875 527 1,402
20 June				100 100 200	5.27 5.00	527 500 1,027	75	5.00	375

Value of issues under LIFO: 250 + 417 + 514 + 1,027 = £2,208.

Value of closing stock: £375

(b)

Date	Received units	Issued units	Balance units	Total stock value	Unit cost
				£	£
Opening stock			300	1,500	5.00
4 June		(50)		(250)	5.00
			250	1,250	5.00
7 June	100			556	5.56
			350	1,806	5.16
10 June		(75)		(387)	5.16
			275	1,419	5.16
11 June		(100)		(516)	5.16
			175	903	5.16
15 June	100			527	5.27
			275	1,430	5.20
20 June		(200)		(1,040)	5.20
			75	390	5.20

Value of issues under AVCO = 250 + 387 + 516 + 1,040
= £2,193

Value of closing stock = £390

6 LIFO is a reasonably accurate method of accounting for inflation provided that closing stock values are periodically reviewed and revalued.

7

Standard time for 340 units (× 2 minutes)	680 minutes
Actual time (8 hours per day) (8 × 60 minutes)	480 minutes
Time saved	200 minutes

	£
Bonus = 75% × 200 minutes × £6 per hour (see note)	15
Basic pay = 8 hours × £6	48
Total labour cost	63

Note: £6 per hour is £0.10 per minute (£6 ÷ 60 = 0.1).

Chapter 3 :

OVERHEAD APPORTIONMENT AND ABSORPTION

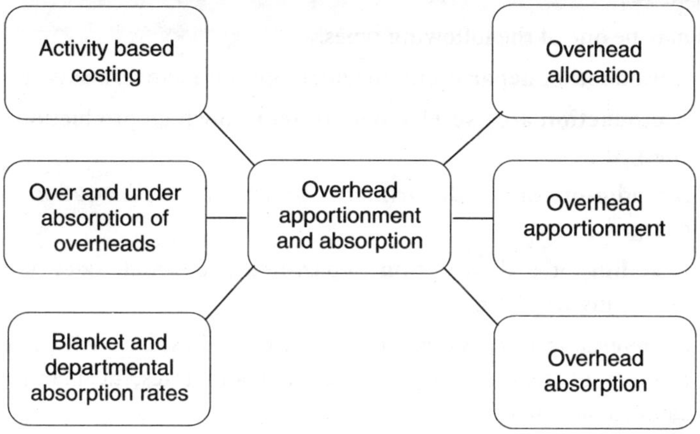

Introduction

There are basically two schools of thought as to the correct method of dealing with overheads: **marginal costing** (which we will be looking at in the next chapter) and **absorption costing**, the topic of this chapter.

Absorption costing is a method for sharing overheads between a number of different products on a fair basis. The chapter begins by looking at the three stages of absorption costing: **allocation, apportionment and absorption**. We then move on to the important issue of **over/under absorption**, a frequently examined topic. The chapter concludes with a brief look at a relatively recent development in the treatment of overheads, **activity based costing**.

Your objectives

In this chapter you will learn about the following.

(a) Overhead allocation

(b) Overhead apportionment

(c) Overhead absorption

(d) Blanket absorption rates and departmental absorption rates

(e) Over and under absorption of overheads

(f) Activity based costing

1 OVERHEAD ALLOCATION

Definition

> **Allocation** is the process by which whole cost items are charged direct to a cost unit or cost centre.

1.1 Cost centres

Cost centres may be one of the following types.

(a) A **production department**, to which production overheads are charged

(b) A **production area service department**, to which production overheads are charged

(c) An **administrative department**, to which administration overheads are charged

(d) A **selling** or a **distribution department**, to which sales and distribution overheads are charged

(e) An **overhead cost centre**, to which items of expense which are shared by a number of departments, such as rent and rates, heat and light and the canteen, are charged

1.2 Allocation

The following are examples of costs which would be charged directly to cost centres via the process of allocation.

(a) The cost of a warehouse security guard will be charged to the warehouse cost centre.

(b) Paper on which computer output is recorded will be charged to the computer department.

EXAMPLE

As an example of overhead allocation, consider the following costs of a company.

Wages of the supervisor of department A	£200
Wages of the supervisor of department B	£150
Indirect materials consumed in department A	£50
Rent of the premises shared by departments A and B	£300

The cost accounting system might include three cost centres.

Cost centre:	101	Department A
	102	Department B
	201	Rent

Overhead costs would be allocated directly to each cost centre, ie £200 + £50 to cost centre 101, £150 to cost centre 102 and £300 to cost centre 201. The rent of the factory will be subsequently shared between the two production departments, but for the purpose of day to day cost recording in this particular system, the rent will first of all be charged in full to a separate cost centre.

NOTES

2 OVERHEAD APPORTIONMENT

2.1 First stage: apportioning general overheads

Overhead apportionment follows on from overhead allocation. The first stage of overhead apportionment is to identify all overhead costs as production department, production area service department, administration or selling and distribution overhead. This means that the costs for heat and light, rent and rates, the canteen and so on (that is, costs which have been allocated to general overhead cost centres) must be shared out between the other cost centres.

2.2 Bases of apportionment

Overhead costs should be shared out on a fair basis. You will appreciate that because of the complexity of items of cost it is rarely possible to use only one method of apportioning costs to the various departments of an organisation. The bases of apportionment for the most usual cases are given below.

Overhead to which the basis applies	Basis
Rent, rates, heating and light, repairs and depreciation of buildings	Floor area occupied by each cost centre
Depreciation, insurance of equipment	Cost or book value of equipment
Personnel office, canteen, welfare, wages and cost offices, first aid	Number of employees, or labour hours worked in each cost centre
Heating, lighting (possible alternative)	Volume of space occupied by each cost centre

WORKED EXAMPLE: OVERHEAD APPORTIONMENT

Millie Ltd has incurred the following overhead costs.

	£'000
Depreciation of factory	100
Factory repairs and maintenance	60
Factory office costs (treat as production overhead)	150
Depreciation of equipment	80
Insurance of equipment	20
Heating	39
Lighting	10
Canteen	90
	549

Information relating to the production and service departments in the factory is as follows.

	Department			
	Production 1	*Production 2*	*Service 100*	*Service 101*
Floor space (square metres)	1,200	1,600	800	400
Volume (cubic metres)	3,000	6,000	2,400	1,600
Number of employees	30	30	15	15
Book value of equipment	£30,000	£20,000	£10,000	£20,000

Determine how the overhead costs should be apportioned between the four departments.

BPP LEARNING MEDIA

ANSWER

Costs are apportioned using the following general formula.

$$\frac{\text{Total overhead cost}}{\text{Total value of apportionent basis}} \times \text{value of apportionment basis of cost centre}$$

So for the factory depreciation, the most reasonable way of sharing the costs would be based on floor area.

	Production 1	*Production 2*	*Service 100*	*Service 101*
Floor space	1,200	1,600	800	400

The total floor area is: 1,200 + 1,600 + 800 + 400 = 4,000 sq metres.

So using the general formula given above the overhead of factory depreciation of £100,000 would be apportioned to the departments as follows.

		Departments			
	Total cost	*1*	*2*	*100*	*101*
	£'000	£'000	£'000	£'000	£'000
Factory depreciation	100	30	40	20	10

Department 1: $\frac{100{,}000}{4{,}000} \times 1{,}200 = 30{,}000$

Department 2: $\frac{100{,}000}{4{,}000} \times 1{,}600 = 40{,}000$

Department 100: $\frac{100{,}000}{4{,}000} \times 800 = 20{,}000$

Department 101: $\frac{100{,}000}{4{,}000} \times 400 = 10{,}000$

Always check to ensure the total of the costs you have apportioned is the same as the total cost. In this example: 30,000 + 40,000 + 20,000 + 10,000 = 100,000 which is the total cost of the factory depreciation. The rest of the table can be completed.

		Total	*To Department*			
Item of cost	*Basis of apportionment*	*cost*	*1*	*2*	*100*	*101*
		£'000	£'000	£'000	£'000	£'000
Factory depreciation	(floor area)	100	30.0	40	20.0	10.0
Factory repairs	(floor area)	60	18.0	24	12.0	6.0
Factory office costs	(number of employees)	150	50.0	50	25.0	25.0
Equipment depreciation	(book value)	80	30.0	20	10.0	20.0
Equipment insurance	(book value)	20	7.5	5	2.5	5.0
Heating	(volume)	39	9.0	18	7.2	4.8
Lighting	(floor area)	10	3.0	4	2.0	1.0
Canteen	(number of employees)	90	30.0	30	15.0	15.0
Total		549	177.5	191	93.7	86.8

2.3 Second stage: service cost centre cost apportionment

The second stage of overhead apportionment concerns the treatment of **service cost centres.** A factory is divided into several production departments and also a number of service departments, but only the production departments are directly involved in the manufacture of the units. In order to be able to add production overheads to unit costs, it is necessary to have all the overheads charged to (or located in) the production departments. The next stage in absorption costing is, therefore, to apportion the costs of service cost centres to the production cost centres. Examples of possible apportionment bases are as follows.

Service cost centre	Possible basis of apportionment
Stores	Number of materials requisitions
Maintenance	Hours of maintenance work done for each cost centre
Production planning	Direct labour hours worked in each production cost centre

WORKED EXAMPLE: APPORTIONING SERVICE COST CENTRE COSTS TO PRODUCTION COST CENTRES

Mac Ltd incurred the following overhead costs.

	Production departments		*Stores*	*Maintenance*
	X	*Y*	*department*	*department*
	£	£	£	£
Allocated costs	6,000	4,000	1,000	2,000
Apportioned costs	2,000	1,000	1,000	500
	8,000	5,000	2,000	2,500

The maintenance department worked 500 hours for department X and 750 hours for department Y. Production department X raised 12,000 material requisitions. Department Y raised 8,000 material requisitions.

Calculate the total production overhead costs of departments X and Y.

ANSWER

The stores cost can be allocated to the production centres using the number of requisitions and the maintenance departments cost can be allocated using maintenance hours.

The formula used in the previous worked example can be used here too.

Stores cost to department X:

$$\frac{\text{Total cost in stores}}{\text{Total number of material requisitions}} \times \text{requisitions by department X}$$

$$\frac{2{,}000}{(12{,}000+8{,}000)} \times 12{,}000 = 1{,}200$$

Stores cost to department Y

$$\frac{\text{Total cost in stores}}{\text{Total number of material requisitions}} \times \text{requisitions by department Y}$$

$$\frac{2{,}000}{(12{,}000+8{,}000)} \times 8{,}000 = 800$$

Similar calculations would be made to reapportion the maintenance department costs to X and Y:

Maintenance to X: $\frac{2{,}500}{(500+750)} \times 500 = 1{,}000$

Maintenance to Y: $\frac{2{,}500}{(500+750)} \times 750 = 1{,}500$

In summary then:

Service department	*Basis of apportionment*	*Total cost*	*Dept X*	*Dept Y*
		£	£	£
Stores	Number of requisitions	2,000	1,200	800
Maintenance	Hours	2,500	1,000	1,500
		4,500	2,200	2,300
Previously allocated and apportioned costs		13,000	8,000	5,000
Total overhead		17,500	10,200	7,300

Never forget to include the directly allocated costs when determining overheads to be apportioned.

NOTES

Activity 1 **(30 minutes)**

Pippin Ltd has three production departments (forming, machines and assembly) and two service departments (maintenance and general).

The following is an analysis of budgeted overhead costs for a twelve-month period.

	£	£
Rent and rates		8,000
Power		750
Light, heat		5,000
Repairs, maintenance:		
Forming	800	
Machines	1,800	
Assembly	300	
Maintenance	200	
General	100	
		3,200
Departmental expenses:		
Forming	1,500	
Machines	2,300	
Assembly	1,100	
Maintenance	900	
General	1,500	
		7,300
Depreciation:		
Plant		10,000
Fixtures and fittings		250
Insurance:		
Plant		2,000
Buildings		500
Indirect labour:		
Forming	3,000	
Machines	5,000	
Assembly	1,500	
Maintenance	4,000	
General	2,000	
		15,500
		52,500

Other available data are as follows.

	Floor area	Plant value	Fixtures & fittings	Effective horse-power	Direct cost for year	Labour hours worked	Machine hours worked
	sq.ft	£	£		£		
Forming	2,000	25,000	1,000	40	20,500	14,400	12,000
Machines	4,000	60,000	500	90	30,300	20,500	21,600
Assembly	3,000	7,500	2,000	15	24,200	20,200	2,000
Maintenance	500	7,500	1,000	5	-	-	-
General	500	-	500	-	-	-	-
	10,000	100,000	5,000	150	75,000	55,100	35,600

Using the data provided, apportion overheads to the five departments.

BPP LEARNING MEDIA

NOTES

Activity 2 **(20 minutes)**

Using your solution to Activity 1 and the following information about the apportionment of service department costs, apportion the costs of the two service departments of Pippin Ltd to the three production departments and hence determine the total overhead for those departments.

	Maintenance	*General*
	%	%
Forming	20	30
Machines	50	60
Assembly	30	10
	100	100

3 OVERHEAD ABSORPTION

Having allocated and/or apportioned all overheads, the next stage in absorption costing is to add them to, or **absorb them into**, the cost of production or sales.

(a) **Production overheads** are added to the prime cost (direct materiais, labour and expenses: see Chapter 1, Para 4.2), the total of the two being the factory cost, or full cost of production. Production overheads are therefore included in the value of stocks of finished goods.

(b) **Administration and selling and distribution overheads** are then added, the sum of the factory cost and these overheads being the total cost of sales. These overheads are not however included in the value of closing stock.

3.1 Use of a predetermined absorption rate

Overheads are not absorbed on the basis of the actual overheads incurred but on the basis of estimated or budgeted figures (calculated prior to the beginning of the period). The rate at which overheads are included in cost of sales (**absorption rate**) is predetermined before the accounting period actually begins for a number of reasons.

(a) Goods are produced and sold throughout the year, but many actual overheads are not known until the end of the year. It would be inconvenient to wait until the year end in order to decide what overhead costs should be.

(b) An attempt to calculate overhead costs more regularly (such as each month) is possible, although estimated costs must be added for occasional expenditures such as rent and rates (incurred once or twice a year). The difficulty with this approach would be that actual overheads from month to month would fluctuate randomly; therefore, overhead costs charged to production would depend to a certain extent on random events and changes. A unit made in one month might be charged with £4 of overhead, in a subsequent month with £5, and in a third month with £4.50. Only units made in winter would be charged with the heating overhead. Such changes are considered misleading for costing purposes and administratively and clerically inconvenient to deal with.

(c) Similarly, production output might vary each month. For example actual overhead costs might be £20,000 per month and output might vary from, say, 1,000 units to 20,000 units per month. The unit rate for overhead would be £20 and £1 per unit respectively, which would again lead to administration and control problems.

3.2 Predetermination

Overhead absorption rates are therefore predetermined as follows.

(a) The overhead **likely to be incurred** during the coming year is estimated.

(b) The total hours, units, or direct costs on which the overhead absorption rates are to be based (activity level) are estimated.

(c) The estimated overhead is divided by the budgeted activity level to arrive at an absorption rate.

3.3 Selecting the appropriate absorption base

There are a number of different **bases of absorption** (or 'overhead recovery rates') which can be used. Examples are as follows.

- A percentage of direct materials cost
- A percentage of direct labour cost
- A percentage of prime cost
- A rate per machine hour
- A rate per direct labour hour
- A rate per unit

The choice of an absorption basis is a matter of judgement and common sense. There are no strict rules or formulae involved, although factors which should be taken into account are set out below. What is required is an absorption basis which realistically reflects the characteristics of a given cost centre and which avoids undue anomalies.

It is safe to assume, for example, that the overhead costs for producing brass screws are similar to those for producing steel screws. The cost of brass is, however, very much greater than that of steel. Consequently, the overhead charge for brass screws would be too high and that for steel screws too low, if a percentage of cost of materials rate were to be used.

Using prime cost as the absorption base would lead to anomalies because of the inclusion of the cost of material, as outlined above.

If the overhead actually attributable to units was incurred on, say a time basis, but one highly-paid employee was engaged on producing one item, while a lower-paid employee was producing another item, the overhead charged to the first item using a percentage of wages rate might be too high while the amount absorbed by the second item might be too low. This method should therefore only be used if similar wage rates are paid to all direct employees in a production department. A direct labour hour rate might be considered 'fairer'.

It is for this reason that many factories use a **direct labour hour rate** or **machine hour rate** in preference to a rate based on a percentage of direct materials cost, wages or prime cost.

(a) A **direct labour** hour basis is most appropriate in a **labour intensive** environment.

(b) A **machine hour** rate would be used in departments where production is controlled or dictated by **machines.** This basis is becoming more appropriate as factories become more heavily automated.

A rate per unit would be effective only if all units were identical.

WORKED EXAMPLE: OVERHEAD ABSORPTION

The budgeted production overheads and other budget data of Calculator Ltd are as follows.

Budget	*Production dept 1*	*Production dept 2*
Overhead cost	£36,000	£5,000
Direct materials cost	£32,000	
Direct labour cost	£40,000	
Machine hours	10,000	
Direct labour hours	18,000	
Units of production		1,000

Calculate the absorption rate using the various bases of apportionment.

ANSWER

(a) Department 1

(i) Percentage of direct materials cost $\frac{£36,000}{£32,000} \times 100\% = 112.5\%$

(ii) Percentage of direct labour cost $\frac{£36,000}{£40,000} \times 100\% = 90\%$

(iii) Percentage of prime cost $\frac{£36,000}{£72,000} \times 100\% = 50\%$

Prime cost = direct materials + direct labour = 32,000 + 40,000 = £72,000

(iv) Rate per machine hour $\frac{£36,000}{10,000 \text{ hrs}} = £3.60$ per machine hour

(v) Rate per direct labour hour $\frac{£36,000}{18,000 \text{ hrs}} = £2$ per direct labour hour

(b) The department 2 absorption rate will be based on units of output.

$\frac{£5,000}{1,000 \text{ units}} = £5$ per unit produced

3.4 Importance of the basis of absorption

The choice of the basis of absorption is significant in determining the cost of individual units, or jobs, produced. Using the previous example, suppose that an individual product has a material cost of £80, a labour cost of £85, and requires 36 labour hours and 23 machine hours to complete. The overhead cost of the product would vary, depending on the basis of absorption used by the company for overhead recovery.

(a) As a percentage of direct materials cost, the overhead cost would be

112.5% × £80 = £90.00

(b) As a percentage of direct labour cost, the overhead cost would be
90% × £85 = £76.50

(c) As a percentage of prime cost, the overhead cost would be
50% × £165 = £82.50

(d) Using a machine hour basis of absorption, the overhead cost would be
23 hrs × £3.60 = £82.80

(e) Using a labour hour basis, the overhead cost would be 36 hrs × £2 = £72.00

In theory, each basis of absorption would be possible, but the company should choose a basis for its own costs which seems to be 'fairest'. In our example, this choice will be significant in determining the cost of individual products, as the following summary shows, but the **total cost** of production overheads is the budgeted overhead expenditure, no matter what basis of absorption is selected. It is the relative share of overhead costs borne by individual products and jobs which is affected by the choice of overhead absorption basis.

3.5 Summary

A summary of the product costs in the previous example is shown below.

	Basis of overhead recovery				
	Percentage of materials cost	*Percentage of labour cost*	*Percentage of prime cost*	*Machine hours*	*Direct labour hours*
	£	£	£	£	£
Direct material	80	80.00	80.00	80.00	80
Direct labour	85	85.00	85.00	85.00	85
Production overhead	90	76.50	82.50	82.80	72
Total production cost	255	241.50	247.50	247.80	237

Activity 3 **(15 minutes)**

Using your solution to Activity 2 and the following information, determine suitable overhead absorption rates for Pippin Ltd's three production departments.

	Forming	*Machines*	*Assembly*
Budgeted direct labour hours per annum	5,556	790	5,240
Budgeted machine hours per annum	1,350	5,626	147

4 BLANKET ABSORPTION RATES AND DEPARTMENTAL ABSORPTION RATES

Definition

A **blanket overhead absorption rate** is an absorption rate used throughout a factory and for all jobs and units of output irrespective of the department in which they were produced.

For example, if total overheads were £500,000 and there were 250,000 direct machine hours during the period, the **blanket overhead rate** would be £2 per direct machine hour and all jobs passing through the factory would be charged at that rate.

Such a rate is not appropriate, however, if there are a number of departments and jobs do not spend an equal amount of time in each department.

It is argued that if a single factory overhead absorption rate is used, some products will receive a higher overhead charge than they ought 'fairly' to bear, whereas other products will be under-charged. By using a separate absorption rate for each department, charging of overheads will be equitable and the full cost of production of items will be more representative of the cost of the efforts and resources put into making them.

Activity 4 **(5 minutes)**

The following data relate to one year in department A.

Budgeted machine hours	25,000
Actual machine hours	21,875
Budgeted overheads	£350,000
Actual overheads	£320,000

Based on the data above, what is the machine hour absorption rate as conventionally calculated?

5 OVER- AND UNDER-ABSORPTION OF OVERHEADS

5.1 Estimates

The rate of overhead absorption is based on **estimates** (of both numerator and denominator) and it is quite likely that either one or both of the estimates will not agree with what *actually* occurs. Actual overheads incurred will probably be either greater than or less than overheads absorbed into the cost of production.

(a) **Over absorption** means that the overheads charged to the cost of production are greater than the overheads actually incurred.

(b) **Under absorption** means that insufficient overheads have been included in the cost of production.

EXAMPLE

Suppose that the budgeted overhead in a production department is £80,000 and the budgeted activity is 40,000 direct labour hours. The overhead recovery rate (using a direct labour hour basis) would be £2 per direct labour hour.

Actual overheads in the period are, say £84,000 and 45,000 direct labour hours are worked.

	£
Overhead incurred (actual)	84,000
Overhead absorbed (45,000 × £2)	90,000
Over-absorption of overhead	6,000

NOTES

In this example, the cost of produced units or jobs has been charged with £6,000 more than was actually spent. An adjustment to reconcile the overheads charged to the actual overhead is necessary and the over-absorbed overhead will be written as a credit to the **profit and loss account** at the end of the accounting period.

Activity 5 **(10 minutes)**

A company has recorded the following information on overheads for a period.

Budgeted information

	Production departments	
	X	*Y*
Allocated overheads	£4,000	£3,000
Apportioned overheads	£2,500	£2,750
	£6,500	£5,750
Direct labour hours	2,500 hrs	1,000 hrs
Machine hours	300 hrs	5,000 hrs
Actual information		
Actual overheads incurred	£7,300	£4,500
Direct labour hours	2,600 hrs	1,300 hrs
Machine hours	400 hrs	4,800 hrs

Calculate the under- or over-absorption of overheads for each of the production departments.

5.2 The reasons for under-/over-absorbed overhead

The overhead absorption rate is **predetermined from budget estimates** of overhead cost and the expected volume of activity. Under or over recovery or absorption of overhead will occur in the following circumstances.

- Actual overhead costs are different from budgeted overheads.
- The actual activity level is different from the budgeted activity level.
- Both actual overhead costs and actual activity level are different from budget.

WORKED EXAMPLE: UNDER- AND OVER-ABSORPTION OF OVERHEADS

Rioch Havery Ltd is a small company which manufactures two products, A and B, in two production departments, machining and assembly. A canteen is operated as a separate production service department.

The budgeted production and sales in the year to 31 March 20X3 are as follows.

	Product A	*Product B*
Sales price per unit	£50	£70
Sales (units)	2,200	1,400
Production (units)	2,000	1,500
Material cost per unit	£14	£12

BPP LEARNING MEDIA

	Product A Hours per unit	Product B Hours per unit
Direct labour:		
Machining department (£4 per hour)	2	3
Assembly department (£3 per hour)	1	2
Machine hours per unit:		
Machining department	3	4
Assembly department	1/2	

Budgeted production overheads are as follows.

	Machining department	*Assembly department*	*Canteen*	*Total*
	£	£	£	£
Allocated costs	10,000	25,000	12,000	47,000
Apportionment of other general production overheads	26,000	12,000	8,000	46,000
	36,000	37,000	20,000	93,000
Number of employees	30	20	1	51
Floor area (square metres)	5,000	2,000	500	7,500

Required

(a) Calculate an absorption rate for overheads in each production department for the year to 31 March 20X3 and the budgeted cost per unit of products A and B.

(b) Suppose that in the year to 31 March 20X3, 2,200 units of Product A are produced and 1,500 units of Product B. Direct labour hours per unit and machine hours per unit in both departments were as budgeted.

Actual production overheads are as follows.

	Machining department	*Assembly department*	*Canteen*	*Total*
	£	£	£	£
Allocated costs	30,700	27,600	10,000	68,300
Apportioned share of general production overheads	17,000	8,000	5,000	30,000
	47,700	35,600	15,000	98,300

Calculate the under- or over-absorbed overhead in each production department and in total.

ANSWER

(a) **Apportion budgeted overheads**

First we need to apportion budgeted overheads to the two production departments. Canteen costs will be apportioned on the basis of the number of employees in each department. (Direct labour hours in each department are an alternative basis of apportionment, but the number of employees seems to be more directly relevant to canteen costs.)

	Machining department	Assembly department	Total
	£	£	£
Budgeted allocated costs	10,000	25,000	35,000
Share of general overheads	26,000	12,000	38,000
Apportioned canteen costs (30:20)	12,000	8,000	20,000
	48,000	45,000	93,000

Notice when reapportioning the canteen cost we have ignored the number of employees in the canteen. The idea of reapportionment is to remove **all** service centre overheads and share them amongst the production departments on a fair basis. It therefore makes sense to ignore the employee working for the canteen, otherwise costs would remain in the canteen service centre. So costs are shared on the ratio of 30:20.

Choose absorption rates

Since machine time appears to be more significant than labour time in the machining department, a machine hour rate of absorption will be used for overhead recovery in this department. On the other hand, machining is insignificant in the assembly department, and a direct labour hour rate of absorption would seem to be the basis which will give the fairest method of overhead recovery.

	Product A		Product B		Total
Total direct labour hours					
Machining department	2 × 2,000	+	3 × 1,500	=	8,500 hours
Assembly department	1 × 2,000	+	2 × 1,500	=	5,000 hours
Total machine hours					
Machining department	3 × 2,000	+	4 × 1,500	=	12,000 hours
Assembly department	½ × 2,000			=	1,000 hours

	Direct labour hours	Machine hours	
Machining	8,500	12,000	Machine intensive
Assembly	5,000	1,000	Labour intensive

Calculate overhead absorption rates

The overhead absorption rates are predetermined, using budgeted estimates. Since the overheads are production overheads, the budgeted activity relates to the volume of production, in units (the production hours required for volume of sales being irrelevant).

	Product A	Product B	Total
Budgeted production (units)	2,000	1,500	
Machining department:			
machine hours	6,000 hrs	6,000 hrs	12,000 hrs
Assembly department:			
direct labour hours	2,000 hrs	3,000 hrs	5,000 hrs

The overhead absorption rates will be as follows.

	Machining department	Assembly department
Budgeted overheads	£48,000	£45,000
Budgeted activity	12,000 hrs	5,000 hrs
Absorption rate	£4 per machine hour	£9 per direct labour hour

Determine a budgeted cost per unit

The budgeted cost per unit would be as follows.

	Product A		Product B	
	£	£	£	£
Direct materials		14		12
Direct labour:				
Machining department (@ £4/hr)	8		12	
Assembly department (@ £3/hr)	3		6	
		11		18
Prime cost		25		30
Production overhead:				
Machining department (@£4/machine hr)	12		16	
Assembly department (@ £9/direct labour hr)	9		18	
		21		34
Full production cost		46		64

(b) **Apportion actual service department overhead to production departments**

When the actual costs are analysed, the 'actual' overhead of the canteen department (£15,000) would be split between the machining and assembly departments.

	Machining department	*Assembly department*	*Total*
	£	£	£
Allocated cost	30,700	27,600	58,300
Apportioned general overhead	17,000	8,000	25,000
Canteen (30:20) (as before)	9,000	6,000	15,000
	56,700	41,600	98,300

Establish the over- or under-absorption of overheads

There would be an over- or under-absorption of overheads as follows.

		Machining department		*Assembly department*	*Total*
		£		£	£
Overheads absorbed					
Product A (2,200 units)	(× £4 × 3hrs)	26,400	(× £9 × 1hr)	19,800	46,200
Product B (1,500 units)	(× £4 × 4hrs)	24,000	(× £9 × 2hrs)	27,000	51,000
		50,400		46,800	97,200
Overheads incurred		56,700		41,600	98,300
Over-/(under)-absorbed overhead		(6,300)		5,200	(1,100)

The total under-absorbed overhead of £1,100 will be written off to the profit and loss account at the end of the year, to compensate for the fact that overheads charged to production (£97,200) were less than the overheads actually incurred (£98,300).

5.3 Recording the under-/over-absorbed overheads in the profit and loss account

Once the under-/over-absorbed overheads have been calculated the amount is recorded in the profit and loss account under cost of sales.

6 ACTIVITY BASED COSTING

Absorption costing appears to be a relatively straightforward way of adding overhead costs to units of production using, more often than not, a volume-related absorption basis (such as direct labour hours or direct machine hours). The assumption that all overheads are related primarily to production volume is implied in this system. Absorption costing was developed at a time when most organisations produced only a narrow range of products and when overhead costs were only a very small fraction of total costs, direct labour and direct material costs accounting for the largest proportion of the costs. Errors made in adding overheads to products were therefore not too significant.

6.1 Development

Nowadays, however, with the advent of **advanced manufacturing technology**, overheads are likely to be far more important and, in fact, direct labour may account for as little as 5% of a product's cost. Moreover, there has been an increase in the costs of **non-volume related support activities**, such as setting-up, production scheduling, inspection and data processing, which assist the efficient manufacture of a wide range of products. These overheads are not, in general, affected by changes in production volume. They tend to vary in the long term according to the **range and complexity** of the products manufactured rather than the volume of output.

Because traditional absorption costing methods tend to allocate too great a proportion of overheads to high volume products (which cause relatively little diversity), and too small a proportion of overheads to low volume products (which cause greater diversity and therefore use more support services), alternative methods of costing have been developed. **Activity based costing (ABC)** is one such development.

6.2 The major ideas behind activity based costing

These are:

(a) **Activities cause costs**. Activities include ordering, materials handling, machining, assembly, production scheduling and despatching.

(b) **Products create demand for the activities.**

(c) Costs are assigned to products **on the basis of a product's consumption of the activities.**

6.3 Outline of an ABC system

An ABC costing system operates as follows.

Step 1. Identify an organisation's major activities.

Step 2. Identify the factors which determine the size of the costs of an activity/cause the costs of an activity. These are known as **cost drivers**. Look at the following examples.

Activity	*Possible cost driver*
Ordering	Number of orders
Materials handling	Number of production runs
Production scheduling	Number of production runs
Despatching	Number of despatches

For those costs that vary with production levels in the short term, ABC uses **volume-related cost drivers** such as labour or machine hours. The cost of oil used as a lubricant on the machines would therefore be added to products on the basis of the number of machine hours since oil would have to be used for each hour the machine ran.

Step 3. Collect the costs of each activity into what are known as **cost pools** (equivalent to cost centres under more traditional costing methods).

Step 4. Charge support overheads to products on the basis of their usage of the activity. A product's usage of an activity is measured by the number of the activity's cost driver it generates.

Suppose, for example, that the cost pool for the ordering activity totalled £100,000 and that there were 10,000 orders (the cost driver). Each product would therefore be charged with £10 for each order it required. A batch requiring five orders would therefore be charged with £50 as its share of the ordering costs for the period.

6.4 Comparison with absorption costing

Absorption costing and **ABC** are similar in many respects. In both systems, direct costs go straight to the product and overheads are allocated to production cost centres/cost pools. The difference lies in the manner in which overheads are absorbed into products.

- **Absorption costing** most commonly uses two **absorption bases** (labour hours and/or machine hours) to charge overheads to products.
- **ABC** uses many **cost drivers** as absorption bases (number of orders, number of despatches and so on).

Absorption rates under ABC should therefore be more closely linked to the causes of overhead costs and hence product costs should be more realistic, especially where support overheads are high.

NOTES

Chapter roundup

- Product costs are built up using absorption costing by a process of allocation, apportionment and absorption.
- The absorption rate is calculated by dividing the budgeted overhead by the budgeted level of activity. For production overheads, the level of activity is often budgeted direct labour hours or budgeted machine hours.
- Management should try to establish an absorption rate that provides a reasonably 'accurate' estimate of overhead costs for jobs, products or services.
- Under- or over-absorbed overhead is inevitable in estimates of absorption costing because the predetermined overhead absorption rates are based on estimates of overhead expenditure and the level, or volume, of activity.
- If overheads absorbed exceed overheads incurred, the cost of production (or sales) will have been too high. The amount of over absorption will be written as a 'favourable' adjustment to the profit and loss account. Similarly, if overheads absorbed are lower than the amount of overheads incurred, the cost of production (or sales) will have been too low. The amount of under absorption will be written as an 'adverse' adjustment to the profit and loss account.
- Activity based costing (ABC) is an alternative to the more traditional absorption costing. ABC involves the identification of the factors (cost drivers) which cause the costs of an organisation's major activities. Support overheads are charged to products on the basis of their usage of an activity.

Quick quiz

1 What is overhead allocation?

2 What basis might be applied to apportion heat and light?

3 What is service cost centre cost apportionment?

4 Why is it common to use *predetermined* overhead absorption rates?

5 What is the problem with using a single factory overhead absorption rate?

6 Why does under- or over-absorbed overhead occur?

7 What is a cost driver?

8 What is a cost pool?

Answers to quick quiz

1 Overhead allocation is the process of charging a cost, in full, directly to a cost centre. (see para 1.2)

2 Volume of space occupied is an appropriate basis for the apportionment of heat and light. (para 2.2)

BPP LEARNING MEDIA

3 Service cost centre cost apportionment is the apportionment of costs allocated or apportioned to a service cost centre to production cost centres directly involved in the production of cost units. (para 2.3)

4 Overhead absorption rates are often predetermined as this avoids two problems.

The value of overheads to be apportioned may not be known until the end of the year, but the cost of the cost unit needs to be ascertained as they are being produced and sold.

Costs and output vary, with a resulting variability in unit cost. This is unhelpful for costing, administration and control purposes. (para 3.1)

5 A single overhead absorption rate will charge unfair amounts of overheads to products unless the product range is homogeneous. A misleading cost will then result. (para 4)

6 Under- and over-absorption of overheads occur because estimates are used of costs and output in the calculation of an overhead absorption rate. The actual overhead costs and activity levels are unlikely to be the same as the estimates. (paras 5.1-5.2)

7 A cost driver is a factor that causes a cost and determines the size of the cost of a major activity in a business. (para 6.3)

8 A cost pool is a collection of all the costs of an activity. (para 6.3)

Answers to activities

1

	Basis	Forming	Machines	Assembly	Maint'nce	General	Total
		£	£	£	£	£	£
Directly allocated overheads:							
Repairs, maintenance	Note 1	800	1,800	300	200	100	3,200
Departmental expenses	Note 1	1,500	2,300	1,100	900	1,500	7,300
Indirect labour	Note 1	3,000	5,000	1,500	4,000	2,000	15,500
Apportionment of other overheads:							
Rent, rates	1	1,600	3,200	2,400	400	400	8,000
Power	2	200	450	75	25	0	750
Light, heat	1	1,000	2,000	1,500	250	250	5,000
Dep'n of plant	3	2,500	6,000	750	750	0	10,000
Dep'n of F & F	4	50	25	100	50	25	250
Insurance of plant	3	500	1,200	150	150	0	2,000
Insurance of buildings	1	100	200	150	25	25	500
Note 2		11,250	22,175	8,025	6,750	4,300	52,500

Basis of apportionment:

1 floor area
2 effective horsepower
3 plant value
4 fixtures and fittings value

NOTES

Notes:

1 Some of the overheads have already been attributed or allocated to a specific department. These costs should just be recorded in that department.

2 Do not forget to include the allocated costs in this total.

2 Maintenance costs are reapportioned using the percentages given so 20% goes to forming, 50% to machines and 30% to assembly.

Forming $6,750 \times 20\% = 1,350$
Machines $6,750 \times 50\% = 3,375$
Assembly $6,750 \times 30\% = 2,025$

Similarly for general.

Service department	*Basis of apportionment*	*Total cost*	*Forming*	*Machines*	*Assembly*
		£	£	£	£
Maintenance	2:5:3	6,750	1,350	3,375	2,025
General	3:6:1	4,300	1,290	2,580	430
		11,050	2,640	5,955	2,455
Previously allocated and apportioned costs		41,450	11,250	22,175	8,025
Total overhead		52,500	13,890	28,130	10,480

3

Forming (labour intensive) $\frac{£13,890}{5,556}$ = £2.50 per direct labour hour

Machines (machine intensive) $\frac{£28,130}{5,626}$ = £5 per machine hour

Assembly (labour intensive) $\frac{£10,480}{5,240}$ = £2 per direct labour hour

Note. Since there are more labour hours than machine hours in the forming department this would be considered a labour intensive department thus an overhead absorption rate per direct labour hour is used.

In the machines department there are considerably more machine hours than labour hours So, being a machine intensive department a machine hour overhead absorption rate is used.

Assembly is clearly labour intensive as the direct labour hours are far more than the machine hours and so a direct labour hour rate is used to absorb overheads.

4 Overhead absorption rate $= \frac{\text{Budgeted overheads}}{\text{Budgeted machine hours}} = \frac{£350,000}{25,000}$

= £14 per machine hour

BPP LEARNING MEDIA

NOTES

5 **Production Department X**

Overhead absorption rate will be based on direct labour hours

$$\text{OAR} = \frac{£6,500}{2,500 \text{ hours}} = £2.60/\text{labour hour}$$

	£
Actual overheads	7,300
Absorbed overheads 2,600 × £2.60	6,760
Under absorbed	540

Production Department Y

Overhead absorption rate will be based on machine hours

$$\text{OAR} = \frac{£5,750}{5,000 \text{ hours}} = £1.15/\text{machine hour}$$

	£
Actual overheads	4,500
Absorbed overheads 4,800 × £1.15	5,520
Over absorbed	1,020

BPP LEARNING MEDIA

Chapter 4 :

MARGINAL AND ABSORPTION COSTING

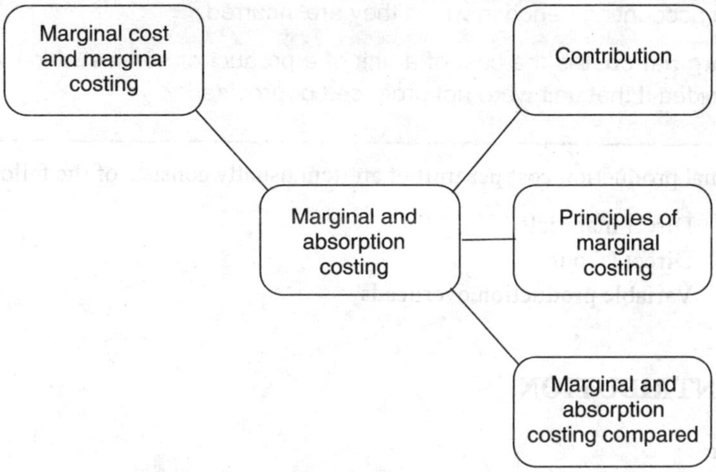

Introduction

In an earlier chapter we introduced the idea of **product costs** and **period costs. Product costs** are costs identified with goods produced or purchased for resale. Such costs are initially identified as part of the value of stock and only become expenses when the stock is sold. In contrast, **period costs** are costs that are deducted as expenses during the current period without ever being included in the value of stock held. In the previous chapter we saw how product costs are absorbed into the cost of units of output.

This chapter describes **marginal costing** and compares it with **absorption costing**. Whereas absorption costing recognises fixed costs (usually fixed production costs) as part of the cost of a unit of output and hence as product costs, marginal costing treats all fixed costs as period costs. Two such different costing methods obviously each have their supporters and we will be looking at the arguments both in favour of and against each method. Each costing method, because of the different stock valuation used, produces a different profit figure and we will be looking at this particular point in detail.

Your objectives

In this chapter you will learn about the following.

- Marginal cost and marginal costing
- Contribution
- The principles of marginal costing
- The differences between marginal costing and absorption costing

1 MARGINAL COSTING AND MARGINAL COST

Definitions

- **Marginal costing** is an alternative method of costing to absorption costing. In marginal costing, only variable costs are charged as a cost of sales and a contribution is calculated which is sales revenue minus the variable cost of sales. Closing stocks of work in progress or finished goods are valued at marginal (variable) production cost. Fixed costs are treated as a period cost, and are charged in full to the profit and loss account of the accounting period in which they are incurred.
- **Marginal cost** is the cost of a unit of a product or service which would be avoided if that unit were not produced or provided.

The marginal production cost per unit of an item usually consists of the following.

- Direct materials
- Direct labour
- Variable production overheads

2 CONTRIBUTION

Definition

Contribution is the difference between sales value and the marginal cost of sales.

Contribution is of fundamental importance in marginal costing, and the term 'contribution' is really short for 'contribution towards covering fixed overheads and making a profit'.

3 THE PRINCIPLES OF MARGINAL COSTING

The principles of marginal costing are as follows.

(a) Period fixed costs are the same for any volume of sales and production (provided that the level of activity is within the 'relevant range'). Therefore, by selling an extra item of product or service the following will happen.

(i) Revenue will increase by the sales value of the item sold.

(ii) Costs will increase by the variable cost per unit.

(iii) Profit will increase by the amount of contribution earned from the extra item.

(b) Similarly, if the volume of sales falls by one item, the profit will fall by the amount of contribution earned from the item.

(c) Profit measurement should therefore be based on an analysis of total contribution. Since fixed costs relate to a period of time, and do not change with increases or decreases in sales volume, it is misleading to charge units of sale with a share of fixed costs. Absorption costing is therefore

NOTES

misleading, and it is more appropriate to deduct fixed costs from total contribution for the period to derive a profit figure.

(d) When a unit of product is made, the extra costs incurred in its manufacture are the **variable production costs.** Fixed costs are unaffected, and no extra fixed costs are incurred when output is increased. It is therefore argued that the valuation of closing stocks should be at variable production cost (direct materials, direct labour, direct expenses (if any) and variable production overhead) because these are the only costs properly attributable to the product.

Before explaining marginal costing principles any further, it will be helpful to look at a numerical example.

WORKED EXAMPLE: MARGINAL COSTING

Water Ltd makes a product, the Splash, which has a variable production cost of £6 per unit and a sales price of £10 per unit. At the beginning of September 20X4, there were no opening stocks and production during the month was 20,000 units. Fixed costs for the month were £45,000 (production, administration, sales and distribution). There were no variable marketing costs.

Required

Calculate the contribution and profit for September 20X4, using marginal costing principles, if sales were as follows.

(a) 10,000 Splashes
(b) 15,000 Splashes
(c) 20,000 Splashes

ANSWER

The first stage in the profit calculation must be to identify the variable costs, and then the contribution. Fixed costs are deducted from the total contribution to derive the profit. All closing stocks are valued at marginal production cost (£6 per unit).

	10,000 Splashes		*15,000 Splashes*		*20,000 Splashes*	
	£	£	£	£	£	£
Sales (at £10)		100,000		150,000		200,000
Opening stock	0		0		0	
Variable production cost	120,000		120,000		120,000	
	120,000		120,000		120,000	
Less value of closing stock (at marginal cost)	60,000		30,000		-	
Variable cost of sales		60,000		90,000		120,000
Contribution		40,000		60,000		80,000
Less fixed costs		45,000		45,000		45,000
Profit/(loss)		(5,000)		15,000		35,000
Profit/(loss) per unit		£(0.50)		£1		£1.75
Contribution per unit		£4		£4		£4

BPP LEARNING MEDIA

NOTES

Conclusions

Note. Closing stock figures are calculated as production minus sales units, so at sales of 10,000 Splashes closing stock would be 10,000 units as 20,000 units were produced. At sales of 15,000 units, 5,000 units will be left in stock at the end of the month. If sales are for 20,000 units then all units produced are sold and no stocks remain.

The conclusions which may be drawn from this example are as follows.

(a) The **profit per unit varies** at differing levels of sales, because the average fixed overhead cost per unit changes with the volume of output and sales.

(b) The **contribution per unit is constant** at all levels of output and sales. Total contribution, which is the contribution per unit multiplied by the number of units sold, increases in direct proportion to the volume of sales.

(c) Since the **contribution per unit does not change,** the most effective way of calculating the expected profit at any level of output and sales would be as follows.

(i) First calculate the total contribution.
(ii) Then deduct fixed costs as a period charge in order to find the profit.

(d) In our example the expected profit from the sale of 17,000 Splashes would be as follows.

	£
Total contribution (17,000 × £4)	68,000
Less fixed costs	45,000
Profit	23,000

3.1 Summary

(a) If total contribution exceeds fixed costs, a profit is made.

(b) If total contribution exactly equals fixed costs, no profit and no loss is made and breakeven point is reached.

(c) If total contribution is less than fixed costs, there will be a loss.

Activity 1 **(10 minutes)**

Plumber Ltd makes two products, the Loo and the Wash. Information relating to each of these products for April 20X4 is as follows.

	Loo		*Wash*
Opening stock	nil		nil
Production (units)	15,000		6,000
Sales (units)	10,000		5,000
	£		£
Sales price per unit	20		30
Unit costs			
Direct materials	8		14
Direct labour	4		2
Variable production overhead	2		1
Variable sales overhead	2		3
Total variable costs per unit	16		20
Fixed costs for the month		£	
Production costs		40,000	
Administration costs		15,000	
Sales and distribution costs		25,000	

Using marginal costing principles, calculate the profit in April 20X4. Use the approach set out in the conclusions above.

4 MARGINAL COSTING AND ABSORPTION COSTING COMPARED

Marginal costing as a cost accounting system is significantly different from absorption costing. It is an **alternative method** of accounting for costs and profit, which rejects the principles of absorbing fixed overheads into unit costs.

4.1 Marginal costing

In marginal costing

(a) Closing stocks are valued at **marginal production cost**.

(b) Fixed costs are charged in full against the profit of the period in which they are incurred.

4.2 Absorption costing

In absorption costing (sometimes referred to as **full costing**)

(a) Closing stocks are valued at full production cost, and include a share of fixed production costs.

(b) This means that the cost of sales in a period will include some fixed overhead incurred in a previous period (in opening stock values) and will exclude some fixed overhead incurred in the current period but carried forward in closing stock values as a charge to a subsequent accounting period.

This distinction between marginal costing and absorption costing is very important and the contrast between the systems must be clearly understood. Work carefully through the following example to ensure that you are familiar with both methods.

WORKED EXAMPLE: MARGINAL AND ABSORPTION COSTING COMPARED

Two Left Feet Ltd manufactures a single product, the Claud. The following figures relate to the Claud for a one-year period.

Activity level		50%	100%
Sales and production (units)		400	800
		£	£
Sales		8,000	16,000
Production costs:	variable	3,200	6,400
	fixed	1,600	1,600
Sales and distribution costs:			
	variable	1,600	3,200
	fixed	2,400	2,400

The normal level of activity for the year is 800 units. Fixed costs are incurred evenly throughout the year, and actual fixed costs are the same as budgeted.

There were no stocks of Claud at the beginning of the year.

In the first quarter, 220 units were produced and 160 units sold.

(a) Calculate the fixed production costs absorbed by Clauds in the first quarter if absorption costing is used.

(b) Calculate the under/over recovery of overheads during the quarter.

(c) Calculate the profit using absorption costing.

(d) Calculate the profit using marginal costing.

(e) Explain why there is a difference between the answers to (c) and (d).

ANSWER

(a) $\dfrac{\text{Budgeted fixed production costs}}{\text{Budgeted output (normal level of activity)}} = \dfrac{£1{,}600}{800 \text{ units}}$

Absorption rate = £2 per unit produced.

During the quarter, the fixed production overhead absorbed was 220 units × £2 = £440.

(b)

	£
Actual fixed production overhead	400 (¼ of £1,600)
Absorbed fixed production overhead	440
Over absorption of overhead	40

(c) Profit for the quarter, absorption costing

	£	£
Sales (160 × £20)		3,200
Production costs		
Variable (220 × £8)	1,760	
Fixed (absorbed overhead (220 × £2))	440	
Total (220 × £10)	2,200	
Less closing stocks (60 × £10)	600	
Production cost of sales	1,600	
Adjustment for over-absorbed overhead	40	
Total production costs		1,560
Gross profit		1,640
Less: sales and distribution costs		
variable (160 × £4)	640	
fixed (1/4 of £2,400)	600	
		1,240
Net profit		400

(d) Profit for the quarter, marginal costing

	£	£
Sales		3,200
Variable production costs	1,760	
Less closing stocks (60 × £8)	480	
Variable production cost of sales	1,280	
Variable sales and distribution costs (Note)	640	
Total variable costs of sales		1,920
Total contribution		1,280
Less:		
Fixed production costs incurred	400	
Fixed sales and distribution costs	600	
		1,000
Net profit		280

Note. Variable sales and distribution costs will be based on units **sold** not produced.

(e) The difference in profit is due to the different valuations of closing stock. In absorption costing, the 60 units of closing stock include absorbed fixed overheads of £120 (60 × £2), which are therefore costs carried over to the next quarter and not charged against the profit of the current quarter. In marginal costing, all fixed costs incurred in the period are charged against profit.

	£
Absorption costing profit	400
Fixed production costs carried forward in stock values (60 × £2)	120
Marginal costing profit	280

4.3 Conclusions

We can draw a number of conclusions from this example.

(a) **Marginal costing** and **absorption costing** are different techniques for assessing profit in a period.

(b) If there are **changes in stocks during a period, marginal costing and absorption costing give different results for profit obtained.**

(i) **If stock levels increase, absorption costing will report the higher profit** because some of the fixed production overhead incurred during the period will be carried forward in closing stock (which reduces cost of sales) to be set against sales revenue in the following period instead of being written off in full against profit in the period concerned (as in the example above).

(ii) **If stock levels decrease, absorption costing will report the lower profit** because as well as the fixed overhead incurred, fixed production overhead which had been brought forward in opening stock is released and is included in cost of sales.

(c) If the opening and closing stock volumes and values are the same, marginal costing and absorption costing will give the same profit figure.

(d) In the long run, total profit for a company will be the same whether marginal costing or absorption costing is used because in the long run, total costs will be the same by either method of accounting. Different accounting conventions merely affect the profit of individual accounting periods.

Activity 2 **(10 minutes)**

The overhead absorption rate for product X is £10 per machine hour. Each unit of product X requires five machine hours. Stock of product X on 1.1.X1 was 150 units and on 31.12.X1 it was 100 units. What is the difference in profit between results reported using absorption costing and results reported using marginal costing?

EXAMPLE: COMPARISON OF TOTAL PROFITS

Let us suppose that a company makes and sells a single product. At the beginning of period 1, there are no opening stocks of the product, for which the variable production cost is £4 and the sales price £6 per unit. Fixed costs are £2,000 per period, of which £1,500 are fixed production costs.

	Period 1	*Period 2*
Sales	1,200 units	1,800 units
Production	1,500 units	1,500 units

What would the profit be in each period using the following methods of costing?

(a) Absorption costing. Assume normal output is 1,500 units per period.

(b) Marginal costing.

ANSWER

It is important to notice that although production and sales volumes in each period are different (and therefore the profit for each period by absorption costing will be different from the profit by marginal costing), over the full period, total production equals sales volume, the total cost of sales is the same, and therefore the total profit is the same by either method of accounting.

(a) **Absorption costing: the absorption rate for fixed production overhead is**

$$\frac{£1,500}{1,500 \text{ units}} = £1 \text{ per unit}$$

	Period 1		*Period 2*		*Total*	
	£	£	£	£	£	£
Sales (× £6)		7,200		10,800		18,000
Opening stock	-		1,500		-	
Production costs						
Variable (× £4)	6,000		6,000		12,000	
Fixed	1,500		1,500		3,000	
	7,500		9,000		15,000	
Less closing stock c/f	1,500		-		-	
Production cost of sales	6,000		9,000		15,000	
(Under-)/over-absorbed overhead (*Note*)	-		-		-	
Total production costs		6,000		9,000		15,000
Gross profit		1,200		1,800		3,000
Other costs		500		500		1,000
Net profit		700		1,300		2,000

Note. **As actual production is the same as the normal output there will not be any under or over absorption of overheads.**

(b) **Marginal costing**

	Period 1		*Period 2*		*Total*	
	£	£	£	£	£	£
Sales		7,200		10,800		18,000
Opening stock	-		1,200		-	
Variable production cost	6,000		6,000		12,000	
	6,000		7,200		12,000	
Less closing stock c/f	1,200		-		-	
Variable production cost of sales		4,800		7,200		12,000
Contribution		2,400		3,600		6,000
Fixed costs		2,000		2,000		4,000
Profit		400		1,600		2,000

Note that the total profit over the two periods is the same for each method of costing, but the profit in each period is different.

Activity 3 **(10 minutes)**

When opening stocks were 8,500 litres and closing stocks 6,750 litres, a firm had a profit of £62,100 using marginal costing.

Assuming that the fixed overhead absorption rate was £3 per litre, what would be the profit using absorption costing?

4.4 Marginal costing and absorption costing compared: which is better?

There are accountants who favour each costing method.

(a) Arguments in favour of **absorption costing** are as follows.

- (i) Fixed production costs are incurred in order to make output; it is therefore 'fair' to charge all output with a share of these costs.
- (ii) Closing stock values, by including a share of fixed production overhead, will be valued on the principle required for the financial accounting valuation of stocks by SSAP 9.
- (iii) A problem with calculating the contribution of various products made by a company is that it may not be clear whether the contribution earned by each product is enough to cover fixed costs, whereas by charging fixed overhead to a product it is possible to ascertain whether it is profitable or not.

(b) Arguments in favour of **marginal costing** are as follows.

- (i) It is simple to operate.
- (ii) There are no apportionments, which are frequently done on an arbitrary basis, of fixed costs. Many costs, such as the managing director's salary, are indivisible by nature.
- (iii) Fixed costs will be the same regardless of the volume of output, because they are period costs. It makes sense, therefore, to charge them in full as a cost to the period.
- (iv) The cost to produce an extra unit is the variable production cost. It is realistic to value closing stock items at this directly attributable cost.
- (v) Under or over absorption of overheads is avoided.
- (vi) Marginal costing information can be used for decision making but absorption costing information is not suitable for decision making.
- (vii) Fixed costs (such as depreciation, rent and salaries) relate to a period of time and should be charged against the revenues of the period in which they are incurred.

NOTES

Activity 4 **(20 minutes)**

Kanga Ltd manufactures a single product, the Roo. Details on the product are given below.

	Roo
	£
Selling price	25
Unit costs	
Direct materials	5
Direct labour	6
Variable production overhead	2
Variable sales overhead	1

Budgeted production for period 500 units

Fixed costs for the month are given below.

	Budgeted costs	*Actual costs*
	£	£
Production overhead	1,500	1,700
Administration costs	900	800
Selling costs	500	625

Budgeted sales for the period were 400 units although actual sales were 500 units. There was no opening stock and actual production for the month was 600 units.

(a) Calculate the net profit using absorption costing.
(b) Calculate the net profit using marginal costing.
(c) Explain the difference between (a) and (b).

BPP LEARNING MEDIA

Chapter roundup

- Absorption costing is most often used for routine profit reporting and must be used for financial accounting purposes. Marginal costing provides better management information for planning and decision making.
- Marginal cost is the variable cost of one unit of product or service (the cost which would be avoided if that unit were not produced).
- Contribution is an important measure in marginal costing, and it is calculated as the difference between sales value and marginal or variable cost.
- In marginal costing, fixed production costs are treated as period costs and are written off as they are incurred. In absorption costing, fixed production costs are absorbed into the cost of units and are carried forward in stock to be charged against sales for the next period. Stock values using absorption costing are therefore greater than those calculated using marginal costing.
- Reported profit figures using marginal costing or absorption costing will differ if there is any change in the level of stocks in the period. If production is equal to sales, there will be no difference in calculated profits using these costing methods.

Quick quiz

1 Define contribution.

2 How are stocks valued in marginal costing?

3 If opening and closing stock volumes and values are the same, does absorption costing or marginal costing give the higher profit?

4 Describe three arguments in favour of absorption costing.

5 What are the arguments in favour of the use of marginal costing?

Answers to quick quiz

1 Contribution is the difference between sales value and the marginal cost of sales. (see para 2)

2 In marginal costing stocks are valued at variable production cost. (para 3)

3 If there is no change in stocks during a period, both methods will give the same profit. (para 4.3)

4 Arguments for absorption costing.

(i) Fixed costs are incurred in order to make output, therefore it is fair to charge output with a share of these costs.

(ii) Stock valuation which includes a share of fixed production cost complies with SSAP 9.

(iii) The calculation of a profit figure for each product shows which products are profitable. (para 4.4)

5 Arguments for marginal costing.

(i) Simple to operate.

(ii) Avoids the arbitrary apportionment of fixed costs.

(iii) Avoids under- and over-absorption of overheads.

(iv) Information produced can be used for decision-making.

(v) It makes sense to charge fixed costs to the period as they do not change with volume of production.

(vi) Closing stock is valued at its directly attributable cost. (para 4.4)

Answers to Activities

1

	£
Contribution from Loos	
(unit contribution = £20 – £16 = £4 × 10,000)	40,000
Contribution from Washes	
(unit contribution = £30 – £20 = £10 × 5,000)	50,000
Total contribution	90,000
Fixed costs for the period (40,000 + 15,000 + 25,000)	80,000
Profit	10,000

2 The key is the change in the volume of stock. Stock levels have decreased therefore absorption costing will report a lower profit.

The correct answer based on the **change** in stock levels × fixed overhead absorption per unit = (150 – 100) × £10 × 5 = £2,500 lower profit, because stock levels decreased.

3 Stock levels reduced, therefore the absorption costing profit would be lower.

Difference in profit = (8,500 – 6,750) × £3 = £5,250
Absorption costing profit = £62,100 – £5,250 = £56,850

4 (a) Profit for the period using absorption costing.

	£	£
Sales (500 × 25)		12,500
Opening stock	-	
Production costs		
Variable production costs		
(600 × (5 + 6 + 2))	7,800	
Fixed production costs		
$(600 \times \left(\frac{1,500}{500}\right)$ Note	1,800	
	9,600	
Closing stock (100 × 16)	(1,600)	
Production cost of sales	8,000	
Adjustment for over absorption (see below)	(100)	
Total production costs		(7,900)
Gross profit		4,600
Administration costs (actual)		(800)
Selling costs:		
Variable (500 × 1)		(500)
Fixed		(625)
Net profit under absorption costing		2,675

Note. Full cost per unit:

	£
Direct materials	5
Direct labour	6
Variable production overhead	2
Fixed production overhead $\left(\frac{1,500}{500}\right) =$	3
	16

	£
Actual production overheads	1,700
Absorbed production overheads (600 × 3)	1,800
Over absorbed	100

(b) Profit for the period using marginal costing.

	£	£
Sales (500 × 25)		12,500
Opening stock	-	
Production costs		
Variable (600 × (5 + 6 + 2))	7,800	
	7,800	
Closing stock (100 × 13)	(1,300)	
Variable production cost of sales	6,500	
Variable sales and distribution costs (500 × 1)	500	
		(7,000)
Total contribution		5,500
Less: Fixed production overheads	1,700	
Fixed administration costs	800	
Fixed selling costs	625	
		(3,125)
Net profit under marginal costing		2,375

NOTES

(c) The difference in profit is caused by the valuation of stock. Under absorption costing fixed production costs are carried forward in closing stock to the next period whereas under marginal costing these fixed production costs are charged in full to the period.

	£
Absorption costing profit	2,675
Fixed production costs carried forward in stock values (100 × 3)	(300)
Marginal costing profit	2,375

BPP LEARNING MEDIA

Chapter : 5

PRICE, VALUE AND QUALITY

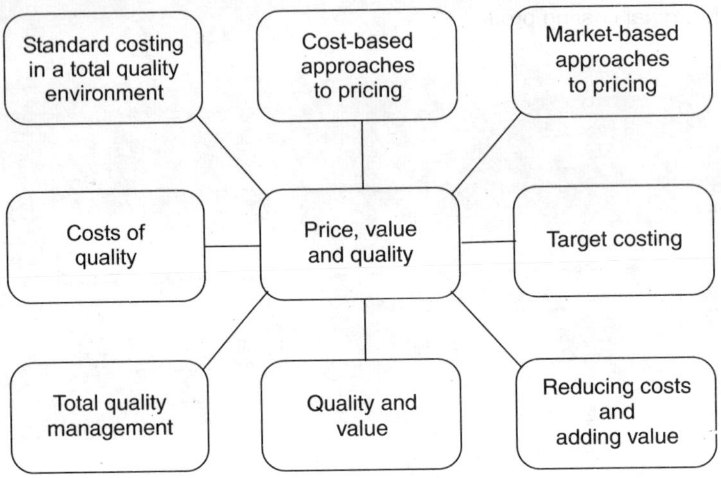

Introduction

Finding the cost of a product or service means, amongst other things, that you have a basis for setting a **selling price** that will earn the business the profit it wants. Recently, however, some businesses have approached the problem from the opposite side: they have decided what the selling price should be in order for the product to sell, and then they deduct the profit they want, which leaves the **target cost**. In this chapter we look at methods of pricing that are based on cost, as well as target costing.

The need to cut costs is something which affects most businesses these days if they want to price their products competitively and remain in business. In this chapter we look at ways in which costs can be reduced and managed. Central to these techniques is the need to maintain and improve **quality** and add **value**.

Your objectives

In this chapter you will learn about the following.

(a) Pricing based on cost

(b) Market-based pricing

(c) Target costing

(d) Cost reduction and value analysis

(e) Total Quality Management

1 COST-BASED APPROACHES TO PRICING

1.1 Full cost-plus pricing

Definition

> **Full cost-plus pricing** is a method of determining the sales price by calculating the full cost of the product and adding a percentage mark-up for profit.

In practice cost is one of the most important influences on price. Many firms base price on simple cost-plus rules (costs are estimated and then a mark-up is added in order to set the price). A traditional approach to pricing is full cost-plus pricing.

The 'full cost' may be a fully absorbed production cost only, or it may include some absorbed administration, selling and distribution overhead.

A business might have an idea of the percentage profit margin it would like to earn, and so might **decide on an average profit mark-up** as a general guideline for pricing decisions. This would be particularly **useful for** businesses that carry out a large amount of **contract work or jobbing work**, for which individual job or contract prices must be quoted regularly to prospective customers. However, the percentage profit **mark-up does not have to be rigid and fixed**, but can be varied to suit the circumstances. In particular, the percentage mark-up can be varied to suit demand conditions in the market.

> **Activity 1** **(5 minutes)**
>
> A product's full cost is £4.70 and is sold at full cost plus 70%.
>
> What is the selling price?

WORKED EXAMPLE: FULL COST-PLUS PRICING

Markup Ltd has begun to produce a new product, Product X, for which the following cost estimates have been made.

	£
Direct materials	27
Direct labour: 4 hrs at £5 per hour	20
Variable production overheads: machining, ½ hr at £6 per hour	3
	50

Fixed production overheads are budgeted at £300,000 per month and, because of the shortage of available machining capacity, the company will be restricted to 10,000 hours of machine time per month. The absorption rate will be a direct labour rate, however, and budgeted direct labour hours are 25,000 per month.

The company wishes to make a profit of 20% on full production cost from product X.

Required

What is the full cost-plus based price?

NOTES

ANSWER

	£
Direct materials	27.00
Direct labour (4 hours)	20.00
Variable production overheads	3.00
Fixed production overheads	
(at $\frac{£300,000}{25,000}$ = £12 per direct labour hour)	48.00
Full production cost	98.00
Profit mark-up (20%)	19.60
Selling price per unit of product X	117.60

Problems with and advantages of full cost-plus pricing

There are several serious **problems** with relying on a full cost approach to pricing.

(a) It **fails to recognise** that demand may be determining price. For many products, the price set will determine the quantity sold. The price we set using this method may not lead to selling the quantity that gives us the biggest profit. In other words, the price we set might not be competitive.

(b) There may be a need to **adjust prices to market and demand conditions.**

(c) **Budgeted output volume** needs to be established. Output volume is a key factor in the overhead absorption rate.

(d) A **suitable basis for overhead absorption** must be selected, especially where a business produces more than one product.

However, it is a **quick, simple and cheap** method of pricing which can be delegated to junior managers (which is particularly important with jobbing work where many prices must be decided and quoted each day) and, since the size of the profit margin can be varied, a decision based on a price in excess of full cost should ensure that a company working at normal capacity will **cover all of its fixed costs and make a profit.**

1.2 Marginal cost-plus pricing

Definition

> **Marginal cost-plus pricing/mark-up pricing** is a method of determining the sales price by adding a profit margin on to either marginal cost of production or marginal cost of sales.

Whereas a full cost-plus approach to pricing draws attention to net profit and the net profit margin, a variable cost-plus approach to pricing **draws attention to gross profit** and the **gross profit margin,** or **contribution.**

BPP LEARNING MEDIA

Activity 2 **(20 minutes)**

A product has the following costs.

	£
Direct materials	5
Direct labour	3
Variable overheads	7

Fixed overheads are £10,000 per month. Budgeted sales per month are 400 units.

What is the mark up on marginal cost if the selling price is £20?

There are several **advantages** of a marginal cost-plus approach to pricing

(a) It is a **simple and easy** method to use.

(b) The **mark-up percentage can be varied**, and so mark-up pricing can be adjusted to reflect demand conditions.

(c) It **draws management attention to contribution**, and the effects of higher or lower sales volumes on profit. In this way, it helps to create a better awareness of the concepts and implications of marginal costing and cost-volume-profit analysis. For example, if a product costs £10 per unit and a mark-up of 150% is added to reach a price of £25 per unit, management should be clearly aware that every additional £1 of sales revenue would add 60 pence to contribution and profit.

(d) In practice, mark-up pricing is used in businesses where there is a readily-identifiable basic variable cost. Retail industries are the most obvious example, and it is quite common for the prices of goods in shops to be fixed by adding a mark-up (20% or 33.3%, say) to the purchase cost.

There are, of course, **drawbacks** to marginal cost-plus pricing.

(a) Although the size of the mark-up can be varied in accordance with demand conditions, it **does not ensure that sufficient attention is paid to demand** conditions, competitors' prices and profit maximisation.

(b) It **ignores fixed overheads** in the pricing decision, but the sales price must be sufficiently high to ensure that a profit is made after covering fixed costs.

1.3 Cost-plus pricing and stock valuation

Many retail businesses price their goods by applying a fixed mark up to their cost. When it comes to stocktaking, it is therefore very convenient to take the selling price of the goods as shown on the price ticket or the price list, and deduct the profit element to arrive at the cost of the goods for stock valuation purposes.

Activity 3 **(5 minutes)**

The price tags on six boxes of cutlery show that the selling price of each is £187.50. The retailer has a uniform mark up on cost of 25%.

What is the cost of the cutlery stock?

2 MARKET-BASED APPROACHES TO PRICING

2.1 Product life cycle

The product life concept is relevant to pricing policy. The concept states that a typical product moves through four stages.

(a) **Introduction**

The product is introduced to the market. Heavy **capital expenditure** will be incurred on product development and perhaps also on the purchase of new fixed assets and building up stocks for sale.

On its introduction to the market, the product will begin to earn some revenue, but initially demand is likely to be small. Potential customers will be unaware of the product or service, and the organisation may have to spend further on **advertising** to bring the product or service to the attention of the market.

(b) **Growth**

The product gains a bigger market as demand builds up. Sales revenues increase and the product begins to make a profit. The initial costs of the **investment** in the new product are gradually **recovered**.

(c) **Maturity**

Eventually, the growth in demand for the product will slow down and it will enter a period of relative maturity. It will continue to be profitable. The product may be **modified or improved, as a means of sustaining its demand.**

(d) **Saturation and decline**

At some stage, the market may reach 'saturation point'. Demand will start to fall. For a while, the product will still be profitable in spite of declining sales, but eventually it will become a **loss-maker** and this is the time when the organisation should decide to stop selling the product or service, and so the product's life cycle should reach its end.

Remember, however, that some mature products will **never decline**: staple food products such as milk or bread are the best example.

Not all products follow this cycle, but it remains a useful tool when considering decisions such as pricing. **The life cycle concept is relevant when considering what pricing policy will be adopted.**

NOTES

2.2 Markets

The price that an organisation can charge for its products will also be influenced by the market in which it operates.

Definitions

- **Perfect competition**: many buyers and many sellers all dealing in an identical product. Neither producer nor user has any market power and both must accept the prevailing market price.
- **Monopoly**: one seller who dominates many buyers. The monopolist can use his market power to set a profit-maximising price.
- **Oligopoly**: relatively few competitive companies dominate the market. Whilst each large firm has the ability to influence market prices, the unpredictable reaction from the other giants makes the final industry price indeterminate.

2.3 Competition

In **established industries** dominated by a few major firms, a price initiative by one firm will usually be countered by a price reaction by competitors. In these circumstances, **prices tend to be stable.**

If a **rival cuts its prices** in the expectation of increasing its market share, a **firm has several options.**

(a) It will **maintain its existing prices** if the expectation is that only a small market share would be lost, so that it is more profitable to keep prices at their existing level. Eventually, the rival firm may drop out of the market or be forced to raise its prices.

(b) It may maintain its prices but respond with a **non-price counter-attack**. This is a more positive response, because the firm will be securing or justifying its current prices with a product change, advertising, or better back-up services.

(c) It may **reduce its prices**. This should protect the firm's market share so that the main beneficiary from the price reduction will be the consumer.

(d) It may **raise its prices** *and respond with a* **non-price counter-attack**. The extra revenue from the higher prices might be used to finance an advertising campaign or product design changes. A price increase would be based on a campaign to emphasise the quality difference between the firm's own product and the rival's product.

2.4 Price leadership

Given that price competition can have disastrous consequences in conditions of oligopoly, it is not unusual to find that large corporations emerge as price leaders. The price leader **indicates to the other firms in the market what the price will be**, and **competitors then set their prices with reference to the leader's price.**

BPP LEARNING MEDIA

2.5 Market penetration pricing

This is a policy of **low prices** when the product is **first launched** in order to obtain sufficient penetration into the market. A penetration policy may be appropriate:

(a) If the firm wishes to **discourage new entrants** into the market.

(b) If the firm wishes to **shorten the initial period of the product's life cycle** in order to enter the growth and maturity stages as quickly as possible.

(c) If there are significant **economies of scale** to be achieved from a high volume of output, so that quick penetration into the market is desirable in order to gain unit cost reductions.

(d) If **demand is likely to increase as prices fall.**

2.6 Market skimming pricing

In contrast, market skimming involves charging **high prices** when a product is **first launched** and **spending heavily on advertising** and sales promotion to obtain sales. As the product moves into the **later stages** of its life cycle (growth, maturity and decline) **progressively lower prices** will be charged. The profitable 'cream' is thus skimmed off in stages until sales can only be sustained at lower prices.

The aim of market skimming is to gain **high unit profits early** in the product's life. High unit prices make it more likely that **competitors** will enter the market than if lower prices were to be charged.

Such a policy is appropriate:

(a) Where the **product is new and different,** so that customers are prepared to pay high prices so as to be one up on other people who do not own it. For example games systems.

(b) Where the strength of **demand** and the sensitivity of demand to price are **unknown**. It is better from the point of view of marketing to start by charging high prices and then reduce them if the demand is insufficient.

(c) Where products may have a **short life cycle**, and so need to recover their development costs and make a profit quickly.

2.7 Differential pricing

In certain circumstances the **same product** can be sold at **different prices** to **different customers.** There are a number of bases on which such prices can be set.

Basis	Example
By **market segment**	A cross-channel ferry company would market its services at different prices in England, Belgium and France, for example. Services such as cinemas and hairdressers are often available at lower prices to old age pensioners and/or juveniles.
By **product version**	Many car models have 'add on' extras which enable one brand to appeal to a wider cross-section of customers. The final price need not reflect the cost price of the add on extras directly: usually the top of the range model would carry a price much in excess of the cost of provision of the extras, as a prestige appeal.

Basis	Example
By place	Theatre seats are usually sold according to their location so that patrons pay different prices for the same performance according to the seat type they occupy.
By time	This is perhaps the most popular type of price discrimination. Railway companies, for example, are successful price discriminators, charging more to rush hour rail commuters whose demand remains the same whatever the price charged at certain times of the day.

2.8 Price and the price elasticity of demand

Economists argue that the higher the price of a good, the lower will be the quantity demanded. We have already seen that in practice it is by no means as straightforward as this (some goods are bought *because* they are expensive, for example), but you know from your personal experience as a consumer that the theory is essentially true.

An important concept in this context is **price elasticity of demand (PED)**.

Definition

> The **price elasticity of demand** measures the extent of change in demand for a good following a change to its price.

Price elasticity (η)is measured as:

$$\frac{\text{\% change in sales demand}}{\text{\% change in sales price}}$$

Demand is said to be **elastic** when a **small change in the price** produces a **large change in the quantity demanded.** The PED is then greater than 1. Demand is said to be **inelastic** when a **small change in the price** produces only a **small change in the quantity demanded.** The PED is then less than 1.

There are two special values of price elasticity of demand.

(a) Demand is **perfectly inelastic (η = 0)**. There is **no change in quantity** demanded, **regardless of the change in price.**

(b) Demand is **perfectly elastic (η = ∞)**. Consumers will want to **buy an infinite amount,** but only **up to a particular price level**. Any price increase above this level will reduce demand to zero.

An awareness of the concept of elasticity can assist management with pricing decisions.

(a) In circumstances of **inelastic demand, prices should be increased** because revenues will increase and total costs will reduce (because quantities sold will reduce).

(b) In circumstances of **elastic demand,** increases in prices will bring decreases in revenue and decreases in price will bring increases in revenue. Management therefore have to **decide whether the increase/decrease in costs will be less than/greater than the increases/decreases in revenue.**

(c) In situations of **very elastic demand**, overpricing can lead to a massive drop in quantity sold and hence a massive drop in profits, whereas underpricing can lead to costly stock outs and, again, a significant drop in profits. **Elasticity must therefore be reduced by creating a customer preference which is unrelated to price** (through advertising and promotional activities).

(d) In situations of **very inelastic demand**, customers are not sensitive to price. **Quality, service, product mix and location are therefore more important** to a firm's pricing strategy.

2.9 The demand-based approach to pricing

Price theory or **demand** theory is based on the idea that a connection can be made between price, quantity demanded and sold, and total revenue. Demand varies with price, and so if an estimate can be made of demand at different price levels, it should be **possible to derive either a profit-maximising price** or a revenue-maximising price.

The theory is dependent on realistic estimates of demand being made at different price levels. Making accurate estimates of demand is often difficult as price is only one of many variables that influence demand. Some larger organisations go to considerable effort to estimate the demand for their products or services at differing price levels by producing estimated demand curves.

For example a large transport authority might be considering an increase in bus fares or underground fares. The effect on total revenues and profit of the increase in fares could be estimated from a knowledge of the demand for transport services at different price levels. If an increase in the price per ticket caused a **large** fall in demand, because demand was price elastic, total revenues and profits would fall whereas a fares increase when demand is price inelastic would boost total revenue, and since a transport authority's costs are largely fixed, this would probably boost total profits too.

Many businesses enjoy something akin to a monopoly position, even in a competitive market. This is because they develop a unique marketing mix, for example a unique combination of price and quality. The significance of a monopoly situation is:

(a) The business does not have to 'follow the market' on price, in other words it is not a 'price-taker', but has more choice and flexibility in the prices it sets.

   (i) At higher prices, demand for its products or services will be less.

   (ii) At lower prices, demand for its products or services will be higher.

(b) There will be a selling price at which the business can maximise its profits.

WORKED EXAMPLE: DEMAND-BASED APPROACH

Moose Ltd sells a product which has a variable cost of £8 per unit. The sales demand at the current sales price of £14 is 3,000 units. It has been estimated by the marketing department that the sales volume would fall by 100 units for each addition of 25 pence to the sales price.

We want to establish whether the current price of £14 is the optimal price which maximises contribution. In order to do this we can look at unit contribution, sales volume and total contribution at different sales prices.

ANSWER

Sales price	*Unit contribution*	*Sales volume*	*Total contribution*
£	£	Units	£
13.00	5.00	3,400	17,000
13.25	5.25	3,300	17,325
13.50	5.50	3,200	17,600
13.75	5.75	3,100	17,825
14.00	*6.00 (14 – 8)*	*3,000*	*18,000*
14.25	6.25	2,900	18,125
14.50	6.50	2,800	18,200
14.75	6.75	2,700	18,225*
15.00	7.00	2,600	18,200

* Contribution would be maximised at a price of £14.75, and sales of 2,700 units.

The current price is not optimal.

3 TARGET COSTING

3.1 The target costing approach

Japanese companies developed target costing as a **response to the problem of controlling and reducing costs over the entire product life cycle**, but **especially** during the **design and development stages**. It has been used successfully **by car manufacturers** in particular, including Toyota and Mercedes Benz.

Target costing requires managers to change the way they think about the relationship between cost, price and profit. The traditional approach is to **develop a product**, **determine the expected standard production cost** of that product and then **set a selling price** (probably **based on cost**), with a **resulting profit or loss**. Costs are **controlled** through **variance analysis** at monthly intervals.

The target costing approach is to **develop a product concept** and the primary specifications for performance and design and then to **determine the price customers would be willing to pay** for that concept. The **desired profit margin** is **deducted from the price, leaving** a figure that represents **total cost**. This is the **target cost**. The product must be capable of being produced for this amount otherwise it will not be manufactured.

During the product's life the **target cost** will be **continuously reviewed and reduced** so that the **price can fall**. Continuous **cost reduction techniques** must therefore be used.

3.2 Achieving the target cost

If the **anticipated product cost** (based on the design specifications) is **above the target cost,** the product must be **modified** so that it is cheaper to produce.

The total target cost can be split into broad cost categories such as development, marketing, manufacturing and so on. A team of designers, engineers, marketing and production staff, as well as the management accountant, should then endeavour to produce a product with planned development, marketing, manufacturing (and so on) costs below the target costs. The cost reduction techniques explored in the next section will need to be used to achieve this.

If any of the target costs cannot be achieved given the product design, other individual targets must be reduced, the product redesigned yet again or scrapped.

4 REDUCING COSTS AND ADDING VALUE

4.1 Cost reduction

Budgetary control and **standard costing** are examples of **cost control techniques.** Cost control is all about **keeping costs within predetermined limits** (usually standard cost). If actual costs differ from planned costs by an excessive amount, cost control action is necessary.

Cost reduction is different. It aims to **reduce costs below a previously accepted level, without adversely affecting the quality of the product** or service being provided.

Significant **cost reduction** can be **achieved** simply by using a **little common sense.** Here are some examples.

(a) **Improve the efficiency of materials usage** by reducing levels of wastage.

(b) **Improve labour productivity** by giving pay incentives or changing work methods to eliminate unnecessary procedures.

(c) **Improve the efficiency of equipment usage** by achieving a better balance between preventive maintenance and machine 'down time' for repairs.

(d) **Reduce material costs** by taking advantage of bulk purchase discounts or by improving stores control.

(e) **Reduce labour costs** by replacing people with machinery or by improving work methods following a work study (see below).

(f) **Save on finance costs** by taking advantage of early payment discounts or reassessing sources of finance.

(g) **Improve control over spending decisions** so that junior managers are not able to commit an organisation without consideration of long-term cost. For example, the hire of two office assistants at wages of £200 per week each would cost £200,000 over a ten-year period. Such a decision might be taken by an office manager whereas the purchase of a piece of machinery for the same cost would probably need board authorisation.

Activity 4 **(10 minutes)**

How can wastage be reduced?

A successful **cost reduction programme** will **cover all aspects** of an organisation's activities, systems and products and will be **supported by senior management**.

As well as the common sense ways of reducing costs, there are a number of formal techniques that can improve products or services, reduce waste, simplify systems and hence reduce costs.

4.2 Value analysis

Value analysis involves **assessing the value of every aspect of a product** (or service) in order to **devise ways** of **achieving** the product's (or service's) **purpose** as **economically** as possible while **maintaining** the required standard of **quality** and **reliability**.

Conventional cost reduction techniques aim to **produce a particular design of a product as cheaply as possible. Value analysis,** on the other hand, tries to **find the least-cost method of making a product that achieves its intended purpose.**

A value analysis assessment is likely to be carried out by a **team of experts** from the engineering, technical production and finance departments. It will involve the systematic investigation of every source of cost and every technique of production with the aim of getting rid of all unnecessary costs. An **unnecessary cost** is a cost that **does not add value**.

Value is **only added** to a product **while it is actually being processed.** Whilst it is being inspected for quality, moving from one part of the factory to another, waiting for further processing and held in store, value is not being added. Non value-adding activities should therefore be eliminated.

A value-adding activity cannot be eliminated without the customer perceiving a deterioration in the performance, function or other quality of a product.

Activity 5 **(5 minutes)**

Which of the following are value-adding activities?

(a) Setting up a machine so that it drills holes of a certain size
(b) Repairing faulty production work
(c) Painting a car, if the organisation manufactures cars
(d) Storing materials

There are some areas of that are of special importance.

(a) **Product design**

At the design stage value analysis is called **value engineering**. The designer should be cost conscious and avoid unnecessary complications. Simple product design can avoid production and quality control problems, thereby resulting in lower costs.

BPP LEARNING MEDIA

NOTES

(b) **Components and material costs**

The purchasing department should beware of lapsing into habit with routine buying decisions. It has a crucial role to play in reducing costs and improving value by procuring the desired quality materials at the lowest possible price.

(c) **Production methods**

These ought to be reviewed continually, on a product-by-product basis, especially with changing technology.

Value analysis typically involves consideration of the following.

(a) **Can the function of the product be achieved in another way**, using less expensive methods?

(b) **Are all the functions of the product essential**, or can some be removed without affecting quality?

(c) **Can a cheaper substitute material be found** which is as good, if not better, than the material currently used?

(d) **Can unnecessary weight or embellishments be removed** without reducing the product's attractions or desirability?

(e) **Can a new product/service be standardised** so it can be produced in conjunction with existing products/services?

(f) **Is it possible to use standardised components** (or to make components to a particular standard) thereby reducing the variety of units used and produced? **Variety reduction (standardisation)** is cost effective because it allows a range of finished products to be produced from a common, relatively small pool of components. In general, if there are fewer product varieties, production is more straight-forward, which makes it easier to automate and so costs are likely to reduce. Fitted kitchens, for example, come in a wide variety of colours and finishes but it is only the cupboard doors that differ; the bodies of the cupboards are standardised.

(g) **Is it possible to reduce the number of components,** for example could a product be assembled safely with a smaller number of screws?

Activity 6 **(15 minutes)**

Standardisation of parts and components might offer enormous cost reduction potential for some manufacturing industries. Can you think why this might be the case? What are the disadvantages of standardisation?

The origins of value analysis were in the engineering industry, but it **can be applied to services or to aspects of office work.**

If applied thoroughly and on a **continuous** basis, value analysis should result in a planned, ongoing search for cost reductions.

BPP LEARNING MEDIA

4.3 Work study

Work study is used to **determine the most efficient methods of using labour, materials and machinery**. There are two main parts to work study.

(a) **Method study** involves **systematically recording** and **critically examining** existing and proposed **ways of doing work**. The aim of this is to **develop** and **apply easier** and **more effective methods**, and so **reduce costs**.

(b) **Work measurement** involves **establishing the time for a qualified worker** to carry out a **specified job** at a **specified level of performance**.

Areas where work study can be applied

(a) Plant facilities, layout and space utilisation

(b) Analysis, design and improvement of work systems (say forms used or the telephone system), work places and work methods

(c) Setting standards

(d) Determining the most profitable, alternative combinations of personnel, materials and equipment

4.4 Organisation and methods (O&M)

Organisation and methods (O&M) is a term for **techniques**, including method study and work measurement, that are used to **examine clerical, administrative and management procedures in order to make improvements**.

O&M is **primarily concerned with office work** and looks in particular at areas such as the following.

- Organisation
- Office layout
- Office mechanisation
- Documentation and the design of forms
- Duties
- Staffing
- Methods of procedure

Work study and O&M are perhaps associated in your mind with establishing standard times for work, but the real aim is to decide the most efficient methods of getting work done. More efficient methods and tighter standards will improve efficiency and productivity, and so reduce costs.

4.5 Difficulties with introducing cost reduction programmes

(a) There may be **resistance from employees** to the pressure to reduce costs, usually because the nature and purpose of the campaign has not been properly explained to them, and because they feel threatened by the change.

(b) The programme may be limited to a small area of the business with the result that **costs are reduced in one cost centre, only to reappear as an extra cost in another**.

(c) Cost reduction campaigns are **often introduced as a rushed, desperate measure** instead of a carefully organised, well thought-out exercise.

(d) **Long-term factors** must be considered. Reduction in expenditure on maintenance, advertising or research and development in the short term could have serious long-term consequences.

(e) It is becoming increasingly apparent that the **key area** for cost reduction is **product design**. Once manufacturing begins there is less scope for reducing costs, especially if production is heavily automated.

5 QUALITY AND VALUE

In the past, many organisations focused on **quantity** – producing as many 'units' as possible as cheaply as possible. **Customers** used to accept late delivery of the same old unreliable products from organisations which appeared to care little for their customers. But **now** they **want more.**

- New products
- High levels of quality
- On-time delivery
- Immediate response to their requests

Businesses **today** are therefore **concentrating** on **quality** in the hope of becoming the success stories of the 21st century.

5.1 Quality

Definition

Quality means 'the **degree of excellence of a thing'** – how well made it is, or how well it is performed if it is a service, how well it serves its purpose, and how it measures up against its rivals.

The quality of a product or service has also been defined as 'its **fitness for the customer's purpose**'.

So if we are looking for an **'excellent' product** or service, we expect it to be **completely satisfactory for its purpose** from the **point of view of the customer.**

The **degree** to which a product or service is **fit for its purpose** will depend on the product or service in question.

(a) **Cost.** Customers expect some products to be cheap because of their short life. Pencils and daily newspapers are examples.

(b) **Life.** Other products are expected to last for longer and to be reliable and hence are more expensive. Televisions are an example.

(c) **Manner of production.** With some products, customers expect the use of highly skilled labour and/or expensive raw materials. A meal in a highly–commended restaurant is an example.

(d) **Esteem.** If a customer is looking for esteem or status from a product, the product is likely to have a high price, a designer label and/or expensive package. An example is designer-label clothing.

A **quality service** is likely to be **efficient**, be provided by **courteous staff** who have **knowledge of the service** and take place within a **pleasant environment**. For example, if a train arrives on time, is clean and comfortable and the guard gives out accurate announcements over the tannoy, many customers would feel they had enjoyed a quality service.

5.2 Value

The **value** of a product or service **to a customer** can therefore be considered in terms of its **fitness for purpose** and the **prestige or esteem attached**. From the **point of view of the producer of the product or the provider of the service,** however, other aspects are important.

(a) All organisations need to control costs and so the **cost of making the product or providing the service** is one aspect.

(b) The other aspect, the product's or service's **selling price** (its **market value),** is of importance to profit-making organisations.

The value of a product therefore has four distinct aspects.

- **Cost value** is the cost of producing and selling an item/providing a service.
- **Exchange value** is the market value of the product or service.
- **Use value** is what the product or service does, the purpose it fulfils.
- **Esteem value** is the prestige the customer attaches to a product.

Activity 7 **(5 minutes)**

Classify the following features of a product, using the types of value set out above.

(a) The product can be sold for £27.50.
(b) The product is available in six colours to suit customers' tastes.
(c) The product will last for ten years.

5.3 Enhancing value

The **producer** of a product or **provider** of a service will want to **increase exchange value** (the selling price) **without increasing cost value. To do this, the value the customer attaches** to the product or service **must be enhanced** (its **use value** or its **esteem value**) so that they will pay the higher price.

(a) Extended opening hours may add to the use value of a local shop.

(b) The esteem value of certain products such as expensive jewellery can be increased by increasing the price!

6 TOTAL QUALITY MANAGEMENT (TQM)

If the level of quality is to be controlled, a **control system** is needed.

Step 1.
Establish **standards of quality** for a product or service.

↓

Step 2.
Establish **procedures or production methods** which ought to ensure that these required standards of quality are met in a suitably high proportion of cases.

↓

Step 3.
Monitor actual quality.

↓

Step 4.
Take **control action** when actual quality falls below standard.

Activity 8 **(5 minutes)**

How is this system of control similar to budgetary control and standard costing control systems?

EXAMPLE

How might the postal service control quality? It might establish a standard that 90% of first class letters will be delivered on the day after they are posted, and 99% will be delivered within two days of posting.

(a) Procedures would have to be established for ensuring that these standards could be met (attending to such matters as frequency of collections, automated letter sorting, frequency of deliveries and number of staff employed).

(b) Actual performance could be monitored, perhaps by taking samples from time to time of letters that are posted and delivered.

(c) If the quality standard is not being achieved, management should take control action (employ more postmen or advertise the use of postcodes again).

Quality management becomes **total *(Total Quality Management (TQM))* when it is applied to everything a business does.**

6.1 Get it right, first time

One of the basic principles of TQM is that the **cost of preventing mistakes is less than the cost of correcting them** once they occur. The aim should therefore be **to get things right first time**. Every mistake, delay and misunderstanding, directly costs an organisation money through **wasted time and effort**, including time taken in pacifying customers. The **lost potential for future sales because of poor customer service must also be taken into account.**

6.2 Continuous improvement

A second basic principle of TQM is dissatisfaction with the *status quo*: the belief that it is **always possible to improve** and so the aim should be to '**get it more right next time**'.

6.3 Quality assurance procedures

Because TQM embraces every activity of a business, quality assurance procedures **cannot be confined to the production process** but must also cover the work of sales, distribution and administration departments, the efforts of external suppliers, and the reaction of external customers.

(a) **Quality assurance of goods inwards**

The quality of output depends on the quality of input materials. Quality control should therefore include **procedures over acceptance and inspection of goods inwards** and **measurement of rejects**. Each supplier can be given a 'rating' for the quality of the goods they tend to supply, and preference with purchase orders can be given to well-rated suppliers. This method is referred to as 'vendor rating'.

Where a **quality assurance scheme** is in place the supplier guarantees the quality of goods supplied and allows the customers' inspectors access while the items are being manufactured. The **onus is on the supplier to carry out the necessary quality checks**, or face cancellation of the contract.

Suppliers' quality assurance schemes are being used increasingly, particularly where extensive sub-contracting work is carried out, for example in the motor industries. One such scheme is **BS EN ISO 9000** certification. A company that gains registration has a certificate testifying that it is operating to a structure of written policies and procedures which are designed to ensure that it can consistently deliver a product or service to meet customer requirements.

(b) **Inspection of output**

This will take place at various key stages in the production process and will provide a continual check that the production process is under control. The aim of inspection is *not* really to sort out the bad products from the good ones after the work has been done. The **aim is to satisfy management that quality control in production is being maintained.**

The **inspection of samples** rather than 100% testing of all items will keep inspection costs down, and smaller samples will be less costly to inspect than larger samples. The greater the confidence in the reliability of production methods and process control, the smaller the samples will be.

(c) **Monitoring customer reaction**

Some sub-standard items will inevitably be produced. Checks during production will identify some bad output, but other items will reach the customer who is the ultimate judge of quality. **Complaints ought to be monitored** in the form of letters of complaint, returned goods, penalty discounts, claims under guarantee, or requests for visits by service engineers. Some companies actually survey customers on a regular basis.

6.4 Employees and quality

Workers themselves are frequently the best source of information about how (or how not) to improve quality. **Empowerment** makes use of this. It has two key aspects.

(a) Allowing workers to have the **freedom to decide how to do** the necessary work, using the skills they possess and acquiring new skills as necessary to be an effective team member.

(b) Making workers **responsible** for achieving production targets and for quality control.

Quality circles can also be used to draw upon the knowledge and experience of the workforce.

A quality circle is a group of employees who meet regularly to discuss **problems of quality** and **quality control** in their area of work, and perhaps to suggest ways of improving quality.

6.5 Quality control and inspection

A distinction should be made between **quality control** and **inspection**.

Quality control involves setting controls for the process of manufacture or service delivery. It is aimed at **preventing the manufacture of defective items** or the provision of defective services.

Inspection is a technique of **identifying when defective items are being produced at an unacceptable level**. Inspection is usually carried out at three main points.

- Receiving inspection – for raw materials and purchased components
- Floor or process inspection for WIP
- Final inspection or testing for finished goods

7 COSTS OF QUALITY

When we talk about quality-related costs you should remember that a concern for **good quality saves money**; it is **poor quality that costs money.** There are four main quality-related costs.

(a) **Prevention costs** are the costs of any action taken to investigate, prevent or reduce defects and failures.

(b) **Appraisal costs** are the costs of assessing the quality achieved.

(c) **Internal failure costs** are the costs arising within the organisation of failing to achieve the required level of quality.

NOTES

(d) **External failure costs** are the costs arising outside the organisation of failing to achieve the required level of quality (after transfer of ownership to the customer).

Quality-related cost	Example
Prevention costs	Quality engineering
	Design/development of quality control/inspection equipment
	Maintenance of quality control/inspection equipment
	Administration of quality control
	Training in quality control
Appraisal costs	Acceptance testing
	Inspection of goods inwards
	Inspection costs of in-house processing
	Performance testing
Internal failure costs	Failure analysis
	Re-inspection costs
	Losses from failure of purchased items
	Losses due to lower selling prices for sub-quality goods
	Costs of reviewing product specifications after failures
External failure costs	Administration of customer complaints section
	Costs of customer service section
	Product liability costs
	Cost of repairing products returned from customers
	Cost of replacing items due to sub-standard products/marketing errors

The introduction of TQM will cause a drop in internal and external failure costs but prevention and appraisal costs will increase. Management need to ensure that the cost savings are never outweighed by the additional costs.

WORKED EXAMPLE: COST OF POOR QUALITY

A manufacturer's inspection procedures indicate that one faulty item out of every 1,000 good items produced is sent to a customer. The management regards this as acceptable, as a replacement will be supplied free of charge. Unit sales are 10,000,000 per year, and each unit costs £20 to manufacture and makes a profit of £5. It is probable that every customer who buys a faulty product will return it, and will thenceforth buy a similar product from another company. The average customer buys two units a year. Marketing costs per new customer are £10 per year.

(a) What is your best estimate of the net cost of this policy for a year?

(b) What name(s) would you give to quality-related costs of this type?

(c) Could the situation be improved by incurring other types of quality-related cost?

ANSWER

(a) Presumed number of bad units delivered a year = 10,000,000/1,000= 10,000

	£
Cost of defects 10,000 × £20	200,000
Cost of free replacement 10,000 × £20	200,000
Manufacturing cost	400,000
Marketing costs for replacement customers £10 × 10,000	100,000
Gross cost of poor quality	500,000
Less income from original sale	250,000
Net cost of poor quality	250,000

Although the cost of the original defective item is recovered, the company **does not get it right first time.** The company has still suffered the cost of the replacement and the cost of replacing the customer by marketing to new customers.

(b) The cost of replacements is an external failure cost; the cost of defects and the new marketing costs are internal failure costs.

(c) It appears that the manufacturer already incurs *appraisal* costs, since there are inspection procedures for goods about to be despatched. The reason(s) for the fault should be established (a further *internal failure* cost) and the extent of the problem should be more precisely ascertained (further *appraisal* costs), since it is not certain that all dissatisfied customers return their goods, though it is highly likely that their business is lost. Once this has been done it will be possible to decide whether, by spending more on *prevention,* the overall cost of poor quality can be reduced.

7.1 Traditional accounting systems and the cost of quality

Traditionally, the **costs** of **scrapped units, wasted materials and reworking** have been **lost within the costs of production** by incorporating the costs of an expected level of loss (a normal loss) to the costs of good production. **Other costs of poor quality have been included within production or marketing overheads.** So such costs are not only **considered as inevitable** but are not highlighted for management attention.

Traditional accounting reports **tend also to ignore the hidden but real costs of excessive stock levels** (held to enable faulty material to be replaced without hindering production) **and the facilities necessary for storing that stock.**

The introduction of a system of **just-in-time (JIT)** purchasing and manufacturing should eradicate such costs. A just-in-time production system is driven by demand from customers for finished products. Components on a production line are only produced when needed for the next stage of production. Stocks of work in progress and finished goods are therefore not needed. In a just-in-time purchasing system, materials are not delivered until they are needed in production, thereby eradicating stock of raw materials.

To **implement a TQM programme, costs of quality** must be **highlighted separately** within accounting reports so that *all* employees are aware of the cost of poor quality.

7.2 Explicit and implicit costs of quality

Explicit costs of quality are those that are recorded in accounting records, to be separately highlighted with the implementation of a TQM programme.

Implicit costs of quality are not recorded in accounting records. They tend to be of two forms.

(a) **Opportunity costs** such as the loss of future sales to a customer dissatisfied with faulty goods

(b) **Costs which tend to be subsumed** within other account headings such as costs which result from the disruptions caused by stockouts due to faulty purchases

Activity 9 **(5 minutes)**

Elyard Ltd defines the cost of quality as the total of all costs incurred in preventing faults in production of its single product, plus the costs involved in correcting faults once they have occurred. It only includes explicit costs of quality.

Task

Determine which of the following costs Elyard Ltd would include in the cost of quality.

(a) Remedial work required as a result of faulty raw material
(b) Cost of customer support department which deals with faulty products
(c) Loss of customer goodwill following delivery of faulty products
(d) Cost of detailed inspection of raw materials due to poor quality of supplies
(e) Cost of products returned by customers due to faults
(f) Sales revenue lost as a result of returns in (e)

8 STANDARD COSTING IN A TOTAL QUALITY ENVIRONMENT

It has been argued that traditional variance analysis is unhelpful and potentially misleading in the modern organisation, and causes managers to focus their attention on the wrong issues.

Standard costing concentrates on **quantity** and ignores other factors contributing to an organisation's effectiveness. In a **total quality** environment, however, quantity is not an issue, **quality** is. Effectiveness in such an environment therefore centres on high quality output (produced as a result of high quality input); the cost of failing to achieve the required level of effectiveness is not measured in variances, but in terms of the **internal and external failure costs** which would not be identified by traditional standard costing analysis.

Standard costing might measure, say, **labour efficiency** in terms of individual tasks and the level of **output**. In a **total quality environment**, the effectiveness of labour is more appropriately measured in terms of **re-working** required, **returns** from customers, **defects** identified in subsequent stages of production and so on.

In a **TQM** environment there are likely to be **minimal rate variances** if the workforce are paid a guaranteed weekly wage. Fixed price contracts, with suppliers guaranteeing levels of quality, are often a feature, and so there are likely to be **few, if any, material price and usage variances.**

BPP LEARNING MEDIA

NOTES

So **can standard costing and TQM exist together?**

(a) Predetermined standards conflict with the TQM philosophy of continual improvement.

(b) Continual improvements should alter quantities of inputs, prices and so on, whereas standard costing is best used in a stable, standardised, repetitive environment.

(c) Standard costs often incorporate a planned level of scrap in material standards. This is at odds with the TQM aim of 'zero defects'.

On the other hand, variance analysis can contribute towards the aim of improved product quality by keeping track of quality control information. This is because variance analysis measures both the planned use of resources and actual use of resources in order to compare the two.

As variance analysis is generally expressed in terms of purely quantitative measures, such as quantity of raw materials used and price per unit of quantity, issues of quality would appear to be excluded from the reporting process. Quality would appear to be an excuse for spending more time, say, or buying more expensive raw materials.

Variance analysis, as it currently stands, therefore needs to be adapted to take account of quality issues.

(a) Variance analysis reports should routinely include measures such as **defect rates**. Although zero defects will be most desirable, such a standard of performance may not be reached at first. However, there should be an expected rate of defects: if this is exceeded then management attention is directed to the excess.

(b) The **absolute number of defects** should be measured *and* their **type**. If caused by certain materials and components this can shed light on, say, a favourable materials price variance which might have been caused by substandard materials being purchased more cheaply. Alternatively, if the defects are caused by shoddy assembly work this can shed light on a favourable labour efficiency variance if quality is being sacrificed for speed.

(c) It should also be possible to provide **financial measures** for the cost of poor quality. These can include direct costs such as the wages of inspection and quality control staff, the cost of time in rectifying the defects, and the cost of the materials used in rectification.

(d) Measures could be built into **materials price** and variance analysis, so that the materials price variance as currently reported includes a factor reflecting the quality of materials purchased.

Activity 10 **(10 minutes)**

Read the following extract from an article in the *Financial Times* and then explain how the bank could monitor the impact of the initiative.

'If you telephone a branch of Lloyds Bank and it rings five times before there is a reply; if the person who answers does not introduce him or herself by name during the conversation; if you are standing in a queue with more people in it than the number of tills, then something is wrong.'

'If any of these things happen then the branch is breaching standards of customer service set by the bank since last July ... the "service challenge" was launched in the bank's 1,888 branches last summer after being tested in 55 branches ...'

'Lloyds already has evidence of the impact. Customers were more satisfied with pilot branches ... than with others.'

Chapter roundup

- In full-cost pricing the sales price is determined by calculating the full cost of the product and then adding a percentage mark-up for profit.
- Marginal cost-plus pricing involves adding a profit margin to the marginal cost of production/sales.
- Cost-plus pricing makes it easy to find the cost for stock valuation purposes of retail goods for which the selling price is available.
- Three alternative pricing strategies for new products are market penetration pricing, market skimming pricing and premium pricing.
- A typical product has a life cycle of four stages.
- The price that an organisation can charge for its products will be determined to a certain extent by the market (perfect competition, monopoly, oligopoly) in which it operates.
- Competition can affect pricing policy.
- A price leader indicates to the other firms in the market what the price will be.
- Differential pricing involves selling the same product at different prices to different customers.
- The price elasticity of demand measure the extent of change in demand for a good following a change in price. Demand can be elastic or inelastic.
- The demand-based approach to pricing involves determining a profit-maximising price.
- The target costing approach is to develop a product concept and the primary specifications for performance and design and then to determine the price customers would be willing to pay for that concept. The desired profit margin is deducted from the price leaving a figure that represents the total cost. This is the target cost. The product must be capable of being produced for this amount otherwise it will not be manufactured.
- Value engineering is cost reduction before production.
- Cost reduction aims to reduce costs below a previously acceptable level, without adversely affecting the quality of the product or service being provided.
- Value analysis involves assessing the value of every aspect of a product (or service) in order to devise ways of achieving the product's (or service's) purpose as economically as possible whilst maintaining the required standard of quality and reliability.
- Other techniques of cost reduction include variety reduction (standardisation), work study and O&M.

NOTES

Quick quiz

1 Fill in the blanks.

Full cost pricing is a method of determining the .... by calculating the .... of the product and adding a .... for profit.

2 Market penetration pricing is appropriate if market research reveals that a small cut in the selling price of the product will lead to a large increase in the quantity demanded. True or False?

3 What are the four stages of the product life cycle?

4 What is an oligopoly?

5 What price is first charged for a product under a policy of market penetration pricing?

6 When target costing is in use, a product concept is developed. What is determined next?

A Profit margin
B Price
C Full cost
D Production cost

7 Choose the correct words from those highlighted.

Cost reduction/control is about regulating the costs of operating a business and keeping costs within acceptable limits whereas **cost reduction/control** is a planned and positive approach to reducing expenditure.

8 The cost of inspecting a product for quality is a value-added cost. True or False?

9 Match the cost to the correct cost category.

Costs

(a) Administration of quality control
(b) Product liability costs
(c) Acceptance testing
(d) Losses due to lower selling prices for sub-quality goods

Cost categories

- Prevention costs
- Appraisal costs
- Internal failure costs
- External failure costs

10 Match the terms to the correct definitions.

Terms

Cost value
Exchange value
Use value
Esteem value

BPP LEARNING MEDIA

Definitions

(a) The prestige the customer attaches to the product
(b) The market value of the product
(c) What the product does
(d) The cost of producing and selling the product

11 Choose the correct word from those highlighted.

Explicit/implicit costs of quality are not recorded in accounting records.

12 Fill in the blanks.

There are two basic principles of TQM.

....

....

Answers to quick quiz

1 Selling price
Full cost
Markup (see para 1.1)

2 True (para 2.5)

3 Introduction, growth, maturity, decline (para 2.1)

4 A market dominated by relatively few competitive companies. (para 2.2)

5 Low prices (para 2.5)

6 B (para 3.1)

7 The first term should be cost control, the second term cost reduction. (para 4.1)

8 False (para 4.2)

9 (a) Prevention costs
(b) External failure costs
(c) Appraisal costs
(d) Internal failure costs (para 7)

10 (a) Esteem value
(b) Exchange value
(c) Use value
(d) Cost value (para 5.2)

11 Implicit (para 7.2)

12 Get it right, first time
Continuous improvement (paras 6.1 and 6.2)

Answers to activities

1 £7.99 (£4.70 × 170%)

2

	£
Selling price	20
Marginal (variable) cost (5 + 3 + 7)	15
	5

$$\text{Mark up} = \frac{\text{Profit}}{\text{Marginal cost}} \times 100\%$$

$$= \frac{5}{15} \times 100\%$$

$$= 33^1/_3\%$$

Note that the fixed overheads are not included in the marginal cost.

3 The selling price is obtained as shown below, firstly in general (%) terms, and than using the actual values.

	%	£	
Cost	100	150.00	(187.5 × 100/125)
Profit	25	37.50	(187.5 × 25/125)
Selling price	125	187.50	

The cost of the stock is £900 (6 × £150) in total.

4 Here are some suggestions

- Changing the specifications for cutting solid materials
- Introducing new equipment that reduces wastage in processing or handling materials
- Identifying poor quality output at an earlier stage in the operational processes
- Using better quality materials

5 All but (c) are **non** value-adding activities.

6 If a manufacturer has fewer types of components to manufacture, he will be able to increase the length of production runs, and so reduce production costs. Non-standard parts tend to be produced in small runs, and unit costs will be higher as a consequence.

Standardisation also helps to cut purchasing cost because there are fewer items to buy and stock. The company can purchase in bulk, and so perhaps obtain bulk purchase discounts. It may also be possible to buy standard parts from more than one supplier, and so purchasing will be more competitive.

The disadvantage of standardisation is that it may result in a loss of sales revenue or customer loyalty.

7 (a) Exchange value
(b) Esteem value
(c) Use value

8 Standard costing and budgetary control systems also require standards to be set, actual results to be monitored and control action to be taken if actual results differ from those expected.

9 (c) and (f) would not be included because they would not be recorded within the accounting records and hence are implicit costs.

10 A wide variety of answers is possible. The article goes on to explain how the bank has monitored the initiative.

(a) It has devised a 100 point scale showing average satisfaction with branch service.

(b) It conducts a 'first impressions' survey of all new customers.

(c) There is also a general survey carried out every six months which seeks the views of a weighted sample of 350 customers per branch.

(d) A survey company telephones each branch anonymously twice a month to test how staff respond to enquiries about products.

(e) A quarter of each branch's staff answer a monthly questionnaire about the bank's products to test their knowledge.

(f) Groups of employees working in teams in branches are allowed to set their own additional standards. This is to encourage participation.

(g) Branches that underperform are more closely watched by 24 managers who monitor the initiative.

Chapter 6 :

COSTING SYSTEMS

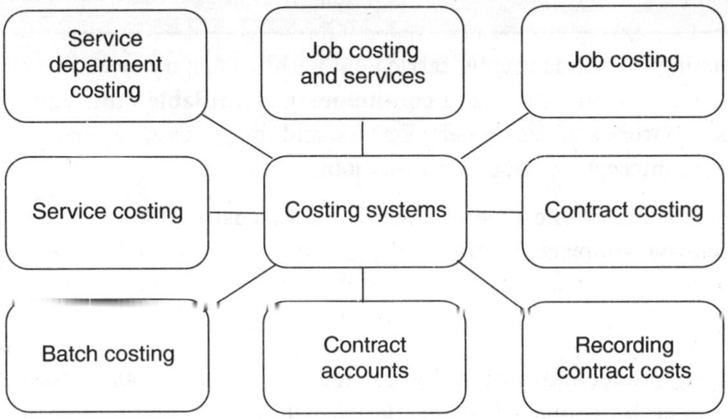

Introduction

A cost accounting method is designed to suit the way goods are processed or manufactured or the way services are provided. Each organisation's cost accounting method will therefore have unique features but costing methods of firms in the same line of business will usually have common aspects. On the other hand, organisations involved in completely different activities, such as hospitals and car part manufacturers, will use very different methods.

This chapter looks at four types of costing system. We will see the circumstances in which each system should be used and how the costs are calculated. A fifth costing system, **process costing**, is dealt with in the next chapter.

Your objectives

In this chapter you will learn about the following.

(a) Job costing

(b) Contract costing

(c) Batch costing

(d) Service costing

1 JOB COSTING

Definitions

A **job** is a cost unit which consists of a single order or contract.

Job costing is a costing method applied where work is undertaken to customers' special requirements and each order is of comparatively short duration.

The work relating to a job is usually carried out within a factory or workshop and moves through processes and operations as a **continuously identifiable unit**. The term job may also be applied to work such as property repairs, and the job costing method may be used in the costing of internal capital expenditure jobs.

Note that job costing is one type of **specific order costing** (another type is **contract costing**, which you will meet shortly).

1.1 Procedure

In job costing, production is usually carried out in accordance with the special requirements of each customer. It is therefore usual for each job to differ in one or more respects from every other job, which means that a separate record must be maintained to show the details of a particular job.

When an **order** is received from a customer, the estimating department will prepare an **estimate** for the job. If the customer accepts the estimate, the job will be given a separate job number, to identify it from all other jobs.

1.2 Collection of job costs

Once work has begun on the job, careful record keeping is necessary to accurately collect the job costs.

(a) **Materials requisitions are sent to stores**. The material requisition note will be used to cost the materials issued to the job concerned, and this cost may then be recorded on a **job cost sheet**, which records all costs relating to a particular job. The cost may include items already in stock, at an appropriate valuation, and/or items specially purchased.

(b) **A job ticket is given to the worker who is to perform the first operation of the job.** The times of his starting and finishing the operation are recorded on the ticket, which is then passed to the person who is to carry out the second operation, where a similar record of the times of starting and finishing is made. When the job is completed, the job ticket is sent to the cost office, where the time spent will be costed and recorded on the job cost sheet.

(c) The job's share of the **factory overhead**, based on the absorption rate(s) in operation, is recorded on the job cost sheet.

(d) The **relevant costs** of materials issued, direct labour performed and direct expenses incurred as recorded on the job cost sheet are charged to the job account in the work in progress ledger. The total value of the jobs in progress will represent the balance on the work in progress control account since each job is represented by an account in the WIP ledger.

(e) **On completion of the job**, the job account is charged with the appropriate administration, selling and distribution overhead, after which the total cost of the job can be ascertained.

(f) The difference between the agreed selling price and the total actual cost will be the supplier's profit (or loss).

1.3 Job cost sheet (or card)

An example of a job cost sheet (or job card) is as follows. It may show the detail of relatively small jobs or may be used to summarise the cost elements for larger jobs.

JOB COST SHEET		Job No. B641
Customer Mr J White	Customer's Order No.	Vehicle make Peugot 205 GTE
Job Description Repair damage to offside front door		Vehicle reg. no. G 614 SOX
Estimate Ref. 2599	Invoice No.	
Quoted price £338.68	Invoice price £355.05	Date to collect 14.6.X3

Material						Labour								Overheads			
Date	Req. No.	Qty.	Price	Cost £	Cost p	Date	Employee	Cost Ctre	Hrs.	Rate	Bonus	Cost £	Cost p	Hrs	OAR	Cost £	Cost p
12.6	36815	1	75.49	75	49	12.6	018	B	1.98	6.50	-	12	87	7.9	2.50	19	75
12.6	36816	1	33.19	33	19	13.6	018	B	5.92	6.50	-	38	48				
12.6	36842	5	6.01	30	05						13.65	13	65				
13.6	36881	5	3.99	19	95												
Total C/F				158	68	Total C/F						65	00	Total C/F		19	75

Expenses				
Date	Ref.	Description	Cost £	Cost p
12.6	-	N. Jolley Panel-beating	50	-
Total C/F			50	-

Job Cost Summary	Actual £	Actual p	Estimate £	Estimate p
Direct Materials B/F	158	68	158	68
Direct Expenses B/F	50	00		
Direct Labour B/F	65	00	180	00
Direct Cost	273	68		
Overheads B/F	19	75		
	293	43		
Admin overhead (add 10%)	29	34		
= Total Cost	322	77	338	68
Invoice Price	355	05		
Job Profit/Loss	32	28		

Comments

Job Cost Card Completed by ____________________

Figure 6.1: Example of a job card

Activity 1 **(20 minutes)**

Frisbee Ltd is a company that carries out jobbing work. One of the jobs carried out in February was job 1357, to which the following information relates.

Direct material Y:	400 kilos were issued from stores at a cost of £5 per kilo.
Direct material Z:	800 kilos were issued from stores at a cost of £6 per kilo.
	60 kilos were returned.
Department P:	320 labour hours were worked, of which 100 hours were done in overtime.
Department Q:	200 labour hours were worked, of which 100 hours were done in overtime.

Overtime work is not normal in Department P, where basic pay is £4 per hour plus an overtime premium of £1 per hour. Overtime work was done in Department Q in February because of a request by the customer of another job to complete his job quickly. Basic pay in Department Q is £5 per hour and overtime premium is £1.50 per hour.

Overhead is absorbed at the rate of £3 per direct labour hour in both departments.

The organisation adds 30% to full production cost to arrive at a price for a job.

Calculate the following.

(a) The direct materials cost of job 1357
(b) The direct labour cost of job 1357
(c) The full production cost of job 1357
(d) The price of job 1357

1.4 Work in progress at the end of an accounting period

At the end of an accounting period any jobs which are still in progress are regarded as work in progress, which is a form of stock. Stock and work in progress need to be valued at the lower of cost and net realisable value for financial accounting purposes. Job cost sheets will provide details of the costs incurred in bringing a job to its present condition. Net realisable value will be the price agreed with the customer, less any further costs to complete the job as per any budgets or estimates made at the time of tendering for the job. Generally, if the job is expected to make a profit the cost per the job sheet will be the value of the incomplete job at the period end.

1.5 Completed jobs

When jobs are completed, job cost sheets are transferred from the work in progress category to finished goods. When delivery is made to the customer, the costs become a cost of sale.

1.6 Job costing and computerisation

Job cost sheets exist in **manual systems**, but it is increasingly likely that in large organisations the job costing system will be **computerised**, using accounting software specifically designed to deal with job costing requirements. A computerised job accounting system is likely to contain the following features.

(a) Every job will be given a job code number, which will determine how the data relating to the job is stored.

(b) A separate set of codes will be given for the type of costs that any job is likely to incur. Thus, 'direct wages', say, will have the same code whichever job they are allocated to.

(c) In a sophisticated system, costs can be analysed both by job (for example all costs related to Job 456), but also by type (for example direct wages incurred on all jobs). It is thus easy to perform control analysis and to make comparisons between jobs.

An example may help to illustrate the way in which the costing of individual jobs fits in with the recording of total costs in control accounts. Study the following example very carefully and make sure that you understand the solution.

WORKED EXAMPLE: JOB COSTING

Pistachio Ltd is a jobbing company. On 1 June 20X2, there was one uncompleted job in the factory. The job cost sheet for this work is summarised as follows.

Job Cost Sheet, Job No 6832

	£
Costs to date	
Direct materials	630
Direct labour (120 hours)	350
Factory overhead (£2 per direct labour hour)	240
Factory cost to date	1,220

During June, three new jobs were started in the factory, and costs of production were as follows.

		£
Direct materials		
Issued to:	job 6832	2,390
	job 6833	1,680
	job 6834	3,950
	job 6835	4,420
Material transfers		£
Job 6834 to job 6833		250
Job 6832 to 6834		620
Materials returned to store		£
From job 6832		870
From job 6835		170
Labour hours recorded		
Job 6832		430 hrs
Job 6833		650 hrs
Job 6834		280 hrs
Job 6835		410 hrs

NOTES

The cost of labour hours during June 20X2 was £3 per hour, and production overhead is absorbed at the rate of £2 per direct labour hour. Production overheads incurred during the month amounted to £3,800. Completed jobs were delivered to customers as soon as they were completed, and the invoiced amounts were as follows.

Job 6832	£5,500
Job 6834	£8,000
Job 6835	£7,500

Administration and marketing overheads are added to the cost of sales at the rate of 20% of factory cost on completion of jobs. Actual costs incurred during June 20X2 amounted to £3,200.

(a) Prepare T-accounts accumulating the production costs for each individual job during June 20X2.

(b) Prepare summaries of the costs of each job, and calculate the profit on each completed job.

ANSWER

(a) **Job accounts**

JOB 6832

	£		£
Balance b/f	1,220	Job 6834 a/c (materials transfer)	620
Materials (stores a/c)	2,390		
Labour (wages a/c)	1,290	Stores a/c (materials returned)	870
Production overhead (o'hd a/c)	860	Cost of sales a/c (balance)	4,270
	5,760		5,760

JOB 6833

	£		£
Materials (stores a/c)	1,680	Balance c/f	5,180
Labour (wages a/c)	1,950		
Production overhead (o'hd a/c)	1,300		
Job 6834 a/c (materials transfer)	250		
	5,180		5,180

JOB 6834

	£		£
Materials (stores a/c)	3,950	Job 6833 a/c (materials transfer)	250
Labour (wages a/c)	840	Cost of sales a/c (balance)	5,720
Production overhead (o'hd a/c)	560		
Job 6832 a/c (materials transfer)	620		
	5,970		5,970

JOB 6835

	£		£
Materials (stores a/c)	4,420	Stores a/c (materials returned)	170
Labour (wages a/c)	1,230	Cost of sales a/c (balance)	6,300
Production overhead (o'hd a/c)	820		
	6,470		6,470

BPP LEARNING MEDIA

(b) **Job costs, summarised**

	Job 6832	*Job 6833*	*Job 6834*	*Job 6835*
	£	£	£	
Materials	*1,530	1,930	**4,320	4,250
Labour	1,640	1,950	840	1,230
Production overhead	1,100	1,300	560	820
Factory cost	4,270	5,180(c/f)	5,720	6,300
Admin & marketing o'hd (20%)	854		1,144	1,260
Cost of sale	5,124		6,864	7,560
Invoice value	5,500		8,000	7,500
Profit/(loss) on job	376		1,136	(60)

* £(630 + 2,390 – 620 – 870) ** £(3,950 + 620 – 250)

Activity 2 **(10 minutes)**

A firm uses job costing and recovers overheads on direct labour.

Three jobs were worked on during a period, the details of which are as follows.

	Job 1	*Job 2*	*Job 3*
	£	£	£
Opening work in progress	8,500	0	46,000
Material in period	17,150	29,025	0
Labour for period	12,500	23,000	4,500

The overheads for the period were exactly as budgeted, £140,000.

Jobs 1 and 2 were the only incomplete jobs.

What was the value of closing work in progress?

2 CONTRACT COSTING

Imagine trying to build up job costs on a job ticket in the way described in the previous section during the excavation of the tunnel under the English Channel or the construction of a skyscraper. It would be impossible. In industries such as building and construction work, civil engineering and shipbuilding, job costing is not usually appropriate. Contract costing is.

NOTES

Definitions

A **contract** is a cost unit or cost centre which is charged with the direct costs of production and an apportionment of head office overheads.

Contract costing is the name given to a method of job costing where the job to be carried out is of such magnitude that a formal contract is made between the customer and supplier. It applies where work is undertaken to customers' special requirements and each order is of long duration (compared with the time to which job costing applies). The work is usually constructional and *in general* the method is similar to job costing, although there are, of course, a few differences.

2.1 Features of contract costing

(a) A **formal contract** is made between customer and supplier.

(b) Work is undertaken to **customers' special requirements.**

(c) The work is for a **relatively long duration**. Large jobs may take a long time to complete, perhaps two or three years. Even when a contract is completed within less than 12 months, it is quite possible that the work may have begun during one financial year and ended during the supplier's next financial year; therefore the profit on the contract will relate to more than one accounting period.

(d) The work is frequently **constructional** in nature.

(e) The method of costing is **similar to job costing.**

(f) The work is frequently **based on site.**

(g) It is not unusual for a site to have its **own cashier and time-keeper.**

2.2 Problems

The problems which may arise in contract costing are as follows.

Problem	Comment
Identifying direct costs	Because of the large size of the job, many cost items which are usually thought of as production overhead are charged as direct costs of the contract (for example supervision, hire of plant, depreciation or loss in value of plant which is owned, sub-contractors' fees or charges and so on).
Low indirect costs	Because many costs normally classed as overheads are charged as direct costs of a contract, the absorption rate for overheads should only apply a share of the cost of those cost items which are not already direct costs. For most contracts the only item of indirect cost would be a charge for head office expenses.
Difficulties of cost control	Because of the size of some contracts and some sites, there are often cost control problems (material usage and losses, pilferage, labour supervision and utilisation, damage to and loss of plant and tools, vandalism and so on).

BPP LEARNING MEDIA

NOTES

Problem	Comment
Dividing the profit between different accounting periods	When a contract covers two or more accounting periods, how should the profit (or loss) on the contract be divided between the periods? This problem is, fortunately, outside the scope of your syllabus.

3 RECORDING CONTRACT COSTS

3.1 Direct materials

The direct materials used on a contract may be obtained from the company's central stores or they may be delivered direct to the site by the company's suppliers. In both cases carefully prepared documentation must ensure that the **correct contract is charged with the correct materials**. A materials requisition note would record the movement of materials from stores; the supplier's invoice supported by a goods received note would document the cost of materials delivered direct to site.

Materials issued from a central store or delivered by a supplier are often in excess of the quantities actually required. The surplus quantities are eventually returned to store, a material returns note prepared and the cost of the materials credited to the contract account.

At the end of an accounting period, a contract may be incomplete and if this is the case, there will probably be materials on site which have not yet been used. (Indeed some of them may never be used, but eventually returned to store.) Materials on site at the end of an accounting period should be carried forward as 'closing stock of materials on site' and brought forward as opening stock at the beginning of the next accounting period.

3.2 Direct labour

Since all the work done by direct labour on a contract site is spent exclusively on a single contract, the direct labour cost of the contract should be easily identified from the wages sheets. If some employees work on several contracts at the same time, perhaps travelling from one site to another, their time spent on each contract will have to be recorded on time sheets, and each contract charged with the cost of these recorded hours. The cost of supervision, which is usually a production overhead in job costing, will be a direct cost of a contract.

3.3 Subcontractors

On large contracts, **much work may be done by subcontractors**. The invoices of subcontractors will be **treated as a direct expense of the contract,** although if the invoiced amounts are small, it may be more convenient to account for them as 'direct materials' rather than as direct expenses.

3.4 The cost of plant

A feature of most contract work is the amount of plant used. Plant used on a contract may be owned by the company, or hired from a plant hire firm.

BPP LEARNING MEDIA

NOTES

Activity 3 **(5 minutes)**

If plant is hired from a plant hire firm, how should the cost be treated?

If the **plant is owned by the company**, a variety of accounting methods may be employed.

(a) **Method one: charging depreciation.** The contract may be charged depreciation on the plant, on a straight line or reducing balance basis. For example if a company has some plant which cost £10,000 and which is depreciated at 10% per annum straight line (to a residual value of nil) and a contract makes use of the plant for six months, a depreciation charge of £500 would be made against the contract. The disadvantage of this simple method of costing for plant is that the contract site foreman is not made directly responsible and accountable for the value of the actual plant in his charge. The foreman must be responsible for receipt of the plant, returning the plant after it has been used and proper care of the plant whilst it is being used.

(b) **Method two: charging the contract with current book value.** A more common method of costing for plant is to charge the contract with the current book value of the plant. A numerical example will help to illustrate this method.

Contract number X795 obtained some plant and loose tools from central store on 1 January 20X2. The book value of the plant was £100,000 and the book value of the loose tools was £8,000. On 1 October 20X2, some plant was removed from the site: this plant had a book value on 1 October of £20,000. At 31 December 20X2, the plant remaining on site had a book value of £60,000 and the loose tools had a book value of £5,000.

CONTRACT X795 ACCOUNT

	£		£
1 January 20X2		*1 October 20X2*	
Plant issued to site	100,000	Plant transferred	20,000
Loose tools issued to site	8,000	*31 December 20X2*	
		Plant value c/f	60,000
		Loose tools value c/f	5,000
		Depreciation (bal fig)	23,000
	108,000		108,000

The difference between the values on the debit and the credit sides of the account (£20,000 for plant and £3,000 for loose tools) is the depreciation cost of the equipment for the year.

(c) **Method three: using a plant account.** A third method of accounting for plant costs is to open a *plant account*, which is debited with the depreciation costs and the running costs (repairs, fuel and so on) of the equipment. A notional hire charge is then made to contracts using the plant, at a rate of £x per day. For example suppose that a company owns some equipment which is depreciated at the rate of £100 per month. Running costs in May 20X3 are £300. The plant is used on 20 days in the month, 12 days on Contract X and 8 days on Contract Y. The accounting entries would be as follows.

BPP LEARNING MEDIA

PLANT ACCOUNT

	£		£
Depreciation	100	Contract X (hire for 12 days)	240
Running costs	300	Contract Y (hire for 8 days)	160
	400		400

CONTRACT X

	£		£
Plant account (notional hire)	240		

CONTRACT Y

	£		£
Plant account (notional hire)	160		

3.5 Overhead costs

Overhead costs are added periodically (for example at the end of an accounting period) and are based on predetermined overhead absorption rates for the period. You may come across examples where a share of head office general costs is absorbed as an overhead cost to the contract, but this should not happen if the contract is unfinished at the end of the period, because only *production* overheads should be included in the value of any closing work in progress.

4 CONTRACT ACCOUNTS

The **account for a contract is a job account, or work in progress account**, and is a record of the direct materials, direct labour, direct expenses and overhead charges on the contract. A typical contract account might appear as shown below. Check the items in the account carefully, and notice how the cost (or value) of the work done emerges as work in progress.

NOTES

EXAMPLE: A CONTRACT ACCOUNT

CONTRACT 794 – TEN-LANE MOTORWAY

	£'000		£'000
Book value of plant on site b/d	14,300	Materials returned to stores or transferred to other sites	2,100
Materials requisition from stores	15,247		
Materials and equipment purchased	36,300	Proceeds from sale of materials on site and jobbing work for other customers	600
Maintenance and operating costs of plant and vehicles	14,444	Book value of plant transferred	4,800
Hire charges for plant and vehicles not owned	6,500	Materials on site c/d	7,194
Tools and consumables	8,570	Book value of plant on site c/d	6,640
Direct wages	23,890		21,334
Supervisors' and engineers' salaries (proportion relating to time spent on the contract)	13,000	Cost of work done c/d (balancing item)	139,917
Other site expenses	12,000		
Overheads (apportioned perhaps on the basis of direct labour hours)	17,000		
	161,251		161,251
Materials on site b/d	7,194		
Book value of plant on site b/d	6,640		
Cost of work done b/d	139,917		

On an unfinished contract, where no profits are taken mid-way through the contract, this cost of work in progress is carried forward as a closing stock balance.

4.1 Progress payments

Because a contract price may run into millions of pounds, a customer is likely to be required under the terms of the contract to make progress payments to the contractor throughout the course of the work so that the contractor does not suffer from significant cash flow problems.

The amount of the payments will be based on the value of work done (as a proportion of the contract price). This value is known as the **value certified** and will be **assessed by an architect or surveyor** (for a building contract) or qualified engineer in his certificate. A certificate provides confirmation that work to a certain value has been completed, and that some payment to the contractor is now due. The **amount of the payment** will be calculated as follows.

	The value of work done and certified by the architect or engineer
minus	**a retention (see below)**
minus	**the payments made to date**
equals	**payment due.**

Thus, if an architect's certificate assesses the value of work done on a contract to be £125,000 and if the retention is 10%, and if £92,000 has already been paid in progress payments the current payment will be:

£125,000 – £12,500 – £92,000 = £20,500

4.2 Retention monies

A customer is unlikely to want to pay the full amount of the value certified in case the contractor fails to complete the work or it later turns out that some of the work is of an unacceptable standard. There is therefore often a retention (usually between 2% and 10% of the certified value). **Retention monies are released when the contract is fully completed and accepted by the customer.** Until then the retention is regarded by the contractor as a debtor.

4.3 Profits on contracts

You may have noticed that the progress payments do not necessarily give rise to profit immediately because of retentions. Let us now turn our attention to how profits are calculated on contracts completed in one accounting period.

If a contract is started and completed in the same accounting period, the calculation of the profit is straightforward, sales minus the cost of the contract. Suppose that contract FM102 has the following costs.

	£'000
Direct materials (less returns)	80
Direct labour	70
Direct expenses	16
Plant costs	12
Overhead	22
	200

The work began on 1 April 20X5 and was completed on 15 October 20X5 in the contractor's same accounting year.

The contract price was £240,000 and on 20 October the inspecting engineer issued the final certificate of work done. At that date the customer had already paid £180,000 and the remaining £60,000 was still outstanding at the end of the contractor's accounting period. The contract accounts would appear as follows.

CONTRACT FM102 ACCOUNT

	£'000		£'000
Materials less returns	80	Cost of sales (P&L)	200
Labour	70		
Expenses	16		
Plant cost	12		
Overhead	22		
	200		200

We need to determine the **turnover figure** to be matched against the cost of sales figure of £200,000. For the purposes of profit reporting, we **take the contract price** of £240,000 (and not the amount already paid).

NOTES

The profit on the contract will therefore be treated in the profit and loss account as follows.

	£'000
Turnover	240
Cost of sales	200
	40

5 BATCH COSTING

Definition

> A **batch** is a cost unit which consists of a separate, readily identifiable group of product units which maintain their separate identity throughout the production process.

The procedures for **costing batches** are very similar to those for costing jobs.

(a) The batch is treated as a **job** during production and the costs are collected in the manner already described in this chapter.

(b) Once the batch has been completed, the **cost per unit** can be calculated as the total batch cost divided by the number of units in the batch.

WORKED EXAMPLE: BATCH COSTING

A company manufactures model cars to order and has the following budgeted overheads for the year, based on normal activity levels.

	Budgeted overheads	*Budgeted activity*
Department	£	
Welding	6,000	1,500 labour hours
Assembly	10,000	1,000 labour hours

Selling and administrative overheads are 20% of factory cost. An order for 250 model cars type XJS1, made as Batch 8638, incurred the following costs.

Materials	£12,000
Labour	100 hours welding shop at £2.50/hour
	200 hours assembly shop at £1/hour

£500 was paid for the hire of special X-ray equipment for testing the welds.

Task

Calculate the cost per unit for Batch 8638.

BPP LEARNING MEDIA

ANSWER

The first step is to calculate the overhead absorption rate for the production departments.

Welding $= \dfrac{£6{,}000}{1{,}500} =$ £4 per labour hour

Assembly $= \dfrac{£10{,}000}{1{,}000} =$ £10 per labour hour

Total cost - Batch no 8638

		£	£
Direct material			12,000
Direct expense			500
Direct labour	100 × 2.50 =	250	
	200 × 1.00 =	200	
			450
Prime cost			12,950
Overheads	100 × 4 =	400	
	200 × 10 =	2,000	
			2,400
Factory cost			15,350
Selling and administrative cost (20% of factory cost)			3,070
Total cost			18,420

Cost per unit $= \dfrac{£18{,}420}{250} = £73.68$

Activity 4 **(30 minutes)**

Lyfsa Kitchen Units Ltd crafts two different sizes of standard unit and a DIY all-purpose unit for filling up awkward spaces. The units are built to order in batches of around 250 (although the number varies according to the quality of wood purchased), and each batch is sold to NGJ Furniture Warehouses Ltd.

The costs incurred in May 20X4 were as follows.

	Big unit	*Little unit*	*All-purpose*
Direct materials purchased	£5,240	£6,710	£3,820
Direct labour			
Skilled (hours)	1,580	1,700	160
Semi-skilled (hours)	3,160	1,900	300
Direct expenses	£1,180	£1,700	£250
Selling price of batch	£33,180	£27,500	£19,500
Completed at 31 May 20X4	100%	80%	25%

The following information is available.

All direct materials for the completion of the batches have been recorded. Skilled labour is paid £5 per hour, semi-skilled £4 per hour. Administration expenses total £4,400 per month and are to be allocated to the batches on the basis of direct labour hours. Direct labour costs, direct expenses and administration expenses will increase in proportion to the total labour hours required to complete the little units and the all-purpose units. On completion of the work the practice of the manufacturer is to divide the calculated profit on each batch 20% to staff as a bonus, 80% to the company. Losses are absorbed 100% by the company.

Required

(a) Calculate the profit or loss made by the company on big units.

(b) Project the profit or loss likely to be made by the company on little units and all-purpose units.

(c) Comment on any matters you think relevant to management as a result of your calculations.

6 SERVICE COSTING

Definition

Service costing is 'Cost accounting for services or functions, eg canteens, maintenance, personnel. These may be referred to as service centres, departments or functions'.

Chartered Institute of Management Accountants Official Terminology

What are service organisations?

Service organisations do not make or sell tangible goods. Profit-seeking service organisations include accountancy firms, law firms, management consultants, transport companies, banks, insurance companies and hotels. Almost all not-for-profit organisations – hospitals, schools, libraries and so on - are also service organisations.

Service costing differs from the other costing methods (product costing methods) for a number of reasons.

(a) With many services, the cost of direct materials consumed will be relatively small compared to the labour, direct expenses and overheads cost. In product costing the direct materials are often a greater proportion of the total cost.

(b) Because of the difficulty of identifying costs with specific cost units in service costing, the indirect costs tend to represent a higher proportion of total cost compared with product costing.

(c) The output of most service organisations is often intangible and hence difficult to define. It is therefore difficult to establish a measurable cost unit.

(d) The service industry includes such a wide range of organisations which provide such different services and have such different cost structures that costing will vary considerably from one service to another.

Specific characteristics of services are **intangibility, simultaneity, perishability** and **heterogeneity.** Consider the service of providing a haircut.

(a) A haircut is **intangible** in itself, and the performance of the service comprises many other intangible factors, like the music in the salon, the personality of the hairdresser, the quality of the coffee.

(b) The production and consumption of a haircut are **simultaneous,** and therefore it cannot be inspected for quality in advance, nor can it be returned if it is not what was required.

(c) Haircuts are **perishable,** that is, they cannot be stored. You cannot buy them in bulk, and the hairdresser cannot do them in advance and keep them stocked away in case of heavy demand. The incidence of work in progress in service organisations is less frequent than in other types of organisation.

(d) A haircut is **heterogeneous** and so the exact service received will vary each time: not only will two hairdressers cut hair differently, but a hairdresser will not consistently deliver the same standard of haircut.

6.1 Unit cost measures

A particular problem with service costing is the difficulty in defining a realistic cost unit that represents a suitable measure of the service provided. Frequently, a **composite cost unit** may be deemed more appropriate if the service is a function of two activity variables. Hotels, for example, may use the '**occupied bed-night**' as an appropriate unit for cost ascertainment and control.

Typical cost units used by companies operating in a service industry are shown below.

Service	Cost unit
Road, rail and air transport services	Passenger-kilometre, tonne-kilometre
Hotels	Occupied bed-night
Education	Full-time student
Hospitals	Patient-day
Catering establishments	Meal served

Each organisation will need to ascertain the cost unit most appropriate to its activities. If a number of organisations within an industry use a common cost unit, valuable **comparisons** can be made between similar establishments. This is particularly applicable to hospitals, educational establishments and local authorities. Unit costs are also useful control measures as we shall see in the examples that follow.

Activity 5 **(10 minutes)**

Suggest cost units that are appropriate to a transport business.

BPP LEARNING MEDIA

6.2 Cost per service unit

Whatever cost unit is decided upon, the calculation of a cost per unit is as follows.

Formula to learn

$$\text{Cost per service unit} = \frac{\text{Total costs for period}}{\text{Number of service units in the period}}$$

The following examples will illustrate the principles involved in service industry costing and the further considerations to bear in mind when costing services.

WORKED EXAMPLE: COSTING AN EDUCATIONAL ESTABLISHMENT

A university offers a range of degree courses. The university organisation structure consists of three faculties each with a number of teaching departments. In addition, there is a university administrative/management function and a central services function.

(a) The following cost information is available for the year ended 30 June 20X3.

(i) **Occupancy costs**

Total £1,500,000

Such costs are apportioned on the basis of area used which is as follows.

	Square metres
Faculties	7,500
Teaching departments	20,000
Administration/management	7,000
Central services	3,000

(ii) **Administrative/management costs**

Direct costs: £1,775,000
Indirect costs: an apportionment of occupancy costs

Direct and indirect costs are charged to degree courses on a percentage basis.

(iii) **Faculty costs**

Direct costs: £700,000
Indirect costs: an apportionment of occupancy costs and central service costs

Direct and indirect costs are charged to teaching departments.

(iv) **Teaching departments**

Direct costs: £5,525,000
Indirect costs: an apportionment of occupancy costs and central service costs plus all faculty costs

Direct and indirect costs are charged to degree courses on a percentage basis.

(v) **Central services**

Direct costs: £1,000,000
Indirect costs: an apportionment of occupancy costs

(b) Direct and indirect costs are charged to users in proportion to the estimated external costs of service provision, as follows.

	£'000
Faculties	240
Teaching departments	800
Degree courses:	
Business studies	32
Mechanical engineering	48
Catering studies	32
All other degrees	448
	1,600

(c) Additional data relating to the degree courses is as follows.

	Business studies	*Degree course Mechanical engineering*	*Catering studies*
Number of undergraduates	80	50	120
Apportioned costs (as % of totals)			
Teaching departments	3.0%	2.5%	7%
Administration/management	2.5%	5.0%	4%

Central services are to be apportioned as detailed in (b) above.

The total number of undergraduates from the university in the year to 30 June 20X3 was 2,500.

Tasks

(a) Calculate the average cost per undergraduate for the year ended 30 June 20X3.

(b) Calculate the average cost per undergraduate for each of the degrees in business studies, mechanical engineering and catering studies, showing all relevant cost analysis.

ANSWER

(a) The average cost per undergraduate is as follows.

	Total costs for university £'000
Occupancy	1,500
Admin/management	1,775
Faculty	700
Teaching departments	5,525
Central services	1,000
	10,500
Number of undergraduates	2,500
Average cost per undergraduate for year ended 30 June 20X3	£4,200

NOTES

(b) Average cost per undergraduate for each course is as follows.

	Business studies	*Mechanical engineering*	*Catering studies*
	£	£	£
Teaching department costs (W1 and using % in question)	241,590	201,325	563,710
Admin/management costs (W1 and using % in question)	51,375	102,750	82,200
Central services (W2)	22,400	33,600	22,400
	315,365	337,675	668,310
Number of undergraduates	80	50	120
Average cost per undergraduate for year ended 30 June 20X3	£3,942	£6,754	£5,569

Workings

1 Cost allocation and apportionment

Cost item	*Basis of apportionment*	*Teaching departments*	*Admin/ management*	*Central services*	*Faculties*
		£'000	£'000	£'000	£'000
Direct costs	allocation	5,525	1,775	1,000	700
Occupancy costs	area used	800	280	120	300
Central services reapportioned	(W2)	560	-	(1,120)	168
Faculty costs reallocated	allocation	1,168	-	-	(1,168)
		8,053	2,055		

2 Central services apportionment of internal costs in proportion to the external costs.

	External costs	*Apportionment of internal central service costs*
	£'000	£'000
Faculties	240	168.0 $(\frac{240}{1,600} \times 1,120)$
Teaching	800	560.0
Degree courses:		
Business studies	32	22.4
Mechanical engineering	48	33.6
Catering studies	32	22.4
All other degrees	448	313.6
	1,600	1,120.0

Note. Some costs will be charged to the degree courses but this has not been considered in this example.

NOTES

Activity 6 **(20 minutes)**

Carry Ltd operates a small fleet of delivery vehicles. Expected costs are as follows.

Loading	1 hour per tonne loaded
Loading costs:	
Labour (casual)	£2 per hour
Equipment depreciation	£80 per week
Supervision	£80 per week
Drivers' wages (fixed)	£100 per man per week
Petrol	10p per kilometre
Repairs	5p per kilometre
Depreciation	£80 per week per vehicle
Supervision	£120 per week
Other general expenses (fixed)	£200 per week

There are two drivers and two vehicles in the fleet.

During a slack week, only six journeys were made.

Journey	*Tonnes carried (one way)*	*One-way distance of journey* Kilometres
1	5	100
2	8	20
3	2	60
4	4	50
5	6	200
6	5	300

What is the expected average full cost per tonne-kilometre for the week?

Activity 7 **(20 minutes)**

Mary Manor Hotel has 80 rooms and these are all either double or twin-bedded rooms offered for either holiday accommodation or for private hire for conferences and company gatherings.

In addition the hotel has a recreation area offering swimming pool, sauna and so on. This area is for the use of all residents with some days being available for paying outside customers.

The restaurant is highly regarded and widely recommended. This is used by the guests and is also open to the general public.

Discuss the possible features of an accounting information system that might be used in this organisation.

BPP LEARNING MEDIA

7 SERVICE DEPARTMENT COSTING

Service department costing is used to establish a specific cost for an '**internal service**' which is a service provided by one department for another, rather than sold externally to customers. Examples of some internal service departments include the following.

- Canteen
- Data processing
- Maintenance

7.1 The purposes of service department costing

The costing of internal services has two basic purposes.

(a) **To control the costs and efficiency in the service department.** If we establish a distribution cost per tonne-km, a canteen cost per employee, a maintenance cost per machine hour, job cost per repair, or a mainframe computer operating cost per hour, we can do the following in order to establish control measures.

(i) Compare actual costs against a target or standard

(ii) Compare actual costs in the current period against actual costs in previous periods

(b) **To control the costs of the user departments, and prevent the unnecessary use of services.** If the costs of services are charged to the user departments in such a way that the charges reflect the use actually made by each user department of the service department's services then the following will occur.

(i) The overhead costs of user departments will be established more accurately. Some service department variable costs might be identified as costs which are directly attributable to the user department.

(ii) If the service department's charges for a user department are high, the user department might be encouraged to consider whether it is making an excessively costly and wasteful use of the service department's service.

(iii) The user department might decide that it can obtain a similar service at a lower cost from an external service company and so the service department will have priced itself out of the market. This is clearly not satisfactory from the point of view of the organisation as a whole.

Service costing also provides a **fairer basis** for charging service costs to user departments, instead of charging service costs as overheads on a broad direct labour hour basis, or similar arbitrary apportionment basis. This is because service costs are related more directly to **use**.

Some examples of situations where the costing of internal services would be useful are as follows.

(a) If repair costs in a factory are costed as jobs with each bit of repair work being given a job number and costed accordingly, repair costs can be charged to the departments on the basis of repair jobs actually undertaken, instead of on a more generalised basis, such as apportionment according to machine hour capacity in each department. Departments with high repair costs could then consider their high incidence of repairs, the age and reliability of their machines, or the skills of the machine operators.

(b) If mainframe computer costs are charged to a user department on the basis of a cost per hour, the user department would make the following assessment.

   (i) Whether it was getting good value from its use of the mainframe computer.

   (ii) Whether it might be better to hire the service of a computer bureau, or perhaps install a stand-alone microcomputer system in the department.

Activity 8 **(5 minutes)**

The maintenance department of FA Ltd charges user departments for its services as follows.

- A predetermined hourly rate for labour hours worked on maintenance jobs
- Specifically identifiable materials are charged at actual cost

The budgeted maintenance labour hours for the latest period were 800 hours, during which maintenance costs of £8,400 were budgeted to be incurred.

During the period, 22 maintenance hours were worked in production department 1, and materials costing £18 were used on these maintenance jobs.

What is the charge to production department 1 for its use of the maintenance service department during the period?

8 JOB COSTING AND SERVICES

Service costing is one of the subdivisions of **continuous operation costing** and as such should theoretically be applied when the services result from a sequence of continuous or repetitive operations or processes. Service costing is therefore ideal for catering establishments, road, rail and air transport services and hotels. However, just because an organisation provides a service, it does not mean that service costing should automatically be applied.

Remember that job costing applies where work is undertaken to customers' special requirements. An organisation may therefore be working in the service sector but may supply one-off services which meet particular customers' special requirements; in such a situation job costing may be more appropriate than service costing. For example, a consultancy business, although part of the service sector, could use job costing.

(a) Each job could be given a separate number.

(b) Time sheets could be used to record and analyse consultants' time.

(c) The time spent against each job number would be shown as well as, for example, travelling time and mileage.

(d) Other costs such as stationery could be charged direct to each job as necessary.

NOTES

Chapter roundup

- Job costing is the costing method used where each cost unit is separately identifiable.
- Each job is given a number to distinguish it from other jobs.
- Costs for each job are collected on a job cost sheet or job card.
- Material costs for each job are determined from material requisition notes.
- Labour times on each job are recorded on a job ticket, which is then costed and recorded on the job cost sheet.
- Overhead is absorbed into the cost of jobs using the predetermined overhead absorption rates.
- Contract costing is a form of job costing which applies where the job is on a large scale and for a long duration. The majority of costs relating to a contract are direct costs.
- Contract costs are collected in a contract account.
- A customer is likely to be required to make progress payments which are calculated as the value of work done and certified by the architect or engineer minus a retention minus the payments made to date.
- Batch costing is similar to job costing in that each batch of similar articles is separately identifiable. The cost per unit manufactured in a batch is the total batch cost divided by the number of units in the batch.
- Service costing can be used by companies operating in a service industry or by companies wishing to establish the cost of services carried out by some of their departments.
- Specific characteristics of services
  - Intangibility
  - Simultaneity
  - Perishability
  - Heterogeneity
- One main problem with service costing is being able to define a realistic cost unit that represents a suitable measure of the service provided. If the service is a function of two activity variables, a composite cost unit may be more appropriate.
- Cost per service unit = $\frac{\text{Total costs for period}}{\text{Number of service units in the period}}$
- Service department costing is also used to establish a specific cost for an internal service which is a service provided by one department for another, rather than sold externally to customers eg canteen, maintenance.

BPP LEARNING MEDIA

NOTES

Quick quiz

1 Describe the procedures by which job costs are collected.

2 How is a job valued at the end of an accounting period if it is incomplete?

3 List the features of contract costing.

4 How is the amount of a progress payment calculated?

5 What are retention monies?

6 How would you calculate the cost per unit of a completed batch?

7 Define service costing.

8 Match up the following services with their typical cost units.

Service	Cost unit
Hotels	Patient-day
Education	Meal served
Hospitals	Full-time student
Catering organisations	Occupied bed-night

9 What is the advantage of organisations within an industry using a common cost unit?

10 Cost per service unit = ______________________

11 Service department costing is used to establish a specific cost for an 'internal service' which is a service provided by one department for another.

True ☐

False ☐

Answers to quick quiz

1 Job costs are collected on a job cost sheet from materials requisitions, which details the materials issued to the job, and job tickets, on which the time spent by each person on the particular job are recorded. The job's share of factory overheads, based on the appropriate absorption rate is also noted on the job sheet. (see para 1.1)

2 Incomplete work at the end of the period is known as Work In Progress, and forms part of stock. It is therefore valued at the lower of cost and net realisable value. The job sheet will detail the cost of bringing the stock to its present location and condition. The net realisable value will be the selling price agreed with the customer, less any further costs to be incurred to complete the job. These details should be obtainable from the estimated costings of the job. (para 1.4)

3 A formal contract is made between customer and supplier
Work is undertaken to the customer's special requirements
The work is for a relatively long duration
It is often construction work
The costing method is similar to job costing
The work is often based on-site
The site may have its own cashier and time-keeper (para 2.1)

BPP LEARNING MEDIA

NOTES

4 The value of work done and certified by the architect or engineer

minus	a retention
minus	the payments made to date
equals	payment due.

(para 4.1)

5 Retention monies are withheld by a customer until the contract is fully completed and accepted by the customer. (para 4.2)

6 $$\frac{\text{Total batch cost}}{\text{Number of units in the batch}}$$ (para 5)

7 Cost accounting for services or functions eg canteens, maintenance, personnel (service centres/functions). (para 6)

8

Service	Cost unit
Hotels	Occupied bed-night
Education	Full-time student
Hospitals	Patient-day
Catering organisations	Meal served

(para 6.1)

9 It is easier to make comparisons. (para 6.1)

10 $$\text{Cost per service unit} = \frac{\text{Total costs for period}}{\text{Number of service units in the period}}$$ (para 6.2)

11 True. (para 7.1)

Answers to activities

1 (a)

	£
Direct material Y (400 kilos × £5)	2,000
Direct material Z (800 – 60 kilcs × £6)	4,440
Total direct material cost	6,440

(b)

	£
Department P (320 hours × £4)	1,280
Department Q (200 hours × £5)	1,000
Total direct labour cost	2,280

Overtime premium will be charged to overhead in the case of Department P, and to the job of the customer who asked for overtime to be worked in the case of Department Q.

(c)

	£
Direct material cost	6,440
Direct labour cost	2,280
Production overhead (520 hours × £3)	1,560
	10,280

(d) Price = £10,280 × 130% = £13,364

2 Total labour cost = £12,500 + £23,000 + £4,500 = £40,000

$$\text{Overhead absorption rate} = \frac{£140,000}{£40,000} \times 100\% = 350\% \text{ of direct labour cost}$$

BPP LEARNING MEDIA

Closing work in progress valuation

		Job 1		*Job 2*	*Total*
		£		£	£
Costs given in question		38,150		52,025	90,175
Overhead absorbed	(12,500 × 350%)	43,750	(23,000 × 350%)	80,500	124,250
					214,425

3 If the plant is hired, the cost will be a direct expense of the contract.

4 (a) Big units

	£	£
Direct materials		5,240
Direct labour		
Skilled 1,580 hours at £5	7,900	
Semi-skilled 3,160 hours at £4	12,640	
		20,540
Direct expenses		1,180
Administrative expenses		
4,740 hours at £0.50 (see below)		2,370
		29,330
Selling price		33,180
Calculated profit		3,850
Divided: staff bonus 20%		£770
profit for company 80%		£3,080

Administration expenses absorption rate $= \frac{£4{,}400}{8{,}800}$ per labour hour

= £0.50 per labour hour

(b)

		Little units			*All-purpose*	
		£	£		£	£
Direct materials			6,710			3,820
Direct labour						
Skilled	1,700 hrs at £5	8,500		160 hrs at £5	800	
Semi-skilled	1,900 hrs at £4	7,600		300 hrs at £4	1,200	
Direct expenses		1,700			250	
Administration expenses:	3,600 hrs at £0.50	1,800		460 hrs at £0.50	230	
		19,600			2,480	
Costs to completion	20/80 × 19,600	4,900		75/25 × 2,480	7,440	
			24,500			9,920
Total costs			31,210			13,740
Selling price			27,500			19,500
Calculated profit/(loss)			(3,710)			5,760
Divided:	Staff bonus 20%		-			1,152
	(Loss)/profit for company		(3,710)			4,608

Note that whilst direct labour costs, direct expenses and administration expenses increase in proportion to the total labour hours required to complete the little units and the all-purpose units, there will be no further material costs to complete the batches.

(c) Little units are projected to incur a loss. There are two possible reasons for the loss.

(i) The estimation process may be inadequate. For example, it may have been incorrect to assume that the make-up of the costs to completion is the same as the make-up of the costs already incurred. It is possible that all of the skilled work has already been carried out and only unskilled labour is required to complete the batch. If the loss is the result of inadequate estimating, the estimation procedure should be reviewed to prevent recurrence.

(ii) It is the result of a lack of cost control. If this is the case, appropriate action should be taken to exercise control in future.

5 The cost unit is the basic measure of control in an organisation, used to monitor cost and activity levels. The cost unit selected must be measurable and appropriate for the type of cost and activity. Possible cost units which could be suggested are as follows.

Cost per kilometre

- Variable cost per kilometre
- Fixed cost per kilometre – however this is not particularly useful for control purposes because it will tend to vary with the kilometres run
- Total cost of each vehicle per kilometre – this suffers from the same problem as above
- Maintenance cost of each vehicle per kilometre

Cost per tonne-kilometre

This can be more useful than a cost per kilometre for control purposes, because it combines the distance travelled and the load carried, both of which affect cost.

Cost per operating hour

Once again, many costs can be related to this cost unit, including the following.

- Total cost of each vehicle per operating hour
- Variable costs per operating hour
- Fixed costs per operating hour – this suffers from the same problems as the fixed cost per kilometre in terms of its usefulness for control purposes.

6 Variable costs

Journey	*1*	*2*	*3*	*4*	*5*	*6*
	£	£	£	£	£	£
Loading labour (£2 per hour, 1 hour per tonne)	10	16	4	8	12	10
Petrol (both ways)	20	4	12	10	40	60
Repairs (both ways)	10	2	6	5	20	30
	40	22	22	23	72	100

NOTES

Total costs

	£
Variable costs (total for journeys 1 to 6 from above)	279
Loading equipment depreciation	80
Loading supervision	80
Drivers' wages (2 drivers)	200
Vehicles depreciation (2 vehicles)	160
Drivers' supervision	120
Other costs	200
	1,119

Journey	*Tonnes*	*One-way distance Kilometres*	*Tonne-kilometres*
1	5	100	500
2	8	20	160
3	2	60	120
4	4	50	200
5	6	200	1,200
6	5	300	1,500
			3,680

Cost per tonne-kilometre $\frac{£1,119}{3,680}$ = £0.304

Note that the large element of fixed costs may distort this measure but that a variable cost per tonne-kilometre of £279/3,680 = £0.076 may be useful for budgetary control.

7 The accounting information system that might be used in this organisation would require the following features.

(a) The hotel should be divided into a number of responsibility centres, with one manager responsible for the performance of each centre. Examples of such centres could be rooms, recreation area and restaurant.

(b) The costing system must be capable of identifying the costs and revenues to be allocated to each responsibility centre.

(c) The system must also include a fair method of apportioning those costs and revenues which cannot be directly allocated to a specific centre.

(d) Each responsibility centre would have a detailed budget against which the actual results would be compared for management control purposes.

(e) The information system must be capable of providing rapid feedback of information to managers so that prompt control action can be taken where appropriate.

(f) Key control measures should also be used, perhaps with standard targets set in advance. Examples include the following.

- Cost per bed per night
- Cost per sauna hour
- Cost per meal in the restaurant

These control measures would also provide the basic information from which a pricing decision can be made.

BPP LEARNING MEDIA

8	Predetermined labour hour rate for maintenance	= £8,400/800
		= £10.50 per hour

∴ Charge to production department 1:

	£
Maintenance labour (22 hours × £10.50)	231
Materials	18
	249

Chapter 7 :
PROCESS COSTING

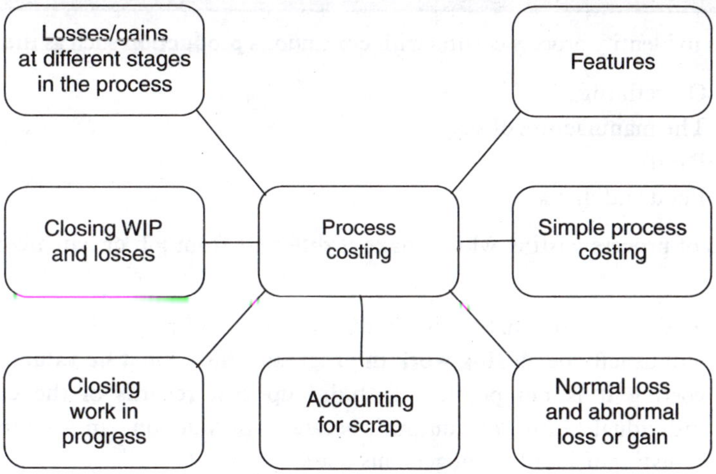

Introduction

We looked at four cost accounting methods, **job costing, contract costing, batch costing** and **service costing** in the previous chapter. In this chapter we will consider another, **process costing**. We will begin from basics and look at how to account for the most simple of processes. We will then move on to how to account for any **losses** which might occur, as well as what to do with any **scrapped units** which are sold. Next we will consider how to deal with **closing work in progress** before examining situations involving closing work in progress and losses. Throughout the chapter we will be looking at how to record process costs in **process accounts** which are simply WIP ledger accounts.

Your objectives

In this chapter you will learn about the following.

(a) The distinguishing features of process costing

(b) Simple process costing

(c) Normal loss and abnormal loss or gain

(d) Accounting for scrap

(e) Closing work in progress

(f) Closing work in progress and losses

(g) Identification of losses/gains at different stages in the process

1 THE DISTINGUISHING FEATURES OF PROCESS COSTING

Definition

> **Process costing** is a costing method used where it is not possible to identify separate units of production, or jobs, usually because of the continuous nature of the production processes involved.

It is common to identify process costing with **continuous production** such as the following.

- Oil refining
- The manufacture of soap
- Paint
- Food and drink

The features of process costing which make it different from job or batch costing are as follows.

(a) The continuous nature of production in many processes means that there will usually be **closing work in progress which must be valued.** In process costing it is not possible to build up cost records of the cost of each individual unit of output because production in progress is an indistinguishable homogeneous mass.

(b) There is often a **loss in process** due to spoilage, wastage, evaporation and so on.

(c) The **output** of one process becomes the **input** to the next until the finished product is made in the final process.

(d) Output from production may be a single product, but there may also be a **by-product** (or by-products) and/or **joint products.**

2 SIMPLE PROCESS COSTING

Before tackling the more complex areas of process costing, we will begin by looking at a very simple process costing example which will illustrate the basic techniques which we will build upon in the remainder of this chapter.

WORKED EXAMPLE

Suppose that Purr and Miaow Ltd make squeaky toys for cats. Production of the toys involves two processes, shaping and colouring. During the year to 31 March 20X3, 1,000,000 units of material worth £500,000 were input to the first process, shaping. Direct labour costs of £200,000 and production overhead costs of £200,000 were also incurred in connection with the shaping process. There were no opening or closing stocks in the shaping department. The process account for shaping for the year ended 31 March 20X3 is as follows.

NOTES

ANSWER

PROCESS 1 (SHAPING) ACCOUNT

	Units	£		Units	£
Direct materials	1,000,000	500,000	Output to Process 2	1,000,000	900,000
Direct labour		200,000			
Production overheads		200,000			
	1,000,000	900,000		1,000,000	900,000

2.1 Double entry

You will see that a **process account** is nothing more than a **ledger account with debit and credit entries** although it does have an additional column on both the debit and credit sides showing **quantity**. When preparing process accounts you are advised to include these memorandum quantity columns and to balance them off (ie ensure they total to the same amount on both sides) **before** attempting to complete the monetary value columns since they will help you to check that you have missed nothing out. This becomes increasingly important as more complications are introduced into questions.

Because process accounts are simply ledger accounts, the double entry works as it does for any other ledger account. For example, the corresponding credit entry of £200,000 for labour in the process 1 account above will be in the **wages and salaries control account**. Students often think process costing is difficult but if you bear in mind that you are simply completing a normal ledger account which is part of a system of double entry cost bookkeeping you will find this topic much more straightforward.

WORKED EXAMPLE

After that slight digression let us go back to Purr and Miaow Ltd. When using process costing, if a series of separate processes is needed to manufacture the finished product, the output of one process becomes the input to the next until the final output is made in the final process. In our example, all output from shaping was transferred to the second process, colouring, during the year to 31 March 20X3. An additional 500,000 units of material, costing £300,000, were input to the colouring process. Direct labour costs of £150,000 and production overhead costs of £150,000 were also incurred. There were no opening or closing stocks in the colouring department. The process account for colouring for the year ended 31 March 20X3 is as follows.

PROCESS 2 (COLOURING) ACCOUNT

	Units	£		Units	£
Materials from process 1	1,000,000	900,000	Output to finished		
Added materials		300,000	goods	1,000,000	1,500,000
Direct labour		150,000			
Production overhead		150,000			
	1,000,000	1,500,000		1,000,000	1,500,000

Direct labour and production overhead may be treated together in some contexts as **conversion cost**.

Notice that although figures are given for the number of units of additional material these are not recorded in the process account. This is because added materials are usually

BPP LEARNING MEDIA

materials which enhance the existing production units – in this example, we would be colouring the squeaky toys from process 1, we are not making any new toys but improving old ones we already have. So we do not need to add any extra units for added material and the number of units of material added are **never** recorded in the process account.

Added materials, labour and overhead in process 2 are usually **added gradually** throughout the process. Materials from process 1, in contrast, will often be **introduced in full at the start of the second process.**

2.2 Framework for dealing with process costing

Process costing is centred around **four key steps**. The exact work done at each step will depend on the circumstances of the question, but the approach can always be used. Don't worry about the terms used. We will be looking at their meaning as we work through the chapter.

Step 1. **Determine output and losses**

- Determine expected output.
- Calculate normal loss and abnormal loss and gain.
- Calculate equivalent units if there is closing work in progress.

Step 2. **Calculate cost per unit of output, losses and WIP**

Calculate cost per unit or cost per equivalent unit.

Step 3. **Calculate total cost of output, losses and WIP**

In some examples this will be straightforward. In cases where there is closing work in progress, a statement of evaluation will have to be prepared.

Step 4. **Complete accounts**

- Complete the process account.
- Write up the other accounts required by the question such as abnormal loss/gain accounts, scrap accounts and so on.

Activity 1 **(15 minutes)**

Palm Ltd manufactures a product, the Wombat, which goes through two separate processes, mixing and shaping.

10,000 units of material costing £30,000 were input into the mixing process along with direct labour costs of £45,000 and production overheads of £22,500.

The output from mixing was transferred to the shaping process where materials were added costing £5,000 for 5,000 units and further direct labour and production overheads were £10,000 and £4,500 respectively.

What was the total value of the output from the shaping process? From this, calculate the full cost per unit.

NOTES

3 NORMAL LOSS AND ABNORMAL LOSS OR GAIN

During a production process, a loss may occur due to wastage, spoilage, evaporation, and so on.

Definitions

Normal loss is the loss expected during a process. It is not given a share of the input costs.

Abnormal loss is the extra loss resulting when actual loss is greater than normal or expected loss, and it is given a share of the input costs.

Abnormal gain is the gain resulting when actual loss is less than the normal or expected loss, and it is given a 'negative cost'.

Since normal loss is not given a cost, the cost of producing these units is borne by the 'good' units of output.

Abnormal loss and gain units are valued at the same unit rate as 'good' units. Abnormal events do not therefore affect the cost of good production. Their costs are **analysed separately** in an **abnormal loss or abnormal gain account.**

WORKED EXAMPLE: ABNORMAL LOSSES AND GAINS

Suppose that input to a process is 1,000 units at a cost of £4,500. Normal loss is 10% and there are no opening or closing stocks. Determine the accounting entries for the cost of output and the cost of the loss if actual output is 860 units.

Before we demonstrate the use of the 'four step framework' we will summarise the way that the losses are dealt with.

(a) Normal loss is given no share of the input cost.

(b) The cost of output is therefore based on the **expected** units of output, which in our example amount to 90% of 1,000 = 900 units.

(c) Abnormal loss is given a cost, which is written off to the profit and loss account via an abnormal loss/gain account.

(d) Abnormal gain is treated in the same way, except that being a gain rather than a loss, it appears as a **debit** entry in the process account (whereas a loss appears as a **credit** entry in this account).

ANSWER

Step 1. **Determine output and losses**

If actual output is 860 units and the actual loss is 140 units:

	Units
Actual loss	140
Normal loss (10% of 1,000)	100
Abnormal loss (balancing figure)	40

BPP LEARNING MEDIA

Step 2. **Calculate cost per unit of output and losses**

The cost per unit of output and the cost per unit of abnormal loss are based on expected output.

$$\frac{\text{Costs incurred}}{\text{Expected output}} = \frac{£4,500}{900 \text{ units}} = £5 \text{ per unit}$$

Step 3. **Calculate total cost of output and losses**

Normal loss is not assigned any cost.

	£
Cost of output (860 × £5)	4,300
Normal loss	0
Abnormal loss (40 × £5)	200
	4,500

Step 4. **Complete accounts**

PROCESS ACCOUNT

	Units	£		Units		£
Cost incurred	1,000	4,500	Normal loss	100		0
			Output (finished goods a/c)	860	(× £5)	4,300
			Abnormal loss	40	(× £5)	200
	1,000	4,500		1,000		4,500

ABNORMAL LOSS ACCOUNT

	Units	£		Units	£
Process a/c	40	200	Profit and loss a/c	40	200

If there is a closing balance in the abnormal loss or gain account when the profit for the period is calculated, this balance is taken to the profit and loss account: an abnormal gain will be a credit to profit and loss and an abnormal loss will be a debit to profit and loss.

Activity 2 **(20 minutes)**

Charlton Ltd manufactures a product in a single process operation. Normal loss is 10% of input. Loss occurs at the end of the process. Data for June are as follows.

Opening and closing stocks of work in progress	Nil
Cost of input materials (3,300 units)	£59,100
Direct labour and production overhead	£30,000
Output to finished goods	2,750 units

What was the full cost of finished output in June?

4 ACCOUNTING FOR SCRAP

4.1 Loss may have a scrap value

The following basic rules are applied in accounting for this value in the process accounts.

(a) **Revenue from scrap is treated, not as an addition to sales revenue, but as a reduction in costs.**

(b) The scrap value of **normal loss** is therefore used to reduce the material costs of the process.

DEBIT Scrap account
CREDIT Process account

with the scrap value of the normal loss.

(c) The scrap value of **abnormal loss** is used to reduce the cost of abnormal loss.

DEBIT Scrap account
CREDIT Abnormal loss account

with the scrap value of abnormal loss, which therefore reduces the write-off of cost to the profit and loss account.

(d) The scrap value of **abnormal gain** arises because the actual units sold as scrap will be less than the scrap value of normal loss. Because there are fewer units of scrap than expected, there will be less revenue from scrap as a direct consequence of the abnormal gain. The abnormal gain account should therefore be debited with the scrap value.

DEBIT Abnormal gain account
CREDIT Scrap account

with the scrap value of abnormal gain.

(e) The **scrap account** is completed by recording the **actual cash received** from the sale of scrap.

DEBIT Cash account
CREDIT Scrap account

with the cash received from the sale of the actual scrap.

The same basic principle therefore applies that only **normal losses** should affect the cost of the good output. The scrap value of **normal loss only** is credited to the process account. The scrap values of abnormal losses and gains are analysed separately in the abnormal loss or gain account.

WORKED EXAMPLE: SCRAP AND ABNORMAL LOSS OR GAIN

A factory has two production processes. Normal loss in each process is 10% and scrapped units sell for £0.50 each from process 1 and £3 each from process 2. Relevant information for costing purposes relating to period 5 is as follows.

	Process 1	*Process 2*
Direct materials added:		
units	2,000	1,250
cost	£8,100	£1,900
Direct labour	£4,000	£10,000
Production overhead	150% of direct labour cost	120% of direct labour cost
Output to process 2/finished goods	1,750 units	2,800 units
Actual production overhead	£17,800	

Required

Prepare the accounts for process 1, process 2, scrap, abnormal loss or gain and production overhead.

ANSWER

Step 1. **Determine output and losses**

	Process 1	*Process 2*
	Units	Units
Output	1,750	2,800
Normal loss (10% of input)	200	300
Abnormal loss (balancing figure)	50	-
Abnormal gain (balancing figure)		(100)
	2,000	3,000*

*** 1,750 units from process 1 + 1,250 units input to process.**

Notice in this example further direct materials have been added in process 2. This will then increase the number of production units. This is very different to the situation where materials are added, remember this type of material enhances the production units and does not increase the number of units.

Step 2. **Calculate cost per unit of output and losses**

		Process 1		*Process 2*
		£		£
Cost of input				
- material		8,100		1,900
- from Process 1		-	(1,750 × £10)	17,500
- labour		4,000		10,000
- overhead	(150% × £4,000)	6,000	(120% × £10,000)	12,000
		18,100		41,400
less: scrap value of **normal loss**	(200 × £0.50)	(100)	(300 × £3)	(900)
		18,000		40,500
Expected output				
90% of 2,000		1,800		
90% of 3,000				2,700
Cost per unit				
£18,000 ÷ 1,800		£10		
£40,500 ÷ 2,700				£15

Step 3. **Calculate total cost of output and losses**

	Process 1		*Process 2*
	£		£
Output (1,750 × £10)	17,500	(2,800 × £15)	42,000
Normal loss (200 × £0.50)*	100	(300 × £3)*	900
Abnormal loss (50 × £10)	500		-
	18,100		42,900
Abnormal gain	-	(100 × £15)	(1,500)
	18,100		41,400

*** Remember that normal loss is valued at scrap value only.**

NOTES

Step 4. **Complete accounts**

PROCESS 1 ACCOUNT

	Units	£		Units	£
Direct material	2,000	8,100	Scrap a/c (normal loss)	200	100
Direct labour		4,000	Process 2 a/c	1,750	17,500
Production overhead a/c		6,000	Abnormal loss a/c	50	500
	2,000	18,100		2,000	18,100

PROCESS 2 ACCOUNT

	Units	£		Units	£
Direct material			Scrap a/c (normal loss)	300	900
From process 1	1,750	17,500	Output	2,800	42,000
Further direct material added	1,250	1,900			
Direct labour		10,000			
Production overhead		12,000			
	3,000	41,400			
Abnormal gain	100	1,500			
	3,100	42,900		3,100	42,900

ABNORMAL LOSS ACCOUNT

	£		£
Process 1 (50 units)	500	Scrap a/c: sale of scrap of extra loss (50 units)	25
		Profit and loss a/c	475
	500		500

ABNORMAL GAIN ACCOUNT

	£		£
Scrap a/c (loss of scrap revenue due to abnormal gain, 100 units × £3)	300	Process 2 abnormal gain (100 units)	1,500
Profit and loss a/c	1,200		
	1,500		1,500

SCRAP ACCOUNT

	£		£
Scrap value of normal loss		Cash a/c - cash received	
Process 1 (200 units)	100	Loss in process 1 (250 units)	125
Process 2 (300 units)	900	Loss in process 2 (200 units)	600
Abnormal loss a/c (process 1)	25	Abnormal gain a/c (process 2)	300
	1,025		1,025

PRODUCTION OVERHEAD ACCOUNT

	£		£
Overhead incurred	17,800	Process 1 a/c	6,000
Over-absorbed overhead a/c (or P & L a/c)	200	Process 2 a/c	12,000
	18,000		18,000

BPP LEARNING MEDIA

NOTES

Activity 3 **(20 minutes)**

JPC Ltd uses a process to manufacture its single product. Details for the latest period were as follows.

	Quantity	£
Direct material input	750	5,175
Direct labour		33,750
Production overheads		2,235

Normal losses are expected to be at 10% of input and JPC Ltd can usually sell any losses for £1.60 per unit. Actual losses for the period were 70 units.

Prepare the ledger account for the process for the period.

5 CLOSING WORK IN PROGRESS

In the examples we have looked at so far we have assumed that opening and closing stocks of work in process have been nil. We must now look at more realistic examples and consider how to allocate the costs incurred in a period between completed output (ie finished units) and partly completed closing stock.

Some examples will help to illustrate the problem, and the techniques used to share out (apportion) costs between finished output and closing work in progress.

WORKED EXAMPLE: VALUATION OF CLOSING STOCK

Trotter Ltd is a manufacturer of processed goods. In March 20X3, in one process, there was no opening stock, but 5,000 units of input were introduced to the process during the month, at the following cost.

	£
Direct materials	16,560
Direct labour	7,360
Production overhead	5,520
	29,440

Of the 5,000 units introduced, 4,000 were completely finished during the month and transferred to the next process. Closing stock of 1,000 units was only 60% complete with respect to materials and conversion costs.

ANSWER

(a) The problem in this example is to divide the costs of production (£29,440) between the finished output of 4,000 units and the closing stock of 1,000 units. It is argued, with good reason, that a division of costs in proportion to the number of units of each (4,000:1,000) would not be 'fair' because closing stock has not been completed, and has not yet 'received' its full amount of materials and conversion costs, but only 60% of the full amount. The 1,000 units of closing stock, being only 60% complete, are the equivalent of 600 fully worked units.

(b) To apportion costs fairly and proportionately, units of production must be converted into the equivalent of completed units, ie into **equivalent units of production**.

Definition

> **Equivalent units** are notional whole units which represent incomplete work, and which are used to apportion costs between work in process and completed output.

Step 1. **Determine output**

For this step in our framework we need to prepare a statement of equivalent units.

STATEMENT OF EQUIVALENT UNITS

	Total units	*Completion*	*Equivalent units*
Fully worked units	4,000	100%	4,000
Closing stock	1,000	60%	600
	5,000		4,600

Step 2. **Calculate cost per unit of output, and WIP**

For this step in our framework we need to prepare a statement of costs per equivalent unit because equivalent units are the basis for apportioning costs.

STATEMENT OF COSTS PER EQUIVALENT UNIT

$$\frac{\text{Total cost}}{\text{Equivalent units}} = \frac{£29,440}{4,600}$$

Cost per equivalent unit £6.40

Step 3. **Calculate total cost of output and WIP**

For this stage in our framework a statement of evaluation may now be prepared, to show how the costs should be apportioned between finished output and closing stock.

STATEMENT OF EVALUATION

Item	*Equivalent units*	*Cost of equivalent unit*	*Valuation*
			£
Fully worked units	4,000	£6.40	25,600
Closing stock	600	£6.40	3,840
	4,600		29,440

NOTES

Step 4. **Complete accounts**

The process account would be shown as follows.

PROCESS ACCOUNT

	Units	£		Units	£
(Stores a/c) Direct materials	5,000	16,560	Output to next process	4,000	25,600
(Wages a/c) Direct labour		7,360	Closing stock c/f	1,000	3,840
(O'hd a/c) Production o'hd		5,520			
	5,000	29,440		5,000	29,440

When preparing a process 'T' account, it might help to make the entries as follows.

(a) **Enter the units first.** The units columns are simply memorandum columns, but they help you to make sure that there are no units unaccounted for (for example as loss).

(b) **Enter the costs of materials, labour and overheads next.** These should be given to you.

(c) **Enter your valuation of finished output and closing stock next.** The value of the credit entries should, of course, equal the value of the debit entries.

5.1 Different rates of input

In many industries, materials, labour and overhead may be added at **different rates** during the course of production.

(a) Output from a previous process (for example, the output from process 1 to process 2) may be introduced into the subsequent process all at once, so that closing stock is 100% complete in respect of these materials.

(b) Further materials may be **added gradually** during the process, so that closing stock is only **partially complete** in respect of these added materials.

(c) Labour and overhead may be 'added' at yet another different rate. When production overhead is absorbed on a labour hour basis, however, we should expect the degree of completion on overhead to be the same as the degree of completion on labour.

When this situation occurs, equivalent units, and a cost per equivalent unit, should be **calculated separately for each type of material, and also for conversion costs.**

WORKED EXAMPLE: EQUIVALENT UNITS AND DIFFERENT DEGREES OF COMPLETION

Suppose that Shaker Ltd is a manufacturer of processed goods, and that results in process 2 for April 20X3 were as follows.

Opening stock	nil
Material input from process 1	4,000 units
Costs of input:	£
material from process 1	6,000
added materials in process 2	1,080
conversion costs	1,720

Output is transferred into the next process, process 3.

NOTES

Closing work in process amounted to 800 units, complete as to:

process 1 material	100%
added materials	50%
conversion costs	30%

Prepare the account for process 2 for April 20X3.

ANSWER

Step 1. **Determine output and losses**

STATEMENT OF EQUIVALENT UNITS (PRODUCTION IN THE PERIOD)

			Equivalent units of production					
			Process 1		*Added*		*Labour and*	
Input	*Output*	*Total*	*material*		*materials*		*overhead*	
Units		Units	Units	%	Units	%	Units	%
4,000	Completed production	3,200	3,200	100	3,200	100	3,200	100
	Closing stock	800	800	100	400	50	240	30
4,000		4,000	4,000		3,600		3,440	

Note. Since 3,200 units were completed these units must be 100% complete for all costs. It is only the closing stock which is partially complete.

Step 2. **Calculate cost per unit of output, losses and WIP**

STATEMENT OF COST (PER EQUIVALENT UNIT)

Input	*Cost*	*Equivalent production in units*	*Cost per unit*
	£		£
Process 1 material	6,000	4,000	1.50
Added materials	1,080	3,600	0.30
Labour and overhead	1,720	3,440	0.50
	8,800		2.30

Step 3. **Calculate total cost of output, losses and WIP**

STATEMENT OF EVALUATION (OF FINISHED WORK AND CLOSING STOCKS)

Production	*Cost element*	*Number of equivalent units*	*Cost per equivalent unit*	*Total*	*Cost*
			£	£	£
Completed production		3,200	2.30		7,360
Closing stock:	process 1 material	800	1.50	1,200	
	added material	400	0.30	120	
	labour and overhead	240	0.50	120	
					1,440
					8,800

BPP LEARNING MEDIA

Step 4. **Complete accounts**

PROCESS ACCOUNT

	Units	£		Units	£
Process 1 material	4,000	6,000	Process 3 a/c	3,200	7,360
Added material		1,080	(finished output)		
Conversion costs		1,720	Closing stock c/f	800	1,440
	4,000	8,800		4,000	8,800

6 CLOSING WORK IN PROGRESS AND LOSSES

The previous paragraphs have dealt separately with the following.

(a) The treatment of **loss** and **scrap**

(b) The use of **equivalent units** as a basis for apportioning costs between units of output and units of **closing stock**

We must now look at a situation where both problems occur together, that is there is closing work in progress, and also losses occurring during the process. We shall begin with an example where loss has no scrap value.

The rules are as follows.

(a) Costs should be **divided** between **finished output, closing stock** and **abnormal loss/gain** using equivalent units as a basis of apportionment.

(b) Units of **abnormal loss/gain** are often taken to be **one full equivalent unit** each, and are valued on this basis.

(c) **Abnormal loss units** are an **addition** to the total equivalent units produced but **abnormal gain units** are **subtracted** in arriving at the total number of equivalent units produced.

(d) Units of normal loss are 'equivalent to' zero equivalent units.

WORKED EXAMPLE: CHANGES IN STOCK LEVEL AND LOSSES

The following data has been collected.

Opening stock	none	Output to finished goods	2,000 units
Input units	2,800 units	Closing stock	450 units, 70% complete
Cost of input	£16,695	Total loss	350 units
Normal loss	10%; nil scrap value		

Required

Prepare the process account for the period.

NOTES

ANSWER

Step 1. **Determine output and losses**

STATEMENT OF EQUIVALENT UNITS

	Total units		*Equivalent units of work done this period*
Completely worked units	2,000	(× 100%)	2,000
Closing stock	450	(× 70%)	315
Normal loss	280		0
Abnormal loss	70	(× 100%)	70
	2,800		2,385

Step 2. **Calculate cost per unit of output, losses and WIP**

STATEMENT OF COST PER EQUIVALENT UNIT

$$\frac{\text{Costs incurred}}{\text{Equivalent units of work done}} = \frac{£16,695}{2,385}$$

Cost per equivalent unit = £7

Step 3. **Calculate total cost of output, losses and WIP**

STATEMENT OF EVALUATION

	Equivalent units	£
Completely worked units	2,000	14,000
Closing stock	315	2,205
Abnormal loss	70	490
	2,385	16,695

Step 4. **Complete accounts**

PROCESS ACCOUNT

	Units	£		Units	£
Input costs	2,800	16,695	Normal loss	280	0
			Finished goods a/c	2,000	14,000
			Abnormal loss a/c	70	490
			Closing stock c/d	450	2,205
	2,800	16,695		2,800	16,695

6.1 Closing work in progress, loss and scrap

When loss has a **scrap value**, the accounting procedures are the same as those previously described. However, if the equivalent units are a different percentage (of the total units) for materials, labour and overhead, it is a convention that the **scrap value of normal loss** is **deducted from the cost of materials** before a cost per equivalent unit is calculated.

BPP LEARNING MEDIA

Activity 4 **(30 minutes)**

Prepare a process account from the following information.

Opening stock	Nil
Input units	10,000
Input costs	
Material	£5,150
Labour	£2,700
Normal loss	5% of input
Scrap value of units of loss	£1 per unit
Output to finished goods	8,000 units
Closing stock	1,000 units
Completion of closing stock	80% for material
	50% for labour

7 IDENTIFICATION OF LOSSES/GAINS AT DIFFERENT STAGES IN THE PROCESS

In our previous examples, we have assumed that loss occurs at the completion of processing, so that units of abnormal loss or abnormal gain count as a full equivalent unit of production. It may be, however, that units are rejected as scrap or 'loss' at an inspection stage **before the completion of processing**. When this occurs, units of abnormal loss should count as a proportion of an equivalent unit, according to the volume of work done and materials added **up to the point of inspection**. An example may help as an illustration.

WORKED EXAMPLE: INCOMPLETE REJECTED ITEMS

Coffee Ltd manufactures product X, and the following information relates to process 3 during September 20X2.

During the month 1,600 units of product X were transferred from process 2, at a valuation of £10,000. Other costs in process 3 were as follows.

Added materials	£4,650
Labour and overhead	£2,920

Units of product X are inspected in process 3 when added materials are 50% complete and conversion cost 30% complete. No losses are normally expected, but during September 20X2, actual loss at the inspection stage was 200 units of product X, which were sold as scrap for £2 each.

Required

Prepare the process 3 account and abnormal loss account for September 20X2.

NOTES

ANSWER

Step 1. **Determine output and losses**

The equivalent units of work done this period are as follows.

STATEMENT OF EQUIVALENT UNITS

Item	*Total units*	*Process 2 material*		*Equivalent units Added material*		*Conversion costs*
Units from process 2	1,600					
Abnormal loss	(200)	200	(50%)	100	(30%)	60
Fully worked units, Sept 20X2	1,400	1,400	(100%)	1,400	(100%)	1,400
		1,600		1,500		1,460

Step 2. **Calculate cost per unit of output, losses and WIP**

STATEMENT OF COST PER EQUIVALENT UNIT

	Process 2 material	*Added material*	*Conversion costs*
Costs incurred, Sept 20X2	£10,000	£4,650	£2,920
Equivalent units	1,600	1,500	1,460
Cost per equivalent unit	£6.25	£3.10	£2

Step 3. **Calculate total cost of output, losses and WIP**

STATEMENT OF EVALUATION

	Process 2 material	*Added material*	*Conversion costs*	*Total*
	£	£	£	£
Fully worked units	8,750	4,340	2,800	15,890
Abnormal loss	1,250	310	120	1,680
	10,000	4,650	2,920	17,570

The only difference between this example and earlier examples is that abnormal loss has been valued at less than one equivalent unit, for added materials and conversion costs.

Step 4. **Complete accounts**

PROCESS 3 ACCOUNT

	Units	£		Units	£
Process 2 output	1,600	10,000	*Output*		
Added materials	-	4,650	Good units	1,400	15,890
Labour and overhead	-	2,920	Abnormal loss	200	1,680
	1,600	17,570		1,600	17,570

ABNORMAL LOSS ACCOUNT

	Units	£		Units	£
Process 3 account	200	1,680	Cash (sale of scrap)	200	400
			Profit and loss a/c		1,280
	200	1,680	Cash (sale of scrap)	200	1,680

BPP LEARNING MEDIA

NOTES

Activity 5 **(30 minutes)**

JM Ltd manufactures a single product, AS, through two continual processes.

Information regarding these processes is given below.

		Process 1	*Process 2*
Direct materials:	units	10,000 units	
	cost	£24,500	
Material added:	units		5,000 units
	cost		£7,460
Direct labour		£15,500	£18,580
Production overheads		£8,260	£6,900
Normal losses:	Expected	10%	5%
	Scrap value	£2 per unit	£5.50 per unit
Output		8,000 units	7,000 units
Closing stock		1,800 units	500 units

Losses in process 1 are noted at the end of the process whereas in process 2 this occurs when 60% of the material is added and it is 30% complete with regard to conversion costs.

Closing stocks are completed as follows.

	Process 1	*Process 2*
Direct material	100%	
Material added		80%
Conversion costs	40%	50%

Prepare the process accounts for the period.

NOTES

Chapter roundup

- Use our suggested four-step approach when dealing with process costing questions.

  Step 1. Determine output and losses
  Step 2. Calculate cost per unit of output, losses and WIP
  Step 3. Calculate total cost of output, losses and WIP
  Step 4. Complete accounts
- Process costing is used where there is a continuous flow of identical units.
- When units are partly complete at the end of a period, it is necessary to calculate the equivalent units of production in order to determine the cost of a complete unit.
- Losses may occur in process. If a certain level of loss is expected, this is known as normal loss. If losses are greater than expected, the extra loss is abnormal loss. If losses are less than expected, the difference is known as abnormal gain.
- The valuation of normal loss is either at scrap value or nil.
- It is conventional for the scrap value of normal loss to be deducted from the cost of materials before a cost per equivalent unit is calculated.
- Abnormal loss and gain units are valued at the same full cost as a good unit of production.
- If units are rejected as scrap or loss before the completion of processing, units of loss should count as a proportion of an equivalent unit, according to the volume of work done and materials added up to the point of inspection.

Quick quiz

1 What are the distinguishing features of process costing?

2 Distinguish between normal loss and abnormal loss.

3 How are normal losses and abnormal losses valued?

4 Is an abnormal gain a debit or credit entry in the process account?

5 What are the different accounting treatments for the scrap value of normal loss and the scrap value of abnormal loss?

6 What is an equivalent unit?

BPP LEARNING MEDIA

Answers to quick quiz

1 Production is continuous

Individual units of output cannot be distinguished

There is often loss in process due to spoilage/wastage/evaporation etc

The output of one process may be the input for another process

Output may be a single product, by products and/or joint products (see para 1)

2 Normal loss is expected during a process, whereas abnormal loss is the unexpected loss over and above the normal loss. (para 3)

3 Normal losses are valued at their scrap value or nil. Abnormal losses are valued at the cost of good production. (paras 3 and 4.1)

4 Debit. (para 4)

5 The scrap value of a normal loss is used to reduce the material costs of the process by debiting the process account. The scrap value of an abnormal loss is used to reduce the value of the abnormal loss by crediting the abnormal loss account. (para 4.1)

6 An equivalent unit is a notional whole unit which represents incomplete work. It is used to apportion costs between work in process and completed output. (para 5)

Answers to activities

1 PROCESS 1: MIXING

	Units	£		Units	£
Direct materials	10,000	30,000	Output to		
Direct labour		45,000	process 2	10,000	97,500
Production overhead		22,500			
	10,000	97,500		10,000	97,500

PROCESS 2: SHAPING

	Units	£		Units	£
Input from process 1	10,000	97,500	Output to		
Added material		5,000	finished goods	10,000	117,000
Direct labour		10,000			
Production overhead		4,500			
	10,000	117,000		10,000	117,000

Total value of output = £117,000

Full cost/unit= $\frac{£117{,}000}{10{,}000}$ = £11.70

2 ***Step 1.*** **Determine output and losses**

	Units
Actual output	2,750
Normal loss (10% × 3,300)	330
Abnormal loss (balancing figure)	220
	3,300

BPP LEARNING MEDIA

NOTES

Step 2. **Calculate cost per unit of output and losses**

$$\frac{\text{Cost of input}}{\text{Expected units of output}} = \frac{£89,100}{3,300 - 330} = £30 \text{ per unit}$$

Step 3. **Calculate total cost of output and losses**

	£
Cost of output (2,750 × £30)	82,500
Normal loss	0
Abnormal loss (220 × £30)	6,600
	89,100

3 ***Step 1.*** ***Determine output and losses***

	Units
Actual loss	70
Normal loss (750 × 10%)	75
Abnormal gain	5

Step 2. **Calculate cost per unit of output and losses**

	£
Cost of input	
Direct materials	5,175
Direct labour	33,750
Production overheads	2,235
	41,160
Less: Normal loss scrap proceeds 75 × 1.60	(120)
	41,040
Expected output 90% × 750	675
Cost per unit £41,040 ÷ 675	£60.80

Step 3. **Calculate total cost of output and losses**

	£
Cost of output (750 – 70) × £60.80	41,344
Normal loss (75 × £1.60)	120
Abnormal gain (5 × £60.80)	(304)
	41,160

Step 4. **Complete account**

PROCESS

	Units	£		Units	£
Direct material	750	5,175	Scrap – normal loss	75	120
Direct labour		33,750	Output	680	41,344
Production overheads		2,235			
Abnormal gain	5	304			
	755	41,464		755	41,464

BPP LEARNING MEDIA

NOTES

4 ***Step 1.*** **Determine output and losses**

STATEMENT OF EQUIVALENT UNITS

		Equivalent units			
	Total	*Material*		*Labour*	
	Units	%	Units	%	Units
Completed production	8,000	100	8,000	100	8,000
Closing stock	1,000	80	800	50	500
Normal loss	500				
Abnormal loss (balancing figure)	500	100	500	100	500
	10,000		9,300		9,000

Step 2. **Calculate cost per unit of output, losses and WIP**

STATEMENT OF COST PER EQUIVALENT UNIT

	Cost	*Equivalent units*	*Cost per equivalent unit*
	£		£
Material (£(5,150 – 500))	4,650	9,300	0.50
Labour	2,700	9,000	0.30
	7,350		0.80

Normal loss scrap proceeds = 500 units × £1 per unit
= £500

Step 3. **Calculate total cost of output, losses and WIP**

STATEMENT OF EVALUATION

	Equivalent units	*Cost per equivalent unit*		*Total*
		£	£	£
Completed production	8,000	0.80		6,400
Closing stock: material	800	0.50	400	
labour	500	0.30	150	
				550
Abnormal loss	500	0.80		400
				7,350

Step 4. **Complete accounts**

PROCESS ACCOUNT

	Units	£		Units	£
Material	10,000	5,150	Completed production	8,000	6,400
Labour		2,700	Closing stock	1,000	550
			Normal loss	500	500
			Abnormal loss	500	400
	10,000	7,850		10,000	7,850

NOTES

5 It is easier in this example to deal with each process separately.

Process 1

Step 1. **Determine output and losses**

The equivalent units of work done for process 1 this period are as follows.

STATEMENT OF EQUIVALENT UNITS

	Total	*Direct material*		*Conversion costs*	
Output	8,000	8,000	100%	8,000	100%
Normal loss	1,000	-		-	
Abnormal gain	(800)	(800)	100%	(800)	100%
Closing stock	1,800	1,800	100%	720	40%
	10,000	9,000		7,920	

Step 2. **Calculate cost per unit of output, losses and WIP**

	Direct material	*Conversion costs*
	£	£
Costs incurred	24,500	15,500 + 8,260
Less scrap proceeds	(2,000)	= £23,760
	£22,500	
Equivalent units	9,000 units	7,920 units
Cost per equivalent unit	£2.50	£3

Step 3. **Calculate total cost of output, losses and WIP**

	Direct material	*Conversion costs*	*Total*
	£	£	£
Output	20,000	24,000	44,000
Abnormal gain	(2,000)	(2,400)	(4,400)
Closing stock	4,500	2,160	6,660

Process 2

Step 1. **Determine output and losses**

	Total	*Process 1 material*		*Material added*		*Conversion costs*	
			%		%		%
Output	7,000	7,000	100	7,000	100	7,000	100
Normal loss	400	-		-		-	
Abnormal loss	100	100	100	60	60	30	30
Closing stock	500	500	100	400	80	250	50
	8,000	7,600		7,460		7,280	

Although the question did not say, closing stock must be 100% for process 1 otherwise it would still be in process 1.

BPP LEARNING MEDIA

NOTES

Step 2. **Calculate cost per unit of output losses and WIP**

	Process 1	Material added	Conversion costs
	£	£	£
Costs incurred	44,000	7,460	25,480
Less: Scrap proceeds	(2,200)		
	41,800		
Equivalent units	7,600	7,460	7,280
Cost per equivalent unit	£5.50	£1.00	£3.50

Step 3. **Calculate total cost of output, losses and WIP**

	Process 1	Material added	Conversion costs	Total
	£	£	£	£
Output	38,500	7,000	24,500	70,000
Abnormal loss	550	60	105	715
Closing stock	2,750	400	875	4,025

Step 4. **Complete accounts**

PROCESS 1

	Units	£		Units	£
Direct materials	10,000	24,500	Scrap: normal loss	1,000	2,000
Direct labour		15,500	Output to process 2	8,000	44,000
Production overheads		8,260	Closing stock	1,800	6,660
Abnormal gain	800	4,400			
	10,800	52,660		10,800	52,660

PROCESS 2

	Units	£		Units	£
From process 1	8,000	44,000	Scrap: normal loss	400	2,200
Materials added		7,460	Output to finished goods	7,000	70,000
Direct labour		18,580	Abnormal loss	100	715
Production overheads		6,900	Closing stock	500	4,025
	8,000	76,940		8,000	76,940

Chapter 8 : BUDGETING

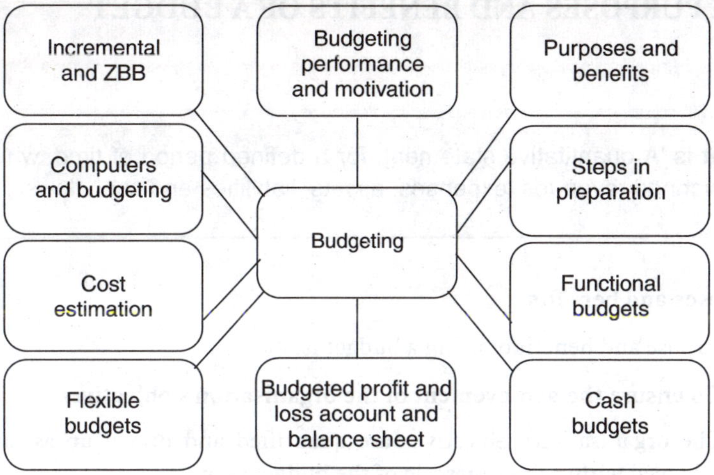

Introduction

The chapter begins by explaining the **reasons** why an organisation might prepare a budget and goes on to detail the **steps in the preparation of a budget**. The method of preparing, and the relationship between the various **functional budgets** is then set out.

The chapter also considers the construction of **cash budgets** and **budgeted profit and loss accounts and balance sheets**, the budgeted profit and loss account and balance sheet making up what is known as a **master budget**. Two different budgeting systems are described: the more traditional **incremental** approach, and a more recent development – **zero-based budgeting (ZBB)**. The difference between these two approaches is that the first builds on the previous year's budgets, whereas ZBB begins from scratch each time the budget is prepared.

Finally, we will look at the way in which budgets can affect the **behaviour** and **performance** of employees, for better and for worse.

Your objectives

In this chapter you will learn about the following.

(a) The purposes and benefits of a budget

(b) Steps in the preparation of a budget

(c) Preparing functional budgets

(d) Cash budgets

(e) Budgeted profit and loss account and balance sheet

(f) Flexible budgets

(g) Cost estimation

(h) Computers and budgeting

(i) Incremental and zero-based budgeting systems

(j) Budgeting, performance and motivation

1 THE PURPOSES AND BENEFITS OF A BUDGET

Definition

> A **budget** is 'A quantitative statement, for a defined period of time, which may include planned revenues, expenses, assets, liabilities and cash flows'.

1.1 Purposes and benefits

The main purpose and benefit of using a budget is:

(a) **To ensure the achievement of the organisation's objectives**

The organisation's objectives are quantified and drawn up as targets to be achieved within the timescale of the budget plan.

Using a budget has six further purposes/benefits, all of which contribute to the main purpose, as listed here.

(b) **To compel planning**

Planning **forces management to look ahead,** to set out detailed plans for achieving the targets for each department, operation and (ideally) each manager and to anticipate problems.

(c) **To communicate ideas and plans**

A **formal system** is necessary to ensure that each person affected by the plans is aware of what he or she is supposed to be doing. Communication might be one-way, with managers giving orders to subordinates, or there might be a two-way dialogue.

(d) **Co-ordinate activities**

The activities of different departments need to be **co-ordinated** to ensure maximum integration of effort towards **common goals.** This implies, for example, that the purchasing department should base its budget on production requirements and that the production budget should in turn be based on sales expectations.

(e) **To provide a framework for responsibility accounting**

Budgets require that managers of budget centres are made **responsible** for the achievement of budget targets for the operations under their personal control.

(f) **To establish a system of control**

Control over actual performance is provided by the comparisons of **actual results against the budget** plan. Departures from budget can then be **investigated** and the reasons for the departures can be found and acted upon

(g) **Motivate employees to improve their performance**

The interest and commitment of employees can be retained if there is a system which lets them know how well or badly they are performing. The identification of controllable reasons for departures from budget with managers responsible provides an **incentive for improving future performance.**

The remainder of the chapter explain further how budgets are used to achieve these benefits. We will being by looking at the planning and control aspects of budgeting.

1.2 Budgets in the context of planning and control

The diagram below represents the planning and control cycle. **Planning** involves making choices between alternatives and is primarily a decision-making activity. The **control** process involves measuring and correcting actual performance to ensure that the strategies that are chosen and the plans for implementing them are carried out. The link between these two is the budget.

The planning and control cycle

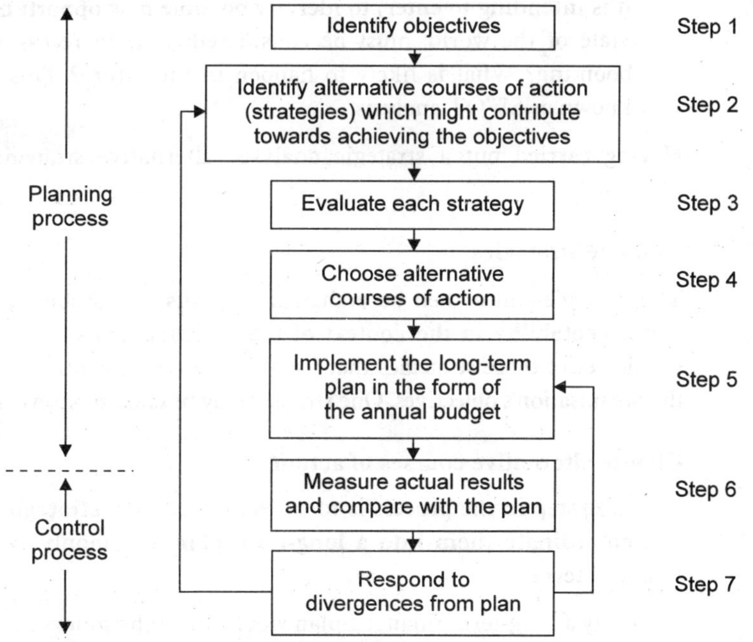

Figure 8.1: Planning and control cycle

Step 1. **Identify objectives**

Objectives establish the direction in which the management of the organisation wish it to be heading. Typical objectives include the following.

- To maximise profits
- To increase market share
- To produce a better quality product than anyone else

Objectives answer the question: **'where do we want to be?'**.

Step 2. **Identify potential strategies**

Once an organisation has decided 'where it wants to be', the next step is to identify a range of possible courses of action or **strategies that might enable the organisation to get there.**

The organisation must therefore carry out an **information-gathering exercise** to ensure that it has a full **understanding of where it is now.** This is known as a **'position audit'** or **'strategic analysis'** and involves **looking** both **inwards** and **outwards.**

(a) The organisation must **gather information from all of its internal parts** to find out what resources it possesses: what its manufacturing capacity and capability is, what is the state of its technical know-how, how well it is able to market itself, how much cash it has in the bank, how much it could borrow and so on.

(b) It must also **gather information externally** so that it can assess its position in the environment. Just as it has assessed its **own strengths and weaknesses,** it must do likewise for its competitors (**threats**). Its market must be analysed (and any other markets that it is intending to enter) to identify possible new **opportunities**. The 'state of the world' must be considered. Is it in recession or is it booming? What is likely to happen in the future? This process is known as SWOT analysis.

Having carried out a strategic analysis, alternative strategies can be identified.

Step 3. **Evaluate strategies**

The strategies must then be evaluated **in terms of suitability, feasibility and acceptability in the context of the strategic analysis**. Management should select those strategies that have the greatest potential for achieving the organisation's objectives. One strategy may be chosen or several.

Step 4. **Choose alternative courses of action**

The next step in the process is to collect the **chosen strategies** together and **co-ordinate them into a long-term plan**, commonly expressed in financial terms.

Typically a long-term financial plan would show the following.

- Projected cash flows
- Projected long-term profits
- Capital expenditure plans
- Balance sheet forecasts
- A description of the long-term objectives and strategies in words

Step 5. **Implement the long-term plan**

The **long-term plan** should then be **broken down into smaller parts.** It is unlikely that the different parts will fall conveniently into successive time periods. Strategy A may take two and a half years, while Strategy B may take five months, but not start until year three of the plan. It is usual, however, to break down the plan as a whole into equal time periods (usually one year). The resulting **short-term plan** is the **budget**.

Steps 6 and 7. **Measure actual results and compare with plan. Respond to divergences from plan**

At the end of the year actual results should be compared with those expected under the long-term plan. The **long-term plan should be reviewed** in the light of this comparison and the progress that has been made towards achieving the organisation's objectives should be assessed. Management can also **consider the feasibility of achieving the objectives** in the light of unforeseen circumstances which have arisen during the year. If the plans are now **no longer attainable then alternative strategies must be considered** for achieving the organisation's objectives, as indicated by the feedback loop (the arrowed line) linking step 7 to step 2. This aspect of control is carried out by senior management, normally on an annual basis.

The control of **day-to-day operations** is exercised by lower-level managers. At frequent intervals they must be provided with **performance reports** which consist of **detailed comparisons of actual results and budgeted results**. Performance reports provide **feedback information** by comparing planned and actual outcomes. Such reports should highlight those activities that do not conform to plan, so that managers can devote their scarce time to focusing on these items. Effective control requires that **corrective action** is taken so that **actual outcomes conform to planned outcomes**, as indicated by the feedback loop linking steps 5 and 7. Isolating past inefficiencies and the reasons for them will enable managers to take action that will avoid the same inefficiencies being repeated in the future. The system that provides reports that compare actual performance with budget figures is known as **responsibility accounting**. We will return to this topic later in the Unit.

2 STEPS IN THE PREPARATION OF A BUDGET

Towards the end of the planning stage, the budget will be prepared. Whilst we need to concentrate here on the mechanics of budget preparation, it is important to appreciate the co-ordinating role of budgets. You will see how the activities of all aspects of the business are brought together in the budget.

2.1 Budget committee

The **co-ordination** and **administration** of budgets is usually the responsibility of a **budget committee** (with the managing director as chairman). The budget committee is assisted by a **budget officer** who is usually an accountant. Every part of the organisation should be represented on the committee, so there should be a representative from sales, production, marketing and so on. Functions of the budget committee include the following.

- **Co-ordination and allocation of responsibility** for the preparation of budgets
- Issuing of the **budget manual**
- **Timetabling**
- **Provision of information** to assist in the preparation of budgets
- **Communication** of final budgets to the appropriate managers
- **Monitoring** the budgeting and planning process by **comparing actual and budgeted results**

2.2 Responsibility for budgets

The responsibility for preparing the budgets should, ideally, lie with the managers who are responsible for implementing them. For example, the preparation of particular budgets might be allocated as follows.

- The sales manager should draft the sales budget and the selling overhead cost centre budgets.
- The purchasing manager should draft the material purchases budget.
- The production manager should draft the direct production cost budgets.

Activity 1 **(5 minutes)**

Which one of the following is the budget committee *not* responsible for?

A Preparing functional budgets
B Timetabling the budgeting operation
C Allocating responsibility for the budget preparation
D Monitoring the budgeting process

2.3 The budget manual

Definition

The **budget manual** is a collection of instructions governing the responsibilities of persons and the procedures, forms and records relating to the preparation and use of budgetary data.

A budget manual may contain the following.

(a) An explanation of the **objectives** of the budgetary process including the following.

(i) The purpose of budgetary planning and control

(ii) The objectives of the various stages of the budgetary process

(iii) The importance of budgets in the long-term planning and administration of the enterprise

(b) **Organisational structures**, including the following

(i) An organisation chart
(ii) A list of individuals holding budget responsibilities

(c) An outline of the **principal budgets** and the **relationship between them**

(d) **Administrative details of budget preparation** such as the following

(i) Membership, and terms of reference of the budget committee
(ii) The sequence in which budgets are to be prepared
(iii) A timetable

(e) **Procedural matters** such as the following

(i) Specimen forms and instructions for their completion
(ii) Specimen reports
(iii) Account codes (or a chart of accounts)
(iv) The name of the budget officer to whom enquiries must be sent

2.4 Steps in budget preparation

The procedures for preparing a budget will differ from organisation to organisation but the steps described below will be indicative of the steps followed by many organisations. The preparation of a budget may take weeks or months and the **budget committee** may meet several times before the **master budget** (budgeted profit and loss account and budgeted balance sheet) is finally agreed. **Functional budgets** (sales budgets, production budgets, direct labour budgets and so on), which are amalgamated into the master budget, may need to be amended many times over as a consequence of discussions between departments, changes in market conditions and so on during the course of budget preparation.

2.5 Identifying the principal budget factor

Definition

> The **principal budget factor** is the factor which limits the activities of an organisation.

The first task in the budgetary process is to identify the principal budget factor. This is also known as the key budget factor or limiting budget factor.

The **principal budget factor** is usually **sales demand**: a company is usually restricted from making and selling more of its products because there would be no sales demand for the increased output at a price which would be acceptable/profitable to the company. The principal budget factor may also be machine capacity, distribution and selling resources, the availability of key raw materials or the availability of cash. Once this factor is defined then the remainder of the budgets can be prepared. For example, if sales are the principal budget factor then the production manager can only prepare his budget after the sales budget is complete.

Once the principal budget factor has been identified, the stages involved in the preparation of a budget can be summarised as follows (assuming that sales are the principal budget factor).

(a) The **sales budget** is prepared in units of product and sales value. The **finished goods stock budget** can be prepared at the same time. This budget decides the planned increase or decrease in finished goods stock levels.

(b) With the information from the sales and stock budgets, the **production budget** can be prepared. This is, in effect, the sales budget in units plus (or minus) the increase (or decrease) in finished goods stock. The production budget will be stated in terms of units.

(c) This leads on logically to budgeting the **resources for production.** This involves preparing a **materials usage budget, machine usage budget and a labour budget.**

(d) In addition to the materials usage budget, a **materials stock budget** will be prepared, to decide the planned increase or decrease in the level of stocks held. Once the raw materials usage requirements and the raw materials stock budget are known, the purchasing department can prepare a **raw materials purchases budget** in quantities and value for each type of material purchased.

(e) During the preparation of the sales and production budgets, the managers of the cost centres of the organisation will prepare their draft budgets for the department **overhead costs.** Such overheads will include maintenance, stores, administration, selling and research and development.

(f) From the above information a **budgeted profit and loss account** can be produced.

(g) In addition several other budgets must be prepared in order to arrive at the **budgeted balance sheet**. These are the **capital expenditure budget** (for fixed assets), the **working capital budget** (for budgeted increases or decreases in the level of debtors and creditors as well as stocks), and a **cash budget**.

3 PREPARING FUNCTIONAL BUDGETS

Having seen the theory of budget preparation, let us look at **functional** (or **departmental**) budget preparation.

WORKED EXAMPLE: PREPARING A MATERIALS PURCHASES BUDGET

ECO Ltd manufactures two products, S and T, which use the same raw materials, D and E. One unit of S uses 3 litres of D and 4 kilograms of E. One unit of T uses 5 litres of D and 2 kilograms of E. A litre of D is expected to cost £3 and a kilogram of E £7.

The sales budget for 20X2 comprises 8,000 units of S and 6,000 units of T; finished goods in stock at 1 January 20X2 are 1,500 units of S and 300 units of T, and the company plans to hold stocks of 600 units of each product at 31 December 20X2.

Stocks of raw material are 6,000 litres of D and 2,800 kilograms of E at 1 January and the company plans to hold 5,000 litres and 3,500 kilograms respectively at 31 December 20X2.

The warehouse and stores managers have suggested that a provision should be made for damages and deterioration of items held in store, as follows.

Product S :	loss of 50 units
Product T :	loss of 100 units
Material D :	loss of 500 litres
Material E :	loss of 200 kilograms

Task

Prepare a material purchases budget for the year 20X2.

ANSWER

To calculate material purchases requirements it is first necessary to calculate the material usage requirements. That in turn depends on calculating the budgeted production volumes.

	Product S Units	*Product T* Units
Production required		
To meet sales demand	8,000	6,000
To provide for stock loss	50	100
For closing stock	600	600
	8,650	6,700
Less stock already in hand	1,500	300
Budgeted production volume	7,150	6,400

	Material D Litres	*Material E* Kgs
Usage requirements		
To produce 7,150 units of S	21,450	28,600
To produce 6,400 units of T	32,000	12,800
To provide for stock loss	500	200
For closing stock	5,000	3,500
	58,950	45,100
Less stock already in hand	6,000	2,800
Budgeted material purchases	52,950	42,300
Unit cost	£3	£7
Cost of material purchases	£158,850	£296,100
Total cost of material purchases	£454,950	

The basics of the preparation of each functional budget are similar to those above.

4 CASH BUDGETS

Definition

A **cash budget** is a statement in which estimated **future cash receipts and payments** are tabulated in such a way as to show the forecast cash balance of a business at defined intervals.

EXAMPLE

For example, in December 20X2 an accounts department might wish to estimate the cash position of the business during the three following months, January to March 20X3. A cash budget might be drawn up in the following format.

	Jan £	*Feb* £	*Mar* £
Estimated cash receipts			
From credit customers	14,000	16,500	17,000
From cash sales	3,000	4,000	4,500
Proceeds on disposal of fixed assets		2,200	
Total cash receipts	17,000	22,700	21,500
Estimated cash payments			
To suppliers of goods	8,000	7,800	10,500
To employees (wages)	3,000	3,500	3,500
Purchase of fixed assets		16,000	
Rent and rates			1,000
Other overheads	1,200	1,200	1,200
Repayment of loan	2,500		
	14,700	28,500	16,200
Net surplus/(deficit) for month	2,300	(5,800)	5,300
Opening cash balance	1,200	3,500	(2,300)
Closing cash balance	3,500	(2,300)	3,000

In the example above (where the figures are purely for illustration) the accounts department has calculated that the cash balance at the beginning of the budget period, 1 January, will be £1,200. Estimates have been made of the cash which is likely to be received by the business (from cash and credit sales, and from a planned disposal of fixed assets in February). Similar estimates have been made of cash due to be paid out by the business (payments to suppliers and employees, payments for rent, rates and other overheads, payment for a planned purchase of fixed assets in February and a loan repayment due in January).

From these estimates it is a simple step to calculate the excess of cash receipts over cash payments in each month. In some months cash payments may exceed cash receipts and there will be a **deficit** for the month; this occurs during February in the above example because of the large investment in fixed assets in that month.

The last part of the cash budget above shows how the business's estimated cash balance can then be rolled along from month to month. Starting with the opening balance of £1,200 at 1 January a cash surplus of £2,300 is generated in January. This leads to a closing January balance of £3,500 which becomes the opening balance for February. The deficit of £5,800 in February throws the business's cash position into **overdraft** and the overdrawn balance of £2,300 becomes the opening balance for March. Finally, the healthy cash surplus of £5,300 in March leaves the business with a favourable cash position of £3,000 at the end of the budget period.

4.1 The usefulness of cash budgets

The cash budget is one of the most important planning tools that an organisation can use. It shows the **cash effect of all plans made within the budgetary process** and hence its preparation can lead to a **modification of budgets** if it shows that there are insufficient cash resources to finance the planned operations.

It can also give management an indication of **potential problems** that could arise and allows them the opportunity to take action to avoid such problems. A cash budget can show **four positions**. Management will need to take appropriate action depending on the potential position. This is part of the process of the management of working capital.

Cash position	Appropriate management action
Short-term surplus	• Pay creditors early to obtain discount • Attempt to increase sales by increasing debtors and stocks • Make short-term investments
Short-term deficit	• Increase creditors • Reduce debtors • Arrange an overdraft
Long-term surplus	• Make long-term investments • Expand • Diversify • Replace/update fixed assets
Long-term deficit	• Raise long-term finance (such as via issue of share capital) • Consider shutdown/disinvestments opportunities

WORKED EXAMPLE: CASH BUDGET

Peter Blair has worked for some years as a sales representative, but has recently been made redundant. He intends to start up in business on his own account, using £15,000 which he currently has invested with a building society. Peter maintains a bank account showing a small credit balance, and he plans to approach his bank for the necessary additional finance. Peter asks you for advice and provides the following additional information.

(a) Arrangements have been made to purchase fixed assets costing £8,000. These will be paid for at the end of September 20X3 and are expected to have a five-year life, at the end of which they will possess a nil residual value.

NOTES

(b) Stocks costing £5,000 will be acquired on 28 September and subsequent monthly purchases will be at a level sufficient to replace forecast sales for the month.

(c) Forecast monthly sales are £3,000 for October, £6,000 for November and December, and £10,500 from January 20X4 onwards.

(d) Selling price is fixed at the cost of stock plus 50%.

(e) Two months' credit will be allowed to customers but only one month's credit will be received from suppliers of stock.

(f) Running expenses, including rent but excluding depreciation of fixed assets, are estimated at £1,600 per month.

(g) Peter intends to make monthly cash drawings of £1,000.

Required

Prepare a cash budget for the six months to 31 March 20X4.

ANSWER

The opening cash balance at 1 October will consist of Peter's initial £15,000 less the £8,000 expended on fixed assets purchased in September. In other words, the opening balance is £7,000. Cash receipts from credit customers arise two months after the relevant sales.

Payments to suppliers are a little more tricky. We are told that cost of sales is 100/150 × sales. Thus for October cost of sales is 100/150 × £3,000 = £2,000. These goods will be purchased in October but not paid for until November. Similar calculations can be made for later months. The initial stock of £5,000 is purchased in September and consequently paid for in October.

Depreciation is not a cash flow and so is *not* included in a cash budget.

The cash budget can now be constructed.

CASH BUDGET FOR THE SIX MONTHS ENDING 31 MARCH 20X4

	Oct	*Nov*	*Dec*	*Jan*	*Feb*	*Mar*
	£	£	£	£	£	£
Payments						
Suppliers	5,000	2,000	4,000	4,000	7,000	7,000
Running expenses	1,600	1,600	1,600	1,600	1,600	1,600
Drawings	1,000	1,000	1,000	1,000	1,000	1,000
	7,600	4,600	6,600	6,600	9,600	9,600
Receipts						
Debtors			3,000	6,000	6,000	10,500
Surplus/(shortfall)	(7,600)	(4,600)	(3,600)	(600)	(3,600)	900
Opening balance	7,000	(600)	(5,200)	(8,800)	(9,400)	(13,000)
Closing balance	(600)	(5,200)	(8,800)	(9,400)	(13,000)	(12,100)

BPP LEARNING MEDIA

NOTES

Activity 2 **(30 minutes)**

You are presented with the budgeted data shown in Annex A for the period November 20X4 to June 20X5 for your firm. It has been extracted from the other functional budgets that have been prepared.

You are also told the following.

(a) Sales are 40% cash, 60% credit. Credit sales are paid two months after the month of sale.

(b) Purchases are paid the month following purchase.

(c) 75% of wages are paid in the current month and 25% the following month.

(d) Overheads are paid the month after they are incurred.

(e) Dividends are paid three months after they are declared.

(f) Capital expenditure is paid two months after it is incurred.

(g) The opening cash balance is £15,000.

The managing director is pleased with these figures as they show sales will have increased by more than 100% in the period under review. In order to achieve this he has arranged a bank overdraft with a ceiling of £50,000 to accommodate the increased stock levels and wage bill for overtime worked.

Annex A

	Nov X4	*Dec X4*	*Jan X5*	*Feb X5*	*Mar X5*	*Apr X5*	*May X5*	*June X5*
	£	£	£	£	£	£	£	£
Sales	80,000	100,000	110,000	130,000	140,000	150,000	160,000	180,000
Purchases	40,000	60,000	80,000	90,000	110,000	130,000	140,000	150,000
Wages	10,000	12,000	16,000	20,000	24,000	28,000	32,000	36,000
Overheads	10,000	10,000	15,000	15,000	15,000	20,000	20,000	20,000
Dividends		20,000						
Capital expenditure			30,000			40,000		

Required

(a) Prepare a cash budget for the 6 month period January to June 20X5.

(b) Comment upon your results in the light of your managing director's comments and offer advice.

4.2 Other working capital budgets

It may also be useful for a business monitoring its cash situation to look at other components of working capital: stock, debtors and creditors. Stock usually gets detailed consideration when the functional budgets are prepared. Debtors budgets and creditors budgets are very straightforward when patterns of payment to creditors and from debtors are considered for the purpose of preparing the cash budget.

BPP LEARNING MEDIA

NOTES

Activity 3 **(15 minutes)**

Using the information in Activity 2 above, calculate the debtors and creditors budgets for January to June 20X5.

5 BUDGETED PROFIT AND LOSS ACCOUNT AND BALANCE SHEET

As well as wishing to forecast its cash position, a business might want to estimate its profitability and its financial position for a coming period. This would involve the preparation of a budgeted profit and loss account and balance sheet, both of which form the **master budget**.

WORKED EXAMPLE: PREPARING A BUDGETED PROFIT AND LOSS ACCOUNT AND BALANCE SHEET

Using the information in the example above involving Peter you are required to prepare Peter Blair's budgeted profit and loss account for the six months ending on 31 March 20X4 and a budgeted balance sheet as at that date.

ANSWER

The profit and loss account is straightforward. The first figure is sales, which can be computed very easily from the information in Paragraph 4.1(c). It is sufficient to add up the monthly sales figures given there; for the profit and loss account there is no need to worry about any closing debtor. Similarly, cost of sales is calculated directly from the information on gross margin contained in the previous example.

FORECAST TRADING AND PROFIT AND LOSS ACCOUNT
FOR THE SIX MONTHS ENDING 31 MARCH 20X4

	£	£
Sales (3,000 + (2 × 6,000) + (3 × 10,500))		46,500
Cost of sales (2/3 × £46,500)		31,000
Gross profit		15,500
Expenses		
Running expenses (6 × £1,600)	9,600	
Depreciation (£8,000 × 20% × 6/12)	800	
		10,400
Net profit		5,100

Stock, debtors and creditors' budgets for each period are not needed; we can find the figures for the balance sheet as follows.

(a) Stock will comprise the initial purchases of £5,000.

(b) Debtors will comprise sales made in February and March (not paid until April and May respectively).

(c) Creditors will comprise purchases made in March (not paid for until April).

(d) The bank overdraft is the closing cash figure computed in the cash budget.

FORECAST BALANCE SHEET AT 31 MARCH 20X4

	£	£
Fixed assets £(8,000 – 800)		7,200
Current assets		
Stocks	5,000	
Debtors (2 × £10,500)	21,000	
	26,000	
Current liabilities		
Bank overdraft	12,100	
Trade creditors (March purchases)	7,000	
	19,100	
Net current assets		6,900
		14,100
Proprietor's interest		
Capital introduced		15,000
Profit for the period	5,100	
Less drawings	6,000	
Deficit retained		(900)
		14,100

Budget questions are often accompanied by a large amount of sometimes confusing detail. This should not blind you to the fact that many figures can be entered very simply from the logic of the trading situation described. For example in the case of Peter Blair you might feel tempted to begin a T-account to compute the closing debtors figure. This kind of working is rarely necessary, since you are told that debtors take two months to pay. Closing debtors will equal total credit sales in the last two months of the period.

Similarly, you may be given a simple statement that a business pays rates at £1,500 a year, followed by a lot of detail to enable you to calculate a prepayment at the beginning and end of the year. If you are preparing a budgeted profit and loss account for the year do not lose sight of the fact that the rates expense can be entered as £1,500 without any calculation at all.

6 FLEXIBLE BUDGETS

Definitions

- A **fixed budget** is a budget which is set for a single activity level.
- A **flexible budget** is 'A budget which, by recognising different cost behaviour patterns, is designed to change as volume of activity changes'.

Master budgets are based on planned volumes of production and sales but do not include any provision for the event that actual volumes may differ from the budget. In this sense they may be described as **fixed budgets**.

A **flexible budget** has two advantages.

(a) At the **planning** stage, it may be helpful to know what the effects would be if the actual outcome differs from the prediction. For example, a company may budget to sell 10,000 units of its product, but may prepare flexible budgets based on sales of, say, 8,000 and 12,000 units. This would enable **contingency plans** to be drawn up if necessary.

(b) At the end of each month or year, actual results may be compared with the relevant activity level in the flexible budget as a **control** procedure.

Flexible budgeting uses the principles of marginal costing. In estimating future costs it is often necessary to begin by looking at cost behaviour in the past. For costs which are wholly fixed or wholly variable no problem arises. But you may be presented with a cost which appears to have behaved in the past as a semi-variable cost (partly fixed and partly variable). A technique for estimating the level of the cost for the future is called the high/low method. We looked at this technique in Chapter 1: attempt the following question to ensure that you can remember what to do.

Activity 4 **(15 minutes)**

The cost of factory power has behaved as follows in past years.

	Units of output produced	*Cost of factory power*
		£
20X1	7,900	38,700
20X2	7,700	38,100
20X3	9,800	44,400
20X4	9,100	42,300

Budgeted production for 20X5 is 10,200 units. Estimate the cost of factory power which will be incurred. Ignore inflation.

We can now look at a full example of preparing a flexible budget.

WORKED EXAMPLE: PREPARING A FLEXIBLE BUDGET

(a) Prepare a budget for 20X6 for the direct labour costs and overhead expenses of a production department at the activity levels of 80%, 90% and 100%, using the information listed below.

(i) The direct labour hourly rate is expected to be £3.75.

(ii) 100% activity represents 60,000 direct labour hours.

(iii) Variable costs

Indirect labour	£0.75 per direct labour hour
Consumable supplies	£0.375 per direct labour hour
Canteen and other welfare services	6% of direct and indirect labour costs

(iv) Semi-variable costs are expected to relate to the direct labour hours in the same manner as for the last five years.

NOTES

Year	*Direct labour hours*	*Semi-variable costs*
		£
20X1	64,000	20,800
20X2	59,000	19,800
20X3	53,000	18,600
20X4	49,000	17,800
20X5	40,000 (estimate)	16,000 (estimate)

(v) Fixed costs

	£
Depreciation	18,000
Maintenance	10,000
Insurance	4,000
Rates	15,000
Management salaries	25,000

(vi) Inflation is to be ignored.

(b) Calculate the budget cost allowance (ie expected expenditure) for 20X6 assuming that 57,000 direct labour hours are worked.

ANSWER

(a)

	80% level	*90% level*	*100% level*
	48,000 hrs	*54,000 hrs*	*60,000 hrs*
	£'000	£'000	£'000
Direct labour	180.00	202.50	225.0
Other variable costs			
Indirect labour	36.00	40.50	45.0
Consumable supplies	18.00	20.25	22.5
Canteen etc	12.96	14.58	16.2
Total variable costs (£5.145 per hour)	246.96	277.83	308.7
Semi-variable costs (W)	17.60	18.80	20.0
Fixed costs			
Depreciation	18.00	18.00	18.0
Maintenance	10.00	10.00	10.0
Insurance	4.00	4.00	4.0
Rates	15.00	15.00	15.0
Management salaries	25.00	25.00	25.0
Budgeted costs	336.56	368.63	400.7

Working

Using the high/low method:

	£
Total cost of 64,000 hours	20,800
Total cost of 40,000 hours	16,000
Variable cost of 24,000 hours	4,800
Variable cost per hour (£4,800/24,000)	£0.20
	£
Total cost of 64,000 hours	20,800
Variable cost of 64,000 hours (× £0.20)	12,800
Fixed costs	8,000

BPP LEARNING MEDIA

Semi-variable costs are calculated as follows.

			£
60,000 hours	(60,000 × £0.20) + £8,000	=	20,000
54,000 hours	(54,000 × £0.20) + £8,000	=	18,800
48,000 hours	(48,000 × £0.20) + £8,000	=	17,600

(b) The budget cost allowance for 57,000 direct labour hours of work would be as follows.

		£
Variable costs	(57,000 × £5.145)	293,265
Semi-variable costs	(£8,000 + (57,000 × £0.20))	19,400
Fixed costs		72,000
		384,665

6.1 Budgetary control

This is the practice of establishing budgets which identify areas of responsibility for individual managers (for example production managers, purchasing managers and so on) and of regularly comparing actual results against expected results. The most important method of budgetary control, for the purpose of your examination, is **variance analysis,** which involves the comparison of actual results achieved during a control period (usually a month, or four weeks) with a flexible budget. The differences between actual results and expected results are called **variances** and these are used to provide a guideline for **control action** by individual managers. We will be looking at variances in some detail later in the following chapter.

The wrong approach to budgetary control is to compare actual results against a fixed budget. Consider the following example.

EXAMPLE

Windy Ltd manufactures a single product, the cloud. Budgeted results and actual results for June 20X2 are shown below.

	Budget	*Actual results*	*Variance*
Production and sales of the cloud (units)	2,000	3,000	
	£	£	£
Sales revenue (a)	20,000	30,000	10,000 (F)
Direct materials	6,000	8,500	2,500 (A)
Direct labour	4,000	4,500	500 (A)
Maintenance	1,000	1,400	400 (A)
Depreciation	2,000	2,200	200 (A)
Rent and rates	1,500	1,600	100 (A)
Other costs	3,600	5,000	1,400 (A)
Total costs (b)	18,100	23,200	5,100
Profit (a) – (b)	1,900	6,800	4,900 (F)

(a) In this example, the variances are meaningless for purposes of control. Costs were higher than budget because the volume of output was also higher; variable costs would be expected to increase above the budgeted costs in the fixed budget. There is no information to show whether control action is needed for any aspect of costs or revenue.

BPP LEARNING MEDIA

(b) For control purposes, it is necessary to know the answers to questions such as the following.

- Were actual costs higher than they should have been to produce and sell 3,000 clouds?
- Was actual revenue satisfactory from the sale of 3,000 clouds?

The correct approach to budgetary control is as follows.

(a) Identify fixed and variable costs.
(b) Produce a flexible budget using marginal costing techniques.

WORKED EXAMPLE: BUDGETARY CONTROL

In the previous example of Windy Ltd, let us suppose that we have the following estimates of cost behaviour.

(a) Direct materials, direct labour and maintenance costs are variable.

(b) Rent and rates and depreciation are fixed costs.

(c) Other costs consist of fixed costs of £1,600 plus a variable cost of £1 per unit made and sold.

ANSWER

The budgetary control analysis should be as follows.

	Fixed budget (a)	*Flexible budget (b)*	*Actual results (c)*	*Budget variance (b) - (c)*
Production & sales (units)	2,000	3,000	3,000	
	£	£	£	£
Sales revenue	20,000	30,000	30,000	0
Variable costs				
Direct materials	6,000	9,000	8,500	500 (F)
Direct labour	4,000	6,000	4,500	1,500 (F)
Maintenance	1,000	1,500	1,400	100 (F)
Semi-variable costs				
Other costs	3,600	4,600	5,000	400 (A)
Fixed costs				
Depreciation	2,000	2,000	2,200	200 (A)
Rent and rates	1,500	1,500	1,600	100 (A)
Total costs	18,100	24,600	23,200	1,400 (F)
Profit	1,900	5,400	6,800	1,400 (F)

Note. (F) denotes a **favourable** variance and (A) an **adverse** or unfavourable variance. Adverse variances are sometimes denoted as (U) for 'unfavourable'.

We can analyse the above as follows.

(a) In selling 3,000 units the expected profit should have been, not the fixed budget profit of £1,900, but the flexible budget profit of £5,400. Instead, actual profit was £6,800 ie £1,400 more than we should have expected. The reason for this £1,400 improvement is that, given output and sales of 3,000 units, overall costs were lower than expected (and sales revenue was exactly as expected). For example the direct material cost was £500 lower than expected.

NOTES

(b) **Another reason for the improvement in profit above the fixed budget profit is the sales volume. Windy Ltd sold 3,000 clouds instead of 2,000 clouds, with the following result.**

	£	£
Budgeted sales revenue increased by		10,000
Budgeted variable costs increased by:		
direct materials	3,000	
direct labour	2,000	
maintenance	500	
variable element of other costs	1,000	
Budgeted fixed costs are unchanged		6,500
Budgeted profit increased by		3,500

Budgeted profit was therefore increased by £3,500 because sales volumes increased. This is the difference in profit between the fixed budget and the flexible budget (5,400 – 1,900 = 3,500).

(c) **A full variance analysis statement would be as follows.**

	£	£
Fixed budget profit		1,900
Variances		
Sales volume	3,500 (F)	
Direct materials cost	500 (F)	
Direct labour cost	1,500 (F)	
Maintenance cost	100 (F)	
Other costs	400 (A)	
Depreciation	200 (A)	
Rent and rates	100 (A)	
		4,900 (F)
Actual profit		6,800

If management believes that any of these variances are large enough to justify it, they will investigate the reasons for them to see whether any corrective action is necessary.

Activity 5 **(5 minutes)**

The budgeted variable cost per unit was £2.75. When output was 18,000 units, total expenditure was £98,000 and it was found that fixed overheads were £11,000 over budget whilst variable costs were in line with budget.

What was the amount budgeted for fixed costs?

7 COST ESTIMATION

It should be obvious that the production of a budget calls for the preparation of **cost estimates** and **sales forecasts**. In fact, budgeting could be said to be as much a test of estimating and forecasting skills than anything else. In this section we will consider various cost estimation techniques.

BPP LEARNING MEDIA

7.1 Cost estimation methods

Cost estimation involves the measurement of **historical costs** to predict **future costs**. Some estimation techniques are more sophisticated than others and are therefore likely to be more reliable but, in practice, the simple techniques are more commonly found and should give estimates that are sufficiently accurate for their purpose. It is these simple techniques which we will be examining here.

7.2 Account-classification method or engineering method

By this method, the manager responsible for estimating costs will go through a list of the individual expenditure items which make up the total costs. Each item will be **classified** as fixed, variable or semi-variable, and values will be assigned to these, probably by reference to the historical cost accounts with an adjustment for estimated cost inflation.

This, in rough terms, is how the direct cost items (materials and labour costs) might be built-up when a budgeted direct cost per unit of output is estimated. It is also commonly used by cost centre managers in budgeting overhead costs and is quick and inexpensive. The technique does, however, depend on the **subjective judgement** of each manager and his skill and realism in estimating costs, and so only an approximate accuracy can be expected from its use.

7.3 High/low method

We met the **high/low method** in Chapter 1 (refer back to this chapter to refresh your memory of how it works). The major drawback to the high/low method is that **only two historical cost records from previous periods are used** in the cost estimation. Unless these two records are a reliable indicator of costs throughout the relevant range of output, which is unlikely, only a 'loose approximation' of fixed and variable costs will be obtained. The advantage of the method is its relative **simplicity**.

7.4 The scattergraph method

You should recall from Chapter 1 that a **graph** can be plotted of the historical costs from previous periods, and from the resulting scatter diagram, a **'line-of-best-fit'** can be drawn by visual estimation.

The advantage of the scattergraph over the high/low method is that a **greater quantity of historical data is used** in the estimation, but its disadvantage is that the cost line is drawn by visual judgement and so is a **subjective approximation**.

8 COMPUTERS AND BUDGETING

The examples we have looked at so far have demonstrated the need for a great number of **numerical manipulations** to produce a budget, be it a cash budget or a master budget. It is highly unlikely that the execution of the steps in the process will be problem free. Functional budgets will be out of balance with each other and will require modification so that they are **compatible**. The revision of one budget may well lead to the revision of all of the budgets. The manual preparation of a master budget and a cash budget in the real world would therefore be daunting to say the very least.

BPP LEARNING MEDIA

8.1 Advantages of computers

Computers, however, can take the hard work out of budgeting: a computerised system will have four basic advantages over a manual system.

(a) A computer has the ability to process a **larger volume of data**.

(b) A computerised system can **process data more rapidly** than a manual system.

(c) Computerised systems tend to be **more accurate** than manual systems.

(d) Computers have the ability to **store large volumes of data** in a readily accessible form.

Such advantages make computers ideal for taking over the manipulation of numbers, leaving staff to get involved in the real planning process.

8.2 Methods

Budgeting is usually computerised using either a computer program written specifically for the organisation or by a commercial spreadsheet package.

Both methods of computerisation of the budgeting process will involve a **mathematical model** which represents the real world in terms of financial values. The model will consist of several, or many, **interrelated variables**, a variable being an item in the model which has a value. For example a cash budgeting model would include variables for sales, credit periods, purchases, wages and salaries and so on.

Once the planning model has been constructed, the same model can be used again and again, simply by changing the values of the variables to produce new results for cash inflows, cash outflows, net cash flows and cash/bank balance.

A major advantage of **budget models** is the ability to evaluate different options and carry out **'what if' analysis**. By changing the value of certain variables (for example altering the ratio of cash sales to credit sales, increasing the amount of bad debts or capital expenditure, increasing the annual pay award to the workforce and so on) management are able to assess the effect of potential changes in their environment.

Computerised models can also incorporate **actual results**, period by period, and carry out the necessary calculations to produce **budgetary control reports**.

The use of a model also allows the **budget for the remainder of the year to be adjusted** once it is clear that the circumstances on which the budget was originally based have changed.

8.3 Spreadsheets

Most organisations do not have budgeting programs written for them but use standard spreadsheet packages.

Definition

'Spreadsheet' has been defined as 'the term commonly used to describe many of the modelling packages available for microcomputers, being loosely derived from the likeness to a "spreadsheet of paper" divided into rows and columns'.

NOTES

The idea behind a spreadsheet is that the model builder should construct a model in rows and columns format.

(a) Variables are represented by a row or column of items, or even by just one 'cell' in the spreadsheet.

(b) Numerical values for the **variables** are derived as follows.

 (i) They can be inserted into the model via **keyboard input**.

 (ii) They can be calculated from other data in the model using **formulae** specified within the construction of the model itself. In other words formulae can be included in the cells of the spreadsheet and referenced to other cells containing numerical information.

 (iii) They can be obtained from data held on **disk file** - in another spreadsheet, for example.

(c) **Text** can also be entered and manipulated to some extent.

The more sophisticated modern packages can handle information in **'3D' format** (a 'pad' of paper, as it were, rather than a single sheet) and can present results as charts or graphs.

To assess the **use of spreadsheets in budgeting** let us consider a cash budget. A cash budget needs frequent updating to reflect current and forecast conditions, changes in credit behaviour and so on. Each period (week, month or whatever) up-to-date information is input and in combination with brought forward file data, the cash budget will be automatically projected forward by the spreadsheet program. Surpluses and deficiencies may well be highlighted.

Both abbreviated and detailed versions of the cash budget may be produced along with graphical representations of the same information.

	A	B	C	D	E	F	G	H
2			Summary Cash Budget (Ref. Details Budgets A-L)					
3								
4			*Jan*	*Feb*	*Mar*	*Apr*	*May*	*June*
5			£'000	£'000	£'000	£'000	£'000	£'000
6	Opening balance		15	22	20	-36	-50	-83
7	add							
8	Total receipts		92	112	122	138	148	162
9	less							
10	Total payments		-85	-114	-178	-152	-181	-235
11	equals							
12	Closing balance		22	20	-36	-50	-83	-156
13								
14	Current overdraft limit		40	40	40	40	60	120
15								
16	Warning indicator					*	*	*
17						*	*	*
18							*	*
19								*

BPP LEARNING MEDIA

NOTES

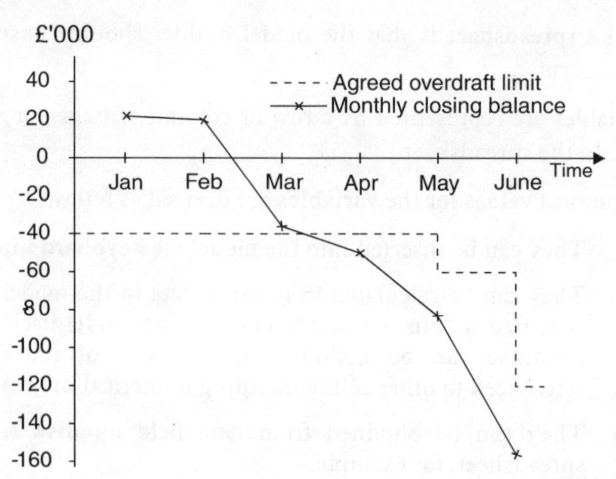

Figure 8.2 Examples of spreadsheets

Perhaps the greatest benefit that can be obtained from a spreadsheet package is its facility to perform **'what if' calculations** at great speed. For example, the consequences throughout the organisation of sales growth per month of nil, $^1/_2$%, 1%, $1^1/_2$% and so on can be calculated at the touch of a button.

9 INCREMENTAL AND ZERO BASED BUDGETING SYSTEMS

9.1 Incremental budgeting

The traditional approach to budgeting is to base next year's budget on the current year's results plus an extra amount for estimated growth or inflation next year. This approach is known as incremental budgeting since it is concerned mainly with the increments in costs and revenues which will occur in the coming period.

Incremental budgeting is a reasonable procedure if current operations are as effective, efficient and economical as they can be, and the organisation and the environment are largely unchanged.

In general, however, it is an **inefficient form of budgeting** as it **encourages slack** and **wasteful spending** to creep into budgets: managers will spend to budget, even if the amount added for inflation proved not to be necessary, so that the level of next year's budget is maintained. The result is that past inefficiencies are perpetuated because cost levels are rarely subjected to close scrutiny.

To ensure that inefficiencies are not concealed, alternative approaches to budgeting have been developed. One such approach is **zero-based budgeting (ZBB)**, the use of which was pioneered by P Pyhrr in the United States in the early 1970s.

9.2 The principles of zero based budgeting

ZBB rejects the assumption inherent in incremental budgeting that next year's budget can be based on this year's costs. Every aspect of the budget is examined in terms of its cost and the benefits it provides and the selection of better alternatives is encouraged.

BPP LEARNING MEDIA

Definition

> **Zero based budgeting** involves preparing a budget for each cost centre from a zero base. Every item of expenditure has then to be justified in its entirety in order to be included in the next year's budget.

9.3 Implementing zero based budgeting

The implementation of ZBB involves a number of steps but of greater importance is the **development of a questioning attitude** by all those involved in the budgetary process. Existing practices and expenditures must be challenged and searching questions, such as the following must be asked.

- Does the activity need to be carried out?
- What would be the consequences if the activity was not carried out?
- Does the activity benefit the organisation?
- Is the current level of provision current?
- Are there alternative ways of providing the function?
- How much should the activity cost?
- Is the expenditure worth the benefits achieved?

The basic approach of ZBB has three steps.

Step 1. **Define decision packages**

A **decision package** is a comprehensive **description of a specific organisational activity which management can use to evaluate the activity and rank it in order of priority against other activities.** Managers prepare decision packages for the activities within the budget centre for which they have responsibility.

There are two types of decision package.

(a) **Mutually exclusive packages** contain **alternative methods of getting the same job done**. The best option among the packages must be selected by comparing costs and benefits and the other packages are then discarded. For example, an organisation might consider two alternative decision packages for the preparation of the payroll: Package 1 might be in-house preparation of the payroll whereas Package 2 could involve the use of an outside agency.

(b) **Incremental packages divide one aspect of an activity into different levels of effort.** The 'base' package will describe the minimum amount of work that must be done to carry out the activity and the other packages describe what additional work could be done, at what cost and for what benefits.

EXAMPLE

Suppose that a cost centre manager is preparing a budget for maintenance costs. He might first consider two mutually exclusive packages. Package A might be to keep a maintenance team of two men per shift for two shifts each day at a cost of £60,000 per annum, whereas package B might be to obtain a maintenance service from an outside contractor at a cost of £50,000. A cost-benefit analysis will be conducted because the quicker repairs obtainable from an in-house maintenance service might justify its extra cost.

If we now suppose that package A is preferred, the budget analysis must be completed by describing the incremental variations in this chosen alternative.

(a) The 'base' package would describe the minimum requirement for the maintenance work. This might be to pay for one man per shift for two shifts each day at a cost of £30,000.

(b) Incremental package 1 might be to pay for two men on the early shift and one man on the late shift, at a cost of £45,000. The extra cost of £15,000 would need to be justified, for example by savings in lost production time, or by more efficient machinery.

(c) Incremental package 2 might be the original preference, for two men on each shift at a cost of £60,000. The cost-benefit analysis would compare its advantages, if any, over incremental package 1.

(d) Incremental package 3 might be for three men on the early shift and two on the late shift, at a cost of £75,000; and so on.

Step 2. **Evaluate and rank packages**

Each activity (decision package) is evaluated and ranked on the basis of its benefit to the organisation.

The ranking process provides managers with a technique to **allocate scarce resources** between different activities. Minimum work requirements (those that are essential to get a job done) will be given high priority and so too will work which meets legal obligations. In the accounting department these would be minimum requirements to operate the payroll, purchase ledger and sales ledger systems, and to maintain and publish a set of accounts which satisfies the external auditors.

The **ranking process can be lengthy** because large numbers of different packages will have been prepared by managers throughout the organisation. In large organisations the number of packages might be so huge that senior management cannot do the ranking unaided. In such circumstances, the following occurs.

(a) Cost centre managers will be asked to rank the packages for their own cost centre.

(b) The manager at the next level up the hierarchy of seniority will consolidate the rankings of his or her subordinates into a single ranking list for the group of cost centres, using the rankings of each cost centre as a guide.

(c) These consolidated rankings will be passed in turn one stage further up the management hierarchy for further consolidation. At higher levels of consolidation, the ranking process might be done by a committee of managers rather than by an individual.

Once a consolidated ranking of packages has been prepared, it should be reviewed to make sure that there is a general agreement that the rankings are reasonable and there are no anomalies in them.

Step 3. **Allocate resources**

Resources in the budget are then **allocated** according to the funds available and the evaluation and ranking of the competing packages. Packages involving small expenditures can be dealt with by junior managers but senior managers must make decisions involving larger amounts of expenditure. The ZBB process must, however, run through the entire management structure.

9.4 The advantages of implementing ZBB

(a) It is possible to identify and **remove inefficient or obsolete operations**.

(b) Cost reductions are possible.

(c) It forces employees to **avoid wasteful expenditure**.

(d) It can **increase motivation**.

(e) It provides a **budgeting and planning tool** for management which responds to changes in the business environment; 'obsolescent' items of expenditure are identified and dropped.

(f) The **documentation** required **provides** all management with a coordinated, in-depth **appraisal of an organisation's operations**.

(g) It **challenges the status quo** and forces an organisation to examine alternative activities and existing expenditure levels.

(h) In summary, ZBB should result in a **more efficient allocation and utilisation of resources** to an organisation's activities and departments.

9.5 The disadvantages of ZBB

The major disadvantage of zero based budgeting is the **time and energy required**. The assumptions about costs and benefits in each package must be continually updated and new packages developed as soon as new activities emerge. The following problems might also occur.

(a) **Short-term benefits** might be **emphasised** to the detriment of long-term benefits.

(b) The **false idea that all decisions have to be made in the budget might be encouraged**. Management must be able to meet unforeseen opportunities and threats at all times, and must not feel restricted from carrying out new ideas simply because they were not approved by a decision package, cost benefit analysis and the ranking process.

(c) It may be a **call for management skills** both in constructing decision packages and in the ranking process **which the organisation does not possess.** Managers may therefore have to be trained in ZBB techniques so that they can apply them sensibly and properly.

(d) It may be **difficult to 'sell' ZBB to managers as a useful technique** for the following reasons.

(i) Incremental costs and benefits of alternative courses of action are hard to quantify accurately.

(ii) Employees or trade union representatives may resist management ideas for changing the ways in which work is done.

(e) The organisation's **information systems may not be capable of providing suitable** incremental cost and incremental benefit **analysis.**

(f) **The ranking process can be difficult**. Managers face three common problems.

(i) A large number of packages may have to be ranked.

(ii) There is often a conceptual difficulty in having to rank packages which managers regard as being equally vital, for legal or operational reasons.

(iii) It is difficult to rank completely different types of activity, especially where activities have qualitative rather than quantitative benefits - such as spending on staff welfare and working conditions - where ranking must usually be entirely subjective.

In summary, perhaps the **most serious drawback to ZBB is that it requires a lot of management time and paperwork**. One way of obtaining the benefits of ZBB but of overcoming the drawbacks is to apply it selectively on a rolling basis throughout the organisation. This year finance, next year marketing, the year after personnel and so on. In this way all activities will be thoroughly scrutinised over a period of time.

9.6 Using zero based budgeting

ZBB can be used by both **profit-making** and **non-profit-making** organisations. It is popular in the US and Canada but its adoption has been slow in the UK.

The procedures of zero base budgeting do not lend themselves easily to direct manufacturing costs where standard costing, work study and the techniques of management planning and control have long been established as a means of budgeting expenditure.

ZBB is best applied to expenditure incurred in **departments that support** the essential production function. These include marketing, finance, quality control, repairs and maintenance, production planning, research and development, engineering design, personnel, data processing, sales and distribution. In many organisations, these expenses make up a large proportion of the total expenditure. These activities are less easily quantifiable by conventional methods and are **more discretionary** in nature.

ZBB can also be successfully applied to **service industries** and **non-profit-making organisations** such as local and central government departments, educational establishments, hospitals and so on.

ZBB can be applied in any organisation where alternative levels of provision for each activity are possible and where the costs and benefits are separately identifiable.

Some particular uses of ZBB are:

(a) **Budgeting for discretionary cost items**, such as advertising, R & D and training costs. The priorities for spending money could be established by ranking activities and alternative levels of spending or service can be evaluated on an incremental basis. For example, is it worth spending £2,000 more to increase the numbers trained on one type of training course by 10%? If so, what priority should this incremental spending on training be given, when compared with other potential training activities?

(b) **Rationalisation measures.** 'Rationalisation' means cutting back on production and activity levels, and cutting costs. ZBB can be used to make rationalisation decisions when an organisation is forced to make spending cuts. (This use of ZBB might explain any unpopularity it might have among managers.)

10 BUDGETING, PERFORMANCE AND MOTIVATION

In this chapter we have concentrated on the importance of the budgeting process for planning and control by management. A further aspect of the budgeting process is the human behavioural aspect, the effect that the budgeting process and resulting budgets has on the performance of managers and employees alike.

10.1 Budgets and motivation

Much has been written about the motivational effect of the budgeting process on managers in a business and there are many conflicting views. However it is well recognised that the budgetary process has the potential to be a powerful motivating tool, but conversely can also quite easily have a de-motivating effect on managers.

The effect of the eventual budgets on the motivation of managers will largely be due to the level of difficulty of the targets set by the budget, and the manner in which the budgets are set – are these imposed budgets or have the managers taken part in the budgeting process?

10.2 Budgets and standards as targets

Once decided, budgets become targets. But **how difficult** should the targets be? And how might people react to targets which are easy to achieve, or difficult to achieve?

The **quantity of material and labour time included in the budget** will **depend on the level of performance** required by management. Four types of performance standard might be set.

Ideal standards are based on **perfect operating conditions**: no wastage, no spoilage, no inefficiencies, no idle time, no breakdowns. Employees will often feel that the goals are unattainable, become demotivated and not work so hard.

Attainable standards are based on the hope that a standard amount of work will be carried out efficiently, machines properly operated or materials properly used. **Some allowance is made for wastage and inefficiencies**. If well-set they provide a useful psychological incentive by giving employees a realistic, but challenging target of efficiency.

Current standards are based on **current working conditions** (current wastage, current inefficiencies). They do not attempt to improve on current levels of efficiency.

Basic standards are kept unaltered over a long period of time, and may be out of date. They are used to show change in efficiency or performance over a long period of time. They are perhaps the least useful and least common type of standard in use.

The impact on employee behaviour of budgets based on these different standards is summarised in the table below.

Type of standard	Impact
Ideal standards:	Some say that they provide employees with an incentive to be more efficient even though it is highly unlikely that the standard will be achieved. Others argue that they are likely to have an unfavourable effect on employee motivation because the differences between standards and actual results will always be adverse. The employees may feel that the goals are unattainable and so they will not work so hard.
Attainable standards:	Might be an incentive to work harder as they provide a realistic but challenging target of efficiency.
Current standards:	Will not motivate employees to do anything more than they are currently doing.
Basic standards:	May have an unfavourable impact on the motivation of employees. Over time they will discover that they are easily able to achieve the standards. They may become bored and lose interest in what they are doing if they have nothing to aim for.

Similar comments apply to budgets.

Budgets and standards are **more likely to motivate** employees if employees accept that the budget or standard is **achievable**. If it can be achieved too easily, it will not provide sufficient motivation. If it is too difficult, employees will not accept it because they will believe it to be unachievable. In extreme circumstances, if employees believe a budget is impossible to achieve, they might be so demotivated that they attempt to prove that the budget is wrong. This is obviously the completely opposite effect to that intended.

The various **research** projects into the behavioural effects of budgeting have given **conflicting views** on certain points. However, there appears to be **general agreement** that a **target must fulfil certain conditions** if it is to motivate employees to work towards it.

- It must be **sufficiently difficult** to be a **challenging** target.
- It must **not be so difficult** that it is not achievable.
- It must be **accepted** by the employees as their personal goal.

10.3 Participation

There are basically two ways in which a budget can be set: from the **top down** (**imposed** budget) or from the **bottom up** (**participatory** budget).

10.4 Imposed style of budgeting

In this approach to budgeting, **top management prepare a budget with little or no input from operating personnel.** This budget is then **imposed** upon the employees who have to work to the budgeted figures.

The times when imposed budgets are **effective** are as follows.

- In newly-formed organisations, because of employees' lack of knowledge
- In very small businesses, because the owner/manager has a complete overview of the business
- When operational managers lack budgeting skills
- When the organisation's different units require precise co-ordination
- When budgets need to be set quickly

They are, of course, advantages and disadvantages to this style of setting budgets.

Advantages

- The aims of long-term plans are more likely to be incorporated into short-term plans.
- They improve the co-ordination between the plans and objectives of divisions.
- They use senior management's overall awareness of the organisation.
- There is less likelihood of input from inexperienced or uninformed lower-level employees.
- Budgets can be drawn up in a shorter period of time because a consultation process is not required.

Disadvantages

- Dissatisfaction, defensiveness and low morale amongst employees who have to work to meet the targets. It is hard for people to be motivated to achieve targets set by somebody else. Employees might put in only just enough effort to achieve targets, without trying to beat them.
- The feeling of team spirit may disappear.
- Organisational goals and objectives might not be accepted so readily and/or employees will not be aware of them.
- Employees might see the budget as part of a system of trying to find fault with their work: if they cannot achieve a target that has been imposed on them they will be punished.
- If consideration is not given to local operating and political environments, unachievable budgets for overseas divisions could be produced.
- Junior management initiative may be stifled if they are not invited to participate.

10.5 Participative style of budgeting

In this approach to budgeting, **budgets are developed by lower-level managers who then submit the budgets to their superiors.** The budgets are based on the lower-level managers' perceptions of what is achievable and the associated necessary resources.

Activity 6 **(10 minutes)**

In what circumstances might participative budgets be effective?

The **advantages** of participative budgets are as follows.

(a) They are based on information from employees most familiar with the department. Budgets should therefore be more realistic.

(b) Knowledge spread among several levels of management is pulled together, again producing more realistic budgets.

(c) Because employees are more aware of organisational goals, they should be more committed to achieving them.

(d) Co-ordination and cooperation between those involved in budget preparation should improve.

(e) Senior managers' overview of the business can be combined with operational-level details to produce better budgets.

(f) Managers should feel that they 'own' the budget and will therefore be more committed to the targets and more motivated to achieve them.

(g) Participation will broaden the experience of those involved and enable them to develop new skills.

Overall, participation in budget setting should give those involved a more positive attitude towards the organisation, which should lead to better performance.

There are, on the other hand, a number of **disadvantages** of participative budgets.

(a) They consume more time.

(b) Any changes made by senior management to the budgets submitted by lower-level management may cause dissatisfaction.

(c) Budgets may be unachievable if managers are not qualified to participate.

(d) Managers may not co-ordinate their own plans with those of other departments.

(e) Managers may include budgetary slack (padding the budget) in their budgets. This means they have over-estimated costs or under-estimated income. Actual results are then more likely to be better than the budgeted target results.

(f) An earlier start to the budgeting process could be required.

The research projects do not appear to provide definite conclusions about the motivational effects of budgeting. The **attitudes of the individuals** involved have an impact.

(a) Some managers may complain that they are too busy to spend time on setting standards and budgeting.

(b) Others may feel that they do not have the necessary skills.

(c) Some may think that any budget they set will be used against them.

In such circumstances participation could be seen as an **added pressure rather than as an opportunity**. For such employees an imposed approach might be better.

10.6 Negotiated style of budgeting

At the two extremes, budgets can be dictated from above or simply emerge from below but, in practice, different levels of management often agree budgets by a process of negotiation.

(a) In the imposed budget approach, operational managers will try to negotiate with senior managers the budget targets which they consider to be unreasonable or unrealistic.

(b) Likewise senior management usually review and revise budgets presented to them under a participative approach through a process of negotiation with lower level managers.

(c) **Final budgets are therefore most likely to lie between what senior management would really like and what junior managers believe is feasible.**

10.7 Creative budgets

In the process of preparing budgets, managers might **deliberately overestimate costs and underestimate sales,** so that they will not be blamed in the future for overspending and poor results.

In controlling actual operations, managers must then **ensure that their spending rises to meet their budget,** otherwise they will be 'blamed' for careless budgeting.

A typical situation is for a manager to **pad the budget** and waste money on non-essential expenses so that he uses all his budget allowances. The reason behind his action is the fear that unless the allowance is fully spent it will be reduced in future periods thus making his job more difficult as the future reduced budgets will not be so easy to attain. Because inefficiency and slack are allowed for in budgets, achieving a budget target means only that costs have remained within the accepted levels of inefficient spending.

Budget bias can **work in the other direction** too. It has been noted that, after a run of mediocre results, some managers **deliberately overstate revenues and understate cost estimates,** no doubt feeling the need to make an immediate favourable impact by promising better performance in the future. They may merely delay problems, however, as the managers may well be censured when they fail to hit these optimistic targets.

10.8 Goal congruence and dysfunctional decision making

Individuals are motivated by personal desires and interests. These desires and interests may tie in with the objectives of the organisation – after all, some people 'live for their jobs'. Other individuals see their job as a chore, and their motivations will have nothing to do with achieving the objectives of the organisation for which they work.

BPP LEARNING MEDIA

NOTES

It is therefore important that **some of the desires, interests and goals motivating employees correspond with the goals of the organisation as a whole.** This is known as **goal congruence**. Such a state would exist, for example, if the manager of department A worked to achieve a 10% increase in sales for the department, this 10% increase being part of the organisation's overall plan to increase organisational sales by 20% over the next three years.

On the other hand, **dysfunctional behaviour** can occur if a **manager's goals are not in line with those of the organisation as a whole**. Attempts to enhance his or her own situation or performance (typically '**empire building**' – employing more staff, cutting costs to achieve favourable variances but causing quality problems in other departments) will be at the expense of the best interests of the organisation as a whole. **Participation is not necessarily the answer**. Goal congruence does not necessarily result from allowing managers to develop their own budgets.

A well designed standard costing and budgetary control system can help to ensure goal congruence: continuous feedback prompting appropriate control action should steer the organisation in the right direction. The next chapter goes on to explore how such systems operate.

Activity 7 **(30 minutes)**

Eskafield Industrial Museum opened ten years ago and soon became a market leader with many working exhibits. In the early years there was a rapid growth in the number of visitors but with no further investment in new exhibits, this growth has not been maintained in recent years.

Two years ago, John Derbyshire was appointed as the museum's chief executive. His initial task was to increase the number of visitors to the museum and, following his appointment, he had made several improvements to make the museum more successful.

Another of John's tasks is to provide effective financial management. This year the museum's Board of Management has asked him to take full responsibility for producing the 20X9 budget. He has asked you to prepare estimates of the number of visitors next year.

Shortly after receiving your notes, John Derbyshire contacts you. He explains that he had prepared a draft budget for the Board of Management based on the estimated numbers for 20X9. This had been prepared on the basis that:

- Most of the museum's expenses such as salaries and rates are fixed costs;
- The museum has always budgeted for a deficit;
- The 20X9 deficit will be £35,000.

At the meeting with the Board of Management, John was congratulated on bringing the deficit down from £41,000 in 20X7 to £37,000 (latest estimate) in 20X8. However, the Board of Management raised two issues.

They felt that the planned deficit of £35,000 should be reduced to £29,000 as this would represent a greater commitment.

They also queried why the budget had been prepared without any consultation with the museum staff, ie a top down approach.

Required

Draft a memo to John Derbyshire. Your memo should:

(a) Discuss the motivational implications of imposing the budget reduction from £35,000 to £29,000;

(b) Consider the arguments for and against using a top-down budgeting approach for the museum.

11 BUDGETING AND QUALITY

Many businesses, both manufacturing and service businesses, are wholly concerned with quality. The concept behind quality control is the principle of 'get it right first time'.

11.1 Total Quality Management (TQM)

Total Quality Management (TQM) is a philosophy that means that quality management is the aim of every part of the organisation. The aim is to 'get it right first time' which means that there is a striving for continuous improvement in order to eliminate faulty work and prevent mistakes. It must apply to every part of the business and every activity that the business undertakes, whether it is in making the product, providing the service, selling the product or general administration. Under TQM each person within the business, in every function of the business, has to recognise that he/she has customers. In some cases these are external customers but in many cases these are internal customers, the employees' colleagues and managers.

11.2 Budgeting and TQM

The budgeting process is about setting standards or targets for all aspects and functions of the business to meet. If the budgeting process is successful it can help in this continuous process of improvement by setting targets that eventually eliminate all unnecessary waste and mistakes.

We looked at TQM in more detail earlier in the Course Book.

Chapter roundup

- The purposes of a budget are as follows.

  1 To ensure the achievement of the organisation's objective
  2 To compel planning
  3 To communicate ideas and plans
  4 To co-ordinate activities
  5 To provide a framework for responsibility accounting
  6 To motivate employees and improve their performance
  7 To establish a system of control

Chapter roundup (continued)

- A budget is a financial or quantitative plan of operations for a forthcoming accounting period.
- The sales budget is usually the first functional budget prepared because sales is usually the principal budget factor. The order of preparation of the remaining budgets could be finished goods stock budget, production budget, budgets for resources of production, materials stock budget, raw materials purchases budget and overhead cost budgets.
- Cash budgets show the expected receipts and payments during a budget period. The usefulness of cash budgets is that they enable management to make any forward planning decisions that may be needed, such as advising their bank of estimated overdraft requirements or strengthening their credit control procedures to ensure that debtors pay more quickly.
- The master budget consists of a budgeted profit and loss account and a budgeted balance sheet.
- Budgeted profit and cash flow for a period are unlikely to be the same.
- Fixed budgets remain unchanged regardless of the level of activity; flexible budgets are designed to flex or change with the level of activity.
- For control purposes, the actual results should be compared with the flexed budget. The differences between the components of the flexed budget and the actual results are budget variances.
- Simple cost estimation techniques include the account classification/ engineering method, the high/low method and the scattergraph method.
- Computers can provide substantial assistance to the budgeting process. 'What if' analysis, budget versus actual comparisons and adjustments to the budget following pertinent changes to the circumstances on which the budget was based are all facilitated.
- Incremental budgeting bases next year's budget on the current year's. Zero-based budgeting prepares each year's budget from a zero base; every item of expenditure has to be justified in its entirety.
- Budgets and standards are most likely to motivate employees if employees accept that the budget/standard is achievable.
- Budgets can be set from the top down (imposed budget) or from the bottom up (participatory budget). You need to be aware of the conditions needed for either one to be the preferred approach.
- Goal congruence occurs when the goals of an individual tie in with the goals of the organisation as a whole. If this is not the case dysfunctional behaviour can occur.

NOTES

Quick quiz

1 Who, ideally, should prepare budgets?

2 What is the master budget?

3 What is the principal budget factor and why is it important in the budgetary planning process?

4 Why are cash budgets useful?

5 What are the advantages of a flexible budget over a fixed budget?

6 Flexible budgets are normally prepared on a marginal costing basis. True or false?

7 What is the wrong approach to budgetary control?

8 What is the correct approach to budgetary control?

9 Match the descriptions to the budgeting style.

Description

(a) Budget allowances are set without the involvement of the budget holder.

(b) All budget holders are involved in setting their own budgets.

(c) Budget allowances are set on the basis of discussions between budget holders and those to whom they report.

Budgeting style

Negotiated budgeting
Participative budgeting
Imposed budgeting

10 Budgetary slack is necessary to ensure that managers are able to meet their targets. True or false?

Answers to quick quiz

1 The managers responsible for the implementation of the budgets should prepare those budgets. (see para 2.2)

2 The master budget comprises a budgeted balance sheet and a budgeted profit and loss account. (para 2.4)

3 The principal budget factor is the factor which limits the activities of an organisation. It is important as it must be identified and a budget for this factor produced first, as all the other budgets will depend on it. (para 2.5)

4 Cash budgets show the cash effects of all the plans, and indicate where potential problems can arise. The organisation can then amend its plans, if necessary, to take advantage of forecast cash surpluses and avoid deficits. (para 4.1)

5 It helps at the planning stage to look at the effects of different activity levels and draw up contingency plans, if necessary

At the year end, actual results will be compared with the flexed budget as a control measure (para 6)

6 True. (para 6)

7 The wrong approach to budgetary control is to compare actual results to the fixed budget. (para 6.1)

8 The correct approach to budgetary control is to compare actual results to the budget flexed to the actual level of activity. (para 6.1)

9 (a) Imposed budgeting
(b) Participative budgeting
(c) Negotiated budgeting (paras 10.4–10.6)

10 False. Budgets should be reviewed to ensure that operational managers have not included slack. (para 10.5)

Answers to activities

1 A is correct because it is the manager responsible for implementing the budget that must prepare it, not the budget committee.

2 Cash budget for January to June 20X5

(a)

	January £'000	*February* £'000	*March* £'000	*April* £'000	*May* £'000	*June* £'000
Receipts						
Sales revenue						
Cash	44	52	56	60	64	72
Credit	48	60	66	78	84	90
	92	112	122	138	148	162
Payments						
Purchases	60	80	90	110	130	140
Wages						
75%	12	15	18	21	24	27
25%	3	4	5	6	7	8
Overheads	10	15	15	15	20	20
Dividends			20			
Capital expenditure			30			40
	85	114	178	152	181	235
b/f	15	22	20	(36)	(50)	(83)
Net cash flow	7	(2)	(56)	(14)	(33)	(73)
c/f	22	20	(36)	(50)	(83)	(156)

(b) The overdraft arrangements are quite inadequate to service the cash needs of the business over the six month period. If the figures are realistic then action should be taken now to avoid difficulties in the near future. The following are possible courses of action.

- Activities could be curtailed.
- Other sources of cash could be explored, for example a long-term loan to finance the capital expenditure and a factoring arrangement to provide cash due from debtors more quickly.
- Efforts to increase the speed of debt collection could be made.
- Payments to creditors could be delayed.
- The dividend payments could be postponed (the figures indicate that this is a small company, possibly owner-managed).

NOTES

- Staff might be persuaded to work at a lower rate in return for, say, an annual bonus or a profit-sharing agreement.
- Extra staff might be taken on to reduce the amount of overtime paid.
- The stockholding policy should be reviewed: it may be possible to meet demand from current production and minimise cash tied up in stocks.

3

Month-end	*Jan X5*	*Feb X5*	*Mar X5*	*Apr X5*	*May X5*	*Jun X5*
	£'000	£'000	£'000	£'000	£'000	£'000
Debtors	126	144	162	174	186	204
Creditors	80	90	110	130	140	150

Example of the calculation of debtors budget:

Debtors at the end of March = 60% × (February sales + March sales)
= 60% × (£130,000 + £140,000)
= £162,000

4

	Units	£
20X3 (highest output)	9,800	44,400
20X2 (lowest output)	7,700	38,100
	2,100	6,300

The variable cost per unit is therefore £6,300/2,100 = £3.

The level of fixed cost can be calculated by looking at any output level.

	£
Total cost of factory power in 20X3	44,400
Less variable cost of factory power (9,800 × £3)	29,400
Fixed cost of factory power	15,000

An estimate of costs is 20X5 is as follows.

	£
Fixed cost	15,000
Variable cost of budgeted production (10,200 × £3)	30,600
Total budgeted cost of factory power	45,600

5

	£
Total expenditure	98,000
Budgeted variable cost (18,000 × £2.75)	49,500
Actual fixed costs incurred	48,500
Fixed overhead expenditure variance	11,000
Budgeted fixed costs	37,500

6 Participative budgets might be effective:

- In well-established organisations, because systems are in place and past experience can be used as a basis for forward planning
- In very large businesses, where senior management do not have enough knowledge of all of the organisation's activities to enable them to draw up budgets
- When operational managers have strong budgeting skills
- When the organisation's different units act autonomously

7 **Tutorial note**. In task (b) you may have felt that the top-down approach to budgeting was more appropriate at the museum. Justify your answer and you will receive marks.

MEMORANDUM

To: John Derbyshire
From: Consultant
Date: 5 October 20X8
Subject: **Behavioural aspects of budgeting**

(a) Motivational implications of imposing the budget reduction

When setting budgets, certain managers establish a budgeted figure and then add on a bit extra (when budgeting costs) or take off a bit (when estimating revenue) 'just in case'. This extra, which is known as **budgetary slack**, is included or deducted 'just in case' they haven't estimated accurately, costs turn out to be higher than expected or revenue lower than expected or there is some other unforeseeable event which stops them meeting their budget target.

This slack **needs to be removed** from the budget. Senior management therefore have to make an estimate of the slack and ask for the budget submitted by the lower-level manager to be adjusted accordingly. If the manager has not incorporated slack, this can be very demotivating; the entire budgeting process has to begin again and costs reduced/revenues increased to the level required. Moreover, the manager is likely to feel no sense of ownership of the budget, it having been imposed on him/her, and hence he or she will be less inclined to make efforts to meet the targets.

The size of the reduction/increase will determine the effect on morale; a small change is likely to have less effect than a large change.

Given that the Board of Management appear to have requested the reduction from £35,000 to £29,000 with no reason to believe that you have incorporated budgetary slack (£35,000 being £2,000 less than the estimated deficit for 20X8), it is likely have a negative impact on both your motivation and that of other museum staff.

(b) Top-down budgeting

In the top-down or **imposed** approach to budgeting, **top management prepare a budget with little or no input from operating personnel** and it is then imposed upon the employees who have to work to the budgeted figures.

In the **bottom-up** or **participatory** approach to budgeting, **budgets are developed by lower-level managers** who then submit the budgets to their superiors. The budgets are based on lower-level managers' perceptions of what is achievable and the associated necessary resources.

Imposed budgets tend to be effective in newly-formed organisations and/or in very small businesses whereas participatory budgets are most often seen in more mature organisations, of medium to large size.

The imposed style of budgeting uses senior management's awareness of total resource availability, decreases the possibility of input from inexperienced or uninformed lower-level employees and ensures that an organisation's strategic plans are incorporated into planned activities.

On the other hand, the bottom-up approach ensures that information from employees most familiar with each department's needs and constraints is included, knowledge spread among several levels of management is pulled together, morale and motivation is improved and acceptance of and commitment to organisational goals and objectives by operational managers is increased. What's more, they tend to be more realistic.

Given that the museum is well established and in view of the advantages set out above, the **bottom-up approach** would seem to be the **more suitable** of the two approaches for the museum.

Chapter 9 :

STANDARD COSTING AND VARIANCE ANALYSIS

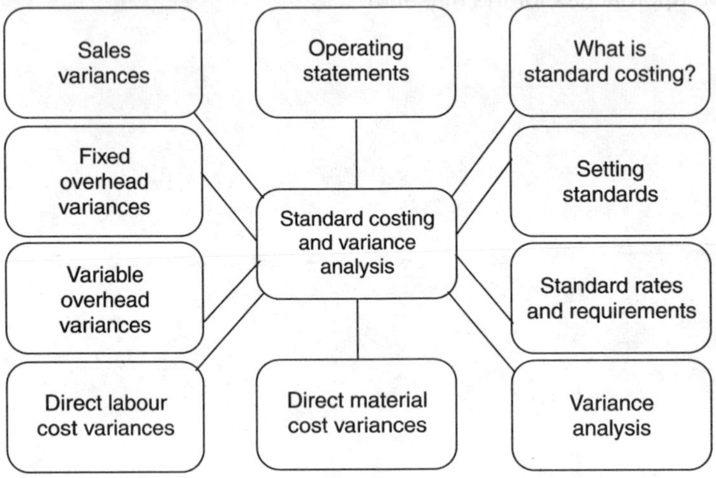

Introduction

Just as there are **standards** for most things in our daily lives (cleanliness in hamburger restaurants, educational achievement of eleven year olds, number of trains running on time), there are standards for the costs of products and services. Moreover, just as the standards in our daily lives are not always met, the standards for the costs of products and services are not always met. We will not, however, be considering the standards of cleanliness of hamburger restaurants in this chapter but we will be looking at standards for **costs,** what they are used for and how they are set.

We will then see how **standard costing** forms the basis of a process called **variance analysis,** which was introduced in the last chapter. Variance analysis is a vital management control tool, and we will spend a large part of this chapter explaining the calculations, and part of the next chapter looking at how the control is actually exercised.

Your objectives

In this chapter you will learn about the following.

(a) Standard costing

(b) Variance analysis

(c) Operating statements

BPP LEARNING MEDIA

NOTES

1 WHAT IS STANDARD COSTING?

The building blocks of standard costing are standard costs and so before we look at standard costing in any detail you really need to know what a standard cost is.

1.1 Standard cost

The standard cost of product 1234 is set out below.

STANDARD COST CARD – PRODUCT 1234

	£	£
Direct materials		
Material X – 3 kg at £4 per kg	12	
Material Y – 9 litres at £2 per litre	18	
		30
Direct labour		
Grade A – 6 hours at £1.50 per hour	9	
Grade B – 8 hours at £2 per hour	16	
		25
Standard direct cost		55
Variable production overhead – 14 hours at £0.50 per hour		7
Standard variable cost of production		62
Fixed production overhead – 14 hours at £4.50 per hour		63
Standard full production cost		125
Administration and marketing overhead		15
Standard cost of sale		140
Standard profit		20
Standard sales price		160

Definition

A **standard cost** is a planned unit cost.

Notice how the total standard cost is built up from standards for each cost element: standard quantities of materials at standard prices, standard quantities of labour time at standard rates and so on. It is therefore determined by management's estimates of the following.

- The expected prices of materials, labour and expenses
- Efficiency levels in the use of materials and labour
- Budgeted overhead costs and budgeted volumes of activity

We will see how management arrives at these estimates in Section 2.

But why should management want to prepare standard costs? Obviously to assist with standard costing, but what is the point of standard costing?

1.2 The uses of standard costing

Standard costing has a variety of uses but its two principal ones are as follows.

(a) To **value stocks** and **cost production** for cost accounting purposes. It is an alternative method of valuation to methods like FIFO and LIFO which we saw earlier in this text.

(b) To act as a **control device** by establishing standards (planned costs), highlighting (via **variance analysis** which we will cover shortly) activities that are not conforming to plan and thus **alerting management** to areas which may be out of control and in need of corrective action.

Activity 1 **(20 minutes)**

Bloggs Ltd makes one product, the Joe. Two types of labour are involved in the preparation of a Joe, skilled and semi-skilled. Skilled labour is paid £10 per hour and semi-skilled £5 per hour. Twice as many skilled labour hours as semi-skilled labour hours are needed to produce a Joe, four semi-skilled labour hours being needed.

A Joe is made up of three different direct materials. Seven kilograms of direct material A, four litres of direct material B and three metres of direct material C are needed. Direct material A costs £1 per kilogram, direct material B £2 per litre and direct material C £3 per metre.

Variable production overheads are incurred at Bloggs Ltd at the rate of £2.50 per direct labour (skilled) hour.

A system of absorption costing is in operation at Bloggs Ltd. The basis of absorption is direct labour (skilled) hours. For the forthcoming accounting period, budgeted fixed production overheads are £250,000 and budgeted production of the Joe is 5,000 units.

Administration, selling and distribution overheads are added to products at the rate of £10 per unit.

A mark-up of 25% is made on the Joe.

Required

Using the above information draw up a standard cost card for the Joe.

Although the use of standard costs to simplify the keeping of cost accounting records should not be overlooked, we will be concentrating on the **control** and **variance analysis** aspect of standard costing.

Definition

Standard costing is 'A control technique which compares standard costs and revenues with actual results to obtain variances which are used to stimulate improved performance'.

Notice that the above definition highlights the control aspects of standard costing.

1.3 Standard costing as a control technique

Standard costing therefore involves the following.

- The establishment of predetermined estimates of the costs of products or services
- The collection of actual costs
- The comparison of the actual costs with the predetermined estimates.

The predetermined costs are known as **standard costs** and the difference between standard and actual cost is known as a **variance**. The process by which the total difference between standard and actual results is analysed in known as **variance analysis.**

Although standard costing can be used in a variety of costing situations (batch and mass production, process manufacture, jobbing manufacture (where there is standardisation of parts) and service industries (if a realistic cost unit can be established)), the greatest benefit from its use can be gained if there is a **degree of repetition** in the production process. It is therefore most suited to **mass production** and **repetitive assembly work.**

2 SETTING STANDARDS

Standard costs may be used in both absorption costing and in marginal costing systems. We shall, however, confine our description to standard costs in absorption costing systems.

As we noted earlier, the standard cost of a product (or service) is made up of a number of different standards, one for each cost element, each of which has to be set by management. We have divided the next section into two: the first part looks at setting the monetary part of each standard, whereas the second part looks at setting the resources requirement part of each standard.

3 STANDARD RATES AND REQUIREMENTS

3.1 Direct material prices

Direct material prices will be estimated by the purchasing department from their knowledge of the following.

- Purchase contracts already agreed
- Pricing discussions with regular suppliers
- The forecast movement of prices in the market
- The availability of bulk purchase discounts

Price inflation can cause difficulties in setting realistic standard prices. Suppose that a material costs £10 per kilogram at the moment and during the course of the next 12 months it is expected to go up in price by 20% to £12 per kilogram. What standard price should be selected?

- The current price of £10 per kilogram
- The average expected price for the year, say £11 per kilogram

Either would be possible, but neither would be entirely satisfactory.

(a) If the **current price** were used in the standard, the reported price variance will become adverse as soon as prices go up, which might be very early in the year. If prices go up gradually rather than in one big jump, it would be difficult to select an appropriate time for revising the standard.

(b) If an **estimated mid-year price** were used, price variances should be favourable in the first half of the year and adverse in the second half of the year, again assuming that prices go up gradually throughout the year. Management could only really check that in any month, the price variance did not become excessively adverse (or favourable) and that the price variance switched from being favourable to adverse around month six or seven and not sooner.

3.2 Direct labour rates

Direct labour rates per hour will be set by discussion with the personnel department and by reference to the payroll and to any agreements on pay rises with trade union representatives of the employees.

(a) A separate hourly rate or weekly wage will be set for each different labour grade/type of employee.

(b) An average hourly rate will be applied for each grade (even though individual rates of pay may vary according to age and experience).

Similar problems when dealing with inflation to those described for material prices can be met when setting labour standards.

3.3 Overhead absorption rates

When standard costs are fully absorbed costs, the **absorption rate** of fixed production overheads will be **predetermined**, usually each year when the budget is prepared, and based in the usual manner on budgeted fixed production overhead expenditure and budgeted production.

For selling and distribution costs, standard costs might be absorbed as a percentage of the standard selling price.

3.4 Standard resource requirements

To estimate the materials required to make each product (**material usage**) and also the labour hours required (**labour efficiency**), **technical specifications** must be prepared for each product by production experts (either in the production department or the work study department).

(a) The '**standard product specification**' for materials must list the quantities required per unit of each material in the product. These standard input quantities must be made known to the operators in the production department so that control action by management to deal with **excess material wastage** will be understood by them.

(b) The '**standard operation sheet**' for labour will specify the expected hours required by each grade of labour in each department to make one unit of product. These standard times must be carefully set (for example by work study) and must be understood by the labour force. Where necessary, **standard procedures** or **operating methods** should be stated.

3.5 Performance standards

The quantity of material and labour time required will depend on the level of performance required by management. Standards may be set at '**attainable levels** which assume efficient levels of operation, but which include **allowances** for normal loss, waste and machine downtime, or at **ideal levels,** which make **no allowance** for the above losses, and are only attainable under the most favourable conditions' (CIMA *Official Terminology).*

When setting standards, managers must be aware of two requirements.

- The need to establish a useful control measure
- The need to set a standard which will have the desired motivational effect.

These two requirements are often conflicting, so that the final standard cost might be a compromise between the two.

3.6 Taking account of wastage, losses etc

If, during processing, the quantity of material input to the process is likely to reduce (due to wastage, evaporation and so on), the quantity input must be greater than the quantity in the finished product and a material standard must take account of this.

Suppose that the fresh raspberry juice content of a litre of Purple Pop is 100ml and that there is a 10% loss of raspberry juice during process due to evaporation. The standard material usage of raspberry juice per litre of Purple Pop will be:

$$100\text{ml} \times \frac{100\%}{(100-10)\%} = 100\text{ml} \times \frac{100\%}{90\%} = 111.11\text{ml}$$

Activity 2 **(10 minutes)**

A unit of product X requires 24 active labour hours for completion. It is anticipated that there will be 20% idle time which is to be incorporated into the standard times for all products. If the wage rate is £10 per hour, what is the standard labour cost of one unit of product X?

3.7 Problems in setting standards

Setting standards is not as straightforward as the above examples might imply. A number of problems can arise.

(a) Deciding how to incorporate **inflation** into planned unit costs

(b) Agreeing on a **performance standard** (attainable or ideal)

(c) Deciding on the **quality** of materials to be used (a better quality of material will cost more, but perhaps reduce material wastage)

(d) Estimating materials **prices** where seasonal price variations or bulk purchase discounts may be significant

(e) Finding sufficient **time** to construct accurate standards as standard setting can be a **time-consuming process**

(f) Incurring the **cost of setting up and maintaining a system** for establishing standards

(g) Dealing with possible **behavioural problems,** managers responsible for the achievement of standards possibly resisting the use of a standard costing control system for fear of being blamed for any adverse variances

Note that standard costing is most difficult in times of inflation but it is still worthwhile.

(a) **Usage and efficiency** variances will still be meaningful

(b) **Inflation is measurable**: there is no reason why its effects cannot be removed from the variances reported.

(c) Standard costs can be **revised** so long as this is **not done too frequently.**

3.8 The advantages of standard costing

The advantages for **control** in having a standard costing system in operation can be summarised as follows.

(a) Carefully planned standards are an **aid to more accurate budgeting.**

(b) Standard costs provide a **yardstick** against which actual costs can be measured.

(c) The **setting of standards** involves determining the best materials and methods which may lead to **economies.**

(d) A **target of efficiency** is set for employees to reach and **cost consciousness** is stimulated.

(e) Variances can be calculated which enable the principle of '**management by exception**' to be operated. Only the variances which exceed acceptable tolerance limits need to be investigated by management with a view to control action.

(f) Standard costs **simplify the process of bookkeeping** in cost accounting, because they are easier to use than LIFO, FIFO and weighted average costs.

(g) Standard times **simplify the process of production scheduling.**

(h) Standard performance levels might provide an **incentive for individuals** to achieve targets for themselves at work.

4 INTRODUCTION TO VARIANCE ANALYSIS

The actual results achieved by an organisation during a reporting period (week, month, quarter, year) will, more than likely, be **different** from the expected results (the expected results being the **standard costs**). Such differences may occur between individual items, such as the cost of labour, and between the total expected profit and the total actual profit.

Management will have spent considerable time and trouble setting **standards** as we have seen. Actual results have differed from the standards. Have costs been controlled? What do wise managers do? Ignore the difference and continue trying to attain the standards? Hopefully not. Wise managers will consider the differences that have occurred and use the results of their considerations in their attempts to attain the standards. The wise manager will use **variance analysis** as a **control** method.

The following sections examine variance analysis and set out the method of calculating material cost variances, labour cost variances, variable and fixed overhead variances and sales variances.

5 VARIANCE ANALYSIS

Definition

> A **variance** is the 'difference between a planned, budgeted, or standard cost and the actual cost incurred. The same comparisons may be made for revenues.'

The process by which the **total** difference between standard and actual results is analysed is known as **variance analysis**. When actual results are better than expected results, we have a **favourable** variance (F). If, on the other hand, actual results are worse than expected results, we have an **adverse** variance (A).

The **total profit variance** (the difference between budgeted profit and actual profit) can be split into three: **sales variances, production cost variances** and **non-production cost variances**. In the remainder of this chapter we will consider production cost variances, both fixed and variable, and sales variances.

6 DIRECT MATERIAL COST VARIANCES

The **total direct material cost variance** (the difference between what the output actually cost and what it should have cost, in terms of material) can be divided into two sub-variances.

(a) **The direct material price variance**

This is the difference between the standard cost and the actual cost for the actual quantity of material used or purchased. In other words, it is the difference between what the material did cost and what it should have cost.

(b) **The direct material usage variance**

This is the difference between the standard quantity of materials that should have been used for the number of units actually produced, and the actual quantity of materials used, valued at the standard cost per unit of material. In other words, it is the difference between how much material should have been used and how much material was used, valued at standard cost.

BPP LEARNING MEDIA

WORKED EXAMPLE: DIRECT MATERIAL COST VARIANCES

Product A has a standard direct material cost as follows.

5 kilograms of material M at £2 per kilogram = £10 per unit of A.

During April 20X3, 100 units of A were manufactured, using 520 kilograms of material M which cost £1,025.

Calculate the following variances.

(a) The total direct material cost variance
(b) The direct material price variance
(c) The direct material usage variance

ANSWER

(a) **The total direct material cost variance**

This is the difference between what 100 units should have cost and what they did cost.

	£
100 units should have cost (× £10)	1,000
but did cost	1,025
Total direct material cost variance	25 (A)

The variance is adverse because the units cost more than they should have cost.

(b) **The direct material price variance**

This is the difference between what 520 kgs should have cost and what 520 kgs did cost.

	£
520 kgs of M should have cost (× £2)	1,040
but did cost	1,025
Material M price variance	15 (F)

The variance is favourable because the material cost less than it should have.

(c) **The direct material usage variance**

This is the difference between how many kilograms of M should have been used to produce 100 units of A and how many kilograms were used, valued at the standard cost per kilogram.

100 units should have used (× 5 kgs)	500 kgs
but did use	520 kgs
Usage variance in kgs	20 kgs (A)
× standard cost per kilogram	× £2
Usage variance in £	£40 (A)

The variance is adverse because more material than should have been used was used.

(d) **Summary**

	£
Material price variance	15 (F)
Material usage variance	40 (A)
Total direct material cost variance	25 (A)

6.1 Material variances and opening and closing stock

Suppose that a company uses raw material P in production, and that this raw material has a standard price of £3 per metre. During one month 6,000 metres are bought for £18,600, and 5,000 metres are used in production. At the end of the month, stock will have been increased by 1,000 metres. In variance analysis, the problem is to decide whether the **material price variance** should be calculated on the basis of **materials purchased** (6,000 metres) or on the basis of **materials used** (5,000 metres).

The answer to this problem depends on how **closing stocks** of the raw materials will be valued.

(a) If they are valued at **standard cost** (1,000 units at £3 per unit) the price variance is calculated on material **purchases** in the period.

(b) If they are valued at **actual cost** *(FIFO)* (1,000 units at £3.10 per unit) the price variance is calculated on materials **used in production** in the period.

A **full standard costing system** is usually in operation and therefore the price variance is calculated on **purchases** in the period. The variance on the full 6,000 metres will be written off to the costing profit and loss account, even though only 5,000 metres are included in the cost of production.

There are two main advantages in extracting the material price variance **at the time of receipt**.

(a) If variances are extracted at the time of receipt they will be **brought to the attention of managers earlier** than if they are extracted as the material is used. If it is necessary to correct any variances then management action can be more timely.

(b) Since variances are extracted at the time of receipt, **all stocks will be valued at standard price**. This is administratively easier and it means that all issues from stocks can be made at standard price. If stocks are held at actual cost it is necessary to calculate a separate price variance on each batch as it is issued. Since issues are usually made in a number of small batches this can be a time consuming task, especially with a manual system.

The price variance would be calculated as follows.

	£
6,000 metres of material P purchased should cost (× £3)	18,000
but did cost	18,600
Price variance	600 (A)

7 DIRECT LABOUR COST VARIANCES

The calculation of **direct labour variances** is very similar to the calculation of direct material variances.

The **total direct labour cost variance** (the difference between what the output should have cost and what it did cost, in terms of labour) can be divided into two sub-variances.

(a) The **direct labour rate variance**

This is similar to the direct material price variance. It is the difference between the standard cost and the actual cost for the actual number of hours paid for.

In other words, it is the difference between what the labour did cost and what it should have cost.

(b) The **direct labour efficiency variance**

This is similar to the direct material usage variance. It is the difference between the hours that should have been worked for the number of units actually produced, and the actual number of hours worked, valued at the standard rate per hour.

In other words, it is the difference between how many hours should have been worked and how many hours were worked, valued at the standard rate per hour.

7.1 Idle time variance

A company may operate a costing system in which any **idle time** is recorded. Idle time may be caused by machine breakdowns or not having work to give to employees, perhaps because of bottlenecks in production or a shortage of orders from customers. When idle time occurs, the labour force is still paid wages for time at work, but no actual work is done. Time paid for without any work being done is unproductive and therefore inefficient. In variance analysis, **idle time is an adverse efficiency variance**.

When idle time is recorded separately, it is helpful to provide control information which identifies the cost of idle time separately and in variance analysis there will be an idle time variance **as a separate part of the labour efficiency variance**. The remaining efficiency variance will then relate only to the productivity of the labour force during the hours spent **actively working**.

WORKED EXAMPLE: LABOUR VARIANCES WITH IDLE TIME

The direct labour cost of product C is as follows.

3 hours of grade T labour at £2.50 per hour = £7.50 per unit of product C.

During June 20X3, 300 units of product C were made, and the cost of grade T labour was £2,200 for 910 hours. During the month, there was a machine breakdown, and 40 hours were recorded as idle time.

Calculate the following variances.

(a) The total direct labour cost variance
(b) The direct labour rate variance
(c) The idle time variance
(d) The direct labour efficiency variance

ANSWER

(a) **The total direct labour cost variance**

	£
300 units of product C should cost (× £7.50)	2,250
but did cost	2,200
Total direct labour cost variance	50 (F)

Actual cost is less than standard cost. The variance is therefore favourable.

(b) **The direct labour rate variance**

The rate variance is a comparison of what the hours paid should have cost and what they did cost.

	£
910 hours of grade T labour should cost (× £2.50)	2,275
but did cost	2,200
Direct labour rate variance	75 (F)

Actual cost is less than standard cost. The variance is therefore favourable.

(c) **The idle time variance**

The idle time variance is the hours of idle time, valued at the standard rate per hour.

Idle time variance = 40 hours (A) × £2.50 = £100 (A)

Idle time is always an adverse variance.

(d) **The direct labour efficiency variance**

The efficiency variance considers the hours actively worked (the difference between hours paid for and idle time hours). In our example, there were (910 – 40) = 870 hours when the labour force was not idle. The variance is calculated by taking the amount of output produced (300 units of product C) and comparing the time it should have taken to make them, with the actual time spent *actively* making them (870 hours). Once again, the variance in hours is valued at the standard rate per labour hour.

300 units of product C should take (× 3 hrs)	900 hrs
but did take (910 – 40)	870 hrs
Direct labour efficiency variance in hours	30 hrs (F)
× standard rate per hour	× £2.50
Direct labour efficiency variance in £	£75 (F)

(e) **Summary**

	£
Direct labour rate variance	75 (F)
Idle time variance	100 (A)
Direct labour efficiency variance	75 (F)
Total direct labour cost variance	50 (F)

Remember that, if idle time is recorded, the actual hours used in the efficiency variance calculation are the **hours worked and not the hours paid for**.

8 VARIABLE OVERHEAD VARIANCES

The total variable overhead variance is the difference between what the output actually cost and what it should have cost, in terms of variable overhead.

Like the materials and labour variances already discussed, the total variable overhead variance can be split into the part relating to a difference in the price of the overheads absorbed (the expenditure variance) and another relating to the quantity of overheads used (the efficiency variance). If overheads are absorbed on the basis of direct labour hours worked, the calculations will be very similar to those used for direct labour variances.

(a) **The variable overhead expenditure variance**

This is the difference between the standard overheads that would have been absorbed over the actual labour hours worked and the actual variable overheads. If there is any idle time then the hours paid will be ignored as variable overheads are only incurred when labour is working.

(b) **The variable overhead efficiency variance**

This is the difference between the actual hours worked and the number of hours that should have been worked for the quantity of output produced, valued at the standard absorption rate.

WORKED EXAMPLE: VARIABLE OVERHEAD VARIANCES

The variable overhead cost of product D is £10 per direct labour hour. Two labour hours are required to make one unit of product D. In July 20X3 225 labour hours were worked to produce 120 units of product D. The total cost for variable overhead was £2,350.

Calculate the following variances.

(a) The total variable overhead variance
(b) The variable overhead expenditure variances
(c) The variable overhead efficiency variance

ANSWER

(a) **The total variable overhead variance**

	£
120 units of product D should have cost (× £10 × 2 hrs)	2,400
but did cost	2,350
Total variable overhead variance	50 (F)

The variance is favourable because the actual cost was less than the standard cost.

Note that variable overheads are assumed to be incurred during active working hours only (and not during hours of idle time).

(b) **The variable overhead expenditure variance**

	£
Overheads should have been incurred at £10 per hr over 225 hrs	2,250
but the actual amount incurred was	2,350
Variable overhead expenditure variance	100 (A)

The variance is adverse because the actual cost of variable overheads was more than would have been expected.

(c) **The variable overhead efficiency variance**

120 units of D should take (× 2 hrs)	240 hrs
but did take	225 hrs
Variable overhead efficiency variance in hours	15 hrs (F)
× standard rate per hour	× £10
Variable overhead efficiency variance	£150 (F)

In many organisations, as in this example, the absorption rate is based on direct labour hours worked. This means that the labour and overheads efficiency variances will always be in the same 'direction' as each other; the efficiency of the workforce is reflected in the efficient use of overheads. This is because the amount of labour hours worked on a product bears a relation to the amount of overhead incurred. So, the longer the workforce works, the more overheads are incurred. A favourable variance therefore means that the workforce has worked fewer hours than expected to produce the goods, and fewer overheads will have been incurred in making those goods.

9 FIXED OVERHEAD VARIANCES

The **total fixed overhead variance** is the difference between the overhead absorbed and the actual cost incurred (where the overhead absorbed is based on the standard number of hours for the units actually produced).

Fixed overheads do not follow the same pattern as the other costs so far considered because of their fixed nature. The total variance can be split into the expenditure and volume variances.

(a) **The fixed overhead expenditure variance**

This is simply the difference between the actual fixed overheads and budgeted fixed overheads that were originally planned (ie not the flexed budget).

(b) **The fixed overhead volume variance**

This looks at the change in the volume of production from the original budgeted level to the actual level. Again, assuming that overheads are absorbed using a labour hours rate, the volume variance is the difference between the budgeted level of production and the actual level of production, valued at the standard overhead absorption rate × standard hours per unit.

If further information is required, the volume variance can be further analysed into capacity and efficiency variances.

(c) **The fixed overhead capacity variance**

This calculates the amount by which the capacity of the workforce has exceeded or fallen short of the budgeted level. It is the difference between the planned hours to be worked and the actual hours worked, valued at the standard fixed overhead absorption rate.

(d) **The fixed overhead efficiency variance**

The efficiency variance is calculated along the same lines as before, to see if more or less hours were used to make the actual level of production, as compared with the standard. It is the difference between the hours that should have been worked for the number of units produced and the actual hours that were worked, valued at the standard fixed overhead absorption rate.

WORKED EXAMPLE: OVERHEAD VARIANCES

A company budgets to produce 1,000 units of product E during August 20X3. The expected time to produce a unit of E is five hours. The budgeted fixed overhead is £20,000 and fixed overheads are absorbed on a labour hours basis. Actual fixed overhead turns out to be £20,450. Actual productive hours during the period were 5,150 and 1,010 units were produced.

Required

Calculate the following variances.

(a) The total fixed overhead variance
(b) The fixed overhead expenditure variance
(c) The fixed overhead volume variance
(d) The fixed overhead capacity variance
(e) The fixed overhead efficiency variance

ANSWER

(a) **The total fixed overhead variance**

We begin by calculating a predetermined overhead absorption rate.

$$\text{Fixed overhead absorption rate} = \frac{\text{Budgeted fixed overheads}}{\text{Budgeted activity level}}$$

$$= \frac{£20{,}000}{1{,}000 \text{ units} \times 5\text{hrs}}$$

$$= £4 \text{ per hour}$$

We can now turn our attention to calculating the total fixed overhead variance.

	£
Actual overhead cost incurred	20,450
Standard overhead absorbed (1,010 × 5 × £4)	20,200
	250 (A)

The variance is adverse since actual overheads were greater than overheads absorbed.

Note how the overhead absorbed is based on the **standard number of hours for actual production.**

(b) **The fixed overhead expenditure variance**

	£	
Actual cost	20,450	
Budgeted cost	20,000	
Fixed overhead expenditure variance	450	(A)

The variance is adverse as the actual cost is greater than that planned in the original budget.

(c) **The fixed overhead volume variance**

Budgeted volume of production	1,000	units
Actual volume	1,010	units
Fixed overhead volume variance in units	10	(F)
× standard hours	× 5	hrs
× standard fixed overhead absorption rate	× £4	
Fixed overhead volume variance	£200	(F)

The volume variance is favourable as the volume of production achieved was greater than the budget.

(d) **The fixed overhead capacity variance**

Budgeted capacity	5,000	hrs
Actual hours worked	5,150	hrs
Fixed overhead capacity variance in hours	150	hrs (F)
× standard rate per hour	× £4	
Fixed overhead capacity variance	£600	(F)

The capacity variance is favourable because the actual capacity achieved is greater than the budgeted capacity of 5,000 hours.

(e) **The fixed overhead efficiency variance**

1,010 units of E should take (× 5 hrs)	5,050	hrs
but did take	5,150	hrs
Variable overhead efficiency variance in hours	100	hrs (A)
× standard rate per hour	× £4	
Fixed overhead efficiency variance	£400	(A)

The efficiency variance is adverse as it has taken longer to produce 1,010 units than was expected.

Activity 3 **(10 minutes)**

Using the information in the example above, calculate the under/over absorption of fixed overheads relating to product E for August 20X3. Be careful to absorb overheads into units of production based on the standard hours per unit and the standard rate per hour.

What do you notice about this figure and the variances above?

NOTES

Activity 4 **(30 minutes)**

Brain Ltd produces and sells one product only, the Blob, the standard cost for one unit being as follows.

	£
Direct material - 10 kilograms at £20 per kg	200
Direct wages - 5 hours at £6 per hour	30
Variable production overhead - 5 hours at £1 per hour	5
Fixed production overhead – 5 hours at £10 per hour	50
Total standard cost	285

The fixed production overhead included in the standard cost is based on an expected monthly output of 900 units.

During April 20X3 the actual results were as follows.

Production	800 units
Direct material	7,800 kg used, costing £159,900
Direct wages	4,200 hours worked for £24,150
Variable production overhead	£4,900
Fixed production overhead	£47,000

Required

(a) Calculate direct material price and usage variances.
(b) Calculate direct labour rate and efficiency variances.
(c) Calculate the variable overhead expenditure and efficiency variances.
(d) Calculate the fixed overhead expenditure and volume variances
(e) Calculate the fixed overhead capacity and efficiency variances

10 SALES VARIANCES

Referring back to our definition of standard costing earlier in this chapter, you will see that revenues are an important part of this control technique. As well as exercising some control over costs, we need to keep an eye on sales and whether they are in line with expectation.

The cost variances we have calculated have all had a direct effect on profit. In other words, any change in the quantity or cost will increase or decrease profit to this extent also. Sales are a little different, however, as an increase in the quantity sold not only increases the sales revenue, but it also means that we bring in all the costs of those extra units sold. We have to take account of this in the calculations, and generally look at the effect on profit of any sales variances.

The total sales variance is the difference between actual sales and budgeted sales, less standard cost in each case. The total variance can be split into two further variances.

(a) **The sales price variance**

This is the difference between the actual selling price and the standard selling price for the actual sales volume in units. The price variance can be calculated in terms of revenue as this will have a direct effect on profit.

(b) **The sales volume variance**

This variance looks at the effect on budgeted profit of selling more or less units than were budgeted-for. It is the difference between the budgeted sales volume and the actual sales volume, valued at the standard profit per unit.

WORKED EXAMPLE: SALES VARIANCES

The sales budget for product F for March 20X4 is 500 units at a price of £25 per unit. Each unit of F has a standard cost of £17.

The actual sales revenue for March 20X4 is £13,260, with 520 units of product F sold.

Calculate the following variances.

(a) The sales price variance
(b) The sales volume variance
(c) The total sales variance

ANSWER

(a) **The sales price variance**

	£	
520 units of F should have sold for (× £25)	13,000	
But did sell for	13,260	
	260	(F)

The variance is favourable as the selling price was higher than expected, at £25.50 (£13,260/520).

Note that this variance can also be calculated in terms of profit; it is not quite such an easy method to remember, but it does tie-in with the total sales variance below.

	£	
Standard selling price – standard cost (£25 – £17)	8.00	
Actual selling price – standard cost (£25.50 – £17)	8.50	
Sales price variance per unit	0.50	
× units sold	× 520	
sales price variance	260	(F)

(b) **The sales volume variance**

Budgeted sales volume	500	units
Actual sales volume	520	units
Sales volume variance in units	20	units
× standard profit per unit (£25 – £17)	× £8	
	160	(F)

The variance is favourable as the sales volume was larger than expected.

(c) **The total sales variance**

	£	
Sales evaluated at the standard profit should be (500 × £8)	4,000	
But actual sales less standard costs were (520 × £8.50)	4,420	
	420	(F)

NOTES

11 OPERATING STATEMENTS

So far, we have considered how variances are calculated without considering how they combine to **reconcile the difference between budgeted profit and actual profit** during a period. This reconciliation is usually presented as a report to senior management at the end of each control period. The report is called an operating statement or statement of variances.

Definition

The Chartered Institute of Management Accountants *Official Terminology* definition of an **operating statement** is 'A regular report for management of actual costs and revenues, as appropriate. Usually compares actual with budget and shows variances'.

WORKED EXAMPLE: VARIANCES AND OPERATING STATEMENTS

Sydney Ltd manufactures one product, and the entire product is sold as soon as it is produced. There are no opening or closing stocks and work in progress is negligible. The company operates a standard costing system and analysis of variances is made every month. The standard cost card for the product, a boomerang, is as follows.

STANDARD COST CARD - BOOMERANG		£
Direct materials	0.5 kilos at £4 per kilo	2.00
Direct wages	2 hours at £2.00 per hour	4.00
Variable overheads	2 hours at £0.30 per hour	0.60
Fixed overhead	2 hours at £3.70 per hour	7.40
Standard cost		14.00
Standard profit		6.00
Standing selling price		20.00

Selling and administration expenses are not included in the standard cost, and are deducted from profit as a period charge.

Budgeted output for the month of June 20X5 was 5,100 units. Actual results for June 20X5 were as follows.

Production of 4,850 units was sold for £95,600.
Materials consumed in production amounted to 2,300 kgs at a total cost of £9,800.
Labour hours paid for amounted to 8,500 hours at a cost of £16,800.
Actual operating hours amounted to 8,000 hours.
Variable overheads amounted to £2,600.
Fixed overheads amounted to £42,300.
Selling and administration expenses amounted to £18,000.

Required

Calculate all variances and prepare an operating statement for the month ended 30 June 20X5.

BPP LEARNING MEDIA

NOTES

ANSWER

(a)	2,300 kg of material should cost (× £4)	£9,200
	but did cost	£9,800
	Material price variance	600 (A)
(b)	4,850 boomerangs should use (× 0.5 kgs)	2,425 kg
	but did use	2,300 kg
	Material usage variance in kgs	125 kg (F)
	× standard cost per kg	× £4
	Material usage variance in £	£ 500 (F)
		£
(c)	8,500 hours of labour should cost (× £2)	17,000
	but did cost	16,800
	Labour rate variance	200 (F)
(d)	4,850 boomerangs should take (× 2 hrs)	9,700 hrs
	but did take (active hours)	8,000 hrs
	Labour efficiency variance in hours	1,700 hrs (F)
	× standard cost per hour	× £2
	Labour efficiency variance in £	£3,400 (F)
(e)	Idle time variance 500 hours (A) × £2	£1,000 (A)
	Hours paid – operating hours	
		£
(f)	8,000 hours incurring variable o/hd expenditure should cost (× £0.30)	2,400
	but did cost	2,600
	Variable overhead expenditure variance	200 (A)
(g)	Variable overhead efficiency variance in hours is the same as the labour efficiency variance:	
	1,700 hours (F) × £0.30 per hour	£ 510 (F)
		£
(h)	Budgeted fixed overhead (5,100 units × 2 hrs × £3.70)	37,740
	Actual fixed overhead	42,300
	Fixed overhead expenditure variance	4,560 (A)
(i)	Actual production volume	4,850 units
	Budgeted production volume	5,100 units
	Fixed overhead volume variance in units	250 units (A)
	× Standard hours × standard fixed overhead absorption rate	× 2 hours
		× £3.70
	Fixed overhead volume variance	1,850 (A)
(j)	Fixed overhead efficiency variance in hours is the same as the labour efficiency variance:	
	1,700 hrs (F) × £3.70 per hour	£6,290 (F)
(k)	Budgeted capacity (5,100 units × 2 hours)	10,200 hrs
	Actual hours of work	8,000 hrs
	Capacity variance in hours	2,200 hrs (A)
	× standard fixed overhead absorption rate per hour	× £3.70
	Fixed overhead capacity variance	£8,140 (A)
(l)	Revenue from 4,850 boomerangs should be (× £20)	97,000
	but was	95,600
	Selling price variance	1,400 (A)

NOTES

(m)	Budgeted sales volume	5,100 units
	Actual sales volume	4,850 units
	Sales volume profit variance in units	250 units
	× standard profit per unit	× £6 (A)
	Sales volume profit variance in £	£1,500 (A)

There are several ways in which an operating statement may be presented. Perhaps the most common format is one which reconciles budgeted profit to actual profit. In this example, sales and administration costs will be introduced at the end of the statement, so that we shall begin with 'budgeted profit before sales and administration costs'.

Sales variances are reported first, and the total of the budgeted profit and the two sales variances results in a figure for 'actual sales minus the standard cost of sales'. The cost variances are then reported, and an actual profit (before sales and administration costs) calculated. Sales and administration costs are then deducted to reach the actual profit.

EXAMPLE

SYDNEY LTD - OPERATING STATEMENT JUNE 20X5

		£	£
Budgeted profit before sales and administration costs (£6 × 5,100)			30,600
Sales volume variance			1,500 (A)
Budgeted profit from actual sales (flexed budget profit)			29,100
Selling price variance			1,400 (A)
Actual sales minus the standard cost of sales			27,700
Cost variances	(F)	(A)	
	£	£	
Material price		600	
Material usage	500		
Labour rate	200		
Labour efficiency	3,400		
Labour idle time		1,000	
Variable overhead expenditure		200	
Variable overhead efficiency	510		
Fixed overhead expenditure		4,560	
Fixed overhead efficiency	6,290		
Fixed overhead capacity		8,140	
	10,900	14,500	3,600 (A)
Actual profit before sales and admin costs			24,100
Sales and administration costs			18,000
Actual profit, June 20X5			6,100

Check	£	£
Sales		95,600
Materials	9,800	
Labour	16,800	
Variable overhead	2,600	
Fixed overhead	42,300	
Sales and administration	18,000	
		89,500
Actual profit		6,100

BPP LEARNING MEDIA

Activity 5 **(45 minutes)**

Bromill Limited makes a single product, LI, using a single raw material AN.

Standard costs relating to LI have been calculated as follows.

Standard cost schedule - LI	*Per unit*
	£
Direct material, AN, 100 kg at £5 per kg	500
Direct labour, 10 hours at £8 per hour	80
Variable production overhead, 10 hours at £2 per hour	20
Fixed production overhead 10 hours at £1 per hour	10
	610

The standard selling price of a LI is £900 and Bromill aim to produce 1,020 units a month.

During December, 1,000 units of LI were produced and sold. Relevant details of this production are as follows.

Direct material AN

90,000 kgs costing £720,000 were bought and used.

Direct labour

8,200 hours were worked during the month and total wages were £63,000.

Variable production overhead

The actual cost for the month was £25,000.

Fixed production overhead

The actual cost for the month was £9,800

Each LI was sold for £975.

Required

Calculate the following for the month of December, and use them to prepare an operating statement.

(a) Direct labour cost variance, analysed into rate and efficiency variances

(b) Direct material cost variance, analysed into price and usage variances

(c) Variable production overhead variance, analysed into expenditure and efficiency variances

(d) Fixed production overhead variance analysed into expenditure, capacity and efficiency

(e) Selling price variance

(f) Sales volume variance

Chapter roundup

- A standard cost is a predetermined estimated unit cost, used for stock valuation and control.
- There are a number of advantages and disadvantages associated with standard costing.
- Variances explain the difference between actual results using actual costs and expected results, at standard cost.
- Management should only receive information of significant variances. This is known as 'management by exception'.
- The total direct material cost variance can be subdivided into the direct material price variance and the direct material usage variance.
- Direct material price variances are extracted at the time of receipt of the materials, not at the time of usage, assuming that stock is valued at standard cost.
- The total direct labour cost variance can be subdivided into the direct labour rate variance and the direct labour efficiency variance.
- If idle time arises, it is usual to calculate a separate idle time variance, and to base the calculation of the efficiency variance on active hours (when labour actually worked) only.
- The total variable overhead variance is the difference between what the total variable overhead cost should have been and what the overhead cost was.
- The total variable overhead variance can be subdivided into the variable overhead expenditure variance and the variable overhead efficiency variance
- The total fixed overhead variance is the difference between the actual fixed overhead incurred and the overhead absorbed (based on standard hours for actual production).
- The total fixed overhead variance can be subdivided into the fixed overhead expenditure variance and the fixed overhead volume variance; the fixed overhead volume variance can be further subdivided into the fixed overhead capacity variance and the fixed overhead efficiency variance.
- The total sales variance can be subdivided into the sales price variance and the sales volume variance.
- An operating statement can be used to reconcile the difference between budgeted profit and actual profit for a period, with variances being the reconciling items.

Quick quiz

1 What is a standard cost?

2 What are the two principal uses of standard costing?

3 What is a standard product specification?

4 Name two types of performance standard.

5 Which two variances subdivide the total direct material cost variance?

6 What are the two main advantages in calculating the material price variance at the time of receipt?

7 Why might idle time occur?

8 What does the total fixed overhead variance measure?

9 Which variance compares budgeted labour hours and actual labour hours and values the difference at the fixed overhead adsorption rate?

10 Which two figures are reconciled in an operating statement?

Answers to quick quiz

1 A standard cost is a planned unit cost. (see para 1.1)

2 To value stocks and cost production.

To act as a control device by analysing the variances between actual and expected results. (para 1.2)

3 A standard product specification lists the different materials and the quantities of each type of material used in the product. (para 3.4)

4 Attainable and ideal standards. (para 3.5)

5 Materials price and materials usage. (para 6)

6 Variances are brought to the attention of managers, and potential problems resolved, earlier.

As the price variance is calculated immediately, all further stock movements will be recorded at standard price which is easier for administrative purposes. (para 6.1)

7 Idle time might occur due to machine breakdown, lack of customer orders or bottlenecks in production. (para 7.1)

8 The total fixed overhead variance measures the difference between overheads actually incurred and overheads absorbed, based on the standard number of hours for the units actually produced. (para 9)

9 The fixed overhead capacity variance (where fixed overheads are recovered using a labour hour rate). (para 9)

10 Budgeted profit and actual profit. (para 11)

NOTES

Answers to activities

1 STANDARD COST CARD – PRODUCT JOE

	£	£
Direct materials		
A: 7 kgs × £1	7	
B: 4 litres × £2	8	
C: 3 m × £3	9	
		24
Direct labour		
Skilled: 8 × £10	80	
Semi-skilled: 4 × £5	20	
		100
Standard direct cost		124
Variable production overhead: 8 × £2.50		20
Standard variable cost of production		144
Fixed production overhead: 8 × £6.25 (W)		50
Standard full production cost		194
Administration, selling and distribution overhead		10
Standard cost of sale		204
Standard profit (25% × 204)		51
Standard sales price		255

Working

$$\text{Overhead absorption rate} = \frac{£250{,}000}{5{,}000 \times 8} = £6.25 \text{ per skilled labour hour}$$

2 The basic labour cost for 24 hours is £240. However with idle time it will be necessary to pay for more than 24 hours in order to achieve 24 hours of actual work, in fact 30 hours will need to be paid for.

$$\text{Standard labour cost} = \text{active hours for completion} \times \frac{125}{100} \times £10$$

$$= 24 \times 1.25 \times £10 = £300$$

3

		£
Fixed overheads for the period		20,450
Fixed overheads absorbed	(1,010 units × 5 hrs per unit × £4 per hr)	20,200
Underabsorption		250

The amount by which the fixed overheads are underabsorbed is the total fixed overhead variance. In dealing with overheads, estimates are made in advance so that an overhead absorption rate can be found and overheads can be recovered as the production process progresses. This is the same process of costing in advance that is used for standard costing. So when we calculate an under or over absorption of overheads, we are basically calculating a variance on fixed overheads.

4 (a) Price variance

	£
7,800 kgs should have cost (× £20)	156,000
but did cost	159,900
Price variance	3,900 (A)

Usage variance

800 units should have used (× 10 kgs)	8,000 kgs
but did use	7,800 kgs
Usage variance in kgs	200 kgs (F)
× standard cost per kilogram	× £20
Usage variance in £	£4,000 (F)

(b) Labour rate

	£
4,200 hours should have cost (× £6)	25,200
but did cost	24,150
Rate variance	1,050 (F)

Labour efficiency

800 units should have taken (× 5 hrs)	4,000 hrs
but did take	4,200 hrs
Efficiency variance in hours	200 hrs (A)
× standard rate per hour	× £6
Efficiency variance in £	£1,200 (A)

(c) Variable overhead expenditure

	£
Overheads should have been incurred at £1 per hr over 4,200 hrs	4,200
but the actual cost was	4,900
Variable overhead expenditure variance	700 (A)

Variable overhead efficiency

800 Blobs should take (× 5 hrs)	4,000 hrs
but did take	4,200 hrs
Variable overhead efficiency variance in hours	200 hrs (A)
× standard rate per hour	× £1
Variable overhead efficiency variance	£200 (A)

(d) Fixed overhead expenditure

	£
Actual cost	47,000
Budgeted cost (900 units × £50 per unit)	45,000
Fixed overhead expenditure variance	2,000 (A)

Fixed overhead volume

Budgeted volume of production	900 units
Actual volume	800 units
Fixed overhead volume variance in units	100 (A)
× standard hours	× 5 hrs
× standard fixed overhead absorption rate	× £10
Fixed overhead volume variance	£5,000 (A)

(e) Fixed overhead capacity

Budgeted capacity (900 Blobs × 5 hrs per Blob)	4,500 hrs
Actual hours worked	4,200 hrs
Fixed overhead capacity variance in hours	300 hrs (A)
× standard rate per hour	× £10
Fixed overhead capacity variance	£3,000 (A)

Fixed overhead efficiency

800 Blobs should take (× 5 hrs)	4,000 hrs
but did take	4,200 hrs
Variable overhead efficiency variance in hours	200 hrs (A)
× standard rate per hour	× £10
Fixed overhead efficiency variance	£2,000 (A)

5 (a) Direct labour cost variances

	£
8,200 hours should cost (× £8)	65,600
but did cost	63,000
Direct labour rate variance	2,600 (F)
1,000 units should take (× 10 hours)	10,000 hrs
but did take	8,200 hrs
Direct labour efficiency variance in hrs	1,800 hrs (F)
× standard rate per hour	× £8
Direct labour efficiency variance in £	£14,400 (F)

Summary	£
Rate	2,600 (F)
Efficiency	14,400 (F)
Total	17,000 (F)

(b) Direct material cost variances

	£
90,000 kg should cost (× £5)	450,000
but did cost	720,000
Direct material price variance	270,000 (A)
1,000 units should use (× 100 kg)	100,000 kg
but did use	90,000 kg
Direct material usage variance in kgs	10,000 kg (F)
× standard cost per kg	× £5
Direct material usage variance in £	£50,000 (F)

Summary	£
Price	270,000 (A)
Usage	50,000 (F)
Total	220,000 (A)

(c) Variable production overhead variances

	£
8,200 hours incurring o/hd should cost (× £2)	16,400
but did cost	25,000
Variable production overhead expenditure variance	8,600 (A)
Efficiency variance in hrs (from (b))	1,800 hrs (F)
× standard rate per hour	× £2
Variable production overhead efficiency variance	£3,600 (F)

Summary	£
Expenditure	8,600 (A)
Efficiency	3,600 (F)
Total	5,000 (A)

NOTES

(d) Fixed overhead variances

	£
Actual cost	9,800
Budgeted cost (1,020 units × £10 per unit)	10,200
Fixed overhead expenditure variance	400 (F)

Budgeted capacity (1,020 units of LI × 10 hrs per LI)	10,200 hrs
Actual hours worked	8,200 hrs
Fixed overhead capacity variance in hours	2,000 hrs (A)
× standard rate per hour	× £1
Fixed overhead capacity variance	£2,000 (A)

1,000 LI should take (× 10 hrs)	10,000 hrs
but did take	8,200 hrs
Fixed overhead efficiency variance in hours	1,800 hrs (F)
× standard rate per hour	× £1
Fixed overhead efficiency variance	£1,800 (F)

Summary

	£
Expenditure	400 (F)
Capacity	2,000 (A)
Efficiency	1,800 (F)
Total	200 (F)

(e) Selling price variance

	£
Revenue from 1,000 units should have been (× £900)	900,000
but was (× £975)	975,000
Selling price variance	75,000 (F)

(f) Sales volume variance

Budgeted sales	1,020 units
Actual sales	1,000 units
Sales volume variance in units	20 units (A)
× standard contribution margin (£(900 – 610))	× £290
Sales volume contribution variance in £	£5,800 (A)

BPP LEARNING MEDIA

BROMILL LIMITED – OPERATING STATEMENT FOR DECEMBER

			£	
Budgeted profit (£290 × 1,020)			295,800	
Sales volume variance			5,800	(A)
Budgeted profit from actual sales			290,000	
Selling price variance			75,000	(F)
Actual sales minus standard cost of sales			365,000	
Cost variances	*(F)*	*(A)*		
	£	£		
Labour rate	2,600			
Labour efficiency	14,400			
Materials price		270,000		
Materials usage	50,000			
Variable production overhead expenditure		8,600		
Variable production overhead efficiency	3,600			
Fixed production overhead expenditure	400			
Fixed production overhead capacity		2,000		
Fixed production overhead efficiency	1,800			
	72,800	280,600	207,800	(A)
Actual profit (£975,000 - £817,800 (Working))			157,200	

Working

	£
Direct material	720,000
Total wages	63,000
Variable production overhead	25,000
Fixed production overhead	9,800
	817,800

Chapter 10 :

RESPONSIBILITY ACCOUNTING

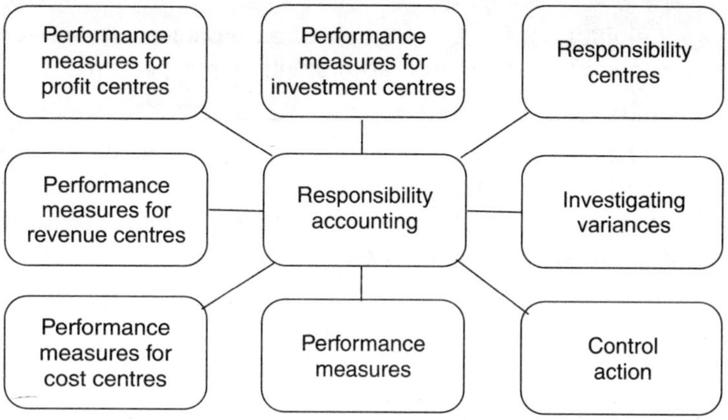

Introduction

In the last chapter we learnt the mechanics of calculating variances and preparing operating statements. But, for the purposes of operating a budgetary control system, this is not the end of the matter. The information must be given to the people responsible for the parts of the organisation that are experiencing variances, so that they can take action to bring the situation under control. Having a set-up which gives this responsibility to managers is known as **responsibility accounting**.

Variances provide one way of highlighting a possible problem area to managers, and is therefore a type of **performance indicator**. We will have a look at other performance indicators, which can be used to monitor the performance of individual departments in the organisation and the organisation as a whole.

Your objectives

In this chapter you will learn about the following.

(a) Responsibility centres

(b) Investigating variances

(c) Control action

(d) Performance indicators

NOTES

1 RESPONSIBILITY CENTRES

Definitions

- **Responsibility accounting** is a system of accounting that **makes revenues and costs the responsibility of particular managers** so that the performance of each part of the organisation can be **monitored** and **assessed**.
- A **responsibility centre** is a **section** of an organisation that is headed by a manager who has **direct responsibility** for its performance.

A budget will be prepared for each responsibility centre, and its manager will be responsible for achieving the budget targets of that centre. The performance of the centre will be monitored, and the manger will be expected to take appropriate action if there are significant variances or other targets are not met.

Responsibility centres are usually divided into different categories. Here we shall describe cost (expense), revenue, profit and investment centres.

1.1 Cost centres

Definition

A **cost** (or **expense**) **centre** is any part of an organisation which incurs costs.

Cost centres can be quite small, sometimes one person or one machine or one expenditure item. They can also be quite big, for example an entire department. An organisation might establish a hierarchy of cost centres. For example, within a transport department, individual vehicles might each be made a cost centre, the repairs and maintenance section might be a cost centre, there might be cost centres for expenditure items such as rent or building depreciation on the vehicle depots, vehicle insurance and road tax. The transport department as a whole might be a cost centre at the top of this hierarchy of sub-cost centres.

To charge actual costs to a cost centre, each cost centre will have a cost code, and items of expenditure will be recorded with the appropriate **cost code**. When costs are eventually analysed, there may well be some apportionment of the costs of one cost centre to other cost centres.

Information about cost centres might be collected in terms of **total actual costs, total budgeted costs** and **total cost variances**. In addition, the information might be analysed in terms of **ratios**, such as cost per unit produced (budget and actual), hours per unit produced (budget and actual) and transport costs per tonne/ kilometre (budget and actual).

1.2 Revenue centres

Definition

> A **revenue centre** is a **section** of an organisation which **raises revenue** but has **no responsibility for production**. A sales department is an example.

The term 'revenue centre' is often used in non-profit-making organisations. Revenue centres are similar to cost centres, except that whereas cost centres are for costs only, revenue centres are for recording revenues only. Information collection and reporting could be based on a comparison of budgeted and actual revenues earned by that centre.

1.3 Profit centres

Definition

> A **profit centre** is any section of an organisation (for example, division of a company) which **earns revenue** and **incurs costs**. The profitability of the section can therefore be measured.

Profit centres differ from cost centres in that they **account for both costs and revenues.** The **key performance measure** of a profit centre is therefore **profit. The manager of the profit centre must be able to influence both revenues and costs** (in other words, have a say in both sales and production policies).

A profit centre manager is likely to be a fairly senior person within an organisation, and a profit centre is likely to cover quite a large area of operations. A profit centre might be an entire division within the organisation, or there might be a separate profit centre for each product, brand or service or each geographical selling area. Information requirements need to be similarly focused.

In the hierarchy of responsibility centres within an organisation, there are likely to be several cost centres within a profit centre.

1.4 Investment centres

Definition

> An **investment centre manager** has some say **in investment policy** in his area of operations as well as **being responsible for costs and revenues.**

Several profit centres might share the same capital items, for example the same buildings, stores or transport fleet, and so investment centres are likely to include several profit centres, and provide a basis for control at a very senior management level, like that of a subsidiary company within a group.

The performance of an investment centre is measured by the **return on capital employed**. It shows how well the investment centre manager has used the resources under his control to generate profit.

Activity 1 **(10 minutes)**

Motorway Minibreaks Limited owns a chain of motels situated at strategic points alongside the major motorways in the UK. It is a high-volume, low-margin business which operates a strict system of budgetary control, central to which is a hierarchy of responsibility centres. Bookings can be made directly with the hotels, or via a central call centre. Each hotel has a restaurant which is open to the public as well as guests. The hotel manager has a capital expenditure budget, although the Head Office makes all decisions regarding the purchase of new hotels.

Suggest which of the following responsibility centres would be categorised as a cost centre, a revenue centre, a profit centre, and an investment centre.

(a) The central bookings call centre.

(b) The Shap Fell Minibreak Hotel

(c) The Bridgeview Restaurant at the Avonmouth Minibreak Hotel

(d) The domestic services (cleaning and maintenance) function in the Tamworth Minibreak Hotel

2 INVESTIGATING VARIANCES

Having identified the areas over which managers have responsibility, each manager will have to decide whether or not to investigate the reasons for the occurrence of a particular variance. There are a number of factors which should be considered.

2.1 Materiality

Small variations in a single period between actual and standard are bound to occur and are unlikely to be significant. Obtaining an 'explanation' of the reasons why they occurred is likely to be time-consuming and irritating for the manager concerned. For such variations further investigation is not worthwhile.

2.2 Controllability

Managers of responsibility centres should only be held responsible for costs over which they have some control. These are known as controllable costs, which are items of expenditure which can be directly influenced by a given manager within a given time span.

If there is a general worldwide price increase in the price of an important raw material there is nothing that can be done internally to control the effect of this. If a central decision is made to award all employees a 10% increase in salary, staff costs in division A will increase by this amount and the variance is not controllable by division A's manager. Uncontrollable variances call for a change in the standard, not an investigation into the past.

2.3 Variance trend

Although small variations in a single period are unlikely to be significant, small variations that occur consistently may need more attention. Variance trend is more important than a single set of variances for one accounting period. The trend provides an indication of whether the variance is fluctuating within acceptable control limits or becoming out of control.

(a) If, say, an efficiency variance is £1,000 adverse in month 1, the obvious conclusion is that the process is out of control and that corrective action must be taken. This may be correct, but what if the same variance is £1,000 adverse every month? The **trend** indicates that the process is in control and the standard has been wrongly set.

(b) Suppose, though, that the same variance is consistently £1,000 adverse for each of the first six months of the year but that production has steadily fallen from 100 units in month 1 to 65 units by month 6. The variance trend in absolute terms is constant, but relative to the number of units produced, efficiency has got steadily worse.

Individual variances should therefore not be looked at in isolation; **variances should be scrutinised for a number of successive periods** if their full significance is to be appreciated.

Activity 2 **(10 minutes)**

What might the following variance trend information indicate?

(a) Regular, perhaps fairly slight, increases in adverse price variances
(b) A rapid, large increase in adverse price variances
(c) Gradually improving labour efficiency variances
(d) Worsening trends in machine running expense variances

2.4 The significance of variances

A variance can be considered significant if it will influence management's actions and decisions. Significant variances usually need investigating.

Variances which are simply random deviations, in other words fluctuations which have arisen by chance, are uncontrollable. This is because a standard cost is really only an *average* expected cost and is not a rigid specification. Some variances either side of this average must be expected to occur and are hence outside management's control.

The problem for both management and the accountant is therefore to decide whether a variation from standard is attributable to chance and hence *not* significant or whether it is due to a controllable cause and therefore significant.

2.5 Control limits and control charts

Because standard costs are only estimates of average costs, it would be incorrect to treat them as being rigid. **Tolerance limits** should be set, and only variances which exceed these limits should be reported as being significant and investigated. The following variances would lie within the tolerance limits.

(a) **Normal variations around average performance**, with variations above and below the average (adverse and favourable variances) cancelling each other out in the course of time.

(b) **Minor operational variances** which are too small to justify the cost of investigation and control action by management. Small variances might 'sort themselves out' in time, and only if they persist and grow larger should investigative action be worthwhile.

(c) A **minor planning error** in the standard cost for the year.

The control limits may be illustrated on a **variance control chart** as follows.

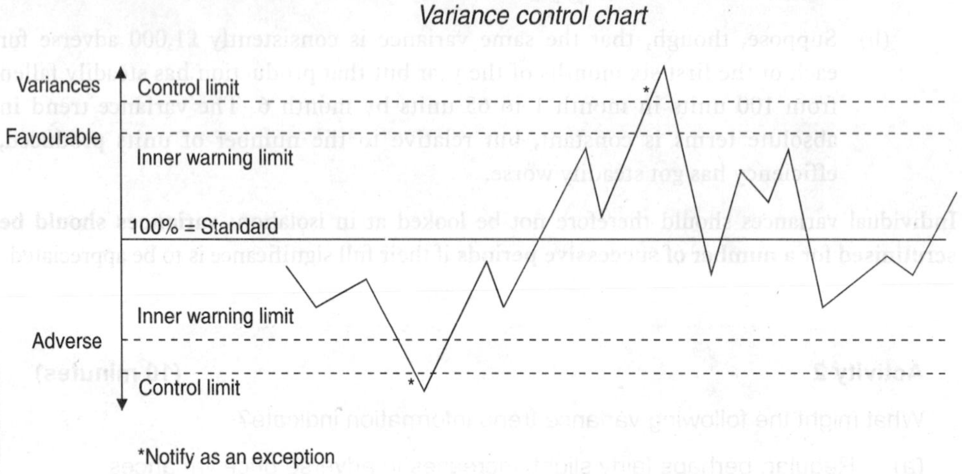

Figure 10.1: Variance control chart

There are several ways of establishing control limits.

(a) Management might establish a rule that any variance should be deemed significant if it exceeds a certain percentage of standard, for example if it exceeds 10% of standard in any one period based on judgement or experience.

(b) Management can use statistics, and estimate not only the standard cost, but the expected standard deviation (a measure of the spread or dispersion) of actual costs around the standard. Variances would then be deemed significant if actual costs were significantly different from standard.

Not all variances which are outside the control limits require detailed investigation. Often the cause is already known. A variance will only be investigated if the expected value of benefits from investigation and any control action exceed the costs of investigation.

For example it may be known from past experience that the cost of investigating a particular variance is £150 and that cost savings amounting to £1,200 can be made if the variance is corrected successfully. However it is also known that there is only a 30% possibility of the variance being corrected once the cause is found.

Expected value of an investigation = (£1,200 × 0.3) – £150 = £210

In this particular case it is worth investigating the variance.

> **Activity 3** **(10 minutes)**
>
> Every month the operating statement of Jefferson Ltd shows a direct material efficiency variance of between £1,500 and £2,500 relating to a product that is only to be produced for a further six months. The company management accountant believes that if the variance is investigated, there is a 70% chance that its cause can eliminated. The cost of the investigation, however, is £5,000.
>
> Should the investigation take place?

Another approach is to **look at the variances over a number of accounting periods,** instead of just looking at variances in a single period.

The variance in each period is added to the total of the variances that have occurred over a longer period of time. If the variances are not significant, the total will simply fluctuate in a random way above and below the average (favourable and unfavourable variances), to give an insignificant total or cumulative sum. If the cumulative sum develops a positive or negative drift, it may exceed a set tolerance limit. Then the situation must be investigated, and control action will probably be required. The cumulative sum of variances over a period of time can be shown on a **cusum chart**.

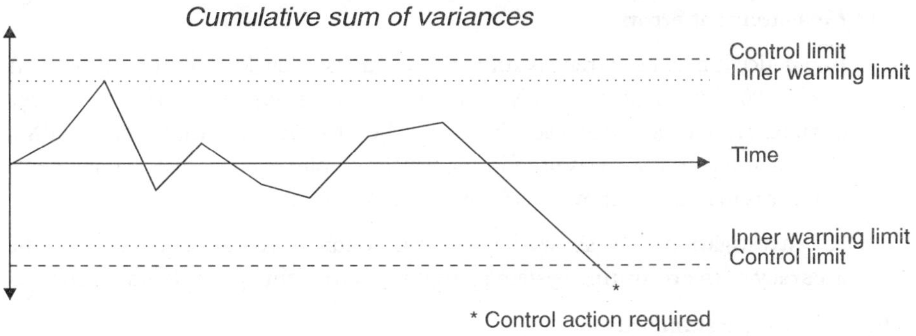

Figure 10.2: Cumulative sum of variances

The advantage of the multiple period approach is that trends are detectable earlier, and control action can be introduced sooner than might have been the case if only current-period variances were investigated.

3 CONTROL ACTION

If a variance is assessed as significant then the responsible manager may need to take control action.

Since a variance compares historical actual costs with standard costs, it is a statement of what has gone wrong (or right) in the past. By taking control action, managers can do nothing about the past, but they can use their analysis of past results to identify where the 'system' is out of control. If the cause of the variance is controllable, action can be taken to bring the system back under control in future. If the variance is uncontrollable, on the other hand, but *not* simply due to chance, it will be necessary to revise forecasts of expected results, and perhaps to revise the budget.

It may be possible for control action to restore actual results back on course to achieve the original budget. For example, if there is an adverse labour efficiency variance in month 1 of 1,100 hours, control action by the production department might succeed in increasing efficiency above standard by 100 hours per month for the next 11 months.

It is also possible that control action might succeed in restoring better order to a situation, but the improvements might not be sufficient to enable the company to achieve its original budget. For example if for three months there has been an adverse labour efficiency in a production department, so that the cost per unit of output was £8 instead of a standard cost of £5. Control action might succeed in improving efficiency, so that unit costs are reduced to £7, £6 or even £5, but the earlier excess spending means that the profit in the master budget will not be achieved.

Depending on the situation and the control action taken, the action may take immediate effect, or it may take several weeks or months to implement. The effect of control action might be short-lived, lasting for only one control period; but it is more likely to be implemented with the aim of long-term improvement.

3.1 Possible control action

The control action which may be taken will depend on the reason why the variance occurred. Some reasons for variances are outlined in the paragraphs below.

(a) **Measurement errors**

In practice it may be extremely difficult to establish that 1,000 units of product A used 32,000 kg of raw material X. Scales may be misread, the pilfering or wastage of materials may go unrecorded, items may be wrongly classified (as material X3, say, when material X8 was used in reality), or employees may make adjustments to records to make their own performance look better.

An investigation may show that control action is required to improve the accuracy of the recording system so that measurement errors do not occur.

(b) **Out of date standards**

Price standards are likely to become out of date when changes to the costs of material, power, labour and so on occur, or in periods of high inflation. In such circumstances an investigation of variances is likely to highlight a general change in market prices rather than efficiencies or inefficiencies in acquiring resources.

Standards may also be out of date where operations are subject to technological development or if learning curve effects have not been taken into account. Investigation of this type of variance will provide information about the inaccuracy of the standard and highlight the need to frequently review and update standards.

(c) **Random or chance fluctuations**

A standard is an average figure. It represents the midpoint of a range of possible values and therefore actual results are likely to deviate unpredictably within the predictable range.

As long as the variance falls within this range, it will be classified as a random or chance fluctuation and control action will not be necessary.

NOTES

(d) **Efficient or inefficient operations**

Spoilage and better quality material/more highly skilled labour than standard are all likely to affect the efficiency of operations and hence cause variances. Investigation of variances in this category should highlight the cause of the inefficiency or efficiency and will lead to control action to eliminate the inefficiency being repeated or action to compound the benefits of the efficiency. For example, stricter supervision may be required to reduce wastage levels. The table below looks at possible reasons for the occurrence of the variances we calculated in the previous chapter.

Variance	Favourable	Adverse
Material price	Unforeseen discounts received More care taken in purchasing Change in material standard	Price increase Careless purchasing Change in material standard
Material usage	Material used of higher quality than standard More effective use made of material Errors in allocating material to jobs	Defective material Excessive waste Theft Stricter quality control Errors in allocating material to jobs
Labour rate of pay	Use of apprentices or other workers at a rate of pay lower than standard	Wage rate increase
Idle time	The idle time variance is always adverse	Machine breakdown Non-availability of material Illness or injury to worker
Labour efficiency (also fixed and variable overhead efficiency where overheads are recovered based on direct labour hours)	Output produced more quickly than expected because of work motivation, training, better quality of equipment or materials Errors in allocating time to jobs	Lost time in excess of standard allowed Output lower than standard set because of deliberate restriction, lack of training, or sub-standard material used Errors in allocating time to jobs
Variable overhead expenditure	Savings in costs incurred More economical use of services	Increase in cost of services used Excessive use of services Change in type of services used
Fixed overhead expenditure	Savings in costs incurred More economical use of services	Increase in cost of services used Excessive use of services Change in type of services used
Sales price	Price increase to cover unforeseen costs Price increase following increased demand	Price cut to stimulate demand due to increase in competition
Sales volume	Increased sales resulting from a new advertising campaign or a change in perception of the product by the public	Unexpected slump in the economy/demand for the product

BPP LEARNING MEDIA

NOTES

3.2 Interdependence between variances

The cause of one variance may be wholly or partly explained by the cause of another variance. Examples could be as follows.

(a) If the purchasing department buys a cheaper material which is poorer in quality than the expected standard, the material price variance will be favourable, but this may cause material wastage and an adverse usage variance.

(b) Similarly, if employees used to do some work are highly experienced, they may be paid a higher rate than the standard wage per hour, but they should do the work more efficiently than employees of 'average' skill. In other words, an adverse rate variance may be compensated by a favourable efficiency variance.

(c) An adverse efficiency variance may be reported following the purchase of cheaper material (favourable material price variance) because operatives find difficulty in processing the cheaper material.

(d) A rise in selling price very often leads to a fall in the volume of goods sold, so sales price and volume variances can be interdependent.

Activity 4 **(25 minutes)**

VARIANCE REPORT: SEPTEMBER 20X5

	Variance (Adverse)	*Variance (Favourable)*	*Total variance*
	£	£	£
Material			–2,000
Usage	5,500		
Price		3,500	
Labour			–1,500
Efficiency	3,000		
Rate		1,500	
Overhead			–500
Expenditure		4,500	
Efficiency	2,000		
Capacity	3,000		

Actual costs for September 20X5 were as follows.

	£
Materials	100,000
Labour	80,000
Overheads	75,000
Total	255,000

The total adverse variance of £4,000 is 1.57% of total costs.

Comment on the possible causes of these variances and whether they warrant investigation.

4 PERFORMANCE MEASURES

Management **measure** the **performance** of an organisation in a number of areas to **see** whether **objectives or targets are being met**.

- In the organisation as a whole
- In each of the main sub-divisions of the organisation
- In individual activities
- In relationships with customers, the market, suppliers and competitors

The process of performance measurement is carried out using a variety of **performance indicators**, which are individual measurements. We look at performance indicators **in general** below before moving on to look at performance indicators **derived from the profit and loss account and balance sheet.** As well as being of use to management, **parties external** to the organisation can use these as a guide to how well the organisation is performing.

4.1 Performance indicators

In the previous section we looked at the analysis of **variances**. Cost variances are examples of performance indicators and can provide assistance to management in a number of ways.

- Monitoring the use of resources
- Controlling the organisation
- Planning for the future

In this section we will look at a wide variety of performance indicators. Let us have a look at some examples and the possible uses they could have.

(a) The direct labour efficiency variance, which could **identify problems** with labour productivity

(b) Distribution costs as a percentage of turnover, which could help with the **control of costs**

(c) Number of hours during which labour are idle, which could indicate **how well resources are being used**

(d) Profit as a percentage of turnover, which could highlight **how well the organisation is being managed**

(e) Number of units returned by customers, which could help with **planning** production and finished stock levels

Given this **wide range of uses**, you should be able to appreciate the importance of performance indictors and their value to managers in allowing them to see where improvements in organisational performance can be made.

A performance indicator is only useful if it is given meaning in relation to something else. Here is a list of **yardsticks** against which indicators can be compared so as to become useful.

(a) **Standards, budgets or targets**

(b) **Trends over time** (comparing last year with this year, say). An upward trend in the number of rejects from a production process, say, would indicate a problem that needed investigating. The effects of inflation would perhaps need to be recognised if financial indicators were being compared over time.

(c) **The results of other parts of the organisation**. Large manufacturing companies may compare the results of their various production departments, supermarket chains will compare the results of their individual stores, while a college may compare pass rates in different departments.

(d) **The results of other organisations.** For example, trade associations or the government may provide details of key indicators based on averages for the industry.

As with all comparisons, it is vital that the performance measurement process compares '**like with like**'. There is little to be gained in comparing the results of a small supermarket in a high street with a huge one in an out-of-town shopping complex. We return to the importance of consistency in comparisons later in this chapter.

4.2 Qualitative and quantitative measures

It is possible to distinguish between quantitative data, which is capable of being expressed in numbers, and qualitative data, which can only be expressed in numerical terms with difficulty.

(a) An example of a **quantitative** performance measure is 'You have been late for work **twice** this week and it's only Tuesday!'.

(b) An example of a **qualitative** performance measure is 'My bed is **very** comfortable'.

The first measure is likely to find its way into a staff appraisal report. The second would feature in a bed manufacturer's customer satisfaction survey. Both are indicators of whether their subjects are doing as good a job as they are required to do.

Qualitative measures are by nature **subjective** and **judgmental** but this does not mean that they are not valuable. They are especially valuable when they are derived from several different sources because then they can be expressed in a mixture of quantitative and qualitative terms which is more meaningful overall.

Consider the statement 'Seven out of ten customers think our beds are very comfortable'. This is a quantitative measure of customer satisfaction as well as a qualitative measure of the perceived performance of the beds. (But it does not mean that only 70% of the total beds produced are comfortable, nor that each bed is 70% comfortable and 30% uncomfortable: 'very' is the measure of comfort.)

4.3 Productivity, efficiency and effectiveness

In general, performance indicators are established to measure productivity, efficiency and effectiveness.

- Effectiveness is about meeting targets and objectives.
- Productivity is a measure of output relative to some form of input.

5 PERFORMANCE MEASURES FOR COST CENTRES

5.1 Productivity

This is the quantity of the product or service produced **(output) in relation to** the resources put in (**input**). For example so many units produced per hour, or per employee, or per tonne of material. It measures **how efficiently resources are being used.**

5.2 Cost per unit

For the manager of a cost centre which is also a production centre one of the most important performance measures will be cost per unit. This is simply the total costs of production divided by the number of units produced in the period.

EXAMPLE: COST PER UNIT

The total costs and number of units produced for a production cost centre for the last two months are as follows:

	May	*June*
Production costs	£128,600	£143,200
Units produced	12,000	13,500
Cost per unit	$\frac{£128,600}{12,000}$	$\frac{£143,200}{13,500}$
	= £10.72	£10.61

5.3 Indices

Indices can be used in order to measure activity.

Indices show **how a particular variable has changed relative to a base value**. The base value is usually the level of the variable at an earlier date. The 'variable' may be just one particular item, such as material X, or several items may be incorporated, such as 'raw materials' generally.

In its simplest form an index is calculated as **(current value ÷ base value) × 100%.**

Thus if materials cost £15 per kg in 20X0 and now (20X3) cost £27 per kg the 20X0 value would be expressed in index form as 100 (15/15 × 100) and the 20X3 value as 180 (27/15 × 100). If you find it easier to think of this as a percentage, then do so.

EXAMPLE: WORK STANDARDS AND INDICES

Standards for work done in a service department could be expressed as an index. For example, suppose that in a sales department, there is a standard target for sales representatives to make 25 customer visits per month each. The budget for May might be for ten sales representatives to make 250 customer visits in total. Actual results in May might be that nine sales representatives made 234 visits in total. Performance could then be measured as:

Budget	100	(Standard = index 100)
Actual	104	(234 ÷ (9 × 25)) × 100)

This shows that 'productivity' per sales representative was actually 4% over budget.

6 PERFORMANCE MEASURES FOR REVENUE CENTRES

Traditionally sales performance is measured against price and volume targets. Other possible measures include revenue targets and target market share. They may be analysed in detail: by country, by region, by individual products, by salesperson and so on.

In a customer-focused organisation the basic information 'Turnover is up by 14%' can be supplemented by a host of other indicators.

(a) **Customer rejects/returns: total sales**. This ratio helps to monitor customer satisfaction, providing a check on the efficiency of quality control procedures.

(b) **Deliveries late: deliveries on schedule**. This ratio can be applied both to sales made to customers and to receipts from suppliers. When applied to customers it provides an indication of the efficiency of production and production scheduling.

(c) **Flexibility measures** indicate how well able a company is to respond to customers' requirements. Measures could be devised to measure how quickly and efficiently **new products** are launched, and how well procedures meet **customer needs**.

(d) **Number of people served and speed of service**, in a shop or a bank for example. If it takes too long to reach the point of sale, future sales are liable to be lost.

(e) **Customer satisfaction questionnaires**, for input to the organisation's management information system.

7 PERFORMANCE MEASURES FOR PROFIT CENTRES

7.1 Profit margin

Definition

> The **profit margin** (profit to sales ratio) is calculated as (profit ÷ sales) × 100%.

The profit margin provides a simple measure of performance for profit centres. Investigation of unsatisfactory profit margins enables control action to be taken, either by reducing excessive costs or by raising selling prices.

Profit margin is usually calculated using operating profit.

NOTES

EXAMPLE: THE PROFIT TO SALES RATIO

A company compares its year 2 results with year 1 results as follows.

		Year 2	Year 1
		£	£
Sales		160,000	120,000
Cost of sales			
Direct materials		40,000	20,000
Direct labour		40,000	30,000
Production overhead		22,000	20,000
Marketing overhead		42,000	35,000
		144,000	105,000
Profit		16,000	15,000
Profit to sales ratio	$\left(\frac{16,000}{160,000}\right) \times 100\%$	10%	
	$\left(\frac{15,000}{120,000}\right) \times 100\%$		12½%

The above information shows that there is a decline in profitability in spite of the £1,000 increase in profit, because the profit margin is less in year 2 than year 1.

7.2 Gross profit margin

The profit to sales ratio above was based on a profit figure which included non-production overheads. The **pure trading activities of a business can be analysed** using the gross profit margin, which is calculated as (gross profit ÷ turnover) × 100%.

For the company in the above example the gross profit margin would be:

$$\text{Year 1: } \left(\frac{(16,000 + 42,000)}{160,000}\right) \times 100\% = 36.25\%$$

$$\text{Year 2: } \left(\frac{(15,000 + 35,000)}{120,000}\right) \times 100\% = 41.67\%$$

7.3 Cost/sales ratios

When target profits are not met, further ratios may be used to shed some light on the problem.

- Production cost of sales ÷ sales
- Distribution and marketing costs ÷ sales
- Administrative costs ÷ sales

Subsidiary ratios can be used to examine problem areas in greater depth. For example, for production costs the following ratios might be used.

- Material costs ÷ sales value of production
- Works labour costs ÷ sales value of production
- Production overheads ÷ sales value of production

NOTES

EXAMPLE: COST/SALES RATIOS

Look back to the previous example. A more detailed analysis would show that higher direct materials are the probable cause of the decline in profitability.

		Year 2	Year 1
Material costs/sales	$\left(\frac{40{,}000}{160{,}000}\right) \times 100\%$	25%	
	$\left(\frac{20{,}000}{120{,}000}\right) \times 100\%$		16.7%

Other cost/sales ratios have remained the same or improved.

Activity 5 **(10 minutes)**

Use the following summary profit and loss account to answer the questions below.

	£
Sales	3,000
Cost of sales	1,800
	1,200
Manufacturing expenses	300
Administrative expenses	200
Operating profit	700

Calculate (a) the profit margin

(b) the gross profit margin

7.4 Resources

Traditional measures for materials compare actual costs with expected costs, looking at differences (or variances) in price and usage. Many traditional systems also analyse **wastage.** Measures used in **modern manufacturing environments** include the number of **rejects** in materials supplied, and the **timing and reliability of deliveries** of materials.

Labour costs are traditionally measured in terms of **standard performance** (ideal, attainable and so on) and rate and efficiency **variances.**

Qualitative measures of labour performance concentrate on matters such as **ability to communicate, interpersonal relationships** with colleagues, **customers' impressions** and **levels of skills** attained.

Managers can expect to be judged to some extent by the performance of their staff. High profitability or tight cost control are not the only indicators of managerial performance!

For variable overheads, differences between actual and budgeted costs (ie variances) are traditional measures. Various time based measures are also available, such as the following.

NOTES

(a) **Machine down time: total machine hours.** This ratio provides a measure of machine usage and efficiency.

(b) **Value added time: production cycle time.** Value added time is the direct production time during which the product is being made. The production cycle time includes non-value-added times such as set-up time, downtime, idle time and so on. The 'perfect' ratio is 100%, but in practice this optimum will not be achieved. A high ratio means non-value-added activities are being kept to a minimum.

7.5 Measures of performance using the standard hour

Sam Ltd manufactures plates, mugs and eggcups. Production during the first two quarters of 20X5 was as follows.

	Quarter 1	*Quarter 2*
Plates	1,000	800
Mugs	1,200	1,500
Eggcups	800	900

The fact that 3,000 products were produced in quarter 1 and 3,200 in quarter 2 does not tell us anything about Sam Ltd's performance over the two periods because plates, mugs and eggcups are so different. The fact that the production mix has changed is not revealed by considering the total number of units produced. The problem of how to **measure output when a number of dissimilar products are manufactured** can be overcome, however, by the **use of the standard hour.**

The standard hour (or standard minute) is the **quantity of work achievable at standard performance, expressed in terms of a standard unit of work done in a standard period of time.**

The standard time allowed to produce one unit of each of Sam Ltd's products is as follows.

	Standard time
Plate	$^1/_2$ hour
Mug	$^1/_3$ hour
Eggcup	$^1/_2$ hour

By measuring the standard hours of output in each quarter, a more useful output measure is obtained.

		Quarter 1		*Quarter 2*	
Product	*Standard hours per unit*	*Production*	*Standard hours*	*Production*	*Standard hours*
Plate	$^1/_2$	1,000	500	800	400
Mug	$^1/_3$	1,200	400	1,500	500
Eggcup	$^1/_4$	800	200	900	225
			1,100		1,125

The output level in the two quarters was therefore very similar.

7.6 Efficiency, activity and capacity ratios

Standard hours are useful in computing levels of **efficiency, activity and capacity**. Any management accounting reports involving budgets and variance analysis should incorporate control ratios. The three main control ratios are the **efficiency, capacity** and **activity** ratios.

BPP LEARNING MEDIA

NOTES

(a) The capacity ratio compares actual hours worked and budgeted hours, and measures the extent to which planned utilisation has been achieved.

(b) The activity or production volume ratio compares the number of standard hours equivalent to the actual work produced and budgeted hours.

(c) The efficiency ratio measures the efficiency of the labour force by comparing equivalent standard hours for work produced and actual hours worked.

WORKED EXAMPLE: RATIOS AND STANDARD HOURS

Given the following information about Sam Ltd for quarter 1 of 20X5, calculate a capacity ratio, an activity ratio and an efficiency ratio and explain their meaning.

Budgeted hours	1,100 standard hours
Standard hours produced	1,125 standard hours
Actual hours worked	1,200

ANSWER

$$\text{Capacity ratio} = \frac{\text{Actual hours worked}}{\text{Budgeted hours}} \times 100\% = \frac{1{,}200}{1{,}100} \times 100\% = 109\%$$

$$\text{Activity ratio} = \frac{\text{Standard hours produced}}{\text{Budgeted hours}} \times 100\% = \frac{1{,}125}{1{,}100} \times 100\% = 102\%$$

The overall activity or production volume for the quarter was 2% greater than forecast. This was achieved by a 9% increase in capacity.

$$\text{Efficiency ratio} = \frac{\text{Standard hours produced}}{\text{Actual hours worked}} \times 100\% = \frac{1{,}125}{1{,}200} \times 100\% = 94\%$$

The labour force worked 6% below standard levels of efficiency.

Activity 6 **(5 minutes)**

If X = Actual hours worked
Y = Budgeted hours
Z = Standard hours produced

What is $\frac{Z}{Y}$?

A Capacity ratio
B Activity ratio
C Efficiency ratio
D Standard hours produced ratio

8 PERFORMANCE MEASURES FOR INVESTMENT CENTRES

8.1 Return on investment (ROI)

Definition

> **Return on investment (ROI)** (also called **Return on capital employed (ROCE)**) is calculated as (profit/capital employed) × 100% and shows how much profit has been made in relation to the amount of resources invested.

ROI is generally used for measuring the performance of investment centres; profits alone do not show whether the return is sufficient when different values of assets are used. Thus if company A and company B have the following results, company B would have the better performance.

	A	*B*
	£	£
Profit	5,000	5,000
Sales	100,000	100,000
Capital employed	50,000	25,000
ROI	10%	20%

The profit of each company is the same but company B only invested £25,000 to achieve that profit whereas company A invested £50,000.

ROI may be calculated in a number of ways, but **profit before interest and tax** is usually used.

Similarly **all assets of a non-operational nature** (for example trade investments and intangible assets such as goodwill) **should be excluded** from capital employed.

Profits should be related to average capital employed. In practice many companies calculate the ratio **using year-end assets.** This can be misleading. If a new investment is undertaken near to the year end, the capital employed will rise but profits will only have a month or two of the new investment's contribution.

What does the ROI tell us? What should we be looking for? There are **two principal comparisons** that can be made.

- The change in ROI from one year to the next
- The ROI being earned by other entities

8.2 Residual income (RI)

An alternative way of measuring the performance of an investment centre, instead of using ROI, is residual income (RI). **Residual income** is a **measure of the centre's profits after deducting a notional or imputed interest cost,** and **depreciation** on capital equipment.

Definition

> **Residual income (RI)** is 'Pre-tax profits less a notional interest charge for invested capital'.

Activity 7 **(10 minutes)**

A division with capital employed of £400,000 currently earns a ROI of 22%. It can make an additional investment of £50,000 for a five-year life with nil residual value. The average net profit from this investment would be £12,000 after depreciation of £2,000. A notional interest charge amounting to 14% of the amount invested is to be charged to the division each year.

Calculate the residual income of the division after the investment.

Chapter roundup

- Responsibility accounting is a system of accounting that segregates revenue and costs into areas of personal responsibility in order to monitor and assess the performance of each part of an organisation.
- A responsibility centre is a function or department of an organisation that is headed by a manager who has direct responsibility for its performance.
- A cost centre is any unit of an organisation to which costs can be separately attributed.
- A profit centre is any unit of an organisation to which both revenues and costs are assigned, so that the profitability of the unit may be measured.
- An investment centre is a profit centre whose performance is measured by its return on capital employed.
- Controllable costs are items of expenditure which can be directly influenced by a given manager within a given time span.
- Materiality, controllability and variance trend should be considered before a decision about whether or not to investigate a variance is taken.
- One way of deciding whether or not to investigate a variance is to only investigate those variances which exceed pre-set tolerance limits.
- Control limits may be illustrated on a control chart.
- A variance should only be investigated if the expected value of benefits from investigation and any control action exceed the costs of investigation.
- If the cause of a variance is controllable, action can be taken to bring the system back under control in future. If the variance is uncontrollable, but not simply due to chance, it will be necessary to review forecasts of expected results, and perhaps to revise the budget.
- Performance measurement aims to establish how well something or somebody is doing in relation to a planned activity.
- Ratios and percentages are useful performance measurement techniques.
- Cost per unit is total costs ÷ number of units produced.
- The profit margin (profit to sales ratio) is calculated as (profit ÷ sales) × 100%.

NOTES

Chapter roundup (continued)

- The gross profit margin is calculated as gross profit ÷ sales × 100%.
- Return on investment (ROI) or return on capital employed (ROCE) shows how much profit has been made in relation to the amount of resources invested.
- Residual income (RI) is an alternative way of measuring the performance of an investment centre. It is a measure of the centre's profits after deducing a notional or imputed interest cost.
- Performance measures for materials and labour include differences between actual and expected (budgeted) performance. Performance can also be measured using the standard hour.

Quick quiz

1 Fill in the blank.

.... is a system of accounting that makes revenues and costs the responsibility of particular managers so that the performance of each part of the organisation can be monitored and assessed.

2 What is the difference between a cost centre and a profit centre?

3 What three types of variance would lie within tolerance limits?

4 What are the four basic reasons why variances occur?

5 What is meant by interdependence between variances?

6 What is the main aim of performance measurement?

7 Fill in the blanks.

To become useful, performance indicators should be compared against yardsticks including .... , ... , ... or ....

8 How do quantitative and qualitative performance measures differ?

9 What types of measure are profit margin and ROCE?

	Profit margin	*ROCE*
A	Of efficiency	Of productivity
B	Of effectiveness	Of effectiveness
C	Of productivity	Of effectiveness
D	Of efficiency	Of efficiency

10 Profit margin = $\frac{C}{D} \times 100\%$

C =...........................

D = ...

11 $ROI = \frac{A}{B} \times 100\%$

A =............................

B = ...

Answers to quick quiz

1 Responsibility accounting. (see para 1)

2 A profit centre collects information on both costs and revenue but a cost centre collects only cost information. (paras 1.1 and 1.3)

3 Normal variations around average performance, minor operational variances and variances due to minor planning errors in the standard cost will lie within tolerance limits. (para 2.5)

4 Variances occur because of measurement errors, out of date standards, efficient or inefficient operations and random/chance fluctuations. (para 3.1)

5 Interdependence between variances means that the cause of one variance can be wholly or partly explained by the cause of another variance. (para 3.2)

6 To establish whether objectives or targets are being met. (para 4)

7 standards, budgets or targets
trends over time
results of other parts of the organisation
results of other organisations (para 4.1)

8 Quantitative measures are expressed in numbers whereas qualitative measures are not. (para 4.2)

9 D (paras 7.2 and 8.1)

10 C = profit
D = sales (para 7.2)

11 A = profit
B = capital employed (para 8.1)

Answers to activities

1 (a) Revenue centre (responsible for revenue from centrally made room bookings only).

(b) Investment centre (responsible for investment in some fixed assets, as well as hotel expenses and income).

(c) Profit centre (the restaurant manager will be responsible for the income and costs of the restaurant).

(d) Cost centre (there will only be costs in relation to cleaning and maintenance).

2 This could indicate that prices are seasonal and perhaps stock could be built up in cheap seasons.

(a) Such variances usually indicate the workings of general inflation.

(b) These variances may indicate a sudden scarcity of a resource. It may soon be necessary to seek out cheaper substitutes.

(c) These may signal the existence of a learning curve, or the success of a productivity bonus scheme.

(d) These may indicate that equipment is deteriorating and will soon need repair or even replacement.

3 Minimum possible cost saving = 6 × £1,500 = £9,000

Expected value of the benefit of investigating the variance	= 70% × £9,000
	= £6,300
Cost of investigation	= £5,000

∴ Expected benefits exceed the costs
∴ The investigation is worthwhile.

4 *Total variance*

The total variance may only be 1.57% of total costs but this total disguises a number of significant adverse and favourable variances which need investigating.

Materials variances

The fact that there is a favourable price variance and an adverse usage variance could indicate interdependence. The purchasing department may have bought cheap materials but these cheaper materials may have been more difficult to work with so that more material was required per unit produced. The possibility of such an interdependence should be investigated. Whether or not there is an interdependence, both variances do require investigation since they represent 5.5% (usage) and 3.5% (price) of the actual material cost for the month.

Labour variances

Again there could be an interdependence between the adverse efficiency variance and the favourable rate variance, less skilled (and lower paid) employees perhaps having worked less efficiently than standard. Discussions with factory management should reveal whether this is so. Both variances do need investigation since they again represent a high percentage (compared with 1.57%) of the actual labour cost for the month (3.75% for the efficiency variance and 1.875% for the rate variance).

Overhead variances

An investigation into the fixed and variable components of the overhead would facilitate control information. The cause of the favourable expenditure variance, which represents 6% of the total overhead costs for the month, should be encouraged.

The adverse overhead variances in total represent 6.67% of actual overhead cost during the month and must therefore be investigated. The capacity variance signifies that actual hours of work were less than budgeted hours of work. The company is obviously working below its planned capacity level. Efforts should therefore be made to increase production so as to eradicate this variance.

CONCLUSION

It is not the total of the monthly variances which should be considered but the individual variances, as a number of them represent significant deviations from planned results. Investigations into their causes should be performed and control action taken to ensure that either performance is back under control in future if the cause of the variance can be controlled, or the forecasts of expected results are revised if the variance is uncontrollable.

5 (a) $\frac{700}{3{,}000} \times 100\% = 23\%$

The profit margin usually refers to operating profit/sales.

(b) $\frac{1{,}200}{3{,}000} \times 100\% = 40\%$

The gross profit margin takes the gross profit/sales.

6 B

7

	£
Divisional profit after investment (400,000 × 22% + 12,000)	100,000
Notional interest (450,000 × 0.14)	63,000
Residual income	37,000

PART B

FINANCIAL REPORTING

Chapter 11 :

THE LEGAL AND REGULATORY FRAMEWORK

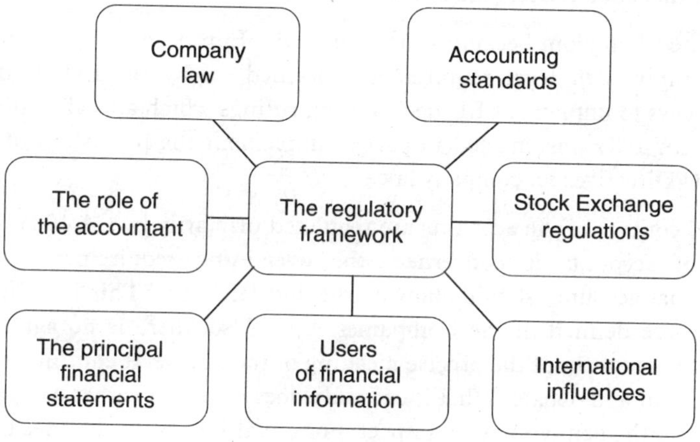

Introduction

The preparation of financial accounts of limited liability companies is closely regulated. The regulation comes from four main sources: company law, accounting standards, international accounting standards and the Stock Exchange requirements. Further pervasive influence comes from the users of the accounts.

The main statute governing the form and content of financial statements is the Companies Act 1985 (CA 1985) as amended by the Companies Act 1989 (CA 1989). A new Companies Act 2006 has been issued, but its provisions will not be fully implemented for some time. The Companies Act 1989 gave the accounting standards the force of law, whereas previously the standards had no legal standing in statute. At the moment, UK standards are issued by the Accounting Standards Board (ASB).

International accounting standards are issued by the International Accounting Standards Board (IASB) and are becoming increasingly important for preparers and users of financial statements in the UK and elsewhere. UK listed groups must now prepare their consolidated financial statements in accordance with International Accounting Standards. UK standards are being brought into line with international standards on a number of issues.

The Stock Exchange requirements apply only to those companies whose shares are traded on the Stock Exchange.

Your objectives

In this chapter you will learn about the following.

(a) The main sources of accounting regulation in the UK

(b) The current structure of the standard-setting process

(c) The differences between SSAPs, SORPs, FRSs, FREDs and UITF statements

(d) The different users of financial statements and their needs

1 COMPANY LAW

Limited companies are required by law to prepare accounts annually for distribution to their shareholders. A copy of these accounts must be lodged with the Registrar of Companies and is available for inspection by any member of the public. For this reason a company's statutory annual accounts are often referred to as its published accounts.

The Companies Act 2006 has consolidated several areas of company law, most notably the Companies Act 1985. The new Act is being introduced in a piecemeal fashion, but as far as possible this book reflects the new legislation.

Since the United Kingdom became a member of the European Union (EU) it has been obliged to comply with legal requirements decided on by the EU. It does this by enacting UK laws to implement EU decisions on rulings which are called directives. For example, the CA 1989 was enacted in part to implement the provisions of the seventh and eighth EU Directives on company law.

The form and content of the accounts are regulated primarily by CA 1985. As far as the preparation of accounts is concerned, the overriding requirement of companies legislation is that accounts should show a 'true and fair view'. This is a slippery phrase which is nowhere defined in the Companies Acts. Also, there is no agreement in the accounting profession about the precise meaning of the phrase. It continues to be a cause of much argument and debate. What it certainly does *not* mean is that company accounts are to be exact to the penny in every respect. For one thing, as we shall see later, many of the figures appearing in a set of accounts are derived at least partly by the exercise of judgement. For another, the amount of time and effort that such a requirement would cost would be out of all proportion to the advantages arising from it.

The legislation also requires that the accounts of any limited company above a certain size must be *audited*. An audit, for this purpose, may be defined as an 'independent examination of, and expression of opinion on, the financial statements of an enterprise'. This means in practice that a limited company must engage a firm of chartered or certified accountants to conduct an examination of its accounting records and its financial statements in order to form an opinion as to whether the accounts which are to be published present a 'true and fair view'. At the conclusion of their audit work, the auditors issue a report (addressed to the owners of the company, ie its members or shareholders) which is published as part of the accounts.

We now look at another source of accounting regulation, namely accounting standards.

2 ACCOUNTING STANDARDS

2.1 The need for accounting standards

Apart from company law, the main regulations affecting accounts in the UK derive from pronouncements issued by the professional accounting bodies. The need for standards arose because of lack of uniformity in the way profit was calculated and presented and financial position measured. Working with the same data, different groups of people could produce very different financial statements. A variety of approaches in the preparation and presentation of financial statements not only made it difficult to compare the financial results of different companies but also allowed deliberate manipulation in order to present accounts in the most favourable light. The accounting standards aim to narrow the areas of difference and choice in financial reporting and improve comparability.

The Accounting Standards Committee (ASC) was set up in January 1970 with the aim of publishing accounting standards in order to crack down on manipulation of published accounts. This was the beginning of a long line of attempts to protect investors in the wake of accounting scandals.

Activity 1 **(10 minutes)**

You will be aware from your reading that such attempts have not yet been entirely successful. For fun, list a few of the more recent accounting scandals you can think of.

The ASC issued 25 Statements of Standard Accounting Practice (SSAPs) before it was replaced by a successor body in 1990, the Accounting Standards Board (ASB). Some SSAPs are still in existence, although they are gradually being replaced.

2.2 Standard setting process

The current system consists of the following four bodies:

(a) the Financial Reporting Council (FRC)
(b) the Accounting Standards Board (ASB)
(c) the Financial Reporting Review Panel (FRRP)
(d) the Urgent Issues Task Force (UITF)

The Financial Reporting Council

This acts as a kind of umbrella organisation to all the bodies involved in standard setting. It is responsible for funding and ensures the smooth running of the standard setting process. It is also responsible for the enforcement of standards, particularly in relation to the Review Panel. Its most important task is to set a general work programme for the ASB, along with a guide to broad policy issues. This role means that it is the FRC which determines what matters should come to the attention of the ASB. It has about 25 members drawn from users, preparers and auditors of accounts. Its chairman is appointed by the Government.

The Accounting Standards Board

The FRC operates through two arms: the FRRP and the ASB. The ASB is, in effect, the successor body to the ASC and is responsible for the issue of accounting standards. Accounting standards issued by the ASB are called **Financial Reporting Standards** (FRSs), of which several have so far been published (see below). Prior to publication, the ASB circulates its proposals in the form of a **Financial Reporting Exposure Draft** (inevitably referred to as a FRED) and invites comments. To avoid chaos, the ASB has 'adopted' those SSAPs still extant, and they therefore remain in force; however, SSAPs are being superseded by the new FRSs. The ASB has a full-time chairperson and technical director. A majority of two thirds of the Board is required to approve a new standard.

The Financial Reporting Review Panel

The FRRP is the second operating arm of the FRC. Its task is to examine accounts published by companies if it appears that Companies Act requirements have been breached – in particular, the requirement that accounts should show a true and fair view. The panel has legal backing: if a company departs from an accounting standard, the panel may go to the courts, which may in turn instruct the company to prepare revised accounts.

The Urgent Issues Task Force

The UITF is an offshoot of the ASB. Its role is to assist the ASB in areas where an accounting standard or Companies Act provision already exists, but where unsatisfactory or conflicting interpretations have developed. As its name suggests, the UITF is designed to act quickly (more quickly than the full standard-setting process is capable of) when an authoritative ruling is urgently needed. The UITF pronouncements, which are called abstracts, are intended to come into effect quickly. They therefore tend to become effective within approximately one month of publication date. The UITF has so far issued over 30 abstracts, some of which have been incorporated into new accounting standards and some of which still stand alone.

Having looked at the standard setting process, we now briefly look at the standards themselves.

2.3 UK accounting standards

The following is the up-to-date list of the UK accounting standards (FRSs are issued by the Accounting Standards Board (ASB); SSAPs were issued by the now defunct Accounting Standards Committee (ASC)).

NUMBER	TITLE
FRSSE	Financial reporting standard for smaller entities
FRS 1	Cash-flow statements
FRS 2	Accounting for subsidiary undertakings
FRS 3	Reporting financial performance
FRS 4	Capital instruments
FRS 5	Reporting the substance of transactions
FRS 6	Acquisitions and mergers
FRS 7	Fair value in acquisition accounting
FRS 8	Related party disclosures
FRS 9	Associates and joint ventures
FRS 10	Goodwill and intangible assets
FRS 11	Impairment of fixed assets and goodwill
FRS 12	Provisions, contingent liabilities and contingent assets
FRS 13	Derivatives and other financial instruments: disclosures
FRS 15	Tangible fixed assets

FRS 16	Current tax
FRS 17	Retirement benefits
FRS 18	Accounting policies
FRS 19	Deferred tax
FRS 20	Share-based payment
FRS 21	Events after the balance sheet date
FRS 22	Earnings per share
FRS 23	The effects of changes in foreign exchange rates
FRS 24	Financial reporting in hyperinflationary economies
FRS 25	Financial instruments: Presentation
FRS 26	Financial instruments: Recognition and measurement
FRS 27	Life assurance
FRS 28	Corresponding amounts
FRS 29	Financial instruments: Disclosures
SSAP 4	Accounting for government grants
SSAP 5	Accounting for value added tax
SSAP 9	Stocks and long-term contracts
SSAP 13	Accounting for research and development
SSAP 19	Accounting for investment properties
SSAP 21	Accounting for leases and hire purchase contracts
SSAP 25	Segmental reporting

As you can see, there are gaps in the above list of UK standards. Some gaps were caused by replacement of old standards with new standards, while some standards were simply withdrawn due to unpopularity or other difficulties.

The ASB adopted all SSAPs extant at 1 August 1990, giving SSAPs the force of law.

The following UITF Abstracts are currently in force.

NO	TITLE
	Foreword to UITF Abstracts
UITF Abstract 4	Presentation of long-term debtors in current assets
UITF Abstract 5	Transfers from current assets to fixed assets
UITF Abstract 15	Disclosure of substantial acquisitions
UITF Abstract 19	Tax on gains and losses on foreign currency borrowings that hedge an investment in a foreign enterprise
UITF Abstract 21	Accounting issues arising from the proposed introduction of the euro
UITF Abstract 22	The acquisition of a Lloyd's business
UITF Abstract 23	Application of the transitional rules in FRS 15

UITF Abstract 24	Accounting for start-up costs
UITF Abstract 25	National Insurance contributions on share option gains
UITF Abstract 26	Barter transactions for advertising
UITF Abstract 27	Revisions to estimates of the useful economic life of goodwill and intangible assets
UITF Abstract 28	Operating lease incentives
UITF Abstract 29	Website development costs
UITF Abstract 31	Exchanges of businesses or other non-monetary assets for an interest in a subsidiary, joint venture or associate
UITF Abstract 32	Employee benefit trusts and other intermediate payment arrangements
UITF Abstract 34	Pre-contract costs
UITF Abstract 35	Death-in-service and incapacity benefits
UITF Abstract 36	Contracts for sales of capacity
UITF Abstract 38	Accounting for ESOP Trusts
UITF Abstract 39	Members' shares in co-operative entities and similar instruments
UITF Abstract 40	Revenue recognition and service contracts
UITF Abstract 41	Scope of FRS 20
UITF Abstract 42	Reassessment of embedded derivatives
UITF Abstract 43	The interpretation of equivalence for the purposes of section 228A of the Companies Act 1985
UITF Abstract 44	FRS 20 Group and treasury share transactions
UITF Abstract 45	Liabilities arising from participating in a specific market – Waste Electrical and Electronic Equipment

FOR DISCUSSION

It has sometimes been suggested that to have too many rules encourages dishonesty as people obey the letter but not the spirit of those rules. Do you agree?

The effectiveness of accounting standards depends on the degree to which organisations comply with the standards. We next look at the 'incentive' organisations have to follow these standards.

2.4 Accounting standards and the law

The Companies Act 1985 requires companies to include a note to the accounts stating that the accounts have been prepared in accordance with applicable accounting standards or, alternatively, giving details of significant departures from those standards, with reasons. The Review Panel and the Secretary of State for Business, Enterprise and Regulatory Reform have the power to apply to the courts for revision of the accounts where non-compliance is not justified. These provisions mean that accounting standards now have the force of law, whereas previously they had no legal standing in statute.

In June 1993, the ASB published its *Foreword to Accounting Standards* in final form. The Foreword contains a legal opinion from Mary Arden QC on the relationship between accounting standards and the Companies Act requirement to show a true and fair view.

Miss Arden considered the changes in the Companies Act which, in her view, strengthen the status of accounting standards. These are the granting of statutory recognition to the existence of standards and the introduction of a procedure whereby the Financial Reporting Review Panel can ask the court to determine whether accounts comply with the true and fair requirement.

'These factors increase the likelihood that the courts will hold that in general compliance with accounting standards is necessary to meet the true and fair requirement.'

The next major source of influence on accounting regulations is the Stock Exchange.

3 THE STOCK EXCHANGE

The Stock Exchange is a market for stocks and shares, and a company whose securities are traded in this market is known as a 'quoted' or 'listed' company.

Shares quoted on the Stock Exchange are said to be 'listed' or to have obtained a 'listing'. When a share is granted a quotation on the Stock Exchange, it appears on the *Official List*, which is published in London for each business day.

In order to receive a listing for its securities, a company must conform with Stock Exchange regulations contained in the *Listing Rules* or *Yellow Book* issued by the Council of the Stock Exchange. The company commits itself to certain procedures and standards, including matters concerning the disclosure of accounting information, which are more extensive than the disclosure requirements of the Companies Act.

Some of the major Stock Exchange requirements with respect to the published accounts of listed companies are:

(a) Companies must issue their annual report and accounts within six months of the end of the accounting year

(b) Companies must prepare half-yearly or interim reports

(c) The accounts must include a statement by the directors explaining the reasons for any significant deviation from accounting standards

(d) The accounts must include a 'segment' analysis of overseas results according to geographical area

(e) The accounts must include short biographical notes on each independent non-executive director.

Many requirements of the *Yellow Book* do not have the backing of law, but the ultimate sanction which can be imposed on a listed company which fails to abide by them is the withdrawal of its securities from the Stock Exchange List: the company's shares would no longer be traded on the market.

NOTES

Activity 2 **(10 minutes)**

One of the Stock Exchange's accounting requirements is that listed companies give financial information regularly. How long do you think a listed company can go without providing some sort of accounts?

The accounting regulations in the UK are also influenced by developments taking place outside the UK. We now look at the international factors affecting UK accounting regulations.

4 INTERNATIONAL INFLUENCES

As mentioned earlier, the UK, being a member of the European Union (EU), is required to implement the Union's legislation. It does this by enacting UK laws to implement, what are called, *Directives*. A number of Directives have been issued but, from the point of view of financial reporting, the two most important ones were the Fourth and the Seventh Directives. The Fourth Directive dealt with the format and content for the published accounts and was originally implemented in the UK via the 1981 Companies Act (later consolidated within the 1985 CA).

The Seventh Directive addressed the issue of financial reporting for companies that come together to form a group and it was incorporated into UK law by the 1989 Companies Act. Both the Fourth and Seventh Directives clearly show that UK accounting is significantly affected by developments on the international accounting scene for it was the Fourth Directive which for the first time laid down, in law, the form and content of final accounts, greatly reducing the flexibility previously enjoyed by UK accountants. Similarly, the Seventh Directive has limited the opportunities for manipulation of group accounts previously available.

Another important influence on financial accounting is the *International Accounting Standards Board* (IASB), which took over from the IASC in April 2001. The IASC was set up in 1973 in an attempt to improve and harmonise accounting standards around the world. It includes representatives from many countries throughout the world, including the USA and the UK.

Both the ASB and the European Union have stated their support for international standards. In the UK, some of the international accounting standards have in fact been incorporated within the UK standards. From 2005 all consolidated financial statements for companies listed in the European Union must comply with International Accounting Standards (IASs) and International Financial Reporting Standards (IFRSs).

From 2005 onwards, all UK companies are now able to choose whether to follow UK standards or IASs and IFRSs when preparing their own (non-consolidated) financial statements.

NOTES

Activity 3 **(10 minutes)**

To ensure you understand which regulations apply to which type of business, fill in the spaces below with a 'yes' where compliance is required and 'no' where it is not.

Type Of Business	*Companies Act*	*FRSs/SSAPs*	*IASs*	*Stock Exchange Listing rules*
Public Listed Company				
Public Listed Group				
Private Limited Company				
Sole Tradership				

Over the last few years the influence of the International Accounting Standards on the UK standard setting process has gradually increased. For example, all UK FRSs state the level of compliance with the relevant International Accounting Standard. Some UK standards are based directly on IASs, or developed jointly with IASs, as happened with FRS 12 and IAS 37, those entitled Provisions, contingent liabilities and contingent assets. The ASB intends to adopt all new IASs as they are issued, so that UK financial reporting practice will eventually converge with IASs and IFRSs.

We will now look at the organisations and people who are interested in the financial information about a business. We will also look at the type of information each of them desires.

5 USERS OF ACCOUNTING INFORMATION

The people who might be interested in financial information about a company may be classified as follows.

(a) **Managers of the company**. These are people appointed by the company's owners to supervise the day-to-day activities of the company. They need information about the company's current financial situation and what it is expected to be in the future. This enables them to manage the business efficiently and to take effective control and planning decisions.

(b) **Shareholders of the company,** ie the company's owners. They will want to assess how effectively management is performing its function. They will want to know how profitably management is running the company's operations and how much profit they can afford to withdraw from the business for their own use.

(c) **Trade contacts,** including suppliers who provide goods to the company on credit and customers who purchase goods or services provided by the company. Suppliers will want to know about the company's ability to pay its debts; customers need to know that the company is a secure source of supply and is in no danger of having to close down.

(d) **Providers of finance** to the company. These might include a bank which permits the company to operate an overdraft, or provides longer-term finance by granting a loan. The bank will want to ensure that the company is able to keep up with interest payments, and eventually to repay the amounts advanced.

(e) **The tax authorities (HM Revenue and Customs)** who will want to know about the business profits in order to assess the tax payable by the company.

(f) **Employees** of the company. They should have a right to information about the company's financial situation, because their future careers and the level of their wages and salaries depend on it.

(g) **Financial analysts and advisers** need information for their clients. For example, stockbrokers will need information to advise investors in stocks and shares; credit agencies will need information to advise potential suppliers of goods to the company; and journalists will need information for their reading public.

(h) **Government and their agencies** are interested in the allocation of resources and therefore in the activities of enterprises. They also require information in order to provide a basis for national statistics.

The purpose of financial statements is to provide useful information to these various groups of people. The regulatory framework does not only prevent preparers of financial statements from misleading users; it has also developed in order to ensure that the information in the financial statements actually does meet users' needs.

6 THE PRINCIPAL FINANCIAL STATEMENTS

The two principal financial statements drawn up by accountants are the **balance sheet** and the **profit and loss account**.

Definition

> The **balance sheet** is simply a list of all the assets owned by a business and all the liabilities owed by a business as at a particular date. It is a snapshot of the financial position of the business at a particular moment. **Assets** are the business's resources so, for example, a business may buy buildings to operate from, plant and machinery, stock to sell and cars for its employees. These are all resources which it uses in its operations. Additionally, it may have bank balances, cash and amounts of money owed to it. These provide the funds it needs to carry out its operations, and are also assets. On the other hand, it may owe money to the bank or to suppliers. These are **liabilities**.

Definition

> A **profit and loss account** is a record of income generated and expenditure incurred over a given period. The period chosen will depend on the purpose for which the statement is produced. The profit and loss account, which forms part of the published annual accounts of a limited company, will be made up for the period of a year, commencing from the date of the previous year's accounts. On the other hand, management might want to keep a closer eye on a company's profitability by making up quarterly or monthly profit and loss accounts. The profit and loss account shows whether the business has had more income than expenditure (a profit) or vice versa (a loss). Organisations which are not run for profit (charities etc) produce a similar statement called an income and expenditure account which shows the surplus of income over expenditure (or a deficit where expenditure exceeds income).

Both the balance sheet and the profit and loss account are summaries of accumulated data. For example, the profit and loss account will show a figure for revenue earned from selling goods to customers. This will be a total amount derived by summing the revenue earned from numerous individual sales made during the period. One of the jobs of an accountant is to devise methods of recording such individual details and eventually to produce summarised financial statements from them.

The balance sheet and the profit and loss account represent the basis of the accounts of most businesses. For limited companies, other information by way of statements and notes must be shown according to company law and accounting standards, for example, a cash flow statement. These will be considered in detail later in this book.

> **Activity 4** **(5 minutes)**
>
> What is the purpose of a profit and loss account? How does it differ from the purpose of a balance sheet?

7 ROLE OF ACCOUNTANT

7.1 Major accounting disciplines

To a greater or lesser extent, accountants aim to satisfy the information needs of all the different groups mentioned earlier. Managers of a business need the most information so they can take their planning and control decisions; and they obviously have 'special' access to information about the business, because they are in a position to tailor-make the internally produced statements. When managers want a large amount of information about the cost and profitability of individual products, or different parts of their business, they can arrange to obtain it through a system of **cost and management accounting**. The preparation of accounting reports for external use is called **financial accounting**. Bookkeeping and costing are the bases of financial and management accounting respectively.

NOTES

7.2 Management accounting

Management accounting refers to the internal reporting function of accounting. This 'branch' of accounting provides managers with information needed for day-to-day operations of the business as well as for short and long-term planning.

Management accounting systems produce detailed information often split between different departments within an organisation (sales, production, finance etc). Although much of the information necessarily deals with past events and decisions, management accountants are also responsible for preparing budgets, helping to set price levels and other decisions about the future activities of a business. Management (or cost) accounting is a management information system which analyses data to provide information as a basis for managerial action. The concern of a management accountant is to present accounting information in the form most helpful to management.

7.3 Financial accounting

Financial accounting is mainly a method of reporting the results and financial position of a business; it is not primarily concerned with providing information as a guide to the more efficient conduct of the business. Although financial accounts may be of interest to management, their principal function is to satisfy the information needs of persons not involved in the day-to-day running of the business.

Financial accounting is usually solely concerned with summarising historical data, often from the same basic records as management accounts, but in a different way. This difference arises partly because external users have different interests from management and have neither the time nor the need for very detailed information, but also because financial statements are prepared under constraints which do not apply to management accounts produced for internal use.

These constraints apply particularly to the accounts of limited companies. As said earlier, the owners of a limited company (the shareholders or members of the company) enjoy limited liability, which means that as individuals they are not personally liable to pay the company's debts. If the company's own assets are not sufficient to do so, the company may have to cease trading, but the shareholders are not obliged to make up any shortfall from their own private assets.

Clearly this system is open to abuse, and one of the safeguards is that limited companies are fenced about with a number of accounting regulations that do not apply to other forms of organisation. For example, they are required by law to prepare financial accounts annually, the minimum content of such accounts being laid down by detailed legal regulations.

In addition, the annual accounts of limited companies must be audited (ie checked) by an independent person with defined qualifications. The auditor must make a report on the accounts, and will highlight any significant areas where they do not comply either with the legal regulations or with other regulations laid down by the accounting profession.

7.4 Auditing

The annual accounts of any limited company which exceeds a certain size must be **audited** by a person independent of the company. In practice, this means that the members of the company appoint a firm of Certified or Chartered Accountants to investigate the accounts prepared by the company. The accountant(s) report as to whether or not the accounts prepared by the company show a true and fair view of the company's results for the year and its financial position at the end of the year.

The accounts of a company do not need to be audited where turnover is less than £5.6 million per annum.

When the auditor has completed his work he (or she) must prepare a report explaining the work that he has done and the opinion he has formed. In simple cases, he will be able to report that he has carried out his work in accordance with auditing standards and that, in his opinion, the accounts show a true and fair view and are properly prepared in accordance with the law. This is described as an **unqualified** (or 'clean') audit report.

Sometimes the auditor may disagree with the directors of the company on a point concerned with the accounts. If he is unable to persuade the directors to change the accounts, and if the item at issue is significant, it is the auditor's duty to prepare a **qualified** report, setting out the matter(s) on which he disagrees with the directors.

The financial statements to which the auditor refers in his report comprise:

(a) The profit and loss account
(b) The balance sheet
(c) The notes to the accounts

In addition he must consider whether the information given in the directors' report is consistent with the audited accounts. If he believes it is not consistent then he must state that fact in his report.

The auditor's report is included as a part of the company's published accounts. It is addressed to the members of the company (not to the directors).

Further information on the role of the auditor is provided within Unit 11.

Chapter roundup

- The development of financial reporting has been influenced by:
  - company law
  - UK accounting standards (SSAPs and FRSs)
  - International accounting standards (IASs and IFRSs)
  - the Stock Exchange Regulations
  - the needs of users.
- Limited companies are required by law to prepare accounts annually for their shareholders.
- Financial statements are required by law to give 'a true and fair view'. This is not defined.
- Accounting standards are issued by the Accounting Standards Board (ASB). It issues Financial Reporting Standards (FRSs) and has also adopted Statements of Standard Accounting Practice (SSAPs) issued by its predecessor, the Accounting Standards Committee (ASC).
- International Accounting Standards (IASs) and International Financial Reporting Standards (IFRSs) are becoming an increasingly important influence on UK financial reporting practice. Listed UK groups must now prepare their consolidated financial statements in accordance with IAS/IFRS.
- Accounting information is required by a wide range of interested parties both within and outside the organisation.
- The principal financial statements of a business are the balance sheet and the profit and loss account.
- Management accounting is primarily concerned with providing information for the efficient running of the business, whereas financial accounting is concerned with reporting results and the financial position.

Quick quiz

1. What are the main factors which have influenced the development of financial accounting?
2. What is the main statute governing the content of limited company accounts in the UK?
3. What is a SSAP?
4. What is the Urgent Issues Task Force?
5. What are FRSs and FREDs?
6. Are companies legally required to comply with accounting standards?
7. What is a 'listed' company?
8. Identify seven user groups who need accounting information.

NOTES

Answers to quick quiz

1 Company law, accounting standards, international accounting standards and Stock Exchange requirements. (see Introduction)

2 Companies Act 1985 (although in due course the Companies Act 2006 will take over). (para 1)

3 Statement of Standard Accounting Practice. (para 2.1)

4 The UITF is an offshoot of the ASB designed to act quickly when an authoritative ruling is needed in respect of unsatisfactory or conflicting interpretations of accounting standards or company law. (para 2.2)

5 Financial Reporting Standards and Financial Reporting Exposure Drafts, produced by the ASB. FRSs are developed from FREDs. (para 2.2)

6 They are required either to comply with accounting standards or to give reasons for significant departures from them. (para 2.4)

7 One quoted on the Stock Exchange. (para 3)

8 Managers, shareholders, trade contacts, providers of finance, tax authorities, employees, financial analysts and advisers. (para 5)

Answers to activities

1 The list is almost endless but among the more recent ones you will have certainly thought of are Enron and WorldCom.

2 Six months. Listed companies are required to publish interim accounts covering the first half of each year as well as amounts covering the whole year. It is common to see statements of six-monthly profit (or loss) figures published by leading companies in the pages of quality newspapers.

3

Type Of Business	*Companies Act*	*FRSs/SSAPs*	*IASs*	*Stock Exchange Listing rules*
Public Listed Company	YES	*	*	YES
Public Listed Group	YES	NO	YES	YES
Private Limited Company	YES	*	*	NO
Sole Tradership	NO	NO	NO	NO

*Public listed companies and private limited companies can chose to follow either UK standards (FRSs and SSAPs) or international standards (IFRSs and IASs).

4 The purpose of a profit and loss account is to show whether a business has made a profit or a loss over a certain period of time. The balance sheet, on the other hand, shows the overall financial position of a business at a given point of time.

Chapter 12 :

THE BALANCE SHEET AND THE PROFIT AND LOSS ACCOUNT

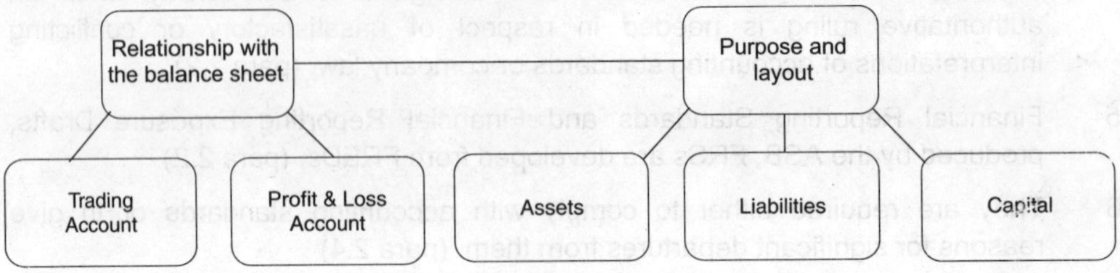

Introduction

The balance sheet shows the assets, liabilities and capital of a business as at the end of the accounting period, to which the financial accounts relate. In other words, it is a statement of the assets, liabilities and capital of a business at a single moment in time – like a snapshot photograph.

One of the items which you will see in the capital section of the balance sheet is the profit earned by the business. The profit and loss account (often called the P and L account) is the statement in which revenues and expenditures are compared to arrive at a figure of a profit or loss. It is a statement which shows in detail how the profit (or loss) for a period has been made. The basic reason for its preparation is that the details in the profit and loss statement enable business managers to exercise effective control over income and expenditure. For limited companies, the format is prescribed in the Companies Act.

Your objectives

In this chapter you will learn about the following.

(a) What a balance sheet is and how it is compiled

(b) The standard layout of a balance sheet

(c) The categories of assets and liabilities found in a typical balance sheet

(d) The profit and loss statement and how it is compiled

(e) How a trading, profit and loss account is usually presented

(f) The main items appearing in a trading, profit and loss account

(g) The difference between capital and revenue items

1 PURPOSE AND LAYOUT

1.1 Purpose

A balance sheet is a list of the assets, liabilities and capital of a business at a given moment. Its purpose is to show the financial position of a business on a certain date.

To emphasise the point that a balance sheet is a listing of balances 'on a particular day' (more accurately, 'at a particular moment'), it is sometimes compared to a kind of snapshot of a business: it captures on paper a still image, frozen at a single moment of time, of something which is as a matter of course dynamic and continually changing. Typically, a balance sheet is prepared to show the liabilities, capital and assets of a business at the end of the accounting period to which the accounts relate.

As you should readily appreciate, a balance sheet is therefore very similar to the accounting equation. In fact, the only differences between a balance sheet and an accounting equation are the:

(a) Manner or format in which the liabilities and assets are presented; and
(b) Extra detail which a balance sheet usually goes into.

Activity 1 **(5 minutes)**

Answer the following questions to make sure you are familiar with the purpose of the balance sheet.

(a) In one sentence describe the balance sheet.
(b) Is the balance sheet included in financial or management accounts?

1.2 Layout

A balance sheet is divided into two halves, usually showing capital in one half and net assets (ie assets less liabilities) in the other.

NAME OF BUSINESS
BALANCE SHEET AS AT (DATE)

	£	£
Fixed assets		xxx
Current assets	xxx	
Current liabilities	(xxx)	
Net current assets		xxx
		xxx
Long-term liabilities		(xxx)
Net assets		xxx
Capital		xxx

The total value of one half of the balance sheet will equal the total value on the other half. You should readily understand this from the accounting equation.

BPP LEARNING MEDIA

NOTES

For many businesses, the way in which assets and liabilities are categorised and presented in a balance sheet is a matter of choice, and you may come across different formats. The format below, with specimen figures, should help you see how a typical balance sheet is compiled.

HARVEY CARD
BALANCE SHEET AS AT 30 JUNE 20X1

	£	£
Fixed assets		
Land and buildings	30,000	
Plant and machinery	20,000	
Fixtures and fittings	17,000	
		67,000
Current assets		
Stocks	6,000	
Debtors	10,000	
Cash in hand	900	
	16,900	
Current liabilities		
Creditors	7,000	
Bank overdraft	300	
	7,300	
Net current assets		9,600
		76,600
Long term loan		(25,000)
Net assets		51,600
Capital		
At 1 July 20X0		43,600
Profit for the year		8,000
At 30 June 20X1		51,600

Activity 2 **(5 minutes)**

Using the figures in the balance sheet above, check that the accounting equation holds good in the form assets = capital + liabilities by putting figures in the appropriate parts of the equation.

At the beginning of the chapter, we said that a major difference between a balance sheet and the accounting equation is the extra details in a balance sheet. We now look at the first category of detail namely, assets.

2 ASSETS

Assets in the balance sheet are divided into fixed and current assets.

2.1 Fixed assets

A fixed asset is an asset acquired for use within the business (rather than for selling to a customer), with a view to earning income or making profits from its use, either directly or indirectly.

Examples

(a) In a manufacturing industry, a production machine would be a fixed asset, because it makes goods which are then sold.

(b) In a service industry, equipment used by employees giving service to customers would be classed as fixed assets (eg the equipment used in a garage, and furniture in a hotel).

These are only examples. You may well have included other assets such as factory premises, office furniture, computer equipment, company cars, delivery vans or pallets in a warehouse.

To be classed as a fixed asset in the balance sheet of a business, an item must satisfy two further conditions.

(a) Clearly, it must be used by the business. For example, the proprietor's own house would not normally appear on the business balance sheet.

(b) The asset must have a 'life' in use of more than one year (strictly, more than one 'accounting period' which might be more or less than one year).

All of the above examples of fixed assets have one thing in common. They have a physical existence. However, not all assets have physical forms.

Definition

- A **tangible fixed asset** is a physical asset, ie one that can be touched. It has a real, 'solid' existence. All of the examples of fixed assets mentioned above are tangible.
- An **intangible fixed asset** is an asset which does not have a physical existence. It cannot be 'touched'. Patents or copyrights or expenses of developing a new product would be classified as an intangible fixed asset.

2.2 Depreciation

Fixed assets might be held and used by a business for a number of years, but they wear out or lose their usefulness over time. Nearly every tangible fixed asset has a limited life. The only exception is freehold land.

The accounts of a business try to recognise that the cost of a fixed asset is gradually consumed as the asset wears out. This is done by gradually writing off the asset's cost over several accounting periods. For example, in the case of a machine costing £1,000 and expected to wear out after ten years, it might be appropriate to reduce the balance sheet value by £100 each year. This process is known as depreciation.

If a balance sheet were drawn up, say, four years after the asset was purchased, the amount of depreciation which would have accumulated would be 4 × £100 = £400. The machine would then appear in the balance sheet as follows:

	£
Machine at original cost	1,000
Less accumulated depreciation	400
Net book value*	600

* ie the value of the asset in the books of account, net of depreciation. After ten years the asset would be fully depreciated and would appear in the balance sheet with a net book value of zero.

Activity 3 **(5 minutes)**

Here is a little test which brings in the concept of residual value. Suppose a business buys a car for £10,000.

It expects to keep the car for three years and then to trade it in at an estimated value of £3,400. How much depreciation should be accounted for in each year of the car's useful life?

In the balance sheet layout in section 1, fixed assets are followed by current assets.

2.3 Current assets

Current assets are either:

(a) items owned by the business with the intention of turning them into cash within one year; or

(b) cash, including money in the bank, owned by the business.

These assets are 'current' in the sense that they are continually flowing through the business.

The definition in (a) above needs explaining further. Let us suppose that a trader, Chris Rhodes, runs a business selling motor cars, and purchases a showroom which he stocks with cars for sale. We will also suppose that he obtains the cars from a manufacturer, and pays for them in cash on delivery.

(a) If he sells a car in a cash sale, the goods are immediately converted into cash. The cash might then be used to buy more cars for re-sale.

(b) If he sells a car in a credit sale, the car will be given to the customer, who then becomes a debtor of the business. Eventually, the debtor will pay what he owes, and Chris Rhodes will receive cash. Once again, the cash might then be used to buy more cars for sale.

In this example the cars, debtors and cash are all current assets. Why?

(a) The cars (goods) held in stock for re-sale are current assets, because Chris Rhodes intends to sell them within one year, in the normal course of trade.

(b) Any debtors are current assets, if they are expected to pay what they owe within one year.

(c) Cash is a current asset.

The transactions described above could be shown as a cash cycle.

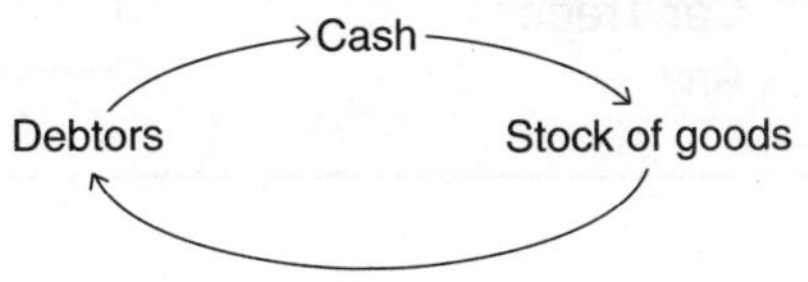

Cash is used to buy goods which are sold. Sales on credit create debtors, but eventually cash is earned from the sales. Some, perhaps most, of the cash will then be used to replenish stocks.

The main items of current assets are therefore:

- Stocks
- Debtors
- Cash

Another item of current asset often found particularly in the balance sheet of large companies is short term investments. These are stocks and shares of other businesses, currently owned, but with the intention of selling them in the near future. For example, if a business has a lot of spare cash for a short time, its managers might decide to buy shares in, say, Marks and Spencer, ICI or British Airways. The shares will later be sold when the business needs the cash again. If share prices rise in the meantime, the business will make a profit from its short term investment.

2.4 The value of current assets in the balance sheet

Current assets must never be valued at more than their net realisable value.

Definition

> **Net realisable value** is the selling price of an item *less* reasonable selling costs; in other words, it is the amount of cash a business will earn when the asset is sold *minus* the further cost required to get it into a condition for sale and to sell it.

Current assets should never be reported in the balance sheet at more than the money the business will make on selling off the asset and after reducing the sales price by the expense incurred in bringing the asset to a saleable condition. Thus, if the historical cost of the asset is more than the net realisable value, then the asset should be reported at the net realisable value.

NOTES

Activity 4 **(5 minutes)**

This activity should help ensure you understand asset classification. Decide which of the following assets falls into the 'fixed' category and which should be treated as 'current'.

ASSET	BUSINESS	CURRENT OR FIXED
Van	Delivery firm	
Machine	Manufacturing Company	
Car	Car Trader	
Investment	Any	

Activity 5 **(5 minutes)**

How would you value (a) debtors and (b) stocks in the balance sheet?

A balance sheet not only lists all the assets of a business, it provides a list of the liabilities of the business as well.

3 LIABILITIES

Just like the assets, the various liabilities should be itemised separately, with a distinction being made between:

(a) Current liabilities, and

(b) Long-term liabilities.

3.1 Current liabilities

Current liabilities are debts of the business that must be paid within a fairly short period of time (by convention, within one year). In the accounts of limited companies, the Companies Act requires use of the term 'creditors: amounts falling due within one year' rather than 'current liabilities' although they mean the same thing.

It is often argued that a bank overdraft is not a current liability, because a business is usually able to negotiate an overdraft facility for a long period of time. If an overdraft thus becomes a more permanent source of borrowing, it is really a long-term liability. However, you should normally expect to account for an overdraft as a current liability, since banks reserve the right to demand repayment at short notice.

3.2 Long-term liabilities

Long-term liabilities (or deferred liabilities) are debts which are not payable within the 'short term' and so any liability which is not current must be long term. Just as 'short term' by convention means one year or less, 'long term' means more than one year. In the accounts of limited companies, the Companies Act requires use of the term: 'Creditors: amounts falling due after more than one year'.

Activity 6 **(5 minutes)**

Try to classify the following items as long-term assets ('fixed assets'), short-term assets ('current assets') or liabilities.

(a) A PC used in the accounts department of a retail store

(b) A PC on sale in an office equipment shop

(c) Wages due to be paid to staff at the end of the week

(d) A van for sale in a motor dealer's showroom

(e) A delivery van used in a grocer's business

(f) An amount owing to a bank for a loan for the acquisition of a van, to be repaid over 9 months

In a balance sheet, liabilities are followed by capital.

4 CAPITAL

The 'capital' section of the balance sheet may vary, depending on the nature of the entity. However, it will include:

- amounts invested by the owner(s) ie capital
  plus
- profit earned by the business
  less
- drawings, if any.

Activity 7 **(15 minutes)**

Prepare a balance sheet for the Sunken Arches Shoes and Boots Shop as at 31 December 20X0, given the information below.

	£
Capital as at 1 January 20X0	47,600
Profit for the year to 31 December 20X0	8,300
Freehold premises, net book value at 31 December 20X0	50,000
Motor vehicles, net book value at 31 December 20X0	9,000
Fixtures and fittings, net book value at 31 December 20X0	8,000
Long term loan (mortgage)	25,000
Bank overdraft *	2,000
Goods held in stock for resale	16,000
Debtors	500
Cash in hand*	100
Creditors	4,700
Drawings	4,000

* A shop might have cash in its cash registers, but still have an overdraft at the bank.

5 THE TRADING, PROFIT AND LOSS ACCOUNT

5.1 Purpose

Any organisation will generate income (or revenue) from one or more sources. A business will sell its goods or services to customers in exchange for cash. A charity will raise money through donations, charitable events and perhaps trading activities. A police force will be granted funds from local or central government, and may also charge for providing its services (for example at sporting events).

The income generated will be used to finance the activities of the organisation: purchasing raw materials for use in manufacturing goods, purchasing ready-made goods for onward sale, purchasing equipment, paying expenses such as staff salaries, stationery, lighting and heating, rent and so on.

Periodically, the organisation will prepare an accounting statement showing the revenue generated and the amounts spent (the 'expenditure' of the organisation). Such a statement is referred to very generally as an income statement, though more specific terms are usually used to describe the income statements of particular forms of organisation.

For businesses, the income statement is referred to as a trading, profit and loss account. The total revenue earned during a period is compared with the expenditure incurred in earning it; the difference is either a profit or a loss.

Thus, the trading, profit and loss account is a statement showing in detail how the profit (or loss) of a period has been made. The owners and managers of a business obviously want to know how much profit or loss has been made, but there is only a limited information value in the profit figure alone. In order to exercise financial control effectively, managers need to know how much income has been earned, what various items of costs have been and whether the performance of sales or the control of costs appears to be satisfactory. This is the basic reason for preparing the trading, profit and loss account.

We next look at the layout of the trading, profit and loss account.

5.2 Layout

As with the balance sheet it may help you to focus on the trading, profit and loss account (also referred to as income statement) if you have an example in front of you. The main sections of the trading, profit and loss account, or income statement, are as follows.

NOTES

NAME OF BUSINESS
TRADING, PROFIT AND LOSS ACCOUNT
FOR THE YEAR ENDED (DATE)

	£
Sales	xxx
Cost of sales	(xxx)
Gross profit	xxx
Expenses	(xxx)
Net profit	xxx

It is usual to distinguish between gross profit (sales revenue less cost of sales) and net profit (being the gross profit less the expenses of selling, distribution, administration etc). If a calculation of gross profit is shown, the statement is usually known as 'trading and profit and loss account'. The reason for this is that many businesses try to distinguish between gross profit earned on trading, and net profit: in the first part of the statement (the trading account) revenue from selling goods is compared with direct costs of acquiring or producing the goods sold to arrive at a gross profit figure; from this, deductions are made in the second half of the statement (the profit and loss account) in respect of indirect costs (expenses). An example is shown below.

EXAMPLE:
HARVEY CARD
TRADING, PROFIT AND LOSS ACCOUNT
FOR THE YEAR ENDED 30 JUNE 20X1

	£	£
Sales		57,010
Cost of sales		30,690
Gross profit		26,320
Selling expenses	5,780	
Distribution expenses	5,150	
Administrative expenses	7,390	
		18,320
Net profit		8,000

The first 'section' of the trading, profit and loss account is the trading account. We now look at this section in more detail.

BPP LEARNING MEDIA

6 TRADING ACCOUNT

The **trading account** shows the gross profit for the accounting period.

6.1 Gross profit

Gross profit is the difference between:

(a) the sales revenue for a given period and

(b) the purchase cost or production cost of the goods that have been actually sold in that period.

Thus, if 20 items were produced in, say, January at a cost of £6 each but only 15 of those items were sold at £10 each, then the gross profit would be as follows.

	£
Sales (£10 × 15) =	150
Cost of sales (£6 × 15) =	90
Gross profit	60

The unsold items (five in this example) would be shown in the balance sheet as 'stock' in the current assets section until such time as they are sold.

In a retail business, the cost of sales (or as it is often called the cost of goods sold) is their purchase cost from the suppliers. In a manufacturing business, the production cost of goods sold is the cost of raw materials in the finished goods, plus the cost of the labour required to make the goods, and certain other costs.

Activity 8 **(5 minutes)**

What does a gross loss signify about the way in which goods are being bought and sold?

The trading account is followed by the profit and loss account. The profit and loss account shows the net profit of the business.

7 PROFIT AND LOSS ACCOUNT

As mentioned above, the profit and loss section of the trading, profit and loss account shows the net profit of the business. The net profit is calculated as follows.

Gross profit – Expenses = Net profit

The expenses in the profit and loss account are the expenses that are incurred in running the business eg advertising, rent on the office etc, which have not been included in the cost of goods sold. (Remember: cost of sales or cost of goods sold are costs incurred in buying and/or producing goods for resale.)

The various expenses in the profit and loss account are mainly classified into three categories: selling, distribution and administrative.

Selling expenses might include any or all of the following.

(a) Salaries of a sales director and sales management

(b) Salaries and commissions of salesmen

(c) Travelling and entertainment expenses of salesmen

(d) Marketing costs (eg advertising and sales promotion expenses)

(e) Discounts allowed to customers for early payment of their debts. For example, a business might sell goods to a customer for £100 and offer a discount of 5% for payment in cash. If the customer takes the discount, the accounts of the business would not record the sales value at £95; they would instead record sales at the full £100, with a cost for discounts allowed of £5

Distribution costs are the costs of getting goods to customers, for example the costs of running and maintaining delivery vans.

Administrative expenses are the expenses of providing management and administration for the business.

An example will show how a trading and profit and loss account is compiled.

EXAMPLE: TRADING AND PROFIT AND LOSS ACCOUNT

On 1 June 20X1, Jock Heiss commenced trading as an ice-cream salesman, selling ice-creams from a van which he drove around the streets of his town.

(a) He rented the van at a cost of £1,000 for three months. Running expenses for the van averaged £300 per month.

(b) He hired a part-time helper at a cost of £100 per month.

(c) He borrowed £2,000 from his bank, and the interest cost of the loan was £25 per month.

(d) His main business was to sell ice-cream to customers in the street, but he also did some special catering arrangements for business customers, supplying ice-creams for office parties. Sales to these customers were usually on credit.

(e) For the three months to 31 August 20X1, his total sales were:

(i) cash sales £8,900;

(ii) credit sales £1,100.

(f) He purchased his ice-cream from a local manufacturer, Floors Ltd. The cost of purchases in the three months to 31 August 20X1 was £6,200, and at 31 August he had sold every item of stock. He still owed £700 to Floors Ltd for unpaid purchases on credit.

(g) He used his own home for his office work. Telephone and postage expenses for the three months to 31 August were £150.

(h) During the three month period he paid himself £300 per month.

BPP LEARNING MEDIA

The trading and profit and loss account for the three months 1 June – 31 August 20X1 will be as follows.

JOCK HEISS
TRADING AND PROFIT AND LOSS ACCOUNT
FOR THE THREE MONTHS ENDED 31 AUGUST 20X1

	£	£
Sales		10,000
Cost of sales		6,200
Gross profit		3,800
Expenses		
Wages	300	
Van rental	1,000	
Van expenses	900	
Telephone and postage	150	
Interest charges	75	
		2,425
Net profit (transferred to the balance sheet)		1,375

Note the following points.

(a) The net profit is the profit for the period, and it is transferred to the balance sheet of the business as part of the proprietor's capital.

(b) Drawings are appropriations of profit and not expenses. They must not be included in the profit and loss account. In this example, the payments that Jock Heiss makes to himself (£900) are drawings.

(c) The cost of sales is £6,200, even though £700 of the costs have not yet been paid and Floors Ltd is still a creditor for £700 in the balance sheet.

The trading, profit and loss account deals with the activities of a business over time. The balance sheet shows the state of a business at a particular point in time. The two statements are connected through the capital section of the balance sheet.

NOTES

8 RELATIONSHIP WITH THE BALANCE SHEET

The relationship between the profit and loss account and the balance sheet is through the capital section of the balance sheet as shown below.

8.1 Profit and loss account and balance sheet

SAMINA SUPERMARKET
TRADING, PROFIT AND LOSS ACCOUNT
FOR THE YEAR ENDED 31 MARCH 20X1

	£	£
Sales		100,000
Cost of goods sold		60,000
Less expenses		40,000
Selling	8,000	
Distribution	5,000	
Administration	7,000	
		20,000
Net profit		20,000

SAMINA SUPERMARKET
BALANCE SHEET
AS AT 31 MARCH 20X1

	£	£
Fixed assets		
Buildings		50,000
Van		15,000
Furniture		10,000
		75,000
Current assets		
Stock	20,000	
Debtors	5,500	
Cash	7,200	
	32,700	
Current liabilities		
Creditors	8,600	
Net current assets		24,100
		99,100
Long-term liabilities		
Loan		(20,000)
		79,100
Capital		
Capital as at 1 April 20X0		62,600
Profit for the year		20,000
		82,600
Less: drawings		(3,500)
Capital as at 31 March 20X1		79,100

BPP LEARNING MEDIA

The owner's investment, ie capital at the beginning of the financial year, stood at £62,600. It increased by the profit made by the business (£20,000). However, the resulting capital total of £82,600 was reduced by drawings of £3,500, resulting in a final balance of £79,100.

8.2 Capital and revenue expenditure

Now that you understand the relationship between the trading, profit and loss account and the balance sheet, you need to be able to decide which items appear in a balance sheet and which appear in a profit and loss account. In order to do this we need to turn our attention to the distinctions between capital and revenue items.

Definition

Capital expenditure is expenditure which results in the acquisition of fixed assets, or an improvement in their earning capacity.

(a) Capital expenditure results in the appearance of a fixed asset in the balance sheet of the business.

(b) Capital expenditure is not charged as an expense in the trading, profit and loss account. Instead, the capital expenditure is gradually reduced in the balance sheet and written-off over a period of time. The amount of the annual write-off is called the depreciation expense (introduced earlier in this chapter) and it is this annual expense (rather than the capital expenditure itself) that appears in the profit and loss account.

Definition

Revenue expenditure is expenditure which is incurred either:

(a) for the purpose of running the business, including expenditure classified as selling and distribution expenses, administration expenses and finance charges eg interest expense; or

(b) to maintain the fixed assets in their present condition (improving the fixed assets is a capital expenditure).

Revenue expenditure is charged to the profit and loss account of a period, provided that it relates to the trading activity and sales of that particular period. For example, if a business buys ten widgets for £200 (£20 each) and sells eight of them during an accounting period, it will have two widgets left in stock at the end of the period. The full £200 is revenue expenditure but only £160 is a cost of goods sold during the period. The remaining £40 (cost of two units) will be included in the balance sheet in the stock of goods held ie as a current asset valued at £40.

Activity 9 **(5 minutes)**

Suppose that a business purchases a building for £30,000. It then adds an extension to the building at a cost of £10,000. The building needs to have a few broken windows mended, its floors polished and some missing roof tiles replaced. These cleaning and maintenance jobs cost £900. Should these three separate amounts be treated as capital or revenue expenditure?

8.3 Capital income and revenue income

Capital income is the proceeds from the sale of non-trading assets (ie proceeds from the sale of fixed assets, including fixed asset investments). The profits (or losses) from the sale of fixed assets are included in the profit and loss account of a business, for the accounting period in which the sale takes place.

Revenue income is income derived from:

(a) the sale of stock; or
(b) interest and dividends received from investments held by the business.

The categorisation of capital and revenue items given above does not mention raising additional capital from the owner(s) of the business, or raising and repaying loans. These are transactions which either:

(a) add to the cash assets of the business, thereby creating a corresponding liability (capital or loan); or

(b) when a loan is repaid, reduce the liabilities (loan) and the assets (cash) of the business.

None of these transactions would be reported through the profit and loss account.

8.4 Why is the distinction between capital and revenue items important?

Since revenue items and capital items are accounted for in different ways, the correct and consistent calculation of profit for any accounting period depends on the correct and consistent classification of items as revenue or capital.

Activity 10 **(5 minutes)**

Complete the missing words to ensure you fully understand the difference between capital and revenue items.

Revenue expenditure results from the purchase of goods and services that will either:

(a) Be ___________ fully in the accounting period in which they are _________, and so be a cost or expense in the trading, profit and loss account; or

(b) Result in a ___________asset as at the end of the accounting period (because the goods or services have not yet been consumed or made use of).

Capital expenditure results in the purchase or improvement of _____________assets, which are assets that will provide benefits to the business in more than ____________ accounting period, and which are not acquired with a view to being resold in the normal course of trade. The cost of purchased fixed assets is not charged _________ to the trading, profit and loss account of the period in which the purchase occurs. Instead, the fixed asset is gradually ____________ over a number of accounting periods.

NOTES

Chapter roundup

- A balance sheet is a statement of the financial position of a business at a given moment. It lists the assets, liabilities and capital of a business in a logical and informative manner.
- A standard layout for the balance sheet is prescribed for limited companies; other entities may adopt other formats.
- The main groupings to remember are: fixed assets; current assets; current liabilities; long term liabilities; capital.
- 'Current' means within one year. Current assets are expected to be converted into cash within one year. Current liabilities are debts which are payable within one year.
- Fixed assets are those acquired for long term use in the business. They are normally valued at cost less depreciation.
- An income statement (called a profit and loss account in the case of an entity trading as a business) shows the revenue generated during a period and the expenditure incurred in earning that revenue. The difference between them is the profit or loss for the period.
- For limited companies, the format of a profit and loss account is defined by the Companies Act 1985. Other organisations have greater flexibility in the way they present their results.
- The trading account shows the gross profit for the period while the profit and loss account shows the net profit of the business.
- Expenses are broadly categorised into three sections: selling costs, distribution costs and administrative costs.
- The trading, profit and loss account is related to the balance sheet through the capital section of the balance sheet.
- The correct accounting treatment of an item depends partly on whether it is of a capital or a revenue nature.

Quick quiz

1 What is the purpose of a balance sheet?

2 List two main categories of fixed assets.

3 What is meant by depreciation?

4 What are the main items of current assets in a balance sheet?

5 Give three examples of current liabilities.

6 What will be included in the capital section of a balance sheet?

7 Identify a source of income other than sale of goods.

8 What are the main categories of expenditure shown in the accounts of a limited company?

9 Where in the financial statements do the proprietor's drawings appear?

NOTES

Answers to quick quiz

1 It shows the financial position of the business on a certain date. (see para 1.1)

2 Intangible, tangible. (para 2.1)

3 A measure of the wearing out of a fixed asset over its life. (para 2.2)

4 Stocks, debtors, short term investments, cash, bank. (para 2.3)

5 Trade creditors, bank overdraft, taxation payable. (para 3.1)

6 Amounts invested and withdrawn by the owner and profits earned by the business. (para 4)

7 Interest and dividends. (para 5.1)

8 Check your answer with the examples given in the chapter. (para 7)

9 As a deduction from net profit in the capital section of the balance sheet. (para 8)

Answers to activities

1 Your answers should have covered the following points.

(a) A balance sheet is a listing of asset and liability balances (including capital) on a certain date.

(b) Both. A balance sheet will be included in financial accounts, showing the position at the year end. A forecast balance sheet may also be used in management decision making.

2

Assets	=	*Capital*	+	*Liabilities*
£(67,000 + 16,900)	=	£51,600	+	£(7,300 + 25,000)
£83,900	=	£83,900		

3 The point in this case is that the car has a residual value of £3,400. It would be inappropriate to account for depreciation in such a way as to write off the asset completely over three years; the aim should be to account only for its loss of value (£10,000 – £3,400 = £6,600), which suggests depreciation of £2,200 per annum.

4

Asset	Business	Current or Fixed
Van	Delivery Firm	*Fixed*
Machine	Manufacturing Company	*Fixed*
Car	Car Trader	*Current*
Investment	Any	*Either**

*The classification of the investment will depend on the purpose for which it is held. If the intention is to make a long term investment it will be a fixed asset, but if it is a short term way of investing spare cash it will be a current asset.

NOTES

5 (a) Debtors are valued at the cash value of the debt – ie at their realisable value.

(b) Stocks of goods are usually valued at historical cost. However, if the net realisable value (NRV) of stocks is less than their cost, the stocks will be valued at NRV instead of cost. In other words, stocks of goods are valued at the lower of their cost and net realisable value. In normal circumstances, the lower of the two amounts is cost.

6 Fixed asset = F Current asset = C Liabilities = L

(a)	A PC used in the accounts department of a retail store	F
(b)	A PC on sale in an office equipment shop	C
(c)	Wages due to be paid to staff at the end of the week	L
(d)	A van for sale in a motor dealer's showroom	C
(e)	A delivery van used in a grocer's business	F
(f)	An amount owing to a bank for a loan for the acquisition of a van, to be repaid over 9 months	L

7

SUNKEN ARCHES BALANCE SHEET
AS AT 31 DECEMBER 20X0

	£	£
Fixed assets at net book value		
Freehold premises		50,000
Fixtures and fittings		8,000
Motor vehicles		9,000
		67,000
Current assets		
Stocks	16,000	
Debtors	500	
Cash	100	
	16,600	
Current liabilities		
Bank overdraft	2,000	
Creditors	4,700	
	6,700	
Net current assets		9,900
		76,900
Long term liabilities		
Loan		(25,000)
Net assets		51,900
Capital		
Capital as at 1 January 20X0		47,600
Profit for the year		8,300
		55,900
Less drawings		(4,000)
		51,900

BPP LEARNING MEDIA

8 A common reason for offering discount is to encourage a higher volume of sales. This is often seen in a retail context ('one ball point pen for 25p or five for £1'), and is common too on a larger scale (for example, a publisher will sell his books to customers, ie bookshops, at a discount level reflecting the purchasing 'clout' of the individual bookshop). By generating more activity the business aims to increase the total amount of profit from the amount it would have earned on a lower activity level.

9 The original purchase (£30,000) and the cost of the extension (£10,000) are capital expenditure because they are incurred to acquire and then improve a fixed asset. The other costs of £900 are revenue expenditure, because these merely maintain the building and thus the 'earning capacity' of the building.

10 The missing words are: used; purchased; current; fixed; one; in full; depreciated.

Chapter 13 : FINANCIAL RECORDS

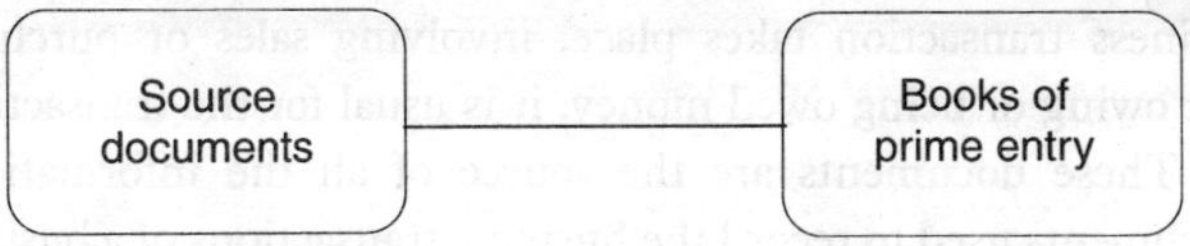

Introduction

The profit and loss account and the balance sheet provide a summary of the activities and the resulting financial position of a business. Accounting needs evidence that these activities and events, called transactions, have taken place. This evidence is provided by a number of documents. These documents are the source of all the information recorded by a business and are therefore called source documents. Examples of source documents are many including sales and purchase invoices.

Records of source documents are kept in 'books of prime entry' which, as the name suggests, are the first stage at which a business transaction enters into the accounting system. The various books of prime entry are discussed in Section 2.

Your objectives

In this chapter you will learn about the following.

(a) The role of source documents

(b) The books of prime entry

(c) The purpose of sales and purchase day books and how they are prepared

(d) The sales and purchases returns day books and how they are prepared

(e) The cash book and how it is prepared

Source documents and books of prime entry were covered in Unit 2, Managing Financial Resources and Decisions. Some of the content of this chapter will therefore be familiar to you from that Unit.

1 SOURCE DOCUMENTS

From the previous chapters you should have grasped some important points about the nature and purpose of accounting. You should have realised that most organisations exist to provide products and services in the ultimate hope of making profit for their owners, which they do by receiving payment in money for goods and services provided. Whenever such activities take place, they need to be recorded. They are recorded on what is called a document.

Whenever a business transaction takes place, involving sales or purchases, receiving or paying money, or owing or being owed money, it is usual for the transaction to be recorded on a document. These documents are the source of all the information recorded by a business. The documents used to record the business transactions of a business includes the:

- Sales order
- Purchase order
- Invoice
- Credit note
- Debit note
- Goods received note

We will now look at each of these documents in turn.

1.1 Sales order

A document showing the goods or services the customer wishes to buy.

1.2 Purchase order

A document sent by a business to a supplier ordering specified goods or services.

1.3 Invoice

An invoice relates to a sales order or a purchase order. When a business sells goods or services on credit to a customer, it sends out an invoice. The details on the invoice should match up with the details on the sales order. The invoice is a request for the customer to pay what he owes. Similarly, when a business buys goods or services on credit it receives an invoice from the supplier. The details on the invoice should match up with the details on the purchase order.

The invoice is primarily a demand for payment, but it is used for other purposes as well. Because it has several uses, an invoice is often produced on multi-part stationery, or photocopied, or carbon-copied. The top copy will go to the customer and other copies will be used by various people within the business.

1.4 What does an invoice show?

Most invoices are numbered, so that the business can keep track of all the invoices it sends out. Information usually shown on an invoice includes the following.

(a) Name and address of the seller and the purchaser

(b) Date of the sale

NOTES

(c) Description of what is being sold

(d) Quantity and unit price of what has been sold (eg 20 pairs of shoes at £25 a pair)

(e) Details of trade discount, if any (eg 10% reduction in cost if buying over 100 pairs of shoes). We shall look at discounts in a later chapter

(f) Total amount of the invoice including (in the UK) any details of VAT

(g) Sometimes, the date by which payment is due, and other terms of sale

1.5 Credit note

A document issued by the seller to show a reduction in the amount owed by the buyer. The reduction could be due to a variety of reasons such as:

(a) Goods were not according to specifications
(b) Goods were damaged during packing or transit
(c) Goods were faulty.

A credit note is sometimes printed in red to distinguish it from an invoice. Otherwise, it will be made out in much the same way as an invoice, but with less detail and 'Credit Note Number' instead of 'Invoice Number'.

1.6 Debit note

A document issued by the buyer to show a reduction in the amount owed to the seller/supplier. More commonly, a debit note is issued by the buyer to the seller as a means of formally requesting a credit note. It may also be issued by the seller to increase the amount already owed by the buyer.

1.7 Goods Received Note (GRN)

This is a document which is filled in to record a receipt of goods, most commonly in a warehouse. It may be used in addition to suppliers' advice notes. Often the accounts department will require to see the relevant GRN before paying a supplier's invoice. Even where GRNs are not routinely used, the details of a consignment from a supplier which arrives without an advice note must always be recorded.

Activity 1 **(5 minutes)**

Answer the following questions to make sure you are familiar with source documents.

(a) Explain how an invoice relates to a sales order.
(b) Why is a credit note issued?
(c) Who fills in the GRNs?

The source documents provide the evidence needed for recording business transactions in the accounting system. The transactions are first recorded in what are called books of prime entry.

2 BOOKS OF PRIME ENTRY

We have seen that in the operation of a business, source documents are created. The details on these source documents need to be summarised, as otherwise the business might forget to ask for some money, or forget to pay some, or even accidentally pay something twice. In other words, it needs to keep records of source documents – of transactions – so that it can keep tabs on what is going on. When a business is small, it can keep all these details in a single binder or book. However, as the firm grows, it becomes impossible to keep all records in just one binder/book. Maintaining separate binders/books for similar transactions, eg a separate book only for credit sales, another one only for credit purchases and so on makes the process of recording and retrieving information far more manageable and efficient (as more than one person can work on recording information at the same time).

Definition

> **Books of prime entry** or **day books** refer to a set of 'books' in which transactions are initially recorded in the accounting system; it is in these 'books' that information is recorded from the source documents at the start of the accounting process. Each of the books record only a particular type of transaction eg credit sales, credit purchases etc.

The main books of prime entry which we need to look at are the:

Sales day book
Purchase day book
Sales returns day book
Purchases returns day book
Journal (described in the next chapter)
Cash book
Petty cash book

It is worth bearing in mind that, for convenience, this chapter describes books of prime entry as if they are actual books. Nowadays, books of prime entry are often not books at all, but rather files hidden in the memory of a computer. However, the principles remain the same whether they are manual or computerised.

2.1 The sales day book

The sales day book is used to keep a list of all invoices sent out to customers each day. An extract from a sales day book might look like this.

SALES DAY BOOK

Date	*Invoice*	*Customer*	*Sales ledger folio*	*Total amount invoiced*
20X1				£
Jan 10	247	Jones & Co	SL 14	105.00
	248	Smith Ltd	SL 8	86.40
	249	Alex & Co	SL 6	31.80
	250	Enor College	SL 9	1,264.60
				1,487.80

BPP LEARNING MEDIA

The column called 'sales ledger folio' is a reference to the sales ledger. We will explain ledger accounting in the next chapter.

Most businesses 'analyse' their sales. For example, suppose that the business sells boots and shoes, and that the sale to Smith was entirely boots, the sale to Alex was entirely shoes, and the other two sales were a mixture of both.

Then the sales day book might look like this.

SALES DAY BOOK

Date	*Invoice*	*Customer*	*Sales ledger folio*	*Total amount invoiced*	*Boot sales*	*Shoe sales*
20X1				£	£	£
Jan 10	247	Jones & Co	SL 14	105.00	60.00	45.00
	248	Smith Ltd	SL 8	86.40	86.40	
	249	Alex & Co	SL 6	31.80		31.80
	250	Enor College	SL 9	1,264.60	800.30	464.30
				1,487.80	946.70	541.10

This sort of analysis gives the managers of the business useful information which helps them to decide how best to run the business.

2.2 The purchase day book

A business also keeps a record in the purchase day book of all the invoices it receives. An extract from a purchase day book might look like this.

PURCHASE DAY BOOK

Date	*Supplier*	*Purchase ledger folio*	*Total amount invoiced*	*Purchases*	*Electricity etc*
20X1			£	£	£
Mar 15	Cook & Co	PL 31	315.00	315.00	
	W Butler	PL 46	29.40	29.40	
	EEB	PL 42	116.80		116.80
	Show Fair Ltd	PL 12	100.00	100.00	
			561.20	444.40	116.80

You should note the following points.

(a) The 'purchase ledger folio' is a reference to the purchase ledger just as the sales ledger folio was to the sales ledger. Again, we will see the purpose of this in the next chapter.

(b) There is no 'invoice number' column, because the purchase day book records other people's invoices, which have all sorts of different numbers.

(c) Like the sales day book, the purchase day book analyses the invoices which have been sent in. In this example, three of the invoices related to goods which the business intends to re-sell (called simply 'purchases') and the fourth invoice was an electricity bill.

2.3 The sales returns day book

When customers return goods for some reason, the returns are recorded in the sales returns day book or as it is sometimes called, the returns inwards journal. An extract from the sales returns day book might look like this.

SALES RETURNS DAY BOOK

Date	*Customer and goods*	*Sales ledger folio*	*Amount*
20X1			£
30 April	Owen Plenty		
	3 pairs 'Texas' boots	SL 82	135.00

Not all sales returns day books analyse what goods were returned, but it makes sense to keep as complete a record as possible.

The source document is the credit note.

2.4 The purchase returns day book

There are no prizes for guessing that the purchase returns day book is kept to record goods which the business sends back to its suppliers. The business might expect a cash refund from the supplier. In the meantime, however, it might issue a debit note to the supplier, indicating the amount by which the business expects its total debt to the supplier to be reduced. An extract from the purchase returns day book might look like this.

PURCHASE RETURNS DAY BOOK

Date	*Supplier and goods*	*Purchase ledger folio*	*Amount*
20X1			£
29 April	Boxes Ltd		
	300 cardboard boxes	PL 123	46.60

Activity 2 **(5 minutes)**

Why do you think businesses maintain separate returns day books rather than recording the returns in the respective sales and purchase day books?

2.5 Journal

Earlier in this chapter, we defined the books of prime entry as the first stage at which a business transaction enters into the accounting system. The journal is one such book of prime entry.

We shall consider the journal in greater detail in chapter 15, once we have introduced double entry bookkeeping.

2.6 The cash book

The cash book is also a day book, which is used to keep a cumulative record of money received and money paid out by the business. The cash book deals with money paid into

NOTES

and out of the business bank account. This could be money received on the business premises in notes, coins and cheques. There are also receipts and payments made by bank transfer, standing order, direct debit and, in the case of bank interest and charges, directly by the bank. Some cash, in notes and coins, is usually kept on the business premises in order to make occasional payments for odd items of expense. This cash is usually referred to as petty cash and is accounted for separately.

One part of the cash book is used to record receipts of cash, and another part is used to record payments. The best way to see how the cash book works is to follow through an example.

EXAMPLE

At the beginning of 1 July 20X1, Robin Plenty had £900 in the bank. On 1 July 20X1, Robin Plenty had the following receipts and payments:

(a) Cash sale – receipt of £80
(b) Payment from credit customer Jo £400 less discount allowed £20
(c) Payment from credit customer Been £720
(d) Payment from credit customer Seed £150 less discount allowed £10
(e) Cheque received for cash to provide a short-term loan from Len Dinger £1,800
(f) Second cash sale – receipts of £150
(g) Cash received for sale of machine £200
(h) Payment to supplier Kew £120
(i) Payment to supplier Hare £310
(j) Payment of telephone bill £400
(k) Payment of gas bill £280
(l) £100 in cash withdrawn from bank for petty cash
(m) Payment of £1,500 to Hess for new plant and machinery

If you look through these transactions, you will see that seven of them are receipts and six of them are payments.

The receipts part of the cash book for 1 July would look like this.

CASH BOOK (RECEIPTS)

Date	*Narrative*	*Folio*	*Total*
20X1			£
1 July	Balance b/d*		900
	Cash sale		80
	Debtor: Jo		380
	Debtor: Been		720
	Debtor: Seed		140
	Loan: Len Dinger		1,800
	Cash sale		150
	Sale of fixed asset		200
			4,370
2 July	Balance b/d*		1,660

* 'b/d' = brought down (ie brought forward from the previous period)

You should note the following points.

(a) There is space on the right hand side of the cash book so that the receipts can be analysed under various headings – for example, 'receipts from debtors', 'cash sales' and 'other receipts'.

BPP LEARNING MEDIA

(b) The cash received in the day amounted to £3,470. Added to the £900 at the start of the day, this comes to £4,370. But this is not, of course, the amount to be carried forward to the next day, because first we have to subtract all the payments made on 1 July.

The payments part of the cash book for 1 July would look like this.

CASH BOOK (PAYMENTS)

Date	*Narrative*	*Folio*	*Total*
20X1			£
1 July	Creditor: Kew		120
	Creditor: Hare		310
	Telephone		400
	Gas bill		280
	Petty cash		100
	Machinery purchase		1,500
	Balance c/d*		1,660
			4,370

*'c/d' = carried down

As you can see, this is very similar to the receipts part of the cash book. The only points to note are as follows.

(a) The analysis on the right would be under headings like 'payments to creditors', 'payments into petty cash', 'wages' and 'other payments'.

(b) Payments during 1 July totalled £2,710. We know that the total of receipts was £4,370. That means that there is a balance of £4,370 – £2,710 = £1,660 to be 'carried down' to the start of the next day. As you can see this 'balance carried down' is noted at the end of the payments column, so that the receipts and payments totals show the same figure of £4,370 at the end of 1 July. And if you look to the receipts part of this example, you can see that £1,660 has been brought down ready for the next day.

With analysis columns completed, the cash book given in the examples above might look as follows.

CASH BOOK (RECEIPTS)

Date	*Narrative*	*Folio*	*Total*	*Debtors*	*Cash sales*	*Other*
20X1			£	£	£	£
1 July	Balance b/d		900			
	Cash sale		80		80	
	Debtor – Jo		380	380		
	Debtor – Been		720	720		
	Debtor – Seed		140	140		
	Loan – Len Dinger		1,800			1,800
	Cash sale		150		150	
	Sale of fixed asset		200			200
			4,370	1,240	230	2,000

NOTES

CASH BOOK (PAYMENTS)

Date	*Narrative*	*Folio*	*Total*	*Creditors*	*Petty cash*	*Wages*	*Other*
			£	£	£	£	£
20X1							
1 July	Creditor – Kew		120	120			
	Creditor – Hare		310	310			
	Telephone		400				400
	Gas bill		280				280
	Petty cash		100		100		
	Machinery purchase		1,500				1,500
	Balance c/d		1,660				
			4,370	430	100	-	2,180

2.7 Petty cash book

Most businesses keep a small amount of cash on the premises to make occasional small payments in cash – eg to pay the milkman, to buy a few postage stamps, to pay the office cleaner, to pay for some bus or taxi fares etc. This is often called the cash float or petty cash account. The cash float can also be the resting place for occasional small receipts, such as cash paid by a visitor to make a phone call, or take some photocopies etc. There are usually more payments than receipts, and petty cash must be 'topped up' from time to time with cash from the business bank account to keep petty cash at an agreed level, say, £100. Expense items are recorded on vouchers as they occur, so that at any time:

	£
Cash remaining in petty cash	X
Plus voucher payments	X
Must equal the agreed sum	X

The balance is made up regularly (to £100, or whatever the agreed sum is) by means of a cash payment from the bank account into petty cash. The amount of the 'top-up' into petty cash will be equal to the total of the voucher payments since the previous top-up.

The format of a petty cash book is much the same as for the cash book, with analysis columns (chiefly for expenditure items, such as travel, postage, cleaning etc).

2.8 Summary

The following table may help you remember the various day books and what is recorded in each book.

Day book		**Transactions recorded**
(a)	Sales day book	credit sales
(b)	Purchase day book	credit purchases
(c)	Sales returns day book (also: returns inwards journal)	returns from customers
(d)	Purchase returns day book (also: returns outwards journal)	returns to suppliers
(e)	Journal	not recorded in the other books (see next chapter)

NOTES

Day book		Transactions recorded
(f)	Cash book	cash receipts and payments
(g)	Petty cash book	small (petty) cash receipts and payments

Activity 3 **(5 minutes)**

State which books of prime entry the following transactions would be entered into.

(a) Your business pays A Brown (a supplier) £450.

(b) You send D Smith (a customer) an invoice for £650.

(c) Your accounts manager asks you for £12 urgently in order to buy some envelopes.

(d) You receive an invoice from A Brown for £300.

(e) You pay D Smith £500.

(f) F Jones (a customer) returns goods to the value of £250.

(g) You return goods to J Green to the value of £504.

(h) F Jones pays you £500.

Chapter roundup

- Business transactions are recorded on source documents. These include:
  - Sales orders
  - Purchase orders
  - Invoices
  - Credit notes
  - Debit notes
  - Goods received notes (GRNs)
- These transactions are recorded in books of prime entry of which there are seven:
  - Sales day book
  - Sales returns day book
  - Purchase day book
  - Purchase returns day book
  - Cash book
  - Petty cash book
  - Journal
- Most businesses keep petty cash on the premises which is topped up from the main bank account.
- You should be aware of which transactions go in a given book of prime entry.

BPP LEARNING MEDIA

NOTES

Quick quiz

1 Name four pieces of information normally shown on an invoice.

2 What is the difference between a debit and a credit note?

3 Name the seven books of prime entry.

4 What information is summarised in the sales day book?

5 What is the purchase returns day book used for?

6 What is the difference between the cash book and the petty cash book?

Answers to quick quiz

1 There are a number of possibilities which you may have chosen and you should refer back to para 1.3 of the chapter to check your answer.

2 A credit note shows a reduction in the amount owed by the buyer, whereas a debit note is a formal way of requesting a credit note. (see paras 1.5 and 1.6)

3 Sales day book, purchase day book, sales returns day book, purchase returns day book, journal, cash book, petty cash book. (para 2)

4 All invoices sent out to customers. (para 2.1)

5 Details of goods sent back to suppliers. (para 2.4)

6 The petty cash book details small amounts of cash relating to cash kept on the premises, usually in a petty cash box and the cash book records all cash received and paid by the business through its bank account. (paras 2.6 and 2.7)

Answers to activities

1 (a) An invoice relates to both a sales order and a purchase order. When a business sells goods or services on credit to a customer, it sends out an invoice. It receives an invoice when it buys goods and services on credit.

(b) A credit note is issued by the seller of goods to the buyer in cases where the buyer is not satisfied with the goods. The credit note shows the allowance that has Leen given to the buyer for the faulty goods. As a result of the credit note, the amount owed by the buyer is reduced by the amount of the credit note.

(c) Goods received notes (GRNs) are filled in by the buyer (receiver) of goods to record the receipt of goods.

2 The maintenance of separate returns day books helps to ensure that goods returned to the business and by the business are separately identified and accounted for rather than being 'lost' (ie netted) in the sales and purchase day books. Returning goods or receiving returned goods involves time and money. By keeping a separate record of such activity, a business is able to keep a close tab on it and be in a position to take preventive measures, when needed.

3 (a) Cash book
(b) Sales day book
(c) Petty cash book
(d) Purchases day book
(e) Cash book
(f) Sales returns day book
(g) Purchase returns day book
(h) Cash book

Chapter 14 : LEDGER ACCOUNTING AND DOUBLE ENTRY

Introduction

Once accounting information has been recorded, it is summarised by means of a nominal or general ledger. The ledger accounts work on the principle of double entry bookkeeping which means that every transaction is recorded twice in the accounts. While some variations are found in practice in the way transactions are recorded using the double entry system, the rules of recording are firmly established.

While transactions can be entered directly into the ledger, they are first recorded in the books of prime entry. The journal is one such book and is used to record those transactions which cannot be recorded in the other books of prime entry discussed in that previous chapter.

Your objectives

In this chapter you will learn about the following.

(a) The need for a nominal ledger

(b) The rules of debit and credit

(c) How to record a variety of transactions in the ledger

(d) The purpose of the sales and purchase ledgers and how they are prepared

(e) The purpose of the journal and how it is prepared.

If you studied Unit 2 under the revised Edexcel guidelines, much of this chapter should be familiar.

1 LEDGER ACCOUNTING

1.1 What is ledger accounting?

In earlier chapters we looked at the profit and loss account and the balance sheet. We saw that by means of the accounting equation and the business equation, it would be possible to prepare a statement of the affairs of a business at any time we like, and that a profit and loss account and a balance sheet could be drawn up on any date, relating to any period of time. A business is continually making transactions, buying and selling etc, and we would not want to prepare a profit and loss account and a balance sheet on completion of every individual transaction. To do so would be a time-consuming and cumbersome administrative task.

However, it is common sense that a business should keep a record of the transactions that it makes, the assets it acquires and liabilities it incurs so that when the time comes to prepare a profit and loss account and a balance sheet, the relevant information can be taken from those records.

Ledger accounting is the process by which business keeps a record of its transactions:

(a) In chronological order, and dated so that transactions can be related to a particular period of time; and

(b) Built up in cumulative totals. For example, a business may build up the total of its sales:

  (i) Day by day (eg total sales on Monday, total sales on Tuesday)
  (ii) Week by week
  (iii) Month by month
  (iv) Year by year.

Every business generates a large amount of financial information. The nominal ledger is a means of summarising such information.

1.2 The nominal ledger

Every business needs a means of summarising information required to meet the needs of internal and external users of accounting information.

Definition

> The **nominal** or **general ledger** is a file, binder, floppy disc or some other device which contains all the separate accounts of a business. In other words, a general ledger is an accounting record which summarises the financial affairs of a business.

The general or nominal ledger contains details of assets, liabilities and capital, income and expenditure and so profit and loss. It consists of a large number of different accounts, each account having its own purpose or 'name' and an identity or code. There may be various subdivisions, whether for convenience, ease of handling, confidentiality, security, or to meet the needs of computer software design.

NOTES

Examples of accounts in the nominal or general ledger include:

- Plant and machinery at cost (fixed asset)
- Motor vehicles at cost (fixed asset)
- Proprietor's capital (liability)
- Stocks – raw materials (current asset)
- Stocks – finished goods (current asset)
- Total debtors (current asset)
- Total creditors (current liability)
- Wages and salaries (expense item)
- Rent and rates (expense item)
- Advertising expenses (expense item)
- Bank charges (expense item)
- Motor expenses (expense item)
- Telephone expenses (expense item)
- Sales (income)
- Total cash or bank overdraft (current asset or liability).

We next look at the layout of a ledger account.

1.3 The format of a ledger account

If a ledger account were to be kept in an actual book rather than as a computer record, its format might be as follows.

ADVERTISING EXPENSES

Date	*Narrative*	*Folio*	£	*Date*	*Narrative*	*Folio*	£
20X0							
15 April	JFK Agency for quarter to 31 March	PL 348	2,500				

Only one entry in the account is shown here, because the example is introduced simply to illustrate the general format of a ledger account.

There are two sides to the account, and an account heading on top. Thus, it is convenient to think in terms of 'T' accounts:

(a) On top of the account is its name eg capital, advertising expense etc;
(b) There is a left hand side, or *debit side*; and
(c) There is a right hand side, or *credit side*.

NAME OR TITLE OF ACCOUNT

Left hand side	£	*Right hand side*	£
DEBIT SIDE		CREDIT SIDE	

The words debit and credit have no other meaning in accounting except the left and the right side of an account respectively. As will be explained later, neither debit nor credit implies good or bad news – they simply mean the left or the right side of an account.

BPP LEARNING MEDIA

Similarly, debiting an account only means recording a transaction on the left side of an account (any account) and crediting an account only means entering a transaction on the right hand side of an account.

FOR DISCUSSION

Are the terms debit and credit either good or bad? Or are they simply factual?

We will now look at the way transactions are recorded, using the system of double-entry accounting, in ledger accounts.

2 DOUBLE ENTRY BOOKKEEPING

2.1 Dual effect

Double entry bookkeeping is the method used to transfer our weekly/monthly totals from our books of prime entry into the nominal ledger.

Central to this process is the idea that every transaction has two effects, the **dual effect.** This feature is not something peculiar to businesses. If you were to purchase a car for £1,000 cash for instance, you would be affected in two ways.

(a) You own a car worth £1,000.
(b) You have £1,000 less cash.

If instead you got a bank loan to make the purchase:

(a) You own a car worth £1,000.
(b) You owe the bank £1,000.

A month later if you pay a garage £50 to have the exhaust replaced:

(a) You have £50 less cash.
(b) You have incurred a repairs expense of £50.

Ledger accounts, with their debit and credit side, are kept in a way which allows the two-sided nature of business transactions to be recorded. This system of accounting is known as the '**double entry**' system of bookkeeping, so called because **every transaction is recorded twice** in the accounts.

2.2 The rules of double entry bookkeeping

The basic rule which must always be observed is that **every financial transaction gives rise to two accounting entries, one a debit and the other a credit**. The total value of debit entries in the nominal ledger is therefore always equal at any time to the total value of credit entries. Which account receives the credit entry and which receives the debit depends on the nature of the transaction.

NOTES

Definitions

- An **increase** in an **expense** (eg a purchase of stationery) or an **increase in an asset** (eg a purchase of office furniture) is a **debit**.
- An **increase** in **income** (eg a sale) or an **increase in a liability** (eg buying goods on credit) is a **credit**.
- A **decrease** in an **asset** (eg making a cash payment) is a **credit**.
- A **decrease** in a **liability** (eg paying a creditor) is a **debit**.

Have a go at the activity below before you learn about this topic in detail.

Activity 1 **(5 minutes)**

Complete the following table relating to the transactions of a bookshop. (The first two are done for you.)

(a) Purchase of books on credit

(i) creditors increase	CREDIT	creditors (increase in liability)
(ii) purchases expense increases	DEBIT	purchases (item of expense)

(b) Purchase of cash register

(i) own a cash register	DEBIT	cash register (increase in asset)
(ii) cash at bank decreases	CREDIT	cash at bank (decrease in asset)

(c) Payment received from a debtor

(i) debtors decrease
(ii) cash at bank increases

(d) Purchase of van

(i) own a van
(ii) cash at bank decreases

How did you get on? Learners coming to the subject for the first time often have difficulty in knowing where to begin. A good starting point is the cash account, ie the nominal ledger account in which receipts and payments of cash are recorded. The rule to remember about the cash account is as follows.

(a) A cash **payment** is a **credit** entry in the cash account. Here the **asset is decreasing.** Cash may be paid out, for example, to pay an expense (such as rates) or to purchase an asset (such as a machine). The matching debit entry is therefore made in the appropriate expense account or asset account.

(b) A cash **receipt** is a **debit** entry in the cash account. Here the **asset is increasing**. Cash might be received, for example, by a retailer who makes a cash sale. The credit entry would then be made in the sales account.

Definition

Double entry bookkeeping is the method by which a business records financial transactions. An account is maintained for every supplier, customer, asset, liability, and income and expense. Every transaction is recorded twice so that for every *debit* there is an equal, corresponding *credit.*

EXAMPLE: DOUBLE ENTRY FOR CASH TRANSACTIONS

In the cash book of a business, the following transactions have been recorded.

(a) A cash sale (ie a receipt) of £2
(b) Payment of a rent bill totalling £150
(c) Buying some goods for cash at £100
(d) Buying some shelves for cash at £200

How would these four transactions be posted to the ledger accounts? For that matter, which ledger accounts should they be posted to? Don't forget that each transaction will be posted twice, in accordance with the rule of double entry.

ANSWER

(a) The two sides of the transaction are:

(i) Cash is received (debit entry in the cash account).
(ii) Sales increase by £2 (credit entry in the sales account).

CASH ACCOUNT

	£		£
Sales a/c	2		

SALES ACCOUNT

	£		£
		Cash a/c	2

(Note how the entry in the cash account is cross-referenced to the sales account and vice-versa. This enables a person looking at one of the accounts to trace where the other half of the double entry can be found.)

(b) The two sides of the transaction are:

(i) Cash is paid (credit entry in the cash account).
(ii) Rent expense increases by £150 (debit entry in the rent account).

CASH ACCOUNT

	£		£
		Rent a/c	150

RENT ACCOUNT

	£		£
Cash a/c	150		

(c) The two sides of the transaction are:

(i) Cash is paid (credit entry in the cash account).

(ii) Purchases increase by £100 (debit entry in the purchases account).

CASH ACCOUNT

	£		£
		Purchases a/c	100

PURCHASES ACCOUNT

	£		£
Cash a/c	100		

(d) The two sides of the transaction are:

(i) Cash is paid (credit entry in the cash account).

(ii) Assets – in this case, shelves – increase by £200 (debit entry in shelves account).

CASH ACCOUNT

	£		£
		Shelves a/c	200

SHELVES (ASSET) ACCOUNT

	£		£
Cash a/c	200		

If all four of these transactions related to the same business, the cash account of that business would end up looking as follows.

CASH ACCOUNT

	£		£
Sales a/c	2	Rent a/c	150
		Purchases a/c	100
		Shelves a/c	200

2.3 Credit transactions

Not all transactions are settled immediately in cash. A business might purchase goods or fixed assets from its suppliers on credit terms, so that the suppliers would be creditors of the business until settlement was made in cash. Equally, the business might grant credit terms to its customers who would then be debtors of the business. Clearly no entries can be made in the cash book when a credit transaction occurs, because initially no cash has been received or paid. Where then can the details of the transactions be entered?

The solution to this problem is to use **debtors and creditors accounts**. When a business acquires goods or services on credit, the credit entry is made in an account designated 'creditors' instead of in the cash account. The debit entry is made in the appropriate expense or asset account, exactly as in the case of cash transactions. Similarly, when a sale is made to a credit customer the entries made are a debit to the total debtors account (instead of cash account) and a credit to sales account.

EXAMPLE: CREDIT TRANSACTIONS

Recorded in the sales day book and the purchase day book are the following transactions.

(a) The business sells goods on credit to a customer Mr A for £2,000.

(b) The business buys goods on credit from a supplier B Ltd for £100.

How and where are these transactions posted in the ledger accounts?

ANSWER

(a)

DEBTORS ACCOUNT

	£		£
Sales a/c	2,000		

SALES ACCOUNT

	£		£
		Debtors account	2,000

(b)

CREDITORS ACCOUNT

	£		£
		Purchases a/c	100

PURCHASES ACCOUNT

	£		£
Creditors a/c	100		

2.4 When cash is paid to creditors or by debtors

What happens when a credit transaction is eventually settled in cash? Suppose that, in the example above, the business paid £100 to B Ltd one month after the goods were acquired. The two sides of this new transaction are:

(a) Cash is paid (credit entry in the cash account)

(b) The amount owing to creditors is reduced (debit entry in the creditors account).

CASH ACCOUNT

	£		£
		Creditors a/c (B Ltd)	100

NOTES

CREDITORS' ACCOUNT

	£		£
Cash a/c	100		

If we now bring together the two parts of this example, the original purchase of goods on credit and the eventual settlement in cash, we find that the accounts appear as follows.

CASH ACCOUNT

	£		£
		Creditors a/c	100

PURCHASES ACCOUNT

	£		£
Creditors a/c	100		

CREDITORS' ACCOUNT

	£		£
Cash a/c	100	Purchases a/c	100

The two entries in the creditors account cancel each other out, indicating that no money is owing to creditors any more. We are left with a credit entry of £100 in the cash account and a debit entry of £100 in the purchases account. These are exactly the entries which would have been made to record a *cash* purchase of £100 (compare example above). This is what we would expect: after the business has paid off its creditors it is in exactly the position of a business which has made cash purchases of £100, and the accounting records reflect this similarity.

Similar reasoning applies when a customer settles his debt. In the example above when Mr A pays his debt of £2,000 the two sides of the transaction are:

(a) Cash is received (debit entry in the cash account)

(b) The amount owed by debtors is reduced (credit entry in the debtors account).

CASH ACCOUNT

	£		£
Debtors a/c	2,000		

DEBTORS' ACCOUNT

	£		£
		Cash a/c	2,000

The accounts recording this sale to, and payment by, Mr A now appear as follows.

CASH ACCOUNT

	£		£
Debtors a/c	2,000		

BPP LEARNING MEDIA

SALES ACCOUNT

	£		£
		Debtors a/c	2,000

DEBTORS' ACCOUNT

	£		£
Sales a/c	2,000	Cash a/c	2,000

The two entries in the debtors account cancel each other out; while the entries in the cash account and sales account reflect the same position as if the sale had been made for cash (see above).

Now try the following activity.

Activity 2 **(15 minutes)**

See if you can identify the debit and credit entries in the following transactions.

(a) Bought a machine on credit from A, cost £8,000.
(b) Bought goods on credit from B, cost £500.
(c) Sold goods on credit to C, value £1,200.
(d) Paid D (a creditor) £300.
(e) Collected £180 from E, a debtor.
(f) Paid wages £4,000.
(g) Received rent bill of £700 from landlord G.
(h) Paid rent of £700 to landlord G.
(i) Paid insurance premium £90.

FOR DISCUSSION

Take a look at your bank statement, which is prepared from the bank's point of view. When your account is in credit, the bank owes you money and *vice versa*. How does this compare with a cash or bank account prepared by a business?

We next look at certain types of accounts which, although not part of the double-entry system, are crucial to the efficient running of a business.

3 PERSONAL AND IMPERSONAL ACCOUNTS

The accounts in the nominal ledger (ledger accounts) relate to types of revenue, expense, asset, liability – rent, rates, sales, debtors, creditors etc – rather than to the person to whom the money is paid or from whom it is received. They are therefore called **impersonal** accounts. However, there is also a need for personal accounts, most commonly for debtors and creditors, and these are contained in the sales ledger and purchase ledger.

3.1 Personal accounts

Personal accounts include details of transactions which have already been summarised in ledger accounts (eg sales invoices are recorded in sales and total debtors, payments to creditors in the cash and creditors accounts). The personal accounts do not therefore form part of the double entry system, as otherwise transactions would be recorded twice over (ie two debits and two credits for each transaction). They are memorandum accounts only.

3.2 The sales ledger

The sales day book provides a chronological record of invoices sent out by a business to credit customers. For many businesses, this might involve very large numbers of invoices per day or per week. The same customer might appear in several different places in the sales day book, for purchases he has made on credit at different times. So at any point in time, a customer may owe money on several unpaid invoices. Therefore, in addition to keeping a chronological record of invoices, a business should also keep a record of how much money each individual credit customer owes, and what this total debt consists of. The need for a personal account for each customer is a practical one.

(a) A customer might telephone, and ask how much he currently owes. Staff must be able to tell him.

(b) It is a common practice to send out statements to credit customers at the end of each month, showing how much they still owe, and itemising new invoices sent out and payments received during the month.

(c) The managers of the business will want to keep a check on the credit position of an individual customer, and to ensure that no customer is exceeding his credit limit by purchasing more goods.

(d) Most important is the need to match payments received against debts owed. If a customer makes a payment, the business must be able to set off the payment against the customer's debt and establish how much he still owes on balance.

Sales ledger accounts are written up as follows.

(a) When entries are made in the sales day book (invoices sent out), they are subsequently also made in the debit side of the relevant customer account in the sales ledger.

(b) Similarly, when entries are made in the cash book (payments received), or in the sales returns day book, they are also made in the credit side of the relevant customer account.

Each customer account is given a reference or code number, and it is that reference which is the 'sales ledger folio' in the sales day book. We say that amounts are posted from the sales day book to the sales ledger. An example of how a sales ledger account is laid out is as follows.

ENOR COLLEGE				A/c no: SL 9
		£		£
Balance b/f		250.00		
10.1.X0	Sales – SDB 48 (invoice no 250)	1,264.60	Balance c/d	1,514.60
		1,514.60		1,514.60
11.1.X0	Balance b/d	1,514.60		

The debit side of this personal account, then, shows amounts owed by Enor College. When Enor pays some of the money it owes it will be entered into the cash book (receipts) and subsequently 'posted' to the credit side of the personal account. For example, if the college paid £250 on 10.1.20X0, it would appear as follows.

ENOR COLLEGE				A/c no: SL 9
		£		£
Balance b/f		250.00	10.1.X0 Cash	250.00
10.1.X0	Sales – SDB 48 (invoice no 250)	1,264.60	Balance c/d	1,264.60
		1,514.60		1,514.60
11.1.X0	Balance b/d	1,264.60		

The opening balance owed by Enor College on 11.1.X0 is now £1,264.60 instead of £1,514.60, because of the £250 receipt which came in on 10.1.X0.

3.3 The purchase ledger (bought ledger)

The purchase ledger, like the sales ledger, consists of a number of personal accounts. These are separate accounts for each individual supplier, and they enable a business to keep a continuous record of how much it owes each supplier at any time. After entries are made in the purchase day book, cash book, or purchase returns day book – ie after entries are made in the books of prime entry – they are also made in the relevant supplier account in the purchase ledger. Again we say that the entries in the purchase day book are posted to the suppliers' personal accounts in the purchase ledger.

Following is an example of how a purchase ledger account is laid out.

COOK & CO				A/c no: SL 31
		£		£
			Balance b/f	200.00
			15.3.X8 Invoice received	
Balance c/d		515.00	PDB 37	315.00
		515.00		515.00
			16.3.X8 Balance b/d	515.00

The credit side of this personal account, then, shows amounts owing to Cook & Co. If the business paid Cook & Co some money, it would be entered into the cash book (payments) and subsequently posted to the debit side of the personal account. For example, if the business paid Cook & Co £100 on 15 March 20X8, it would appear as follows:

COOK & CO				A/c no: SL 31
		£		£
15.3.X8	Cash	100.00	Balance b/f	200.00
			15.3.X8 Invoice received	
	Balance c/d	415.00	PDB 37	315.00
		515.00		515.00
			16.3.X8 Balance b/d	415.00

NOTES

The opening balance owed to Cook & Co on 16.3.X8 is now £415.00 instead of £515.00 because of the £100 payment made during 15.3.X8.

The roles of the sales day book and purchases day book are very similar, with one book dealing with invoices sent out and the other with invoices received. The sales ledger and purchases ledger also serve similar purposes, with one consisting of personal accounts for credit customers (debtors) and the other consisting of personal accounts for creditors.

Transactions can be recorded directly in the ledger accounts. However, with a large number of transactions, detecting errors or following individual transactions through the accounting system can be very difficult. It is the journal where unusual movement between accounts is first recorded.

3.4 The journal

In the previous chapter, we defined the books of prime entry as the first stage at which a business transaction enters into the accounting system. The journal is one such book of prime entry.

Definition

> A **journal** is a book of prime entry in which are entered those transactions which cannot be recorded in chronological order. Such transactions are generally non-routine in nature such as sale or purchase of fixed assets, correction of errors and so on.

Whatever type of transaction is being recorded, the format of a journal entry is:

Date	*Folio*	*Debit*	*Credit*
		£	£
Account to be debited		X	
Account to be credited			X
(Narrative to explain transaction)			

Remember: in due course, the ledger accounts will be written up to include the transactions listed in the journal.

A narrative explanation must accompany each journal entry. It is required for audit and control.

EXAMPLES: JOURNAL ENTRIES

The following is a summary of the transactions of Jo's hairdressing business of which Jo Ruth is the sole proprietor and which Jo started on 1 January.

1 January	Put in cash of £2,000 as capital
	Purchased brushes and combs for cash £50
	Purchased hair driers from Z Ltd on credit £150

BPP LEARNING MEDIA

The journal entries for these transactions would be as follows.

JOURNAL

			£	£
1 January	DEBIT	Cash	2,000	
	CREDIT	Jo Ruth – capital account		2,000
	Initial capital introduced			
1 January	DEBIT	Brushes and combs account	50	
	CREDIT	Cash		50
	The purchase for cash of brushes and combs as fixed assets			
1 January	DEBIT	Hair dryer account	150	
	CREDIT	Sundry creditors account*		150
	The purchase on credit of hair driers as fixed assets			

* Note: Creditors who have supplied fixed assets are included amongst sundry creditors, as distinct from creditors who have supplied raw materials or goods for resale, who are trade creditors. It is quite common to have separate 'total creditors' accounts, one for trade creditors and another for sundry other creditors.

Activity 3 **(5 minutes)**

Prepare journal entries for the following transactions for Hacker who commenced business as a retail butcher on 1 February 20X1.

1 Feb Put in cash of £4,000 as capital

10 Feb Bought a delivery van at a cost of £900 for cash

NOTES

Chapter roundup

- A general or nominal ledger is a file, binder, computer disc or floppy containing all the accounts of a business.
- In its most basic form, an account has three elements: a title, the left hand or the debit side and the right hand or the credit side.
- The only meaning of the term debit is the left side of the account and similarly the only meaning of the term credit is the right side of the account.
- In a double entry system, every transaction must be entered in the ledger accounts twice: once as a debit and once as an equal and opposite credit.
- The rules of double entry bookkeeping are:

Account 'type'	*Debit*	*Credit*
Asset	Increase	Decrease
Expense	Increase	Decrease
Liability	Decrease	Increase
Capital	Decrease	Increase
Income/Revenue	Decrease	Increase

- The rules of double entry bookkeeping are best learnt by considering the cash book. In the cash book a credit entry indicates a payment made by the business; the matching debit entry is then made in an account denoting an expense paid, an asset purchased or a liability settled. A debit entry in the cash book indicates cash received by the business; the matching credit entry is then made in an account denoting revenue received, a liability created or a debt paid off.
- Some accounts in the nominal ledger represent the total of very many smaller balances. For example, the debtors account represents all the balances owed by individual customers of the business, while the creditors account represents all amounts owed by the business to its suppliers.
- To keep track of individual customer and supplier balances, it is common to maintain subsidiary ledgers (called the sales ledger and the purchase ledger respectively). Each account in these ledgers represents the balance owed by or to an individual customer or supplier. These subsidiary ledgers are kept purely for reference and are therefore known as memorandum records. They do not normally form part of the double entry system.
- The journal is a book of prime entry where non-routine transactions which cannot be recorded in other books are recorded.

NOTES

Quick quiz

1 What do the terms debit and credit mean?

2 List the rules of debit and credit bookkeeping.

3 What is the double entry to record a cash sale of £50?

4 What is the double entry to record a purchase of office chairs for £1,000 cash?

5 What is the double entry to record a credit sale?

6 What is the difference between the creditors account in the nominal ledger and the purchase ledger?

Answers to quick quiz

1 They relate to the two sides of ledger accounts. (see para 1.3)

2 Every debit must have a corresponding credit in the double entry system and the chapter gives further details depending on the type of transaction. (para 2.2)

3 DEBIT: Cash £50
CREDIT: Sales £50. (para 2.2)

4 DEBIT: Office furniture (or similar account) £1,000
CREDIT: Cash £1,000. (para 2.2)

5 DEBIT: Debtors
CREDIT: Sales. (para 2.3)

6 The creditors account in the nominal ledger represents amounts owed by the business to suppliers and the purchase ledger provides memorandum entries for each individual creditor. (para 3)

Answers to activities

1 (c) Payment received from a debtor

(i) debtors decrease	CREDIT	debtors (decrease in asset)
(ii) cash at bank increases	DEBIT	cash at bank (increase in asset)

(d) Purchase of van

(i) own a van	DEBIT	van (increase in asset)
(ii) cash at bank decreases	CREDIT	cash at bank (decrease in asset)

BPP LEARNING MEDIA

NOTES

2

			£	£
(a)	DEBIT	Machine account (fixed asset)	8,000	
	CREDIT	Creditors (A)		8,000
(b)	DEBIT	Purchases account	500	
	CREDIT	Creditors (B)		500
(c)	DEBIT	Debtors (C)	1,200	
	CREDIT	Sales		1,200
(d)	DEBIT	Creditors (D)	300	
	CREDIT	Cash		300
(e)	DEBIT	Cash	180	
	CREDIT	Debtors (E)		180
(f)	DEBIT	Wages account	4,000	
	CREDIT	Cash		4,000
(g)	DEBIT	Rent account	700	
	CREDIT	Creditors (G)		700
(h)	DEBIT	Creditors (G)	700	
	CREDIT	Cash		700
(i)	DEBIT	Insurance costs	90	
	CREDIT	Cash		90

3

	JOURNAL		£	£
1 February	DEBIT	Cash	4,000	
	CREDIT	Hacker – Capital		4,000
	Initial capital introduced			
10 February	DEBIT	Delivery van	900	
	CREDIT	Cash		900
	The purchase of delivery van for cash			

BPP LEARNING MEDIA

Chapter 15 :
PREPARATION OF ACCOUNTS FROM A TRIAL BALANCE

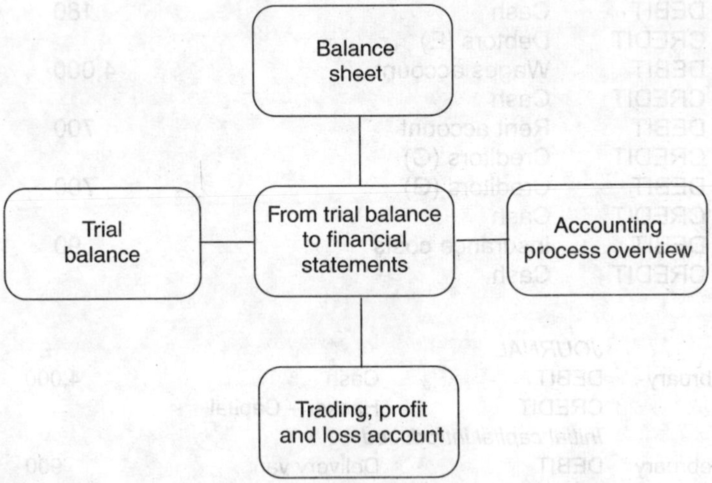

Introduction

You have learned the principles of double entry and how to post the ledger accounts. Once all the transactions have been posted, it is usual to test the accuracy of double entry bookkeeping records by preparing a trial balance. Its preparation also provides a convenient stepping stone to the preparation of the final accounts (and the related financial statements).

The trial balance is prepared by taking the balance of each and every account and aggregating separately the accounts with debit balances and those with credit balances. If the two totals equal, it will show that the basic principle of double entry has been correctly applied. Although such equality does not guarantee error-free accounting, it is possible to prepare final accounts directly from a trial balance without going through the time consuming process of referring to the ledger accounts. Once the final accounts have been prepared, preparation of financial statements is merely a matter of rearranging the information.

Your objectives

In this chapter you will learn about the following.

(a) The purpose of a trial balance and how it is prepared

(b) The circumstances when a trial balance might balance despite certain types of errors

(c) How to prepare a trading, profit and loss account from the trial balance

(d) How to balance accounts and prepare a balance sheet

(e) All the accounting steps involved from entering transactions in the ledger accounts to preparing the financial statements

1 TRIAL BALANCE

The earlier chapter on double entry would have shown you the following.

(a) Each transaction is entered at least twice in the ledger: once as a debit and once as a credit.

(b) The £ amounts of debit and credit entered for each transaction are equal.

Since equal £ amounts of debits and credits are recorded for each and every transaction, it follows that if all the debits in the ledger are added up, they must equal the total of all the credits in the ledger.

Total debit £ amount = Total credit £ amount

It is desirable that this equality is proven after all the transactions have been posted to the ledger but before the final accounts and the related financial statements are prepared. This proof of equality of debits and credits is obtained through the preparation of a trial balance.

The steps involved in preparing a trial balance are as follows.

(a) Find the balance on the ledger accounts

(b) Record the ledger account balances in the appropriate column of the trial balance

(c) Total each column

(d) Compare the totals of the two columns of the trial balance

Before you draw up a trial balance, you will have a collection of ledger accounts, such as below.

CASH

	£		£
Capital – Ron Knuckle	7,000	Rent	3,500
Bank loan	1,000	Shop fittings	2,000
Sales	10,000	Trade creditors	5,000
Debtors	2,500	Bank loan interest	100
		Incidental expenses	1,900
		Drawings	1,500
			14,000
		Balancing figure	6,500
	20,500		20,500

CAPITAL (RON KNUCKLE)

	£		£
		Cash	7,000

BANK LOAN

	£		£
		Cash	1,000

PURCHASES

	£		£
Trade creditors	5,000		

TRADE CREDITORS

	£		£
Cash	5,000	Purchases	5,000

RENT

	£		£
Cash	3,500		

SHOP FITTINGS

	£		£
Cash	2,000		

SALES

	£		£
		Cash	10,000
		Debtors	2,500
			12,500

DEBTORS

	£		£
Sales	2,500	Cash	2,500

BANK LOAN INTEREST

	£		£
Cash	100		

OTHER EXPENSES

	£		£
Cash	1,900		

DRAWINGS ACCOUNT

	£		£
Cash	1,500		

Given a series of accounts in which transactions have been recorded, the process of preparing a trial balance is as follows.

1.1 *Step 1:* Finding the balance on the ledger accounts

At the end of an accounting period all ledger accounts are 'balanced'. This means finding the balance in each account by going through the following procedure.

(a) Total all the debits in the account, ie find the total of the left side of the account.

(b) Total all the credits on the account, ie total the right side of the account.

(c) Subtract the lower side total from the higher side total.

(d) If the higher side is the debit side, ie if total debits exceed total credits, the account has a debit balance.

(e) If, on the other hand, the higher side is the credit side, ie if total credits exceed total debits, the account has a credit balance.

(f) If the debit and credit sides of an account are equal, the account has a zero balance.

In our example of Ron Knuckle, there is very little balancing to do.

(a) The trade creditors account and the debtors account balance off to zero.
(b) The cash account has a debit balance of £6,500.
(c) The total on the sales account is £12,500, which is a credit balance.

The remaining accounts have only one entry each, so there is no totalling to do.

1.2 *Step 2:* Recording the balances

Once all the accounts have been 'balanced', a list of all the accounts along with their balances is prepared. The crucial thing is that the debit balances are entered in the debit column and the credit balances are recorded in the credit column of the trial balance. This is illustrated below for Ron Knuckle's accounts.

	Debit	*Credit*
	£	£
Cash	6,500	
Capital		7,000
Bank loan		1,000
Purchases	5,000	
Trade creditors	-	-
Rent	3,500	
Shop fittings	2,000	
Sales		12,500
Debtors	-	-
Bank loan interest	100	
Other expenses	1,900	
Drawings	1,500	

1.3 *Step 3:* Totalling each column

After all the accounts and their balances have been entered in the proper columns (debit balances in the left-hand column and credit balances in the right-hand column), the two columns are then totalled.

	Debit	*Credit*
	£	£
Cash	6,500	
Capital		7,000
Bank loan		1,000
Purchases	5,000	
Trade creditors	-	-
Rent	3,500	
Shop fittings	2,000	
Sales		12,500
Debtors	-	-
Bank loan interest	100	
Other expenses	1,900	
Drawings	1,500	
	20,500	20,500

1.4 *Step 4:* Comparing the totals

The final step in preparing the trial balance is to make sure that the totals of the debit and the credit columns are equal.

In our example, the two columns do total to £20,500. But what if the trial balance shows unequal debit and credit balances?

If the two columns of the trial balance are not equal, this means that there are error(s) in recording the transactions in the accounts or that mistake(s) have been made in entering the balances in the trial balance. These errors need to be corrected before going any further.

However, it is possible for the trial balance to balance, ie for debit and credit column totals to be equal, and still to have errors present. The errors that a trial balance will not disclose are the following.

(a) The complete omission of a transaction, because neither a debit nor a credit is made

(b) The posting of a debit or credit to the correct side of the ledger, but to a wrong account, eg debiting furniture account as opposed to cash

(c) Compensating errors, eg an error of £100 is exactly cancelled by another £100 error elsewhere

(d) Errors of principle, eg cash received from debtors being debited to the debtors account and credited to cash instead of the other way round

---

EXAMPLE

As at 30.3.20X1, your business has the following balances on its ledger accounts.

Accounts	*Balance*
	£
Bank loan	12,000
Cash	11,700
Capital	13,000
Rates	1,880
Trade creditors	11,200
Purchases	12,400
Sales	14,600
Sundry creditors	1,620
Debtors	12,000
Bank loan interest	1,400
Other expenses	11,020
Vehicles	2,020

During the next day the business made the following transactions.

(a) Bought materials for £1,000, half for cash and half on credit.
(b) Made £1,040 sales, £800 of which was for credit.
(c) Paid wages to shop assistants of £260 in cash.

We will now draw up a trial balance showing the balances as at the end of 31.3.X1.

First it is necessary to put the original balances into a trial balance – ie decide which are debit and which are credit balances.

Account	*Debit*	*Credit*
	£	£
Bank loan		12,000
Cash	11,700	
Capital		13,000
Rates	1,880	
Trade creditors		11,200
Purchases	12,400	
Sales		14,600
Sundry creditors		1,620
Debtors	12,000	
Bank loan interest	1,400	
Other expenses	11,020	
Vehicles	2,020	
	52,420	52,420

1.5 The Rule of Thumb

With practice you will be able to distinguish between debit and credit balances at a glance. What may help you in the beginning is a simple rule of thumb: **accounts are likely to reflect the balance on the side on which increases are recorded in that account.** In other words, if the increases in an account are recorded on the debit side, the account is likely to have a debit balance and similarly if the increases are recorded on the credit side, the account will show a credit balance. In the above example, cash is shown as having a debit balance. Cash is an asset and hence increases are recorded on the debit side. Trade creditors, on the other hand, is a liability account. Increases in liability accounts are recorded on the credit side and hence trade creditors is showing a credit balance (as are sundry creditors).

Now we must take account of the effects of the three transactions which took place on 31.3.X1:

			£	£
(a)	DEBIT	Purchases	1,000	
	CREDIT	Cash		500
		Trade creditors		500
(b)	DEBIT	Cash	240	
		Debtors	800	
	CREDIT	Sales		1,040
(c)	DEBIT	Other expenses	260	
	CREDIT	Cash		260

When these figures are included in the trial balance, it becomes:

Account	*Debit*	*Credit*
	£	£
Bank loan		12,000
Cash (11,700 – 500 + 240 – 260)	11,180	
Capital		13,000
Rates	1,880	
Trade creditors (11,200 + 500)		11,700
Purchases (12,400 + 1,000)	13,400	
Sales (14,600 + 1,040)		15,640
Sundry creditors		1,620
Debtors (12,000 + 800)	12,800	
Bank loan interest	1,400	
Other expenses (11,020 + 260)	11,280	
Vehicles	2,020	
	53,960	53,960

Activity 1 **(15 minutes)**

S Trader carries on a small business. The following balances have been extracted from his books on 30 September 20X0.

	£
Capital	24,239
Office furniture	1,440
Drawings	4,888
Stock	14,972
Purchases	167,760
Sales	184,269
Rent	1,350
Lighting and heating	475
Insurance	304
Salaries	6,352
Debtors	19,100
Creditors	8,162
Petty cash in hand	29

Prepare a trial balance as at 30 September 20X0.

Now that you understand how a trial balance is prepared and what it is supposed to do, we will give you a concise definition of a trial balance, something we have avoided doing so far.

Definition

A **trial balance** is a schedule which lists all the accounts of the ledger along with their balances in the appropriate debit or credit column. It is used to ensure that the equality of debits and credits has been maintained in preparing the ledger accounts.

NOTES

Once a trial balance has been balanced, the next step is to start preparing the financial statements. We start by looking at the trading, profit and loss account.

2 TRADING, PROFIT AND LOSS ACCOUNT

The first step in the process of preparing the financial statements is to open up another ledger account, for the trading, profit and loss account. In it a business summarises its results for the period by gathering together all the ledger account balances relating to income and expenses. This account is still part of the double entry system, so the basic rule of double entry still applies: every debit must have an equal and opposite credit entry. This trading, profit and loss account however is not the financial statement we are aiming for, even though it has the same name. The difference between the two is not very great, because they contain the same information. However, the financial statement lays it out differently and may be much less detailed.

So what do we do with this new ledger account? The first step is to look through the ledger accounts and identify which ones relate to income and expenses. In the case of Ron Knuckle, the income and expense accounts are the following.

(a) Purchases
(b) Sales
(c) Rent
(d) Bank loan interest
(e) Other expenses

The balances on these accounts are transferred to the new trading, profit and loss account. For example, the purchases account has a debit balance of £5,000. To transfer this balance we need to make a credit entry of £5,000 to the account. However, we cannot write £5,000 on the credit side of the purchases account without making a debit entry somewhere else in the ledger (it would be against the rules of double entry). The debit entry would go to the new trading, profit and loss account. In this way, the purchase account balance has been transferred to the trading, profit and loss account. If we do the same thing with all the income and expense accounts of Ron Knuckle, the result will be as follows.

PURCHASES

	£		£
Trade creditors	5,000	Trading, P & L a/c	5,000

RENT

	£		£
Cash	3,500	Trading, P & L a/c	3,500

TRADING, PROFIT AND LOSS ACCOUNT

	£		£
Purchases	5,000	Sales	12,500
Rent	3,500		
Bank loan interest	100		
Other expenses	1,900		

NOTES

BANK LOAN INTEREST

	£		£
Cash	100	Trading, P&L a/c	100

OTHER EXPENSES

	£		£
Cash	1,900	Trading, P & L a/c	1,900

SALES

	£		£
Trading, P & L a/c	12,500	Cash	10,000
		Debtors	2,500
	12,500		12,500

(Note that the trading, profit and loss account has not yet been balanced off but we will return to that later.)

If you look at the items we have gathered together in the trading, profit and loss account, they should strike a chord in your memory. They are the same items that we need to draw up the trading, profit and loss account in the form of a financial statement. With a little rearrangement they could be presented as follows:

RON KNUCKLE: TRADING, PROFIT AND LOSS ACCOUNT

	£	£
Sales		12,500
Cost of sales (= purchases in this case)		(5,000)
Gross profit		7,500
Expenses		
Rent	3,500	
Bank loan interest	100	
Other expenses	1,900	
		(5,500)
Net profit		2,000

The trading, profit and loss account is followed by the preparation of the balance sheet.

3 THE BALANCE SHEET

Look back at the ledger accounts of Ron Knuckle. Now that we have dealt with those relating to income and expenses, which ones are left? The answer is that we still have to find out what to do with cash, capital, bank loan, trade creditors, shop fittings, debtors and the drawings account.

Are these the only ledger accounts left? No: don't forget there is still the last one we opened up, called the trading, profit and loss account. The balance on this account represents the profit earned by the business, and if you go through the arithmetic, you will find that it has a credit balance – a profit – of £2,000. (Not surprisingly, this is the figure that is shown in the trading, profit and loss account financial statement.) These remaining accounts must also be balanced and ruled off.

However, since these accounts represent assets and liabilities of the business (not income and expenses) their balances are not transferred to the trading, profit and loss account. Instead they are carried down in the books of the business. This means that they become opening balances for the next accounting period and indicate the value of the assets and liabilities at the end of one period and the beginning of the next. This should be contrasted with the income and expenses accounts which are closed off at the end of the accounting period and transferred to trading, profit and loss account. This means that at the start of each accounting period, income and expenditure accounts always have a zero starting balance.

The conventional method of ruling off a ledger account at the end of an accounting period is illustrated by the bank loan account in Ron Knuckle's books.

BANK LOAN ACCOUNT

	£		£
Balance carried down (c/d)	1,000	Cash	1,000
		Balance brought down (b/d)	1,000

Ron Knuckle therefore begins the new accounting period with a credit balance of £1,000 on this account. A credit balance brought down denotes a liability. An asset would be represented by a debit balance brought down.

One further point is worth noting before we move on to complete this example. You will remember that a proprietor's capital comprises any cash introduced by him, plus any profits made by the business, less any drawings made by him. At the stage we have now reached these three elements are contained in different ledger accounts:

(a) Cash introduced of £7,000 appears in the capital account

(b) Drawings of £1,500 appear in the drawings account

(c) £2,000 profit made by the business is reflected by the credit balance in the trading, profit and loss account.

It is convenient to gather together all these amounts into one capital account, in the same way as we earlier gathered together income and expense accounts into one trading and profit and loss account. If we go ahead and gather the three amounts together, the results are as follows.

DRAWINGS

	£		£
Cash	1,500	Capital a/c	1,500

CAPITAL

	£		£
Drawings	1,500	Cash	7,000
Balance c/d	7,500	Trading, P & L a/c	2,000
	9,000		9,000
		Balance b/d	7,500

TRADING, PROFIT AND LOSS ACCOUNT

	£		£
Purchases	5,000	Sales	12,500
Rent	3,500		
Bank loan interest	100		
Other expenses	1,900		
Capital a/c	2,000		
	12,500		12,500

A re-arrangement of these balances will complete Ron Knuckle's simple balance sheet.

RON KNUCKLE
BALANCE SHEET AT END OF FIRST TRADING PERIOD

	£
Fixed assets	
Shop fittings	2,000
Current assets	
Cash	6,500
Total assets	8,500
Liabilities	
Bank loan	(1,000)
Net assets	7,500
Proprietor's capital	7,500

When a balance sheet is drawn up for an accounting period which is not the first one, it ought to show the capital at the start of the accounting period and the capital at the end of the accounting period.

> **Activity 2** **(5 minutes)**
>
> If you totalled up a trading, profit and loss account and found that it had a debit balance, what would that mean? Where would that balance go?

We next briefly review all the accounting steps involved from the moment transactions enter the accounting system until the preparation of financial statements.

4 ACCOUNTING PROCESS OVERVIEW

The accounting process described to this point may be summarised in the following eight steps.

Step 1 Enter the transactions in the books of prime or original entry.

Step 2 Post the transactions to the nominal ledger.

Step 3 Prepare a trial balance.

Step 4 Make any non-routine or special entries using the journal eg correcting the errors etc.

Step 5 Close all income and expenditure accounts by transferring their balance to trading, profit and loss account.

Step 6 Balance all asset, liabilities and capital accounts.

Step 7 Clear profit and drawings balances to the capital account.

Step 8 Prepare the financial statements.

NOTES

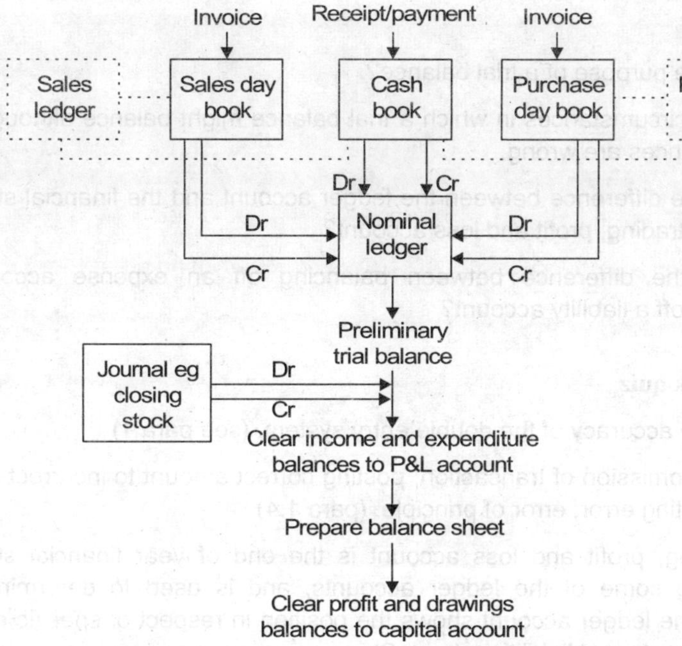

Figure 15.1: Accounting process overview

Chapter roundup

- At suitable intervals, the entries in each ledger account are totalled and a balance is struck. Balances are usually collected in a trial balance which is then used as a basis for preparing a profit and loss account and a balance sheet.
- A trial balance can be used to test the accuracy of the double entry accounting records. It works by listing the balances on ledger accounts, some of which will be debits and some credits, to see if they balance off to zero.
- The balancing off of the trial balance does not mean that the accounting process, so far, has been error free. There are a number of errors which are not revealed by a balanced-off trial balance.
- A trading, profit and loss ledger account is opened up to gather all items relating to income and expenses. When rearranged, the items make up the profit and loss financial statement.
- The balances on all remaining ledger accounts (including the trading, profit and loss account) can be listed and rearranged to form the balance sheet.

BPP LEARNING MEDIA

NOTES

Quick quiz

1 What is the purpose of a trial balance?

2 Give four circumstances in which a trial balance might balance although some of the balances are wrong.

3 What is the difference between the ledger account and the financial statement called the trading, profit and loss account?

4 What is the difference between balancing off an expense account and balancing off a liability account?

Answers to quick quiz

1 To test the accuracy of the double entry system. (see para 1)

2 Complete omission of transaction; posting correct amount to incorrect account; compensating error; error of principle. (para 1.4)

3 The trading, profit and loss account is the end of year financial statement comprising some of the ledger accounts, and is used to determine profit, whereas the ledger account shows the position in respect of specific expense, income, assets and liabilities. (para 2)

4 An expense account is 'closed' at the end of the financial year by a transfer to the trading, profit and loss account and a liability account remains 'open' for the next accounting period and appears in the balance sheet. (para 3)

Answers to activities

1 TRADER
TRIAL BALANCE
30 SEPTEMBER 20X0

	Dr	*Cr*
	£	£
Capital		24,239
Office furniture	1,440	
Drawings	4,888	
Stock	14,972	
Purchases	167,760	
Sales		184,269
Rent	1,350	
Lighting and heating	475	
Insurance	304	
Salaries	6,352	
Debtors	19,100	
Creditors		8,162
Petty cash	29	
	216,670	216,670

2 A debit balance in trading, profit and loss account would show that the business has suffered a loss for that period.

The debit balance will be transferred to the capital account of the business by crediting the trading, profit and loss account and debiting the capital account.

BPP LEARNING MEDIA

Chapter 16 :

PERIOD END ADJUSTMENTS

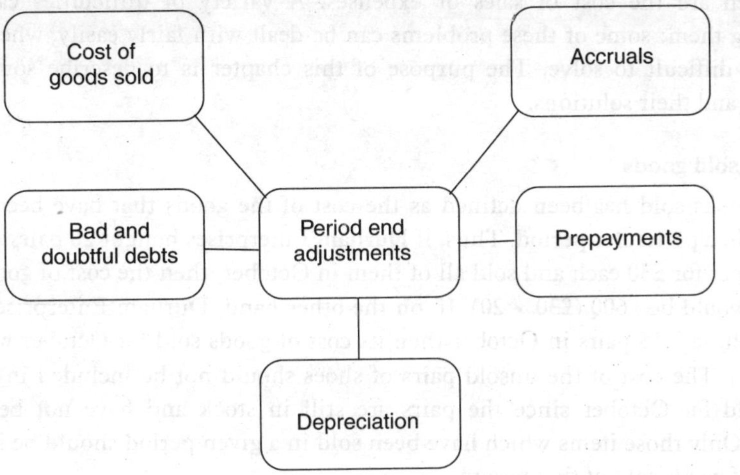

Introduction

The trial balance lists the balances on the ledger accounts at the period end date. It does not take into account various items which can only be calculated right at the end of the period once the final position is known. These adjustments include the cost of goods sold, accruals (expenditure incurred which has not yet been invoiced or paid) prepayments (payments made, some of which relate to the next accounting period) depreciation (the consumption of fixed assets) and bad and doubtful debts (debts due to the business which may or may not be paid).

It is important that these items are treated correctly in the accounts, to avoid the profit or loss for the year from being over or under estimated.

Your objectives

In this chapter you will learn about the following.

(a) The accruals concept

(b) Accrued expenses and prepayments and their accounting treatment

(c) The main differences between bad debts and doubtful debts

(d) How to write off a bad debt and create a provision for doubtful debts

(e) How to adjust the provision for doubtful debts

(f) Accounting for depreciation at the period end

1 COST OF GOODS SOLD

1.1 Definition

When we looked at the trading, profit and loss account earlier in this book, we defined profit as:

Sales *less* **Cost of sales** *less* **Expenses**

This definition might seem simple enough; however, it is not always immediately clear how much are the cost of sales or expenses. A variety of difficulties can arise in measuring them: some of these problems can be dealt with fairly easily, whereas others are more difficult to solve. The purpose of this chapter is to describe some of these problems and their solutions.

1.2 Unsold goods

Cost of goods sold has been defined as the cost of the goods that have been sold by a business in a particular period. Thus, if Durham Enterprises bought 20 pairs of shoes in, say, October for £30 each and sold all of them in October, then the cost of goods sold for October would be £600 (£30 × 20). If, on the other hand, Durham Enterprises was only able to sell, say, 15 pairs in October then its cost of goods sold for October will be £450 (£30 × 15). The cost of the unsold pairs of shoes should not be included in the cost of goods sold for October since the pairs are still in stock and have not been sold in October. Only those items which have been sold in a given period should be included in the cost of goods sold of that period.

EXAMPLE: CLOSING STOCK

Suppose that Perry P Louis, trading as the Umbrella Shop, ends his financial year on 30 September each year. On 1 October 20X0 he had no goods in stock. During the year to 30 September 20X1, he purchased 30,000 umbrellas costing £60,000 from umbrella wholesalers and suppliers. He resold the umbrellas for £5 each, and sales for the year amounted to £100,000 (20,000 umbrellas). At 30 September there were 10,000 unsold umbrellas left in stock, valued at £2 each.

Perry P Louis's cost of goods sold for the year can be calculated as follows.

Cost of each umbrella is £2 (£60,000 ÷ 30,000)

Umbrellas sold: 20,000	=	Purchases	–	Unsold
		30,000		10,000

Therefore, cost of goods sold = £40,000 (£2 × 20,000)

We can put this calculation in a more formal way as follows.

	£
Purchases	60,000
Closing stock	20,000
Cost of goods sold	40,000

Purchases in accounting refers to goods bought for resale to customers; it reflects only those goods which have been acquired for resale. Assets acquired for use in the business such as buildings, office supplies etc are recorded by debiting the appropriate asset account, not the purchases account.

Stock unsold at the end of the year (or at the end of any period) is called *closing stock*. Thus, the correct way of presenting the above information is as follows:

	£
Purchases	60,000
Closing stock	20,000
Cost of goods sold	40,000

You already know that gross profit is calculated as follows:

Sales – Cost of goods sold

The gross profit for Umbrella shop for the year ending 30 September 20X1 can be calculated as follows.

	£	£
Sales (20,000 × £5)		100,000
Purchases	60,000	
Closing stock	20,000	
Cost of goods sold		40,000
Gross profit		60,000

We shall continue the example of the Umbrella Shop into its next accounting year, 1 October 20X1 to 30 September 20X2. Suppose that during the course of this year, Perry P Louis purchased 40,000 umbrellas at a total cost of £95,000. During the year he sold 45,000 umbrellas for £230,000. At 30 September 20X2 he had 5,000 umbrellas left in stock, which had cost £12,000. Let us now calculate his gross profit for the year.

In this accounting year, he purchased 40,000 umbrellas to add to the 10,000 he already had in stock at the start of the year. He sold 45,000, leaving 5,000 umbrellas in stock at the year end. Once again, gross profit should be calculated by matching the value of 45,000 units of sales with the cost of those 45,000 units.

The cost of sales is the value of the 10,000 umbrellas in stock at the beginning of the year, plus the cost of the 40,000 umbrellas purchased, less the value of the 5,000 umbrellas in stock at the year end.

	£	£
Sales (45,000 units)		230,000
Opening stock (10,000 units)*	20,000	
Add purchases (40,000 units)	95,000	
	115,000	
Less closing stock (5,000 units)	12,000	
Cost of sales (45,000 units)		103,000
Gross profit		127,000

*Taken from the closing stock value of the previous accounting year.

The cost of goods sold

The cost of goods sold is found by applying the following formula.

	£
Opening stock	X
Add cost of purchases	X
	X
Less closing stock	(X)
Equals cost of goods sold	X

In other words, to match 'sales' and the 'cost of goods sold', it is necessary to adjust the cost of goods purchased to allow for increases or reduction in stock levels during the period.

Activity 1 **(5 minutes)**

On 1 January 20X1, the Grand Union Food Stores had goods in stock valued at £6,000. During 20X1 its proprietor, who ran the shop, purchased supplies costing £50,000. Sales turnover for the year to 31 December 20X1 amounted to £80,000. The cost of goods in stock at 31 December 20X1 was £12,500.

Calculate the gross profit for the year.

Sometimes the buyer pays the delivery costs on his purchases. In such cases, the delivery charges become part of the cost of goods sold.

1.3 Carriage inwards and outwards

'Carriage' refers to the cost of transporting purchased goods from the supplier to the premises of the business which has bought them. Someone has to pay for these delivery costs: sometimes the supplier pays, and sometimes the purchaser pays.

Definitions

Carriage inwards is the cost to the purchaser of having goods transported to his business. It is paid by the purchaser.

Carriage outwards is the cost to the seller, paid by the seller, of having goods transported to the customer.

Carriage inwards is usually added to the cost of purchases, and is therefore included in the trading account while the cost of carriage outwards is a selling and distribution expense in the profit and loss account.

EXAMPLE: CARRIAGE COSTS

Gwyn Tring, trading as Clickety Clocks, imports and resells cuckoo clocks and grandfather clocks. He must pay for the costs of delivering the clocks from his supplier in Switzerland to his shop in Wales.

He resells the clocks to other traders throughout the country, paying the costs of carriage for the consignments from his business premises to his customers.

On 1 July 20X0, he had clocks in stock valued at £17,000. During the year to 30 June 20X1, he purchased more clocks at a cost of £75,000. Carriage inwards amounted to £2,000. Sales for the year were £162,100. Other expenses of the business amounted to £56,000 excluding carriage outwards which cost £2,500. Gwyn Tring took drawings of £20,000 from the business during the course of the year. The value of the goods in stock at the year end was £15,400.

The trading, profit and loss account of Clickety Clocks for the year ended 30 June 20X1 would be as follows.

CLICKETY CLOCKS
TRADING, PROFIT AND LOSS ACCOUNT
FOR THE YEAR ENDED 30 JUNE 20X1

	£	£
Sales		162,100
Opening stock	17,000	
Purchases	75,000	
Carriage inwards	2,000	
	94,000	
Less closing stock	15,400	
Cost of goods sold		78,600
Gross profit		83,500
Carriage outwards	2,500	
Other expenses	56,000	
		58,500
Net profit (transferred to balance sheet)		25,000

1.4 Goods written off or written down

A trader might be unable to sell all the goods that he purchases, because a number of things might happen to the goods before they can be sold. For example:

(a) goods might be lost or stolen;

(b) goods might be damaged, and so become worthless. Such damaged goods might be thrown away;

(c) goods might become obsolete or out of fashion. These might have to be thrown away, or possibly sold off at a very low price in a clearance sale.

When goods are lost, stolen or thrown away as worthless, the business will make a loss on those goods because their 'sale value' will be nil. Similarly, when goods lose value because they have become obsolete or out of fashion, the business will make a loss if their clearance sales value is less than their cost. For example, if goods which originally cost £500 are now obsolete and could only be sold for £150, the business would suffer a loss of £350.

If, at the end of an accounting period, a business still has goods in stock which are either worthless or worth less than their original cost, the value of the stocks should be written down to:

(a) zero, if they are worthless; or
(b) their net realisable value, if this is less than their original cost.

This means that the loss will be reported as soon as it is foreseen, even if the goods have not yet been thrown away or sold off at a cheap price.

The costs of stock written off or written down should not usually cause any problems in calculating the gross profit of a business, because the cost of goods sold will include the cost of stocks written off or written down, as the following example shows.

EXAMPLE: STOCKS WRITTEN OFF AND WRITTEN DOWN

Lucas Wagg, trading as Fairlock Fashions, ends his financial year on 31 March. At 1 April 20X0 he had goods in stock valued at £8,800. During the year to 31 March 20X1, he purchased goods costing £48,000. Fashion goods which cost £2,100 were still held in stock at 31 March 20X1, and Lucas Wagg believes that these could only now be sold at a sale price of £400. The goods still held in stock at 31 March 20X1 (including the fashion goods) had an original purchase cost of £7,600. Sales for the year were £81,400.

The calculation of gross profit of Fairlake Fashion would be a two-step process:

Step 1.

Initial calculation of closing stock values:

STOCK COUNT

	At cost	*Realisable value*	*Amount written down*
	£	£	£
Fashion goods	2,100	400	1,700
Other goods (balancing figure)	5,500	5,500	-
	7,600	5,900	1,700

Step 2.

FAIRLOCK FASHIONS
TRADING ACCOUNT FOR THE YEAR ENDED 31 MARCH 20X1

	£	£
Sales		81,400
Value of opening stock	8,800	
Purchases	48,000	
	56,800	
Less closing stock	5,900	
Cost of goods sold		50,900
Gross profit		30,500

Just as cost of goods sold for a period needs to be matched with the revenue for that period to calculate gross profit, similarly expenses need to be matched with revenue to calculate net profit. We now look at those situations where matching is not completely straightforward.

2 ACCRUALS AND PREPAYMENTS

It has already been stated that the gross profit for a period should be calculated by matching sales and the cost of goods sold. In the same way, the net profit for a period should be calculated by charging the expenses which relate to that period only. For example, in preparing the profit and loss account of a business for a period of, say, six months, it would be appropriate to charge only six months' expenses for rent and rates, insurance costs, telephone costs etc.

2.1 Introduction

It is quite possible that certain expenses might not be paid for during the period to which they relate. For example, if a business rents a shop for £20,000 per annum, it might pay the full annual rent on, say, 1 April each year. Now if we were to calculate the profit of the business for the first six months of the year 20X1, the correct charge for rent in the profit and loss account would be £10,000 even though the rent payment would be £20,000 in that period. Similarly, the rent charge in a profit and loss account for the

NOTES

business in the second six months of the year would be £10,000, even though no rent payment would be made in that six month period.

Definitions

- **Accruals** or accrued expenses are expenses which have been incurred by a business but have not yet been paid for.
- **Prepayments** are payments which have been made in advance for such expenses as rent, light and heat etc.

2.2 Examples

Accruals and prepayments might seem difficult at first, but the following examples might help to clarify the principle involved, that expenses should be matched against the period to which they relate.

EXAMPLE: ACCRUALS

Horace Goodrunning, trading as Goodrunning Motor Spares, ends his financial year on 28 February each year. His telephone was installed on 1 April 20X0 and he receives his telephone account quarterly at the end of each quarter. He pays it promptly as soon as it is received. On the basis of the following data, let us calculate the telephone expense to be charged to the profit and loss account for the year ended 28 February 20X1.

Goodrunning Motor Spares – telephone expense for the three months ended:

	£
30.6.20X0	23.50
30.9.20X0	27.20
31.12.20X0	33.40
31.3.20X1	36.00

The telephone expenses for the year ended 28 February 20X1 are:

	£
1 March–31 March 20X0 (no telephone)	0.00
1 April–30 June 20X0	23.50
1 July–30 September 20X0	27.20
1 October–31 December 20X0	33.40
1 January–28 February 20X1 (two months)	24.00
	108.10

The charge for the period 1 January – 28 February 20X1 is two-thirds of the quarterly charge received on 31 March. As at 28 February 20X1, no telephone bill has been received for the quarter because it is not due for another month. However, it would be inappropriate to ignore the telephone expenses for January and February, and so an accrued charge of £24 should be made, being two-thirds of the quarter's bill of £36.

As far as financial statements are concerned, the rules on accruals are as follows.

(a) **Total expense (including accrual)** → **Profit and loss (as expense)**

(b) **Accrued expense** → **Balance sheet (as current liability)**

Thus, in the case of Goodrunning Motor Spares, £108.10 would appear on the P&L as an expense while the accrued expense of £24 would be classified in the balance sheet as a current liability.

EXAMPLE: PREPAYMENTS

The Square Wheels Garage pays fire insurance annually in advance on 1 June each year. The firm's financial year end is 28 February. From the following record of insurance payments, we will calculate the charge to profit and loss for the financial year to 28 February 20X2.

Insurance paid	£
1.6.20X0	600
1.6.20X1	700

Insurance cost for year end 28 February 20X2:	£
(a) the 3 months, 1 March – 31 May 20X1 (3/12 × £600)	150
(b) the 9 months, 1 June 20X1 – 28 February 20X2 (9/12 × £700)	525
Insurance cost for the year, charged to the P & L account	675

At 28 February 20X2 there is a prepayment for fire insurance, covering the period 1 March – 31 May 20X2. This insurance premium was paid on 1 June 20X2, but only nine months worth of the full annual cost is chargeable to the accounting period ended 28 February 20X2. The prepayment of (3/12 × £700) £175 as at 28 February 20X2 will appear as a current asset in the balance sheet of the Square Wheels Garage as at that date.

In the same way, there was a prepayment of (3/12 × £600) £150 in the balance sheet one year earlier as at 28 February 20X1.

Summary

	£
Prepaid insurance premiums as at 28 February 20X1	150
Add insurance premiums paid 1 June 20X1	700
	850
Less insurance costs charged to the P&L account for the year ended 28 February 20X2	675
Equals prepaid insurance premiums as at 28 February 20X2	175

This diagram summarises the situation.

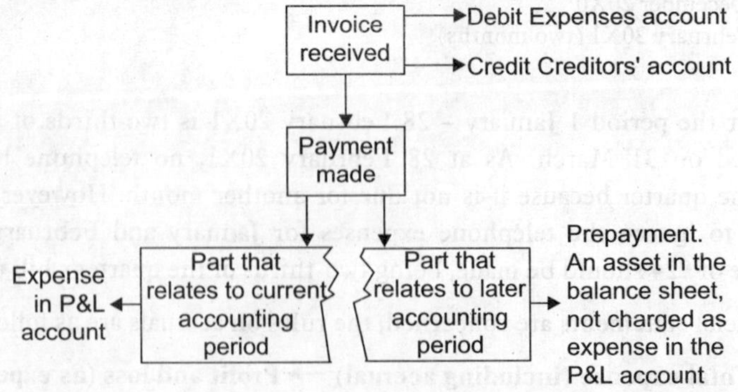

BPP LEARNING MEDIA

In the next period, charge the profit and loss account with the amount of the prepayment brought forward.

Activity 2 **(5 minutes)**

Included in the balance sheet of Kate's Coffee House at 30 June 20X0 were the following.

	£
Prepayment (insurance)	450
Accrual (electricity)	80

The following invoices were received and paid during the year to 30 June 20X1.

Date paid		£
5.9.20X0	Electricity (quarter to 31 August 20X0)	309
8.12.20X0	Electricity (quarter to 30 November 20X0)	320
2.1.20X1	Insurance (year to 31 December 20X1)	1,000
7.3.20X1	Electricity (quarter to 28 February 20X1)	340
6.6.20X1	Electricity (quarter to 31 May 20X1)	321

Calculate the electricity and insurance expenses for the year ended 30 June 20X1.

FURTHER EXAMPLE: ACCRUALS

Suppose that Willie Woggle opens a shop on 1 May 20X1 to sell hiking and camping equipment. The rent of the shop is £12,000 per annum, payable quarterly in arrears (with the first payment on 31 July 20X1). Willie decides that his accounting period should end on 31 December each year.

The rent account as at 31 December 20X1 will record only two rental payments (on 31 July and 31 October) and there will be two months' accrued rental expenses for November and December 20X1 (£2,000) since the next rental payment is not due until 31 January 20X2. Since the charge to the P&L account for the period to 31 December 20X1 will be for 8 months' rent (May-December inclusive), it follows that the total rental cost should be £8,000.

So far, the rent account appears as follows.

RENT ACCOUNT

		£			£
20X1			*20X1*		
31 Jul	Cash	3,000			
31 Oct	Cash	3,000	31 Dec	P&L account	8,000

BPP LEARNING MEDIA

NOTES

To complete the picture, the accruals of £2,000 have to be put in, not only to balance the account, but also to have an opening balance of £2,000 ready for next year. So the accrued rent of £2,000 is debited to the rent account as a balance to be carried down, and credited to the rent account as a balance brought down.

RENT ACCOUNT

		£			£
20X1			*20X1*		
31 Jul	Cash	3,000			
31 Oct	Cash*	3,000	31 Dec	P&L account	8,000
31 Dec	Balance c/d (accruals)	2,000			8,000
		8,000			
			20X2		
			1 Jan	Balance b/d	2,000

* The corresponding credit entry would be cash if rent is paid without the need for an invoice – eg with payment by standing order or direct debit at the bank. If there is always an invoice where rent becomes payable, the double entry would be:

DEBIT	Rent account	£2,000	
CREDIT	Creditors		£2,000

Then when the rent is paid, the ledger entries would be:

DEBIT	Creditors	£2,000	
CREDIT	Cash		£2,000

The rent account for the *next* year to 31 December 20X2, assuming no increase in rent in that year, would be as follows.

RENT ACCOUNT

		£			£
20X2			*20X2*		
31 Jan	Cash	3,000	1 Jan	Balance b/d	2,000
30 Apr	Cash	3,000			
31 Jul	Cash	3,000			
31 Oct	Cash	3,000			
31 Dec	Balance c/d (accruals)	2,000	31 Dec	P&L account	12,000
		14,000			14,000
			20X3		
			1 Jan	Balance b/d	2,000

Here, you will see that for a full year, a full 12 months' rental charges are taken as an expense to the P&L account.

Activity 3 **(5 minutes)**

At 1 January 20X1, the accounts of John Smith showed accrued rent payable of £500. During the year, he pays rent bills totalling £2,550, including one bill for £750 in respect of the quarter ending 31 January 20X2.

What is the profit and loss charge for rent for the year ended 31 December 20X1?

BPP LEARNING MEDIA

NOTES

FURTHER EXAMPLE: PREPAYMENTS

Prepayments are expenses which have been paid in advance (or for which an invoice demanding payment has been received) but which relate to a future accounting period, and so should be an expense in the P&L account of that future period.

Suppose that Terry Trunk commences business as a landscape gardener on 1 September 20X0. He immediately decides to join his local trade association, the Confederation of Luton Gardeners, for which the annual membership subscription is £180, payable annually in advance. He paid this amount on 1 September. Terry decides that his account period should end on 30 June each year.

In the first period to 30 June 20X1 (10 months), a full year's membership will have been paid, but only ten twelfths of the subscription should be charged to the period (ie 10/12 × £180 = £150). There is a prepayment of two months of membership subscription ie 2/12 × £180 = £30. It is therefore necessary to recognise the prepayment in the ledger account for subscriptions. This is done in much the same way as accounting for accruals, by using the balance carried down/brought down technique.

DEBIT	Subscriptions account with the same balance b/d	£30
CREDIT	Subscription with prepayment as a balance c/d	£30

The remaining expenses in the subscriptions account should then be taken to the P&L account. The balance on the account (ie the prepayment) will appear as a current asset (prepaid subscriptions) in the balance sheet as at 30 June 20X1.

SUBSCRIPTIONS ACCOUNT

		£			£
20X0			*20X1*		
1 Sep	Cash	180	30 Jun	P&L account	150
			30 Jun	Balance c/d (prepayment)	30
		180			180
20X1					
1 Jul	Balance b/d	30			

The subscriptions account for the next year, assuming no increase in the annual charge and that Terry Trunk remains a member of the association, will be:

SUBSCRIPTIONS ACCOUNT

		£			£
20X1			*20X2*		
1 Jul	Balance b/d	30	30 Jun	P&L account	180
1 Sept	Cash	180	30 Jun	Balance c/d (prepayment)	30
		210			210
20X2					
1 Jul	Balance b/d	30			

Again, we see that for a full accounting year, the charge to the P&L account is for a full year's subscriptions.

3 BAD AND DOUBTFUL DEBTS

3.1 Bad debts

Customers who buy goods on credit might fail to pay for them, perhaps out of dishonesty or perhaps because they have gone bankrupt and cannot pay. Customers in another country might be prevented from paying by the unexpected introduction of foreign exchange control restrictions by their country's government during the credit period. For one reason or another, a business might decide to give up expecting payment and to write the debt off as a 'lost cause'.

Definition

> A **bad debt** is a debt which a business finds it impossible to collect from the customer.

3.2 Accounting treatment

When a business decides that a particular debt is unlikely ever to be repaid, the amount of the debt should be 'written off' as an expense in the profit and loss account. For example, if Alfred's Mini-Cab Service sends an invoice for £300 to a customer who subsequently does a 'moonlight flit' from his office premises, never to be seen or heard of again, the debt of £300 must be written off. It might seem sensible to record the business transaction as:

Sales £(300 – 300) = £0.

However, bad debts written off are accounted for as follows.

(a) Sales continue to be shown at their invoice value in the trading account. The fact that a debt has gone 'bad' has no effect whatsoever on sales.

(b) The bad debt written off is shown as an expense in the profit and loss account.

(c) The debtors account in the balance sheet is reduced by the amount of bad debt written off, ie the debtors in the balance sheet is shown net of bad debts.

3.3 Bad debts written off and subsequently paid

A bad debt which has been written off might occasionally be unexpectedly paid. The only accounting problem to consider is when a debt written off as bad in one accounting period is subsequently paid in a later accounting period.

The amount paid should be recorded as additional income in the profit and loss account of the period in which the payment is received. For example, a trading, profit and loss account for the Blacksmith's Forge for the year to 31 December 20X1 could be prepared as shown below from the following information.

	£
Stocks of goods in hand, 1 January 20X1	6,000
Purchases of goods	122,000
Stocks of goods in hand, 31 December 20X1	8,000
Cash sales	100,000
Credit sales	70,000
Discounts allowed	1,200
Discounts received	5,000
Bad debts written off	9,000
Debts paid in 20X1 which were previously written off as bad in 20X0	2,000
Other expenses	31,800

BLACKSMITH'S FORGE
TRADING, PROFIT AND LOSS ACCOUNT FOR THE YEAR ENDED 31.12.20X1

	£	£
Sales		170,000
Opening stock	6,000	
Purchases	122,000	
	128,000	
Less closing stock	8,000	
Cost of goods sold		120,000
Gross profit		50,000
Add: discounts received		5,000
Debts paid, previously written off as bad		2,000
		57,000
Expenses		
Discounts allowed	1,200	
Bad debts written off	9,000	
Other expenses	31,800	
		42,000
Net profit		15,000

Whether or not a business actually incurs a bad debt, it always faces the possibility that some of its customers may not pay. This possibility is reflected in the accounting records by means of a provision for doubtful debts.

3.4 A provision for doubtful debts

When bad debts are written off, specific debts owed to the business are identified as unlikely ever to be collected. However, because of the risks involved in selling goods on credit, it might be accepted that a certain percentage of outstanding debts at any time are unlikely to be collected. But although it might be estimated that, say, 5% of debts will turn out bad, the business will not know until later which specific debts are bad.

Definition

The **provision for doubtful debts** shows the estimated portion of the debts which is unlikely to be collected.

The following information is available for Niel's Hardware Store after the first year of operation to 30 June 20X1.

	£
Credit sales during the year	300,000
Add debtors at 1 July 20X0	0
Total debts owed to the business	300,000
Less cash received from credit customers	244,000
	56,000
Less bad debts written off	6,000
Debtors outstanding at 30 June 20X1	50,000

Now, some of these outstanding debts might turn out to be bad. The business does not know on 30 June 20X1 which specific debts in the total £50,000 owed will be bad, but it might guess (from experience perhaps) that 5% of debts will eventually be found to be bad.

When a business expects bad debts amongst its current debtors, but does not yet know which specific debts will be bad, it can make a provision for doubtful debts. A 'provision' is a 'providing for' and so a provision for doubtful debts provides for future bad debts, as a prudent precaution by the business.

(a) When a provision is first made

Profit and loss account	*Balance sheet*
Initial provision charged as expense	Initial provision shown as a reduction from debtors in the current asset section
Example A 5% provision in the above example would lead to an expense of £2,500 being shown in the P&L for the year ending 30 June 20X1	*Example* Debtors 50,000 less: doubtful debts 2,500 47,500

(b) An existing provision is increased

Profit and loss account	*Balance sheet*
The amount of the increase in provision is charged as expense to the P&L	The new higher total of the provision is shown as a deduction from debtors

Example

Assume no change is debtors balance of £50,000; provision is increased from 5% to 7% for the year ending 30 June 20X2

Charged as expense to P&L for the year ending 30 June 20X2: £1,000		Balance sheet as at 30 June 20X2	
Calculation	£		£
		Debtors	50,000
		less: doubtful debts	3,500
New total provision	3,500 (7% × 50,000)	Balance sheet value	46,500
Existing provision	2,500		
Amount of increase	1,000		

(c) An existing provision is decreased

Profit and loss account	*Balance sheet*
The amount of decrease in the provision is recorded as an item of 'income' in the P&L	The new reduced total is shown as a deduction from debtors

NOTES

EXAMPLE: PROVISION FOR DOUBTFUL DEBTS

Corin Flakes owns and runs the Aerobic Health Foods Shop in Dundee. He commenced trading on 1 January 20X1, selling health foods to customers, most of whom make use of a credit facility that Corin offers. (Customers are allowed to purchase up to £200 of goods on credit but must repay a certain proportion of their outstanding debt every month.)

This credit system gives rise to a large number of bad debts, and Corin Flake's results for his first three years of operations are as follows.

Year to 31 December 20X1

Gross profit	£27,000
Bad debts written off	£8,000
Debts owed by customers as at 31 December 20X1	£40,000
Provision for doubtful debts	2½ % of outstanding debtors
Other expenses	£20,000

Year to 31 December 20X2

Gross profit	£45,000
Bad debts written off	£10,000
Debts owed by customers as at 31 December 20X2	£50,000
Provision for doubtful debts	2½ % of outstanding debtors
Other expenses	£28,750

Year to 31 December 20X3

Gross profit	£60,000
Bad debts written off	£11,000
Debts owed by customers as at 31 December 20X3	£30,000
Provision for doubtful debts	3% of outstanding debtors
Other expenses	£32,850

For each of these three years we would prepare the profit and loss account of the business, and state the value of debtors appearing in the balance sheet as at 31 December as follows.

AEROBIC HEALTH FOODS SHOP
PROFIT AND LOSS ACCOUNTS FOR THE YEARS ENDED 31 DECEMBER

	20X1		*20X2*		*20X3*	
	£	£	£	£	£	£
Gross profit		27,000		45,000		60,000
Sundry income:						
Reduction in						
provision for doubtful debts*						350
						60,350
Expenses:						
Bad debts written off	8,000		10,000		11,000	
Increase in provision						
for doubtful debts*	1,000		250		-	
Other expenses	20,000		28,750		32,850	
		29,000		39,000		43,850
Net (loss)/profit		(2,000)		6,000		16,500

* At 1 January 20X1 when Corin began trading the provision for doubtful debts was nil. At 31 December 20X1 the provision required was 2.5% of £40,000 = £1,000. The increase in the provision is therefore £1,000.

BPP LEARNING MEDIA

At 31 December 20X2 the provision required was 2.5% of £50,000 = £1,250. The provision must therefore be increased by £250. At 31 December 20X3 the provision required is 3% × £30,000 = £900. The 20X2 provision is therefore reduced by £350.

VALUE OF DEBTORS IN THE BALANCE SHEET

	As at 31.12.20X1	*As at 31.12.20X2*	*As at 31.12.20X3*
	£	£	£
Total value of debtors	40,000	50,000	30,000
Less provision for doubtful debts	1,000	1,250	900
Balance sheet value	39,000	48,750	29,100

Activity 4 **(5 minutes)**

At 31 December 20X0, the ledger of X included a £1,270 provision for doubtful debts. During 20X1, bad debts of £680 were written off. Debtors balances at 31 December 20X1 totalled £60,500 and X wished to carry forward a general provision of 2%. Which of the following is the charge for bad and doubtful debts in the profit and loss account for 20X1?

(a) £620
(b) £740
(c) £1,800
(d) £1,890

3.5 Bad debts written off: ledger accounting entries

For bad debts written off, there is a bad debts account. The double-entry bookkeeping is fairly straightforward, but there are two separate transactions to record.

(a) *When it is decided that a particular debt will not be paid*

DEBIT Bad debts account (expense)
CREDIT Debtors account

(b) *At the end of the accounting period*

At the end of the year, the balance on the bad debts account is transferred to the P&L ledger account (like all other expense accounts):

DEBIT P&L account
CREDIT Bad debts account

EXAMPLE: BAD DEBTS WRITTEN OFF

At 1 October 20X0 a business had total outstanding debts of £8,600. During the year to 30 September 20X1:

(a) Credit sales amounted to £44,000
(b) Payments from various debtors amounted to £49,000

NOTES

(c) Two debts, for £180 and £420, were declared bad and the customers are no longer purchasing goods from the company. These are to be written off.

The debtors account and the bad debts account for the year will be as follows.

DEBTORS

	£		£
Opening balance b/f	8,600	Cash	49,000
Sales	44,000	Bad debts	180
		Bad debts	420
		Closing balance c/d	3,000
	52,600		52,600
Opening balance b/d	3,000		

BAD DEBTS

	£		£
Debtors	180	P&L a/c	600
Debtors	420		
	600		600

In the sales ledger, personal accounts of the customers whose debts are bad will be taken off the ledger. The business should then take steps to ensure that it does not sell goods on credit to those customers again.

The accounting entries for doubtful debts are different from those for bad debts.

3.6 Provision for doubtful debts: ledger accounting entries

A provision for doubtful debts is rather different. A business might know from past experience that, say, 2% of debtors' balances are unlikely to be collected. It would then be considered prudent to make a general provision of 2%. It may be that no particular customers are regarded as suspect and so it is not possible to write off any individual customer balances as bad debts. The procedure is then to leave the total debtors balances completely untouched, but to open up a provision account by the following entries.

DEBIT Doubtful debts account (expense)
CREDIT Provision for doubtful debts

When preparing a balance sheet, the credit balance on the provision account is deducted from the total debit balances in the debtors ledger.

In subsequent years, adjustments may be needed to the amount of the provision. The procedure to be followed then is:

(a) Calculate the new provision required

(b) Compare it with the existing balance on the provision account (ie the balance b/f from the previous accounting period)

(c) Calculate increase or decrease required.

 (i) *If a higher provision is required:*

 DEBIT P&L account
 CREDIT Provision for doubtful debts

 with the amount of the increase.

BPP LEARNING MEDIA

NOTES

(ii) *If a lower provision than before is needed:*

DEBIT	Provision for doubtful debts
CREDIT	P&L account

with the amount of the decrease.

Activity 5 **(5 minutes)**

Select the appropriate option to complete the following sentence. A decrease in the provision for doubtful debts would result in:

(a) an increase in liabilities
(b) a decrease in net assets
(c) a decrease in net profits
(d) an increase in net profits

EXAMPLE: ACCOUNTING ENTRIES FOR PROVISION FOR DOUBTFUL DEBTS

Alex Gullible has total debtors' balances outstanding at 31 December 20X0 of £28,000. He believes that about 1% of these balances will not be collected and wishes to make an appropriate provision. Before now, he has not made any provision for doubtful debts at all.

On 31 December 20X1 his debtors balances amount to £40,000. His experience during the year has convinced him that a provision of 5% should be made.

Let us consider what accounting entries Alex should make on 31 December 20X0 and 31 December 20X1, and what figures for debtors will appear in his balance sheets as at those dates.

At 31 December 20X0

Provision required = 1% × £28,000 = £280

Alex will make the following entry.

DEBIT	P&L account (doubtful debts expense)	£280	
CREDIT	Provision for doubtful debts		£280

In the balance sheet debtors will appear as follows under current assets.

	£
Sales ledger balances	28,000
Less provision for doubtful debts	280
	27,720

At 31 December 20X1

Following the procedure described above, Alex will calculate the provision as follows.

	£
Provision required now (5% × £40,000)	2,000
Existing provision	(280)
∴ Additional provision required	1,720

NOTES

He will now make the following entry:

DEBIT	P&L account (doubtful debts)	£1,720	
CREDIT	Provision for doubtful debts		£1,720

The provision account will by now appear as follows.

PROVISION FOR DOUBTFUL DEBTS

		£			£
20X0			*20X0*		
31 Dec	Balance c/d	280	31 Dec	P&L account	280
20X1			*20X1*		
31 Dec	Balance c/d	2,000	1 Jan	Balance b/d	280
			31 Dec	P&L account	1,720
		2,000			2,000
			20X2		
			1 Jan	Balance b/d	2,000

For the balance sheet at 31 December 20X1, debtors will be valued as follows.

	£
Sales ledger balances	40,000
Less provision for doubtful debts	2,000
	38,000

In practice, it is unnecessary to show the total debtors balances and the provision as separate items in the balance sheet. A balance sheet would normally show only the net figure (£27,720 in 20X0, £38,000 in 20X1). However, it might be good practice at this stage in your studies to show the provision in the balance sheet.

4 DEPRECIATION

4.1 Definition

A fixed asset is acquired for use within a business with a view to earning profits. Its life extends over more than one accounting period, and so it earns profits over more than one period. With the exception of land, every fixed asset eventually wears out over time. Machines, cars and other vehicles, fixtures and fittings, and even buildings do not last for ever. When a business acquires a fixed asset, it will have some idea about how long its useful life will be, and it might decide either to:

(a) Keep on using the fixed asset until it becomes completely worn out, useless, and worthless; or

(b) Sell off the fixed asset at the end of its useful life, either by selling it as a second-hand item or as scrap.

Since a fixed asset has a cost and a limited useful life, and its value eventually declines, it follows that a charge should be made in the trading, profit and loss account to reflect the use that is made of the asset by the business.

BPP LEARNING MEDIA

Definition

> **Depreciation** (depreciation expense) is the allocation of the cost of a fixed asset to trading, profit and loss account over the estimated useful life of the asset.

Suppose that a business buys a machine for £40,000. Its expected life is four years, and at the end of that time it is expected to be worthless.

Since the fixed asset is used to make profits for four years, it would be reasonable to charge the cost of the asset over those four years (perhaps by charging £10,000 per annum) so that at the end of the four years the total cost of £40,000 would have been charged against profits. The key points to remember about the definition for depreciation are as follows.

(a) Depreciation is a measure of the wearing out or depletion of a fixed asset through use, time or obsolescence.

(b) Depreciation charges should be spread fairly over a fixed asset's life, and so allocated to the accounting periods which are expected to benefit (ie make profits) from the asset's use.

The total charge for depreciation: the depreciable amount

The total amount to be charged over the life of a fixed asset ('the depreciable amount') is usually:

Cost less residual value

Residual value is the value a business expects to receive at the end of the useful life of the asset by selling or trading-in the asset. It is also sometimes referred to as **salvage value** or **scrap value**.

EXAMPLES

(a) A fixed asset costing £20,000 which has an expected life of five years and an expected residual value of nil would have the depreciable amount of £20,000.

(b) A fixed asset costing £20,000 which has an expected life of five years and an expected residual value of £3,000 should be depreciated by £17,000 in total over the five year period.

4.2 Accounting for depreciation

When a fixed asset is depreciated, two things must be accounted for.

(a) The depreciation charge which is an expense of the period and hence is charged to the profit and loss account.

(b) The wearing out and lowering in value of the fixed asset. Therefore, the value of the fixed asset in the balance sheet must be reduced by the amount of depreciation charged.

The depreciation charge, calculated for each accounting period during the life of an asset, is accounted for like any other business expense.

EXAMPLE: DEPRECIATION

Let us assume that Jo McGowan bought a used car on 1 January 20X0 for £1,200 cash. She planned to use it for four years while she attended university. Jo does not expect the car to have any salvage value after four years.

With a depreciable amount of £1,200 (1,200 – 0) and a useful life of four years, the depreciation expense would be £300 (1,200 ÷ 4) per year.

The accounting entry would be as follows.

(a) The debit is to the depreciation expense account.

DEPRECIATION EXPENSE

	£		
31 Dec 20X0	300		

At the end of the accounting period, the depreciation expense will be transferred to the profit and loss account.

The credit is not as straightforward. You may think the credit should be to the 'automobile' or 'motor vehicle' account since depreciation represents a reduction in value of the fixed asset. While remaining faithful to the idea that the value of the fixed asset should be reduced by the amount of depreciation, accounting practice requires that the credit should not be to the asset account (in this case, 'automobile' or 'motor vehicle' account) but to a provision for depreciation account.

PROVISION FOR DEPRECIATION

	£		£
		31 Dec 20X0	300

At the year end, the balance in the provision for depreciation will be brought forward as the opening balance for next year. This is because the provision account is used to accumulate the depreciation on the asset and the account will continue to do so as long as the particular asset is being depreciated. Only when the asset is disposed of, will the related provision for depreciation account be 'closed'.

Continuing with Jo McGowan's example will help to understand this point.

(b) Entries at year-end 20X0

DEPRECIATION EXPENSE

	£		£
31 Dec 20X0 Provision for dep'n	300	31 Dec 20X0 Profit & Loss	300

PROVISION FOR DEPRECIATION

	£		£
31 Dec 20X0 Bal c/d	300	31 Dec 20X0 Dep'n expense	300
		1 Jan 20X1 Bal b/d	300

(c) Entries at year-end 20X1

The depreciation expense for 20X1 is also £300.

DEPRECIATION EXPENSE

	£		£
31 Dec 20X1 Provision for dep'n	300	31 Dec 20X1 Profit & loss	300

PROVISION FOR DEPRECIATION

	£		£
31 Dec 20X1 Bal c/d	600	1 Jan 20X1 Bal b/d	300
		31 Dec 20X1 Dep'n expense	300
	600		600
		1 Jan 20X2 Bal b/d	600

While the depreciation expense account shows only the depreciation charge for the year, the provision account shows the total depreciation charged on that asset since its acquisition by the business. Depreciation will continue to be credited to the provision account until the asset is completely written off or disposed of.

In Jo's example, depreciation will be charged for another two years (20X2 and 20X3) at which time the total depreciation shown by the provision account will be £1,200. Even though the asset would be completely depreciated by the end of 20X3 and no more depreciation will be charged, the provision for depreciation account will stay on the accounting books, as pointed out earlier, until the car is disposed of. The fact that an asset is fully depreciated does not mean that a business stops using the asset. A business can continue to use an asset as long as it deems fit. So long as the asset is being used by the business, the provision account for that asset will stay on the books.

As for the fixed asset account, it continues to show the asset at cost. Fixed asset accounts are unaffected by depreciation. Thus, in Jo's example, the motor vehicle account will appear as follows.

MOTOR VEHICLE

	£		£
1 Jan 20X0 Cash	1,200	31 Dec 20X0 Bal c/d	1,200
1 Jan 20X1 Bal b/d	1,200	31 Dec 20X1 Bal c/d	1,200
1 Jan 20X2 Bal b/d	1,200		

At year-end 20X3, the car would finish its expected useful life of four years. However, just like the provision for depreciation account, until the fixed asset is sold off or scrapped, it will remain in the ledger, showing the asset at cost.

If the fixed asset account is not reduced by depreciation expense in the ledger, how is the reduction in value of the fixed asset reflected?

The answer is very simple. It is done in the balance sheet. In the balance sheet, the fixed assets are shown at their **net book value** (NBV) which is defined as:

Cost *less* accumulated depreciation

Accumulated depreciation is the total depreciation that has been charged on an asset since the asset was acquired by the business. Depreciation is accumulated by the provision for depreciation account.

NOTES

Thus, another way to look at net book value is:

Cost *less* provision for depreciation

In Jo McGowan's example the car would appear in the balance sheet as follows.

MOTOR VEHICLE

	Cost	*Accumulated depreciation*	*NBV*
	£	£	£
At year end 20X0	1,200	300	900
At year end 20X1	1,200	600	600
At year end 20X2	1,200	900	300
At year end 20X3	1,200	1,200	0

Thus, we see that the value of the fixed asset is reduced in every accounting period by the amount of depreciation. The key thing to remember is that the reduction takes place indirectly through the provision account.

If Jo continues to use the car in 20X4 and beyond, the balance sheet in each of those years will continue to show the motor vehicle as a fixed asset with zero net book value. Only when the fixed asset is disposed of will it stop being listed on the balance sheet.

To summarise:

(a) There is a separate provision for depreciation account for each category of fixed asset, for example, plant and machinery, land and buildings, fixtures and fittings etc.

(b) The depreciation charge for an accounting period is a charge against profit. It is accounted for as follows:

DEBIT P&L account (depreciation expense)
CREDIT Provision for depreciation account

with the depreciation charge for the period.

(c) The balance on the provision for depreciation account is the total accumulated depreciation. This is always a credit balance brought forward in the provision for depreciation account.

(d) The fixed asset accounts are unaffected by depreciation. Fixed assets are recorded in these accounts at cost.

(e) In the balance sheet of the business, the total balance on the provision for depreciation account (ie accumulated depreciation) is subtracted from the value of fixed asset accounts (ie fixed assets at cost) to derive the net book value of the fixed assets.

While the accounting treatment of depreciation expense is always the same, there are several methods to calculate the expense itself.

BPP LEARNING MEDIA

NOTES

4.3 Methods of depreciation

There are several different methods of depreciation. The three methods covered in this Course Book are:

(a) The straight-line method;
(b) The reducing balance method; and
(c) The machine hour method (sometimes called the units of output method).

4.4 The straight-line method

This is the technical name of the method of depreciation we have used so far. It is the most commonly used method of all. The total depreciable amount is charged in equal instalments to each accounting period over the expected useful life of the asset. (In this way, the net book value of the fixed asset declines at a steady rate, or in a 'straight line' over time.)

The formula for the annual depreciation charge is as follows.

$$\frac{\text{Cost of asset minus residual value}}{\text{Expected useful life of the asset}}$$

The depreciation charge on an asset is the same each year.

EXAMPLE: STRAIGHT-LINE DEPRECIATION

(a) A fixed asset costing £20,000 with an estimated life of 10 years and no residual value would be depreciated at the rate of:

$$\frac{\pounds 20{,}000}{10 \text{ years}} = \pounds 2{,}000 \text{ per annum}$$

(b) A fixed asset costing £60,000 has an estimated life of five years and a residual value of £7,000. The annual depreciation charge using the straight line method would be:

$$\frac{\pounds(60{,}000 - 7{,}000)}{5 \text{ years}} = \pounds 10{,}600 \text{ per annum}$$

The net book value of the fixed asset would be:

	After 1 year	*After 2 years*	*After 3 years*	*After 4 years*	*After 5 years*
	£	£	£	£	£
Cost of the asset	60,000	60,000	60,000	60,000	60,000
Accumulated depreciation	10,600	21,200	31,800	42,400	53,000
Net book value	49,400	38,800	28,200	17,600	7,000*

* ie its estimated residual value.

Since the depreciation charge per annum is the same amount every year with the straight line method, it is often convenient to state that depreciation is charged at the rate of x per cent per annum on the cost of the asset. In the example in '(a)' above, the depreciation charge per annum is 10% of cost (ie 10% of £20,000 = £2,000).

The straight line method of depreciation is a fair allocation of the total depreciable amount between the different accounting periods, provided that it is reasonable to assume that the business enjoys equal benefits from the use of the asset in every period throughout its life.

NOTES

Activity 6 **(5 minutes)**

Can you name two assets which are likely to be depleted or worn out on a constant basis?

4.5 Assets acquired in the middle of an accounting period

A business can purchase new fixed assets at any time during the course of an accounting period. It might therefore seem fair to charge an amount for depreciation in the period when the purchase occurs. This will then reflect the limited amount of use the business has had from the asset in that period.

Suppose that a business which has an accounting year which runs from 1 January to 31 December purchases a new fixed asset on 1 April 20X0, at a cost of £24,000. The expected life of the asset is four years, and its residual value is nil. What should be the depreciation charge for 20X0?

The annual depreciation charge will be $\frac{\text{£24,000}}{\text{4 years}} = \text{£6,000 per annum}$

However, since the asset was acquired on 1 April 20X0, the business has only benefited from the use of the asset for 9 months instead of a full 12 months. It would therefore seem fair to charge depreciation in 20X0 of only:

$$\frac{9}{12} \times \text{£6,000} = \text{£4,500}$$

However, in practice, many businesses ignore the niceties of part-year depreciation, and charge a full year's depreciation on fixed assets in the year of their purchase (regardless of the point in time during the year at which they were acquired) and no depreciation in the year of sale/disposal of the asset.

4.6 The reducing balance method

The reducing balance method of depreciation calculates the annual depreciation charge as a fixed percentage of the net book value of the asset, as at the end of the previous accounting period. (This should not be confused with the straight-line method where annual depreciation charge is a fixed percentage of the cost of the asset.)

For example, suppose that a business purchases a fixed asset at a cost of £10,000. Its expected useful life is 3 years and its estimated residual value is £2,160. The business wishes to use the reducing balance method to depreciate the asset, and calculates that the rate of depreciation should be 40% of the reducing (net book) value of the asset. (The method of deciding that 40% is a suitable annual percentage is a problem of mathematics, not financial accounting, and is not described here.)

The total depreciable amount is £(10,000 – 2,160) = £7,840.

BPP LEARNING MEDIA

NOTES

The depreciation charge per annum and the net book value of the asset as at the end of each year will be as follows.

		Accumulated depreciation
	£	£
Asset at cost	10,000	
Depreciation in year 1 (40%)	4,000	4,000
Net book value at end of year 1	6,000	
Depreciation in year 2		6,400
(40% of reducing balance ie £6,000)	2,400	(4,000+2,400)
Net book value at end of year 2	3,600	
Depreciation in year 3 (40%)	1,440	7,840
		(6,400+1,440)
Net book value at end of year 3	2,160	

You should note that with the reducing balance method, the annual charge for depreciation is higher in the earlier years of the asset's life, and lower in the later years. In the example above, the annual charges for years 1, 2 and 3 are £4,000, £2,400 and £1,440 respectively (as compared to a constant charge per annum under straight line).

The reducing balance method might therefore be used when it is considered fair to allocate a greater proportion of the total depreciable amount to the earlier years and a lower proportion to later years, on the assumption that the benefits obtained by the business from using the asset decline over time.

Activity 7 **(5 minutes)**

In the above example (cost £10,000; residual value £2,160), what will be the depreciation charge under the straight line method?

4.7 The machine hour method of depreciation

As the name of this method implies, it is a method of depreciation which might be considered suitable for plant and machinery, where it is assumed that the fixed asset wears out through use rather than over time. Instead of calculating a depreciation charge relating to a period of time, depreciation is calculated according to the number of hours of use made of the machine by the business during the course of the period.

The life of the asset is estimated in hours (or miles or other conventional units) and each unit is given a money value for depreciation purposes. The rate of depreciation in a particular year is calculated as:

$$\frac{\text{Cost of asset minus estimated residual value}}{\text{Expected useful life of the asset in hours}} \times \text{Hours used that year}$$

EXAMPLE: THE MACHINE HOUR METHOD

A business purchases a machine at a cost of £45,000. Its estimated useful life is 8,000 hours of running time, and its estimated residual value is £5,000.

NOTES

The rate of depreciation by the machine hour method will be:

$$\frac{£(45{,}000 - 5{,}000)}{8{,}000 \text{ hours}} = £5 \text{ per machine hour}$$

Suppose that the actual use of the machine each year is:

	Hours
Year 1	3,000
Year 2	1,500
Year 3	2,500
Year 4	1,000
	8,000

We can calculate the annual depreciation charge and net book value of the machine as at the end of each year as follows.

Year	*Depreciation charge in the P&L account of the year*	*Accumulated depreciation as at end of the year*	*Fixed asset at cost*	*Net book value as at end of the year*
	£	£	£	£
Start of life			45,000	45,000
Year 1 (3,000 × £5)	15,000	15,000	45,000	30,000
Year 2 (1,500 × £5)	7,500	22,500	45,000	22,500
Year 3 (2,500 × £5)	12,500	35,000	45,000	10,000
Year 4 (1,000 × £5)	5,000	40,000	45,000	5,000
	40,000			

This method is sometimes modified so as to calculate each year's depreciation on the number of units produced by the machine in that year, rather than on the number of hours in which the machine is active. In this case the depreciation method is referred to as the units of output method.

4.8 Applying a depreciation method consistently

It is up to the business concerned to decide which method of depreciation to apply to its fixed assets. Once that decision has been made, however, it should not be changed – the chosen method of depreciation should be applied consistently from year to year. This is an instance of the consistency concept. This however does not mean that a business can never alter its depreciation method. A business can change its depreciation policy provided there are sound reasons for it. Similarly, it is up to the business to decide what a sensible life span for a fixed asset should be. Again, once that life span has been chosen, it should not be changed unless something unexpected happens to the fixed asset.

It is permissible for a business to depreciate different categories of fixed assets in different ways. For example, if a business owns three cars, then each car would normally be depreciated in the same way (eg by the straight line method) but another category of fixed asset, say, photocopiers, might be depreciated using a different method (eg by the machine hour method).

Regardless of the depreciation method chosen, changes in circumstances may require adjustments to the depreciation charge.

4.9 Changes to depreciation expense

(a) **A fall in the value of a fixed asset**

When the recoverable value of a fixed asset falls so that it is worth less than its net book value, the asset should be written down to its new low market value. The reduction in value should then be charged to the profit and loss account. This is known as an impairment.

	£
Net book value at the beginning of the period	X
Less: new reduced value	(X)
Equals: the charge to the P&L for reduction in the asset's value	X

EXAMPLE: FALL IN ASSET VALUE

A business purchases a building on 1 January 20X0 at a cost of £100,000. The building has a 20 year life. After five years' use, on 1 January 20X5, the business decides that since property prices have fallen sharply, the building is now worth only £60,000, and that the value of the asset should be reduced in the accounts of the business.

The building was being depreciated at the rate of 5% per annum on cost.

Before the asset is reduced in value, the annual depreciation charge is:

$$\frac{£100{,}000}{20 \text{ years}} = £5{,}000 \text{ per annum } (= 5\% \text{ of } £100{,}000)$$

After five years, the accumulated depreciation would be £25,000 (£5,000 × 5), and the net book value of the building £75,000, which is £15,000 more than the new asset value. This £15,000 should be written off as:

(i) a charge for depreciation; or

(ii) fall in the asset's value in year 5, so that the total charge in year 5 is:

	£
Net book value of the building after 4 years £(100,000-20,000)	80,000
Revised asset value at end of year 5	60,000
Charge against profit in year 5	20,000

An alternative method of calculation is:

	£
'Normal' depreciation charge per annum	5,000
Impairment charge	15,000
Charge against profit in year 5	20,000

The building has a further 15 years to run, and its value is now £60,000. From year 6 to year 20, the annual charge for depreciation will be:

$$\frac{£60{,}000}{15 \text{ years}} = £4{,}000 \text{ per annum}$$

NOTES

(b) **Change in expected life of an asset**

The depreciation charge on a fixed asset depends not only on the cost (or value) of the asset and its estimated residual value, but also on its estimated useful life.

Suppose, for example, that a business purchased a fixed asset costing £12,000 with an estimated life of four years and no residual value. If it used the straight line method of depreciation, it would make an annual provision of 25% of £12,000 = £3,000.

Now what would happen if the business decided after two years that the useful life of the asset has been underestimated, and it still had five more years in use to come (making its total life seven years)?

For the first two years, the asset would have been depreciated by £3,000 per annum, so that its net book value after two years would be £(12,000 – 6,000) = £6,000. If the remaining life of the asset is now revised to five more years, the remaining amount to be depreciated (here £6,000) should be spread over the remaining life. This would give an annual depreciation charge for the final five years of:

$$\frac{\text{Net book value at time of life readjustment, minus residual value}}{\text{New estimate of remaining useful life}}$$

$$= \frac{£60,000}{5 \text{ years}} = £1,200 \text{ per annum}$$

NOTES

Chapter roundup

- This chapter has illustrated how the amount of profit is calculated when:
  - There are opening or closing stocks of goods in hand
  - There is carriage inwards and/or carriage outwards
  - Stocks are written off or written down in value
  - There are accrued charges
  - There are prepayments of expenses.
- The cost of goods sold is calculated by adding the value of opening stock in hand to the cost of purchases and subtracting the value of closing stock.
- Accrued expenses are expenses which relate to an accounting period but have not yet been paid for. They are a charge against the profit for the period and are shown in the balance sheet as at the end of the period as a current liability.
- Prepayments are expenses which have already been paid but relate to a future accounting period. They are not charged against the profit of the current period and are shown in the balance sheet as at the end of the period as a current asset.
- Accruals and prepayments are aspects of the accruals concept which is one of the fundamental concepts in accounting (see later chapter).
- Bad debts written off are an expense in the profit and loss account.
- An increase in the provision for doubtful debts is an expense in the profit and loss account whereas a decrease in the provision for doubtful debts is shown as 'other income' in the P&L account.
- Debtors are valued in the balance sheet after deducting any provision for doubtful debts.
- Depreciation is the allocation of the cost of a fixed asset to trading, profit and loss account over its estimated useful life.
- The depreciation charge is an expense in the profit and loss account.
- The value of the fixed asset in the balance sheet is reduced by the amount of depreciation charged.
- Commonly used methods of depreciation are: the straight-line method; the reducing balance method; and the machine hour method.

Quick quiz

1 How is the cost of goods sold calculated?

2 Distinguish between carriage inwards and carriage outwards.

3 How is carriage inwards treated in the trading, profit and loss account?

4 Give three reasons why goods purchased might have to be written off.

5 If a business has paid rates of £1,000 for the year on 1 January 20X1, what is the prepayment in the accounts for the year to 31 March 20X1?

6 Define an accrual.

NOTES

7 Where are the prepayments reported in the financial statements?

8 If a doubtful debts provision is increased, what is the effect on the P&L account?

Answers to quick quiz

1 Opening stock plus purchases less closing stock and any other appropriate adjustments associated with stock. (see para 1)

2 Carriage inwards is the delivery cost of goods purchased, carriage outwards is the delivery cost of goods sold. (para 1.3)

3 Added to the cost of purchases. (para 1.3)

4 They may be lost or stolen, damaged or obsolete or out of fashion. (para 1.4)

5 £750 (3/4 × £1,000). (para 2.1)

6 An expense incurred by a business but which has not yet been paid for. (para 2.1)

7 Under current assets. (para 2.2)

8 The increase is included as an expense in the profit and loss account. (para 3.4)

Answers to activities

1 **GRAND UNION FOOD STORES**
TRADING ACCOUNT FOR THE YEAR ENDED 31 DECEMBER 20X0

	£	£
Sales		80,000
Opening stocks	6,000	
Add purchases	50,000	
	56,000	
Less closing stocks	12,500	
Cost of goods sold		43,500
Gross profit		36,500

2

	£
Electricity paid:	309
	320
	340
	321
Add closing accrual (321 × 1/3)	107
Less opening accrual	(80)
	1,317

3 £1,800.

John paid £2,550 of which £500 was applicable to the previous year. Therefore only £2,050 out of £2,550 was applicable to the year ended 31 December 20X1. However, £2,050 needs to be reduced by the amount applicable to the quarter ending 31 January 20X2, ie by one month's rent of £250 (1/3 × £750). The profit and loss charge is therefore £1,800 £(2,050 – 250).

NOTES

4 (a):£620

	£
Bad debts written off	680
Less: decrease in the provision for doubtful debts £1,270 – (2% × 60,500)	(60)
	620

5 (d): an increase in net profits because lowering the provision is a credit to the P&L account.

6 Assets likely to be worn out on a constant basis and which hence might be suitable for straight line depreciation are:

(a) furniture
(b) buildings
(c) fixtures and fittings.

7 $\frac{10,000 - 2,160}{3}$ = £2,613.33 per annum

Chapter 17 :

PREPARING ACCOUNTS FROM INCOMPLETE RECORDS

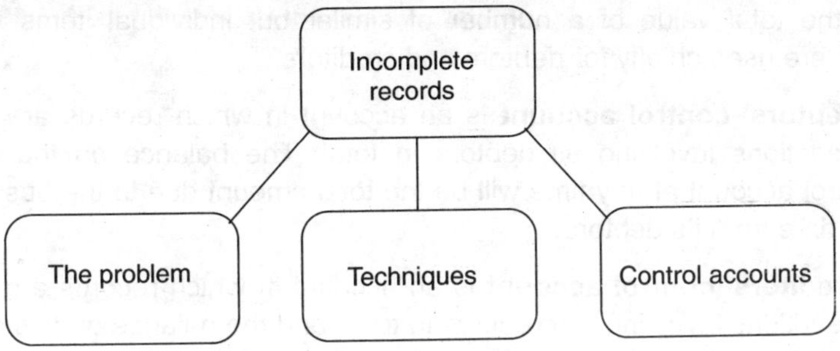

Introduction

Incomplete records problems occur when a business does not have a full set of accounting records. The problems can arise for two reasons.

(a) The proprietor of the business does not keep a full set of accounts, ie it has **limited accounting records.**

(b) Some of the business accounts are **accidentally lost or destroyed.**

However, as long as there is some basic information, it is often possible to reconstruct the accounting records and then from those draw up the accounts themselves.

There are several specific techniques which can be applied, depending on the availability of information.

Your objectives

In this chapter you will learn about the following.

(a) The use of control accounts

(b) The differences between limited and incomplete accounting records

(c) How to calculate the net asset position and the profit for a sole trader business which has incomplete accounting records

1 CONTROL ACCOUNTS

Control accounts are a useful tool if you have to write up accounts from incomplete records.

1.1 What are control accounts?

Definitions

A **control account** is an account in the nominal ledger in which a record is kept of the total value of a number of similar but individual items. Control accounts are used chiefly for debtors and creditors.

- A **debtors' control account** is an account in which records are kept of transactions involving all debtors in total. The balance on the debtors control account at any time will be the total amount due to the business at that time from its debtors.
- A **creditors' control account** is an account in which records are kept of transactions involving all creditors in total, and the balance on this account at any time will be the total amount owed by the business at that time to its creditors.

Although control accounts are used mainly in accounting for debtors and creditors, they can also be kept for other items, such as stocks of goods, wages and salaries. The first important idea to remember, however, is that a control account is an account which keeps a **total record for a collective item** (eg debtors) which in reality consists of many individual items (eg individual debtors).

A control account is an **(impersonal) ledger account** which will appear in the nominal ledger. Before we look at the reasons for having control accounts, we will first look at how they are made up.

1.2 Control accounts and personal accounts

The personal accounts of individual debtors are kept in the **sales ledger**, and the amount owed by each debtor will be a balance on his personal account. The amount owed by all the debtors together will be a balance on the **debtors control account**.

At any time the balance on the debtors control account should be **equal** to the sum of the individual balances on the personal accounts in the sales ledger.

EXAMPLE

For example, if a business has three debtors, H Duckworth who owes £200, T Carter who owes £450 and J Matthews who owes £320, the debit balances on the various accounts would be:

Sales ledger (personal accounts)

	£
H Duckworth	200
T Carter	450
J Matthews	320
Nominal ledger – debtors control account	970

What has happened here is that the three entries of £200, £450 and £320 were first entered into the sales day book. They were also recorded in the three personal accounts of Duckworth, Carter and Matthews in the sales ledger - but remember that this is not part of the double entry system.

Later, the **total** of £970 is posted from the sales day book into the debtors (control) account. It is fairly obvious that if you add up all the debit figures on the personal accounts, they also should total £970.

2 THE OPERATION OF CONTROL ACCOUNTS

2.1 Accounting for debtors

It will be useful first of all to see how transactions involving debtors are accounted for by means of an illustrative example. Folio numbers are shown in the accounts to illustrate the cross-referencing that is needed, and in the following example folio numbers beginning:

(a) SDB, refer to a page in the sales day book
(b) SL, refer to a particular account in the sales ledger
(c) NL, refer to a particular account in the nominal ledger
(d) CB, refer to a page in the cash book.

EXAMPLE: ACCOUNTING FOR DEBTORS

At 1 September 20X0, the Earthminder Garden Business had no debtors at all. During September, the following transactions affecting credit sales and customers occurred.

(a) Sept 3 Invoiced H Duckworth for the sale on credit of plants: £170

(b) Sept 11 Invoiced T Carter for the sale on credit of garden tools: £260

(c) Sept 15 Invoiced J Matthews for the sale on credit of plants: £330

(d) Sept 10 Received payment from H Duckworth of £150, in settlement of his debt in full, having taken a permitted discount of £20 for payment within seven days

(e) Sept 18 Received a payment of £108 from T Carter in part settlement of £120 of his debt. A discount of £12 was allowed for payment within seven days of invoice

(f) Sept 28 Received a payment of £200 from J Matthews, who was unable to claim any discount

Account numbers are as follows.

SL 028	Personal account: H Duckworth
SL 105	Personal account: T Carter
SL 017	Personal account: J Matthews
NL 200	Debtors control account
NL 207	Discounts allowed
NL 401	Sales: plants
NL 402	Sales: garden tools
NL 100	Cash control account

Required

Write up all the accounts listed above for the transactions which took place in September.

ANSWER

The accounting entries, suitably dated, would be as follows.

SALES DAY BOOK — SDB 090

Date	*Name*	*Folio*	*Total*	*Plants*	*Garden tools*
20X0			£	£	£
Sept 3	H Duckworth	SL 028 Dr	170.00	170.00	
11	T Carter	SL 105 Dr	260.00		260.00
15	J Matthews	SL 017 Dr	330.00	330.00	
			760.00	500.00	260.00
			NL 200 Dr	NL 401 Cr	NL 402 Cr

Note. The personal accounts in the sales ledger are debited on the day the invoices are sent out. The double entry in the ledger accounts might be made at the end of each day, week or month; here it is made at the end of the month, by posting from the sales day book as follows.

			£	£
DEBIT	NL 200	Debtors control account	760	
CREDIT	NL 401	Sales: plants		500
	NL 402	Sales: garden tools		260

CASH BOOK EXTRACT

RECEIPTS CASH BOOK: SEPTEMBER 20X0 — CB 079

Date	*Narrative*	*Folio*	*Total*	*Discount*	*Debtors*
20X0			£	£	£
Sept 10	H Duckworth	SL 028 Cr	150.00	20.00	170.00
18	T Carter	SL 105 Cr	108.00	12.00	120.00
28	J Matthews	SL 017 Cr	200.00	-	200.00
			458.00	32.00	490.00
			NL 100 Dr	NL 207 Dr	NL 200 Cr

The personal accounts in the sales ledger are memorandum accounts, because they are not a part of the double entry system.

Memorandum sales ledger

H DUCKWORTH — A/c no: SL 028

Date	*Narrative*	*Folio*	£	*Date*	*Narrative*	*Folio*	£
20X0				*20X0*			
Sept 3	Sales	SDB 090	170.00	Sept 10	Cash	CB 079	150.00
					Discount	CB 079	20.00
			170.00				170.00

NOTES

T CARTER — A/c no: SL 105

Date	Narrative	Folio	£	Date	Narrative	Folio	£
20X0				20X0			
Sept 11	Sales	SDB 090	260.00	Sept 18	Cash	CB 079	108.00
					Discount	CB 079	12.00
				Sept 30	Balance	c/d	140.00
			260.00				260.00
Oct 1	Balance	b/d	140.00				

J MATTHEWS — A/c no: SL 017

Date	Narrative	Folio	£	Date	Narrative	Folio	£
20X0				20X0			
Sept 15	Sales	SDB 090	330.00	Sept 28	Cash	CB 079	200.00
				Sept 30	Balance	c/d	130.00
			330.00				330.00
Oct 1	Balance	b/d	130.00				

In the nominal ledger, the accounting entries can be made from the books of prime entry to the ledger accounts, in this example at the end of the month.

Nominal ledger (extract)

TOTAL DEBTORS (SALES LEDGER CONTROL ACCOUNT) — A/c no: NL 200

Date	Narrative	Folio	£	Date	Narrative	Folio	£
20X0				20X0			
Sept 30	Sales	SDB 090	760.00	Sept 30	Cash and discount	CB 079	490.00
				Sept 30	Balance	c/d	270.00
			760.00				760.00
Oct 1	Balance	b/d	270.00				

Note. At 30 September the closing balance on the debtors control account (£270) is the same as the total of the individual balances on the personal accounts in the sales ledger (£0 + £140 + £130).

DISCOUNT ALLOWED — A/c no: NL 207

Date	Narrative	Folio	£	Date	Narrative	Folio	£
20X0							
Sept 30	Debtors	CB 079	32.00				

CASH CONTROL ACCOUNT — A/c no: NL 100

Date	Narrative	Folio	£	Date	Narrative	Folio	£
20X0							
Sept 30	Cash received	CB 079	458.00				

SALES: PLANTS — A/c no: NL 401

Date	Narrative	Folio	£	Date	Narrative	Folio	£
				20X0			
				Sept 30	Debtors	SDB 090	500.00

SALES: GARDEN TOOLS — A/c no: NL 402

Date	Narrative	Folio	£	Date	Narrative	Folio	£
				20X0			
				Sept 30	Debtors	SDB 090	260.00

If we took the balance on the accounts shown in the above example as at 30 September 20X0 the trial balance (insofar as it is appropriate to call these limited extracts by this name) would be as follows.

TRIAL BALANCE

	Debit	*Credit*
	£	£
Cash (all receipts)	458	
Debtors	270	
Discount allowed	32	
Sales: plants		500
Sales: garden tools		260
	760	760

The trial balance is shown here to emphasise the point that a trial balance **includes the balances on control accounts, but excludes the balances on the personal accounts** in the sales ledger and purchase ledger.

2.2 Accounting for creditors

If you were able to follow the example above dealing with the debtors control account, you should have no difficulty in dealing with similar examples relating to purchases/creditors. If necessary refer back to revise the entries made in the purchase day book and purchase ledger personal accounts.

2.3 Entries in control accounts

Typical entries in the control accounts are listed below. Folio reference Jnl indicates that the transaction is first lodged in the journal before posting to the control account and other accounts indicated. References SRDB and PRDB are to sales returns and purchase returns day books.

SALES LEDGER (DEBTORS) CONTROL

	Folio	£		*Folio*	£
Opening debit balances	b/d	7,000	Opening credit balances (if any)	b/d	200
Sales	SDB	52,390	Cash received	CB	52,250
Dishonoured bills or cheques	Jnl	1,000	Discounts allowed	CB	1,250
Cash paid to clear credit balances	CB	110	Returns inwards from debtors	SRDB	800
Closing credit balances	c/d	120	Bad debts	Jnl	300
			Closing debit balances	c/d	5,820
		60,620			60,620
Debit balances b/d		5,820	Credit balances b/d		120

Notes. Opening credit balances are unusual in the debtors control account. They represent debtors to whom the business owes money, probably as a result of the over payment of debts or for advance payments of debts for which no invoices have yet been sent.

NOTES

PURCHASES LEDGER (CREDITORS) CONTROL

	Folio	£		Folio	£
Opening debit balances (if any)	b/d	70	Opening credit balances	b/d	8,300
Cash paid	CB	29,840	Purchases and other expenses	PDB	31,000
Discounts received	CB	30	Cash received clearing debit balances	CB	20
Returns outwards to suppliers	PRDB	60	Closing debit balances (if any)	c/d	80
Closing credit balances	c/d	9,400			
		39,400			39,400
Debit balances	b/d	80	Credit balances	b/d	9,400

Note. Opening debit balances in the creditors control account would represent suppliers who owe the business money, perhaps because debts have been overpaid or because debts have been prepaid before the supplier has sent an invoice.

Posting from the journal to the memorandum sales or bought ledgers and to the nominal ledger may be effected as in the following example, where J Matthews has returned goods with a sales value of £100.

Journal entry	*Folio*	*Dr* £	*Cr* £
Sales	NL 401	100	
To debtors' control	NL 200		100
To J Matthews (memorandum)	SL 017	-	100

Return of electrical goods inwards

Activity 1 **(10 minutes)**

A creditors' control account contains the following entries:

	£
Bank	83,000
Credit purchases	86,700
Discounts received	4,130
Contra with debtors control account	5,200
Balance c/f at 31 December 20X0	13,700

There are no other entries in the account. What was the opening balance brought forward at 1 January 20X0?

BPP LEARNING MEDIA

NOTES

Activity 2 **(15 minutes)**

On examining the books of Archright Ltd, you ascertain that on 1 October 20X0 the debtors' ledger balances were £20,347 debit and £228 credit, and the creditors' ledger balances on the same date £18,024 credit and £319 debit.

For the year ended 30 September 20X1 the following particulars are available.

	£
Sales	176,429
Purchases	108,726
Cash received from debtors	148,481
Cash paid to creditors	95,184
Discount received	2,798
Discount allowed	5,273
Returns inwards	3,180
Returns outwards	1,417
Bad debts written off	1,079
Cash received in respect of debit balances in creditors' ledger	319
Amount due from customer as shown by debtors' ledger, offset against amount due to the same firm as shown by creditors' ledger (settlement by contra)	949
Allowances to customers on goods damaged in transit	553

On 30 September 20X1 there were no credit balances in the debtors' ledger except those outstanding on 1 October 20X0, and no debit balances in the creditors' ledger.

You are required to write up the following accounts recording the above transactions bringing down the balances as on 30 September 20X1:

(a) Debtors' control account; and
(b) Creditors' control account.

3 THE PURPOSE OF CONTROL ACCOUNTS

3.1 Accuracy check

Control accounts provide a **check on the accuracy of entries made in the personal accounts** in the sales ledger and purchase ledger. It is very easy to make a mistake in posting entries, because there might be hundreds of entries to make. Figures might get transposed. Some entries might be omitted altogether, so that an invoice or a payment transaction does not appear in a personal account as it should. By comparing:

(a) the total balance on the debtors control account with the total of individual balances on the personal accounts in the sales ledger; and

(b) the total balance on the creditors control account with the total of individual balances on the personal accounts in the purchase ledger;

it is possible to identify the fact that errors have been made.

3.2 Discovering errors

The control accounts could also assist in the **location of errors**, where postings to the control accounts are made daily or weekly, or even monthly. If a clerk fails to record an invoice or a payment in a personal account, or makes a transposition error, it would be a formidable task to locate the error or errors at the end of a year, say, given the hundreds or thousands of transactions during the year. By using the control account, a comparison with the individual balances in the sales or purchase ledger can be made for every week or day of the month, and the error found much more quickly than if control accounts did not exist.

3.3 Internal check

Where there is a separation of clerical (bookkeeping) duties, the control account provides an **internal check**. The person posting entries to the control accounts will act as a check on a different person whose job it is to post entries to the sales and purchase ledger accounts.

3.4 Provides a total balance

To provide debtors' and creditors' balances more quickly for producing a trial balance or balance sheet. A single balance on a control account is obviously **extracted more simply and quickly** than many individual balances in the sales or purchase ledger. This means also that the number of accounts in the double entry bookkeeping system can be kept down to a manageable size, since the personal accounts are memorandum accounts only and the control accounts instead provide the accounts required for a double entry system.

However, particularly in **computerised systems**, it may be feasible to use sales and purchase ledgers without the need for operating separate control accounts. In such a system, the sales or purchase ledger printouts produced by the computer constitute the list of individual balances as well as providing a total balance which represents the control account balance.

3.5 Balancing and agreeing control accounts with sales and purchase ledgers

The control accounts should be **balanced regularly** (at least monthly), and the balance on the account agreed with the sum of the individual debtors' or creditors' balances extracted from the sales or bought ledgers respectively. It is one of the sad facts of an accountant's life that more often than not the balance on the control account does not agree with the sum of balances extracted, for one or more of the following reasons.

(a) An **incorrect amount** may be **posted** to the control account because of a miscast of the total in the book of prime entry (ie adding up incorrectly the total value of invoices or payments). The nominal ledger debit and credit postings will then balance, but the control account balance will not agree with the sum of individual balances extracted from the (memorandum) sales ledger or purchase ledger. A journal entry must then be made in the nominal ledger to correct the control account and the corresponding sales or expense account.

(b) A **transposition** error may occur in posting an individual's balance from the book of prime entry to the memorandum ledger, eg the sale to J Matthews of £330 might be posted to his account as £303. This means that the sum of balances extracted from the memorandum ledger must be corrected. No accounting entry would be required to do this, except to alter the figure in J Matthews's account.

(c) A transaction may be recorded in the control account and not in the memorandum ledger, or vice versa. This requires an entry in the ledger that has been **missed out** which means a double posting if the control account has to be corrected, and a single posting if it is the individual's balance in the memorandum ledger that is at fault.

(d) The sum of balances extracted from the memorandum ledger may be **incorrectly extracted** or **miscast**. This would involve simply correcting the total of the balances.

Reconciling the control account balance with the sum of the balances extracted from the (memorandum) sales ledger or bought ledger should be done in two stages.

(a) Correct the total of the balances extracted from the memorandum ledger. (The errors must be located first of course.)

	£	£
Sales ledger total		
Original total extracted		15,320
Add difference arising from transposition error (£95 written as £59)		36
		15,356
Less		
Credit balance of £60 extracted as a debit balance (£60 × 2)	120	
Overcast of list of balances	90	
		210
		15,146

(b) Bring down the balance before adjustments on the control account, and adjust or post the account with correcting entries.

DEBTORS CONTROL

	£		£
Balance before adjustments	15,091	Petty cash: posting omitted	10
		Returns inwards: individual posting omitted from control account	35
Undercast of total invoices issued in sales day book	100	Balance c/d (now in agreement with the corrected total of individual balances in (a))	15,146
	15,191		15,191
Balance b/d	15,146		

4 THE PROBLEM

The problem is to **prepare a set of year-end accounts** for the business; a trading, profit and loss account, and a balance sheet. Since the business does not have a full set of accounts, preparing the final accounts is not a simple matter of closing off accounts and transferring balances to the trading, profit and loss account, or showing outstanding balances in the balance sheet. Preparing the final accounts involves the following tasks.

NOTES

(a) Establishing the cost of **purchases and other expenses**

(b) Establishing the total amount of **sales**

(c) Establishing the amount of **creditors, accruals, debtors and prepayments** at the end of the year

Questions may take incomplete records problems a stage further, by introducing an 'incident' such as fire or burglary which leaves the owner of the business uncertain about how much **stock has been destroyed or stolen.**

To understand what incomplete records are about, it will obviously be useful now to look at what exactly might be incomplete. We shall consider the following items in turn.

- The opening balance sheet
- Credit sales and debtors
- Purchases and trade creditors
- Purchases, stocks and the cost of sales
- Stolen goods or goods destroyed
- The cash book
- Accruals and prepayments
- Drawings (for a sole trader)

5 THE OPENING BALANCE SHEET

In practice there should not be any missing item in the opening balance sheet of the business, because it should be available from the preparation of the previous year's final accounts. However, a problem might provide information about the assets and liabilities of the business at the beginning of the period under review, but then leave the balancing figure unspecified. This **balancing figure** represents the opening balance of the proprietor's business capital.

EXAMPLE: OPENING BALANCE SHEET

For example, a business has the following assets and liabilities as at 1 January 20X0.

	£
Fixtures and fittings at cost	7,000
Provision for depreciation, fixtures and fittings	4,000
Motor vehicles at cost	12,000
Provision for depreciation, motor vehicles	6,800
Stock in trade	4,500
Trade debtors	5,200
Cash at bank and in hand	1,230
Trade creditors	3,700
Prepayment	450
Accrued rent	2,000

Required

Prepare a balance sheet for the business inserting a balancing figure for proprietor's capital.

ANSWER

The balance sheet of the business can be prepared and the balancing figure is the proprietor's capital at the balance sheet date.

BPP LEARNING MEDIA

	£	£
Fixtures and fittings at cost	7,000	
Less accumulated depreciation	4,000	
		3,000
Motor vehicles at cost	12,000	
Less accumulated depreciation	6,800	
		5,200
		8,200
Current assets		
Stock in trade	4,500	
Trade debtors	5,200	
Prepayment	450	
Cash	1,230	
	11,380	
Current liabilities		
Trade creditors	3,700	
Accrual	2,000	
	5,700	
Net current assets		5,680
		13,880
Capital		
Proprietor's capital as at 1.1.X0 (balancing figure)		13,880

The opening balance sheet should now provide some of the information needed to prepare the final accounts for the current period.

6 CREDIT SALES AND DEBTORS

If a business does not keep a record of its **sales on credit**, the value of these sales can be derived from the opening balance of trade debtors, the closing balance of trade debtors, and the payments received from trade debtors during the period.

6.1 Credit sales

Credit sales are calculated as follows.

Definition

	£
Credit sales	
Payments received from trade debtors	X
Plus closing balance of trade debtors (since these represent sales in the current period for which cash payment has not yet been received)	X
Less opening balance of trade debtors (unless these become bad debts, they will pay what they owe in the current period for sales in a previous period)	(X)
Credit sales during the period	X

For example, suppose that a business had trade debtors of £1,750 on 1 April 20X0 and trade debtors of £3,140 on 31 March 20X1. If payments received from trade debtors during the year to 31 March 20X1 were £28,490, and if there are no bad debts, then credit sales for the period would be as follows.

NOTES

	£
Cash received from debtors	28,490
Plus closing debtors	3,140
Less opening debtors	(1,750)
Credit sales during the period	29,880

If there are **bad debts** during the period, the value of sales will be increased by the amount of bad debts written off, no matter whether they relate to opening debtors or credit sales during the current period.

The same calculation could be made in a ledger account, with credit sales being the balancing figure to complete the account.

DEBTORS

	£		£
Opening balance b/f	1,750	Cash received	28,490
Credit sales (balancing figure)	29,880	Closing balance c/f	3,140
	31,630		31,630

The same interrelationship between credit sales, cash from debtors, and opening and closing debtors balances can be used to derive a missing figure for cash from debtors, or opening or closing debtors, given the values for the three other items. For example, if we know that opening debtors are £6,700, closing debtors are £3,200 and credit sales for the period are £69,400, then cash received from debtors during the period would be as follows.

DEBTORS

	£		£
Opening balance	6,700	Cash received (balancing figure)	72,900
Sales (on credit)	69,400	Closing balance c/f	3,200
	76,100		76,100

There is an alternative way of presenting the same calculation.

	£
Opening balance of debtors	6,700
Plus credit sales during the period	69,400
Total money owed to the business	76,100
Less closing balance of debtors	3,200
Equals cash received during the period	72,900

6.2 Control account

You may be asked to **reconcile control accounts** in an incomplete records question or assessment. You should also remember the complications which might arise in a sales ledger control account, which might include the following.

SALES LEDGER CONTROL ACCOUNT

	£		£
Opening debit balances	X	Opening credit balances (if any)	X
Sales	X	Cash received	X
Dishonoured bills or cheques	X	Discounts allowed	X
Cash paid to clear credit balances	X	Returns inwards	X
Bad debts recovered	X	Bad debts	X
Closing credit balances	X	Cash from bad debts recovered	X
		Contra with P/L control a/c	X
		Allowances on goods damaged	X
		Closing debit balances	X
	X		X

BPP LEARNING MEDIA

If you have to find a balancing figure in the sales ledger control account, you may have to consider all the above items.

Activity 3 **(10 minutes)**

A debtors control account contains the following entries:

	£
Balance b/f 1 January	42,800
Bank	204,000
Discounts allowed	16,250
Credit sales	240,200

Assuming there are no other entries into the account, what is the closing balance at 31 December?

7 PURCHASES AND TRADE CREDITORS

A similar relationship to that discussed above exists between **purchases of stock** during a period, the opening and closing balances for trade creditors, and amounts paid to trade creditors during the period.

If we wish to calculate an unknown amount for purchases, the amount would be derived as follows.

Definition

	£
Payments to trade creditors during the period	X
Plus closing balance of trade creditors (since these represent purchases in the current period for which payment has not yet been made)	X
Less opening balance of trade creditors (these debts, paid in the current period, relate to purchases in a previous period)	(X)
Purchases during the period	X

EXAMPLE

Suppose that a business had trade creditors of £3,728 on 1 October 20X0 and trade creditors of £2,645 on 30 September 20X1. If payments to trade creditors during the year to 30 September 20X1 were £31,479, then purchases during the year can be derived as follows.

	£
Payments to trade creditors	31,479
Plus closing balance of trade creditors	2,645
Less opening balance of trade creditors	(3,728)
Purchases	30,396

NOTES

The same calculation could be made in a ledger account, with purchases being the balancing figure to complete the account.

CREDITORS

	£		£
Cash payments	31,479	Opening balance b/f	3,728
Closing balance c/f	2,645	Purchases (balancing figure)	30,396
	34,124		34,124

7.1 Control account

Once again, various complications can arise in the purchase ledger control account which you may have to consider.

PURCHASE LEDGER CONTROL ACCOUNT

	£		£
Opening debit balances (if any)	X	Opening credit balances	X
Cash paid	X	Purchases and other expenses	X
Discounts received	X	Cash received clearing debit balances	X
Returns outwards	X	Closing debit balances	X
Contras with S/L control a/c	X		
Allowances on goods damaged	X		
Closing credit balances	X		
	X		X

8 PURCHASES, STOCKS AND COST OF SALES

8.1 Purchases

When the **value of purchases is not known**, a different approach might be required to find out what they were, depending on the nature of the information given to you.

One approach would be to use information about the cost of sales, and opening and closing stocks. This means that you would be using the **trading account** rather than the trade creditors account to find the cost of purchases.

Definition

		£
Since	opening stocks	X
	plus purchases	X
	less closing stocks	(X)
	equals the cost of goods sold	X
then	the cost of goods sold	X
	plus closing stocks	X
	less opening stocks	(X)
	equals purchases for the period	X

EXAMPLE

Suppose that the stock in trade of a business on 1 July 20X0 has a balance sheet value of £8,400, and a stock taking exercise at 30 June 20X1 showed stock to be valued at £9,350. Sales for the year to 30 June 20X1 are £80,000, and the business makes a mark up of $33^1/_3$% on cost for all the items that it sells. What were the purchases during the year?

ANSWER

The cost of goods sold can be derived from the value of sales, as follows.

		£
Sales	($133^1/_3$%)	80,000
Gross profit	($33^1/_3$%)	20,000
Cost of goods sold	(100%)	60,000

The cost of goods sold is 75% (100% ÷ $133^1/_3$%) of sales value.

	£
Cost of goods sold	60,000
Plus closing stock	9,350
Less opening stock	(8,400)
Purchases during the period	60,950

Activity 4 **(10 minutes)**

An extract from a company's trading account stood as follows for the year ended 31 March 20X0.

	£	£
Sales		150,000
Opening stock	12,000	
Purchases	114,500	
	126,500	
Closing stock	14,000	
		112,500

(a) Calculate the gross profit as a percentage of cost of sales.

(b) Calculate the gross profit as a percentage of sales.

8.2 Stolen goods or goods destroyed

A similar type of calculation might be required to derive the value of goods stolen or destroyed. An example will show how to determine the cost of an unknown quantity of goods lost.

EXAMPLE: STOCK LOST IN A FIRE

Fairmount Boutique is a shop which sells fashion clothes. On 1 January 20X0, it had stock in trade which cost £7,345. During the nine months to 30 September 20X0, the business purchased goods from suppliers costing £106,420. Sales during the same period were £154,000. The shop makes a mark-up of 40% on cost for everything it sells. On 30 September 20X0, there was a fire in the shop which destroyed most of the stock in it. Only a small amount of stock, known to have cost £350, was undamaged and still fit for sale.

How much stock was lost in the fire?

ANSWER

		£
(a)	Sales (140%)	154,000
	Gross profit (40%)	44,000
	Cost of goods sold (100%)	110,000
(b)	Opening stock, at cost	7,345
	Plus purchases	106,420
		113,765
	Less closing stock, at cost	350
	Equals cost of goods sold and goods lost	113,415
		£
(c)	Cost of goods sold and lost	113,415
	Cost of goods sold	110,000
	Cost of goods lost	3,415

EXAMPLE: STOCK STOLEN

Ashley Guerrard runs a jewellery shop in the High Street. On 1 January 20X0, his stock in trade, at cost, amounted to £4,700 and his trade creditors were £3,950.

During the six months to 30 June 20X0, sales were £42,000. Ashley Guerrard makes a gross profit of $33^{1}/_{3}\%$ on the sales value of everything he sells.

On 30 June, there was a burglary at the shop, and all the stock was stolen.

In trying to establish how much stock had been taken, Ashley Guerrard was able to provide the following information.

(a) He knew from his bank statements that he had paid £28,400 to creditors in the six month period to 30 June 20X0.

(b) He currently owes creditors £5,550.

Required

(a) Calculate how much stock was stolen.

(b) Prepare a trading account for the six months to 30 June 20X0.

ANSWER

Step 1. We must establish some 'unknowns' before we can calculate how much stock was stolen. The first 'unknown' is the amount of purchases during the period. This is established by the method previously described in this chapter.

CREDITORS

	£		£
Payments to creditors	28,400	Opening balance b/f	3,950
Closing balance c/f	5,550	Purchases (balancing figure)	30,000
	33,950		33,950

Step 2. **The cost of goods sold is also unknown, but this can be established from the gross profit margin and the sales for the period.**

		£
Sales	(100%)	42,000
Gross profit	($33^1/_3$%)	14,000
Cost of goods sold	($66^2/_3$%)	28,000

Step 3. The cost of the goods stolen is as follows.

	£
Opening stock at cost	4,700
Purchases	30,000
	34,700
Less closing stock (after burglary)	0
Cost of goods sold and goods stolen	34,700
Cost of goods sold (see (ii) above)	28,000
Cost of goods stolen	6,700

Step 4. **The cost of the goods stolen will not be a charge in the trading account, and so the trading account for the period is as follows.**

ASHLEY GUERRARD
TRADING ACCOUNT FOR THE SIX MONTHS TO 30 JUNE 20X0

	£	£
Sales		42,000
Less cost of goods sold		
Opening stock	4,700	
Purchases	30,000	
	34,700	
Less stock stolen	6,700	
		28,000
Gross profit		14,000

8.3 Term used

You may have noticed that we have used two terms for the relationship between gross profit and either cost or sales.

(a) **Mark-up** is where the gross profit is calculated as a percentage of cost, for example the company makes a mark up of 30% on cost.

(b) **Gross profit margin** is usually used to denote the relationship between profit and sales, for example the company makes a gross profit of 25% on sales.

	Mark-up	*Gross profit percentage*
	%	%
Sales	130	100
Cost of sales	100	75
Mark up/gross profit margin	30	25

8.4 Accounting for stock lost

When stock is stolen, destroyed or otherwise lost, the loss must be accounted for somehow. Since the loss is **not a trading loss**, the cost of the goods lost is not included in the trading account, as the previous example showed. The credit side of the accounting double entry *is* made in the trading account, but instead of showing the cost of the loss as a credit, it is usually shown as a deduction on the debit side of the trading account, which is the same as a 'plus' on the credit side.

There are two possible accounts that could be **debited** with the other side of the accounting double entry, depending on whether or not the lost goods were insured.

(a) If the lost goods were **not insured** the business must bear the loss and the loss is shown in the profit and loss account.

DEBIT	Profit and loss
CREDIT	Trading account

(b) If the lost goods were **insured** the business will not suffer a loss because the insurance will pay back the cost of the lost goods. This means that there is no charge at all in the profit and loss account, and the appropriate double entry for the cost of the loss is as follows.

DEBIT	Insurance claim account (debtor account)
CREDIT	Trading account

The insurance claim will then be a current asset, and shown in the balance sheet of the business as such. When the claim is paid, the account is then closed.

DEBIT	Cash
CREDIT	Insurance claim account

Activity 5 **(10 minutes)**

Janey Jennings's business had opening stock of £71,300. Purchases and sales for 20X0 were £282,250 and £455,000 respectively. The gross profit margin is a constant 40% on sales. On 31 December 20X0 a fire destroyed all the stock on Janey Jennings's premises, except for small sundry items with a cost of £1,200.

Required

Calculate the cost of the stock destroyed.

9 THE CASH BOOK

The construction of a cash book (**largely from bank statements** showing receipts and payments of a business during a given period) is often an important feature of incomplete records problems. The purpose of an incomplete records exercise is largely to test your understanding about how various items of receipts or payments relate to the preparation of a final set of accounts for a business.

We have already seen in this chapter that information about cash receipts or payments might be needed to establish the amount of credit sales or of purchases during a period. Other receipts or payments figures might be needed to establish the following amounts.

- Cash sales
- Certain expenses in the profit and loss account
- Drawings by the business proprietor

It might therefore be helpful, if a business does not keep a cash book on a daily basis, to **construct a cash book** at the end of an accounting period. A business which typically might not keep a daily cash book is a shop.

(a) Many sales, if not all sales, are cash sales and payment is received in the form of notes and coins, cheques, or credit cards at the time of sale.

(b) Some payments are made in notes and coins out of the till rather than by payment out of the business bank account by cheque.

Where there appears to be a sizeable volume of receipts and payments in cash then it is also helpful to construct a **two column cash book**. This is a cash book with one column for receipts and payments, and one column for money paid into and out of the business bank account.

EXAMPLE: PREPARING A CASH BOOK

Franklin George owns and runs a bookshop, making a gross profit of 25% on the cost of everything he sells. He does not keep a cash book.

On 1 January 20X0 the balance sheet of his business was as follows.

	£	£
Net fixed assets		20,000
Stock	10,000	
Cash in the bank	3,000	
Cash in the till	200	
	13,200	
Trade creditors	1,200	
		12,000
		32,000
Proprietor's capital		32,000

You are given the following information about the year to 31 December 20X0.

(a) There were no sales on credit.

(b) £41,750 in receipts were banked.

(c) The bank statements of the period show these payments.

(i)	To trade creditors	£36,000
(ii)	Sundry expenses	£5,600
(iii)	In drawings	£4,400

(d) Payments were also made in cash out of the till.

(i)	To trade creditors	£800
(ii)	Sundry expenses	£1,500
(iii)	In drawings	£3,700

At 31 December 20X0, the business had cash in the till of £450 and trade creditors of £1,400. The cash balance in the bank was not known and the value of closing stock has not yet been calculated. There were no accruals or prepayments. No further fixed assets were purchased during the year. The depreciation charge for the year is £900.

(a) Prepare a two-column cash book for the period.

(b) Prepare the trading, profit and loss account for the year to 31 December 20X0 and the balance sheet as at 31 December 20X0.

ANSWER

A two-column cash book is completed as follows.

Step 1. Enter the opening cash balances.

Step 2. Enter the information given about cash payments (and any cash receipts, if there had been any such items given in the problem).

Step 3. The cash receipts banked are a 'contra' entry, being both a debit (bank column) and a credit (cash in hand column) in the same account.

Step 4. Enter the closing cash in hand (cash in the bank at the end of the period is not known).

CASH BOOK

	Cash in hand	*Bank*		*Cash in hand*	*Bank*
	£	£		£	£
Balance b/f	200	3,000	Trade creditors	800	36,000
Cash receipts banked (contra)		41,750	Sundry expenses	1,500	5,600
			Drawings	3,700	4,400
Sales	*48,000		Cash receipts banked (contra)	41,750	
Balance c/f		*1,250	Balance c/f	450	
	48,200	46,000		48,200	46,000
* Balancing figures					

Step 5. The closing balance of money in the bank is a balancing figure.

Step 6. Since all sales are for cash, a balancing figure that can be entered in the cash book is sales, in the cash in hand (debit) column.

It is important to notice that since not all receipts from cash sales are banked, the value of cash sales during the period is as follows.

	£
Receipts banked	41,750
Plus expenses and drawings paid out of the till in cash £(800 + 1,500 + 3,700)	6,000
Plus any cash stolen (here there is none)	0
Plus the closing balance of cash in hand	450
	48,200
Less the opening balance of cash in hand	(200)
Equals cash sales	48,000

The cash book constructed in this way has enabled us to establish both the closing balance for cash in the bank and also the volume of cash sales. The trading, profit and loss account and the balance sheet can also be prepared, once a value for purchases has been calculated.

CREDITORS

	£		£
Cash book: payments from bank	36,000	Balance b/f	1,200
Cash book: payments in cash	800	Purchases (balancing figure)	37,000
Balance c/f	1,400		
	38,200		38,200

The mark-up of 25% on cost indicates that the cost of the goods sold is £38,400, as follows.

	£
Sales (125%)	48,000
Gross profit (25%)	9,600
Cost of goods sold (100%)	38,400

The closing stock amount is now a balancing figure in the trading account.

FRANKLIN GEORGE TRADING, PROFIT AND LOSS ACCOUNT
FOR THE YEAR ENDED 31 DECEMBER 20X0

	£	£
Sales		48,000
Less cost of goods sold		
Opening stock	10,000	
Purchases	37,000	
	47,000	
Less closing stock (balancing figure)	8,600	
		38,400
Gross profit (25/125 × £48,000)		9,600
Expenses		
Sundry £(1,500 + 5,600)	7,100	
Depreciation	900	
		8,000
Net profit		1,600

NOTES

FRANKLIN GEORGE
BALANCE SHEET AS AT 31 DECEMBER 20X0

	£	£
Net fixed assets £(20,000 – 900)		19,100
Stock	8,600	
Cash in the till	450	
	9,050	
Bank overdraft	1,250	
Trade creditors	1,400	
	2,650	
Net current assets		6,400
		25,500
Proprietor's capital		
Balance b/f		32,000
Net profit for the year		1,600
		33,600
Drawings £(3,700 + 4,400)		(8,100)
Balance c/f		25,500

9.1 Theft of cash from the till

When cash is stolen from the till, the amount stolen will be a credit entry in the cash book, and a debit in either the profit and loss account or insurance claim account, depending on whether the business is **insured**. The missing figure for cash sales, if this has to be calculated, must take account of cash received but later stolen.

9.2 Using debtors account to calculate both cash sales and credit sales

Another point which needs to be considered is how a missing value can be found for **cash sales and credit sales**, when a business has both, but takings banked by the business are not divided between takings from cash sales and takings from credit sales.

EXAMPLE: DETERMINING THE VALUE OF SALES DURING THE PERIOD

Suppose that a business had, on 1 January 20X0, trade debtors of £2,000, cash in the bank of £3,000, and cash in hand of £300.

During the year to 31 December 20X0 the business banked £95,000 in takings. It also paid out the following expenses in cash from the till.

Drawings	£1,200
Sundry expenses	£800

On 29 August 20X0 a thief broke into the shop and stole £400 from the till.

At 31 December 20X0 trade debtors amounted to £3,500, cash in the bank £2,500 and cash in the till £150.

What was the value of sales during the year?

ANSWER

If we tried to prepare a debtors account and a two column cash book, we would have insufficient information, in particular about whether the takings which were banked related to cash sales or credit sales.

DEBTORS

	£		£
Balance b/f	2,000	Payments from debtors	
Credit sales	*Unknown*	(credit sales)	*Unknown*
		Balance c/f	3,500

CASH BOOK

	Cash	*Bank*		*Cash*	*Bank*
	£	£		£	£
Balance b/f	300	3,000	Drawings	1,200	
			Sundry expenses	800	
Debtors: payments		*Unknown*	Cash stolen	400	
Cash sales		*Unknown*	Balance c/f	150	2,500

All we do know is that the combined sums from debtors and cash takings banked is £95,000.

The value of sales can be found instead by using the debtors account, which should be used to record cash takings banked as well as payments by debtors. The balancing figure in the debtors account will then be a combination of credit sales and some cash sales. The cash book only needs to have single columns.

DEBTORS

	£		£
Balance b/f	2,000	Cash banked	95,000
Sales to trading account	96,500	Balance c/f	3,500
	98,500		98,500

CASH (EXTRACT)

	£		£
Balance in hand b/f	300	*Payments in cash*	
Balance in bank b/f	3,000	Drawings	1,200
Debtors a/c	95,000	Expenses	800
		Other payments	?
		Cash stolen	400
		Balance in hand c/f	150
		Balance in bank c/f	2,500

The remaining 'undiscovered' amount of cash sales is now found as follows.

	£
Payments in cash out of the till	
Drawings	1,200
Expenses	800
	2,000
Cash stolen	400
Closing balance of cash in hand	150
	2,550
Less opening balance of cash in hand	(300)
Further cash sales	2,250
Total sales for the year	£
From debtors account	96,500
From cash book	2,250
Total sales	98,750

BPP LEARNING MEDIA

NOTES

10 ACCRUALS AND PREPAYMENTS

Where there is an accrued expense or a prepayment, the charge to be made in the profit and loss account for the item concerned should be found from the opening balance b/f, the closing balance c/f, and cash payments for the item during the period. The charge in the profit and loss account is perhaps most easily found as the balancing figure in a ledger account.

EXAMPLE: ACCRUALS AND PREPAYMENTS

For example, suppose that on 1 April 20X0 a business had prepaid rent of £700 which relates to the next accounting period. During the year to 31 March 20X1 it pays £9,300 in rent, and at 31 March 20X1 the prepayment of rent is £1,000. The cost of rent in the profit and loss account for the year to 31 March 20X1 would be the balancing figure in the following ledger account. (Remember that a prepayment is a current asset, and so is a debit balance brought forward.)

RENT

	£		£
Prepayment: balance b/f	700	P&L account (balancing figure)	9,000
Cash	9,300	Prepayment: balance c/f	1,000
	10,000		10,000
Balance b/f	1,000		

Similarly, if a business has accrued telephone expenses as at 1 July 20X0 of £850, pays £6,720 in telephone bills during the year to 30 June 20X1, and has accrued telephone expenses of £1,140 as at 30 June 20X1, then the telephone expense to be shown in the profit and loss account for the year to 30 June 20X1 is the balancing figure in the following ledger account. (Remember that an accrual is a current liability, and so is a credit balance brought forward.)

TELEPHONE EXPENSES

	£		£
Cash	6,720	Balance b/f (accrual)	850
Balance c/f (accrual)	1,140	P&L a/c (balancing figure)	7,010
	7,860		7,860
		Balance b/f	1,140

11 DRAWINGS

In the case of a sole trader, drawings would normally represent no particular problem at all in preparing a set of final accounts from incomplete records, but it is not unusual for questions to involve the following situations.

(a) The business owner **pays income into his bank account** which has nothing whatever to do with the business operations. For example, the owner might pay dividend income or other income from investments into the bank, from stocks and shares which he owns personally, separate from the business itself.

(b) The business owner **pays money out of the business bank account** for items which are not business expenses, such as life insurance premiums or a payment for his family's holidays.

(c) The owner takes stock for his personal use.

BPP LEARNING MEDIA

11.1 Accounting treatment

These personal items of receipts or payments should be dealt with as follows.

(a) **Receipts should be set off against drawings**. For example, if a business owner receives £600 in dividend income from investments not owned by the business and pays it into the business bank account, then the accounting entry is as follows.

DEBIT	Cash
CREDIT	Drawings

(b) Payments of cash for personal items should be charged to drawings.

DEBIT	Drawings
CREDIT	Cash

(c) **Goods taken for personal use (drawings of stock)**: the traditional way of dealing with this has been to charge the goods to drawings at cost. The required entries are:

DEBIT	Drawings
CREDIT	Purchases

However, the recommended treatment, according better with modern practice and the requirements of HM Revenue and Customs, is as follows.

DEBIT	Drawings at selling price (including VAT)
CREDIT	Sales
CREDIT	VAT

12 COMPREHENSIVE APPROACH

A suggested approach to dealing with incomplete records problems brings together the various points described so far in this chapter. The nature of the 'incompleteness' in the records will vary from problem to problem, but the approach, suitably applied, should be successful in arriving at the final accounts whatever the particular characteristics of the problem might be.

12.1 The approach

The approach is as follows.

Step 1 If it is not already known, establish the opening balance sheet and the brought forward profit and loss account balance if possible.

Step 2 Open up four accounts.

- A trading account (if you wish, leave space underneath for entering the profit and loss account later)
- A cash book, with two columns if cash sales are significant and there are payments in cash out of the till
- A debtors' account
- A creditors' account

Step 3 Enter the opening balances in these accounts.

Step 4 Work through the information you are given line by line. Each item should be entered into the appropriate account if it is relevant to one or more of these four accounts.

You should also try to recognise each item as a 'profit and loss account income or expense item' or a 'closing balance sheet item'.
It may be necessary to calculate an amount for drawings and an amount for fixed asset depreciation.

Step 5 Look for the balancing figures in your accounts. In particular you might be looking for a value for credit sales, cash sales, purchases, the cost of goods sold, the cost of goods stolen or destroyed, or the closing bank balance. Calculate these missing figures and make any necessary double entry (for example to the trading account from the creditors account for purchases, to the trading account from the cash book for cash sales, and to the trading account from the debtors account for credit sales).

Step 6 Now complete the profit and loss account and balance sheet. Working ledger accounts might be needed where there are accruals or prepayments.

Chapter roundup

- Preparation of accounts from incomplete records may be necessary where a business has limited accounting records or where accounting information has been accidentally lost or destroyed.
- Control accounts are usually used for debtors and creditors and they record all relevant transactions on a totals basis.
- The opening balance sheet can be reconstructed using the information available.
- Writing up the trading account and using gross profit percentages or mark up can help to provide missing figures.
- Reconstruction of a two column cash book is another technique.

Quick quiz

1 In the absence of a sales account or sales day book, how can a figure of sales for the year be computed?

2 In the absence of a purchase account or purchases day book, how can a figure of purchases for the year be computed?

3 What is the accounting double entry to record the loss of stock by fire or burglary?

4 If a business proprietor pays his personal income into the business bank account, what is the accounting double entry to record the transaction?

Answers to quick quiz

1 Sales can be found using the formula: (see para 6.1)

	£
Payments received from trade debtors	X
Plus closing balance of trade debtors	X
Less opening balance of trade debtors	(X)
Credit sales	X

2 Again, the following formula can be used. (para 7)

	£
Payments to trade creditors	X
Plus closing balance of trade creditors	X
Less opening balance of trade creditors	(X)
Credit purchases	X

3 (a) If the goods are not insured: (para 8.4)

DEBIT Profit and loss
CREDIT Trading account

(b) If the loss is insured: (para 8.4)

DEBIT Insurance claim a/c
CREDIT Trading account

4 For a receipt from a proprietor, the double entry is:

DEBIT Cash
CREDIT Drawings (para 11)

Answers to activities

1

		£	£
Amounts due to creditors at 1 January (balancing figure)			19,330
Purchases in year			86,700
			106,030
Less:	cash paid to creditors in year	83,000	
	discounts received	4,130	
	contra with debtors control	5,200	
			92,330
Amounts still unpaid at 31 December			13,700

NOTES

2 (a)

DEBTORS' CONTROL ACCOUNT

20X0		£	*20X0*		£
Oct 1	Balances b/f	20,347	Oct 1	Balances b/f	228
20X1			*20X1*		
Sept 30	Sales	176,429	Sept 30	Cash received from debtors	148,481
	Balances c/f	228		Discount allowed	5,273
				Returns	3,180
				Bad debts written off	1,079
				Transfer creditors control account	949
				Allowances on goods damaged	553
				Balances c/f	37,261
		197,004			197,004

(b)

CREDITORS' CONTROL ACCOUNT

		£			£
20X0			*20X0*		
Oct 1	Balances b/f	319	Oct 1	Balances b/f	18,024
20X1			*20X1*		
Sept 30	Cash paid to creditors	95,184	Sept 30	Purchases	108,726
	Discount received	2,798		Cash	319
	Returns outwards	1,417			
	Transfer debtors control account	949			
	Balances c/f	26,402			
		127,069			127,069

3 The ledger account will look like this.

DEBTORS' CONTROL ACCOUNT

	£		£
1 January balance b/f	42,800	Bank	204,000
Sales	240,200	Discounts allowed	16,250
		31 December balance c/f	62,750
	283,000		283,000

4 The gross profit is £150,000 – £112,500 = £37,500.

(a) The gross profit as a percentage of cost of sales is:

$$\frac{£37{,}500}{£112{,}500} \times 100\% = 33^1/_3\%$$

(b) The gross profit as a percentage of sales is:

$$\frac{£37{,}500}{£150{,}000} \times 100\% = 25\%$$

BPP LEARNING MEDIA

NOTES

5 The trading account of Jennings Ltd will appear as follows.

	£	£
Sales		455,000
Less cost of sales		
Opening stock	71,300	
Purchases	282,250	
	353,550	
Closing stock (balance)	80,550	
		273,000
Gross profit (40% × £455,000)		182,000

Cost of stock destroyed = £80,550 – £1,200 = £79,350.

Chapter 18 :
LIMITED COMPANY ACCOUNTS

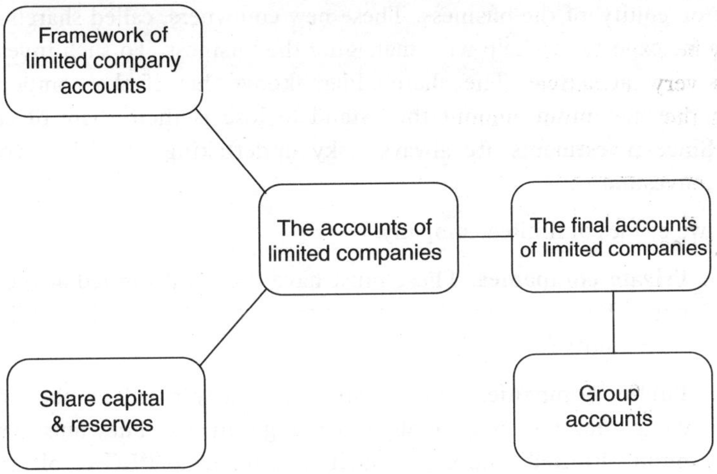

Introduction

So far we have dealt mainly with the accounts of businesses in general. In this chapter, we shall turn our attention to the accounts of limited companies. Limited companies are businesses whose owners are called shareholders and who offer limited liability for their owners. It will come as no surprise to you that the accounting rules and conventions for recording the business transactions and preparing the final accounts of limited companies are much the same as for sole traders. There is, however, extensive legislation governing the activities of limited companies including that concerned with the layout and disclosure of accounting information. For example, the capital is shown differently from that of a sole trader.

This chapter will highlight the main features of the accounts of limited companies and provide a detailed worked example.

Your objectives

In this chapter you will learn about the following.

(a) The nature of limited liability and the legal safeguards that surround it

(b) The capital structure of limited companies

(c) The main features of the accounts of limited companies

1 FRAMEWORK OF LIMITED COMPANY ACCOUNTS

Sole traders and partnerships are, with some significant exceptions, generally fairly small concerns. The amount of capital involved may be modest, and the proprietors of the business usually participate in managing it.

As a business grows, it needs more capital to finance its operations, and significantly more than the people currently managing the business can provide themselves. One way of obtaining more capital is to invite investors from outside the business to invest in the ownership or 'equity' of the business. These new co-owners, called shareholders, would not usually be expected to help with managing the business. To such investors, limited liability is very attractive. The shareholders know that if the company goes into liquidation the maximum amount they stand to lose is their share of capital in the business. Since investments are always risky undertakings, this is a very attractive prospect to investors.

There are two classes of limited company.

(a) **Private companies.** These must have the word limited at the end of their name. Being private, they cannot invite members of the public to invest in their equity (ownership).

(b) **Public companies**. These are much fewer in number than private companies, but are generally much larger in size. They must have the words **public limited company**, usually shortened to PLC or plc, at the end of their name. Public companies can invite members of the general public to invest in their equity, and the 'shares' of these companies are usually traded on the Stock Exchange, (that is to say, public companies are usually also listed companies, though this is not always the case).

The accounting rules and conventions for recording the business transactions of limited companies, and then preparing their final accounts, are much the same as for sole traders. For example, companies will have basic accounting records similar to a sole trader. They also prepare a profit and loss account annually, and a balance sheet at the end of the accounting year.

There are, however, some differences in the accounts of limited companies. The legislation governing the activities of limited companies is very extensive. Amongst other things, the Companies Acts define certain minimum accounting records which must be maintained by companies. In addition, a copy of the annual accounts of a limited company must be filed with the Registrar of Companies. This is so that accounts are available for public inspection. Companies legislation also contains detailed requirements on the minimum information which must be disclosed in a company's accounts.

Activity 1 **(5 minutes)**

Mark the following statements as true or false.

(a) Where there are numerous owners of an enterprise it will always be incorporated.

(b) The capital of a company is shown differently from that of a sole trader.

(c) Sole traders usually manage their businesses on a day-to-day basis, unlike shareholders.

(d) Shareholders may appropriate profits through drawings.

(e) Shareholders receive annual published accounts prepared according to the Companies Acts.

One of the main differences between the accounts of a sole trader and a limited company is in the area of capital accounts.

2 SHARE CAPITAL AND RESERVES

2.1 Share capital

The proprietors' capital in a limited company consists of share capital. When a company is set up for the first time, it issues shares, which are paid for by investors, who then become shareholders of the company. Shares are denominated in units of 25 pence, 50 pence, £1 or whatever seems appropriate. This 'face value' of the shares is called their *nominal value*.

Activity 2 **(5 minutes)**

Fill in the gaps in the following table.

Number of shares	Nominal value	Total value £
100,000		100,000
	50p	100,000
500,000	40p	
	10p	85,000

The nominal value is set by the company and is not the same as the market value, which is the price someone is prepared to pay for the share.

A distinction is made between authorised and issued share capital.

Definitions

- The **authorised share capital** is the maximum amount of share capital that a company can issue. It is also sometimes known as nominal capital.
- The **issued share capital** is the amount of authorised share capital that has already been issued to the shareholders.

The issued share capital obviously cannot exceed the authorised share capital. It can be equal to the authorised capital if all of the authorised share capital has been issued.

Shareholders expect to earn a return on their investment. However, before any profit can be distributed to the shareholders, companies must pay taxes.

2.2 Taxes

Companies pay what is called corporation tax on the profits they earn. The amount of tax is based on the amounts of profits made – the larger the profit, the higher the tax.

The important thing to remember at this point is that, for limited companies, tax is not an expense. Rather it is an appropriation of profits. While sole traders and partnerships do not show the tax they owe on the profit of their businesses (it is treated as part of drawings), limited companies have to show the amount of corporation tax owed to the government.

(a) The amount of corporation tax on profits for the year is shown as a deduction from profits, prior to appropriating the dividends.

	£
Profit before tax	X
Tax	(X)
Profit after tax	X

(b) In the balance sheet, tax payable to the government is generally shown as a current liability as it is usually due nine months after the year end.

A portion or all of the profit left after payment of taxes can be distributed to the shareholders. Profit paid out to shareholders is called dividends.

2.3 Dividends

Shareholders in a company are rewarded in the form of a dividend.

Definition

Dividends are that portion of the profit after tax that is distributed to the shareholders.

A company might pay dividends in two stages during the course of its accounting year.

(a) In mid year, after the half-year financial results are known, the company might pay an **interim dividend.**

(b) After the end of the year, the company might pay a further **final dividend.**

The total dividend for the year is:

Interim plus final

However, do remember that not all companies pay an interim dividend. Interim dividends are, however, commonly paid out by listed companies.

At the end of an accounting year a company's directors will often propose a final divided payment. If this is proposed after the year end then it is not a liability of the company at the year end and therefore does not appear in the financial statements. However the amount of the proposed dividend should be disclosed in a note to the financial statements.

The dividend paid during the accounting period (often last year's proposed final dividend plus the current year interim dividend) is not shown as a deduction from profit in the profit and loss account but is instead deducted directly from the accumulated profits of the company.

The terminology of dividend payments can be confusing, since they may be expressed either in the form:

(a) x pence per share eg 2p per share
(b) y per cent eg 5% per share

In the latter case, the meaning is always 'y per cent of the nominal value of the shares in issue'. For example, suppose a company's issued share capital consists of 100,000 50p ordinary shares. The company's balance sheet would include the following.

Issued share capital: 100,000 50p ordinary shares £50,000

If the directors wish to pay a dividend of £5,000, they may propose either:

(a) A dividend of 5p per share (100,000 × 5p = £5,000); or
(b) a dividend of 10% (10% × £50,000 = £5,000).

Dividends are paid to shareholders who may own more than one type of share, each with its own rights and privileges.

2.4 Ordinary and preference shares

At this stage it is relevant to distinguish between the two types of shares most often encountered, preference shares and ordinary shares.

Preference shares carry the right to a final dividend which is expressed as a percentage of their nominal value: eg a 6% £1 preference share carries a right to an annual dividend of 6p. Preference dividends have priority over ordinary dividends. If the directors of a company wish to pay a dividend (which they are not obliged to do) they must pay any preference dividend first. Otherwise, no ordinary dividend may be paid.

Ordinary shares are by far the most common. They carry no right to a fixed dividend but are entitled to all profits left after payment of any preference dividend. Generally however, only a part of such remaining profits is distributed, the rest being kept in reserve (see below). The amount of ordinary dividends fluctuates although there is a general expectation that it will increase from year to year. Should the company be wound up, any surplus is shared between the ordinary shareholders.

Ordinary shares normally carry voting rights, and in effect ordinary shareholders are the effective owners of the company. They own the 'equity' of the business, and any reserves of the business (described later) belong to them. Ordinary shareholders are sometimes referred to as **equity shareholders.**

It should be emphasised that the precise rights attached to preference and ordinary shares vary from company to company; the distinctions noted above are generalisations.

Activity 3 **(5 minutes)**

The share capital of X Ltd is as follows.

	Authorised	*Issued*
	£	£
7% preference shares of £1 each	20,000	12,000
Ordinary shares of 20p each	100,000	80,000
	120,000	92,000

The directors declare an ordinary dividend for the year of 12%. How much in total will be paid out by the company in dividends?

One of the key differences between ordinary and preference shareholders not mentioned above, is the fact that ordinary shareholders own what are called reserves.

2.5 Reserves

The ordinary shareholders' total investment in a limited company is called the *equity* and consists of share capital plus reserves. Reserves are difficult to define since different reserves arise for different reasons, but one way of defining them is:

Reserves = net assets less share capital

The total amount of reserves in a company varies, according to changes in the net assets of the business. The important point to note is that all reserves are owned by the *ordinary* shareholders.

A distinction should be made between two types of reserves.

(a) **Non-distributable reserves** are reserves established in circumstances defined by companies legislation. They are not available for distribution as dividends. Companies legislation restricts the amounts that companies are allowed to pay out to their shareholders in order to protect the claims of creditors.

(b) **Distributable reserves** are reserves consisting of profits which are distributable as dividends, if the company so wishes.

NOTES

Profit and loss reserve (retained profits)

This is the most significant distributable reserve, and it is variously described as:

- Revenue reserve
- Retained profits
- Retained earnings
- Undistributed profits
- Profit and loss account
- Unappropriated profits.

These are profits earned by the company and not appropriated by dividends, taxation or transfer to another reserve account.

Assuming the company is making profits, this reserve generally increases from year to year, as most companies do not distribute all their profits as dividends.

Dividends can be paid from it: even if a loss is made in one particular year, a dividend can be paid from previous years' retained profits. For example, if a company makes a loss of £100,000 in one year, yet has unappropriated profits from previous years totalling £250,000, it can pay a dividend not exceeding £150,000 (ie £250,000 – £100,000).

One reason for retaining some profit each year is to enable the company to pay dividends even when profits are low (or non-existent). Another reason is usually shortage of cash. Very occasionally, you might come across a debit balance on the profit and loss account. This would indicate that the company has accumulated losses.

2.6 Other distributable reserves

The company directors may choose to set up other reserves. These may have a specific purpose (for example plant and machinery replacement reserve) or not (for example general reserve).

Profits are transferred to these reserves by making an appropriation out of profits, usually profits for the year. Typically, you might come across the following.

EXAMPLE

	£	£
Profit and loss reserve b/f		250,000
Net profit for the year		100,000
Appropriations of profit		
Dividend	60,000	
Transfer to general reserve	10,000	
		(70,000)
Profit and loss reserve carried forward		280,000

There is no real significance about the creation of separate distributable reserves. After all, there is little difference between the following two balance sheet extracts.

BPP LEARNING MEDIA

(a)

	£	£
Net assets		3,500
Share capital		2,000
Reserves: general (distributable as dividend)	1,000	
Retained profits (distributable)	500	
		1,500
		3,500

(b)

	£
Net assets	3,500
Share capital	2,000
Reserves: retained profits (distributable)	1,500
	3,500

The establishment of a 'plant and machinery replacement reserve' (or something similar) indicates an intention by a company to keep funds in the business to replace its plant and machinery. However, the reserve would still, legally, represent distributable profits, and the existence of such a reserve does not guarantee the company's ability to replace its fixed assets in the future.

2.7 The share premium account

There are a number of non-distributable reserves, the most important of which at this stage is the **share premium account**.

Definition

> **Share premium**: Whenever shares are issued at a price in excess of their nominal value, the excess is called share premium and it is credited to a share premium account.

A share premium arises when a company sells shares for a price which is higher than their nominal value. By 'premium' is meant the difference between the issue price of the share and its nominal value.

For example, if X Ltd issues 1,000 £1 ordinary shares at £2.60 each the proceeds will be recorded as follows.

Accounts	*Debit*	*Credit*
	£	£
Cash	2,600	
Ordinary share capital		1,000
Share premium account		1,600

In the balance sheet, they would be classified as follows.

	£
Share capital	1,000
Share premium	1,600

A share premium account only comes into being when a company, at the time of issue of shares, receives money in excess of their nominal value. The market price of the shares, once they have been issued, has no bearing at all on the company's accounts, and so if their market price goes up or down, the share premium account would not be affected at all.

Activity 4 **(5 minutes)**

Here are extracts from a company's balance sheet at 30 June 20X0 and 30 June 20X1.

	20X1	*20X0*
	£	£
Capital reserves		
Issued share capital: 50p ordinary shares	9,000	7,500
Share premium account	3,500	2,000

How many shares were issued during the year, and at what price?

2.8 Revaluation reserve

A revaluation reserve must be created when a company revalues one or more of its fixed assets. Revaluations frequently occur with freehold property, as the market value of property rises or falls. The company's directors might wish to show a more 'reasonable' value of the asset in their balance sheet, to avoid giving a misleading impression about the financial position of the company.

When an asset is revalued, the revaluation reserve is credited with the difference between the revalued amount of the asset, and its net book value before the revaluation took place.

EXAMPLE: REVALUATION RESERVE

X Ltd bought freehold land and buildings for £20,000 ten years ago; their net book value (after depreciation of the buildings) is now £19,300. A professional valuation of £390,000 has been given, and the directors wish to reflect this in the accounts.

(a) The revaluation surplus is £390,000 – £19,300 = £370,700.

(b) In the balance sheet:

- freehold land and buildings will be restated to reflect the revaluation;
- revaluation reserve of £370,700 will appear in the share capital section.

(c) The revaluation has no immediate effect on the profit and loss account.

An unrealised capital profit (such as the £370,700 above) is generally not distributable, whereas a realised capital profit (ie if the property is actually sold for £390,000) usually is distributable.

Having looked at some of the unique features of the accounts of limited companies, we now look at the final accounts of limited companies.

NOTES

3 THE FINAL ACCOUNTS OF LIMITED COMPANIES

3.1 Format of the final accounts

The preparation and publication of the final accounts of limited companies in the UK are governed by the Companies Act 1985 which consolidates, and replaces, the provisions of the previous Companies Acts. A number of amendments to the provisions of the Companies Act 1985 are contained in the Companies Act 1989, and further amendments will follow when the Companies Act 2006 is implemented. The detailed regulations laid down by these Acts are beyond the scope of this course book. However, the general format of the balance sheet and profit and loss account of a limited company are shown below.

TYPICAL COMPANY LIMITED BALANCE SHEET AS AT ...

	£	£	£
Fixed assets			
Intangible assets			
Concessions, patents, licences, trademarks		15,000	
Goodwill		4,000	
			19,000
Tangible assets			
Land and buildings		75,000	
Plant and machinery		24,000	
Fixtures, fittings, tools and equipment		8,000	
Motor vehicles		13,000	
			120,000
Investments			2,500
			141,500
Current assets			
Stocks		6,000	
Debtors and prepayments		8,500	
Investments		1,500	
Cash at bank and in hand		300	
		16,300	
Creditors: amounts falling due within one year (ie current liabilities)			
Debenture loans (nearing their repayment date)	4,000		
Bank loans and overdrafts	1,300		
Trade creditors	6,200		
Taxation	2,800		
Accruals	800		
Proposed dividend	1,000		
		16,100	
Net current assets			200
Total assets less current liabilities			141,700
Creditors: amounts falling due after more than one year			
Debenture loans			(8,000)
			133,700

BPP LEARNING MEDIA

NOTES

Capital and reserves		
Ordinary shares	20,000	
Preference shares	5,000	
		25,000
Reserves		
Share premium account	11,000	
Revaluation reserve	15,000	
Other reserves	6,000	
Profit and loss account (retained profits)	76,700	
		108,700
		133,700

TYPICAL COMPANY LIMITED
PROFIT AND LOSS ACCOUNT FOR THE YEAR ENDED...

	£	£
Turnover		91,700
Cost of sales		(32,000)
Gross profit		59,700
Distribution costs	17,000	
Administrative expenses	24,000	
		(41,000)
		18,700
Other operating income	1,000	
Income from fixed asset investments	200	
Other interest receivable and similar income	500	
		1,700
		20,400
Interest payable		(3,200)
Profit before taxation		17,200
Tax		(3,500)
Net profit for the year		13,700

Intangible assets

These are assets that do not have a physical existence. If a company purchases some patent rights, or a concession from another business, or the right to use a trademark, the cost of the purchase can be accounted for as the purchase of an intangible fixed asset. These assets must then be amortised (depreciated) over their economic life.

Investments

Investments are fixed assets if the company intends to hold on to them for a long time, and current assets if they are only likely to be held for a short time before being sold.

Creditors: amounts falling due within one year

The term 'creditors: amounts falling due within one year' was introduced by the Companies Act 1981 as a phrase meaning 'current liabilities'.

Debenture loans

Limited companies may issue debenture stock ('debentures') or loan stock. These are long-term liabilities.

Interest is calculated on the nominal value of debenture, regardless of its market value. If a company has £700,000 (nominal value) 12% debentures in issue, interest of £84,000 will be charged in the profit and loss account per year. Interest is usually paid half-yearly. There may be a current liability in the balance sheet for interest due but not yet paid at the year end.

For example, assume a company has issued £700,000 of 12% debentures on which it pays interest on 30 June and 31 December each year. The company ends its accounting year on 30 September. Therefore there would be an accrual of three months' unpaid interest (3/12 × £84,000 = £21,000) at the end of each accounting year so long as the debentures are still in issue.

We now pull together several of the items described in this chapter into a comprehensive example.

EXAMPLE OF LIMITED COMPANY ACCOUNTS

The accountant of Tehreem Ltd has prepared the following list of balances as at 31 December 20X0.

	£'000
50p ordinary shares	350
7% £1 preference shares	100
10% debentures	200
Retained profit 1 January 20X0	92
General reserve 1 January 20X0	71
Freehold land and buildings 1 January 20X0	430
Plant and machinery 1 January 20X0 (cost)	830
Provision for depreciation:	
freehold buildings 1 January 20X0	20
plant and machinery 1 January 20X0	222
Sales	2,695
Cost of sales	2,156
Preference dividend paid	7
Ordinary dividend (interim) paid	8
Debenture interest paid	10
Wages and salaries	274
Light and heat	14
Sundry expenses	107
Suspense account	420
Debtors	179
Creditors	195
Cash	126

Notes

(a) The suspense account is in respect of the following items.

	£'000
Proceeds from the issue of 100,000 ordinary shares	120
Proceeds from the sale of plant	300
	420

BPP LEARNING MEDIA

NOTES

(b) The freehold property was acquired some years ago. The buildings element of the cost was estimated at £100,000 and the estimated useful life of the assets was fifty years at the time of purchase. As at 31 December 20X0 the property is to be revalued at £800,000.

(c) The plant which was sold had cost £350,000 and had a net book value of £274,000 as on 1 January 20X0. £36,000 depreciation is to be charged on plant and machinery for 20X0.

(d) The debentures have been in issue for some years.

(e) The directors wish to provide for:

   (i) debenture interest due
   (ii) a transfer to general reserve of £16,000
   (iii) audit fees of £4,000.

(f) Stock as at 31 December 20X0 was valued at £224,000 (cost). The cost of sales has been adjusted for this stock. There was no stock at 1 January 20X0.

(g) Taxation is to be ignored.

Now, let us prepare the final accounts of Tehreem Ltd.

Approach

(a) The debenture interest accrued is calculated as follows.

	£'000
Charge needed in P&L account (10% × £200,000)	20
Amount paid so far, as shown in trial balance	10
Accrual – presumably six months' interest now payable	10

(b) Depreciation on the freehold building is calculated as = £2,000.

The net book value of the freehold property is then £430,000 – £20,000 – £2,000 = £408,000 at the end of the year. When the property is revalued a reserve of £800,000 – £408,000 = £392,000 is then created.

(c) The profit on disposal of plant is calculated as proceeds £300,000 (per suspense account) less net book value £274,000, ie £26,000. The cost of the remaining plant is calculated at £830,000 – £350,000 = £480,000. The depreciation provision at the year end is made up of the following.

	£'000
Balance 1 January 20X0	222
Charge for 20X0	36
Less depreciation on disposal (350-274)	(76)
	182

(d) The other item in the suspense account is dealt with as follows.

	£'000
Proceeds of issue of 100,000 ordinary shares	120
Less nominal value 100,000 × 50p	50
Excess of consideration over nominal value (= share premium)	70

(e) The transfer to general reserve increases that reserve to £71,000 + £16,000 = £87,000.

BPP LEARNING MEDIA

TEHREEM LIMITED: PROFIT AND LOSS ACCOUNT

	£'000	£'000
Sales		2,695
Less cost of sales		2,156
Gross profit		539
Profit on disposal of plant		26
		565
Less expenses		
Wages and salaries	274	
Sundry expenses	107	
Light and heat	14	
Depreciation: freehold building	2	
plant	36	
Audit fees	4	
Debenture interest	20	
		457
Net profit		108

TEHREEM LIMITED: BALANCE SHEET

	Cost/val'n £'000	*Dep'n* £'000	*NBV* £'000
Fixed assets			
Tangible assets			
Freehold property	800	-	800
Plant and machinery	480	182	298
	1,280	182	1,098
Current assets			
Stock		224	
Debtors		179	
Cash		126	
		529	
Creditors: amounts falling due within one year			
Creditors	195		
Accrued audit fee	4		
Accrued debenture interest	10		
		209	
Net current assets			320
Total assets less current liabilities			1,418
Creditors: amounts falling due after more than one year			
10% debentures			200
			1,218
Capital and reserves			
Share capital			
50p ordinary shares		400	
7% £1 preference shares		100	
			500
Reserves			
Share premium		70	
Revaluation reserve		392	
General reserve		87	
Profit and loss account (92 + 108 – 7 – 8 – 16)		169	
			718
			1,218

3.2 Notes to the accounts

The published accounts of limited companies are required to include a large number of supporting notes. These analyse the total figures in more detail or provide additional information or explanations. The accounts of other types of organisations such as sole traders may also include notes.

Some examples of common notes to limited company accounts are shown below.

NOTES TO THE ACCOUNTS

1 *Operating profit*

	£
Operating profit is stated after charging:	
Depreciation	12,500
Exceptional items	1,500
Directors' remuneration	9,500
Staff costs	12,500

2 *Tangible fixed assets*

	Land and Buildings £	*Plant and machinery* £	*Fixtures and fittings* £	*Motor vehicles* £	*Total* £
Cost (or valuation)					
At the beginning of the year	66,000	31,000	10,000	24,000	131,000
Additions	-	9,000	1,000	4,000	14,000
Revaluations	10,000	-	-	-	10,000
Disposals	-	(3,000)	-	-	(3,000)
At the end of the year	76,000	37,000	11,000	28,000	152,000
Depreciation					
At the beginning of the year	5,000	10,000	2,500	9,000	26,500
Charge for the year	1,000	5,000	500	6,000	12,500
Revaluation	(5,000)	-	-	-	(5,000)
Disposals	-	(2,000)	-	-	(2,000)
At the end of the year	1,000	13,000	3,000	15,000	32,000
Net book value					
At the end of the year	75,000	24,000	8,000	13,000	120,000
At the beginning of the year	61,000	21,000	7,500	15,000	104,500

3 *Reserves*

	Share premium £	*Revaluation reserve* £	*Other reserves* £	*Profit and loss* £	*Total* £
At the beginning of the year	11,000	-	6,000	65,000	82,000
Net profit for the year	-	-	-	11,700	11,700
Revaluations	-	15,000	-	-	15,000
Dividends	-	-	-	(1,700)	(1,700)
At the end of the year	11,000	15,000	6,000	75,000	107,000

We now look briefly at some other aspects of limited company financial statements.

BPP LEARNING MEDIA

3.3 Statement of total recognised gains and losses

Definition

> The **statement of total recognised gains and losses** brings together the profit as shown in the profit and loss account and other gains or losses.

It is important to understand that the profit and loss account can only deal with **realised** profits. An example of realised profits might be profits resulting from the sale proceeds already received or about to be received.

A company can also make substantial unrealised profits and losses, for example through changes in the **value** of its fixed assets. These are recognised, in the case of asset revaluation, by increasing the value or the assets in the balance sheet, the double entry being to a revaluation reserve included in shareholders' funds (as in the example in the previous section).

> **Activity 5** **(5 minutes)**
>
> Can you think of another type of gains and losses which might be recognised during a period but which are not realised and do not pass through the profit and loss account?

Generally speaking, realised profits and losses have been recognised in the profit and loss account; unrealised profits and losses may be recognised in the balance sheet. FRS 3 argues that users of accounts need to know about the unrealised movements. The statement brings all the information together.

The ASB regards the statement of total recognised gains and losses as very important, and accords it the status of a primary statement. This means that it must be presented with the same prominence as the balance sheet and the profit and loss account. Below is a specimen statement.

STATEMENT OF TOTAL RECOGNISED GAINS AND LOSSES

	£m
Profit for the financial year (ie profit after tax)	29
Unrealised surplus on revaluation of properties	4
Unrealised loss on trade investment	(3)
	30
Foreign currency translation differences	(2)
Total gains and losses recognised since last annual report	28

The statement is, as you can see, fairly brief, but it is useful in that it brings together information from different sources: the profit and loss account, the balance sheet and the supporting notes for the asset revaluations.

3.4 The annual report

The annual report is the name sometimes given to the published financial statements of a limited company.

All companies are required by law to prepare a profit and loss account, balance sheet and supporting notes. Accounting standards require two further statements: the statement of total recognised gains and losses (described above) and the cash flow statement (which will be covered in a later chapter). The published financial statements of most companies also include a directors' report and an auditors' report (there are exemptions available for small companies).

For most private companies, the financial statements are only 'published' in the sense that they are distributed to the shareholders and filed with the Registrar of Companies. However, most public companies treat the annual report as an important way of advertising the company to potential investors, the financial press, and the general public. The report is normally attractively designed and printed and contains much more information than the minimum required by law, for example:

- a Chairman's Statement;
- highlights and summary indicators (key figures showing trends over a number of years);
- environmental and social reports (these are sometimes issued as separate documents).

Often an Operating and Financial Review is also included, which is a discussion of the main factors underlying a company's performance and financial position. It is intended to help users of the financial statements to assess the future performance of the company. It includes non-financial information, such as the objectives of the business, the risks that it faces, the influences on its performance and factors likely to affect it in future. Environmental and social reports contain information about the way in which the company has interacted with the natural environment and the wider community.

This additional information can be very useful and often provides a more balanced picture of a company's performance and activities than the financial statements by themselves. However, it is important to remember that, unlike the financial statements, it is not audited. Companies can publish whatever information they wish and inevitably the directors will wish to present the company in the best possible light.

So far, we have only considered the financial statements of single companies. We will now explain how to prepare the financial statements of a group of companies.

4 GROUPS OF COMPANIES

4.1 Parent and subsidiary

You will probably know that many large businesses actually consist of several companies controlled by one central or administrative company. Together these companies are called a **group**. The controlling company, called the parent or **holding company**, will own some or all of the shares in the other companies, called subsidiary and associated companies.

There are many reasons for businesses to operate as groups; for the goodwill associated with the names of the subsidiaries, for tax or legal purposes and so forth. Company law requires that the results of a group should be presented as a whole.

BPP LEARNING MEDIA

In traditional accounting terminology, a **group of companies** consists of a **holding company** (or parent company) and one or more **subsidiary companies** which are controlled by the holding company.

The legal definitions of parent companies (called parent undertakings) and subsidiaries (called subsidiary undertakings) are very detailed, but the basic idea behind them is simple. A company is a parent undertaking of another undertaking (a subsidiary undertaking) if it can control that undertaking. Control is the ability to direct the financial and operating policies of another company with a view to gaining economic benefits from its activities.

There are several ways in which one company can gain control of another, but the most common ways are:

(a) by holding a majority of voting rights; or

(b) by holding shares in the company and having the right to appoint or remove directors holding a majority of the voting rights at meetings of the board.

In practice, if a company holds more than 50% of the equity (ordinary) shares in another company it is normally able to control that company.

4.2 The consolidated balance sheet

The preparation of a consolidated balance sheet, in a very simple form, consists of two procedures.

(a) Take the individual accounts of the holding company and each subsidiary and **cancel out items** which appear as an asset in one company and a liability in another.

(b) **Add together all the uncancelled assets and liabilities** throughout the group.

Items requiring cancellation may include the following.

(a) The asset '**shares in subsidiary companies**' which appears in the parent company's accounts will be matched with the liability 'share capital' in the subsidiaries' accounts.

(b) There may be **inter-company trading** within the group. For example, S Ltd may sell goods to H Ltd. H Ltd would then be a debtor in the accounts of S Ltd, while S Ltd would be a creditor in the accounts of H Ltd.

EXAMPLE: H GROUP

H Ltd regularly sells goods to its one subsidiary company, S Ltd. The balance sheets of the two companies on 31 December 20X0 are given below.

NOTES

H LIMITED
BALANCE SHEET AS AT 31 DECEMBER 20X0

		£	£	£
Fixed assets				
Tangible assets				35,000
40,000 £1 shares in S Ltd at cost				40,000
				75,000
Current assets				
Stocks			16,000	
Debtors:	S Ltd	2,000		
	Other	6,000		
			8,000	
Cash at bank			1,000	
			25,000	
Current liabilities				
Creditors			14,000	
				11,000
				86,000
Capital and reserves				
70,000 £1 ordinary shares				70,000
Reserves				16,000
				86,000

S LIMITED
BALANCE SHEET AS AT 31 DECEMBER 20X0

	£	£	£
Fixed assets			
Tangible assets			45,000
Current assets			
Stocks		12,000	
Debtors		9,000	
		21,000	
Current liabilities			
Bank overdraft		3,000	
Creditors: H Ltd	2,000		
Other	2,000		
		4,000	
		7,000	
			14,000
			59,000
Capital and reserves			
40,000 £1 ordinary shares			40,000
Reserves			19,000
			59,000

Prepare the consolidated balance sheet of H Ltd.

ANSWER

The cancelling items are:

(a) H Ltd's asset 'investment in shares of S Ltd' (£40,000) cancels with S Ltd's liability 'share capital' (£40,000);

(b) H Ltd's asset 'debtors: S Ltd' (£2,000) cancels with S Ltd's liability 'creditors: H Ltd' (£2,000).

The remaining assets and liabilities are added together to produce the following consolidated balance sheet.

BPP LEARNING MEDIA

NOTES

H LIMITED
CONSOLIDATED BALANCE SHEET AS AT 31 DECEMBER 20X0

	£	£
Fixed assets		
Tangible assets		80,000
Current assets		
Stocks	28,000	
Debtors	15,000	
Cash at bank	1,000	
	44,000	
Current liabilities		
Bank overdraft	3,000	
Creditors	16,000	
	19,000	
		25,000
		105,000
Capital and reserves		
70,000 £1 ordinary shares		70,000
Reserves		35,000
		105,000

Notes on the example

(a) H Ltd's bank balance is not netted off with S Ltd's bank overdraft. To offset one against the other would be less informative and would conflict with the statutory principle that assets and liabilities should not be netted off.

(b) The share capital in the consolidated balance sheet is the share capital of the parent company alone. This must **always** be the case, no matter how complex the consolidation, because the share capital of subsidiary companies must **always** be a wholly cancelling item.

4.3 Minority interests

It was mentioned earlier that the total assets and liabilities of subsidiary companies are included in the consolidated balance sheet, even in the case of subsidiaries which are only partly owned. A proportion of the net assets of such subsidiaries in fact belongs to investors from outside the group (minority interests).

In the consolidated balance sheet it is necessary to distinguish this proportion from those assets attributable to the group and financed by shareholders' funds.

The net assets of a company are financed by share capital and reserves. The consolidation procedure for dealing with partly owned subsidiaries is to **calculate the proportion of ordinary shares and reserves attributable to minority interests.**

EXAMPLE: MINORITY INTERESTS

H Ltd has owned 75% of the share capital of S Ltd since the date of S Ltd's incorporation. Their latest balance sheets are given below.

BPP LEARNING MEDIA

H LIMITED
BALANCE SHEET

	£	£
Fixed assets		
Tangible assets	50,000	
30,000 £1 ordinary shares in S Ltd at cost	30,000	
		80,000
Net current assets		25,000
		105,000
Capital and reserves		
80,000 £1 ordinary shares		80,000
Reserves		25,000
		105,000

S LIMITED
BALANCE SHEET

	£
Tangible fixed assets	35,000
Net current assets	15,000
	50,000
Capital and reserves	
40,000 £1 ordinary shares	40,000
Reserves	10,000
	50,000

Prepare the consolidated balance sheet.

ANSWER

All of S Ltd's net assets are consolidated despite the fact that the company is only 75% owned. The amount of net assets attributable to minority interests is calculated as follows.

	£
Minority share of share capital (25% × £40,000)	10,000
Minority share of reserves (25% × £10,000)	2,500
	12,500

Of S Ltd's share capital of £40,000, £10,000 is included in the figure for minority interest, while £30,000 is cancelled with H Ltd's asset 'investment in S Limited'.

The consolidated balance sheet can now be prepared.

H GROUP
CONSOLIDATED BALANCE SHEET

	£
Tangible fixed assets	85,000
Net current assets	40,000
	125,000
Share capital	80,000
Reserves £(25,000 + (75% × 10,000))	32,500
Shareholders' funds	112,500
Minority interest	12,500
	125,000

In this example we have shown minority interest on the 'capital and reserves' side of the balance sheet to illustrate how some of S Ltd's net assets are financed by shareholders' funds, while some are financed by outside investors.

4.4 Goodwill arising on consolidation

In the examples we have looked at so far the cost of shares acquired by the parent company has always been equal to the nominal value of those shares. This is seldom the case in practice. To begin with, **we will examine the entries made by the parent company in its own balance sheet when it acquires shares.**

When a company H Ltd wishes to **purchase shares** in a company S Ltd it must pay the previous owners of those shares. Suppose H Ltd purchases all 40,000 £1 shares in S Ltd and pays £60,000 cash to the previous shareholders in consideration. The entries in H Ltd's books would be:

DEBIT	Investment in S Ltd at cost	£60,000	
CREDIT	Bank		£60,000

The amount which H Ltd records in its books as the cost of its investment in S Ltd may be more or less than the book value of the assets it acquires. Suppose that S Ltd in the previous example has nil reserves, so that its share capital of £40,000 is balanced by net assets with a book value of £40,000. For simplicity, assume that the book value of S Ltd's assets is the same as their market or fair value.

Now when the directors of H Ltd agree to pay £60,000 for a 100% investment in S Ltd they must believe that, in addition to its tangible assets of £40,000, S Ltd must also have intangible assets worth £20,000. This amount of £20,000 paid over and above the value of the tangible assets acquired is called **goodwill arising on consolidation** (sometimes **premium on acquisition**).

Following the normal cancellation procedure the £40,000 share capital in S Ltd's balance sheet could be cancelled against £40,000 of the 'investment in S Limited' in the balance sheet of H Ltd. This would leave a £20,000 debit uncancelled in the parent company's accounts and this £20,000 would appear in the consolidated balance sheet under the caption 'Intangible fixed assets. Goodwill arising on consolidation.'

4.5 Goodwill and pre-acquisition profits

Up to now we have assumed that S Ltd had nil reserves when its shares were purchased by H Ltd. Assuming instead that S Ltd had earned profits of £8,000 in the period before acquisition, its balance sheet just before the purchase would look as follows.

	£
Net tangible assets	48,000
Share capital	40,000
Reserves	8,000
	48,000

If H Ltd now purchases all the shares in S Ltd it will acquire net tangible assets worth £48,000 at a cost of £60,000. Clearly in this case S Ltd's intangible assets (goodwill) are being valued at £12,000. It should be apparent that any **reserves** earned by the subsidiary **prior to its acquisition** by the parent company must be **incorporated in the cancellation** process so as to arrive at a figure for goodwill arising on consolidation. In other words, not only S Ltd's share capital, but also its pre-acquisition reserves, must be cancelled against the asset 'investment in S Ltd' in the accounts of the parent company. The uncancelled balance of £12,000 appears in the consolidated balance sheet.

The consequence of this is that **any pre-acquisition reserves of a subsidiary company are not aggregated with the parent company's reserves** in the consolidated balance sheet. The figure of consolidated reserves comprises the reserves of the parent company plus the post-acquisition reserves only of subsidiary companies. The post-acquisition reserves are simply reserves now less reserves at acquisition.

EXAMPLE: GOODWILL AND PRE-ACQUISITION PROFITS

Sing Ltd acquired the ordinary shares of Wing Ltd on 31 March when the draft balance sheets of each company were as follows.

SING LIMITED
BALANCE SHEET AS AT 31 MARCH

	£
Fixed assets	
Investment in 50,000 shares of Wing Ltd at cost	80,000
Net current assets	40,000
	120,000
	£
Capital and reserves	
Ordinary shares	75,000
Revenue reserves	45,000
	120,000

WING LIMITED
BALANCE SHEET AS AT 31 MARCH

Net current assets	60,000
Share capital and reserves	
50,000 ordinary shares of £1 each	50,000
Revenue reserves	10,000
	60,000

Prepare the consolidated balance sheet as at 31 March.

ANSWER

The technique to adopt here is to produce a new working: 'Goodwill'.

	£	£
Cost of investment		80,000
Share of net assets acquired as represented by:		
Ordinary share capital	50,000	
Revenue reserves on acquisition	10,000	
	60,000	
Group share 100%		60,000
Goodwill		20,000

SING LIMITED
CONSOLIDATED BALANCE SHEET AS AT 31 MARCH

	£
Fixed assets	
Goodwill arising on consolidation	20,000
Net current assets	100,000
	120,000
Capital and reserves	
Ordinary shares	75,000
Revenue reserves	45,000
	120,000

Activity 6 **(10 minutes)**

Under UK law, companies with subsidiaries are required to publish group accounts. Why do you think this is? Do group accounts have any limitations?

4.6 Consolidated profit and loss account

The principles are exactly the same as for the consolidated balance sheet.

EXAMPLE

H Ltd acquired 75% of the ordinary shares of S Ltd on that company's incorporation. The summarised profit and loss accounts of the two companies for the year ending 31 December 20X0 are set out below.

	H Ltd	*S Ltd*
	£	£
Turnover	75,000	38,000
Cost of sales	30,000	20,000
Gross profit	45,000	18,000
Administrative expenses	14,000	8,000
Profit before taxation	31,000	10,000
Taxation	10,000	2,000
Net profit for the year	21,000	8,000

The brought forward reserves of H Ltd and S Ltd at 1 January 20X0 were £87,000 and £17,000 respectively.

Required

Prepare the consolidated profit and loss account.

ANSWER

H LIMITED
CONSOLIDATED PROFIT AND LOSS ACCOUNT
FOR THE YEAR ENDED 31 DECEMBER 20X0

	£
Turnover (75 + 38)	113,000
Cost of sales (30 + 20)	50,000
Gross profit	63,000
Administrative expenses (14 + 8)	22,000
Profit before taxation	41,000
Taxation (10 + 2)	12,000
Profit after taxation	29,000
Minority interest (25% × £8,000)	2,000
Group net profit for the year	27,000

Notice how the minority interest is dealt with.

(a) Down to the line '**profit after taxation**' the **whole** of S Ltd's results is included without reference to group share or minority share. A **one-line adjustment** is then inserted to deduct the minority's share of S Ltd's profit after taxation.

(b) The minority's share (£4,250) of S Ltd's retained profits brought forward is excluded. This means that the carried forward figure of £126,750 is the figure which would appear in the balance sheet for group retained reserves (see below).

This last point may be clearer if we revert to our balance sheet technique and construct the working for group reserves.

Group reserves

	£
H Ltd (87,000 + 21,000)	108,000
Share of S Ltd's PARR (75% × £25,000 (17,000 + 8,000))	18,750
	126,750

The minority share of S Ltd's reserves comprises the minority interest in the £17,000 profits brought forward plus the minority interest (£2,000) in £8,000 retained profits for the year. (*Note*. PARR = Post acquisition retained reserves.)

Notice that a consolidated profit and loss account links up with a consolidated balance sheet exactly as in the case of an individual company's accounts: the figure of retained profits carried forward that can be calcualted from the profit and loss account appears as the figure for retained profits in the balance sheet.

Chapter roundup

- The accounting records and financial statements of a limited company are strictly regulated by statue.
- Ordinary shareholders are in effect the owners of the company.
- Profits paid out to shareholders are called dividends; profits not paid out in the form of dividends and taxation are kept in the profit and loss reserve.
- The total amount of reserves in a company varies according to changes in the net assets of the business.
- Share premium is the cash received by a company in excess of the nominal value of shares at the time of issue of the shares.
- The difference between the net book value of an asset before revaluation and the revalued amount of the asset is credited to the revaluation reserve.
- The net assets side of a company's balance sheet is similar to that of a sole trader. The capital side consists of share capital and reserves owned by the equity shareholders.
- Where one company controls another, that company has a subsidiary. Group accounts present the results, assets and liabilities of a holding (parent) company and its subsidiaries as if they were a single company.

Quick quiz

1 Who owns a limited company? Who manages its day-to-day activities?

2 What are the two classes of limited company?

3 A public limited company is the same as a listed company. True or false?

4 Who receives dividends?

5 Distinguish between a preference share and an ordinary share.

6 Name two kinds of non-distributable reserve.

7 What is a debenture loan?

8 What is 'goodwill arising on consolidation'?

Answers to quick quiz

1 Shareholders own a limited company and directors manage the day-to-day activities. (see para 1)

2 Public and private. (para 1)

3 False, as not all public companies need to be listed. (para 1)

4 Shareholders. (para 2.3)

5 Preference shares have a right to a fixed level of dividend prior to dividends for ordinary shareholders. (para 2.4)

6 Share premium account and revaluation reserve. (para 2.5)

7 A long-term liability arising from the issue of debenture stock by a company. (para 3.1)

8 The amount paid over and above the fair value of the net assets acquired. (para 4.4)

Answers to activities

1 True.

(b) Yes, and similarly the appropriation account of a company is different.

(c) True. With companies, the owners (shareholders) appoint directors to be responsible for management. However, even if shareholders and directors are the same people there is a legal distinction between the two roles. Where a director receives a salary he is an employee and his salary is an expense; as a shareholder he receives a dividend which is an appropriation.

(e) Yes.

False.

(a) Generally where there are numerous owners an enterprise will be incorporated, the obvious exception being partnerships.

(d) Shareholders receive dividends rather than take drawings from the business. Both dividends and drawings are appropriations.

2

Number of shares	Nominal value	Total value £
100,000	£1	100,000
200,000	50p	100,000
500,000	40p	200,000
850,000	10p	85,000

3 To begin with, ignore the figures for authorised capital: dividends are paid only on shares actually in issue.

If an ordinary dividend is proposed, the preference dividends will also have to be paid. The total to be paid is therefore as follows:

	£
Preference dividend (7% × £12,000)	840
Ordinary dividend (12% × £80,000)	9,600
	10,440

4 Issued share capital has increased from £7,500 to £9,000; this means that 3,000 shares (nominal value 50p each) have been issued. The amount received for the shares was £1,500 nominal value, plus £1,500 share premium (£3,500 – £2,000), ie £3,000 in total. The issue price was therefore £1 per share.

5 Gains or losses arising on the translation of foreign currency, for example with overseas investments.

NOTES

6 The object of annual accounts is to help shareholders exercise control over their company by providing information about how its affairs have been conducted. The shareholders of a holding company would not be given sufficient information from the accounts of the holding company on its own, because not enough would be known about the nature of the assets, income and profits of all the subsidiary companies in which the holding company has invested. The primary purpose of group accounts is to provide a true and fair view of the position and earnings of the holding company group as a whole, from the standpoint of the shareholders in the holding company.

A number of arguments have been put forward, however, which argue that group accounts have certain limitations.

(a) Group accounts may be misleading.

(i) The solvency (liquidity) of one company may hide the insolvency of another.

(ii) The profit of one company may conceal the losses of another.

(iii) They imply that group companies will meet each others' debts (this is certainly not true: a parent company may watch creditors of an insolvent subsidiary go unpaid without having to step in).

(b) Where a group consists of widely diverse companies in different lines of business, a set of group accounts may obscure much important detail unless supplementary information about each part of the group's business is provided.

Chapter 19 :
FUNDAMENTAL ACCOUNTING CONCEPTS

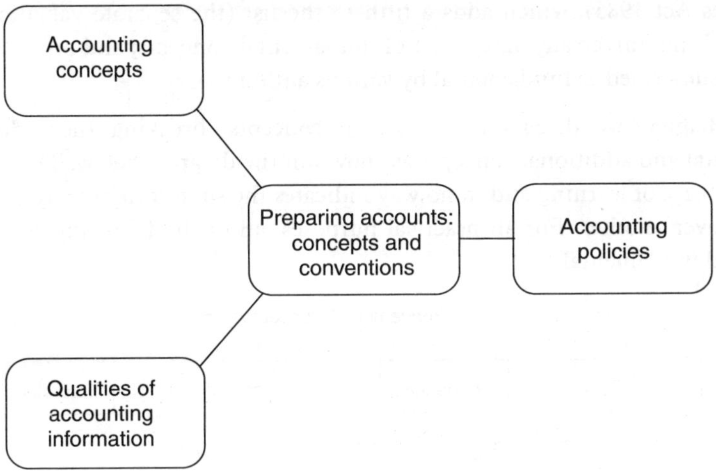

Introduction

Accounting standards, called FRSs and SSAPs, are one of the major sources of accounting regulation. Accountants have traditionally regarded four concepts as being fundamental to the preparation of accounting information: they are going concern, prudence, accruals and consistency. In addition to these four concepts, a number of additional concepts and ideas have been highlighted by various people as being important to accounting. In terms of conventions, historical cost accounting is by far the most widely accepted and practical.

Whereas the concepts and conventions are designed to help in the preparation of accounts, the accounting information itself is expected to have certain qualities. Four such qualities have been identified.

Your objectives

In this chapter you will learn about the following.

(a) The more widely accepted concepts underlying the preparation of accounts

(b) Some of the main conventions applied in the preparation of accounts

(c) The desirable qualities of accounting information

BPP LEARNING MEDIA

1 ACCOUNTING CONCEPTS

Accounting practice developed gradually over a period of centuries. Many of its commonly accepted procedures and concepts are by no means self-evident, nor are they the only possible concepts which could be used to build up an accounting framework.

Our first step is to look at some of the more important concepts which are taken for granted in preparing accounts. Accountants have traditionally regarded four concepts as fundamental accounting concepts: they are going concern, prudence, accruals and consistency. These four are also identified as fundamental by companies legislation (the Companies Act 1985), which adds a fifth to the list (the separate valuation principle). But there is no universally agreed list of fundamental concepts, and others besides these have been described as fundamental by various authors.

In this chapter, we discuss a number of concepts, breaking them down between fundamental and additional concepts as shown in the diagram below. This breakdown is simply for ease of learning and in no way indicates the superiority of any one or group of concepts over another. For all practical purposes, all of the following concepts may be considered fundamental.

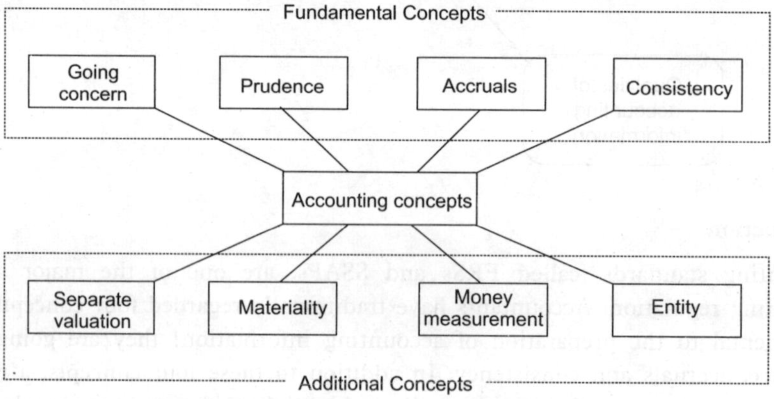

1.1 Fundamental concepts

The following concepts are defined as being fundamental by the Companies Act:

(a) Going concern concept

(b) Prudence concept

(c) Accruals concept

(d) Consistency concept

We will now discuss each of these concepts separately.

NOTES

1.2 The going concern concept

Definition

> The **going concern** concept implies that the business will continue to operate for the foreseeable future, and that there is no intention to close the company down or to make drastic cutbacks to the scale of operations.

The main significance of the going concern concept is that the assets of the business should not be valued at their 'break-up' value, which is the amount that they would sell for if they were sold off piecemeal and the business were thus broken up.

EXAMPLE

Suppose, for example, that Brenda acquires a Corgi-making machine at a cost of £60,000 which is expected to last six years. Since the asset has an estimated useful life of six years, it is normal to gradually write off the cost of the asset over this time. This practice of gradually writing off the cost of an asset over its useful life helps to ensure that as the asset physically or operationally deteriorates, its cost in the accounting records is also reduced to reflect the physical/operational deterioration. The yearly reduction in the cost of the asset is called depreciation. In this example the depreciation will be £10,000 per year (£60,000 ÷ 6 years).

Using the going concern concept, it would be presumed that the business will continue its operations and so the asset will live out its full six years in use. A depreciation charge of £10,000 will be made each year, and the value of the asset will be reduced each year by the amount of yearly depreciation. After one year, the value of the asset would therefore appear in the accounting records as £(60,000 – 10,000) = £50,000, after two years it would be £40,000, after three years £30,000 and so on, until it has been written down to a value of 0 after 6 years.

Now suppose that this asset has no other operational use outside the business, and in a forced sale, it would only sell for scrap. After one year of operation, its scrap value might be, say, £8,000. What would the value be after one year?

The value of the asset in the accounting records, applying the going concern concept, would be £50,000 after one year, but its immediate sell-off value is only £8,000. It might be argued that the asset is over-valued at £50,000 and that it should be written down to its break-up value. However, provided that the going concern concept is valid, it will be assumed that the asset will continue to be used; hence, it will not be written down to its sell off value but will gradually be reduced in value over time.

Activity 1 **(5 minutes)**

Your friend John has just started a business on 1 January. He bought a stock of 20 second-hand washing machines, each costing £100. During the year he sold 17 machines at £150 each.

John is not completely happy with this venture and is considering closing down the business. However, before he can make up his mind, John has asked for your help in determining the value of the remaining machines on 31 December.

John has asked you to calculate the value of the remaining machines if:

(a) He is forced to close down his business at the end of the year and the remaining machines will realise only £60 each in a forced sale; or

(b) He intends to continue his business into the next year.

How will you respond to John's request for help?

1.3 The prudence concept

Definition

Historically, the **prudence concept** has been seen to mean that in selecting between alternative procedures, or alternative valuations, the one selected should be the one which gives the most cautious presentation of the business financial position or results.

However, FRS 18 *Accounting policies* has subtly changed its emphasis. FRS 18 states that prudence should be applied in conditions of uncertainty to ensure that more confirmatory evidence is required about the existence of an asset or gain than is required about the existence of a liability or loss. It is not necessary to exercise prudence if there is no uncertainty.

Thus, for example, in the case of John's washing machines (Activity 1), the washing machines will be recorded in the accounting records at £100 each (their original cost) rather than £150 each (the selling price). This is simply an aspect of the prudence concept: to record the machines at £150 before they have been sold would be to anticipate a profit before the profit has actually been made.

On the other hand, in the case where a loss can be foreseen, it should be anticipated and taken into account immediately. If a business purchases stock for £1,200 but because of a sudden slump in the market only £900 is likely to be realised when the stock is sold, the prudence concept dictates that the stock should be valued at £900. It is not enough to wait until the stock is sold, and then recognise the £300 loss; it must be recognised as soon as it is foreseen.

1.4 Revenue recognition

The prudence concept raises the issue of when revenue should be recognised (ie recorded) in the accounting records. Let us suppose that John sold his washing machines (Activity 1) on credit. Should John be allowed to show a revenue of £2,550 (£150 × 17)?

Would allowing John to show the revenue be prudent, given that the customers have purchased on credit and have not yet paid cash to John?

Sales revenue should only be 'realised' and so 'recognised' in the trading, profit and loss account when:

(a) The sale transaction is for a specific quantity of goods at a known price, so that the sales value of the transaction is known for certain;

(b) The sale transaction has been completed, or else it is certain that it will be completed (eg in the case of long-term contract work, when the job is well under way but not yet completed by the end of an accounting period);

(c) The critical event in the sale transaction has occurred. The critical event is the event after which either:

  (i) It becomes virtually certain that cash will eventually be received from the customer; or

  (ii) Cash is actually received.

Usually, revenue is 'recognised' either:

(a) When a cash sale is made; or

(b) When the customer promises to pay on or before a specified future date, and the debt is legally enforceable.

The prudence concept is applied here in the sense that revenue should not be anticipated, and included in the trading, profit and loss account, before it is reasonably certain to 'happen'.

1.5 The accruals or matching concept

Definition

> The **accruals concept** states that, in computing profit, revenue earned must be matched against the expenditure incurred in earning it.

Assume that it costs Brenda £5 to produce a Corgi and she sells them for £10 each. If she made 20 Corgis in a month and sold all of them in the same month, her profit for the month would be (£200 – £100) = £100. If, however, Brenda had only sold 18 Corgis, it would be incorrect to calculate her profit as follows.

	£
Revenue (£10 × 18) =	180
Expenses (£5 × 20) =	100
Incorrect profit	80

The above calculation goes against the matching concept because the revenue earned on 18 Corgis is being matched not against the expenditure in earning that revenue (ie 18 Corgis) but against the expenditure incurred on producing 20 Corgis. The sales revenue of 18 Corgis should be matched with the purchase cost of identical number of Corgis (£90), leaving her with a profit of £90 (180 – 90).

In this example, the concepts of going concern and matching are linked. If Brenda decided to give up selling Corgis, how would the two Corgis in the balance sheet be valued?

If Brenda decided to give up selling Corgis, then the going concern concept would no longer apply and the value of the two Corgis would be a break-up valuation rather than cost. Similarly, if the two unsold Corgis were now unlikely to be sold at more than their cost of £5 each (say, because of damage or a fall in demand) then they should be recorded at their net realisable value (ie the likely eventual sales price less any expenses to be incurred to make them saleable, eg paint) rather than cost. This shows the application of the prudence concept.

1.6 The consistency concept

Accounting is not an exact science. There are many areas in which judgement must be exercised in attributing money values to items appearing in accounts. Over the years certain procedures and principles have come to be recognised as good accounting practice, but within these limits there are often various acceptable methods of accounting for similar items.

The consistency concept states that in preparing accounts consistency should be observed in two respects.

(a) Similar items within a single set of accounts should be given similar accounting treatment.

(b) The same treatment should be applied from one period to another in accounting for similar items. This enables valid comparisons to be made from one period to the next.

Activity 2 **(5 minutes)**

Peter Axon has a trading year which runs from 1 January to 31 December. In the year to 31 December 20X0, he sold goods, produced in his industrial unit, for £30,000 and expects to earn a similar revenue for 20X1.

Peter pays rent for a year in advance on 1 July annually. On 1 July 20X0 he paid £2,400 rent and on 1 July 20X1 £3,000.

(a) How much rent should Peter include in his accounts for the year ended 31 December 20X1?

(b) If Peter's landlord agreed, could he alter his payment date for rent to 1 January or would this conflict with the consistency concept?

1.7 Clashes between accounting concepts

Sometimes inconsistencies arise between the different accounting concepts. Consider the following two examples.

(a) **Accruals and prudence**. The accruals concept requires future income (eg in relation to credit sales) to be accrued. The prudence concept dictates that caution should be exercised, so that if there is doubt about the subsequent receipt, no accrual should be made.

(b) **Consistency and prudence**. If circumstances change, prudence may conflict with the consistency concept, which requires the same treatment year after year.

We next look at certain other accounting concepts considered equally fundamental by various authors.

1.8 Additional concepts

Company law recognises the above four fundamental concepts, although it describes them not as concepts but as accounting principles. The Act also mentions a fifth principle which may be called the separate valuation principle. This, and some other important concepts which are described below, are:

(a) The separate valuation principle
(b) The materiality concept
(c) The money measurement concept
(d) The entity concept

1.9 The separate valuation principle

The separate valuation principle states that, in determining the amount of an asset or liability in the balance sheet, each component item of the asset or liability must be valued separately. These separate valuations must then be aggregated to arrive at the total figure. For example, if a company's stock comprises 50 separate items, a valuation must (in theory) be arrived at for each item separately; the 50 figures must then be aggregated and the total is the stock figure which should appear in the accounting records.

1.10 The materiality concept

As we stated above in discussing the consistency concept, accounts preparation is not an exact science. Apart from the possibility of downright error, there will be many areas where two different accountants would come up with different figures for the same item. The materiality concept is relevant in this context.

Definition

> **Materiality** has been formally defined as: 'An expression of the relative significance or importance of a particular matter in the context of the financial statements as a whole. A matter is material if its omission or misstatement would reasonably influence the decisions of a [reader of the accounts].'

An error which is too trivial to affect anyone's understanding of the accounts is referred to as immaterial (ie insignificant). In preparing accounts it is important to assess what is

NOTES

material (ie significant) and what is not, so that time and money are not wasted in the pursuit of excessive detail.

1.11 Deciding on materiality

Determining whether or not an item is material is a very subjective exercise. There is no absolute measure of materiality. It is common to apply a convenient rule of thumb (for example, to define material items as those with a value greater than 5% of the profit disclosed by the accounts). But some items disclosed in accounts are regarded as particularly sensitive and even a very small misstatement of such an item would be regarded as a material error. An example might be the amount of remuneration paid to directors of the company.

In assessing whether or not an item is material, it is not only the amount of the item which needs to be considered. The context is also important.

(a) If a company shows assets of £2 million and stocks of £30,000, an error of £20,000 in the asset valuation might not be regarded as material, whereas an error of £20,000 in the stock valuation would be. In other words, the total of which the erroneous item forms part must be considered.

(b) If a business has a bank loan of £50,000 and a £55,000 balance on bank deposit account, it might well be regarded as a material misstatement if these two amounts were netted and the total shown as 'cash at bank £5,000'. (These two items should be shown separately, even though the net effect of showing separately or netting would be identical.) In other words, incorrect presentation may amount to material misstatement even if there is no monetary error.

Activity 3 **(5 minutes)**

You have recently paid £4.95 for a waste paper bin which should have a useful life of about five years. Should you treat it as a fixed asset and capitalise it in the balance sheet?

1.12 The money measurement concept

This concept states that accounts will only deal with those items to which a monetary value can be attributed. For example, monetary values can be attributed to such assets as machinery (eg the original cost of the machinery; or the amount it would cost to replace the machinery) and stocks of goods (eg the original cost of the goods, or, theoretically, the price at which the goods are likely to be sold).

However, a business may have assets such as the flair of a good manager or the loyalty of its workforce which although important are difficult to quantify. These may be important enough to give it a clear superiority over an otherwise identical business, but because they cannot be evaluated in monetary terms they do not appear anywhere in the accounts.

The fact that some assets cannot be expressed in monetary terms and therefore are not recorded in the accounting records does not mean that they are less important than the

BPP LEARNING MEDIA

assets which can be expressed in monetary terms. In fact, recognising the importance of non-quantifiable assets, accountants in recent years have tried to come up with ways of attributing values to them. These methods are beyond the scope of this text, but you should at least be aware of the problems such attempts try to address.

1.13 The entity concept

Briefly, the concept is that accountants regard a business as a separate entity, distinct from its owners or managers. The concept applies whether the business is a limited company (and so recognised in law as a separate entity) or a sole proprietorship or partnership (in which case the business is not separately recognised by the law).

Acceptance of this concept has important practical consequences, particularly in the case of a small business run by a single individual where the owner's personal affairs and business affairs may appear to be inextricably linked.

WORKED EXAMPLE: ENTITY CONCEPT

Suppose, for example, John runs a DIY shop but at times keeps some of the stock at home. In preparing the business accounts, it is essential to distinguish his private activities and keep them separate from the business activities.

Suppose that John withdraws some paint boxes from his stock to give to friends. How would this be reflected in the accounts?

ANSWER

The correct accounting treatment is to regard John as having purchased the goods from the business, which is a completely separate entity; the subsequent gift to his friends is then a private transaction and is not recorded anywhere in the books of the business. John should pay for the paint by taking money from his own purse and putting it into the till, or he should regard the taking of the paint boxes as a partial withdrawal of the investment he has made in the business. Otherwise, the accounts will give a misleading picture.

Activity 4 **(5 minutes)**

This activity will help to ensure that you have understood the concepts and conventions covered so far in this chapter.

Are the following statements true or false?

(a) The entity concept is that accountants regard a business as a separate legal entity, distinct from its owners or managers.

(b) Accounts deal only with items to which a monetary value can be attributed.

2 ACCOUNTING POLICIES

Accounting policies are the principles, conventions and rules that a business applies in order to specify the way in which particular items are reflected in the accounts. For example, if a business decides to depreciate its fixed assets using the straight line method rather than the reducing balance method, this is its accounting policy.

A business should adopt accounting policies that enable its financial statements to give a true and fair view. Those accounting policies should be consistent with the requirements of accounting standards, UITF Abstracts and companies legislation, if these apply to the business.

If it is necessary to choose between accounting policies, the business should select the policy that is most appropriate to its particular circumstances for the purpose of giving a true and fair view.

The accounting policies chosen should enable the information in the financial statements to have the following qualities:

(a) Relevance
(b) Reliability
(c) Comparability, and
(d) Understandability.

These qualities are discussed later in the chapter.

A business should not change its accounting policies unless a new policy would give a fairer presentation of its results and financial position. This is because frequent changes would make it more difficult for users to compare a business's financial statements with those of earlier periods. However, a business should review its accounting policies regularly to ensure that they are still appropriate.

The financial statements should include a description of each of the accounting policies adopted by the business, where these have a material effect on the financial statements. Details of any changes to the accounting policies that were followed in the preceding period should also be disclosed.

3 QUALITIES OF ACCOUNTING INFORMATION

The following are the key characteristics of useful information.

(a) **Relevance**. The information provided should be that which is required to satisfy the needs of information users. In the case of company accounts, clearly a wide range of information will be needed to satisfy the interested parties already identified.

(b) **Reliability**. Information is reliable if:

(i) Users can depend upon it to represent what it is supposed to represent and it reflects the substance of the transactions that have taken place;

(ii) It is free from bias and material error and is complete; and

(iii) I#t has been prudently prepared.

(c) **Comparability**. Information should be produced on a consistent basis so that valid comparisons can be made with information from previous periods and with information produced by other sources (for example the accounts of similar companies operating in the same line of business).

(d) **Understandability**. Information needs to be capable of being understood by users who have a reasonable knowledge of business and economic activities and accounting and are willing to study the information provided with reasonable diligence.

There are two other qualities of information which should be considered.

(a) **Objectivity**. The usefulness of information will be enhanced if it contains a minimum of subjective judgement. In the context of preparing accounts, where many decisions must be based on judgement rather than objective facts, this problem often arises. Management are often inclined to paint a rosy picture of a company's profitability to make their own performance look impressive, while the auditor responsible for verifying the accounts is inclined to take a more prudent view so that he cannot be held liable by, say, a supplier misled into granting credit to a shaky company.

(b) **Timeliness**. The usefulness of information is reduced if it does not appear until long after the period to which it relates, or if it is produced at unreasonably long intervals. What constitutes a long interval depends on the circumstances: management of a company may need very frequent (perhaps daily) information on cash flows to run the business efficiently; but shareholders are normally content to see accounts produced annually.

FOR DISCUSSION

Some of these qualities may not be compatible, for example timeliness and reliablity. If you try to produce a financial report, essay or any other piece of work to a tight deadline, you may well leave something out. Another potential conflict exists between prudence and objectivity. How do you think any incompatability between qualities should be resolved?

Chapter roundup

- In preparing financial statements, certain fundamental concepts are adopted as a framework.
- Accountants have traditionally regarded the following four concepts as fundamental.
  - The going concern concept. Unless there is evidence to the contrary, it is assumed that a business will continue to trade normally for the foreseeable future.
  - The prudence concept. Where alternative accounting procedures are acceptable in conditions of uncertainty, choose the one which gives the less optimistic view of profitability and asset values.
  - The accruals or matching concept. Revenue earned must be matched against expenditure incurred in earning it.
  - The consistency concept. Similar items should be accorded similar accounting treatments.
- A number of other concepts may be regarded as fundamental.
  - The entity concept. A business is an entity distinct from its owner(s).
  - The money measurement concept. Accounts only deal with items to which monetary values can be attributed.
  - The separate valuation principle. Each component of an asset or liability must be valued separately.
  - The materiality concept. Only items material in amount or in their nature will affect the true and fair view given by a set of accounts.
- The accounting information is expected to possess a number of qualities.
- They are, among others, relevance, reliability, comparability and understandability.

Quick quiz

1 List the four accounting concepts traditionally identified as fundamental.

2 Briefly re-cap what is meant by: the entity concept; the money measurement concept; the going concern concept; the prudence concept; the accruals concept; the consistency concept; the separate valuation principle; and the materiality concept.

3 At what stage is it normal to recognise the revenue arising from a credit sale?

4 What are the qualities of useful accounting information?

Answers to quick quiz

1 Accruals, consistency, going concern, prudence. (see para 1.1)

2 Check your answers in respect of these concepts in the chapter.

3 Refer to the various aspects detailed. (para 1.4)

4 Check the various qualities in the chapter. (para 3)

Answers to activities

1 (a) If the business is to be closed down, the remaining three machines must be valued at the amount they will realise in a forced sale, ie 3 × £60 = £180.

(b) If the business is regarded as a going concern, the stock unsold at 31 December will be carried forward into the following year, when the cost of the three machines will be matched against the eventual sale proceeds in computing that year's profits. The three machines will therefore appear in the balance sheet at 31 December at cost, 3 × £100 = £300.

2 (a) The matching concept is applied so that £1,200 rent applies to the first half of the year and £1,500 to the second half of the year – a total of £2,700.

(b) Consistency is concerned with the application of accounting concepts, bases and policies and so long as matching and accruals are applied, it does not matter when the actual payment of rent takes place.

3 No, because of the materiality concept. The cost of the bin is very small. Rather than cluttering up the balance sheet for five years, treat the £4.95 as an expense in this year's profit and loss account.

4 (a) False. Although it is certainly true that the entity concept is that accountants regard a business as a separate entity, it is not always a legal difference. For example, legally a sole trader is not separate from his business.

(b) True, although attempts have been made to account for a number of non-monetary items.

Chapter 20 :
CASH FLOW STATEMENTS

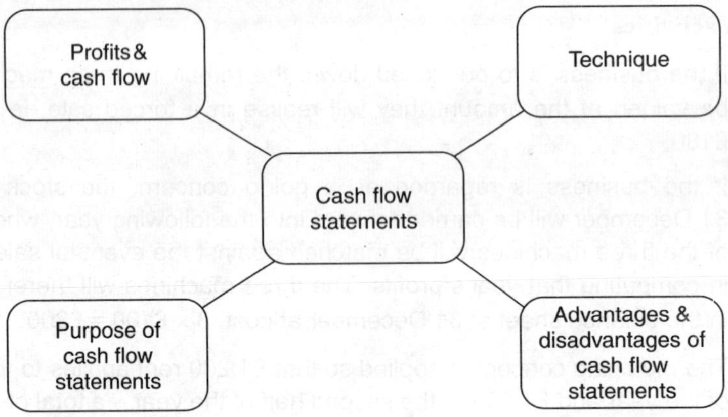

Introduction

If a firm is unable to pay its bills when they are due it can be forced into liquidation, regardless of how profitable the firm may happen to be. In the long run, profit will result in an increase in the company's cash balance but, as Keynes observed, 'in the long run we are all dead'. In the short run, the making of a profit will not necessarily result in an increased cash balance.

This observation leads us to two questions. The first relates to the importance of the distinction between cash and profit. The second is concerned with the usefulness of the information provided by the balance sheet and profit and loss account in the problem of deciding whether the company has, or will be able to generate, sufficient cash to finance its operations.

The importance of the distinction between cash and profit and the scant attention paid to this by the profit and loss account has resulted in the development of cash flow statements. Section 1 of this chapter discusses the distinction between profit and cash while the preparation of cash flow statements is covered in Section 2.

Your objectives

In this chapter you will learn about the following.

(a) The differences between profits and cash surpluses

(b) The purpose of cash flow statements and show how they are prepared

(c) The strengths and weaknesses of cash flow accounting

NOTES

1 PROFITS AND CASH FLOW

To be successful in business, an enterprise must make a profit. Profits are needed to pay dividends to shareholders and to reward partners or proprietors. Some profits are retained within the business as reserves to finance the development and growth of the business. We can therefore say that although a firm may be able to bear occasional losses, it must be profitable in the long term.

In addition to being **profitable,** in order to survive and grow, it is also necessary for a firm to 'pay its way': to **pay cash** for the goods and services and capital equipment it buys, the workforce it employs and the other expenses (such as rent, rates and taxation) that it incurs. If a firm does not pay its bills when they are due, it will first of all lose the goodwill of its suppliers or workforce and may then be driven into liquidation. **It is therefore necessary to be not just profitable, but also capable of obtaining cash to meet demand for payments.**

Activity 1 **(5 minutes)**

Profits and cash surpluses are not the same thing for a number of reasons. For example, cash may be obtained from a transaction which has nothing to do with profit or loss, such as a share issue. Fill in the missing entries in the following table to ensure you understand the impact on cash flow and profit of the items listed.

Item	*Effect on cash flow*	*Effect on profit*
Fixed asset purchased two years ago		
New issue of shares for cash		
Increase in bank loan		
New fixed asset purchased for cash		
Fixed asset sold during year		

The profit and loss account reports the total sales in a year. If goods are sold on credit, the cash receipts will differ from sales. The relationship between sales and receipts is as follows, with illustrative figures.

	£
Debtors owing money at the start of the year	20,000
Sales during the year	300,000
Total money due from customers	320,000
Less debtors owing money at the end of the year	30,000
Cash receipts from debtors during the year	290,000

Similarly, the profit and loss account reports the cost of goods sold during the year. However, if materials are bought on credit, the cash payments to suppliers will be different from the value of materials purchased.

NOTES

	£
Payments owed to creditors at the start of the year	6,000
Add purchases during the year	70,000
	76,000
Less payments still owing to creditors at the end of the year	4,000
Equals cash payments to creditors during the year	72,000

Information about cash receipts and payments can add to our understanding of a firm's operations and financial stability. Whereas a profit and loss statement reports on profitability, cash flow statements report on the ability of the firm to pay its bills.

It can be argued that 'profit' does not always give a useful or meaningful picture of a company's operations. Readers of a company's financial statements might even be misled by a reported profit figure. Shareholders, employees and creditors might interpret a company's making profit in different ways.

(a) **Shareholders** might believe that if a company makes a profit after tax, of say, £100,000 then this is the amount which it could afford to pay as a dividend. Unless the company has sufficient cash available to stay in business and also to pay a dividend, the shareholders' expectation would be wrong.

(b) **Employees** might believe that if a company makes profits, it can afford to pay higher wages next year. This opinion may not be correct: the ability to pay wages depends on the availability of cash.

(c) **Creditors** might consider that a profitable company is a going concern. But this may not be so. For example, if a company builds up large amounts of stock, their cost would not be chargeable against profits. However, cash would have been used up in making them, thus weakening the company's liquid resources.

Moreover, the profit and loss account and balance sheet are subject to manipulation by the use of different accounting policies, eg different stock valuation methods, depreciation methods, etc.

The survival of a business entity therefore depends not so much on profits as on its ability to pay its debts when they fall due. Such payments might include 'profit and loss' items such as material purchases, wages, interest and taxation etc, but also capital payments for new fixed assets and the repayment of a loan when it falls due.

From these examples, it is apparent that a company's performance and prospects depend not so much on the 'profits' earned in a period, but more realistically on cash flows.

Since cash flows are so vital to the survival and growth of a business, regulatory bodies require that information about cash flows be made available to external users as well.

2 PURPOSE OF CASH FLOW STATEMENTS

2.1 Aims

In September 1991, the Accounting Standards Board (ASB) published FRS 1 *Cash flow statements* (revised 1996). The standard requires most medium and large companies to produce a cash flow statement.

The main purpose of the statement is to provide information about a company's cash receipts and cash payments during an accounting year. Some of the information provided by the cash flow statement can be obtained by analysing the profit and loss statement and the balance sheet. However, it is the cash flow statement that brings together all those transactions which affect a company's cash position.

The aim of a cash flow statement is to assist users to:

(a) Assess the enterprise's ability to generate positive net cash flows in the future

(b) Assess its ability to meet its obligations to service loans, pay dividends etc

(c) Assess the reasons for differences between reported profit and cash flows

(d) Assess the effect on its finances of major transactions in the year

(e) Compare the cash flow performance of different businesses

The statement should therefore show changes in cash. Cash is cash in hand, plus any deposits repayable on demand less overdrafts. Deposits repayable on demand include the company's current account with the bank plus any other accounts that are repayable without penalty within 24 hours.

2.2 Classifying cash flows

The statement should list cash flows for the period classified under the following standard headings.

(a) Operating activities
(b) Returns on investments and servicing of finance
(c) Taxation
(d) Capital expenditure
(e) Equity dividends paid
(f) Management of liquid resources
(g) Financing

The use of these standard headings enables users of the accounts to compare the cash flow statements of different businesses and those of the same business over time.

Activity 2 **(10 minutes)**

The cash flow statement should classify cash receipts and payments according to their nature. Try classifying the following receipts and payments.

(a) Purchase of an asset for cash
(b) Cash repayment of a loan
(c) Issue of shares for cash
(d) Borrowing money
(e) Receipts from customers

Before we start looking at how to construct a cash flow statement, an example will help our understanding of the issues discussed so far.

2.3 Example of a cash flow statement

Flail Ltd commenced trading on 1 January 20X0 with a medium-term loan of £21,000 and a share issue which raised £35,000. The company purchased fixed assets for £21,000 cash, and during the year to 31 December 20X0 entered into the following transactions.

(a) Purchases from suppliers were £19,500, of which £2,550 was unpaid at the year end.

(b) Wages and salaries amounted to £10,500, of which £750 was unpaid at the year end.

(c) Interest on the loan of £2,100 was fully paid in the year and a repayment of £5,250 was made.

(d) Sales turnover was £29,400, including £900 debtors at the year end.

(e) Interest on cash deposits at the bank amounted to £75.

(f) A dividend of £4,000 was proposed as at 31 December 20X0.

The cash flow statement for the year ended 31 December 20X0 will be as follows.

NOTES

FLAIL LIMITED
CASH FLOW STATEMENT FOR THE YEAR ENDED 31 DECEMBER 20X0

	£	£
Operating activities		
Cash received from customers (£29,400 – £900)	28,500	
Cash paid to suppliers (£19,500 – £2,550)	(16,950)	
Cash paid to and on behalf of employees (£10,500 – £750)	(9,750)	
Cash flow from operating activities		1,800
Returns on investments and servicing of finance		
Interest paid	(2,100)	
Interest received	75	
		(2,025)
Capital expenditure		
Purchase of fixed assets		(21,000)
Cash flow before financing		(21,225)
Financing		
Issue of shares	35,000	
Proceeds from medium-term loan	21,000	
Repayment of medium-term loan	(5,250)	
Cash flow from financing		50,750
Net increase in cash		29,525
Cash at 1 January 20X0		-
Cash at 31 December 20X0		29,525

Note that the dividend is only proposed and so there is no related cash flow in 20X0.

Preparing a cash flow statement is straightforward. We next look at the various steps involved in preparing the statement.

3 TECHNIQUE

3.1 Categories of cash flows

Operating activities include the cash receipts and payments for those activities which a business undertakes in the normal course of operation. Examples of inflows and outflows that fall under operating activities are shown in the diagram below.

Operating activities

Inflows

- Cash sales
- Receipts from debtors

Outflows

- Cash payment for selling expenses
- Cash payment for distribution expenses
- Cash payment for administration expenses
- Payment to creditors

BPP LEARNING MEDIA

Returns on investments and servicing of finance. These cash flows include receipts of dividends and interest and payments of interest and non-equity dividends (dividends on preference shares).

Taxation is the payment of corporation tax to HM Revenue and Customs.

Capital expenditure. This heading includes receipts from the sale of fixed assets and payments for the purchase of fixed assets. It may also include receipts and payments relating to the sale and purchase of fixed asset investments (if this is the case, the heading should be 'capital expenditure and financial investment').

Equity dividends paid. These are dividends paid on equity (ordinary) shares.

Management of liquid resources. Liquid resources are current asset investments (in other words, investments intended to be held for a short time). For example, if a company temporarily has more cash than it needs for its day to day operations it may put the cash on deposit in order to earn interest. Short term deposits and investments are not cash because they are not repayable on demand. This heading includes withdrawals from and payments into short term deposits and payments or receipts in respect of other short term investments.

Financing. These cash flows include receipts from the issue of shares and debentures and from borrowings (eg, long term loans) and repayments of debentures and loans.

3.2 Cash flow from operations

The key areas to look at when 'converting' a profit and loss account into a statement of cash flow from operating activities are as follows.

(a) **Changes in debtors**. An increase in the debtor balance over an accounting period means that cash receipts have been less than the sales for the period (no change in debtor balance over a period means that cash receipts from sales were exactly equal to sales).

Since the profit for the year includes all sales (whether for cash or credit), it is important that the profit figure is adjusted for changes in debtors to arrive at cash flow from operations.

		Profit + decrease in debtors
To arrive at cash flow from operations	=	**or**
		Profit – increase in debtors

This somewhat confusing rule holds good because a decrease in debtors means that cash receipts from sales were greater than the sales for the period. As profit only includes the sales for the period, we need to add the excess cash collections (excess of cash receipts over sales shown by the decrease in debtors) to the profit in order to include all the cash receipts for the period in our calculations.

The opposite applies, of course, if debtor balances have increased over the year.

(b) **Changes in creditors**. The situation here is the reverse of that described under debtors. Thus, the rule is:

		Profit – decrease in creditors
To arrive at cash flow from operations	=	**or**
		Profit + increase in creditors

The reason for an increase in creditors being added to the profit is that not all purchases are being bought for cash. In fact, cash is being retained and not used to pay off creditors.

(c) **Changes in stock**. Stock in the balance sheet at the year end represents an asset for which money has been paid, but which has not been charged against profits for the period. To the extent that closing stock exceeds opening stock the profit and loss account therefore, understates the amount of cash paid out to suppliers. To compensate for this, the increase in stock over the year is shown as a deduction in reconciling operating profit to net cash flow from operating activities.

Once again, it is obvious that a decrease in stock levels over the year would be a positive item in the reconciliation.

		Profit – decrease in creditors
To arrive at cash flow from operations	=	**or**
		Profit + increase in creditors

The following are some other important things you need to keep in mind when preparing a cash flow statement.

(a) **Depreciation**. To arrive at our figure of operating profit we would deduct an amount to reflect depreciation of our fixed assets. But although this is correctly shown as a reduction in profit, it is not a cash outflow. If cash flows are what we are interested in, we must add back amounts deducted in respect of depreciation.

		Profit – decrease in creditors
To arrive at cash flow from operations	=	**or**
		Profit + increase in creditors

(b) **Fixed asset disposal**. The above logic also applies to any gain or loss on disposal of fixed assets (if these are included in operating profit; sometimes they are separately disclosed below operating profit, in which case no adjustment needs to be made).

		Profit – decrease in creditors
To arrive at cash flow from operations	=	**or**
		Profit + increase in creditors

NOTES

Activity 3 **(10 minutes)**

The summarised balance sheets of Cashflow Ltd at 30 June 20X0 and 20X1 are given below. Calculate the net cash flow from operating activities for the year ended 30 June 20X1, assuming no tax or dividends.

	30 June 20X0	30 June 20X1
	£	£
Fixed assets: cost	12,000	13,600
Depreciation	6,500	7,800
	5,500	5,800
Stock	4,000	5,200
Debtors	6,000	4,700
Cash	1,800	850
	17,300	16,550
Creditors	(4,300)	(1,850)
Shareholders' funds	13,000	14,700

To reinforce your understanding of this area let's work through a more detailed example.

WORKED EXAMPLE: CASH FLOW STATEMENT

The balance sheets of Outflow Ltd at 30 June 20X0 and 20X1 are set out below.

	20X1		20X0	
	£	£	£	£
Freehold property (revalued in 20X1)		30,000		16,000
Plant and machinery				
Cost at 1 July 20X0	8,000		8,000	
Acquisitions at cost	4,500		0	
Disposals at cost	(2,200)		0	
	10,300		8,000	
Depreciation	2,800		1,900	
		7,500		6,100
		37,500		22,100
Stock	12,000		7,800	
Debtors	7,600		5,900	
Balance at bank	0		850	
		19,600		14,550
		57,100		36,650
Bank overdraft	3,500		0	
Loan	0		1,000	
Creditors	5,250		5,000	
		8,750		6,000
		48,350		30,650
Share capital		10,000		8,500
Share premium account		1,000		0
Revaluation reserve		14,000		0
Profit and loss reserve		23,350		22,150
		48,350		30,650

The machinery disposed of had a net book value of £550 and was sold for £800.

BPP LEARNING MEDIA

NOTES

ANSWER

The cash flow statement for the year ended 30 June 20X1 will be as follows.

OUTFLOW LIMITED
CASH FLOW STATEMENT FOR THE YEAR ENDED 30 JUNE 20X1

Reconciliation of operating profit to net cash outflow from operating activities

	£
Operating profit (£23,350-£22,150)	1,200
Depreciation (£2,800-(£1,900-£1,650))	2,550
Profit on sale of tangible fixed assets	(250)
Increase in stocks	(4,200)
Increase in debtors	(1,700)
Increase in creditors	250
	(2,150)

	£	£
Net cash outflow from operating activities		(2,150)
Capital expenditure		
Payments to acquire tangible fixed assets	(4,500)	
Receipts from sale of tangible fixed assets	800	
Net cash outflow from capital expenditure		(3,700)
Net cash flow before financing		(5,850)
Financing		
Issue of share capital	2,500	
Repayment of loan	(1,000)	
Net cash outflow from financing		1,500
Decrease in cash (3,500 + 850)		(4,350)

Activity 4 **(10 minutes)**

Check your understanding of the above example. Are you sure you know how the figures were derived for:

(a) issue of share capital; and
(b) depreciation?

Preparing a cash flow statement takes time. In business, time is money. Why does a business then spend time preparing such a statement?

4 ADVANTAGES AND DISADVANTAGES OF CASH FLOW STATEMENTS

The advantages of cash flow accounting are as follows.

(a) Survival in business depends on the ability to generate cash. Cash flow accounting directs attention towards this critical issue.

(b) Cash flow is more objective than 'profit'. In other words, it is less 'dependent' on somewhat arbitrary accounting conventions and concepts.

BPP LEARNING MEDIA

(c) Creditors (long and short-term) are more interested in an entity's ability to repay them than in its profitability. Whereas 'profits' might indicate that cash is likely to be available, cash flow accounting is more direct with its message.

(d) Cash flow reporting provides a better means of comparing the results of different companies than traditional profit reporting, since profit can be easily manipulated by choosing the more favourable accounting policies.

(e) Cash flow reporting satisfies the needs of all users better:

  (i) For management, it provides the sort of information on which decisions should be taken; traditional profit accounting does not help with decision making;

  (ii) For shareholders and auditors, cash flow accounting can provide a satisfactory basis for judging the performance of management;

  (iii) As described previously, the information needs of creditors and employees will be better served by cash flow accounting.

(f) Cash flow forecasts are easier to prepare, as well as more useful, than profit forecasts.

(g) Cash is an easy, familiar concept for users to understand.

FOR DISCUSSION

You should give some thought to the possible disadvantages of cashflow accounting which are essentially the advantages of accruals accounting. There is also the practical problem that few businesses keep historical cash flow information in the form needed to prepare a historical cash flow statement and so extra record keeping is likely to be necessary.

Chapter roundup

- Cash is vital to the survival of a business.
- Profits are not the same as cash flows. A company can have healthy profits, but poor cash flow or *vice versa*.
- Whereas profit and loss accounts report on profitability, cash flow statements report on a firm's ability to pay its bills.
- A cash flow statement shows changes in cash over a period.
- The statement classifies receipts and payments under standard headings: operating activities; returns on investments and servicing of finance; taxation; capital expenditure; equity dividends paid; management of liquid resources; and financing.
- The possible disadvantages of cash flow accounting are essentially the advantages of accrual accounting.

BPP LEARNING MEDIA

Quick quiz

1 List four examples of transactions which affect profit differently from their effect on cash flow.

2 Explain the limitations of a profit figure for:

(a) Shareholders
(b) Employees
(c) Creditors
(d) Management

3 What are the aims of a cash flow statement?

4 Why is an increase in stock treated as negative in a cash flow statement?

Answers to quick quiz

1 Check your answer against the details given in para 1 of the chapter.

2 Compare your answer with the chapter. (see para 1)

3 To assist users to assess the enterprise's ability to generate net cash flows in the future, to meet its obligations to service loans, pay dividends, the reasons for differences between reported profit and cash flows and the effect on its finances of major transaction in the year. (para 2.1)

4 To compensate for impact of stock in the profit calculation. (para 3.2)

Answers to activities

1

	Effect on cash flow	*Effect on profit*
Fixed asset purchased two years ago	None	Depreciation charge
New issue of shares for cash	Cash inflow	None
Increase in bank loan	Cash inflow	Increase in interest charges
New fixed asset purchased for cash	Cash outflow	Depreciation charge
Fixed asset sold during year	Cash inflow	Profit or loss on sale

2 You should have included (a) capital expenditure, (b), (c) and (d) as financing and (e) as a cash flow from operating activities. Cash flows from operating activities also include payments to employees and suppliers and any other cash flows from transactions not classified as investing or financing.

3

	£
Profit for the year (14,700 – 13,000)	1,700
Depreciation (7,800 – 6,500)	1,300
Increase in stock	(1,200)
Decrease in debtors	1,300
Decrease in creditors	(2,450)
	650

4 (a) The share capital account has risen from £8,500 to £10,000 over the year. This, however, only reflects the *nominal* value of the shares issued. It is clear that the amount actually *received* for the shares exceeded this nominal value by £1,000: that is how the balance on share premiurn account arose. The total received is therefore £10,000+£1,000-£8,500=£2,500.

(b)

	£	£
Accumulated depreciation at 30 June 20X0		1,900
Depreciation eliminated on disposal:		
Cost of asset disposed of	2,200	
Net book value of asset disposed of	550	
Accumulated depreciation on asset disposed of		1,650
		250
Accumulated depreciation at 30 June 20X1		2,800
∴ Depreciation charged for the year		2,550

Chapter 21 :
PARTNERSHIPS

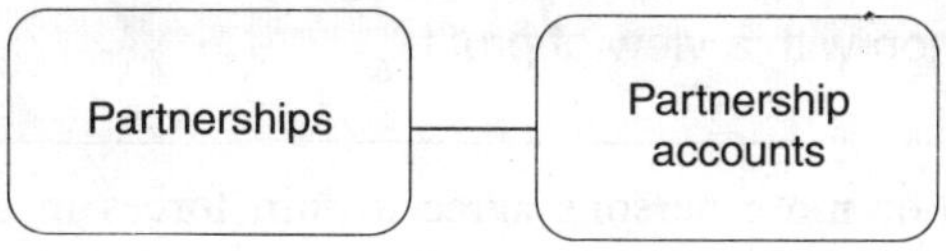

Introduction

The Edexel Guidelines make it clear that you are expected to be able to prepare and present financial statements for sole traders, limited companies and partnerships. So far we have concentrated on the first two of those three, so this chapter introduces partnership accounting.

Your objectives

In this chapter, you will learn about the following.

(a) The nature of a partnership

(b) Partnership accounts

1 PARTNERSHIP ACCOUNTS

1.1 What is a partnership?

This is defined by the **Partnership Act 1890**.

Definition

A **partnership** is the relationship which subsists between persons carrying on a business in common with a view of profit.

In other words, if two or more persons agree to join forces in some kind of business venture, then a partnership is the usual result. In a partnership:

(a) The **personal liability** of each partner for the firm's debts is **unlimited**, and so an individual's personal assets may be used to meet any partnership liabilities in the event of partnership bankruptcy.

(b) All partners usually **participate in the running of the business**, rather than merely providing the capital.

(c) Profits or losses of the business are **shared** between the partners.

(d) A **partnership deed** is usually (though not always) drawn up detailing the provisions of the contract between the partners.

Activity 1 **(5 minutes)**

Try to think of reasons why a business should be conducted as a partnership rather than:

(a) As a sole trader
(b) As a company

1.2 Preparation of partnership accounts

In this book we are primarily concerned with the accounting aspects of partnership, rather than the details of partnership law. However, in the absence of an agreement, express or implied, between the partners, or where an agreement is silent on particular points, certain provisions of the Partnership Act 1890 will apply. The most important of these are as follows.

(a) Partners share equally in the profits and losses of the partnership

(b) Partners are not entitled to receive salaries

(c) Partners are not entitled to interest on their capital

(d) Partners may receive interest at 5% per annum on any advances over and above their agreed capital

(e) A new partner may not be introduced without the consent of all the existing partners

NOTES

(f) A retiring partner is entitled to receive interest at 5% per annum on his share of the partnership assets (his capital) retained within the partnership after his retirement

(g) On the dissolution of a partnership the assets of the firm must be used (in the following order)

(i) To repay outside creditors
(ii) To repay partners' advances
(iii) To repay partners' capital
(iv) To distribute any residue to the partners in profit sharing ratio

When working partnership accounting problems, the above provisions should be applied unless contrary clauses of a partnership agreement are detailed in the question. In fact, partnership accounts are in many respects identical to those of sole traders, the principal **differences** being that:

(a) The partnership capital is contributed not by one, but by several proprietors, and **each partner's contribution** must be identified in the accounts.

(b) The net profit, once calculated, has to be **appropriated** between the partners.

1.3 Partnership capital

Just as capital contributed by a sole trader to his business is recorded in his capital account, the capital contributed to a partnership is recorded in a series of **capital accounts, one for each partner**. The amount of each partner's contribution usually depends upon the partnership agreement, and since each partner is ultimately entitled to repayment of his capital it is vital to keep a continuous record of his interest in the firm. Sometimes partners may be required to contribute equally to the capital fund.

With one or two exceptions (dealt with below) each partner's capital account balance normally **remains constant** from year to year.

1.4 Current accounts

A **current account** for each partner is maintained to record a wide range of items on a continuous basis, for example, to charge drawings and other personal benefits and to credit salaries, interest on capital, share of profits etc. In effect, a partner's current account is merely an extension of his capital account, its balance representing further funds invested by the partner in the firm.

Sometimes, as in sole traders' accounts, a **drawings account** is kept to record each partner's withdrawals (in money or money's worth) throughout the year.

		£	£
DEBIT	Drawings account (or current account)	X	
CREDIT	Bank account (or other asset accounts)		X
	Purchases (or cost of sales)		X

Being withdrawal of cash (drawings and/or salaries) or other assets (including goods originally purchased for resale) by the partner

The balance on the partner's drawings account is **debited to his current account at the end of the year**. If he has withdrawn more than his profit share the current account may show a debit balance. This disadvantages the other partners who have credit balances and who have to find the excess. To overcome this problem, the partnership agreement could be altered to give partners interest on their current accounts and/or charge interest where debit balances are outstanding at the end of the year.

1.5 Loans to the partnership

Where an existing or previous partner makes a **loan to the partnership** he becomes a **creditor** of the partnership.

(a) If the partnership is short of cash (which often happens) and the existing partners do not wish to contribute further capital which would be tied up in the business for many years, one or more of them may be prepared to enter into a formal loan agreement for a specified period and at a realistic interest rate.

(b) When a partner retires, if there is insufficient cash to pay the balance owed to him (the total of his capital and current account balances), the amount which he cannot yet be paid is usually transferred to a loan account.

In the partnership balance sheet a loan is shown separately as a long-term liability (unless repayable within 12 months), whether or not the loan creditor is also an existing partner. Remember that any such loan attracts interest at 5% per annum (Partnership Act 1890) unless there is agreement to the contrary.

1.6 Presentation of capital accounts

When preparing the partnership accounts, the **assets employed** (assets less liabilities) side of the balance sheet is presented in the same way as in a sole trader's set of accounts. However, the **funds employed** (partnership capital) side is shown in the following way.

	£	£
Capital accounts		
Jill	10,000	
Susan	6,000	
		16,000
Current accounts		
Jill	2,500	
Susan	(1,000)	
		1,500
		17,500

Note that, unlike in a sole trader's balance sheet, the profit and drawings figures are not shown separately. They have been absorbed into the current accounts and only the balances appear on the final accounts.

1.7 Appropriation of net profits

When a sole trader's net profit has been ascertained it is appropriated by him, ie credited to his capital account. He may or may not remove it from the business in the form of drawings. The net profit of a partnership is appropriated by the partners, according to whatever formula they choose, and the sharing out of profit between them is detailed in a **profit and loss appropriation account**. The following factors have to be taken into consideration.

NOTES

(a) **Interest**. Partners can agree to credit themselves with interest on capital account balances and, more rarely, interest may be allowed (or charged) on current accounts. This is a means of compensating partners for funds tied up in the business that could be earning interest if invested elsewhere. However, the rate of interest agreed upon often bears little relation to current market rates.

(b) **Salaries**. Partners can agree to credit one or more partners with fixed salaries. This can be a means of compensating a partner for particularly valuable services rendered, especially if his share of profits is otherwise small.

(c) **Share of residual profits (or losses).** After allowing any interest and salaries, partners share remaining profits (or losses) according to their profit sharing ratio. Unless fixed by the partnership agreement they are divided equally.

All these appropriations of profit (or loss) are credited (or debited) to the partners' current accounts.

Interest on a loan account represents an expense charged against profit, whereas **interest on a capital account** is an appropriation of profit. Loan interest must therefore be deducted before arriving at the figure of net profit available for appropriation.

1.8 Format of partnership accounts

It is preferable to present details of partners' capital and current ledger accounts side by side, in **columnar form**. In practice, of course, a separate ledger account would be maintained for each account for each partner, but in the subsequent examples the columnar format is adopted.

EXAMPLE: PARTNERSHIP ACCOUNTS

Crossly, Steels and Nabs are partners in a music business, sharing profits in the ratio 5:3:2 respectively. Their capital and current account balances on 1 January 20X1 were as follows.

	Capital accounts	*Current accounts*
	£	£
Crossly	24,000	2,000
Steels	18,000	(1,000) Dr
Nabs	13,000	1,500

Interest at 10% per annum is given on the fixed capitals, and salaries of £8,000 per annum are credited to Steels and Nabs. Expansion of the business was hindered by lack of working capital, so Crossly made a personal loan of £20,000 on 1 July 20X1. The loan was to be repaid in full on 30 June 20X4 and loan interest at the rate of 15% per annum was to be credited to Crossly's account every half year. The partnership profit (before charging loan interest) for the year ended 31 December 20X1 was £63,000 and the partners had made drawings of: Crossly £16,000; Steels £16,500; Nabs £19,000, during the year.

NOTES

Prepare the profit and loss appropriation account, the partners' capital and current accounts and the partnership balance sheet in respect of the year ended 31 December 20X1.

ANSWER

PROFIT AND LOSS APPROPRIATION ACCOUNT
FOR THE YEAR ENDED 31 DECEMBER 20X1

	£	£
Net profit*		61,500
Interest on capital accounts		
Crossly	2,400	
Steels	1,800	
Nabs	1,300	
	5,500	
Salaries		
Steels	8,000	
Nabs	8,000	
	16,000	
		21,500
		40,000
Partners' shares of balance		
Crossly (5/10)		20,000
Steels (3/10)		12,000
Nabs (2/10)		8,000
		40,000

	£
*Profit per question	63,000
Less loan interest to Crossly: 15% × £20,000 × 1/2	1,500
Net profit available for appropriation	61,500

PARTNERS' CAPITAL ACCOUNTS

	Crossly	Steels	Nabs		Crossly	Steels	Nabs
	£	£	£		£	£	£
				Balances b/f	24,000	18,000	13,000

PARTNERS' CURRENT ACCOUNTS

	Crossly	Steels	Nabs		Crossly	Steels	Nabs
	£	£	£		£	£	£
Balances b/f	-	1,000	-	Balances b/f	2,000	-	1,500
Drawings (cash)	16,000	16,500	19,000	Loan interest	1,500	-	-
Balances c/d	9,900	4,300	-	Profit & loss appropriation a/c			
				Interest	2,400	1,800	1,300
				Salary	-	8,000	8,000
				Balance	20,000	12,000	8,000
				Balance c/d			200
	25,900	21,800	19,000		25,900	21,800	19,000

BALANCE SHEET AS AT 31 DECEMBER 20X1

	£
Total assets less current liabilities (balancing figure)	89,000
Creditor: amount falling due after more than one year	
Crossly: loan	20,000
	69,000

BPP LEARNING MEDIA

	£	£
Partners' capital accounts		
Crossly	24,000	
Steels	18,000	
Nabs	13,000	
		55,000
Partners' current accounts		
Crossly	9,900	
Steels	4,300	
Nabs	(200)	
		14,000
		69,000

It is possible that salaries and interest on capital may **exceed the partnership profit**, or indeed, increase a partnership loss. The usual treatment is to credit the partners with their salaries, interest on capital etc and divide the total loss between them in the usual profit sharing ratio.

Activity 2 **(10 minutes)**

Suppose Bill and Ben are partners sharing profit in the ratio 2:1 and that they agree to pay themselves a salary of £10,000 each. If profits before deducting salaries are £26,000, how much income would each partner receive?

Chapter roundup

- This chapter has introduced the basic principles of accounting for partnerships. In general, a profit and loss account may be prepared for a partnership in exactly the same way as for a sole trader. In the profit and loss appropriation account the net profit is then apportioned between the partners according to the partnership agreement.
- In the partnership balance sheet, net assets are financed by partners' capital and current accounts. Current accounts must be credited with the profits appropriated to each partner for the year, and debited with partners' drawings. It is essential to remember that drawings, salaries and interest on capital are *not* expenses. Drawings only affect the balance sheet. Salaries and interest on capital are appropriations of profit.

Quick quiz

1 In the absence of any agreement to the contrary, what financial arrangements are presumed to apply between partners in respect of:

(a) partnership salaries;
(b) interest on partners' capital?

2 In the balance sheet of a partnership, how is a loan from a partner disclosed?

3 Interest on a loan made by a partner is shown as an appropriation of profit, not as an expense. True or false?

Answers to quick quiz

1 (a) Partners are not entitled to receive salaries.

(b) Partners are not entitled to interest on their capital. (see para 1.2)

2 A loan from a partner is shown separately as a long-term liability. (para 1.5)

3 False. Interest on a loan is an expense charged against profit. (para 1.7)

Answers to activities

1 (a) The main problem with trading as a sole trader is the limitation on resources it implies. As the business grows, there will be a need for:

(i) Additional capital. Although some capital may be provided by a bank, it would not be desirable to have the business entirely dependent on borrowing;

(ii) Additional expertise. A sole trader technically competent in his own field may not have, for example, the financial skills that would be needed in a larger business;

(iii) Additional management time. Once a business grows to a certain point, it becomes impossible for one person to look after all aspects of it without help.

(b) The main disadvantage of incorporating is the regulatory burden faced by limited companies. In addition, there are certain 'businesses' which are not allowed to enjoy limited liability; you may have read about the Lloyd's 'names' who face personal bankruptcy because the option of limited liability was not available to them.

There are also tax factors to consider, but these are beyond the scope of this book.

2 First, the two salaries are deducted from profit, leaving £6,000 (£26,000 – £20,000).

This £6,000 has to be distributed between Bill and Ben in the ratio 2:1. In other words, Bill will receive twice as much as Ben. You can probably work this out in your head and see that Bill will get £4,000 and Ben £2,000, but we had better see how this is calculated properly.

Add the 'parts' of the ratio together. For our example, 2 + 1 = 3. Divide this total into whatever it is that has to be shared out. In our example, £6,000 ÷ 3 = £2,000. Each 'part' is worth £2,000, so Bill receives 2 × £2,000 = £4,000 and Ben will receive 1 × £2,000 = £2,000.

So the final answer to the question is that Bill receives his salary plus £4,000 and Ben his salary plus £2,000. This could be laid out as follows:

	Bill	*Ben*	*Total*
	£	£	£
Salary	10,000	10,000	20,000
Share of residual profits (ratio 2:1)	4,000	2,000	6,000
	14,000	12,000	26,000

Chapter 22 :

INTERPRETING FINANCIAL STATEMENTS

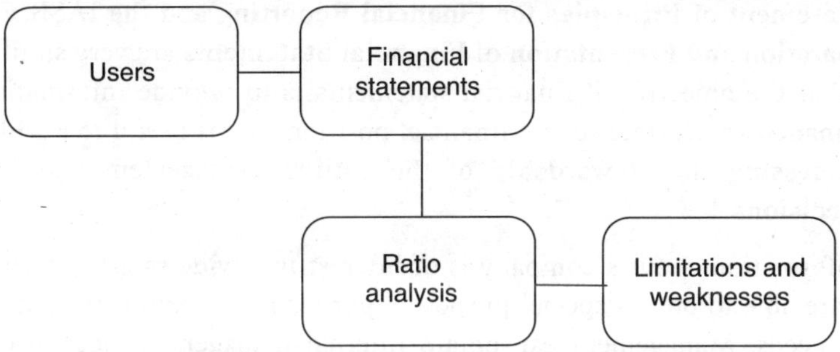

Introduction

Financial statements are prepared for a reason: to provide information. Users need information in order to make decisions about a business. For example, shareholders of a limited company often need to decide whether to sell their shares or continue to hold them.

Users and their advisers must interpret the figures in the financial statements. How do they decide whether a company is performing well or badly? Or whether it is a safe investment or a risky investment? What do they look at in the figures in the profit and loss account and the balance sheet to help them to make their judgement?

Ratio analysis is the main technique used to interpret a set of financial statements. It involves comparing one figure with another to calculate a ratio and then assessing whether the ratio indicates a weakness or a strength.

In this chapter we concentrate on ratio analysis: the main ratios and what they measure; how to interpret them; how to report your conclusions; and the limitations of this type of analysis.

Your objectives

In this chapter, you will learn about the following.

(a) User needs and how they relate to ratio analysis

(b) Calculating ratios that reflect profitability, liquidity, efficiency and gearing

(c) Comparing these ratios with other ratios and interpreting the results

(d) The limitations of ratio analysis

1 USERS OF THE FINANCIAL STATEMENTS AND THEIR INFORMATION NEEDS

1.1 Purpose of financial statements

Both the ASB and the IASB have developed and published statements that explain the purpose of financial statements and the general principles that should be followed in preparing and presenting financial statements. Accounting standards reflect these principles.

The ASB **Statement of Principles for Financial Reporting** and the IASB **Framework for the Preparation and Presentation of Financial Statements** are very similar. Both of them state that the objective of financial statements is to provide information about a company's financial performance and financial position that is useful to a **wide range of users** for **assessing the stewardship** of the entity's management and for **making economic decisions.**

Financial information about a company is of interest to a wide range of users. Some of these users are able to obtain special-purpose reports about a company specific to their information needs. Management can obtain internal management accounting reports, and on occasion, someone else, such as a lending bank or the tax authorities, can obtain specially-prepared reports. Many users of accounts, however, do not have access to special-purpose reports, and must rely for their information on general purpose financial statements, normally the company's published financial statements.

1.2 Users of financial statements

Both the ASB and the IASB identify a number of different groups of users of financial statements

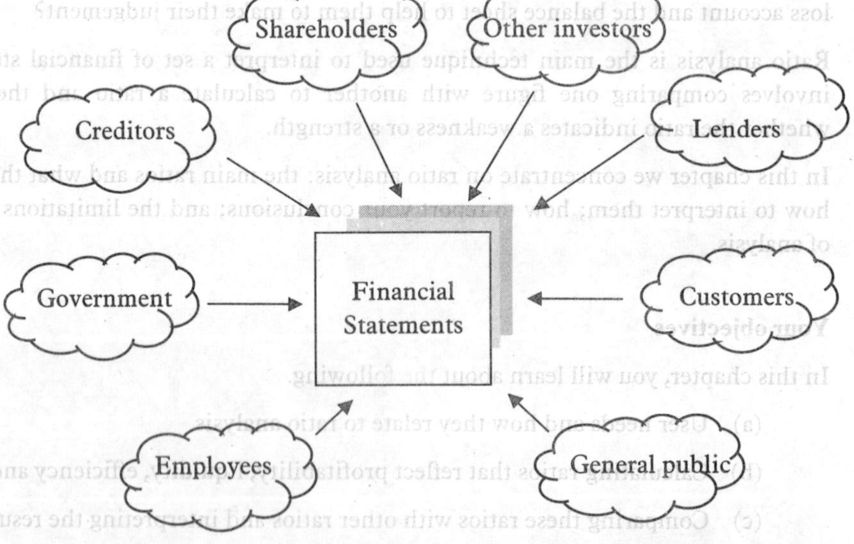

The ASB and the IASB suggest that although there are many different users of general purpose financial statements, the needs of all these users will be met if the information provided in the statements meets the requirements of present and future investors in the company.

1.3 Financial statements for assessing stewardship

Management is accountable to investors for the stewardship of the company. To understand this, you might find it useful to think of the stewardship of an estate, which involves looking after the assets and condition of the estate, and managing it in the interest of the owner. In much the same way, managers are responsible for the safeguarding of the assets and other resources of the company, and for putting these resources to an efficient and profitable use. Investors will be interested in any **information that helps them to judge how well management has carried out their stewardship responsibility.**

1.4 Using financial statements to make economic decisions

Various groups make use of a company's financial statements to make economic decisions.

(a) Present and potential **investors** in the company will consider their investment decision. Should they buy shares in the company? Should they sell their shares? To make an investment decision, the investor needs information about profitability and the ability to generate cash to pay dividends, and also about the risks in the investment. Financial statements should help an investor to assess both the cash-generating capabilities of a company, and also its ability to respond to risks and change (its financial adaptability).

(b) **Lenders** to a company will be interested in any information that helps them to assess whether the company will have the ability to meet its obligations: to pay interest and repay the loan principal on time. Potential lenders need similar information to decide whether to lend to the company, and if so, how much and on what terms.

(c) **Suppliers** to the company and other **trade creditors** need to know how reliable the company will be in paying its debts, and how much credit can safely be given.

(d) **Employees** want information about the financial stability and profitability of their employer, particularly in the part of the company's business where they work. Their decision to remain with the company will depend to a large extent on the ability of the company to continue to offer them secure and well-paid employment. They will also be interested in how much the company is earning in order to reach a view on what remuneration levels should be.

(e) **Customers** are interested in the financial performance and position of a company in order to decide whether to continue buying from it. Where a customer relies on a long-term warranty, or expects to purchase replacement parts from the company over a long period, it will want reassurance that the company is financially stable, with good long-term future prospects.

(f) The **government** (and its agencies) can often obtain the information it needs from a company from special-purpose reports. Even so, general purpose financial statements can provide additional useful information. For example, the tax authorities are provided with specially-prepared information about the company's trading and profits to determine how much tax is payable. A comparison with general purpose financial statements can then help the tax authorities to assess whether the amounts payable in tax seem consistent with the published information. They would certainly be interested if a company declares profits of several million pounds but pays no corporation tax.

(g) A company's activities have an influence on the **community at large**. A major employer in a local community, for example, will help to boost the local economy and stimulate business and employment. Members of the general public might therefore use the financial statements of a company to assess trends and recent developments in its business, and the implications these might have in the future.

1.5 Types of financial information available to users

The information needs of different users are not the same. Financial statements do not provide all the information that individuals need, or would like, to make their decisions, and the **limitations** of a company's report and accounts should be understood. Financial statements are **backward-looking,** reporting what has happened in the past, when users are more often concerned with the **future**. They also report on the company in purely **financial** terms, and do not properly address **non-financial** matters.

Managers responsible for the running of a business are likely to find **detailed management accounts** showing actual performance against budget, usually on a monthly basis, to be more useful than statutory financial statements. Moreover, these are likely to be used alongside **business plans** projected into the future usually over a period of three to five years.

1.6 Investor focus

In reaching their decisions about what financial statements should disclose, the ASB and IASB take the view that **investors are the 'defining class of user'**. Investors need information about the ability of a company to generate profits and cash flows from its operations and on the company's financial adaptability (ie its ability to respond to unexpected events and new opportunities). Essentially, other user groups are interested in the same information. 'Therefore, in preparing financial statements, it is assumed that financial statements that **focus on the interest** that **investors** have in the company's financial performance and financial position will, in effect, also be focusing on the common interest that all users have in the company's financial performance and financial position.'

1.7 The information required by investors

Investors need information about a company's financial performance and financial position.

(a) **Financial performance** relates to the **return** that the company has made on the **resources** at its disposal. Information about performance provides an account of the **stewardship** by management, and can also be used to assess the ability of the company to **generate** cash from its **existing resources**. Information about historical performance can help investors to make judgements about future prospects.

(b) The **financial position** of a company relates to the assets that it owns (including its cash position), the liabilities it owes and the amount of capital invested. This information helps investors to assess the **stewardship of management.** It also helps them to understand how the **future cash flows** generated by the business will be distributed among those with an interest in or a claim on the company (eg lenders, trade creditors, employees and shareholders). Information about the cash position and liquidity helps investors to assess the **ability** of the company to **meet** its **financial obligations** as they fall due. Information about the **risk profile** of a company will help them to judge the **financial adaptability** of the company, and its ability to deal with **unexpected future setbacks and opportunities.**

(c) The extent to which a company needs to be **financially adaptable** depends on the **risks** that it faces, and the appetite of its shareholders for risk in their investment. Financial adaptability can be provided in several ways, but many relate to the **ability** of the company to **raise new cash** should the need arise. For example, a company is financially adaptable if it is able to raise new capital at **short notice**, for example by borrowing or issuing new debt securities. Alternatively, financial adaptability exists if the company could **sell off assets quickly** without disrupting its **continuing business operations**, or if it can achieve a **rapid improvement** in its ability to generate cash flows from its **ongoing business operations.**

(d) The financial statements consist of the **balance sheet**, a **profit and loss account** for the period under review and a **cash flow statement** for the same period. In broad terms, profits and cash flow information can be used to assess the **ability of the company to generate cash.** A balance sheet provides information about the **financial position**. Taken together, they provide information on **performance** and the **stewardship of management.**

Activity 1 **(10 minutes)**

It is easy to see how 'internal' people get hold of accounting information. A senior manager, for example, can just go along to the accounts department and ask the staff there to prepare whatever accounting statements he needs. But external users of accounts cannot do this. How, in practice, can (a) a business contact, (b) a financial analyst, (c) a bank or (d) an employee of the company obtain financial statements about the company?

2 THE BROAD CATEGORIES OF RATIOS

Broadly speaking, basic ratios can be grouped into five categories.

(a) Profitability and return
(b) Long-term solvency and stability
(c) Short-term solvency and liquidity
(d) Efficiency (turnover ratios)
(e) Shareholders' investment ratios

NOTES

Within each heading we will identify a number of standard measures or ratios that are normally calculated and generally accepted as meaningful indicators. One must stress however that each individual business must be considered separately, and a ratio that is meaningful for a manufacturing company may be completely meaningless for a financial institution. Try not to be too mechanical when working out ratios and constantly think about what you are trying to achieve.

The key to obtaining meaningful information from ratio analysis is **comparison**. This may involve comparing ratios over time within the same business to establish whether things are improving or declining, and comparing ratios between similar businesses to see whether the company you are analysing is better or worse than average within its specific business sector.

It must be stressed that ratio analysis **on its own is not sufficient for interpreting** company accounts, and that there are other items of information which should be looked at, for example:

(a) Comments in the Chairman's report and directors' report

(b) The age and nature of the company's assets

(c) Current and future developments in the company's markets, at home and overseas

(d) Any other noticeable features of the report and accounts, such as notes describing events after the balance sheet date, a qualified auditors' report, the company's taxation position, and so on

EXAMPLE: CALCULATING RATIOS

To illustrate the calculation of ratios, the following balance sheet and profit and loss account figures will be used.

BETATEC PLC PROFIT AND LOSS ACCOUNT
FOR THE YEAR ENDED 31 DECEMBER 20X8

	Notes	*20X8*	*20X7*
		£	£
Turnover	1	3,095,576	1,909,051
Operating profit	1	359,501	244,229
Interest	2	17,371	19,127
Profit on ordinary activities before taxation		342,130	225,102
Taxation on ordinary activities		74,200	31,272
Profit on ordinary activities after taxation		267,930	193,830
Dividend for the year		41,000	16,800
Earnings per share		12.8p	9.2p

BPP LEARNING MEDIA

BETATEC PLC BALANCE SHEET
AS AT 31 DECEMBER 20X8

	Notes	*20X8* £	*20X7* £
Fixed assets			
Tangible fixed assets		802,180	656,071
Current assets			
Stocks and work in progress		64,422	86,550
Debtors	3	1,002,701	853,441
Cash at bank and in hand		1,327	68,363
		1,068,450	1,008,354
Creditors: amounts falling due within one year	4	881,731	912,456
Net current assets		186,719	95,898
Total assets less current liabilities		988,899	751,969
Creditors: amounts falling due after more than one year			
10% Debenture stock 20Y4/20Y9		(100,000)	(100,000)
Provision for liabilities		(20,000)	(10,000)
		868,899	641,969
Capital and reserves			
Called up share capital	5	210,000	210,000
Share premium account		48,178	48,178
Profit and loss account		610,721	383,791
		868,899	641,969

NOTES TO THE ACCOUNTS

1 *Turnover and profit*

		20X8 £	*20X7* £
(i)	Turnover	3,095,576	1,909,051
	Cost of sales	2,402,609	1,441,950
	Gross profit	692,967	467,101
	Administration expenses	333,466	222,872
	Operating profit	359,501	244,229
(ii)	Operating profit is stated after charging:		
	Depreciation	151,107	120,147
	Auditors' remuneration	6,500	5,000
	Leasing charges	47,636	46,336
	Directors' emoluments	94,945	66,675

2 *Interest*

	20X8 £	*20X7* £
Payable on bank overdrafts and other loans	8,115	11,909
Payable on debenture stock	10,000	10,000
	18,115	21,909
Receivable on short-term deposits	744	2,782
Net payable	17,371	19,127

3 *Debtors*

	20X8 £	*20X7* £
Amounts falling due within one year		
Trade debtors	981,581	805,981
Amounts falling due after more than one year		
Trade debtors	21,120	47,460
Total debtors	1,002,701	853,441

4 *Creditors: amounts falling due within one year*

	20X8	20X7
	£	£
Trade creditors	627,018	545,340
Accruals and deferred income	81,279	280,464
Corporation tax	108,000	37,200
Other taxes and social security costs	65,434	49,452
	881,731	912,456

5 *Called up share capital*

	20X8	20X7
	£	£
Authorised ordinary shares of 10p each	1,000,000	1,000,000
Issued and fully paid ordinary shares of 10p each	210,000	210,000

3 PROFITABILITY AND RETURN ON CAPITAL

3.1 PBIT

In our example, the company made a profit in both 20X8 and 20X7, and there was an increase in profit on ordinary activities between one year and the next:

- Of 52% before taxation
- Of 39% after taxation

Profit on ordinary activities ***before* taxation** is generally thought to be a **better** figure to use **than profit after taxation,** because there might be unusual variations in the tax charge from year to year which would not affect the underlying profitability of the company's operations.

Another profit figure that should be calculated is **PBIT, profit before interest** and tax. This is the amount of profit which the company earned before having to pay interest to the providers of loan capital. By providers of loan capital, we usually mean longer-term loan capital, such as debentures and medium-term bank loans, which will be shown in the balance sheet as 'creditors: amounts falling due after more than one year'.

Profit before interest and tax is therefore:

- Profit on ordinary activities before taxation; PLUS
- Interest charges on long-term loan capital

Published accounts do not always give sufficient detail on interest payable to determine how much is interest on long-term finance. We will assume in our example that the whole of the interest payable (£18,115, note 2) relates to long-term finance.

PBIT in our example is therefore:

	20X8	20X7
	£	£
Profit on ordinary activities before tax	342,130	225,102
Interest payable	18,115	21,909
PBIT	360,245	247,011

This shows a 46% growth between 20X7 and 20X8.

NOTES

3.2 Return on capital employed (ROCE)

It is impossible to assess profits or profit growth properly without relating them to the amount of funds (capital) that were employed in making the profits. The most important profitability ratio is therefore return on capital employed (ROCE), which states the profit as a percentage of the amount of capital employed.

Definitions

$$\text{ROCE} = \frac{\text{Profit on ordinary activities before interest and taxation}}{\text{Capital employed}}$$

Capital employed = Shareholders' funds plus 'creditors: amounts falling due after more than one year' plus any long-term provision for liabilities (*or* total assets less current liabilities).

The underlying principle is that we must compare like with like, and so if capital means share capital and reserves plus long-term liabilities and debt capital, profit must mean the profit earned by all this capital together. This is PBIT, since interest is the return for loan capital.

EXAMPLE: ROCE

In our example, capital employed = 20X8 868,899 + 100,000 + 20,000 = £988,899
20X7 641,969 + 100,000 + 10,000 = £751,969

These total figures are the total assets less current liabilities figures for 20X8 and 20X7 in the balance sheet.

		20X8	*20X7*
ROCE	=	$\frac{360,245}{988,899} = 36.4\%$	$\frac{247,011}{751,969} = 32.8\%$

What does a company's ROCE tell us? What should we be looking for? There are three comparisons that can be made.

(a) The change in ROCE from one year to the next can be examined. In this example, there has been an increase in ROCE by about 10% or 11% from its 20X7 level.

(b) The ROCE being earned by other companies, if this information is available, can be compared with the ROCE of this company. Here the information is not available.

(c) A **comparison** of the ROCE with **current market borrowing** rates may be made.

(i) What would be the cost of extra borrowing to the company if it needed more loans, and is it earning a ROCE that suggests it could make profits to make such borrowing worthwhile?

(ii) Is the company making a ROCE which suggests that it is getting value for money from its current borrowing?

BPP LEARNING MEDIA

(iii) Companies are in a risk business and commercial borrowing rates are a good independent yardstick against which company performance can be judged.

In this example, if we suppose that current market interest rates, say, for medium-term borrowing from banks, are around 10%, then the company's actual ROCE of 36% in 20X8 would not seem low. On the contrary, it might seem high.

However, it is **easier to spot a low ROCE than a high one,** because there is always a chance that the company's **fixed assets**, especially property, **are undervalued** in its balance sheet, and so the capital employed figure might be unrealistically low. If the company had earned a ROCE, not of 36%, but of, say only 6%, then its return would have been below current borrowing rates and so disappointingly low.

3.3 Return on shareholders' capital (ROSC)

Another measure of profitability and return is the return on shareholders' capital (ROSC):

Definition

$$\textbf{ROSC} = \frac{\text{Profit on ordinary activities before tax}}{\text{Share capital and reserves}}$$

It is intended to focus on the return being made by the company for the benefit of its shareholders, and in our example, the figures are:

20X8	*20X7*
$\frac{342{,}130}{868{,}899} = 39.4\%$	$\frac{225{,}102}{641{,}969} = 35.1\%$

These figures show an improvement between 20X7 and 20X8, and a return which is clearly in excess of current borrowing rates.

ROSC is not a widely-used ratio, however, because there are more useful ratios that give an indication of the return to shareholders, such as earnings per share, dividend per share, dividend yield and earnings yield, which are described later.

3.4 Analysing profitability and return in more detail: the secondary ratios

We often sub-analyse ROCE, to find out more about why the ROCE is high or low, or better or worse than last year. There are two factors that contribute towards a return on capital employed, both related to sales turnover.

(a) **Profit margin**. A company might make a high or low profit margin on its sales. For example, a company that makes a profit of 25p per £1 of sales is making a bigger return on its turnover than another company making a profit of only 10p per £1 of sales.

(b) **Asset turnover**. Asset turnover is a measure of how well the assets of a business are being used to generate sales. For example, if two companies each

NOTES

have capital employed of £100,000 and Company A makes sales of £400,000 per annum whereas Company B makes sales of only £200,000 per annum, Company A is making a higher turnover from the same amount of assets (twice as much asset turnover as Company B) and this will help A to make a higher return on capital employed than B. Asset turnover is expressed as 'x times' so that assets generate x times their value in annual turnover. Here, Company A's asset turnover is 4 times and B's is 2 times.

Profit margin and asset turnover together explain the ROCE and if the ROCE is the primary profitability ratio, these other two are the secondary ratios. The relationship between the three ratios can be shown mathematically.

Definition

Profit margin × Asset turnover = ROCE

$$\therefore \quad \frac{\text{PBIT}}{\text{Sales}} \times \frac{\text{Sales}}{\text{Capital employed}} = \frac{\text{PBIT}}{\text{Capital employed}}$$

In our example:

	Profit margin		*Asset turnover*		*ROCE*
(a) 20X8	$\frac{360{,}245}{3{,}095{,}576}$	×	$\frac{3{,}095{,}576}{988{,}899}$	=	$\frac{360{,}245}{988{,}899}$
	11.64%	×	3.13 times	=	36.4%
(b) 20X7	$\frac{247{,}011}{1{,}909{,}051}$	×	$\frac{1{,}909{,}051}{751{,}969}$	=	$\frac{247{,}011}{751{,}969}$
	12.94%	×	2.54 times	=	32.8%

In this example, the company's improvement in ROCE between 20X7 and 20X8 is attributable to a higher asset turnover. Indeed the profit margin has fallen a little, but the higher asset turnover has more than compensated for this.

It is also worth commenting on the change in sales turnover from one year to the next. You may already have noticed that Betatec plc achieved sales growth of over 60% from £1.9 million to £3.1 million between 20X7 and 20X8. This is very strong growth, and this is certainly one of the most significant items in the P&L account and balance sheet.

3.5 A warning about comments on profit margin and asset turnover

It might be tempting to think that a high profit margin is good, and a low asset turnover means sluggish trading. In broad terms, this is so. But there is a **trade-off between profit margin and asset turnover**, and you cannot look at one without allowing for the other.

(a) A high profit margin means a high profit per £1 of sales, but if this also means that sales prices are high, there is a strong possibility that sales turnover will be depressed, and so asset turnover lower.

BPP LEARNING MEDIA

NOTES

(b) A high asset turnover means that the company is generating a lot of sales, but to do this it might have to keep its prices down and so accept a low profit margin per £1 of sales.

Consider the following.

Company A		*Company B*	
Sales	£1,000,000	Sales	£4,000,000
Capital employed	£1,000,000	Capital employed	£1,000,000
PBIT	£200,000	PBIT	£200,000

These figures would give the following ratios.

Company A		Company B	
ROCE	$= \frac{200,000}{1,000,000} = 20\%$	ROCE	$= \frac{200,000}{1,000,000} = 20\%$
Profit margin	$= \frac{200,000}{1,000,000} = 20\%$	Profit margin	$= \frac{200,000}{4,000,000} = 5\%$
Asset turnover	$= \frac{1,000,000}{1,000,000} = 1$	Asset turnover	$= \frac{4,000,000}{1,000,000} = 4$

The companies have the same ROCE, but it is arrived at in a very different fashion. Company A operates with a low asset turnover and a comparatively high profit margin whereas company B carries out much more business, but on a lower profit margin. Company A could be operating at the luxury end of the market, whilst company B is operating at the popular end of the market (Fortnum and Masons v Sainsbury's).

Activity 2 **(5 minutes)**

Which one of the following formulae correctly expresses the relationship between return on capital employed (ROCE), profit margin (PM) and asset turnover (AT)?

A $PM = \frac{AT}{ROCE}$

B $ROCE = \frac{PM}{AT}$

C $AT = PM \times ROCE$

D $PM = \frac{ROCE}{AT}$

3.6 Gross profit margin, net profit margin and profit analysis

Depending on the format of the P&L account, you may be able to calculate the gross profit margin as well as the net profit margin. Looking at the two together can be quite informative.

For example, suppose that a company has the following summarised profit and loss accounts for two consecutive years.

NOTES

	Year 1	Year 2
	£	£
Turnover	70,000	100,000
Cost of sales	42,000	55,000
Gross profit	28,000	45,000
Expenses	21,000	35,000
Net profit	7,000	10,000

Although the net profit margin is the same for both years at 10%, the gross profit margin is not.

In year 1 it is: $\frac{28,000}{70,000} = 40\%$

and in year 2 it is: $\frac{45,000}{100,000} = 45\%$

The improved gross profit margin has not led to an improvement in the net profit margin. This is because expenses as a percentage of sales have risen from 30% in year 1 to 35% in year 2.

4 LIQUIDITY, GEARING AND WORKING CAPITAL

4.1 Long-term solvency: debt and gearing ratios

Debt ratios are concerned with **how much the company owes in relation to its size,** whether it is getting into heavier debt or improving its situation, and whether its debt burden seems heavy or light.

(a) When a company is heavily in debt banks and other potential lenders may be unwilling to advance further funds.

(b) When a company is earning only a modest profit before interest and tax, and has a heavy debt burden, there will be very little profit left over for shareholders after the interest charges have been paid. And so if interest rates were to go up (on bank overdrafts and so on) or the company were to borrow even more, it might soon be incurring interest charges in excess of PBIT. This might eventually lead to the liquidation of the company.

These are two big reasons why companies should keep their debt burden under control. There are four ratios that are particularly worth looking at, the **debt** ratio, **gearing** ratio, **interest cover** and **cash flow** ratio.

4.2 Debt ratio

The **debt ratio** is the ratio of a **company's total debts to its total assets.**

Assets consist of fixed assets at their balance sheet value, plus current assets. Debts consist of all creditors, whether amounts falling due within one year or after more than one year.

You can ignore long-term provisions and liabilities.

There is no absolute guide to the maximum safe debt ratio, but as a **very general guide,** you might regard **50% as a safe limit** to debt. In practice, many companies operate successfully with a higher debt ratio than this, but 50% is nonetheless a helpful

NOTES

benchmark. In addition, if the debt ratio is over 50% and getting worse, the company's debt position will be worth looking at more carefully.

In the case of Betatec plc the debt ratio is as follows.

	20X8	*20X7*
Total debts	(681,731 + 100,000)	(912,456 + 100,000)
Total assets	(802,180 + 1,068,450)	(656,071 + 1,008,354)
	= 52%	= 61%

In this case, the debt ratio is quite high, mainly because of the large amount of current liabilities. However, the debt ratio has fallen from 61% to 52% between 20X7 and 20X8, and so the company appears to be improving its debt position.

4.3 Gearing ratio

Capital gearing is concerned with a company's **long-term capital structure**. We can think of a company as consisting of fixed assets and net current assets (ie working capital, which is current assets minus current liabilities). These assets must be financed by **long-term capital** of the company, which is **one of two** things.

(a) **Share capital and reserves** (shareholders' funds) which can be divided into:

  (i) Ordinary shares plus reserves
  (ii) Preference shares

(b) **Long-term debt capital**: 'creditors: amounts falling due after more than one year'

Preference share capital is not debt. It would certainly not be included as debt in the debt ratio. However, like loan capital, preference share capital **has a prior claim over profits** before interest and tax, ahead of ordinary shareholders. Preference dividends must be paid out of profits before ordinary shareholders are entitled to an ordinary dividend, and so we refer to preference share capital and loan capital as prior charge capital.

The **capital gearing ratio** is a measure of the proportion of a company's capital that is prior charge capital. It is measured as follows.

Definition

$$\textbf{Capital gearing ratio} = \frac{\text{prior charge capital}}{\text{total capital}}$$

(a) **Prior charge capital** is capital carrying a right to a fixed return. It will include preference shares and debentures.

(b) **Total capital** is ordinary share capital and reserves plus prior charge capital plus any long-term liabilities or provisions. In group accounts we would also include minority interests. It is easier to identify the same figure for total capital as total assets less current liabilities, which you will find given to you in the balance sheet.

BPP LEARNING MEDIA

NOTES

As with the debt ratio, there is no absolute limit to what a gearing ratio ought to be. A company with a gearing ratio of **more than 50%** is said to be **high-geared** (whereas low gearing means a gearing ratio of less than 50%). Many companies are high geared, but if a high geared company is becoming increasingly high geared, it is likely to have difficulty in the future when it wants to borrow even more, unless it can also boost its shareholders' capital, either with retained profits or by a new share issue.

A similar ratio to the gearing ratio is the **debt/equity ratio**, which is calculated as follows.

Definition

$$\textbf{Debt/equity ratio} = \frac{\text{prior charge capital}}{\text{ordinary share capital and reserves}}$$

This gives us the same sort of information as the gearing ratio, and a ratio of 100% or more would indicate high gearing.

In the example of Betatec plc, we find that the company, although having a high debt ratio because of its current liabilities, has a low gearing ratio. It has no preference share capital and its only long-term debt is the 10% debenture stock.

	20X8	*20X7*
Gearing ratio	$\frac{100{,}000}{988{,}899} = 10\%$	$\frac{100{,}000}{751{,}969} = 13\%$
Debt/equity ratio	$\frac{100{,}000}{868{,}899} = 12\%$	$\frac{100{,}000}{641{,}969} = 16\%$

4.4 The implications of high or low gearing

We mentioned earlier that gearing is, amongst other things, an attempt to quantify the **degree of risk** involved in holding equity shares in a company, risk both in terms of the company's ability to remain in business and in terms of expected ordinary dividends from the company. The problem with a high geared company is that by definition there is a lot of debt. Debt generally carries a fixed rate of interest (or fixed rate of dividend if in the form of preference shares), hence there is a given (and large) amount to be paid out from profits to holders of debt before arriving at a residue available for distribution to the holders of equity. The riskiness will perhaps become clearer with the aid of an example.

	Company A	*Company B*	*Company C*
	£'000	£'000	£'000
Ordinary share capital	600	400	300
Profit and loss account	200	200	200
Revaluation reserve	100	100	100
	900	700	600
6% preference shares	-	-	100
10% loan stock	100	300	300
Capital employed	1,000	1,000	1,000
Gearing ratio	10%	30%	40%

Now suppose that each company makes a profit before interest and tax of £50,000, and the rate of corporation tax is 30%. Amounts available for distribution to equity shareholders will be as follows.

	Company A	*Company B*	*Company C*
	£'000	£'000	£'000
Profit before interest and tax	50	50	50
Interest	10	30	30
Profit before tax	40	20	20
Taxation at 30%	12	6	6
Profit after tax	28	14	14
Preference dividend	-	-	6
Available for ordinary shareholders	28	14	8

If in the subsequent year profit before interest and tax falls to £40,000, the amounts available to ordinary shareholders will become:

	Company A	*Company B*	*Company C*
	£'000	£'000	£'000
Profit before interest and tax	40	40	40
Interest	10	30	30
Profit before tax	30	10	10
Taxation at 30%	9	3	3
Profit after tax	21	7	7
Preference dividend	-	-	6
Available for ordinary shareholders	21	7	1

Note the following.

Gearing ratio	10%	30%	40%
Change in PBIT	– 20%	– 20%	– 20%
Change in profit available for ordinary shareholders	– 25%	– 50%	– 87.5%

The more highly geared the company, the greater the risk that little (if anything) will be available to distribute by way of dividend to the ordinary shareholders.

(a) The example clearly displays this fact in so far as the more highly geared the company, the greater the percentage change in profit available for ordinary shareholders for any given percentage change in profit before interest and tax.

(b) The relationship similarly holds when profits increase, and if PBIT had risen by 20% rather than fallen, you would find that once again the largest percentage change in profit available for ordinary shareholders (this means an increase) will be for the highly geared company.

(c) This means that there will be greater volatility of amounts available for ordinary shareholders, and presumably therefore greater volatility in dividends paid to those shareholders, where a company is highly geared. That is the risk: you may do extremely well or extremely badly without a particularly large movement in the PBIT of the company.

The risk of a company's ability to remain in business was referred to earlier. Gearing is relevant to this. A high geared company has a large amount of interest to pay annually (assuming that the debt is external borrowing rather than preference shares). If those borrowings are 'secured' in any way (and debentures in particular are secured), then the

NOTES

holders of the debt are perfectly entitled to force the company to realise assets to pay their interest if funds are not available from other sources. Clearly the more highly geared a company the more likely this is to occur when and if profits fall. **Higher gearing may mean higher returns, but also higher risk.**

4.5 Interest cover

The interest cover ratio shows whether a company is earning enough profits before interest and tax to pay its interest costs comfortably, or whether its interest costs are high in relation to the size of its profits, so that a fall in PBIT would then have a significant effect on profits available for ordinary shareholders.

Definition

$$\textbf{Interest cover} = \frac{\text{profit before interest and tax}}{\text{interest charges}}$$

An interest cover of 2 times or less would be low, and should really exceed 3 times before the company's interest costs are to be considered within acceptable limits.

Returning first to the example of Companies A, B and C, the interest cover was as follows.

	Company A	*Company B*	*Company C*
(a) When PBIT was £50,000 =	$\frac{50{,}000}{10{,}000}$	$\frac{50{,}000}{30{,}000}$	$\frac{50{,}000}{30{,}000}$
	5 times	1.67 times	1.67 times
(b) When PBIT was £40,000 =	$\frac{40{,}000}{10{,}000}$	$\frac{40{,}000}{30{,}000}$	$\frac{40{,}000}{30{,}000}$
	4 times	1.33 times	1.33 times

Note. Although preference share capital is included as prior charge capital for the gearing ratio, it is usual to exclude preference dividends from 'interest' charges. We also look at all interest payments, even interest charges on short-term debt, and so interest cover and gearing do not quite look at the same thing.

Both B and C have a low interest cover, which is a warning to ordinary shareholders that their profits are highly vulnerable, in percentage terms, to even small changes in PBIT.

Activity 3 **(5 minutes)**

Returning to the example of Betatec plc above, what is the company's interest cover?

BPP LEARNING MEDIA

4.6 Cash flow ratio

The **cash flow ratio** is the ratio of a company's net cash inflow to its total debts.

(a) Net cash inflow is the amount of cash which the company has coming into the business from its operations. A suitable figure for net cash inflow can be obtained from the cash flow statement.

(b) Total debts are short-term and long-term creditors, together with provisions for liabilities. A distinction can be made between debts payable within one year and other debts and provisions.

Obviously, a company needs to be earning enough cash from operations to be able to meet its foreseeable debts and future commitments, and the cash flow ratio, and changes in the cash flow ratio from one year to the next, provide a useful indicator of a company's cash position.

4.7 Short-term solvency and liquidity

Profitability is of course an important aspect of a company's performance and debt or gearing is another. Neither, however, addresses directly the key issue of **liquidity**.

Liquidity is the amount of cash a company can put its hands on quickly to settle its debts (and possibly to meet other unforeseen demands for cash payments too).

Liquid funds consist of:

(a) Cash

(b) Short-term investments for which there is a ready market

(c) Fixed-term deposits with a bank or building society, for example, a six month high-interest deposit with a bank

(d) Trade debtors (because they will pay what they owe within a reasonably short period of time)

In summary, **liquid assets** are current asset items that will or could soon be **converted into cash, and cash itself**. Two common definitions of liquid assets are:

(a) All current assets without exception
(b) All current assets with the exception of stocks

A company can obtain liquid assets from sources other than sales, such as the issue of shares for cash, a new loan or the sale of fixed assets. But a company cannot rely on these at all times, and in general, obtaining liquid funds depends on making sales and profits. Even so, profits do not always lead to increases in liquidity. This is mainly because funds generated from trading may be immediately invested in fixed assets or paid out as dividends. You should refer back to the chapter on cash flow statements to examine this issue.

The reason why a company needs liquid assets is so that it can meet its debts when they fall due. Payments are continually made for operating expenses and other costs, and so there is a cash cycle from trading activities of cash coming in from sales and cash going out for expenses. This is illustrated by the diagram below.

4.8 The cash cycle

To help you to understand liquidity ratios, it is useful to begin with a brief explanation of the cash cycle. The cash cycle describes the flow of cash out of a business and back into it again as a result of normal trading operations.

Cash goes out to pay for supplies, wages and salaries and other expenses, although payments can be delayed by taking some credit. A business might hold stock for a while and then sell it. Cash will come back into the business from the sales, although customers might delay payment by themselves taking some credit.

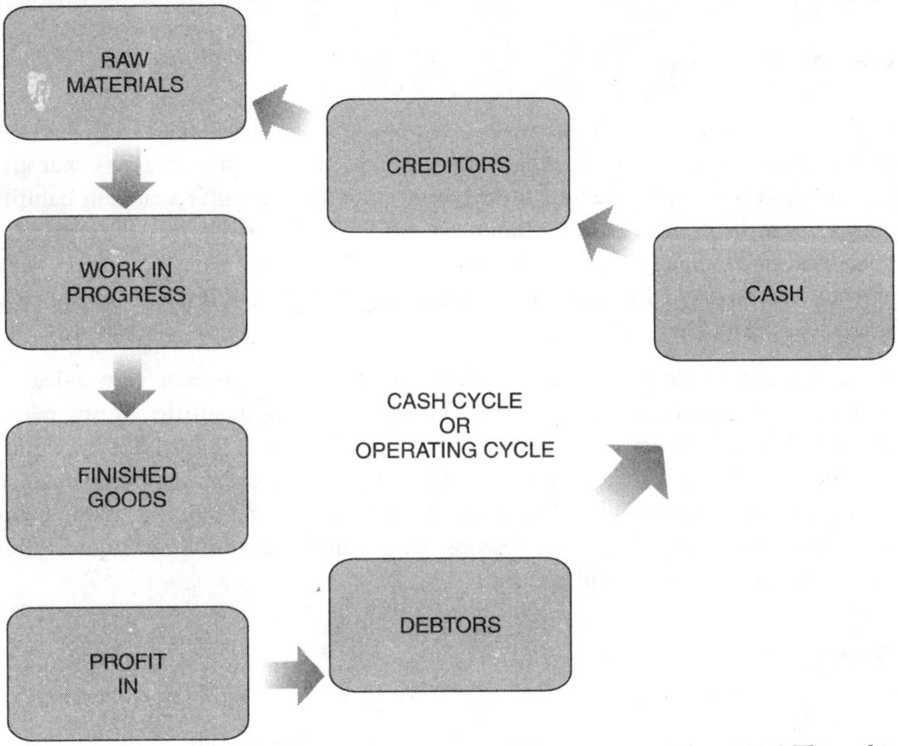

Figure 22.1 The cash cycle

The main points about the cash cycle are as follows.

(a) The **timing of cash flows in and out of a business does not coincide with the time when sales and costs of sales occur**. Cash flows out can be postponed by taking credit. Cash flows in can be delayed by having debtors.

(b) **The time between making a purchase and making a sale also affects cash flows.** If stocks are held for a long time, the delay between the cash payment for stocks and cash receipts from selling them will also be a long one.

(c) Holding stocks and having debtors can therefore be seen as two reasons why cash receipts are delayed. Another way of saying this is that **if a company invests in working capital, its cash position will show a corresponding decrease.**

(d) Similarly, **taking credit from creditors can be seen as a reason why cash payments are delayed.** The company's liquidity position will worsen when it has to pay the creditors, unless it can get more cash in from sales and debtors in the meantime.

The liquidity ratios and working capital turnover ratios are used to test a company's liquidity, length of cash cycle, and investment in working capital.

4.9 Liquidity ratios: current ratio and quick ratio

The 'standard' test of liquidity is the **current ratio**. It can be obtained from the balance sheet, and is calculated as follows.

Definition

$$\textbf{Current ratio} = \frac{\text{current assets}}{\text{current liabilities}}$$

The idea behind this is that a company should have enough current assets that give a promise of 'cash to come' to meet its future commitments to pay off its current liabilities. Obviously, a **ratio in excess of 1** should be expected. Otherwise, there would be the prospect that the company might be unable to pay its debts on time. In practice, a ratio comfortably in excess of 1 should be expected, but what is 'comfortable' varies between different types of businesses.

Companies are not able to convert all their current assets into cash very quickly. In particular, some manufacturing companies might hold large quantities of raw material stocks, which must be used in production to create finished goods stocks. Finished goods stocks might be warehoused for a long time, or sold on lengthy credit. In such businesses, where stock turnover is slow, most stocks are not very 'liquid' assets, because the cash cycle is so long. For these reasons, we calculate an additional liquidity ratio, known as the **quick ratio** or **acid test** ratio.

Definition

The **quick ratio**, or **acid test ratio** is: $\dfrac{\text{current assets less stocks}}{\text{current liabilities}}$

This ratio should ideally be at least 1 for companies with a slow stock turnover. For companies with a fast stock turnover, a quick ratio can be comfortably less than 1 without suggesting that the company should be in cash flow trouble.

Both the current ratio and the quick ratio offer an indication of the company's liquidity position, but the absolute figures should not be interpreted too literally. It is often theorised that an acceptable current ratio is 1.5 and an acceptable quick ratio is 0.8, but these should only be used as a guide.

EXAMPLE

Different businesses operate in very different ways. At the time of writing, for example, Budgens (the supermarket group) had a current ratio of 0.52 and a quick ratio of 0.17. Budgens has low debtors (people do not buy groceries on credit), low cash (good cash management), medium stocks (high stocks but quick turnover, particularly in view of perishability) and very high creditors (Budgens buys its supplies of groceries on credit).

Compare the Budgens ratios with the Tomkins group which had a current ratio of 1.44 and a quick ratio of 1.03. Tomkins is a manufacturing and retail organisation and operates with liquidity ratios closer to the standard. At the same date, Tate & Lyle's figures gave a current ratio of 1.18 and a quick ratio of 0.80.

What is important is the **trend** of these ratios. From this, one can easily ascertain whether liquidity is improving or deteriorating. If Budgens has traded for the last 10 years (very successfully) with current ratios of 0.52 and quick ratios of 0.17 then it should be supposed that the company can continue in business with those levels of liquidity. If in the following year the current ratio were to fall to 0.38 and the quick ratio to 0.09, then further investigation into the liquidity situation would be appropriate. It is the relative position that is far more important than the absolute figures.

Don't forget the other side of the coin either. **A current ratio and a quick ratio can get bigger than they need to be.** A company that has large volumes of stocks and debtors might be over-investing in working capital, and so tying up more funds in the business than it needs to. This would suggest poor management of debtors (credit) or stocks by the company.

4.10 Efficiency ratios: control of debtors and stock

A rough measure of the average length of time it takes for a company's debtors to pay what they owe is the 'debtor days' ratio, or **average debtors' payment period**.

Definition

$$\textbf{Debtors payment period} = \frac{\text{trade debtors}}{\text{sales}} \times 365 \text{ days}$$

The estimated average **debtors' payment period** is calculated as follows.

The figure for sales should be taken as the turnover figure in the P&L account. The trade debtors are not the total figure for debtors in the balance sheet, which includes prepayments and non-trade debtors. The trade debtors figure will be itemised in an analysis of the debtors total, in a note to the accounts.

The estimate of debtor days is only approximate.

(a) The balance sheet value of debtors might be abnormally high or low compared with the 'normal' level the company usually has.

(b) Turnover in the P&L account is exclusive of VAT, but debtors in the balance sheet are inclusive of VAT. **We are not strictly comparing like with like.**

NOTES

(Some companies show turnover inclusive of VAT as well as turnover exclusive of VAT, and the 'inclusive' figure should be used in these cases.)

Sales are usually made on 'normal credit terms' of payment within 30 days. Debtor days significantly in excess of this might be representative of poor management of funds of a business. However, **some companies must allow generous credit terms to win customers**. Exporting companies in particular may have to carry large amounts of debtors, and so their average collection period might be well in excess of 30 days.

The **trend** of the collection period (debtor days) **over time is probably the best guide.** If debtor days are increasing year on year, this is indicative of a poorly managed credit control function (and potentially therefore a poorly managed company).

EXAMPLE: DEBTOR DAYS

Using the same examples as before, the debtor days of those companies were as follows.

Company	*Trade debtors* / *Turnover*		*Debtor days* (× 365)	*Previous year*		*Debtor days* (× 365)
Budgens	£5,016k / £284,986k	=	6.4 days	3,977k / £290,668k	=	5.0 days
Tomkins	£458.3m / £2,059.5m	=	81.2 days	£272.4m / £1,274.2m	=	78.0 days
Tate & Lyle	£304.4m / £3,817.3m	=	29.3 days	£287.0m / £3,366.3m	=	31.1 days

The differences in debtor days reflect the differences between the types of business. Budgens has hardly any trade debtors at all, whereas the manufacturing companies have far more. The debtor days are fairly constant from the previous year for all three companies.

4.11 Stock turnover period

Another ratio worth calculating is the **stock turnover period,** or **stock days.** This is another estimated figure, obtainable from published accounts, which indicates the average number of days that items of stock are held for. As with the average debt collection period, however, it is only an approximate estimated figure, but one which should be reliable enough for comparing changes year on year.

Definition

The number of **stock days** is calculated as:

$$\frac{\text{Stock}}{\text{Cost of sales}} \times 365$$

The reciprocal of the above fraction, ie:

$$\frac{\text{cost of sales}}{\text{stock}}$$

is termed the stock turnover, and is another measure of how vigorously a business is trading. A lengthening stock turnover period from one year to the next indicates one of two things:

(a) A slowdown in trading

(b) A build-up in stock levels, perhaps suggesting that the investment in stocks is becoming excessive

Presumably if we add together the stock days and the debtor days, this should give us an indication of how soon stock is convertible into cash. Both debtor days and stock days therefore give us a further indication of the company's liquidity.

EXAMPLE

Returning once more to our first example, the estimated stock turnover periods for Budgens were as follows.

Company	$\frac{\textit{Stock}}{\textit{Cost of sales}}$	*Stock turnover period (days × 365)*	*Previous year*
Budgens	$\frac{£15{,}554K}{£254{,}751K}$	22.3 days	$\frac{£14{,}094K}{£261{,}368K} \times 365 = 19.7$ days

The figures for cost of sales were not shown in the accounts of either Tate & Lyle or Tomkins.

Activity 4 **(5 minutes)**

Butthead Ltd buys raw materials on six weeks credit, holds them in store for three weeks and then issues them to the production department. The production process takes two weeks on average, and finished goods are held in store for an average of four weeks before being sold. Debtors take five weeks credit on average.

Calculate the length of the cash cycle.

Activity 5 **(5 minutes)**

During a year a business sold stock which had cost £60,000. The stock held at the beginning of the year was £6,000 and at the end of the year £10,000.

What was the annual rate of stock turnover?

Activity 6 **(10 minutes)**

Calculate liquidity and working capital ratios from the accounts of the BET Group, a business which provides service support (cleaning etc) to customers worldwide.

	20X7	20X6
	£'000	£'000
Turnover	2,176.2	2,344.8
Cost of sales	1,659.0	1,731.5
Gross profit	517.2	613.3
Current assets		
Stocks	42.7	78.0
Debtors (note 1)	378.9	431.4
Short-term deposits and cash	205.2	145.0
	626.8	654.4
Creditors: amounts falling due within one year		
Loans and overdrafts	32.4	81.1
Corporation tax	67.8	76.7
Dividend	11.7	17.2
Creditors (note 2)	487.2	467.2
	599.1	642.2
Net current assets	27.7	12.2

Notes

		20X7	20X6
1	Trade debtors	295.2	335.5
2	Trade creditors	190.8	188.1

BET Group is a service company and hence it would be expected to have very low stock and a very short stock turnover period. The similarity of debtors' and creditors' turnover periods means that the group is passing on most of the delay in receiving payment to its suppliers.

Creditors' turnover is ideally calculated by the formula:

$$\frac{\text{Trade creditors}}{\text{Purchases}} \times 365$$

However, it is rare to find purchases disclosed in published accounts and so cost of sales serves as an approximation. The creditors' turnover ratio often helps to assess a company's liquidity; an increase in creditor days is often a sign of lack of long-term finance or poor management of current assets, resulting in the use of extended credit from suppliers, increased bank overdraft and so on.

BET's current ratio is a little lower than average but its quick ratio is better than average and very little less than the current ratio. This suggests that stock levels are strictly controlled, which is reinforced by the low stock turnover period. It would seem that working capital is tightly managed, to avoid the poor liquidity which could be caused by a high debtors' turnover period and comparatively high creditors.

NOTES

5 INVESTMENT RATIOS

5.1 Information provided by investment ratios

These are the ratios that help shareholders and other investors to assess the value and quality of an investment in the ordinary shares of a company. The value of an investment in ordinary shares in a listed company is its market value, and so investment ratios must have regard not only to information in the company's published accounts, but also to the current price. The market price of the company's shares is used to calculate some of these ratios.

5.2 Earnings per share

Earnings per share (EPS) is often regarded as the most important single measure of a company's performance. It is used to compare the results of a company over a period of time and to compare the performance of one company's shares against the performance of another company's shares (and also against the returns obtainable from loan stock and other forms of investment). It shows the amount of residual profit available to the holder of one ordinary share.

Definition

$$\text{EPS} = \frac{\text{Profit for the year available for ordinary shareholders}}{\text{Number of ordinary shares in issue}}$$

The profit which 'belongs' to ordinary shareholders is the profit that is left after all other appropriations have been made: interest on debt; taxation; and preference dividends (if any). It can be paid out directly in the form of ordinary dividends or retained in the company (where, hopefully, it will help to generate increased profits in future periods).

Returning to our example of Betatec plc, earnings per share is as follows:

20X8	*20X7*
$\frac{£267,930}{2,100,000} = 12.8\text{p}$	$\frac{£193,830}{2,100,000} = 9.2\text{p}$

5.3 Dividend cover

Dividend cover is an indicator of how secure shareholders can expect to be in terms of their dividend being paid. It measures the number of times the current dividend could have been paid from available earnings.

Definition

$$\text{Dividend cover} = \frac{\text{Earnings per share}}{\text{Net dividend per ordinary share}}$$

In practice, the simplest way to calculate this is by dividing the profit available to ordinary shareholders by the ordinary dividend paid for the year.

For Betatec plc, dividend cover is as follows:

20X8	*20X7*
$\frac{267,930}{41,000} = 6.5$ times	$\frac{193,830}{16,800} = 11.5$ times

Although earnings per share has increased, dividend cover has fallen. This is because the dividend paid has gone up by 244.1% over this period when the net profit after tax has only increased by 38.2%.

5.4 Price earnings ratio (P/E ratio)

Definition

The **price earnings ratio (P/E ratio)** = $\frac{\text{Share price}}{\text{Earnings per share}}$

A high P/E ratio indicates strong shareholder confidence in the company and its future (for example, profits are likely to increase) and a lower P/E ratio indicates lower confidence. The P/E ratio of one company can be compared with other companies in the same business sector and with other companies generally. It is generally used by investment analysts and other experts.

Suppose that the market price of a share in Betatec plc is 45p per share. The P/E ratio for 20X8 is:

$$\frac{45}{12.8} = 3.5$$

6 PRESENTATION OF A RATIO ANALYSIS REPORT

6.1 Basic approach

You should begin your report with a heading showing who it is from, the name of the addressee, the subject of the report and a suitable date.

A good approach is often to head up a **schedule of ratios** which will form an **appendix to the main report**. Calculate the ratios in a logical sequence, dealing in turn with operating and profitability ratios, use of assets (eg turnover periods for stocks and debtors), liquidity and gearing.

As you calculate the ratios you are likely to be struck by **significant fluctuations and trends.** These will form the basis of your comments in the body of the report. The report should begin with some introductory **comments,** setting out the scope of your analysis and mentioning that detailed figures have been included in an appendix. You should then go on to present your analysis under any categories called for by the question (eg separate sections for management, shareholders and creditors, or separate sections for profitability and liquidity).

Finally, look out for opportunities to **suggest remedial action** where trends appear to be unfavourable.

6.2 Focusing on user needs

Users of financial information are likely to fall into a few key categories:

- shareholders and potential investors
- creditors
- bankers and other providers of finance.

Most users are interested in a range of performance indicators. However, they are likely to interpret them from their own perspective, based on their own particular needs and interests. For example, shareholders will focus on profitability and return on investment, whereas a bank manager may be more concerned with a company's cash flow and its ability to pay debts as they fall due.

When preparing a report, ask yourself the following questions:

- Who are the users of the report and what are their interests?
- What is the purpose of the report?
- What is wanted, definite recommendations or less specific advice?

Ratio analysis is not foolproof. There are many problems in trying to identify trends and make comparisons.

7 LIMITATIONS OF RATIO ANALYSIS

7.1 General limitations

(a) Financial statements are based on historic information, not forecast information. They may be several months out of date by the time that they are published.

(b) Financial statements normally ignore the effects of inflation (although some fixed assets may be measured at current value). This means that trends can be distorted.

(c) Information in published accounts is generally summarised information, so that analysis based on published information alone is likely to be superficial. (However, proper analysis of ratios should identify areas about which more information is needed.)

7.2 Comparing different businesses

It can be useful to compare the ratios of a business with industry averages, or with ratios for another business in the same industry sector. However, such a comparison may be misleading.

(a) Ratios may not always be calculated in the same way. For example, there are several different ways of calculating the return on capital. It can be calculated based on total capital employed or on ordinary shareholders' capital. It can be based on average capital employed, rather than on the closing figure.

BPP LEARNING MEDIA

NOTES

(b) The businesses may adopt different accounting policies. For example, if a business that revalues fixed assets is compared with one that measures them at historic cost, ratios such as ROCE, profit margin and gearing will not be strictly comparable.

(c) A small business may not be directly comparable with a large company, because it is probably managed in a completely different way. For example, a large company is likely to be able to take advantage of extended credit terms and trade discounts for bulk buying which may not be available to a smaller business.

(d) Businesses within the same industry sector can operate in completely different markets. For example, one clothes store may sell a very large number of cheap items at low margins, while another may sell a relatively small number of expensive items.

Activity 7 **(1 hour)**

Bimbridge Hospitals Trust has just lost its supplier of bandages. The company that has been supplying it for the last five years has gone into liquidation. The Trust is concerned to select a new supplier which it can rely on to supply it with its needs for the foreseeable future. You have been asked by the Trust managers to analyse the financial statements of a potential supplier of bandages. You have obtained the latest financial statements of the company, in summary form, which are set out below.

PATCH LIMITED
SUMMARY PROFIT AND LOSS ACCOUNT
FOR THE YEAR ENDED 30 SEPTEMBER 20X8

	20X8	*20X7*
	£'000	£'000
Turnover	2,300	2,100
Cost of sales	1,035	945
Gross profit	1,265	1,155
Expenses	713	693
Net profit before interest and tax	552	462

BPP LEARNING MEDIA

NOTES

PATCH LIMITED
SUMMARY BALANCE SHEET
AS AT 30 SEPTEMBER 20X8

	20X8		20X7	
	£'000	£'000	£'000	£'000
Fixed assets		4,764		5,418
Current assets				
Stocks	522		419	
Debtors	406		356	
Cash	117		62	
	1,045		837	
Current liabilities				
Trade creditors	305		254	
Taxation	170		211	
	475		465	
Net current assets		570		372
Long-term loan		(1,654)		(2,490)
		3,680		3,300
Share capital		1,100		1,000
Share premium		282		227
Profit and loss account		2,298		2,073
		3,680		3,300

You have also obtained the relevant industry average ratios which are as follows:

	20X8	20X7
Return on capital employed	9.6%	9.4%
Net profit percentage	21.4%	21.3%
Quick ratio/acid test	1.0:1	0.9:1
Gearing (debt/capital employed)	36%	37%

Tasks

Prepare a report for the managers of Bimbridge Hospitals Trust recommending whether or not to use Patch Ltd as a supplier of bandages. Use the information contained in the financial statements of Patch Ltd and the industry averages supplied.

Your answer should:

(a) Comment on the company's profitability, liquidity and financial position
(b) Consider how the company has changed over the two years
(c) Include a comparison with the industry as a whole

The report should include calculation of the following ratios for the two years.

(a) Return on capital employed
(b) Net profit percentage
(c) Quick ratio/acid test
(d) Gearing

BPP LEARNING MEDIA

NOTES

Chapter roundup

- The ASB and the IASB have identified several different groups of users of financial statements; each with particular information needs. Investors are assumed to be the most important group of users.
- Profitability is measured by:
  - return on capital employed
  - net profit as a percentage of sales
  - asset turnover ratio
  - gross profit as a percentage of sales
- Debt and gearing are measured by:
  - debt ratio
  - gearing ratio
  - interest cover
  - cash flow ratio
- Liquidity and efficiency are measured by:
  - current ratio
  - quick ratio (acid test ratio)
  - debtor days (average debt collection period)
  - average stock turnover period
- Investment ratios include earnings per share, dividend cover and the price earnings (P/E) ratio
- Ratios provide information through comparison:
  - **trends** in a company's ratios from one year to the next, indicating an improving or worsening position;
  - in some cases, against a **'norm'** or 'standard';
  - in some cases, against the **ratios of other companies**, although differences between one company and another should often be expected.
- Ratio analysis is not foolproof. There are several **problems** inherent in making comparisons over time and between organisations.

Quick quiz

1 List three groups of people who might be interested in a company's financial statements.

2 Why might a bank be interested in the financial statements of a company?

3 Apart from ratio analysis, what other information might be helpful in interpreting a company's accounts?

4 What is the usual formula for ROCE?

5 ROCE can be calculated as the product of two other ratios. What are they?

6 Define the 'debt ratio'.

7 Give two formulae for calculating gearing.

8 What are the formulae for:

(a) The current ratio?
(b) The quick ratio?
(c) The debtors payment period?
(d) The stock turnover period?

Answers to quick quiz

1 Managers of the company, shareholders, trade contacts, providers of finance, tax authorities, employees, financial analysts and advisers, government agencies, the public. (see para 1.2)

2 In order to satisfy itself as to the company's financial position before giving it a loan. (para 1.4)

3 (a) Comments in the Chairman's report and directors' report. (para 2)
(b) The age and nature of the company's assets.
(c) Current and future developments in the company's markets.
(d) Post balance sheet events, contingencies, qualified audit report and so on.

4 $\frac{\text{Profit on ordinary activities before interest and tax}}{\text{Capital employed}}$ (para 3.2)

5 Asset turnover and profit margin. (para 3.4)

6 The ratio of a company's total debts to its total assets. (para 4.2)

7 (a) Capital gearing ratio $= \frac{\text{Prior charge capital}}{\text{Total capital}}$

(b) Debt/equity ratio $= \frac{\text{Prior charge capital}}{\text{Ordinary share capital and reserves}}$ (para 4.3)

8 (a) $\frac{\text{Current assets}}{\text{Current liabilities}}$

(b) $\frac{\text{Current assets less stock}}{\text{Current liabilities}}$

(c) $\frac{\text{Trade debtors}}{\text{Sales}} \times 365$

(d) $\frac{\text{Stock}}{\text{Cost of sales}} \times 365$ (para 4.9)

Answers to activities

1 Any of these user groups could obtain the latest filed statutory accounts for the company from the Registrar of Companies. If the company is small or medium-sized, however, the accounts may be in an abbreviated form. Public companies whose shares are traded on the London Stock Exchange are required to provide copies of their most recent published accounts to anyone who asks for them.

There is a greater problem in obtaining financial information from private companies. A trade contact, such as a supplier, can demand to see financial statements as a condition of doing business with the company. Similarly, a bank can demand to see financial information as a condition of granting a loan or overdraft facility.

Employees, as members of the public, are entitled to see the statutory accounts of their company employer. Some companies choose to provide financial statements prepared specifically for the benefit of their employees, but this is not a legal requirement.

2 $\text{ROCE} = \frac{\text{Profit}}{\text{Capital employed}}$

$\text{PM} = \frac{\text{Profit}}{\text{Sales}}$

$\text{AT} = \frac{\text{Sales}}{\text{Capital employed}}$

It follows that ROCE = PM × AT, which can be re-arranged to the form given in option D.

3 Interest payments should be taken gross, from the note to the accounts, and not net of interest receipts as shown in the P & L account.

	20X8	*20X7*
$\frac{\text{PBIT}}{\text{Interest payable}}$	$\frac{360,245}{18,115}$	$\frac{247,011}{21,909}$
	= 20 times	= 11 times

Betatec plc has more than sufficient interest cover. In view of the company's low gearing, this is not too surprising and so we finally obtain a picture of Betatec plc as a company that does not seem to have a debt problem, in spite of its high (although declining) debt ratio.

4 The cash cycle is the length of time between paying for raw materials and receiving cash from the sale of finished goods. In this case Butthead Ltd stores raw materials for three weeks, spends two weeks producing finished goods, four weeks storing the goods before sale and five weeks collecting the money from debtors: a total of 14 weeks. However, six weeks of this period is effectively financed by the company's creditors so that the length of the cash cycle is eight weeks.

5 $\text{Stock turnover} = \frac{\text{Cost of goods sold}}{\text{Average stock}} = \frac{£60,000}{£8,000}$

= 7.5 times

6

	20X7		*20X6*	
Current ratio	$\frac{626.8}{599.1}$	= 1.05	$\frac{654.4}{642.2}$	= 1.02
Quick ratio	$\frac{584.1}{599.1}$	= 0.97	$\frac{576.4}{642.2}$	= 0.90
Debtors' payment period	$\frac{295.2}{2,176.2} \times 365$	= 49.5 days	$\frac{335.5}{2,344.8} \times 365$	= 52.2 days

NOTES

	1997	1996
Stock turnover period	$\frac{42.7}{1,659.0} \times 365 = 9.4$ days	$\frac{78.0}{1,731.5} \times 365 = 16.4$ days
Creditors' turnover period	$\frac{190.8}{1,659.0} \times 365 = 42.0$ days	$\frac{188.1}{1,731.5} \times 365 = 40.0$ days

7 **Note**. Do not be put off by the fact that you are writing to the managers of a hospitals trust – this is ratio analysis in its normal form. Don't forget – you need to *comment* on the ratios as well as calculating them correctly.

REPORT

To: The Managers, Bimbridge Hospitals Trust
From: Business Adviser
Date: 20 November 20X8

Performance and position of Patch Ltd

As requested, I have analysed the performance and position of Patch Ltd with special reference to selected accounting ratios. The calculation of the ratios is shown in the Appendix attached to this report. The purpose of the analysis is to determine whether we should use Patch Ltd as a supplier of bandages.

General comments

Both turnover and profits have increased over the two years. The company is clearly expanding, although not at an exceptionally fast rate. The growth seems to have been achieved without investing heavily in fixed assets, the fall in this figure presumably being due to depreciation. Shares were issued in 20X8 at a premium, while a sizeable portion of the long-term loan has been paid off. Expansion appears to be financed by share capital and profits.

Return on capital employed

This has increased from 8% in 20X7 to 10.3% in 20X8. It had also gone from being below the industry average in 20X7 to above it in 20X8. These are encouraging signs. As indicated above, the company has not invested significantly in fixed assets to finance its expansion – the assets/capital employed is simply working harder.

Net profit percentage

This has also increased from 22% in 20X7 to 24% in 20X8. In both years it was higher than the industry average. This is obviously good news. Sometimes when a company grows, it is at the expense of lower margins, but this is clearly not the case for Patch Ltd.

Quick ratio or acid test

The quick ratio shows how many assets, excluding stock, are available to meet the current liabilities. Stock is excluded because it is not always readily convertible into cash. The quick ratio or acid test is therefore a better indicator of a company's true liquidity than the current ratio which does not exclude stock. Patch Ltd's quick ratio is healthy (around 1) in both years, and has in fact improved from) 0.9:1 to 1.1:1. While Patch's quick ratio was the same as the industry average in 20X7, it was better than average in 20X8.

These are encouraging signs. Sometimes growth can lead to overtrading to the detriment of liquidity, but Patch Ltd has not fallen into this trap.

Gearing

The gearing ratio is also favourable. This can be calculated in two ways: debt/capital employed and debt/equity. Debt/capital employed shows a fall from 43% in 20X7 to 31% in 20X8. In 20X7 it was higher than the industry average, but in 20X8 it is lower. Calculated as debt/equity, the ratio shows an even more significant decline.

This is reassuring. A high geared company is more risky than a low geared one in that, if profits are falling, it is more difficult for a high geared company to meet interest payments. A high geared company is therefore more likely to go into liquidation, as our last supplier of bandages did.

Conclusion

On the basis of the above analysis, I see every reason to use Patch Ltd as our supplier. The company's profitability and liquidity are improving and the gearing is at a lower level than last year. In addition the company compares favourably with other companies operating in the same sector.

APPENDIX – CALCULATION OF RATIOS

	20X8	*Industry average 20X8*	*20X7*	*Industry average 20X7*
Return on capital employed	$\frac{552}{5,334} = 10.3\%$	9.6%	$\frac{462}{5,790} = 8.0\%$	9.4%
Net profit percentage	$\frac{552}{2,300} = 24\%$	21.4%	$\frac{462}{2,100} = 22\%$	21.3%
Quick ratio/acid test	$\frac{1,045 - 522}{475} = 1.1:1$	1.0:1	$\frac{837 - 419}{465} = 0.9:1$	0.9:1
Gearing:				
Debt/capital employed	$\frac{1,654}{5,334} = 31\%$	36%	$\frac{2,490}{5,790} = 43\%$	37%
Debt/equity	$\frac{1,654}{3,680} = 45\%$		$\frac{2,490}{3,300} = 75\%$	

PART C

FINANCIAL SYSTEMS AND AUDITING

Chapter 23 : ACCOUNTING SYSTEMS

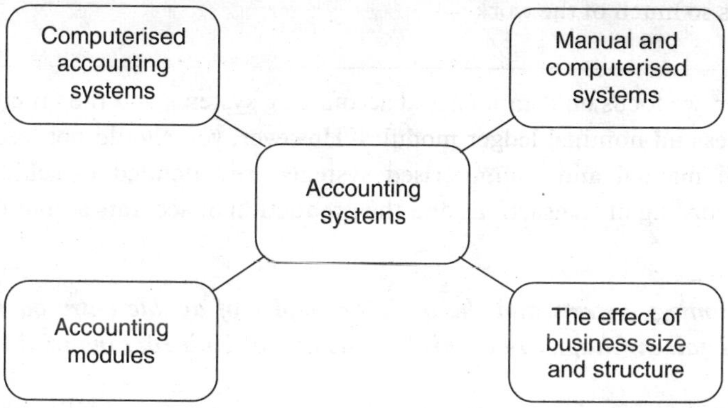

The Edexcel Guidelines include accounting records and fundamental accounting concepts under the heading of Accounting Systems. These topics are covered in Chapters 13 and 19 as part of Unit 10, Financial Reporting, as an understanding of them is also required for that unit.

Introduction

These days most accounting systems are computerised. Hence, a sound knowledge of computer applications in accounting is very important, even for a beginner. While using a computer package does require a certain level of specialist knowledge about the unique characteristics of the system, the good news is that the principles of computerised accounting are the same as those of manual accounting. Even the accounting functions retain the same names in computerised systems as in more traditional written records.

This chapter starts by introducing you to accounting packages and then it takes a somewhat detailed look at the operation of the programs available to deal individually with the various parts of the accounting system such as the sales ledger, purchase ledger etc. Such programs are called modules and are discussed in Section 3.

A modern computer generally consists of a keyboard, a television-like screen, a box-like disk drive which contains all the necessary electronic components for data processing, and a printer. This is the computer hardware. Computer programs are the instructions that tell the electronics how to process data. The general term used for these is software. Software is what we are concerned with in this Course Book.

Your objectives

In this chapter you will learn about the following.

(a) The major features of accounting packages

(b) The functioning of the sales, purchase and nominal ledger modules

(c) The effect of business size and structure on the accounting system.

1 MANUAL AND COMPUTERISED SYSTEMS

FOR DISCUSSION

As most accounting systems are computerised, why do you think we learn bookkeeping as though they were manual? Do we really need to learn bookkeeping at all when the computer does so much of the work?

In this chapter, we focus on computerised accounting systems and the functioning of the sales, purchases and nominal ledger modules. However, you should not lose sight of the fact that both manual and computerised systems are intended to achieve the same results: the recording of transactions and the production of accurate accounts.

Manual accounting systems and the basic principles of double entry bookkeeping are explained in detail in Chapter 14 of this book as part of Unit 10, Financial Reporting.

2 COMPUTERISED ACCOUNTING SYSTEMS

2.1 What are accounting packages?

'Software' can be defined as computer programs that tell the hardware what to do.

Definitions

> **Accounting packages** are collections of computer programs or software designed to carry out specific accounting tasks. They may be customised or bought 'off-the-shelf'.
>
> An **accounting suite** is a set of accounting modules or programs.

Examples of accounting packages are packages for payroll, sales and purchase ledger packages and fixed assets register. Small businesses are more likely to purchase 'off-the-shelf' packages as this is normally a more cost effective option. Larger organisations may develop 'bespoke' software.

FOR DISCUSSION

Which accounting packages are you familiar with? What are they used for? Are they 'off-the-shelf' or 'bespoke'?

One of the most important facts to remember about computerised accounting is that in principle, it is exactly the same as manual accounting. Even the accounting functions retain the same names in computerised systems as in more traditional written records. Computerised accounting still uses the familiar ideas of day books, ledger accounts, double entry, trial balance and financial statements. The principles of working with computerised sales, purchase and nominal ledgers are exactly what would be expected in the manual methods they replace. The only difference is that these various books of account have become invisible. Ledgers are now computer files which are held in a computer-sensible form, ready to be called upon.

2.2 Coding

Computers are used more efficiently if vital information is expressed in the form of codes. For example, nominal ledger accounts will be coded individually, perhaps by means of a two-digit code: eg

05	Profit and loss account
15	Purchases
22	Debtors ledger control account
41	Creditors ledger control account
42	Interest

In the same way, individual accounts must be given a unique code number in the sales ledger and purchase ledger.

When an invoice is received from a supplier (code 1234) for £3,000 for the purchase of raw materials, the transaction might be coded for input to the computer as:

	Nominal ledger		*Stock*		
Supplier code	*Debit*	*Credit*	*Value*	*Code*	*Quantity*
1234	15	41	£3,000	56742	150

Code 15 might represent purchases and code 41 the creditors control account. This single input could be used to update the purchase ledger, the nominal ledger, and the stock ledger. The stock code may enable further analysis to be carried out, perhaps allocating the cost to a particular department or product. Thus the needs of both financial accounting and cost accounting can be fulfilled at once.

2.3 Using an accounting package

When a user begins to work with an accounting package he or she will usually be asked to key in a password. Separate passwords can be used for different parts of the system, for example for different ledgers if required. This prevents access by unauthorised personnel. The user will then be presented with a 'menu' of options such as 'enter new data' or 'print report'. By selecting and keying in the appropriate option number or letter the user will then be guided through the actions needed to enter the data or generate the report.

Activity 1 **(5 minutes)**

Give some examples, from your own experience, of the use of passwords.

Although accounting packages are, in principle, exactly the same as manual accounting, they do have certain distinctive advantages and disadvantages.

NOTES

2.4 Advantages and disadvantages of accounting packages

The main advantages of accounting packages are as follows.

(a) The packages can be used by non-specialists as use of codes for input means that correct accounts will be updated.

(b) A large amount of data can be processed very quickly.

(c) Computerised systems are more accurate than manual systems.

(d) A computer is capable of handling and processing large volumes of data.

(e) The ability to integrate systems or modules prevents wasteful repetition as one entry may update several records.

(f) Once the data has been input, computerised systems can analyse data rapidly to present useful control information for managers such as a trial balance or a debtors schedule.

Although the advantages of computerised accounting systems far outweigh the disadvantages, particularly for large businesses, they still suffer from certain disadvantages. The main ones are as follows.

(a) The initial time and costs involved in installing the system, training personnel and so on.

(b) The need for security checks to make sure that unauthorised personnel do not gain access to data files.

(c) The necessity to develop a system of coding and checking.

(d) Lack of 'audit trail'. It is not always easy to see where a mistake has been made.

(e) Possible resistance on the part of staff to the introduction of the system.

We next look at the 'building blocks' of the accounting package namely, modules.

3 ACCOUNTING MODULES

3.1 What are they?

An accounting package will consist of several modules.

Definition

> A **module** is a program which deals with one particular part of a business accounting system.

A simple accounting package might consist of only one module (in which case it is called a stand-alone module), but more often it will consist of several modules. The name given to a set of several modules is a suite.

NOTES

An accounting package, therefore, might have separate modules for:

- Invoicing
- Stock
- Sales ledger
- Purchase ledger
- Nominal ledger
- Payroll
- Cash book
- Fixed asset register
- Report generator

and so on.

Linking modules in such a way that data input into one module can then be transferred automatically to all other relevant modules can increase efficiency and reduce errors.

3.2 Integrated software

Each module may be integrated with the others, so that data entered in one module will be passed automatically or by simple operator request through into any other module where the data is of some relevance to form an integrated accounting system. For example, if there is an input into the invoicing module authorising the despatch of an invoice to a customer, there might be automatic links to:

(a) The sales ledger, to update the file by posting the invoice to the customer's account

(b) The stock module, to update the stock file by:

  (i) Reducing the quantity and value of stock in hand
  (ii) Recording the stock movement

(c) The nominal ledger, to update the file by posting the sale to the sales account

(d) The report generator, to update the sales analysis and sales totals which are on file and awaiting inclusion in management reports.

The advantages of integrated software are as follows.

(a) It becomes possible to make just one entry in one of the ledgers which automatically updates the others.

(b) Users can specify reports, and the software will automatically extract the required data from all the relevant files.

(c) Both of the above simplify the workload of the user, and the irritating need to constantly load and unload disks is eliminated.

There are some disadvantages of integrated software as well. They are as follows.

(a) Usually, it requires more computer memory than separate (stand-alone) systems – which means there is less space in which to store actual data.

(b) Because one program is expected to do everything, the user will often find that an integrated package has fewer facilities than a set of specialised modules. In effect, an integrated package could be 'Jack of all trades but master of none'.

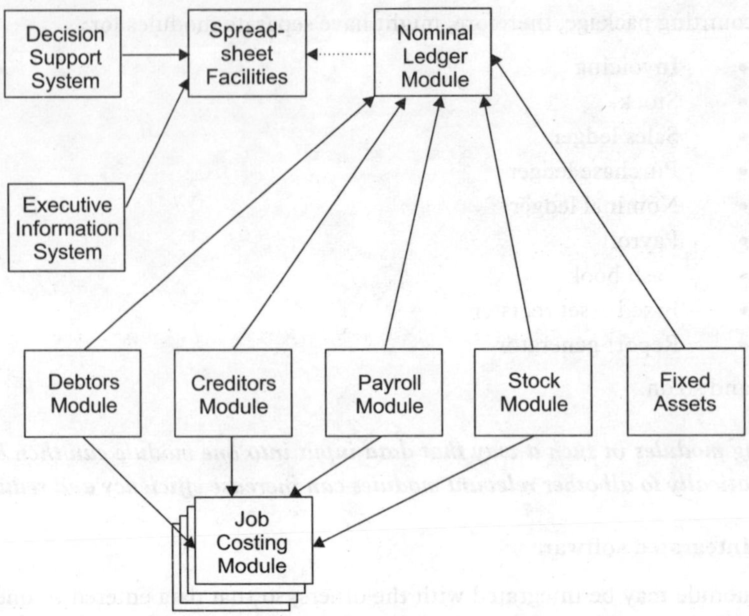

Figure 23.1: Integrated accounting system

FOR DISCUSSION

What are the benefits and disadvantages of different computer accounting packages you have used?

Now that you understand the general nature of accounting modules we look at some of the accounting modules in more detail, starting with the sales ledger.

3.3 Accounting for debtors

A computerised sales ledger will be expected to keep the sales ledger up to date, and also it should be able to produce certain output (eg statements, sales analysis reports, responses to file interrogations etc). The output might be produced daily (eg day book listings), monthly (eg statements), quarterly (eg sales analysis reports) or periodically (eg responses to file interrogations, or customer name and address lists printed on adhesive labels for despatching circulars or price lists).

What we need to do is to have a closer look at the form that input, output and processing take within a sales ledger. We will begin by thinking about what data we would expect to see in a sales ledger.

3.4 Data held on a sales ledger file

The sales ledger file will consist of individual records for each customer account. Some of the data held on the record will be standing data (ie it will change infrequently).

Typical items of standing data are:

- Customer account number
- Customer name
- Address
- Credit limit
- Account sales analysis code
- Account type (there are two different types of account – open item or balance forward – which we will look at shortly).

Each of these items is referred to as a field of information.

Other data held on a customer record will change as the sales ledger is updated. Such data is called variable data, and will include:

- Transaction data
- Transaction description (eg sale, credit note etc)
- Transaction code (eg to identify payment period allowed)
- Debits
- Credits
- Balance

The file which contains these customer records – the sales ledger – is an example of a master file. If it is updated from another file containing various transactions, then that file is called a transactions file.

Activity 2 **(5 minutes)**

What is the relationship between a file, a field and a record?

3.5 Input to a sales ledger system

Bearing in mind what we expect to find in a sales ledger, we can say that typical data input into a sales ledger system is as follows.

(a) Amendments:

(i) Amendments to customer details, eg change of address, change of credit limit, etc

(ii) Insertion of new customers

(iii) Deletion of old 'non-active' customers.

(b) Transaction data relating to:

(i) Sales transactions, for invoicing
(ii) Customer payments
(iii) Credit notes
(iv) Adjustments (debit or credit items).

Some computerised sales ledgers produce invoices, so that basic sales data is input into the system. But other businesses might have a specialised invoicing module, so that the sales ledger package is not expected to produce invoices. The invoice details are already available (as output from the specialised module) and are input into the sales ledger system rather than basic sales data. So item (b)(i) of the list of typical data should read as follows.

(b) (i) Sales transactions, for invoicing (if the sales ledger is expected to produce invoices) or invoice details (if already available from a specialised invoicing module).'

3.6 Processing in a sales ledger system

The primary action involved in updating the sales ledger is modifying the amount outstanding on the customer's account. How the amount is modified depends on what data is being input (ie whether it is an invoice, credit note, remittance etc).

When processing starts, the balance on an account is called the brought-forward balance. When processing has finished, the balance on the account is called the carried-forward balance. These terms are often abbreviated to b/f and c/f. What a computer does is to add or subtract whatever you tell it to from the b/f balance, and end up with a c/f balance. This is the same principle which applies to manual accounting.

	£	£
Brought forward account balance		X
Add:		
Invoice value	X	
Adjustments (+)	X	
		X
		X
Deduct:		
Credit note value	X	
Adjustments (–)	X	
Remittances	X	
		(X)
Carried forward account balance		X

This method of updating customer accounts is called the **balance forward method**.

Alternatively, the computer might use the **open item method** of processing the data. Under this method, the computer identifies specific invoices, and credits individual payments against specific invoices. Late payments of individual invoices can be identified and chased up. The customer's outstanding balance is the sum of the unpaid open items.

3.7 Outputs from a sales ledger system

Typical outputs in a computerised sales ledger are as follows.

(a) **Day book listing**. A list of all transactions posted each day. This provides an audit trail – ie it is information which the auditors of the business can use when carrying out their work

(b) **Invoices** (if the package is one which is expected to produce invoices)

(c) **Statements**. End of month statements for customers

(d) **Sales analysis reports**. These will analyse sales according to the sales analysis codes on the sales ledger file. They may be by customer or by the type of product sold. They may also do it by region or sales office

NOTES

(e) **Debtors reminder letters.** Letters can be produced automatically to chase late payers when the due date for payment goes by without payment having been received

(f) **Customer lists** (or perhaps a selective list). The list might be printed on to adhesive labels, for sending out customer letters or marketing material

(g) **Responses to enquiries**, perhaps output on to a screen rather than as printed copy, for fast response to customer enquiries

(h) **Output on to disk file for other modules** – eg to the stock control module and the nominal ledger module, if these are also used by the organisation, and the package is not an integrated one

3.8 The advantages of a computerised debtor system

The advantages of such a system, in addition to the advantages of computerised accounting generally, are its ability to assist in sales administration and marketing by means of outputs such as those listed above.

3.9 Purchase ledger

A computerised purchase ledger will certainly be expected to keep the purchase ledger up to date, and also it should be able to output various reports requested by the user. In fact, a computerised purchase ledger is much the same as a computerised sales ledger, except that it is a sort of mirror image as it deals with purchases rather than sales.

3.10 Inputs to a purchase ledger system

Bearing in mind what we expect to see held on a purchase ledger, typical data input into a purchase ledger system is:

(a) Details of purchases recorded on invoices
(b) Details of returns to suppliers for which credit notes are received
(c) Details of payments to suppliers
(d) Adjustments.

3.11 Processing in a purchase ledger system

The primary action involved in updating the purchase ledger is adjusting the amounts outstanding on the supplier accounts. These amounts will represent money owed to the suppliers. The computer will adjust the owed brought-forward balance by adding or deducting the value of transactions as you tell it to. The carried-forward balance becomes the new balance recorded on the suppliers account. This processing is identical to updating the accounts in the sales ledger, except that the sales ledger balances are debits (debtors) and the purchase ledger balances are credits (creditors).

3.12 Outputs from a purchase ledger system

Typical outputs in a computerised purchase ledger are as follows.

(a) Lists of transactions posted – produced every time the system is run.

BPP LEARNING MEDIA

(b) An analysis of expenditure for nominal ledger purposes. This may be produced every time the system is run or at the end of each month.

(c) List of creditors balances together with a reconciliation between the total balance brought forward, the transactions for the month and the total balance carried forward.

(d) Copies of creditors' accounts. This may show merely the balance b/f, current transactions and the balance c/f. If complete details of all unsettled items are given, the ledger is known as an open-ended ledger. (This is similar to the open item or balance forward methods with a sales ledger system.)

(e) Any purchase ledger system can be used to produce details of payments to be made. For example:

(i) Remittance advices (usually a copy of the ledger account)
(ii) Cheques
(iii) Credit transfer listings

(f) Other special reports may be produced for:

(i) Costing purposes
(ii) Updating records about fixed assets
(iii) Comparisons with budget

The last accounting module we will look at is the nominal ledger. This module enables a business's profit or loss to be calculated. If you have already studied Unit 10 you will have seen the nominal ledger in Chapter 14.

3.13 Nominal ledger

The nominal ledger (or general ledger) is an accounting record which summarises the financial affairs of a business. It is the nucleus of an accounting system. It contains details of assets, liabilities and capital, income and expenditure and thus enables the profit or loss to be calculated.

The nominal ledger consists of a large number of different accounts, each account having its own purpose or 'name' and an identity or code. Some nominal ledgers are separately structured, but others are posted automatically from related modules (eg sales ledger module, purchase ledger module). This difference in the types of computerised nominal ledger which exist has implications for what is input into the system, as we shall see.

A nominal ledger will consist of a large number of coded accounts. For example, part of a nominal ledger might be as follows.

Account code	Account name
100200	Plant and machinery (cost)
100300	Motor vehicles (cost)
100201	Plant and machinery depreciation
100301	Motor vehicies depreciation
300000	Total debtors
400000	Total creditors
500130	Wages and salaries

Account code	**Account name**
500140	Rent and rates
500150	Advertising expenses
500160	Bank charges
500170	Motor expenses
500180	Telephone expenses
600000	Sales
700000	Cash

A business will, of course, choose its own codes for its nominal ledger accounts. The codes given in this table are purely for illustrative purposes.

It is important to remember that a computerised nominal ledger works in exactly the same way as a manual nominal ledger, although there are some differences in terminology. For instance, in a manual system, the sales and debtors accounts were posted from the sales day book (not the sales ledger) (see Chapter 14). But in a computerised system, the sales day book is automatically produced as part of the 'sales ledger module'. So it may sound as if you are posting directly from the sales ledger, but in fact the day book is part of a computerised sales ledger.

3.14 Inputs to the nominal ledger

Inputs depend on whether the accounting system is integrated or not.

(a) If the system is integrated, then as soon as data is put into the sales ledger module (or anywhere else for that matter), the relevant nominal ledger accounts are updated. There is nothing more for the system user to do.

(b) If the system is not integrated then the output from the sales ledger module (and anywhere else) has to be input into the nominal ledger. This is done by using journal entries. For instance:

Accounts	*Debit*	*Credit*
	£	£
A/c 300000	3,000	
A/c 600000		3,000

Where 600000 is the nominal ledger code for sales, and 300000 is the code for debtors. However, regardless of whether the system is integrated or not, the actual data needed by the nominal ledger package to be able to update the ledger accounts includes:

(a) Date
(b) Description
(c) Amount
(d) Account codes (sometimes called distinction codes)

3.15 Outputs from the nominal ledger

The main outputs apart from listings of individual nominal ledger accounts are:

(a) The trial balance (see Chapter 15)
(b) Financial statements (see Chapter 18)

NOTES

FOR DISCUSSION

As most accounting systems are computerised, why do you think we learn bookkeeping as if they were manual? Do we really need to learn bookkeeping at all when the computer does so much of the work?

4 THE EFFECT OF BUSINESS SIZE AND STRUCTURE

The Edexcel Guidelines require you to assess the factors which influence the nature and structure of accounting systems. The main factors are the effect of the business size and structure.

The structure of businesses is covered in depth in Mandatory Unit 3, Organisations and Behaviour. You should refer back to your work for that unit in order to revise the main types of business structure.

We now turn to consider the finance function and authority within the organisation.

4.1 The finance function and authority

The finance function is part of the technostructure of an organisation and therefore we must consider how the authority of departments in the technostructure is exercised over the middle line and the operating core. The types of authority that a manager or a department may have are line authority, staff authority and functional authority.

Definitions

- **Line authority** is the authority a manager has over a subordinate.
- **Staff authority** is the authority one manager or department may have in giving specialist advice to another manager or department, over which there is no line authority. Staff authority does not entail the right to make or influence decisions in the advisee department.
- **Functional authority** is a hybrid of line and staff authority, whereby the technostructure manager or department has the authority, in certain circumstances, to direct, design or control activities or procedures of another department. An example is where a finance manager has authority to require timely reports from line managers.

Activity 3 **(10 minutes)**

What sort of authority is exercised:

(a) By the financial controller over the chief accountant?
(b) By the production manager over the production workforce?
(c) By the financial controller over the production manager?

4.2 Problems with authority

Problem	Possible solution
The technostructure can **undermine** the **line managers**' authority, by empire building.	**Clear** demarcations of line, staff and functional authority should be created.
Lack of seniority: middle line managers may be more senior in the hierarchy than technostructure advisers.	Use **functional authority** (through procedures). Experts should be seen as a resource, not a threat.
Expert managers may **lack realism**, going for technically perfect, but commercially impractical, solutions.	Technostructure planners should **be fully aware** of **operations issues**.
Technostructure experts **lack responsibility** for the success of their ideas.	Technostructure experts should be involved in **implementing** their suggestions and should take responsibility for their success.

4.3 Dangers of a weak technostructure

(a) **Legal** restrictions, such as the Companies Act, might be broken by the line managers.

(b) **Increased risk**: expert advice might be ignored or not sought.

(c) **Important work** not directly involved with day-to-day operations, such as personnel planning, new technology and management techniques **might be ignored**.

4.4 Dangers of an over-strong technostructure

(a) Professional specialists sometimes have **divided loyalties** between their organisation and their profession. Computer specialists, for example, might want to introduce state of the art computer systems when these might not be the most appropriate for the organisation.

(b) **Instability.** Many professional specialists have skills which can be marketed to other organisations, so that their careers are not necessarily tied to one organisation.

(c) The technostructure **introduces rules and procedures** such as control systems, job evaluation and appraisal systems, and these tend to **hamper operations**.

(d) Different departments or levels in the technostructure might have **conflicting expertise.**

(e) It may be **difficult to measure the benefits** to the organisation of various aspects of technostructural work as these benefits are indirect.

4.5 The accountant's role

In many companies, the finance function is one of the most important expert roles in the organisation. The roles of the management accountant and financial accountant are technostructural roles but are different. The **financial accountant** is likely to play a less direct role in the operational running of the business than the **management accountant,** but is crucial to a company's effective boundary management with shareholders.

4.6 Information

The **financial accountant** classifies accounting information and is responsible for presenting this to **external shareholders**. The need to provide financial accounting information to shareholders has a necessary impact on the activities of the strategic apex, middle line and operating core.

(a) A business's performance is **measured in money terms**. Business decisions impact on the firm's financial results. 'What will shareholders think?'

(b) The **timing** of business transactions is important for financial reporting purposes.

Financial reporting is not an optional extra. The published accounts are an important source of communication with outsiders. Reported levels of profit determine the return that investors can receive. They also indirectly affect the company's cost of capital (although this is more determined by expectations of future benefits) by affecting the share price. Published financial information therefore affects the cost of one of the organisation's most important resources, money.

The **management accountant** is even nearer the policy making and management process. This is because the management accountant is not primarily interested in reporting to interested parties external to the organisation. After all, the requirements of external users of accounts may be different to those involved in managing and running the business in several respects.

- Level of detail
- Aggregation of information
- Classification of data
- The period covered

Internally, accountants therefore provide information for **planning and controlling** the business.

- Past cost information
- Product profitability
- Cost/profit centre performance
- Desirability of investments
- Competitors performance
- Sensitivity analysis
- Alternative options

The accountant provides information essential for the current management and decision-making of the business. If line decisions are assessed in accounting terms, even in part, then the accountant will be involved in them. Accountants assess the future financial consequences of certain decisions.

4.7 Control and stewardship

The accounting staff's authority is generally expressed in procedures and rules. For example, capital investment is analysed in financial terms. People have formal expenditure limits. In many respects, money and funds are a business's lifeblood, and monitoring their flow is a necessary precaution. If the flow of funds dries up a business can fail very easily. Proper financial control ensures that the business is adequately financed to meet its obligations.

Chapter roundup

- Computer software used in accounting may be divided into two types:
  - Dedicated accounting packages;
  - General software, the uses of which include accounting amongst many others.
- In principle, computerised accounting is the same as manual accounting, but a computerised approach has certain advantages, the principal one being improved efficiency.
- An accounting package consists of a number of 'modules' which perform all the tasks needed to maintain a normal accounting function like purchase ledger or payroll. The modules may or may not be integrated with each other.
- The size and structure of an organisation will have a considerable impact on the operation of the finance function.

Quick quiz

1. What is an accounting suite?
2. What is coding?
3. What are the advantages of integrated software?
4. What sort of data is input into a sales ledger system?
5. What is the open item method of processing?
6. What are the typical outputs from a purchase ledger system?

Answers to quick quiz

1. A set of accounting modules or programs. (see para 2.1)
2. A way of labelling accounts for ease of recognition and posting. (para 2.2)
3. One entry to an account will automatically update others; users can specify reports; work of the user is simplified. (para 3.2)
4. Amendments to customer details. New customer information. Transaction data. (para 3.4)

5 The computer identifies specific invoices, and credits specific payments against specific invoices allowing late payments of invoices to be identified and chased up. (para 3.6)

6 List of transactions posted; analysis of expenditure; list of creditor balances; copies of creditor accounts; other information on payments; special reports. (para 3.12)

Answers to activities

1 Some of the more common examples for using passwords are to prevent/limit access to:

(i) Personnel records
(ii) Accounting records
(iii) Future plans
(iv) Product formulae

2 A file is made up of records which are made up of fields. Make sure you learn any new terminology like this, because it will make your answers far more convincing in an assessment.

3 (a) Line authority
(b) Line authority
(c) Functional authority

Chapter 24 :
MANAGEMENT CONTROL

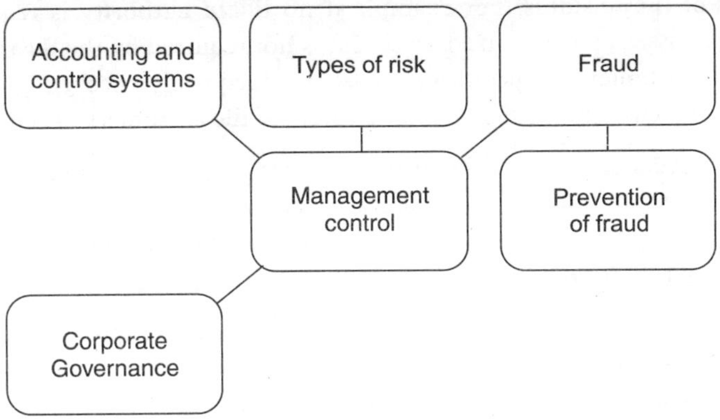

Introduction

The environment within which a business operates and the systems it adopts are critical in determining the degree of control exercised by management of the business over the accounting and other functions.

Management are usually keen to ensure that an adequate system of control is in place, to ensure that nothing should go wrong in the running of the business and there should be no scope for fraud.

Management control is closely related to business risk, in that management try to eliminate the impact of uncertainty in making business decisions. 'Risk' is sometimes used to describe situations where outcomes are not known, but their probabilities can be estimated.

Business risk is covered in the BPP Learning Media Business Essentials Course Book on Business Strategy.

Your objectives

In this chapter you will learn about the following.

(a) Types of risk

(b) Features of accounting and control systems

(c) Types of internal control

(d) The inherent limitations of internal control

(e) Fraud

(f) Value for money auditing

(g) Corporate governance

1 TYPES OF RISK

There are three types of risk mentioned by the Edexcel Guidelines for Unit 11, being operational risk, financial risk and compliance risk. These make up business risk.

1.1 Operational, financial and compliance risk

Operating risk can be defined as the chances of errors or mistakes being made within the operations of the business. For example if no Board authority is required for the purchase of fixed assets, a major fixed asset that is not required by the business might be purchased, or if customer job specifications are not adequately checked, goods might be manufactured for a customer which are not entirely to the customers' specification.

Financial risk covers all of the risks of incorrect payments being made or not all due receipts being collected. For example if there are not adequate payroll control systems it might be possible for 'dummy' employees to be paid and the additional wages taken by a member of the payroll department.

Compliance risk is the overall risk that a company will not comply with all of the legal requirements laid out in the Companies Act. One key area here is the requirement for the directors of a company to keep proper accounting records.

Definition

Companies Act requirements can be explained as follows.

The responsibility for installing and maintaining a **satisfactory accounting system** rests, in the case of a company, with the directors. The Companies Act 1985 (CA 85 s 221) requires that companies shall keep accounting records which are sufficient to show and explain the company's transactions and are such that they:

(a) Disclose with reasonable accuracy, at any time, the financial position of the company at that time.

(b) Enable the directors to ensure that any balance sheet and profit and loss account prepared under this Part complies with the requirements of this Act.

1.2 Accounting records: statutory requirements

S 221 goes on to state that the accounting records should show how **monies** have been **received** and **expended** and **record** the **assets** and **liabilities** of the company. If the company deals in goods, records should show **statements** of **stock held** at the **year end** and also **stocktake records** that form the basis of statements of stock held.

Officers of a company are liable to imprisonment or a fine (or both) if found guilty of knowingly failing to comply with the above sections.

1.3 Business risk

Business risk cannot be eliminated, but must be **managed** by the company.

NOTES

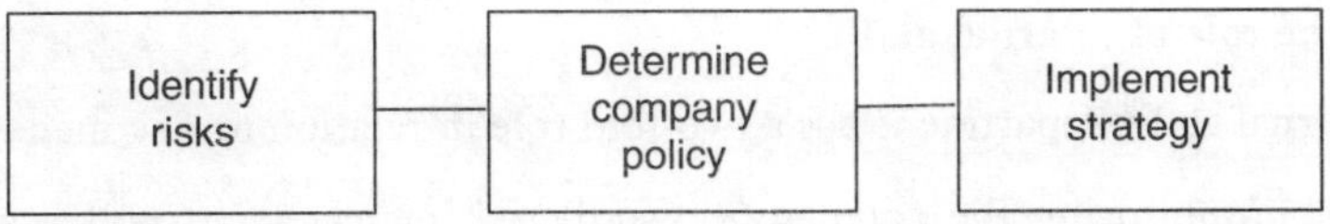

1.4 Responses to given risks

Broadly speaking, there are four potential responses a company can take to any given risk:

- Accept risk (ie live with it – only acceptable if it is a low risk)
- Reduce risk (by instituting a system of internal control or protection)
- Avoid risk (by not engaging in that activity or not accepting a contract)
- Transfer risk (by taking out insurance)

Risks to the business can exist on an individual department and individual level and also on a higher, strategic level. Employees at all levels should be involved in identifying risks.

Depending on the risk identified, company policy may be set at a department or at Board level.

Activity 1 **(10 minutes)**

For the following two departments, think of (a) a risk that the company might face and (b) what policy they might adopt in respect of it.

(i) Purchasing department
(ii) Human resources department

Designing and operating internal control systems is a key part of a company's risk management. This will often be done by employees in their various departments, although sometimes (particularly in the case of specialised computer systems) the company will hire external expertise to design systems.

1.5 The role of internal audit

The internal audit department has a two-fold role in relation to risk management.

- Monitoring the company's overall risk management policy and ensuring it operates effectively.
- Monitoring the strategies implemented to ensure that they continue to operate effectively.

Going back to the diagram in Paragraph 1.3, this can be shown as:

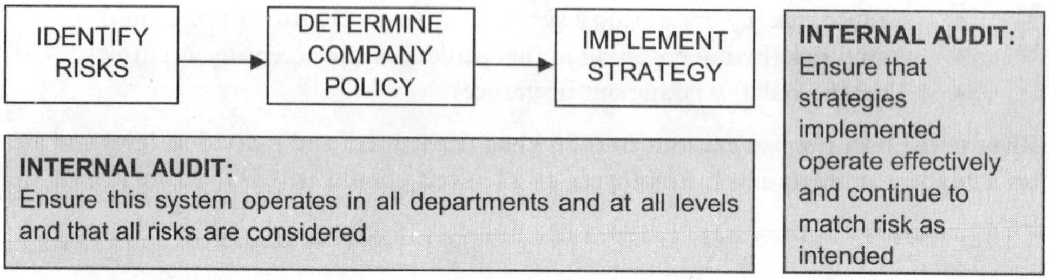

As a significant risk management policy in companies is to implement internal controls to reduce them, internal audit have a key role in assessing systems and testing controls.

Internal audit may assist in the development of systems. However, their key role will be in **monitoring the overall process** and in **providing assurance** that the **systems** which the departments have designed **meet objectives** and **operate effectively**.

It is important that the internal audit department retain their **objectivity** towards these aspects of their role, which is another reason why internal audit would generally not be involved in the assessment of risks and the design of the system.

2 FEATURES OF ACCOUNTING AND CONTROL SYSTEMS

Definition

> An **internal control system** comprises the control environment and control procedures. It includes all the policies and procedures (internal controls) adopted by the directors and management of an entity to ensure, as far as practicable, the orderly and efficient conduct of its business, including adherence to internal policies, the safeguarding of assets, the prevention and detection of fraud and error, the accuracy and completeness of the accounting records, and the timely preparation of reliable financial information. Internal controls may be incorporated within computerised accounting systems. However the internal control system extends beyond those matters which relate directly to the accounting system.

International Standard on Auditing 315 (ISA 315) *Obtaining an understanding of the entity and its environment and assessing the risks of material misstatement* covers the whole area of controls. ISAs are issued by the Auditing Practices Board on all aspects of auditing. You will become familiar with some of them while you are working on this Unit.

2.1 Control environment

The control environment is the framework within which controls operate. The control environment is very much determined by the management of a business.

Definition

> **Control environment** includes the governance and management functions and the attitudes, awareness and actions of those charged with governance and management concerning the entity's internal control and its importance in the entity.

The ISA adds to the definition of the control environment that a strong control environment does not, by itself, ensure the effectiveness of the overall internal control system. However, aspects of the control environment (such as management attitudes towards control) will be a significant factor in determining **how controls operate**. Controls are more likely to operate well in an environment where they are treated as being important. In addition consideration of the control environment will, as shown above, mean considering whether certain controls (internal audits, budgets) actually exist.

The following factors will be reflected in the control environment.

Communication and enforcement of integrity and ethical values	Control systems can only be effective where managers and staff have integrity and follow a system of ethics. The ethical system provides guidance on 'right' and 'wrong' – in other words it is ethically correct to follow control systems. Without ethics, controls may not be followed and managers/staff would not see this was incorrect.
Commitment to competence	Competence is the skills and knowledge necessary for each individual to carry out jobs. The company needs to ensure that each individual does have the necessary skill and knowledge so that the control system can be run effectively.
Participation by those charged with governance	The control system will be reviewed by staff independent of that system ie those charged with governance. In a large company this will be the audit committee and internal audit department; in a smaller company this may be a manager outside of the accounting department.
Management's philosophy and operating style	Management must show a pro-active approach to risk management. This provides a lead for the rest of the company to follow. If management appeared not to be interested in controls then staff would also be less inclined to follow control systems.

BPP LEARNING MEDIA

Organisational structure	The company's organisational structure provides the framework within which the control system works. The structure must therefore provide appropriate communication and reporting systems to enable the control system to be effective.
Assignment of authority and responsibility	Authority and responsibility are assigned appropriately within the company. This means staff know when they have to implement/follow controls and how to report control weaknesses to an appropriate manager.
Human resource policies and practices	These relate to the recruitment, training, evaluation, promoting and paying of staff. Basically, policies should be in place to ensure that appropriate staff are hired and that they are trained so that the control system can be operated effectively.

The ISA identifies five elements of an internal control system, as follows.

1. The control environment
2. The entity's risk assessment process
3. The information system
4. Control activities
5. Monitoring of controls

These elements are explained below.

2.2 Risk assessment process

Definition

The **risk assessment process** is the entity's process of identifying business risks relevant to the financial reporting objectives and deciding about the actions to address those risks and the results thereof.

The auditor will enquire with management to ensure that risks that could affect the business have been identified and appropriate controls put into place to minimise the impact of those risks. The fact that management have carried out a risk assessment will provide the auditor with some confidence that company systems will not have errors in them.

2.3 Information system

Definition

An **information system** is the system that processes information within an organisation. It includes not only the processing of information but also the procedures to initiate, record, process and report on financial statements, both manual and computerised.

The auditor will review the information system to ensure information can be processed completely and accurately. Where this takes place, then the auditor gains confidence that the financial statements will also be complete and accurate.

2.4 Control activities

Definition

Control activities are specific activities within an organisation which are designed to address risks and therefore help ensure that management directives are carried out.

Examples of specific controls include:

Authorisation controls

Transactions should be **approved** by an appropriate person (eg overtime being approved by departmental managers). Important aspects of documentation are:

(a) **Multi-part documents**. Copies are sent to everyone who needs to know about the event recorded in the document.

(b) **Pre-numbering of documents**. Missing numbers in a sequence may indicate that operations have not been **recorded** or have **not** been **processed** further, for example outstanding orders.

(c) **Standardisation of documents**. Each document should be in a standard format showing clearly the required information.

Performance reviews

Review of staff to ensure they have been operating the control system effectively.

Information processing

Controls over information processing systems to ensure that:

(a) All information is processed (completeness of processing)

(b) Information is accurately processed

(c) Appropriate authorisation is obtained for the processing of each item of information

Physical controls

Authorised personnel alone should have access to certain assets, particularly those which are valuable or portable. An example would be ensuring the stock store is only open when the stores personnel are there, and is locked at other times.

Restricting access to records can be a particular problem in computerised systems as we shall discuss in the next chapter.

Segregation of duties

Segregation of duties is a vital aspect of the internal control system. Segregation of duties implies a **number of people** being involved in the accounting process. Hence it is more difficult for fraudulent transactions to be processed (since a number of people would have to collude in the fraud), and it is also more difficult for accidental errors to be processed (since the more people are involved, the more checking there can be). Segregation should take place in various ways.

(a) **Segregation of function**. The key functions that should be assigned to different people are the **carrying out** of a transaction, **recording** that transaction in the accounting records and **maintaining custody** of assets that arise from the transaction.

(b) The various **steps** in carrying out the transaction should also be segregated.

(c) The **carrying out** of various **accounting operations** should be segregated. For example the same staff should not record transactions and carry out the reconciliations at the period-end.

2.5 Monitoring of controls

Definition

The auditor should obtain an understanding of the major types of activities that the company uses to **monitor internal control** over financial reporting and how the entity initiates corrective actions to its controls.

Ongoing monitoring means that management is continually assessing the effectiveness of the company's internal control systems. Monitoring may be undertaken by the company's senior managers or in some situations by the internal audit department of the company. Where internal audit are involved, the external auditor will also carry out limited monitoring of the internal audit function.

2.6 Limitations of internal control systems

Any internal control system can only provide the directors with **reasonable assurance** that their objectives are reached, because of **inherent limitations.** These include the following.

- The costs of control not outweighing their benefits
- The potential for human error
- Collusion between employees

- The possibility of controls being by-passed or overridden by management
- Controls being designed to cope with routine but not non-routine transactions

Activity 2 **(15 minutes)**

Consider the accounting function of the organisation where you work, or any organisation of which you have had experience. Which of these types of internal control do you think have proved most effective?

3 FRAUD

3.1 What is fraud?

Give an employee responsibility, and he may manage the resources under his control dishonestly. The incidence of **financial fraud**, including fraud in a computer environment, appears to be increasing fast. This trend, together with the increasing sophistication of fraudsters, creates difficult problems for management and for **internal auditors.**

The mere presence of internal auditors will serve to discourage fraudsters for fear of being discovered, although the public's expectations tend to go much further. Everyone has their own idea of where an acceptable bending of the rules ends and fraud begins, so it is appropriate to start with a definition of fraud.

Definitions

Fraud comprises both the use of deception to obtain an unjust or illegal financial advantage, and intentional misrepresentation by management, employees or third parties.

An **error**, in contrast, is an unintentional mistake.

3.2 Types of fraud

Some of the most common methods of fraud are described briefly in the following paragraphs.

FOR DISCUSSION

Can you think of any famous 'big name' frauds which have happened over the last few years?

3.3 Ghost employees

These are imaginary employees for whom the wages department prepare wage packets which are distributed amongst the fraudsters. This type of fraud arises when there is extensive reliance on casual workers, and minimal record keeping for such workers. Inflated overtime claims can also result from poor time recording systems.

3.4 Miscasting of the payroll

This fraud often succeeds due to its simplicity. If there are twenty employees, each to be paid £100, then the computer program for the payroll could be adjusted so that an extra £50 is added to the total added up for the amounts to be paid. Thus management approve a payment of £2,050 for the period's wages, each employee gets his £100 and the fraudster collects his extra £50. Manual payroll systems can be manipulated in a similar way. When employees are paid in cash, this type of fraud can be hard to trace.

3.5 Stealing unclaimed wages

This is effectively confined to wages paid in cash and can occur when an employee leaves without notice or is away sick. In the case of a subsequent claim for unpaid wages, it could be claimed that the cash in the original pay packet was paid back into the bank.

3.6 Collusion with external parties

This could involve suppliers, customers or their staff. Possible frauds are overcharging on purchase invoices, undercharging on sales invoices or the sale of confidential information (eg customer lists, expansion plans) to a competitor. Management should watch out for unusual discounts or commissions being given or taken, or for an excessive zeal on the part of an employee to handle all business with a particular company.

3.7 Teeming and lading

This is a 'rolling' fraud rather than a 'one-off' fraud. It occurs when a clerk has the chance to misappropriate payments from debtors or to creditors. Cash received by the company is 'borrowed' by the cashier rather than being kept as petty cash or banked. (It is also possible, although riskier and more difficult to organise, to misappropriate cheques made payable to the company.) When the cashier knows that a reconciliation is to be performed, or audit visit planned, he pays the money back so that everything appears satisfactory at that point, but after the audit the teeming and lading starts again. Surprise visits by auditors and independent checking of cash balances should discourage this fraud.

A common fraud, arising when one employee has sole control of the sales ledger and recording debtors' cheques, is to pay cheques into a separate bank account, either by forged endorsement or by opening an account in a name similar to the employer's.

The clerk has to allocate cheques or cash received from other debtors against the account of the debtor whose payment was misappropriated. This prevents other staff from asking why the account is still overdue or from sending statements etc to the debtors. However, the misallocation has to continue as long as the money is missing. This fraud, therefore, never really stops. It can be detected by independent verification of debtors balances (eg by circulation) and by looking at unallocated payments, if the sales ledger is organised to show this. In addition, sending out itemised monthly statements to debtors should act as a deterrent, although in a really elaborate fraud the clerk may be keeping two sets of books, so that the statements show the debtor's own analysis of amounts due and paid off in the month, but do not agree with the books.

FOR DISCUSSION

Discuss with your tutor and fellow learners which types of business you think might be more prone to frauds such as teeming and lading.

3.8 Altering cheques and inflating expense claims

These are self-explanatory.

3.9 Stealing assets

Using the company's assets for personal gain and stealing fully depreciated assets are both encountered in practice. Whether or not the private use of company telephones and photocopiers is a serious matter is up to the company to judge, but it may still be fraudulent. More serious examples include the sale by employees of unused time on the computer, which is a growing fraud.

3.10 Issuing false credit notes

Another way of avoiding detection when cash and cheques received from debtors have been misappropriated is to issue a credit note which is not sent to the customer (who has paid his account) but is recorded in the books. Again, the issue of itemised statements monthly should show this up, as the customer would query the credit note. A similar tactic is to write a debt off as bad to cover up the disappearance of the payment.

3.11 Failing to record all sales

A very elaborate fraud may be perpetrated in a business with extremely poor controls over sales recording and minimal segregation of duties. In such circumstances, a dishonest bookkeeper may invoice customers but fail to record the invoices so that the customer's payments never have to be recorded and the misappropriation is not missed.

3.12 The role of the internal auditors

The internal auditors should start their work by identifying the areas of the business most susceptible to fraud. These will include areas where cash is involved, and the other areas where the auditors' judgement is that the internal controls are insufficient to safeguard the assets. The existence of a properly functioning system of internal controls will diminish the incidence of frauds, so the auditors' opinion on the internal control system is of fundamental importance. Whenever a fraud is discovered, the auditors should judge whether a weakness in internal controls has been highlighted, and if so what changes are needed.

4 PREVENTION OF FRAUD

Fraud will only be prevented successfully if potential fraudsters perceive the risk of detection as being high, and if personnel are adequately screened before employment and given no incentive to turn against the company once employed. The following safeguards should therefore be implemented:

(a) A good internal control system
(b) Continuous supervision of all employees
(c) Surprise audit visits
(d) Thorough personnel procedures

4.1 Comparisons

The work of employees must be monitored as this will increase the perceived risk of being discovered. Actual results must regularly be compared against budgeted results, and employees should be asked to explain significant variances.

4.2 Surprise audit visits

Surprise audit visits are a valuable contribution to preventing fraud. If a cashier is carrying out a teeming and lading fraud and is told that an audit visit is due the following week, he may be able to square up the books before the visit so that the auditors will find nothing wrong. But if the threat of a surprise visit is constantly present, the cashier will not be able to carry out a teeming and lading fraud without the risk of being discovered, and this risk is usually sufficient to prevent the fraud. The auditors do not need to carry out any sophisticated audit tests during their surprise visit. The fraud deterrent effect on the employee is highly significant, because the employee thinks that every figure is being checked.

4.3 Personnel procedures

Finally, **personnel procedures** must be adequate to prevent the occurrence of frauds.

(a) Whenever a fraud is discovered, the fraudster should be dismissed and the police should be informed. Too often an employee is 'asked to resign' and then moves on to a similar job where the fraud is repeated, often because management fear loss of face or investor confidence. This is a self-defeating policy.

(b) All new employees should be required to produce adequate references from their previous employers.

(c) If an employee's lifestyle changes dramatically, explanations should be sought.

(d) Every employee must be made to take his annual holiday entitlement. Often in practice the employee who is 'so dedicated that he never takes a holiday' is in fact not taking his leave for fear of his fraud being discovered by his replacement worker while he is away.

(e) Pay levels should be adequate and working conditions of a reasonable standard. If employees feel that they are being paid an unfairly low amount or 'exploited', they may look for ways to supplement their pay dishonestly.

5 MANAGEMENT FRAUD

So far, we have concentrated on employee fraud. However, arguably more serious (and very much more difficult to prevent and detect) is the growing problem of **management fraud**.

5.1 Reasons for management fraud

While employee fraud is usually undertaken purely for the employee's financial gain, management fraud is often undertaken to improve the company's apparent performance, to reduce tax liabilities or to improve the manager's promotion prospects. Managers are often in a position to override internal controls and to intimidate their subordinates into collusion or turning a blind eye. This makes it difficult to detect such frauds. In addition, where the company is benefiting financially rather than the manager, it can be difficult to persuade staff that any dishonesty is involved.

This clash of interest between loyalty to an employer and professional integrity can be difficult to resolve and can compromise an internal auditor's independence. Management fraud often comes to light after a takeover or on a change of audit staff or practices. Its consequences can be far reaching for the employing company in damaging its reputation or because it results in legal action. Because management usually have access to much larger sums of money than more lowly employees, the financial loss to the company can be immense.

6 RESPONSIBILITY FOR REPORTING FRAUD TO MANAGEMENT

A company's **external auditors** are required to report all instances of fraud that they find to the company's management, unless they suspect management of being involved in the fraud. If they uncover fraud by management, they should report the matter to the appropriate **public authorities** or seek **legal advice**. The external auditors should also report to management any material (ie significant) **weakness in the company's systems of accounting and internal control.**

If **internal auditors** uncover instances of fraud, they should also report this to executive management. If they discover management fraud, they should make use of lines of communication to the company's **audit committee**, which should be in place as a matter of good corporate governance practice. The audit committee should have the authority to take appropriate action, which is likely to include discussion of the matter with the external auditors.

7 CONTROL PROCEDURES FOR REDUCING FRAUD RISK

Maintaining key control procedures reduces the risk of fraud occurring and increases the risk of detection. Controls over cash are particularly important. These procedures are summarised below.

7.1 Cash receipts

Segregation of duties between the various functions listed below is particularly important. In other words, more than one person should have responsibilities within each particular area.

Receipts by post

- Safeguards to prevent interception of mail between receipt and opening
- Appointment of responsible person to supervise mail
- Protection of cash and cheques (restrictive crossing)

Control over cash sales and collections

- **Restrictions** on **receipt of cash** (by cashiers only, or by salespeople etc)
- **Evidencing** of receipt of cash (numbered receipt forms/sealed till rolls)
- **Clearance** of cash offices and registers
- **Agreement** of **cash collections** with cash and sales records
- **Investigation** of cash shortages and surpluses

Recording

- Maintenance of records
- Limitation of duties of receiving cashiers
- Holiday arrangements
- Giving and recording of receipts
  - Retained copies
  - Serially numbered receipts books
  - Custody of receipt books
  - Comparisons with cash records and bank paying in slips

Paying into bank

- Daily bankings
- Make-up and comparison of paying-in slips against receipt records and cash book
- Banking of receipts intact/control of disbursements

Cash and bank balances

- Restrictions on opening new bank accounts
- Limitations on cash floats held
- Restrictions on payments out of cash received
- Restrictions on access to cash registers and offices
- Independent checks on cash floats
- Surprise cash counts
- Custody of cash outside office hours
- Safeguarding of IOUs, cash in transit
- Insurance arrangements
- Control of funds held in trust for employees
- Bank reconciliations
  - Issue of bank statements
  - Frequency of reconciliations by independent person
  - Reconciliation procedures
  - Treatment of longstanding unpresented cheques
  - Stop payment notice
  - Sequence of cheque numbers
  - Comparison with cash books

NOTES

7.2 Cash payments

The arrangements for controlling payments will depend to a great extent on the nature of business transacted, the volume of payments involved and the size of the company.

Cheque payments

(a) **Custody** over **supply** and issue of cheques
(b) **Preparation** of **cheques** restricted
(c) **Cheque requisitions**
  (i) Presentation to cheque signatories
  (ii) Cancellation (crossing/recording cheque number)
(d) **Authority** to sign cheques
  (i) Limitations on authority
  (ii) Number of signatories
  (iii) Prohibitions over signing of blank cheques
(e) Safeguards over **mechanically signed cheques**/cheques carrying printed signatures
(f) **Restrictions** on issue of **blank** or **bearer** cheques
(g) **Prompt despatch** of signed **cheques**
(h) **Obtaining** of paid **cheques** from **banks**

Cash payments

(a) Authorisation of expenditure
(b) Cancellation of vouchers to ensure cannot be paid twice
(c) Limits on disbursements
(d) Rules on cash advances to employees, IOUs and cheque cashing

7.3 Cheque and cash payments generally

The cashier should generally not be concerned with keeping or writing-up books of account other than those recording disbursements nor should he have access to, or be responsible for the custody of, securities, title deeds or negotiable instruments belonging to the company. (This is an example of **segregation of duties**.)

The person responsible for preparing cheques or traders' credit lists should not himself be a cheque signatory. Cheque signatories in turn should not be responsible for recording payments. (This is another example of **segregation of duties**.)

NOTES

Activity 3 **(20 minutes)**

PCs (personal computers) have been marketed for small and medium sized businesses that have previously been using manual or mechanical systems for bookkeeping and accounting functions. In reviewing computer controls in this environment, the auditor is likely to find general control weaknesses which would not be anticipated in larger computer installations using for example an on-line, real-time system.

Why do you think the auditors are likely to find weaknesses in the controls over a PC-based accounting system in a small company?

8 ISA 240 ON FRAUD

ISA 240 emphasises that it is the responsibility of the directors to take reasonable steps to prevent and detect fraud. It is also their responsibility to prepare financial statements which give a true and fair view of the entity's affairs. The UK Combined Code on Corporate Governance has made a variety of suggestions to help directors fulfil their responsibilities.

In an appendix to the ISA there is a list of examples of conditions or events which may increase the risk of either fraud or error or both.

It is the responsibility of the external auditor to report on all instances of fraud that they find to management, unless they suspect management of being involved in the fraud. It is not the auditor's responsibility actively to search for fraud, although an efficient and well-designed audit should detect a material fraud.

8.1 Conditions and events

Conditions and events which may be indicative of fraud include the following.

Fraud and error	
Previous experience or incidents which **call into question** the **integrity** or **competence** of **management**	Management dominated by one person (or a small group) and no effective oversight board or committee Complex corporate structure where complexity does not seem to be warranted High turnover rate of key accounting and financial personnel Personnel (key or otherwise) not taking holidays Significant and prolonged under-staffing of the accounting department Frequent changes of legal advisers or auditors

NOTES

Fraud and error	
Particular financial reporting pressures within an entity	Industry volatility Inadequate working capital due to declining profits or too rapid expansion Deteriorating quality of earnings, for example increased risk taking with respect to credit sales, changes in business practice or selection of accounting policy alternatives that improve income The entity needs a rising profit trend to support the market price of its shares due to a contemplated public offering, a takeover or other reason Significant investment in an industry or product line noted for rapid change Pressure on accounting personnel to complete financial statements in an unreasonably short period of time Dominant owner-management Performance-based remuneration
Weaknesses in the **design** and **operation** of the **accounting and internal controls system**	A weak control environment within the entity Systems that, in their design, are inadequate to give reasonable assurance of preventing or detecting error or fraud Inadequate segregation of responsibilities in relation to functions involving the handling, recording or controlling of the entity's assets Indications that internal financial information is unreliable Evidence that internal controls have been overridden by management Ineffective monitoring of the operation of systems which allows control overrides, breakdown or weakness to continue without proper corrective action Continuing failure to correct major weakness in internal control where such corrections are practicable and cost effective
Unusual transactions	Unusual transactions, especially near the year end, that have a significant effect on earnings Complex transactions or accounting treatments Unusual transactions with related parties Payments for services (for example to lawyers, consultants or agents) that appear excessive in relation to the services provided

Fraud and error	
Problems in obtaining sufficient appropriate audit evidence	Inadequate records, for example incomplete files, excessive adjustments to accounting records, transactions not recorded in accordance with normal procedures and out-of-balance control accounts
	Inadequate documentation of transactions, such as lack of proper authorisation, supporting documents not available and alteration to documents (any of these documentation problems assume greater significance when they relate to large or unusual transactions)
	An excessive number of differences between accounting records and third party confirmations, conflicting audit evidence and unexplainable changes in operating ratios
	Evasive, delayed or unreasonable responses by management to audit inquires
	Inappropriate attitude of management to the conduct of the audit, eg time pressure, scope limitation and other constraints
Some factors unique to an **information systems environment** which relate to the conditions and events described above	Inability to extract information from computer files due to lack of, or non-current, documentation of record contents or programs
	Large numbers of program changes that are not documented, approved and tested
	Inadequate overall balancing of computer transactions and data bases to the financial accounts

9 CORPORATE GOVERNANCE

9.1 Introduction

Definition

'Corporate governance is the system by which companies are directed and controlled'. *Cadbury Committee report*

'Good governance ensures that constituencies (stakeholders) with a relevant interest in the company's business are fully taken into account. ' *Hampel Committee report*

The issue of corporate governance has existed since companies began to be used commonly as part of business. However, in the late twentieth century, some high profile frauds and questionable business practices led to **public and government attention** being firmly fixed on **business management**. In the late 1990s, a series of committees were set up to consider the matter.

The key committees were:

- Cadbury Committee 1992 (corporate governance)
- Greenbury Committee 1995 (directors' remuneration)
- Hampel Committee 1995 (corporate governance)
- Turnbull Committee 1999 (corporate governance)
- Higgs report and new Combined Code – 2004

These committees made various **recommendations** about how companies should be run and monitored to provide **safeguards** to shareholders.

> **Activity 4** **(5 minutes)**
>
> Based on your knowledge of company law, which type of company do you think is most likely to be affected by the need for good corporate governance measures?

Although the issues raised in considering the answer to the activity above are generalisations, corporate governance issues have **historically** tended to be **directed** at **listed, public limited companies.**

In 2004, the Stock Exchange issued a revised **Combined Code** (updating the 1998 code) of corporate governance requirements drawn from the recommendations of the Higgs report. Following this Code is **mandatory** for **companies listed on the Stock Exchange** (who have to disclose their reasoning for any non-compliance) but can be seen as **good practice** for **any UK company**.

9.2 Combined Code

Provisions of the Combined Code	
Directors' responsibilities	
The board	Should **meet regularly**, and have a **formal schedule of matters** reserved to it for its decision. There should be clear division of responsibilities between chairman and chief executive. **Non-executive directors** should comprise 50% of the board with the Chairman having a casting vote. Directors should submit themselves for re-election every three years and NEDs should not normally exceed two three-year terms of office.
The AGM	Companies should propose **separate resolutions** at the AGM on each substantially different issue. The chairman should ensure that members of the audit, remuneration and nomination committees are available at the AGM to **answer questions**. Notice of AGMs should be sent out at least 20 days before the meeting.

Provisions of the Combined Code	
Remuneration	There should be remuneration committees composed of non-executive directors to set directors' pay, which should provide pay which attracts, retains and motivates quality directors but avoids paying more than is necessary for the purpose. The company's annual report should contain a statement of remuneration policy and details of the remuneration of each director.
Accountability and audit	The directors should **explain** their **responsibility for preparing accounts**. They should **report that the business is a going concern**, with supporting assumptions and qualifications as necessary.
Internal control	The directors should review the **effectiveness of internal control** systems, at least annually, and also **review the need for an internal audit function.**
Audit committee	The board **should establish an audit committee.**
Auditors' responsibilities	
Statement of responsibilities	The auditors **should include** in their report a statement of their reporting responsibilities.
Directors' remuneration	Under the Directors' Remuneration Regulations of 2002, auditors are also required to check the accuracy of disclosure in the financial statements of some elements of directors' remuneration.

9.3 Turnbull recommendations

The Turnbull Report adds some additional guidelines in relation to internal control systems.

Definition

An **internal control system** comprises the control environment and control procedures. It includes all the policies and procedures (internal controls) adopted by the directors and management of an entity to ensure, as far as practicable, the orderly and efficient conduct of its business, including adherence to internal policies, the safeguarding of assets, the prevention and detection of fraud and error, the accuracy and completeness of the accounting records, and the timely preparation of reliable financial information. Internal controls may be incorporated within computerised accounting systems. However the internal control system extends beyond those matters which relate directly to the accounting system.

TURNBULL GUIDELINES Have a **defined process** for the **review** of effectiveness of **internal control.**
Review **regular** reports on **internal control.**
Consider **key risks** and how they have been **managed.**
Check the **adequacy** of **action taken** to remedy weaknesses and incidents.
Consider the **adequacy** of **monitoring.**
Conduct an **annual assessment** of risks and the effectiveness of internal control.
Make a **statement** on this process in the **annual report.**

9.3 Assurance provision

As you can see from the above tables, many of the requirements in relation to corporate governance necessitate **communication** between the directors and the shareholders.

By law, **directors** of all companies are **required to produce financial statements** annually which give a **true and fair view** of the affairs of the company and its profit or loss for the period. They are also **encouraged** to **communicate with shareholders** on matters relating to **directors' pay** and benefits (this is required by law in the case of public limited companies), **going concern** and **management of risks.**

But how are the shareholders to know whether the directors' communications are **accurate,** or present a **fair picture?** Part of the auditor's duty is to provide a report on the financial statements prepared by the directors. As the auditor is independent of the directors, the shareholders can then rely on this report to confirm that the directors are running their company correctly. In other words, an audit is an 'assurance' engagement.

Definition

> An **assurance engagement** is one where a professional accountant evaluates or measures a subject matter that is the responsibility of another party against suitable criteria, and expresses an opinion which provides the intended user with a level of assurance about that subject matter.

Chapter roundup

- Business risk comprises operational, financial and compliance risk.
- It is the responsibility of the directors to install and maintain a satisfactory accounting system to minimise business risk.
- An internal control system comprises the control environment and control procedures. It extends beyond those matters which relate directly to the accounting system.
- **ISA 315** covers accounting and internal control systems and audit risk assessments.
- Segregation of duties is a vital aspect of the control system.
- Fraud is the use of deception to obtain advantage, while an error is an unintentional mistake.
- There are many control procedures for reducing the risk of fraud.
- Corporate governance is a contributory factor in the elimination of fraud.

Quick quiz

1 What should a company's accounting records be able to do, according to the Companies Act 1985?

2 What is the control environment?

3 What is meant by segregation of duties?

4 Give two examples of controls over documents.

5 What is 'teeming and lading'?

6 What are the main safeguards to prevent fraud?

7 What is the responsibility of the external auditor with regard to fraud?

Answers to quick quiz

1 (a) Disclose with reasonable accuracy at any time the financial position of the company.

(b) Enable the directors to ensure that any balance sheet and profit and loss account complies with the requirements of the Act. (see para 1.1)

2 The framework within which controls operate. (para 2.1)

3 It is segregation of function and the segregation of staff carrying out various accounting operations. (para 2.3)

4 Multi-part documents
Pre-numbering of documents
Standardisation of documents (para 2.4)

5 It is a fraud whereby a cashier steals money from the company and then applies money received later on from someone else to cover up the original theft. It is a 'rolling fraud'. (para 3.7)

6 A good system of internal control
Continuous supervision of all employees
Surprise audit visits
Thorough personnel procedures (para 4)

7 To report all instances of fraud that they find to management, unless they suspect management of being involved in the fraud. (para 8)

Answers to activities

1 *Purchasing department*

A key risk is the risk that suppliers will not deliver goods when the company needs them in order to be able to produce goods on time for its customers.

The company can reduce this risk by setting up a system of internal control in respect of contracting with suppliers and ensuring that it does not contract with suppliers unless they have certain quality standards in place.

Human resources department

A key risk is the risk that the HR will recruit staff who are not capable of carrying out their roles in the organisation.

The company can reduce this risk by setting up a system of internal control so that no one is employed until they have provided evidence of their qualifications and references from previous employers.

2 This will depend very much on the type of organisation involved. You would certainly expect to see a good handful of those controls in operation, although bear in mind that it is often more difficult for a small company with few employees to operate a cohesive system of internal controls.

3 Reasons for weaknesses in small company PC-based systems include the following.

(a) Small companies generally have few accounting staff, so that it will often be difficult to create good conditions for segregation of duties. The accountant, for instance, may be the only person in the company fully conversant with the accounting system. This weakens security and problems may arise if the computer 'expert' is ill or away on holiday. If one person has specialised programming knowledge not shared by others, s/he may easily be able to put through unauthorised program changes undetected.

(b) Controls over access to the system may be poor or non-existent. In a small office, it will probably be difficult to create physical security by putting the computer in a secure area. Controls over programs and disks may also be poor.

(c) Clerical staff in a small company may be required to use the computer for routine processing without an understanding of the system or of its possible risks and pitfalls. If a malfunction occurs or if an error is made, untrained staff may not be able to take proper corrective action, and there is a risk that files may be corrupted or data lost as a result.

NOTES

(d) Poor access controls, combined with real-time processing, may result in poor control over input; there is a risk that data may be input twice or not at all.

(e) Small companies with few resources may not have adequate provision for maintenance or stand-by equipment in case of breakdown or damage.

4 Clearly, it is in the interest of all shareholders that all companies are well-managed so as to maximise returns from their investment. However, in the UK, only public limited companies are entitled to sell shares to the general public. This means that in **many** cases (although not all), shareholders in private (Ltd) companies will be more closely connected to the directors than in public limited company (plcs). In fact, many Ltd companies in the UK are 'owner-managed', in other words, their shareholders and directors are one and the same. This is not always the case, and some Ltd companies are large affairs where owners and managers are very clearly distinct from one another.

While all public limited companies are entitled to sell shares to the public, in practice, the public are most likely to invest in shares that are **listed** on an exchange, for example, the Stock Exchange. This makes them key candidates for the need of good corporate governance.

Chapter 25 :

THE ROLE OF THE AUDITOR AND THE AUDITING ENVIRONMENT

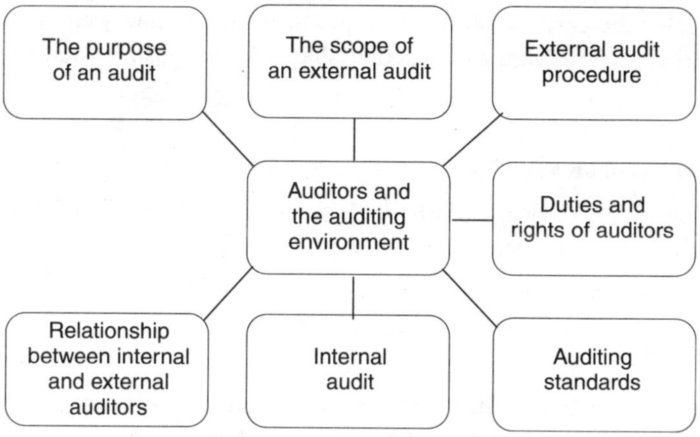

Introduction

The Edexcel guidelines require you to appreciate the distinction between and the importance of both internal and external audit. Although this chapter refers to internal audit, it is mainly concerned with the law and professional standards relating to external audit, in order for you to fulfil the learning outcome 'explain the environment in which the audit of a business organisation takes place'.

You should appreciate that although it is only large limited companies which are required by law to undergo an audit, many other business organisations do so on a voluntary basis. These include partnerships, sole traders, clubs and societies. The main reason for this is the fact that a set of audited accounts is of great value in supporting applications for finance and in providing credibility to the organisation as a whole.

Your objectives

In this chapter you will learn about the following.

(a) The purpose of an audit and the responsibilities of the various parties involved

(b) The scope of external audit

(c) The procedure for the conduct of an external audit

(d) The duties and rights of the external auditor

(e) The role of International Standards on Auditing (ISAs)

(f) The role and scope of internal audit and the relationship between external and internal audit

BPP LEARNING MEDIA

1 THE PURPOSE OF AN AUDIT

1.1 The role of the auditors

In the modern commercial environment, businesses which are operated as companies with limited liability need to produce accounts in order to show their owners how their investment has been used, and how successfully the businesses are performing. However the owners of a business require something more than accounts because the managers responsible for preparing them may, either unintentionally or by deliberate manipulation, produce accounts which are misleading (put another way, there is **information risk** about the accounts). An independent examination of the accounts is needed so that the owners of the business can assess how well management have discharged their stewardship and whether shares in the business remain a worthwhile investment.

1.2 Definition of an audit

The Auditing Practices Board (APB) is the main standard setting body in the United Kingdom. The APB gives general guidance on what constitutes an audit.

Definition

> According to ISA 200: The objective of an **audit** of financial statements is to enable the auditor to express an opinion whether the financial statements are prepared, in all material respects, in accordance with an applicable financial reporting framework. The phrases used to express the auditor's opinion are 'give a true and fair view' or 'present fairly, in all material respects' which are equivalent terms.

This wording follows very closely that of the auditors' report on financial statements, which we will look at later.

First of all, though, we need to look at what an audit is really about. This is the subject matter of the APB's ISA 200 *Objective and general principles governing an audit of financial statements*.

1.3 ISA 200

In undertaking an audit of financial statements auditors should:

(a) Conduct an audit in accordance with the ISAs.

(b) Plan and perform an audit with an attitude of professional scepticism – in other words the auditor should realise that circumstances may exist which cause the financial statements to be materially misstated.

(c) Carry out procedures designed to obtain sufficient appropriate audit evidence, in accordance with Auditing Standards contained in ISAs, to determine with reasonable confidence whether the financial statements are free of **material** misstatement.

NOTES

Materiality is discussed in detail in Chapter 26.

(d) Evaluate the overall presentation of the financial statements, in order to ascertain whether they have been prepared in accordance with relevant legislation and accounting standards.

(e) Issue a report containing a clear expression of their opinion on the financial statements.

The ISAs explanatory material highlights the credibility given to financial statements by the auditors' opinion; it provides '**reasonable assurance** from an **independent** source that they present a true and fair view'. That is to say the audit report reassures readers of the accounts that the accounts have been examined by a **knowledgeable, impartial** professional. ISA 200 goes on to stress further the importance of auditors acting **independently** and **ethically.**

There are provisos, of course. Remember that the auditors' opinion is *not:*

- A guarantee of the future viability of the entity, or
- An assurance of the management's effectiveness and efficiency

1.4 Responsibility of directors

Most importantly, the standard makes clear that the auditors do not bear any responsibility for the preparation and presentation of the financial statements.

The responsibility for the preparation and presentation of the financial statements is that of the management of the entity, with oversight from those charged with governance. Auditors are responsible for forming and expressing an opinion on the financial statements. The audit of the financial statements does not relieve the directors of any of their responsibilities.

1.5 Limitations of audit

The assurance auditors give is governed by the fact that auditors use **judgement** in deciding what audit procedures to use and what conclusions to draw, and also by the limitations of every audit.

(a) The fact that auditing is **not** a purely **objective** exercise. Auditors have to make judgements in a number of areas including risk assessment, what constitutes a significant error, what tests to perform and ultimately what opinion to give.

(b) The fact that **auditors do not check every item** in the accounting records. We shall see that for many tests auditors only check a sample of items.

(c) The **limitations** of **accounting** and **internal control systems.** For example the systems may not be able to deal with unusual transactions, and may not be flexible enough to cope well with changing circumstances.

(d) The possibility that **client management or staff** might **not tell the truth,** or **collude in fraud.** One important control may be a division of responsibilities so that one member of staff checks another's work, but the control will be ineffective if the two collude.

(e) The fact that audit **evidence indicates** what is **probable** rather than what is **certain.** Some figures in the accounts are estimates, some require a significant degree of judgement and some are affected by uncertainty.

(f) The fact that auditors are **reporting** generally **some months after** the balance sheet date. The client's position may be changing, and the position shown in the accounts at the last year-end may be significantly different from the up-to-date position. If on the other hand auditors do report soon after the balance sheet date, evidence about certain figures in the balance sheet may be insufficient.

(g) The **limitations** of the audit report. Although work has been done to make the report more informative, the standard format is unlikely to reflect all aspects of the audit.

Hence auditors can only express an opinion; they cannot certify whether accounts are completely correct.

Material misstatements may exist in financial statements and auditors will plan their work on this basis, ie with **professional scepticism**. ISA 200 makes it clear that, even where auditors assess the risk of litigation or adverse publicity as very low, they must still perform sufficient procedures according to auditing standards, ie there can never be a reason for carrying out an audit of a lower quality than that demanded by the auditing standards.

1.6 The expectations gap

Definition

> The **expectations gap** is the 'gap' between the role of the auditor as laid down by statute and the Auditing Standards, and the public's perception of the role of the auditor, which usually encompasses being responsible for finding frauds.

There are some common misconceptions in relation to the role of the auditors, even among 'financially aware' people, including the following examples.

(a) Many people think that the auditors report to the directors of a company, rather than the members.

(b) Some think that a qualified audit report is more favourable than an unqualified audit report, whereas the converse is true.

(c) There is a perception that it is the auditors' duty to detect fraud, when in fact the detection of fraud is the responsibility of the directors.

These findings highlight the 'expectations gap' between what auditors do and what people in general think that they do. Add the fact that many 'financially aware' people do not look at the report and accounts of a company they are considering investing in, and you have some sobering facts for the auditors to contemplate!

Some of the recent large company collapses have emphasised the need to reduce the expectation gap. For this reason, reports such as those of the Cadbury and Hampel Committee reports on corporate governance have been published. They aim to reduce the expectations gap by laying out a code of conduct for directors, as well as making suggestions for the content of company reports.

2 THE SCOPE OF EXTERNAL AUDIT

2.1 Statutory and non-statutory audits

Audits are required under statute in the case of a large number of undertakings, including the following.

Undertaking	Principal Act
Limited companies	Companies Act 1985 (being replaced by the Companies Act 2006 during 2007 and 2008)
Building societies	Building Societies Act 1986
Trade unions and employer associations	Trade Union and Labour Relations Act 1974
Housing Associations	Various Acts depending on the legal constitution of the housing association, including: Industrial and Provident Societies Act 1965; Friendly and Industrial and Provident Societies Act 1968; Housing Act 1980; Companies Act 1985; Housing Association Act 1985.
Certain charities	Various Acts depending on the status of the charity, including special Acts of Parliament.
Unincorporated investment businesses	Regulations made under the Financial Services and Markets Act 2000

Non-statutory audits are performed by independent auditors because the owners, proprietors, members, trustees, professional and governing bodies or other interested parties want them, rather than because the law requires them.

2.2 External and internal audit

We have discussed auditing in particular in the context of the APB definition in section 1.2. The definition relates to the work of **external** auditors, independent persons brought in from outside an organisation to review the accounts prepared by management. **Internal auditors** perform a different role.

The management of an organisation will wish to establish systems to ensure that business activities are carried out efficiently. They will institute clerical, administrative and financial controls.

Larger organisations may appoint full-time staff whose function is to monitor and report on the running of the company's operations. **Internal** audit staff members are one type of control. Although some of the work carried out by internal auditors is similar to that performed by external auditors, there are important distinctions between the nature of the two functions.

We shall look at internal audit in more detail later in this chapter.

BPP LEARNING MEDIA

3 THE EXTERNAL AUDIT PROCEDURE

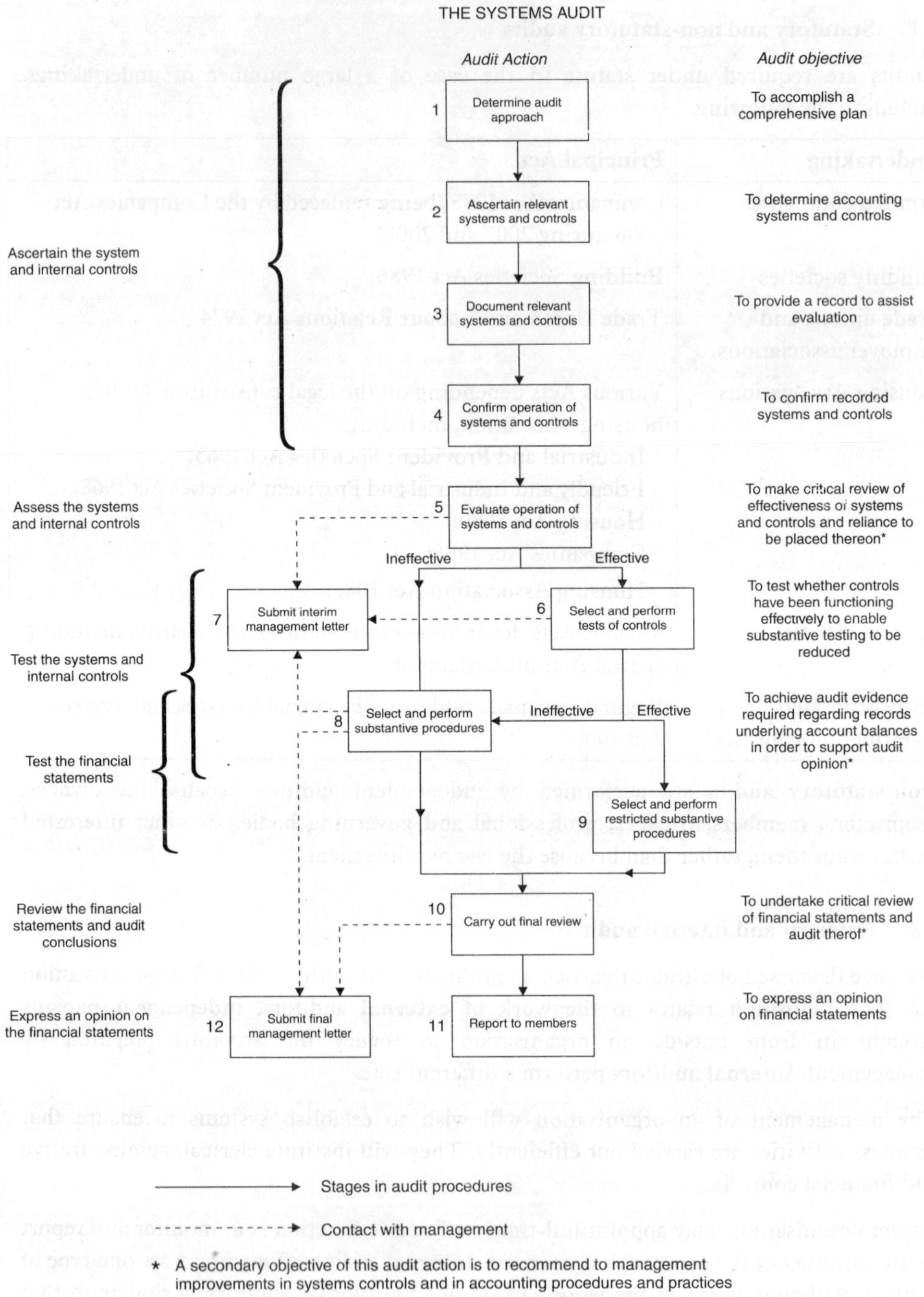

Figure 25.1: The external audit procedure

4 DUTIES AND RIGHTS OF AUDITORS

The duties and rights of auditors are enshrined in law, indicating their importance.

4.1 Duties

The principal statutory duties of auditors in respect of the audit of a limited company are set out in ss 235 and 237 CA 1985 (soon to be ss. 475 and 495–498 CA 2006). Auditors are required to report on the **truth and fairness** of every balance sheet and profit and loss account laid before the company in general meeting, and also report whether these accounts have been **properly prepared in accordance with the Companies Act 1985**.

The Companies Act lists other factors which auditors must consider.

(a) **Proper accounting records** have been kept and proper returns adequate for the audit received from branches not visited.

(b) The **accounts** agree with the **accounting records** and **returns**.

(c) **All information and explanations** have been **received** as the auditors think necessary and they have had access at all times to the company's books, accounts and vouchers.

(d) **Details** of **directors' emoluments** and **other benefits** have been correctly **disclosed** in the financial statements.

(e) Particulars of **loans** and **other transactions** in favour of **directors** and others have been correctly disclosed in the financial statements.

(f) The **information** given in the **directors' report** is **consistent** with the **accounts.**

Auditors must report if any of (a) to (f) is not true.

4.2 Rights

The principal statutory rights auditors have, excepting those dealing with resignation or removal, are set out in the table below. All references are to the Companies Act 1985. Some of these rights will change under the Companies Act 2006 as limited companies (as compared to public companies) will no longer be required to hold general meetings).

s 389A(1)	*Access to records*	A right of access at all times to the books, accounts and vouchers of the company
s 389A(1)	*Information and explanations*	A right to require from the company's officers such information and explanations as they think necessary for the performance of their duties as auditors
s 390(1)(a) and (b)	*Attendance at/notices of general meetings*	A right to attend any general meetings of the company and to receive all notices of and communications relating to such meetings which any member of the company is entitled to receive
s 390(1)(c)	*Right to speak at general meetings*	A right to be heard at general meetings which they attend on any part of the business that concerns them as auditors
s 381B(2)-(4)	*Rights in relation to written resolutions*	A right to receive a copy of any written resolution proposed
s 253	*Right to require laying of accounts*	A right to give notice in writing requiring that a general meeting be held for the purpose of laying the accounts and reports before the company (if elective resolution dispensing with laying of accounts is in force)

5 AUDITING STANDARDS

5.1 The APB and International Standards on Auditing (ISAs)

Auditing standards are initially set by the International Auditing and Assurance Standards Board in New York. These standards are then tailored for use in the UK and Ireland by the Auditing Practices Board (APB).

(a) The APB can issue auditing standards in its own right without having to obtain the approval of all the professional accounting bodies.

(b) It has strong representation from outside the accounting profession.

(c) It has a commitment to openness, with agenda papers being circulated to interested parties, and an annual report being published.

5.2 Scope of ISAs

The APB issued a document in June 2006 entitled *Statement of scope and authority of APB pronouncements*. The APB makes several categories of pronouncement.

- The auditors' code
- International Standards on Auditing (ISAs)
- Quality control standards
- Ethical Standards for Auditors
- Practice Notes
- Bulletins

The auditors' code contains the fundamental principles that apply to all auditors and the work they carry out.

Quality control standards and ISAs contain basic principles and essential procedures ('Auditing Standards') which are indicated by bold type and with which auditors are required to comply, except where otherwise stated in the ISA concerned, in the conduct of any audit of financial statements.

The ethical standards explain the ethical principles that apply to all work undertaken by accountants with specific standards relating to different areas of service provided including non-audit services.

Apart from statements in bold type, ISAs also contain other material which is not prescriptive but which is designed to help auditors interpret and apply auditing standards. The APB document also states that auditing standards need not be applied to immaterial items (items which are not significant to the accounts).

The authority of ISAs is defined as follows.

> 'Apparent failures by auditors to comply with APB standards are liable to be investigated by the relevant accountancy body. Auditors who do not comply with auditing standards when performing company or other audits make themselves liable to regulatory action which may include the withdrawal of registration and hence of eligibility to perform company audits.'

5.3 Other documents

Practice Notes are issued 'to assist auditors in applying Auditing Standards of general application to particular circumstances and industries'.

Bulletins are issued 'to provide auditors with timely guidance on new or emerging issues'.

Practice Notes and Bulletins are persuasive rather than prescriptive, but they indicate good practice and have a similar status to the explanatory material in ISAs. Both Practice Notes and Bulletins may be included in later ISAs.

6 INTERNAL AUDIT

The management of an organisation will wish to establish systems to ensure that business activities are carried out efficiently. They will institute clerical, administrative and financial controls. Even in very small businesses with simple accounting systems it will be found that some limited checks and controls are present.

6.1 Differences between internal and external audit

Larger organisations may appoint full-time **internal audit** staff whose function is to monitor and report on the running of the company's operations. Internal audit staff are one kind of control. Although some of the work carried out by internal auditors is similar to that performed by external auditors, there are important distinctions between the nature of the two functions.

(a) External auditors are independent of the organisation, whereas internal auditors (as employees) are responsible to the management.

(b) The responsibility of external auditors is fixed by statute, but internal auditors' responsibilities are decided by management.

(c) External auditors report to the members, not to the management (directors), as in the case of internal auditors.

(d) External auditors perform work to enable them to express an opinion on the truth and fairness of the accounts. Internal auditors' work may range over many areas and activities, both operational and financial, as determined by management.

NOTES

Definition

Internal audit is an appraisal or monitoring activity established by management and directors for the review of the accounting and internal control systems as a service to the entity. It functions by, amongst other things, examining, evaluating and reporting to management and the directors on the adequacy and effectiveness of components of the accounting and internal control systems.

Internal audit was originally concerned entirely with the financial records, checking for weaknesses in the accounting systems and errors in the accounts. The function of internal audit has now been extended to the monitoring of all aspects of an organisation's activities.

Activity 1 **(10 minutes)**

What consequences do you think the above differences have for the scope of internal and external auditors' work? Which difference do you think is most important?

6.2 Objectives of internal audit

The Institute of Internal Auditors states:

> 'The objective of internal auditing is to assist members of the organisation in the effective discharge of their responsibilities. To this end internal auditing furnishes them with analyses, appraisals, recommendations, counsel and information concerning the activities reviewed.'

The role of the internal auditor has expanded in recent years as internal auditors seek to add value to their organisation. The work of the internal auditor is still prescribed by management, but it may cover the following broad areas.

(a) **Monitoring of internal control.** The establishment of adequate accounting and internal control systems is a responsibility of management and the directors which demands proper attention on a continuous basis. Often, internal audit is assigned specific responsibility for:

(i) Reviewing the design of the systems
(ii) Monitoring operation of the systems
(iii) Recommending improvements

(b) **Examination of financial and operating information.** This may include review of the means used to identify, measure, classify and report such information and specific enquiry into individual items including detailed testing of transactions, balances and procedures.

(c) **Review of the economy, efficiency and effectiveness of operations** (often called a 'value for money' audit) including non-financial controls of an organisation.

(d) **Review of compliance** with laws, regulations and other external requirements and with internal policies and directives and other requirements including appropriate authorisation of transactions.

(e) **Special investigations** into particular areas, for example suspected fraud.

6.3 Essential criteria for internal auditors

(a) The internal auditors should have the **independence** in terms of organisational status and personal objectivity which permits the proper performance of their duties.

(b) Like external audit teams, the internal audit unit should be **appropriately staffed** in terms of numbers, grades, qualifications and experience, having regard to its responsibilities and objectives. Training should be a planned and continuing process at all levels.

(c) The internal auditors should seek to foster constructive **working relationships** and mutual understanding with management, with external auditors, with any other review agencies and, where one exists, with the audit committee.

(d) The internal auditors cannot be expected to give total assurance that control weaknesses or irregularities do not exist, but they should exercise **due care** in fulfilling their responsibilities.

(e) Like the external auditors, the internal auditors should adequately **plan, control and record** their work. As part of the planning process the internal auditors should identify the whole range of systems within the organisation.

(f) The internal auditors should identify and evaluate **the organisation's internal control system** as a basis for reporting upon its adequacy and effectiveness.

(g) The internal auditors should obtain **sufficient, relevant and reliable evidence** on which to base reasonable conclusions and recommendations.

(h) For **reporting and follow-up**, the internal auditors should ensure that findings, conclusions and recommendations arising from each internal audit assignment are communicated promptly to the appropriate level of management and they should actively seek a response.

7 RELATIONSHIP BETWEEN INTERNAL AND EXTERNAL AUDIT

Co-ordination between the external and internal auditors of an organisation will minimise duplication of work and encourage a wide coverage of audit issues and areas. This co-ordination will involve:

(a) Periodic meetings to plan the overall audit to ensure adequate coverage
(b) Periodic meetings to discuss matters of mutual interest
(c) Mutual access to audit programmes and working papers
(d) Exchange of audit reports and management letters
(e) Common development of audit techniques, methods and terminology

NOTES

Where the external auditors wish to rely on the work of the internal auditors, then the external auditors must assess the internal audit function, as with any part of the system of internal control.

Although the reliability of records and adequacy of the reporting and accounting systems are interests shared by both types of auditor:

(a) Internal audit must not be seen merely as a service to the external audit and internal audit work should not be so distorted in order to fit with external audit needs that its own function is lost, and

(b) Internal audit is not always a cheaper way of carrying out an external audit function because:

   (i) The internal role extends into many other areas, and

   (ii) The special position of the external auditors makes them more effective and appropriate sometimes.

Activity 2 **(15 minutes)**

Explain why the internal and external auditors' review of internal control procedures differ in purpose.

Chapter roundup

- The purpose of an audit is to enable auditors to give an opinion as to whether the financial statements give a true and fair view.
- There are common misconceptions as to the role of the auditor, known as the expectation gap.
- Internal audit is designed to assure management that the controls of the business are operating effectively.
- The external audit has a precise procedure involving testing both of controls and transactions.
- Auditors have specific duties and rights which are laid down by statute.
- Auditing standards (ISAs) are issued by the Auditing Practices Board, and auditors are expected to follow them unless there are extremely valid reasons for not doing so.

Quick quiz

1 What is an audit?

2 What is the expectation gap?

3 List three statutory rights of the auditor.

4 To whom does the internal auditor report?

Answers to quick quiz

1 An exercise whose objective is to enable the auditor to express an opinion as to whether the financial statements give a true and fair view. (see para 1.2)

2 The difference between the role of the auditor as laid down by statute and auditing standards, and the public perception of that role. (para 1.6)

3 Access to records
Receive information and explanations
Receive notice of and attend general meetings
Speak at general meetings
Require laying of accounts before members (para 4.2)

4 Management of the organisation. (para 6.1)

Answers to activities

1 The difference in objectives is particularly important, although internal and external auditors use many similar methods to achieve their respective objectives. Every definition of internal audit suggests that it has a much wider scope than external audit, which has the objective of considering whether the accounts give a true and fair view of the organisation's financial position.

2 The internal auditors review and test the system of internal control and report to management in order to improve the information received by managers and to help in their task of running the company. The internal auditors will recommend changes to the system to make sure that the management receives objective information which is efficiently produced. The internal auditors will also have a duty to search for and discover fraud.

The external auditors review the system of internal control in order to determine the extent of the substantive work required on the year end accounts. The external auditors report to the shareholders rather than the managers or directors.

External auditors usually however issue a letter of weakness to the managers, laying out any areas of weakness and recommendations for improvement in the system of internal control. The external auditors report on the truth and fairness of the financial statements, not directly on the system of internal control. The auditors do not have a specific duty to detect fraud, although they should plan their audit procedures so as to detect any material misstatement in the accounts on which they give an opinion.

Chapter 26 : PLANNING THE AUDIT

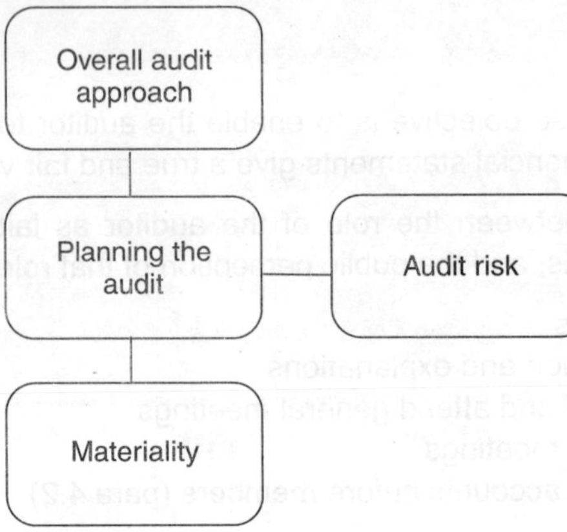

Introduction

Audit planning is a critical part of the audit process as it is at this stage that the key decisions are made including the assessment of risk and materiality. Information obtained will determine the overall approach or audit strategy as well as the detailed audit procedures which will be performed.

Your objectives

In this chapter you will learn about the following.

(a) How to determine the audit approach

(b) The implications of the assessment of controls

(c) The components of audit risk

(d) The importance of materiality

NOTES

1 OVERALL AUDIT APPROACH

1.1 Scope

The first stage in any audit should be to determine its scope and the auditors' general approach. For statutory audits the scope is clearly laid down in the Companies Act as expanded by auditing standards.

1.2 Audit strategy

Auditors should prepare an **audit strategy** to be placed on the audit file. The purpose of this document is to provide a record of the major areas to which the auditors attach special significance and to highlight any particular difficulties or points of concern peculiar to the audit client.

1.3 Documenting accounting systems

The auditor should obtain an understanding of the entity and its environment, including its internal control, sufficient to identify and assess the risks of material misstatement of the financial statements whether due to fraud or error, and sufficient to design and perform further audit procedures. (ISA 315.2)

This **understanding** of the accounting system must enable auditors to identify and understand:

- Major classes of transactions in the entity's operations
- How such transactions are initiated
- Significant accounting records, supporting documents and accounts
- The accounting and financial reporting process

The factors affecting the **nature, timing and extent** of the **procedures** performed in order to understand the systems include:

(a) The auditor's judgement regarding **materiality**

(b) The **size** of the entity

(c) The **nature of the entity's business**, including its organisation and ownership characteristics

(d) The **diversity and complexity** of the entity's operations

(e) Applicable **legal and regulatory requirements**

(f) The nature and complexity of the systems that are a part of the entity's **internal control**, including the use of service organisations

1.4 Ascertain the system and internal controls

The objective at this stage is to determine the **flow of documents** and **extent of controls** in existence. This is very much a fact-finding exercise, achieved by discussing the accounting system and document flow with all the relevant departments, including typically, sales, purchases, cash, stock and accounts personnel. It is good practice to make a rough record of the system during this fact-finding stage, which will be converted to a formal record.

The objective here is to prepare a **comprehensive record** to facilitate evaluation of the systems. Records may be in various formats.

- Charts, for example organisation charts and records of the books of account
- Narrative notes
- Internal control questionnaires
- Flowcharts

The auditors' objective here is to confirm that the **system recorded** is the same as that in **operation**.

After completion of the preparation (or update) of the systems records the auditors will confirm their understanding of the system by performing **walk-through** tests. These involve tracing literally a handful of transactions of each type through the system and observing the operation of controls over them. This procedure will establish whether the accounting system operates in the manner ascertained and recorded.

The need for this check arises as the client's staff will occasionally tell the auditors what they should be doing (the established procedures) rather than what is actually being done in practice.

1.5 Assess the system and internal controls

The purpose of **evaluating the systems** is to gauge their reliability and formulate a basis for testing their effectiveness in practice. Following the evaluation, the auditors will be able to recommend improvements to the system and determine the extent of the further tests to be carried out as described.

1.6 Test the system and internal controls

Given effective controls, the objective is to select and perform tests designed to establish compliance with the system. One of the most important points underlying modern auditing is that, if the controls are strong, the records should be reliable and consequently the amount of detailed testing can be reduced.

Auditors should however check that the controls are as effective in practice as they are on paper. They will therefore carry out **tests of controls**. These are like walk-through checks in so far as they are concerned with the workings of the system. There are a number of differences between the two.

- Tests of control are concerned only with those areas subject to effective control.
- Tests of control cover a representative sample of transactions throughout the period.
- Tests of control are likely to cover a larger number of items than walk-through tests.

The conclusion drawn from the results of a test of controls may be either that:

(a) The **controls are effective**, in which case the auditors will only need to carry out restricted substantive procedures.

(b) The **controls are ineffective** in practice, although they had appeared strong on paper, in which case the auditors will need to carry out more extensive substantive procedures.

These procedures should only be carried out if the controls are evaluated at Stage 5 as being effective. If the auditors know that the controls are ineffective then there is no point in carrying out tests of controls which will merely confirm what is already known. Instead the auditors should go straight on to carry out full substantive procedures.

Having assessed the accounting system and control environment, the auditors can make a **preliminary assessment** of whether the system is capable of producing reliable financial statements and of the likely mix of tests of control and substantive procedures (see Chapter 28).

2 AUDIT RISK

Definition

> **Audit risk** is the risk that auditors may give an inappropriate opinion on the financial statements.

2.1 Components of audit risk

Audit risk has three components: inherent risk, control risk and detection risk.

Audit risk is the risk that the auditors give an unqualified opinion on the accounts when they should have given a qualified opinion (or *vice versa*) **or** they give an opinion qualified for a particular reason where that reason was not justified.

In recent years there has been a shift towards risk-based auditing. This refers to the development of auditing techniques which are responsive to **risk factors** in an audit. Auditors apply judgement to determine what level of risk pertains to different areas of a client's system and devise appropriate audit tests. This approach should ensure that the greatest audit effort is directed at the riskiest areas, so that the chance of detecting errors is improved and excessive time is not spent on 'safe' areas.

The increased use of risk-based auditing reflects two factors.

(a) The growing **complexity** of the business environment increases the danger of fraud or misstatement. Factors such as the developing use of computerised systems and the growing internationalisation of business are relevant here.

(b) Pressures are increasingly exerted by audit clients for the auditors to keep **fee levels down** while providing an improved level of service.

Risk-based auditing is responsive to both factors.

ISA 200 *Objective and general principles governing an audit of financial statements* introduces audit risk. ISA 315 provides more detail on how to plan to miminise that risk to an acceptable level.

Auditors should:

(a) Obtain an understanding of the entity and its environment including its internal control, sufficient to identify and assess the risks of material misstatement of the financial statements whether due to fraud or error, and sufficient to design and perform further audit tests (ISA 315.2); and

(b) Plan and perform the audit to reduce audit risk to an acceptably low level that is consistent with the objective of the audit (ISA 200.15).

Audit risk can never be completely eliminated. The auditors are called upon to make subjective judgements in the course of forming an opinion and so fraud or error may possibly go undetected.

A **risk-based approach** gives the auditors an overall measure of risk, but at the same time it provides a quantification of each stage of the audit. The extent of detailed testing required is determined by a purely risk-based perspective. A diagrammatic view of the risk-based approach is given here.

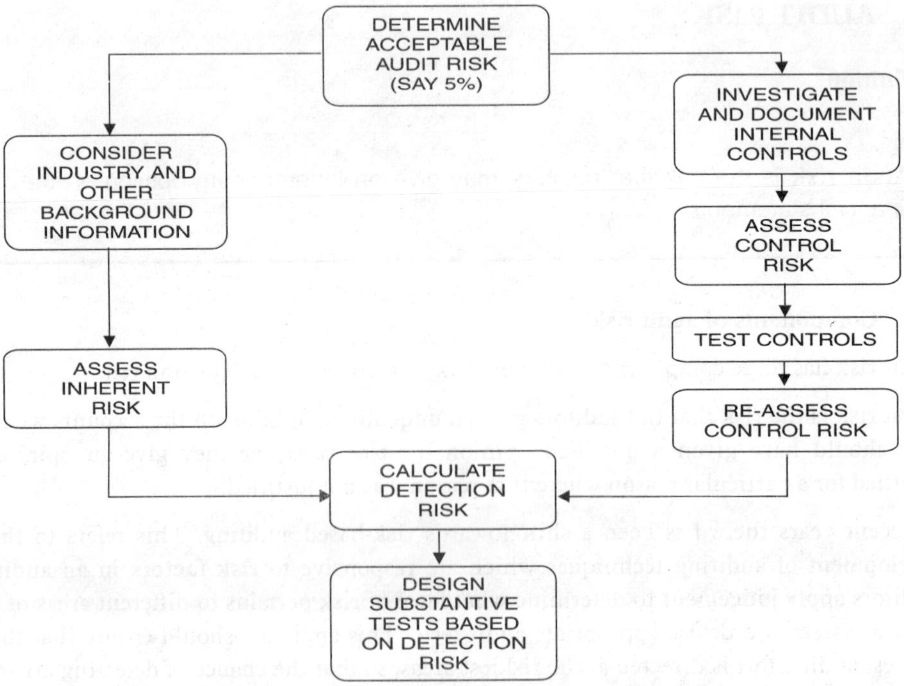

Figure 26.1: Risk-based approach

2.2 Inherent risk

Definition

Inherent risk is the susceptibility of an assertion to a misstatement that could be material, either individually or when aggregated with other misstatements, assuming that there are no related controls (ISA 200.20).

Inherent risk is the risk that items will be misstated due to characteristics of those items, such as the fact they are **estimates** or that they are **important** items in the accounts. The auditors must use their professional judgement and all available knowledge to assess inherent risk. If no such information or knowledge is available then the inherent risk is **high.**

The results of the assessment must be properly documented and, where inherent risk is assessed as not high, then audit work may be reduced.

In developing their audit approach and detailed procedures, auditors should assess inherent risk in relation to financial statement assertions about material account balances and classes of transactions, taking account of factors relevant both to the entity as a whole and to the specific assertions. For more detail on audit assertions, see chapter 28. Factors that indicate higher risk are set out in the tables below. ISA 315 Appendix 3 contains a similar list although this is not split by client and individual account balances.

FACTORS AFFECTING CLIENT AS A WHOLE	
Integrity and **attitude to risk** of directors and management	Domination by a single individual can cause problems
Management experience and **knowledge**	Changes in management and quality of financial management
Unusual pressures on management	Examples include tight reporting deadlines, or market or financing expectations
Nature of business	Potential problems include technological obsolescence or over-dependence on a single product
Industry factors	Competitive conditions, regulatory requirements, technology developments, changes in customer demand
Information technology	Problems include lack of supporting documentation, concentration of expertise in a few people, potential for unauthorised access

FACTORS AFFECTING INDIVIDUAL ACCOUNT BALANCES OR TRANSACTIONS	
Financial statement **accounts prone to misstatement**	Accounts which require adjustment in previous period, require high degree of estimation or judgement, or which may significantly affect profitability or liquidity
Complex accounts	Accounts which require expert valuations or are subjects of current professional discussion
Assets at risk of being **lost or stolen**	Cash (consider opportunities for unauthorised payments), stock, portable fixed assets (computers)
High volume of **transactions**	Accounting system may have problems coping
Quality of **accounting systems**	Strength of individual departments (sales, purchases, cash etc)
Unusual transactions	Transactions for large amounts, with unusual names, not settled promptly (particularly important if they occur at period-end)
	Transactions that do not go through the system, that relate to specific clients or processed by certain individuals
Staff	Staff changes or areas of low morale

2.3 Control risk

Definition

Control risk is the risk that a misstatement that could occur in an assertion and that could be material, either individually or when aggregated with other misstatements, will not be prevented, or detected and corrected, on a timely basis by the entity's internal control (ISA 200.20).

Control risk is the risk that client controls fail to detect material misstatements. The most important point is that the ISA requires a **preliminary assessment** of **control risk** at the planning stage of the audit if the auditors intend to rely on their assessment to reduce the extent of their substantive procedures. This assessment should be supported subsequently by tests of control (see Chapter 28).

2.4 Detection risk

Definition

Detection risk is the risk that the auditor will not detect a misstatement that exists in an assertion that could be material, either individually, or when aggregated with other misstatements (ISA 200.22).

Detection risk is the risk that audit procedures will fail to detect material errors. Detection risk relates to the inability of the auditors to examine all evidence. Audit evidence is usually persuasive rather than conclusive so some detection risk is usually present, allowing the auditors to seek 'reasonable confidence'.

Auditors should consider the assessed levels of inherent and control risk in determining the nature, timing and extent of substantive procedures required to reduce audit risk to an acceptable level.

The auditors' **inherent and control risk assessments** influence the **nature, timing and extent of substantive procedures** required to reduce detection risk and thereby audit risk.

(a) Auditors need to be careful when relying on their **assessment** of **control risk,** as good controls may impact upon some but not other aspects of audit areas. For example, good controls over the recording of sales and debtors would not reduce audit testing on bad debts, as the amounts recorded may represent amounts that will not be collected.

(b) To design an efficient audit strategy, auditors should not just consider reducing the number of items they test substantively, the **extent** of testing, if inherent and control risks are low. They may also alter the tests they do, the **design** of testing, by placing for instance more reliance on analytical procedures. They may also change the **timing** of tests, for example carrying out certain procedures such as circularisation at a date that is not the year-end, and placing reliance upon internal controls functioning at the year-end.

NOTES

Misstatements discovered in substantive procedures may cause the auditors to modify their previous assessment of control risk.

Regardless of the assessed levels of inherent and control risks, auditors should perform some substantive procedures for financial statement assertions of material account balances and transaction classes.

Substantive procedures can never be abandoned entirely because control and inherent risk can never be assessed at a low enough level, although substantive procedures may be restricted to analytical procedures if appropriate.

Where the auditors' assessment of the components of audit risk changes during the audit, they should modify the planned substantive procedures based on the revised risk levels.

When both inherent and control risks are assessed as high, the auditors should consider whether substantive procedures can provide sufficient appropriate audit evidence to reduce detection risk, and therefore audit risk, to an acceptably low level. For example, they may not be able to obtain sufficient evidence about the completeness of income in the absence of some internal controls. If sufficient evidence cannot be obtained, auditors may have to qualify their audit report.

Activity 1 **(20 minutes)**

Hippo Ltd is a long established client of your firm. It manufactures bathroom fittings and fixtures, which it sells to a range of wholesalers in the UK, on credit.

You are the audit senior and have recently been sent the following extract from the draft balance sheet by the finance director.

	Budget		*Actual*	
	£'000s	£'000s	£'000s	£'000s
Fixed assets		453		367
Current assets				
Trade debtors	1,134		976	
Bank	-		54	
Current liabilities				
Trade creditors	967		944	
Bank overdraft	9		-	
Net current assets		58		86
Total assets		611		453

During the course of conversation with the finance director, you establish that a major new customer the company had included in its budget went bankrupt during the year.

Identify any potential risks for the audit of Hippo and explain why you believe they are risks.

BPP LEARNING MEDIA

3 MATERIALITY

3.1 What is materiality?

Definition

> **Materiality** is an expression of the relative significance or importance of a particular matter in the context of financial statements as a whole, or of individual financial statements. A matter is material if its omission or misstatement could influence the economic decisions of users taken on the basis of the financial statements. Materiality depends on the size of the item or error judged in the particular circumstances of its omission or misstatement. Thus, materiality provides a threshold or cut-off point rather than being a primary qualitative characteristic which information must have if is to be useful. (ISA 320.3)

Although the definition refers to the decision of the user of the financial statements (that is, the members of the company), their decisions may well be influenced by how the accounts are used. For example if the accounts are to be used to secure a bank loan, what is significant to the bank will influence the way members act. The views of other users of the accounts must be taken into account.

3.2 ISA 320 Audit materiality

ISA 320 states that auditors should consider materiality and its relationship with audit risk when conducting an audit.

Auditors plan and perform the audit to be able to provide reasonable assurance that the financial statements are free of material misstatement and give a true and fair view. The assessment of what is material is a matter of professional judgement.

Small amounts should be considered if there is a risk that they could occur more than once and together add up to an amount which is material in total. As well as quantitative aspects, qualitative aspects must also be considered, for example the inaccurate and therefore misleading description of an accounting policy.

Materiality considerations will differ depending on the aspect of the financial statements being considered.

Materiality is considered at both the overall financial statement level and in relation to individual account balances, classes of transactions and disclosures.

A good example is directors' pay which make normal materiality considerations irrelevant, because it **must** be disclosed by the auditors if they are not disclosed correctly by the directors in the financial statements.

Materiality considerations during **audit planning** are extremely important. The assessment of materiality when determining the nature, timing and extent of audit procedures should be based on the most recent and reliable financial information and will help to determine an effective and efficient audit approach. Materiality assessment in conjunction with risk assessment will help the auditors to make a number of decisions.

- What items to examine
- Whether to use sampling techniques (see Chapter 28)
- What level of error is likely to lead to an opinion that the accounts do not give a true and fair view

The resulting combination of audit procedures should help to reduce detection risk to an appropriately low level.

3.3 Practical implications

Because many users of accounts are primarily interested in the **profitability** of the company, the materiality level is often expressed as a proportion of its profits before tax. Some argue, however, that materiality should be thought of in terms of the **size** of the business. Hence, if the company remains a fairly constant size, the materiality level should not change; similarly if the business is growing, the level of materiality will increase from year to year.

The **size** of a company can be measured in terms of turnover and total assets before deducting any liabilities (sometimes referred to in legislation as 'the balance sheet total') both of which tend not to be subject to the fluctuations which may affect profit. The auditors will often calculate a range of values, such as those shown below, and then take an average or weighted average of all the figures produced as the materiality level.

Value	%
Profit before tax	5
Gross profit	½–1
Turnover	½–1
Total assets	1–2
Net assets	2–5
Profit after tax	5–10

The effect of planning materiality on the audit process is shown in the diagram below.

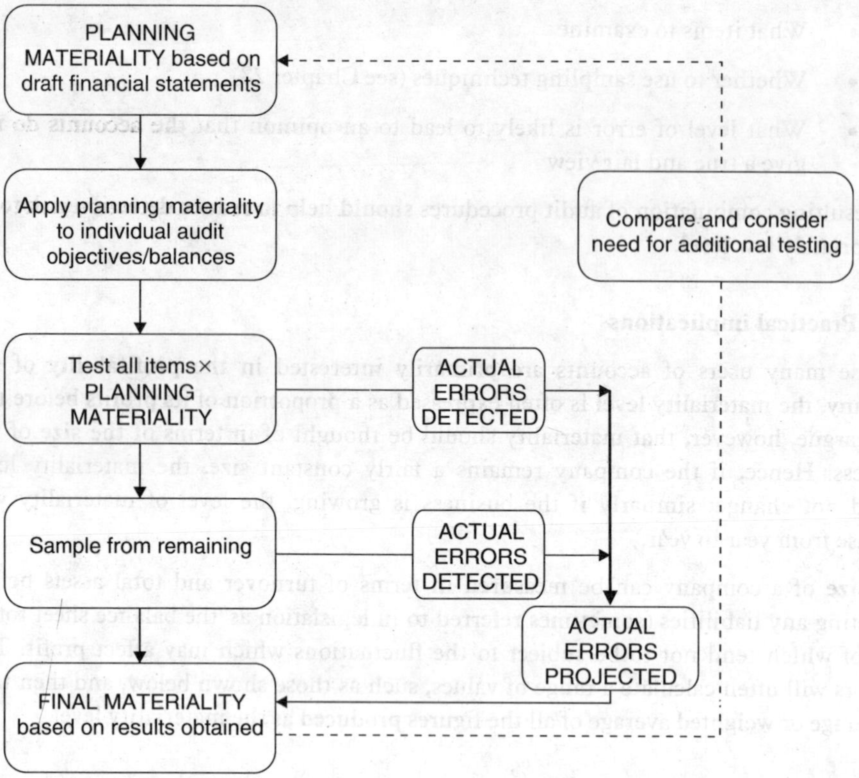

Figure 26.2: Effect of planning materiality on audit process

3.4 Changes to the level of materiality

The level of materiality must be reviewed constantly as the audit progresses. Changes to audit procedures may be required for various reasons.

(a) **Draft accounts are altered (due to material error and so on) and therefore overall materiality changes.**

(b) **External factors cause changes in the control or inherent risk estimates.**

(c) **Changes are caused by errors found during testing.**

Activity 2 **(10 minutes)**

Which measures of the business would an audit firm use when setting a level of materiality:

(a) If the client had a stable asset base, steady turnover over the last few years, but had only made a small pre-tax profit this year owing to a large one-off expense?

(b) If the directors had expressed concern over declining profits over the last few years?

Chapter roundup

- The auditor will formulate an overall audit plan which will be translated into a detailed audit programme for audit staff to follow.
- The audit programme documents the nature, timing and extent of planned audit procedures.
- There is no single accepted approach to audit. The more commonly used approach is the systems based audit, which has evolved into a risk-based approach.

Quick quiz

1 What is a systems audit?

2 What is risk based auditing?

3 What are the components of audit risk?

4 Which factors affecting the client as a whole increase inherent risk?

5 What impact does the auditor's assessment of inherent risk and control risk have on audit planning?

6 Why cannot substantive procedures be abandoned entirely?

7 What decisions are made on the basis of the materiality assessment?

8 At which levels should materiality be considered?

Answers to quick quiz

1 The audit of internal controls within a system. (see paras 1.3–1.4)

2 The use of auditing techniques which are responsive to risk factors in an audit, so that the greatest audit effort is directed at the riskiest areas. (para 2.1)

3 Inherent risk
Control risk
Detection risk (para 2.1)

4 Integrity and attitude of management
Unusual pressures
Nature of business
Industry factors
Information technology problems (para 2.2)

5 It influences the nature, timing and extent of substantive procedures. (paras 1.3 and 2.2)

6 Control risk and inherent risk cannot be eliminated entirely. (para 2.4)

7
- How many and what items to examine
- Whether to use sampling techniques
- What level of error is likely to lead to a qualified audit report. (para 3.2)

8
- Overall financial statement level
- Individual accounts balance level (para 3.2)

Answers to activities

1 **Potential risks relevant to the audit of Hippo**

(1) **Credit sales**. Hippo makes sales on credit. This increases the risk that Hippo's sales will not be converted into cash. Debtors is likely to be a risky area and the auditors will have to consider what the best evidence that debtors are going to pay their debts is likely to be.

(2) **Related industry**. Hippo manufactures bathroom fixtures and fittings. These are sold to wholesalers, but it is possible that Hippo's ultimate market is the building industry. This is a notoriously volatile industry, and Hippo may find that their results fluctuate too, as demand rises and falls. This suspicion is added to by the bankruptcy of the wholesaler in the year. The auditors must be sure that accounts which present Hippo as a viable company are in fact correct.

(3) **Controls**. The fact that a major new customer went bust suggests that Hippo did not undertake a very thorough credit check on that customer before agreeing to supply them. This implies that the controls at Hippo may not be very strong.

(4) **Variance**. The actual results are different from budget. This may be explained by the fact that the major customer went bankrupt, or it may reveal that there are other errors and problems in the reported results, or in the original budget.

(5) **Debtors**. There is a risk that the result reported contains debt from the bankrupt wholesaler, which is likely to be irrecoverable.

2 (a) Because the business is stable, auditors are likely to base overall materiality on a % of turnover or gross assets, or possibly an average of both. Profit before tax is unlikely to be used overall as its fluctuation does not appear to be significant. However a different materiality level may be set when considering the one-off expense, since it may be particularly significant to readers of the accounts.

(b) Auditors are likely here to pay some attention to the level of profit when setting materiality, because the outside members regard profit as significant. However the auditors are also likely to take into account gross and net assets. Low profits will be of less significance if the business has a strong asset base, but of more significance if the business is in long-term financial difficulty.

Chapter 27 :

RECORDING AUDIT WORK

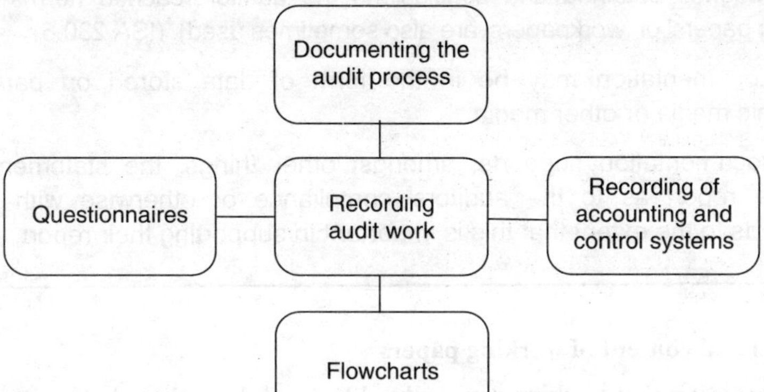

Introduction

Recording audit work is a vital part of the audit procedure, as it provides documentary evidence of how the audit has been carried out, what work has been done and what conclusions have been reached. This is essential should the auditor subsequently have to justify his audit opinion on the financial statements.

Adequate recording of audit work can also be helpful in subsequent years, as it is common practice for the auditor to look back at last year's files to see what work was done and problems found, in case they should impact on the current year's work.

Your objectives

In this chapter you will learn about the following.

(a) Working papers and their different forms

(b) The different ways of recording accounting and control systems

(c) Flowcharting techniques

(d) Questionnaires

NOTES

1 DOCUMENTING THE AUDIT PROCESS

All audit work must be documented: the working papers are the tangible evidence of the work done in support of the audit opinion. ISA 230 *Audit documentation* covers this area.

Definition

> **Audit documentation** means the record of audit procedures performed, relevant audit evidence obtained and conclusions the auditor reached (terms such as 'working papers' or 'workpapers' are also sometimes used). (ISA 230.6)
>
> Audit documentation may be in the form of data stored on paper, film, electronic media or other media.
>
> Audit documentation supports, amongst other things, the statement in the auditors' report as to the auditors' compliance or otherwise with Auditing Standards to the extent that this is important in supporting their report.

1.1 Form and content of working papers

ISA 230.2 indicates that working papers should record the auditors' planning, the nature, timing and extent of the audit procedures performed, and the conclusions drawn from the audit evidence obtained.

Auditors should record in their working papers their reasoning on all significant matters which require the exercise of judgement, and their conclusions thereon.

Auditors cannot record everything they consider. Therefore judgement must be used as to the extent of working papers, based on the following test.

> What would be necessary to provide an experienced auditor, with no previous connection with the audit, with an understanding of the audit procedures performed, the results of those procedures and the audit evidence obtained and the conclusions reached on each significant matter?

The form and content of working papers are affected by various matters.

(a) The nature of the audit procedures performed

(b) The identified risks of material misstatement

(c) The extent of judgement required in performing the work and evaluating the results

(d) The significance of the audit evidence obtained

(e) The nature and extent of exceptions identified

(f) The need to document a conclusion or the basis for a conclusion not readily determinable from the documentation of the work performed or audit evidence obtained, and

(g) The audit methodology tools used.

Standardised working papers, eg checklists, standard audit programmes, specimen letters can be used as they may improve the efficiency with which such working papers are prepared and reviewed. But while they facilitate the delegation of work and provide a means to control its quality, it is never appropriate to follow mechanically a standard approach to the conduct and documentation of the audit without regard to the need to exercise professional judgement.

While auditors may utilise schedules, analyses etc prepared by the entity, they require evidence that such information is properly prepared.

1.2 Typical contents of working papers

These include the following.

- Information concerning the legal and organisational structure of the client
- Information concerning the client's industry, economic and legal environment
- Evidence of the planning process
- Evidence of the auditors' understanding of the accounting and internal control systems
- Evidence of inherent and control risk assessments and any revisions
- Analyses of transactions and balances
- Analyses of significant ratios and trends
- A record of the nature, timing, extent and results of auditing procedures
- Copies of communications with other auditors, experts and other third parties
- Copies of correspondence with the client
- Reports to directors or management
- Notes of discussions with the entity's directors or management
- A summary of the significant aspects of the audit
- Copies of the approved financial statements and auditors' reports

1.3 Format of working papers

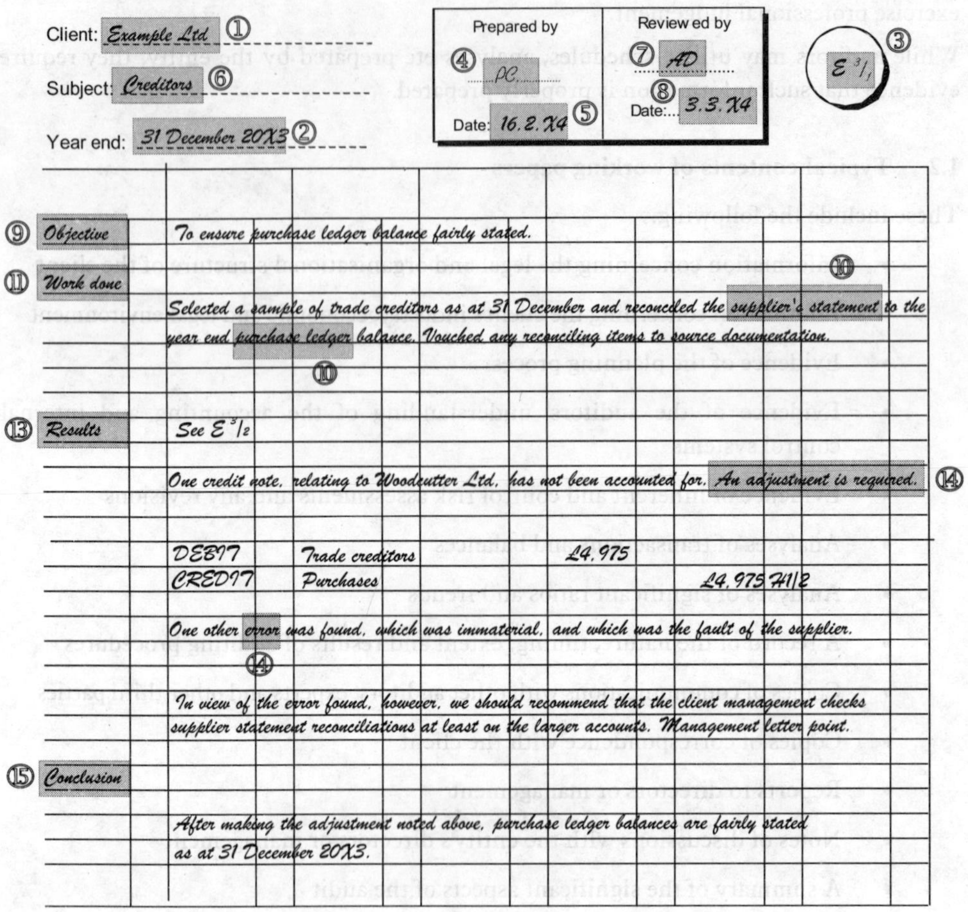

Client: *Example Ltd* ①

Subject: *Creditors* ⑥

Year end: *31 December 20X3* ②

Prepared by	Reviewed by
④ *PC*	⑦ *AD*
Date: *16.2.X4* ⑤	⑧ Date: *3.3.X4*

③ *E 3/1*

⑨ **Objective** — *To ensure purchase ledger balance fairly stated.*

⑪ **Work done** — ⑩ *Selected a sample of trade creditors as at 31 December and reconciled the supplier's statement to the year end purchase ledger balance. Vouched any reconciling items to source documentation.* ⑩

⑬ **Results** — *See E 3/2*

One credit note, relating to Woodcutter Ltd, has not been accounted for. An adjustment is required. ⑭

DEBIT	*Trade creditors*	*£4,975*	
CREDIT	*Purchases*		*£4,975 H1/2*

One other error was found, which was immaterial, and which was the fault of the supplier. ⑭

In view of the error found, however, we should recommend that the client management checks supplier statement reconciliations at least on the larger accounts. Management letter point.

⑮ **Conclusion** — *After making the adjustment noted above, purchase ledger balances are fairly stated as at 31 December 20X3.*

NOTES

Client: *Example Ltd*

Subject: *Creditors*

Year end: *31 December 20X3*

Prepared by	Reviewed by
PC	*AD*
Date: *16.2.X4*	Date: *3.3.X4*

E 3/2

Client	*Purchase ledger* £	*Supplier statement* £	*Difference*	*Agreed*	*Reconciling item*	
A Ltd	↘ 300 00	300 00	-	✓	-	
B Ltd	↘ 747 00	732 00	15 00	✗	15 00	*Credit note not yet received*
	1,047 00 ^					

⑫ *Key*

✓ *Agreed*
✗ *Not agreed*
^ *Adds checked*
↘ *Agreed to purchase ledger*

KEY

① The **name** of the **client**

② The balance sheet **date**

③ The **file reference** of the working paper

④ The **name** of the **person** preparing the working paper

⑤ The **date** the working paper was **prepared**

⑥ The **subject** of the working paper

⑦ The **name** of the person **reviewing** the working paper

⑧ The **date** of the **review**

⑨ The **objective** of the work done

⑩ The **sources of information**

⑪ The **work done**

⑫ A **key** to any audit ticks or symbols

⑬ The **results obtained**

⑭ **Analysis** of **errors** or other significant observations

⑮ The **conclusions drawn**

Figure 27.1: Format of working papers

1.4 Computerised working papers

Automated working paper packages have been developed which can make the documenting of audit work much easier. These are automatically cross referenced and balanced by the computer. Whenever an adjustment is made, the computer will automatically update all the necessary schedules.

The **advantages** of automated working papers are as follows.

(a) The **risk** of **errors** is **reduced**.

(b) The **working papers** will be **neater** and **easier to review.**

(c) The **time saved** will be **substantial** as adjustments can be made easily to all working papers, including working papers summarising the key analytical information.

(d) **Standard** forms **do not have** to be **carried** to audit locations. Forms can be designed to be called up and completed on the computer screen.

(e) **Audit working papers** can be **transmitted** for review via a computer network, or fax facilities (if both the sending and receiving computers have fax boards and fax software).

1.5 Confidentiality, safe custody and ownership

Auditors should adopt appropriate procedures for maintaining the confidentiality and safe custody of their working papers.

Working papers are the property of the auditors. They are not a substitute for, nor part of, the client's accounting records.

Auditors must follow ethical guidance on the confidentiality of audit working papers. They may, at their discretion, release parts of or whole working papers to the client, as long as disclosure does not undermine 'the independence or validity of the audit process'. Information should not be made available to third parties without the permission of the entity.

1.6 Audit files

For recurring audits, working papers may be split between permanent and current audit files.

(a) **Permanent audit files** are updated with new information of continuing importance such as legal documents, background information and correspondence with the client of relevance for a number of years. The file should also contain a copy of each year's final accounts.

(b) **Current audit files** contain information relating primarily to the audit of a single period.

Activity 1 **(15 minutes)**

The auditing standard ISA 230 *Audit documentation* states the following regarding audit documentation.

'Auditors base their judgement as to the extent of working papers upon what would be necessary to provide an experienced auditor, with no previous connection with the audit, with an understanding of the work performed and the basis of the decisions taken.'

Task

Describe four benefits that auditors will obtain from working papers that meet the above requirement in ISA 230.

Activity 2 **(10 minutes)**

(a) With what details should working papers of audit tests performed be headed?

(b) What other details should working papers covering audit tests contain?

2 RECORDING OF ACCOUNTING AND CONTROL SYSTEMS

There are several techniques for recording accounting and internal control systems.

- Narrative notes
- Flowcharts
- Questionnaires (eg ICQ)
- Checklists

Often a combination may be used, with narrative notes and/or flowcharts recording the accounting system, and questionnaires recording controls.

Whatever method of recording the system is used, the record will usually be retained on the permanent file and updated each year.

2.1 Narrative notes

Narrative notes have the advantage of being simple to record. However they are awkward to change if written manually. Editing in future years will be easier if they are computerised. The purpose of the notes is to **describe** and **explain** the **system**, at the same time making any comments or criticisms which will help to demonstrate an intelligent understanding of the system.

For each system notes need to deal with the following questions.

- What functions are performed and by whom?
- What documents are used?
- Where do the documents originate and what is their destination?
- What sequence are retained documents filed in?
- What books are kept and where?

Narrative notes can be used to support flowcharts.

3 FLOWCHARTS

There are two methods of flowcharting in regular use.

- Document flowcharts
- Information flowcharts

3.1 Document flowcharts

Document flowcharts are more commonly used because they are relatively easy to prepare.

- *All* documents are followed through from 'cradle to grave'.
- *All* operations and controls are shown.

We shall concentrate on document flowcharts.

3.2 Information flowcharts

Information flowcharts are prepared in the reverse direction from the flow: they start with the entry in the accounting records and work back to the actual transaction. They concentrate on significant information flows and key controls and ignore any unimportant documents or copies of documents.

3.3 Advantages and disadvantages of flowcharts

Advantages include the following.

(a) After a little experience they can be **prepared quickly**.

(b) As the information is presented in a standard form, they are fairly **easy to follow** and to review.

(c) They generally ensure that the system is **recorded in its entirety,** as all document flows have to be traced from beginning to end. Any 'loose ends' will be apparent from a quick examination.

(d) They **eliminate** the need for **extensive narrative** and can be of considerable help in highlighting the salient points of control and any weaknesses in the system.

On the other hand, flowcharts do have some **disadvantages**.

(a) They are **only really suitable for describing standard systems**. Procedures for dealing with unusual transactions will normally have to be recorded using narrative notes.

(b) They are useful for recording the flow of documents, but once the **records** or the assets to which they relate have **become static** they **can no longer be used for describing the controls** (for example over fixed assets).

(c) Major **amendment is difficult** without redrawing.

(d) **Time** can be **wasted** by **charting areas** that are of no **audit significance** (a criticism of *document* not information flowcharts).

3.4 Design of flowcharts

Flowcharts should be kept simple, so that the overall structure or flow is clear at first sight.

(a) There must be **conformity of symbols**, with each symbol representing one and only one thing.

(b) The direction of the flowchart should be from **top to bottom** and from **left to right**.

(c) There must be no **loose ends**.

(d) The main flow should finish at the **bottom right hand corner**, not in the middle of the page.

(e) Connecting lines should cross *only* where absolutely necessary to preserve the chart's simplicity.

3.5 Flowcharting symbols

Basic symbols will be used for the charting of all systems, but where the client's system involves mechanised or computerised processing, then further symbols may be required to supplement the basic ones. The basic symbols used are shown below.

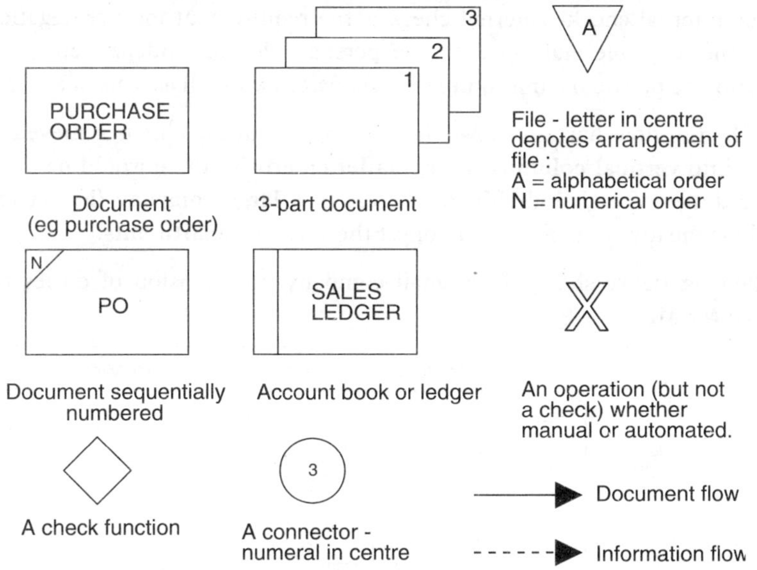

Figure 27.2: Flow chart symbols

Preparation of a basic flowchart will involve the procedures laid out in the next few paragraphs.

3.6 Document flows

The symbols showing the sequence of operations taking place within the one department are joined by a vertical line as illustrated in the figure below.

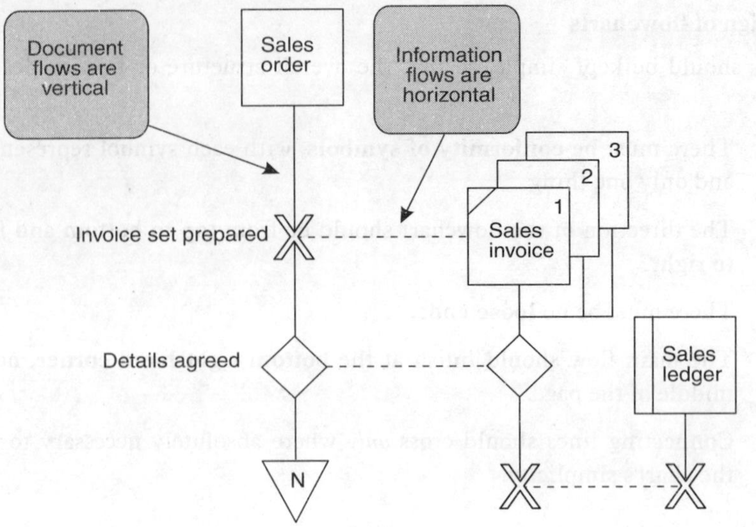

Figure 27.3: Document flows

3.7 Division of duties

One of the key features of any good system of internal control is that there should be a system of 'internal check'. Internal check is the requirement for a segregation of duties amongst the available staff so that one person's work is independently reviewed by another, no one person having complete responsibility for all aspects of a transaction.

This method of flowcharting shows the division of duties. This is achieved by dividing the chart into **vertical columns**. In a **smaller** enterprise there would be one column to show the duties of each **individual,** whereas in a **large** company the vertical columns would show the division of duties amongst the various **departments**.

The following figure shows, in a small company, the division of duties between Mr Major and Mr Minor.

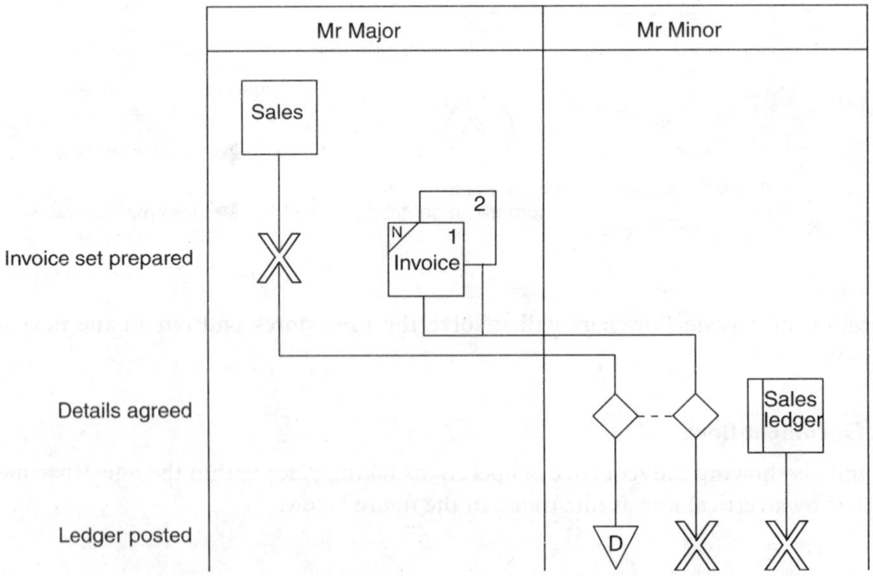

Figure 27.4 Division of duties

3.8 Sequence and description of operations

To facilitate ease of reference each operation shown on the chart is numbered in sequence on the chart, a separate column being used for this purpose.

Finally, the chart will be completed by the inclusion of a narrative column which will describe significant operations. Narrative should be kept to a minimum and only included where in fact it is required.

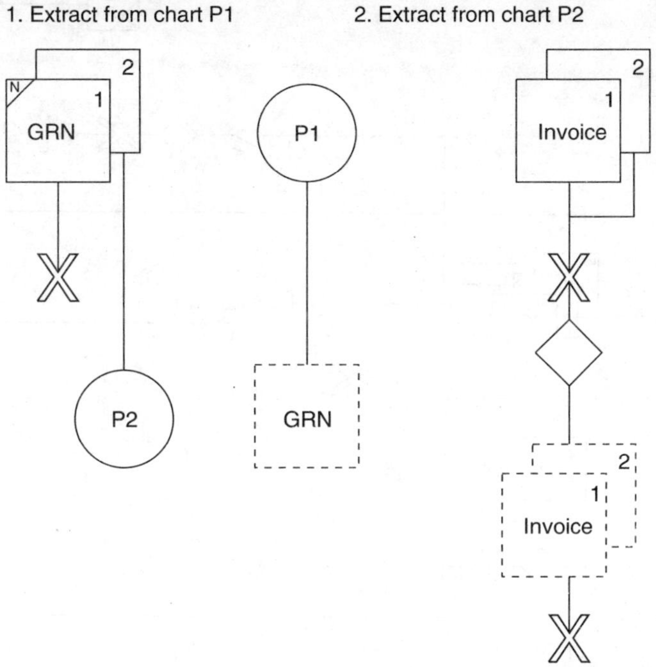

Figure 27.5: Sequence and description of operations

On the following pages you will find two charts which illustrate typical procedures in a company's purchasing system.

- Ordering and receiving of goods
- Approval of invoices

NOTES

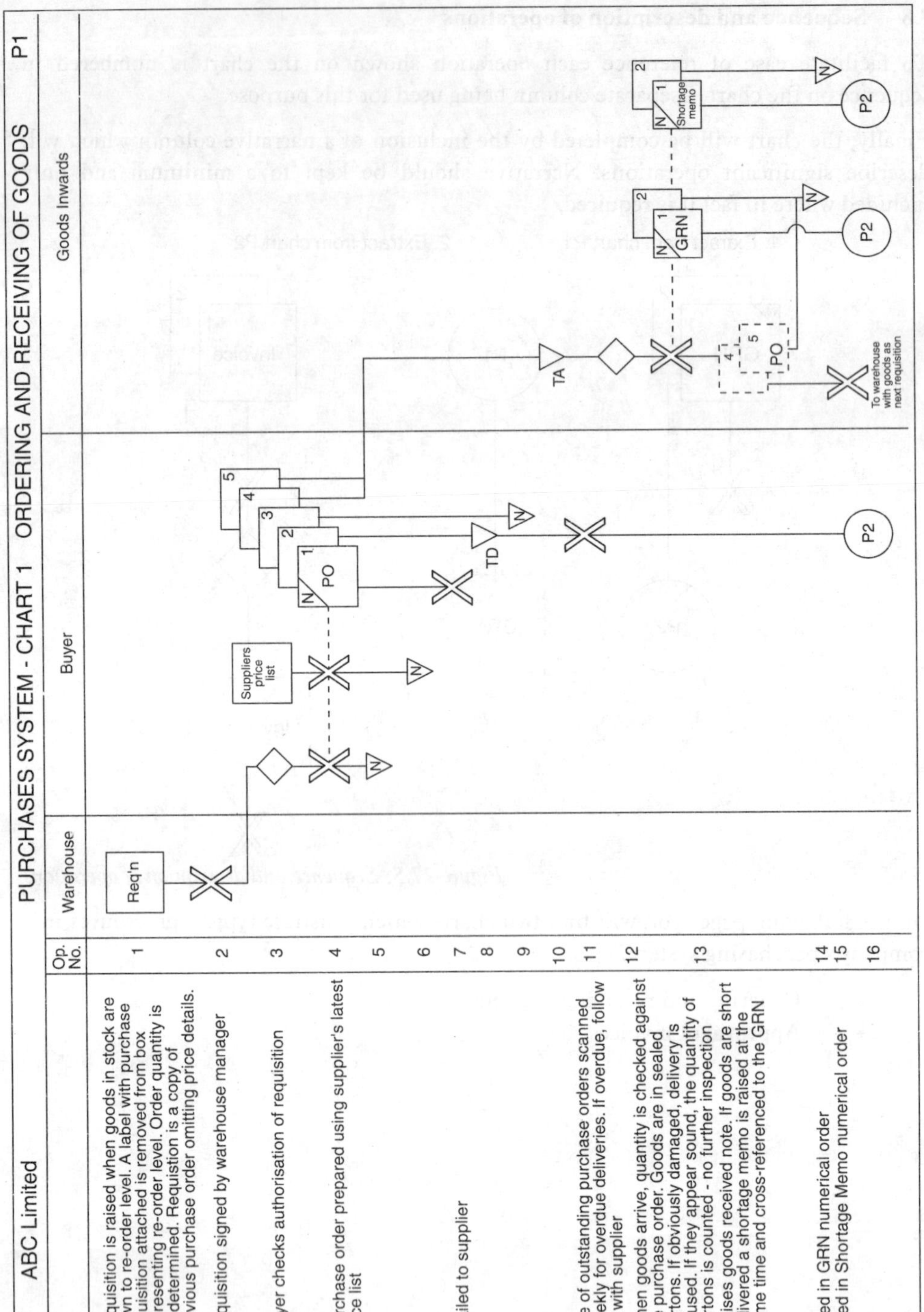

Figure 27.6: Ordering and receiving of goods

BPP LEARNING MEDIA

NOTES

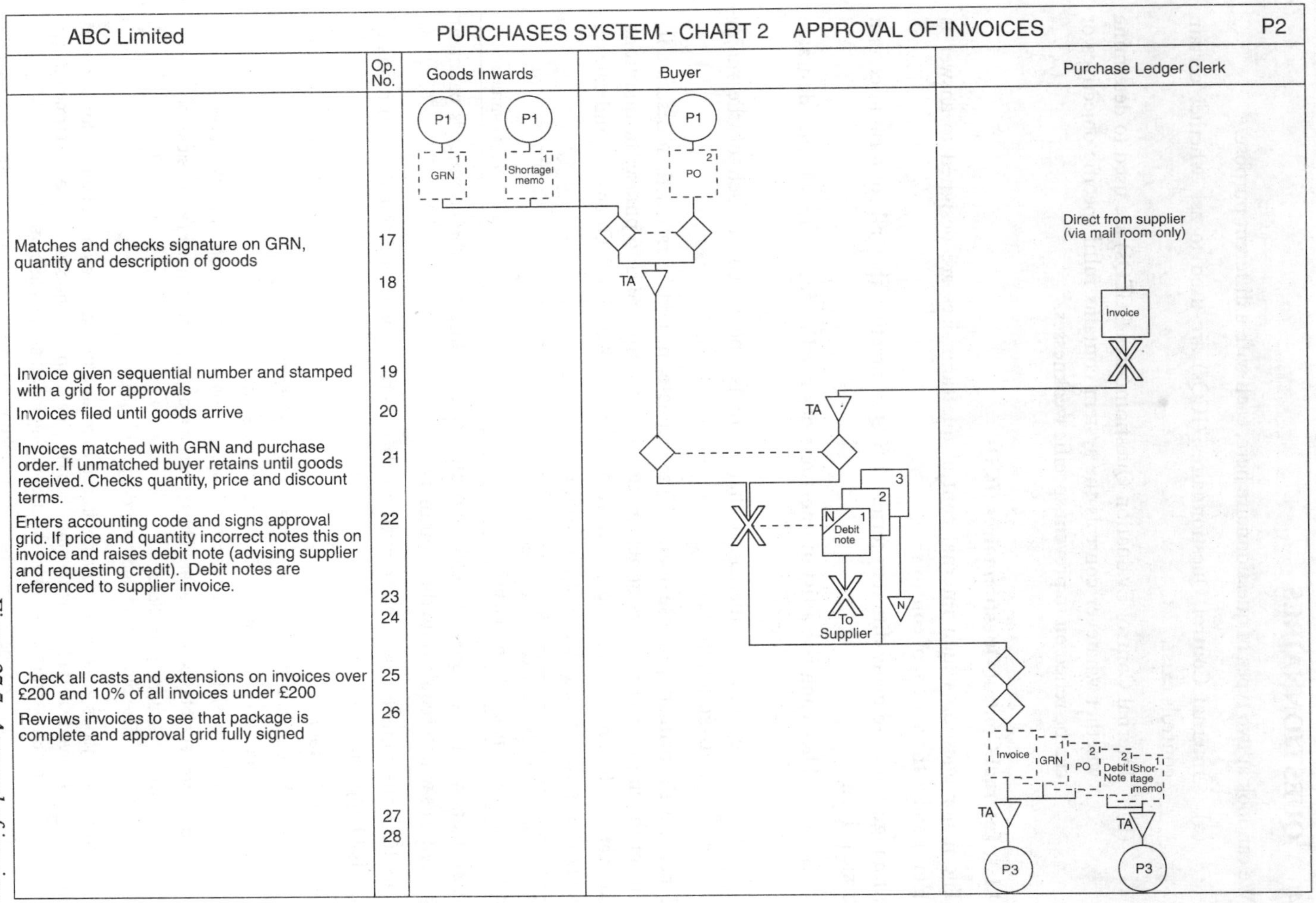

Figure 27.7: Approval of invoices

4 QUESTIONNAIRES

We can look at two types of questionnaire here, each with a different purpose.

(a) Internal Control Questionnaires (ICQs) are used to ask whether certain controls exist.

(b) Internal Control Evaluation Questionnaires (ICEQs) are used to determine whether whatever controls the system contains fulfil specific objectives or can be relied on to prevent specific weaknesses.

4.1 Internal Control Questionnaires (ICQs)

The major question which internal control questionnaires are designed to answer is 'How good is the system of controls?'

Although there are many different forms of ICQ in practice, they all conform to certain basic principles.

(a) They comprise a **list of questions** designed to determine whether desirable controls are present.

(b) They are formulated so that there is one to cover each of the **major transaction cycles**.

Since it is the primary purpose of an ICQ to evaluate the system rather than describe it, one of the most effective ways of designing the questionnaire is to phrase the questions so that all the answers can be given as 'YES' or 'NO' and a 'NO' answer indicates a weakness in the system. An example would be:

Are purchase invoices checked to goods received notes before being passed for payment?	YES/NO/Comments

A 'NO' answer to that question clearly indicates a weakness in the company's payment procedures which requires further comment.

The ICQ questions below dealing with goods inward provide additional illustrations of the ICQ approach.

Goods inward

(a) Are supplies examined on arrival as to quantity and quality?

(b) Is such an examination evidenced in some way?

(c) Is the receipt of supplies recorded, perhaps by means of goods inwards notes?

(d) Are receipt records prepared by a person independent of those responsible for:
   (i) Ordering functions
   (ii) The processing and recording of invoices

(e) Are goods inwards records controlled to ensure that invoices are obtained for all goods received and to enable the liability for unbilled goods to be determined (by pre-numbering the records and accounting for all serial numbers)?

(f) (i) Are goods inward records regularly reviewed for items for which no invoices have been received?
   (ii) Are any such items investigated?

(g) Are these records reviewed by a person independent of those responsible for the receipt and control of goods?

Each situation must therefore be judged on its own merits and hence, although the ICQs often take the form of a standard pre-printed pack, they should be used with imagination.

As using ICQs is a skilled and responsible task, the evaluation should be performed by a senior member of the audit team.

4.2 Advantages and disadvantages of ICQs

ICQs have various advantages.

(a) If drafted thoroughly, they can ensure **all controls** are **considered.**

(b) They are **quick** to **prepare.**

(c) They are **easy** to **use** and **control**. A manager or partner reviewing the work can easily see what has been done.

However they also have disadvantages:

(a) The client may be able to **overstate controls.**

(b) They may contain a large number of **irrelevant controls.**

(c) They can give the impression that all controls are of **equal weight**. In many systems one 'no' answer (for example lack of segregation of duties) may cancel the apparent value of a string of 'yes' answers).

(d) They may not include unusual controls, which are nevertheless effective in particular circumstances.

4.3 Internal Control Evaluation Questionnaires (ICEQs)

In recent years many auditing firms have developed and implemented an evaluation technique more concerned with assessing whether specific errors (or frauds) are possible rather than establishing whether certain desirable controls are present.

This is achieved by reducing the control criteria for each transaction stream down to a handful of key questions (or control questions). The characteristic of these questions is that they concentrate on criteria that the controls present should fulfil.

The nature of an ICEQ can be illustrated by the following example.

Internal control evaluation questionnaire: control questions

The sales cycle

Is there reasonable assurance that:

(a) Sales are properly authorised?

(b) Sales are made to reliable payers?

(c) All goods despatched are invoiced?

(d) All invoices are properly prepared?

(e) All invoices are recorded?

(f) Invoices are properly supported?

(g) All credits to customers' accounts are valid?

(h) Cash and cheques received are properly recorded and deposited?

(i) Slow payers will be chased and that bad and doubtful debts will be provided against?

(j) All transactions are properly accounted for?

(k) Cash sales are properly dealt with?

(l) Sundry sales are controlled?

(m) At the period end the system will neither overstate nor understate debtors?

The purchases cycle

Is there reasonable assurance that:

(a) Goods or services could not be received without a liability being recorded?

(b) Receipt of goods or services is required in order to establish a liability?

(c) A liability will be recorded:

 (i) Only for authorised items; and
 (ii) At the proper amount?

(d) All payments are properly authorised?

(e) All credits due from suppliers are received?

(f) All transactions are properly accounted for?

(g) At the period end liabilities are neither overstated nor understated by the system?

(h) The balance at the bank is properly recorded at all times?

(i) Unauthorised cash payments could not be made and that the balance of petty cash is correctly stated at all times?

Each key control question is supported by detailed control points to be considered. For example, the detailed control points to be considered in relation to key control question (b) for the expenditure cycle (Is there reasonable assurance that receipt of goods or services is required to establish a liability?) are as follows.

(1) Is segregation of duties satisfactory?

(2) Are controls over relevant master files satisfactory?

(3) Is there a record that all goods received have been checked for:

- Weight or number?
- Quality and damage?

(4) Are all goods received entered in the detailed stock ledgers:

- By means of the goods received note?
- Or by means of purchase invoices?
- Are there, in a computerised system, sensible control totals (hash totals, money values and so on) to reconcile the stock system input with the creditors system?

(5) Are all invoices initialled to show that:

- Receipt of goods has been checked against the goods received records?
- Receipt of services has been verified by the person using it?
- Quality of goods has been checked against the inspection?

(6) In a computerised invoice approval system are there print-outs (examined by a responsible person) of:

- Cases where order, GRN and invoice are present but they are not equal ('equal' within predetermined tolerances of minor discrepancies)?
- Cases where invoices have been input but there is no corresponding GRN?

(7) Is there adequate control over direct purchases?

(8) Are receiving documents effectively cancelled (for example cross-referenced) to prevent their supporting two invoices?

Alternatively, ICEQ questions can be phrased so that the weakness which should be prevented by a key control is highlighted, such as the following.

Question	**Answer**	**Comments or explanation of 'yes' answer**
Can goods be sent to unauthorised suppliers?		

In these cases a 'yes' answer would require an explanation, rather than a 'no' answer.

4.4 Advantages and disadvantages of ICEQs

ICEQs have various advantages:

(a) Because they are drafted in terms of **objectives** rather than specific controls, they are easier to apply to a variety of systems than **ICQs**.

(b) Answering ICEQs should enable auditors to **identify the most important controls** which they are most likely to test during control testing.

(c) ICEQs can **highlight areas of weakness** where extensive substantive testing will be required.

However, the principal disadvantage is that they can be **drafted vaguely**, hence **misunderstood** and important controls not identified.

When the auditor discovers weaknesses or failings in the system, he will produce a report to management (sometimes called a management letter), which will point out the problems, the risks arising from it and the auditor's recommendations to eliminate the weakness. We cover these in detail in Chapter 29.

Chapter roundup

- The proper completion of working papers is fundamental to the recording of audits. They should show:
  - When and by whom the audit work was performed and reviewed
  - Details of the client
  - The year-end
  - The subject of the paper
- Working papers should also show:
  - The objectives of the work done
  - The sources of information
  - How any sample was selected and the sample size determined
  - The work done
  - A key to any audit ticks or symbols
  - Results obtained
  - Errors or other significant observations
  - Conclusions drawn
  - Key points highlighted
- Computerised working papers are being used more by auditors. Their main advantages are that they are neat and easy to update and the risk of errors is reduced.
- Auditors can use a number of methods to record accounting and control systems.
  - Narrative notes
  - Flowcharts
  - ICQs (which ask if various controls exist)
  - ICEQs (which ask if controls fulfil key objectives)
  - Checklists

Quick quiz

1 What is the main danger of using standardised working papers?

2 What does ISA 230 say about the confidentiality of working papers?

3 What is the main disadvantage of recording systems by means of manual narrative notes?

4 In what directions should a flowchart be prepared?

5 What is the main difference between ICQs and ICEQs?

Answers to quick quiz

1 The main danger of using standardised working papers is that they can mean auditors mechanically follow a standard approach to the audit without using professional judgement. (see para 1.1)

2 ISA 230 states that auditors should adopt appropriate procedures for maintaining the confidentiality and safe custody of working papers. (para 1.5)

3 The main disadvantage of manual narrative notes is that they can be difficult to change. (para 2.1)

4 Flowcharts should be prepared going from top to bottom and left to right on a page. (para 3.4)

5 ICQs concentrate on whether specific controls exist, whereas ICEQs concentrate on whether the control system has specific strengths or can prevent specific weaknesses. (para 4)

Answers to activities

1 Four benefits that auditors will obtain from preparing working papers that meet the requirement stated in the ISA are as follows.

(a) They provide a sufficient and appropriate record of the basis for the auditor's report.

(b) Evidence that the work was carried out in accordance with ISAs and applicable legal and regulatory requirements.

(c) Assisting the review and evaluation of the audit evidence obtained.

(d) Assisting the audit team to plan and perform the audit

(e) Assisting members of the audit team responsible for supervision to direct and supervise the audit work, and to discharge their review responsibilities

(f) Enabling the audit team to be accountable for its work

(g) Retaining a record of matters of continuing significance to future audits

(h) Enabling an experienced auditor to conduct quality control reviews and inspections

(i) Enabling an experienced auditor to conduct external inspections in accordance with applicable legal, regulatory or other requirements.

2 (a) Working papers should be headed with:

(i) The name of the client
(ii) The balance sheet date
(iii) The file reference of the working paper
(iv) The name of the person preparing the working paper
(v) The date the working paper was prepared
(vi) The subject of the working paper
(vii) The name of the person reviewing the working paper
(viii) The date of the review

BPP LEARNING MEDIA

NOTES

(b) Working papers should also show:

(i) The objective of the work done
(ii) The source of information
(iii) How any sample was selected and the sample size determined
(iv) The work done
(v) A key to any audit ticks or symbols
(vi) The results obtained
(vii) Analysis of errors or other significant observations
(viii) The conclusions drawn
(ix) The key points highlighted

Chapter 28 :

AUDIT EVIDENCE AND AUDIT PROCEDURES

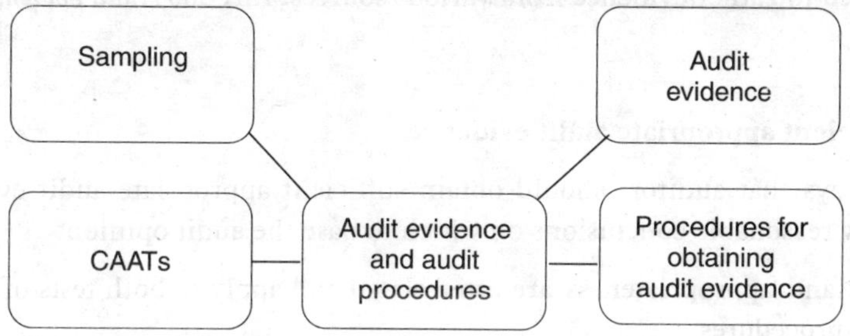

Introduction

It is the procedures carried out during the audit, and the obtaining of audit evidence, which ultimately enable the auditor to form an opinion and produce an audit report. The degree of evidence required and the procedures to be carried out will have been determined at the planning stage, as discussed in the previous chapter.

It is important to realise that the procedures and amount of evidence needed to come to a conclusion will differ from audit to audit (depending on the auditor's assessment of risk and materiality) and the auditor needs to be flexible and adaptable in his approach.

Learning objectives

In this chapter you will learn about the following.

(a) The different kinds of audit evidence

(b) The distinction between tests of control (compliance tests) and substantive procedures

(c) Tests of control and substantive procedures for a variety of accounting areas

(d) How computer assisted audit techniques can be used in the audit

(e) The factors considered when choosing a sample size and how to select an appropriate sample

BPP LEARNING MEDIA

1 AUDIT EVIDENCE

Definition

Audit evidence is the information auditors obtain in arriving at the conclusions on which their report is based.

In order to reach a position in which they can express a professional opinion, the auditors need to gather evidence from various sources. ISA 500 *Audit evidence* covers this area.

1.1 Sufficient appropriate audit evidence

ISA 500.2 says that auditors should obtain sufficient appropriate audit evidence to be able to draw reasonable conclusions on which to base the audit opinion.

'Sufficiency' and 'appropriateness' are interrelated and apply to both tests of controls and substantive procedures.

- **Sufficiency** is the measure of the **quantity** of audit evidence.
- **Appropriateness** is the measure of the **quality** or **reliability** of the audit evidence.

What constitutes sufficient appropriate audit evidence for the different types of audit tests - tests of control and substantive tests - relates to what auditors are trying to assess when carrying out these tests.

Definitions

Tests of control are tests to obtain audit evidence about the effective operation of the accounting and internal control systems, that is, that properly designed controls identified in the preliminary assessment of control risk exist in fact and have operated effectively throughout the relevant period.

Substantive procedures are tests to obtain audit evidence to detect material misstatements in the financial statements. They are generally of two types:

(a) Analytical procedures

(b) Other substantive procedures such as tests of detail of transactions and balances, review of minutes of directors' meetings and enquiry.

Activity 1 **(10 minutes)**

Can you state which of the following tests are tests of control and which are substantive procedures?

(a) Checking that invoices have been approved by the managing director

(b) Attending the year-end stocktake

(c) Reviewing accounting records after the year-end for events that affect this year's accounts

(d) Obtaining confirmation from the bank of balances held at the year-end

(e) Checking how unauthorised personnel are prevented from entering stock-rooms

(f) Checking if references are sought for all new major customers

Thus auditors are essentially looking for enough reliable audit evidence. Audit evidence usually indicates what is probable rather than what is definite (is usually persuasive rather then conclusive) so different sources are examined by the auditors. Auditors can only give reasonable assurance that the financial statements are free from misstatement, as not *all* sources of evidence will be examined.

The auditors' judgement as to what is sufficient appropriate audit evidence is influenced by various factors.

- Assessment of risk
- The nature of the accounting and internal control systems
- The materiality of the item being examined
- The experience gained during previous audits.
- The auditors' knowledge of the business and industry
- The results of audit procedures
- The source and reliability of information available

If they are unable to obtain sufficient appropriate audit evidence, the auditors may have to consider the effect on their audit report.

1.2 Tests of control

In seeking to obtain audit evidence from tests of control, auditors should consider the sufficiency and appropriateness of the audit evidence to support the assessed level of control risk.

There are two aspects of the relevant parts of the accounting and internal control systems about which auditors should seek to obtain audit evidence.

(a) **Design**: the accounting and internal control systems are designed so as to be capable of preventing or detecting material misstatements.

(b) **Operation**: the systems exist and have operated effectively throughout the relevant period.

For example, the auditor might carry out the following tests on ordering and granting of credit in the sales system.

- Check that references are being obtained for all new customers.
- Check that all new accounts on the sales ledger have been authorised by senior staff.
- Check that orders are only accepted from customers who are within their credit terms and credit limits.
- Check that customer orders are being matched with production orders and despatch notes.

1.3 Substantive procedures

In seeking to obtain audit evidence from substantive procedures, auditors should consider the extent to which that evidence together with any evidence from tests of controls supports the relevant financial statement assertions.

Substantive procedures are designed to obtain evidence about the financial statement assertions which are basically what the accounts say about the assets, liabilities and transactions of the client, and the events that affect the client's accounts.

Financial statement assertions are the representations of the directors that are embodied in the financial statements. By approving the financial statements, the directors are making representations about the information therein. These representations or assertions may be described in general terms in a number of ways.

ISA 500 states that 'the auditor should use assertions for **classes of transactions, account balances,** and **presentation and disclosures** in sufficient detail to form a basis for the assessment of risks of material misstatement and the design and performance of further audit procedures'. It gives examples of assertions in these areas.

Assertions used by the auditor	
Assertions about **classes of transactions** and events for the period under audit	**Occurrence**: transactions and events that have been recorded have occurred and pertain to the entity. **Completeness**: all transactions and events that should have been recorded have been recorded. **Accuracy**: amounts and other data relating to recorded transactions and events have been recorded appropriately. **Cut-off**: transactions and events have been recorded in the correct accounting period. **Classification**: transactions and events have been recorded in the proper accounts.
Assertions about **account balances** at the period-end	**Existence**: assets, liabilities and equity interests exist. **Rights and obligations**: the entity holds or controls the rights to assets, and liabilities are the obligations of the entity. **Completeness**: all assets, liabilities and equity interests that should have been recorded have been recorded. **Valuation and allocation**: assets, liabilities, and equity interests are included in the financial statements at appropriate amounts and any resulting valuation or allocation adjustments are appropriately recorded.

NOTES

Assertions used by the auditor	
Assertions about **presentation and disclosure**	**Occurrence and rights and obligations**: disclosed events, transactions and other matters have occurred and pertain to the entity. **Completeness**: all disclosures that should have been included in the financial statements have been included. **Classification and understandability**: financial information is appropriately presented and described, and disclosures are clearly expressed. **Accuracy and valuation**: financial and other information are disclosed fairly and at appropriate amounts.

1.4 Reliability of evidence

(i) *Evidence originated by the auditors*

Evidence originated by the auditors is in general the most reliable type of audit evidence because there is little risk that it can be manipulated by management.

Examples

(1) Analytical procedures, such as the calculation of ratios and trends in order to examine unusual variations

(2) Physical inspection or observation, such as attendance at physical stock counts

(3) Re-performance of calculations making up figures in the accounts, such as the computation of total stock values

(ii) *Evidence created by third parties*

Third party evidence is more reliable than client-produced evidence to the extent that it is obtained from independent sources. Its reliability will be reduced if it is obtained from sources which are not independent, or if there is a risk that client personnel may be able to and have reason to suppress or manipulate it. This, for instance, is an argument against having replies to circularisations sent to the client instead of the auditors.

Examples

(1) Circularisation of trade debtors or creditors, confirmation of bank balances.

(2) Reports produced by experts, such as property valuations, actuarial valuations, legal opinions. In evaluating such evidence, the auditors need to take into account the expert's qualifications, independence and the terms of reference for the work.

(3) Documents held by the client which were issued by third parties, such as invoices, price lists and statements. These may sometimes be manipulated by the client and so are less reliable than confirmations received directly.

BPP LEARNING MEDIA

(iii) *Evidence created by management*

The auditors cannot place the same degree of reliance on evidence produced by client management as on that produced outside the company. However, it will often be necessary to place some reliance on such evidence. The auditors will need to obtain audit evidence that the information supplied is complete and accurate, and apply judgement in doing so, taking into account previous experience of the client's reliability and the extent to which the client's representations appear compatible with other audit findings, as well as the materiality of the item under discussion.

Examples

(1) The company's accounting records and supporting schedules. Although these are prepared by management, the auditors have a statutory right to examine such records in full: this right enhances the quality of this information.

(2) The client's explanations of, for instance, apparently unusual fluctuations in results. Such evidence requires interpretation by the auditors and, being oral evidence, only limited reliance can be placed upon it.

(3) Information provided to the auditors about the internal control system. The auditors need to check that this information is accurate and up-to-date, and that it does not simply describe an idealised system which is not adhered to in practice.

(b) **General considerations in evaluating audit evidence**

Audit evidence will often not be wholly conclusive. The auditors must obtain evidence which is **sufficient and appropriate** to form the basis for their audit conclusions. The evidence gathered should also be **relevant** to those conclusions, and sufficiently **reliable** to form the basis for the audit opinion. The auditors must exercise skill and judgement to ensure that evidence is correctly interpreted and that only valid inferences are drawn from it.

Certain general principles can be stated. **Written evidence** is preferable to oral evidence; **independent evidence** obtained from outside the organisation is more reliable than that obtained internally; and **evidence generated by the auditors** is more reliable than that obtained from others.

2 PROCEDURES FOR OBTAINING AUDIT EVIDENCE

2.1 How evidence is obtained

Audit evidence is usually obtained for assets, liabilities and transactions to support each financial statement assertion and evidence from one does not compensate for failure to obtain evidence for another. However, audit procedures may provide audit evidence of more than one assertion.

NOTES

Auditors obtain evidence by one or more of the following procedures.

PROCEDURES	
Inspection of assets	Inspection of assets that are recorded in the accounting records confirms existence, gives evidence of valuation, but does not confirm rights and obligations. Confirmation that assets seen are recorded in accounting records gives evidence of completeness.
Inspection of documentation	Confirmation to documentation of items recorded in accounting records confirms that an asset exists or a transaction occurred. Confirmation that items recorded in supporting documentation are recorded in accounting records tests completeness. Cut-off can be verified by inspecting the reverse population ie checking transactions recorded after the balance sheet date to supporting documentation to confirm that they occurred after the balance sheet date. Inspection also provides evidence of valuation/measurement, rights and obligations and the nature of items (presentation and disclosure). It can also be used to compare documents (and hence test consistency of audit evidence) and confirm authorisation.
Observation	This involves watching a procedure being performed (for example, post opening). It is of limited use, as it only confirms the procedure took place when the auditor was watching.
Inquiry	This involves seeking information from client staff or external sources. Strength of evidence depends on the knowledge and integrity of the source of the information.
Confirmation	This involves seeking confirmation from another source of details in client's accounting records eg, confirmation from bank of bank balances.
Recalculation	Checking arithmetic of client's records for example, adding up ledger account.
Reperformance	Independently executing procedures or controls, either manually or through the use of computer assisted audit techniques (CAATs, see next section).
Analytical procedures	Evaluating and comparing financial and/or non-financial data for plausible relationships.

Activity 2 **(30 minutes)**

The examination of evidence is fundamental to the audit process. ISA 500 *Audit evidence* states that: 'the auditors should obtain sufficient appropriate audit evidence to be able to draw reasonable conclusions on which to base the audit opinion'. Evidence is available to the auditors from sources under their own control, from the management of the company and from third parties. Each of these sources presents the auditors with differing considerations as to the quality of the evidence so produced.

Tasks

(a) Discuss the quality of the following types of audit evidence, giving two examples of each form of evidence.

(i) Evidence originated by the auditors
(ii) Evidence created by third parties
(iii) Evidence created by the management of the client

(b) Describe the general considerations which the auditors must bear in mind when evaluating audit evidence.

3 COMPUTER-ASSISTED AUDIT TECHNIQUES (CAATs)

Computer-based accounting systems allow auditors to use either the client's computer or another computer during their audit work. Techniques performed with computers in this way are known as Computer Assisted Audit Techniques (CAATs).

There is no mystique about using CAATs to help with auditing.

(a) Most modern accounting systems allow data to be manipulated in various ways and extracted into a **report**.

(b) Even if reporting capabilities are limited, the data can often be exported directly into a **spreadsheet** package (sometimes using simple Windows-type cut and paste facilities in modern systems) and then analysed.

(c) Most systems have **searching** facilities that are much quicker to use than searching through print-outs by hand.

There are a variety of packages specially designed either to ease the auditing task itself, or to carry out audit interrogations of computerised data automatically. There are also a variety of ways of testing the processing that is carried out.

Auditors can use PCs such as laptops that are independent of the organisation's systems when performing CAATs.

3.1 Types of CAAT

There are various types of CAAT.

(a) **Audit interrogation software** is a computer program used for audit purposes to examine the content of the client's computer files.

(b) **Test data** is data used by the auditors for computer processing to test the operation of the client's computer programs.

(c) **Embedded audit facilities** are elements set up by the auditor which are included within the client's computer system. They allow the possibility of continuous checking.

3.2 Audit interrogation software

Interrogation software performs the sort of checks on data that auditors might otherwise have to perform by hand. Its use is particularly appropriate during substantive testing of transactions and especially balances. By using audit software, the auditors may scrutinise large volumes of data and concentrate skilled manual resources on the investigation of results, rather than on the extraction of information.

3.3 Test data

An obvious way of seeing whether a system is **processing** data in the way that it should be is to input some test data and see what happens. The expected results can be calculated in advance and then compared with the results that actually arise.

The problem with test data is that any resulting corruption of the data files has to be corrected. This is difficult with modern real-time systems, which often have built in (and highly desirable) controls to ensure that data entered *cannot* easily be removed without leaving a mark. Consequently test data is used less and less as a CAAT.

3.4 Embedded audit facilities

The results of using test data would, in any case, be completely distorted if the programs used to process it were not the ones *normally* used for processing. For example a fraudulent member of the IT department might substitute a version of the program that gave the correct results, purely for the duration of the test, and then replace it with a version that siphoned off the company's funds into his own bank account.

To allow a **continuous** review of the data recorded and the manner in which it is treated by the system, it may be possible to use CAATs referred to as 'embedded audit facilities'.

An embedded facility consists of audit modules that are incorporated into the computer element of the enterprise's accounting system.

EXAMPLES OF EMBEDDED AUDIT FACILITIES	
Integrated test facility (ITF)	Creates a **fictitious entity** within the company application, where transactions are posted to it alongside regular transactions, and actual results of fictitious entity compared with what it should have produced
Systems control and review file (SCARF)	Allows auditors to have transactions above a **certain amount** from **specific ledger account** posted to a file for later auditor review

3.5 Simulation

Simulation (or 'parallel simulation') entails the preparation of a separate program that simulates the processing of the organisation's real system. Real data can then be passed not only through the system proper but also through the simulated program. For example the simulation program may be used to re-perform controls such as those used to identify any missing items from a sequence.

3.6 Knowledge-based systems

Decision support systems and expert systems can be used to assist with the auditors' own judgement and decisions.

3.7 Planning CAATs

In certain circumstances the auditors will need to use CAATs in order to obtain the evidence they require, whereas in other circumstances they may use CAATs to improve the efficiency or effectiveness of the audit.

In choosing the appropriate combination of CAATs and manual procedures, the auditors will need to take the following points into account.

(a) Computer programs often perform functions of which **no visible evidence** is available. In these circumstances it will frequently not be practicable for the auditors to perform tests manually.

(b) In many audit situations the auditors will have the choice of performing a test either **manually** or with the **assistance of a CAAT**. In making this choice, they will be influenced by the respective efficiency of the alternatives, which is influenced by a number of factors.

   (i) The extent of tests of controls or substantive procedures achieved by both alternatives

   (ii) The pattern of cost associated with the CAAT

   (iii) The ability to incorporate within the use of the CAAT a number of different audit tests

(c) Sometimes auditors will need to report within a comparatively **short time-scale**. In such cases it may be more efficient to use CAATs because they are quicker to apply.

(d) If using a CAAT, auditors should ensure that the **required computer facilities, computer files** and **programs are available**.

(e) The operation of some CAATs requires **frequent attendance** or access by the auditors.

3.8 Controlling CAATs

Where CAATs are used, however, particular attention should be paid to the need to **co-ordinate the work of staff** with specialist computer skills with the work of others engaged on the audit. The **technical work** should be **approved** and **reviewed** by someone with the necessary computer expertise.

3.9 Audit trails

The original purpose of an **audit trail** was to preserve details of all stages of processing on *paper*. This meant that transactions could be followed stage-by-stage through a system to ensure that they had been processed correctly.

3.10 Around the computer?

Traditionally, therefore, it was widely considered that auditors could fulfil their function without having any detailed knowledge of what was going on inside the computer.

The auditors would commonly audit '**round the computer**', ignoring the procedures which take place within the computer programs and concentrating solely on the input and corresponding output. Audit procedures would include checking authorisation, coding and control totals of input and checking the output with source documents and clerical control totals.

3.11 Through the computer

The 'round the computer approach' is now frowned upon. Typical audit problems that arise as audit trails move further away from the hard copy trail include testing computer generated totals when no detailed analysis is available and testing the completeness of output in the absence of control totals. One of the principal problems facing the auditors is that of acquiring an understanding of the workings of electronic data processing and of the computer itself.

Auditors now customarily audit '**through the computer**'. This involves an examination of the detailed processing routines of the computer to determine whether the controls in the system are adequate to ensure complete and correct processing of all data. In these situations it will often be necessary to employ computer assisted audit techniques.

Activity 3 **(15 minutes)**

(a) What is meant by the term 'loss of audit trail' in the context of computerised accounting procedures?

(b) How can auditors gain assurance about the operation of computerised accounting procedures given the 'loss of audit trail'?

4 AUDIT SAMPLING

ISA 530 *Audit sampling and other means of testing* covers this topic in depth.

This ISA is based on the premise that auditors do not normally examine all the information available to them; it would be impractical to do so and using audit sampling will produce valid conclusions.

Definition

Audit sampling is the application of audit procedures to less than 100% of the items within an account balance or class of transactions such that all the sampling units have an equal chance of selection. This will enable the auditor to obtain and evaluate audit evidence about some characteristic of the items selected in order to form or assist in forming a conclusion concerning the population from which the sample is drawn. Audit sampling can use either a statistical or non-statistical approach.

NOTES

Definitions

Sampling units are the individual items constituting the population.

Error is an unintentional mistake in the financial statements.

Tolerable error is the maximum error in the population that the auditors are willing to accept.

Sampling risk is the possibility that the auditors' conclusion, based on a sample, may be different from the conclusion that would be reached if the entire population was subject to the same audit procedure.

Non-sampling risk arises from factors that cause the auditor to reach an erroneous conclusion for any reason not related to the size of the sample.

The ISA points out that some testing procedures do *not* involve sampling.

(a) Testing 100% of items in a population (this should be obvious)

(b) Testing all items with a certain characteristic (eg over a certain value) as selection is not representative

The ISA distinguishes between **statistically based sampling,** which invoives the use of techniques from which mathematically constructed conclusions about the population can be drawn, and **non-statistical or judgmental methods,** from which auditors draw a judgmental opinion about the population. However, the principles of the ISA apply to both methods.

4.1 Design of the sample

Audit objectives

Auditors must consider the **specific audit objectives** to be achieved and the audit procedures which are most likely to achieve them.

The auditors also need to consider the **nature and characteristics** of the **audit evidence** sought and **possible error conditions**. This will help them to define what constitutes an error and what population to use for sampling.

Furthermore auditors must consider the **level of error** they are prepared to accept and **how confident** they wish to be that the population does not contain an error rate greater than what is acceptable.

Thus for a test of controls auditors may wish to be 95% confident that controls have failed to work on no more than 3 occasions. For a substantive test of fixed assets, they may wish to be 90% confident that fixed assets are not mis-stated by more than £10,000.

The % confidence auditors wish to have is the '**confidence level**' and it is related to the degree of audit risk auditors are prepared to accept.

Population

The population from which the sample is drawn must be **appropriate** and **complete** for the specific audit objectives.

BPP LEARNING MEDIA

4.2 Sample size

When determining sample sizes, auditors should consider sampling risk, the amount of error that would be acceptable and the extent to which they expect to find errors.

4.3 Sampling risk

Sampling risk is encountered by the auditors in both tests of control and substantive procedures. It is the risk of drawing a **wrong conclusion** from audit sampling. It is part of detection risk.

For tests of control, drawing a wrong conclusion means making an **incorrect assessment** (too high or too low) of **control risk**. For substantive procedures it means either stating a population is **materially mis-stated when it is not**, or stating a population is **not materially mis-stated when it is.**

The **greater** their reliance on the results of the procedure in question, the **lower** the sampling risk auditors will be willing to accept and the **larger** the sample size needs to be.

Thus if inherent risk is high, control risk is high and sampling is the only substantive procedure auditors are carrying out, then auditors are placing maximum reliance on sampling. Hence the level of sampling risk auditors will be prepared to accept will be at minimum, and sample sizes will be high.

4.4 Tolerable error

For **tests of control,** the tolerable error is the **maximum rate of deviation** from a control that auditors are willing to accept in the population and still conclude that the preliminary assessment of control risk is valid. Often this rate will be very low, since the auditor is likely to be concentrating on testing important controls.

Sometimes even a single failure of an important control will cause auditors to reject their assessment of control risk. If for example, an important control is that all major capital expenditure is approved by the board, failure to approve expenditure on one item may be an unacceptable deviation as far as the auditors are concerned.

For substantive procedures, the **tolerable error** is the **maximum monetary error** in an account balance or class of transactions, that auditors are willing to accept so that when the results of all audit procedures are considered, they are able to conclude with reasonable assurance, that the financial statements are not materially mis-stated.

Sometimes the tolerable error rate will be the materiality rate. Some accounting firms set tolerable error as being a fixed percentage of materiality, say 50% or 70% for reasons of prudence.

4.5 Expected error

Larger samples will be required when errors are expected than would be required if none were expected, in order to conclude that the *actual* error is *less* than the *tolerable* error. If the expected error rate is high then sampling may not be appropriate and auditors may have to examine 100% of a population.

4.6 Selection of the sample

Auditors should select sample items in such a way that the sample can be expected to be representative of the population in respect of the characteristics being tested.

For a sample to be representative of the population, all items in the population are required to have an equal or known probability of being selected.

There are a number of selection methods available, but the ISA identifies four that are commonly used.

(a) Use of a computerised **random number generator** ensures that all items in the population have an equal chance of selection, alternatively random number tables can be used.

(b) **Systematic selection** (or interval sampling) involves selecting items using a constant interval between selections, the first interval having a random start.

Suppose the auditors decide to pick every 50th item and start at random at item number 11. They will then pick item number 61 (11 + 50), item number 111 (11 + (50 × 2)), item number 161 (11 + (50 × 3)) and so on. Auditors must when using this method, guard against the risk of errors occurring systematically in such a way as not to be detected by sampling. In our example this could be errors occurring at item number 41, 91, 141, 191 etc.

(c) **Haphazard selection** involves auditors choosing items subjectively without using formal random methods but also avoiding bias. The biggest danger of haphazard selection is that bias does in fact occur. Auditors may for example end up choosing items that are easily located, and these may not be representative. Haphazard selection is more likely to be used when auditors are using judgmental rather than statistical sampling.

(d) **Block selection** involves selecting a block of contiguous items from within the population. However, this method is not recommended as it is not statistically based which means that results from testing cannot be used to determine any population error.

In addition the auditors may also consider for certain tests:

(a) **Stratification.** This involves division of the population into a number of parts. Each sampling unit can only belong to one, specifically designed, stratum. The idea is that each stratum will contain items which have significant characteristics in common. This enables the auditors to direct audit effort towards items which, for example, contain the greatest potential monetary error.

(b) **Selection by value** is selecting the largest items within a population. This will only be appropriate if auditors believe that the size of the item is related to the risk of the item being seriously misstated.

(c) **Sequence sampling** may be used to check whether certain items have particular characteristics. For example an auditor may use a sample of 50 consecutive cheques to check whether cheques are signed by authorised signatories rather than picking 50 single cheques throughout the year.

Sequence sampling may however produce samples that are not representative of the population as a whole particularly if errors occurred only during a certain part of the year.

Certain items may be tested because they are considered unusual, for example debit balances on a purchase ledger or a nil balance with a major supplier.

4.7 Statistical and judgmental sampling

As mentioned above, auditors need to decide when sampling whether to use statistical or non-statistical methods. Statistical sampling means using statistical theory to measure the impact of sampling risk and evaluate the sample results. Non-statistical sampling relies on judgement to evaluate results.

Whether statistical or non-statistical methods are used, auditors will still have to take account of risk, tolerable and expected error, and population value for substantive tests when deciding on sample sizes.

If these conditions are present, **statistical sampling** normally has the following **advantages**.

(a) At the conclusion of a test the auditors are able to state with a **definite level of confidence** that the whole population conforms to the sample result, within a stated precision limit.

(b) **Sample size** is **objectively determined**, having regard to the degree of risk the auditors are prepared to accept for each application.

(c) The process of fixing required precision and confidence levels compels the auditors to consider and **clarify their audit objectives**.

(d) The **results of tests** can be **expressed** in precise **mathematical terms**.

(e) **Bias is eliminated**.

4.8 Evaluation of sample results

Having carried out, on each sample item, those audit procedures which are appropriate to the particular audit objective, auditors should:

(a) analyse any errors detected in the sample; and
(b) draw inferences for the population as a whole.

4.9 Analysis of errors in the sample

To begin with, the auditors must consider whether the items in question are **true errors**, as they defined them before the test, eg a misposting between customer accounts will not count as an error as far as total debtors are concerned.

Assuming the problems are errors, auditors should consider the **nature and cause** of the error and any possible **effects** the error might have on other parts of the audit.

4.10 Inferences to be drawn from the population as a whole

The auditors should project the error results from the sample on to the relevant population. The projection method should be consistent with the method used to select the sampling unit. The auditors will estimate the **probable error** in the population by extrapolating the errors found in the sample. They will then estimate any **further error** that might not have been detected because of the imprecision of the sampling technique (in addition to consideration of the nature and effects of the errors).

The auditors should then compare the **projected population error** (net of adjustments made by the entity in the case of substantive procedures) to the **tolerable error,** taking account of other audit procedures relevant to the specific control or financial statement assertion.

If the projected population error *exceeds* tolerable error, then the auditors should **re-assess sampling risk**. If it is unacceptable, they should consider **extending auditing procedures** or **performing alternative procedures,** either of which may result in a proposed adjustment to the financial statements.

4.11 Summary

Key stages in the sampling process are as follows.

- Determining objectives and population
- Determining sample size
- Choosing method of sample selection
- Analysing the results and projecting errors

Activity 4 **(15 minutes)**

Describe three commonly-used methods of sample selection and describe the main risks involved in using each method.

Chapter roundup

- The auditors must be able to evaluate all types of audit evidence in terms of its sufficiency and appropriateness.
- Evidence can be in the form of tests of controls or substantive procedures.
- Tests of control concentrate on the design and operation of controls.
- Substantive testing aims to test all the financial statement assertions, including:
  - Existence
  - Rights and obligations (ownership)
  - Occurrence
  - Completeness
  - Valuation
  - Measurement
  - Presentation and disclosure

  These can be applied to specific account balances eg fixed assets.
- The reliability of audit evidence is influenced by its source and by its nature eg circularisation of debtors provides third party evidence.

Chapter roundup continued

- Audit evidence can be obtained by the following techniques.
  - Inspection
  - Observation eg attendance at a stocktake
  - Enquiry and confirmation
  - Computation
  - Analytical procedures
- Auditors may use a number of computer assisted audit techniques including audit interrogation software, test data and embedded audit facilities.
- The main stages of audit sampling are:
  - Design of the sample
  - Selection of the sample
  - Evaluation of sample results
- Sample sizes for tests of control are influenced by sampling risk, tolerable error rate and expected error rate.
- Sample sizes for substantive tests are influenced by inherent, control and detection risk, tolerable error rate, expected error rate, population value and stratification.
- Sample items can be picked by a variety of means including random selection, systematic selection and haphazard selection.
- When evaluating results, auditors should:
  - Analyse any errors considering their amount and the reasons why they have occurred
  - Draw conclusions for the population as a whole

Quick quiz

1 What does ISA 500 say about the evidence that auditors should obtain?

2 When auditors are testing controls, about which two aspects are they seeking evidence?

3 Of which type of audit procedure are the following examples?

(a) Physical check of fixed assets

(b) Watching the payment of wages

(c) Receiving a letter from the client's bank concerning balances held at the bank by the client

(d) Adding up the client's trial balance

4 What tasks are most important in controlling the use of CAATs?

5 What is the difference between auditing round the computer and auditing through the computer?

6 Define:

(a) Error
(b) Tolerable error
(c) Sampling risk

7 Summarise the factors that affect sample sizes for substantive tests.

Answers to quick quiz

1 ISA 500 states that auditors should obtain sufficient appropriate audit evidence to be able to draw reasonable conclusions on which to base their opinion. (see para 1.1)

2 When testing controls, auditors are concentrating on their design and operation. (para 1.2)

3 (a) Inspection
(b) Observation
(c) Confirmation
(d) Computation (para 2)

4 The most important tasks in controlling the use of CAATs are:

(a) Co-ordination of the work of specialist computer staff with the rest of the audit team

(b) Approval and review of the work by someone with the necessary computer experience (para 3.8)

5 Auditing 'round the computer' involves comparisons of input and output, neglecting procedures that take place within the computer.

Auditing 'through the computer' involves examination of the detailed routines that take place within the computer. (para 3.10)

6 (a) An error is an unintentional mistake in the financial statements.

(b) Tolerable error is the maximum error in the population that auditors are willing to accept and still conclude the audit objectives have been achieved.

(c) Sampling risk is the risk that the auditors' conclusion, based on a sample, may be different from the conclusion that would be reached if the entire population was subject to the audit procedure. (para 4)

7 Factors that affect the sample sizes of substantive tests are:

(a) Inherent risk
(b) Control risk
(c) Detection risk
(d) Tolerable error rate
(e) Expected error rate
(f) Population value
(g) Number of items (in small population) (para 4)

Stratification may also lead to smaller sample sizes.

Answers to activities

1 (a) Control
(b) Substantive
(c) Substantive
(d) Substantive
(e) Control
(f) Control

2 (a) (i) There is little risk that evidence originated by the auditors can be manipulated by management. It is therefore, in general, the most reliable type of audit evidence. Examples include the following.

(1) Analytical procedures, such as the calculation of ratios and trends in order to examine unusual variations

(2) Physical inspection or observation, such as attendance at physical stocktakes or inspection of a fixed asset

(3) Re-performance of calculations making up figures in the accounts, such as the computation of total stock values

(ii) Third party evidence is more reliable than client-produced evidence to the extent that it is obtained from sources independent of the client. Its reliability will be reduced if it is obtained from sources which are not independent, or if there is a risk that client personnel may be able to and have reason to suppress or manipulate it. This, for instance, is an argument against having replies to circularisations sent to the client instead of the auditors.

Examples of third party evidence include the following.

(1) Circularisation of debtors or creditors and other requests from the auditors for confirming evidence, such as requests for confirmation of bank balances.

(2) Reports produced by experts, such as property valuations, actuarial valuations, legal opinions. In evaluating such evidence, the auditors need to take into account the qualifications of the expert, his or her independence of the client and the terms of reference under which the work was carried out.

(3) Documents held by the client which were issued by third parties, such as invoices, price lists and statements. These may sometimes be manipulated by the client, to the extent that items may be suppressed or altered, and to this extent they are less reliable than confirmations received direct.

(iii) The auditors cannot place the same degree of reliance on evidence produced by client management as on that produced outside the client organisation. It will, however, often be necessary to place some reliance on the client's evidence. The auditors will need to apply judgement in doing so, taking into account previous experience of the client's reliability and the extent to which the client's representations appear compatible with other audit findings, as well as the materiality of the item under discussion. Examples of evidence originating from client management include the following.

(1) The company's accounting records and supporting schedules. Although these are prepared by management, the auditors have a statutory right to examine such records in full: this right enhances the quality of this information.

(2) The client's explanations of, for instance, apparently unusual fluctuations in results. Such evidence requires interpretation by the auditors and, being oral evidence, only limited reliance can be placed upon it.

(3) Information provided to the auditors about the internal control system. The auditors need to check that this information is accurate and up-to-date, and that it does not simply describe an idealised system which is not adhered to in practice.

(b) Audit evidence will often not be wholly conclusive. The auditors must obtain evidence which is sufficient and appropriate to form the basis for their audit conclusions. The evidence gathered should also be relevant to those conclusions, and sufficiently reliable ultimately to form the basis for the audit opinion. The auditors must exercise skill and judgement to ensure that evidence is correctly interpreted and that only valid inferences are drawn from it.

Certain general principles can be stated. Written evidence is preferable to oral evidence; independent evidence obtained from outside the organisation is more reliable than that obtained internally; and that evidence generated by the auditors is more reliable than that obtained from others.

3 (a) Loss of audit trail means that auditors do not have full details of the accounting process that goes on within the computer, and cannot therefore check that process for accuracy. In addition auditors cannot be sure that the output of the computer is complete. Certain procedures may also take place entirely within the computer without any visible evidence.

(b) Auditors can overcome the loss of audit trail in the following ways.

(i) Placing reliance on application and general controls. Application controls such as check digit verification or record counts can give assurance on the completeness and accuracy of processing. General controls can give assurance that the programs run have been developed properly and access to those programs is limited.

(ii) Audit interrogation software can be used to reperform reconciliations, analyse accounts and identify items which do not fulfil criteria set down by the auditors and may therefore be subject to fraud.

(iii) Test data can be used to see whether the system produces the results expected.

(iv) Likewise an integrated test facility, involving the creation of a fictitious department, can be used to test the operation of processes.

(v) The results of processing can be subject to analytical review, comparisons with previous years, budgets etc.

(vi) Similarly the results of processing can be compared with other audit evidence, for example computer stock balances being compared with actual stock counts.

(vii) Procedures can be reperformed manually but this is very time-consuming.

4 (a) **Random selection** involves using random number tables or other methods to select items. Random selection means that bias cannot affect the sample chosen; it means that all items in the population have an equal chance of being chosen.

However, if the auditors are more concerned about some items than others, they can modify their approach, either by selecting certain items automatically because they are above a certain value, and selecting the rest of the sample by random numbers, or by stratifying the sample.

(b) **Systematic selection** involves selecting items using a constant interval between selections, the first interval having a random start.

The main danger is that errors occur systematically in a pattern that means that none of the items in error will be selected.

(c) **Haphazard selection** involves auditors choosing items subjectively without using formal random methods but avoiding bias.

The main danger is that bias (conscious or unconscious) does affect the auditor's judgement, and that certain items are selected because for example they are easy to obtain.

Chapter 29 :
AUDIT REPORTS AND AUDITORS' LIABILITY

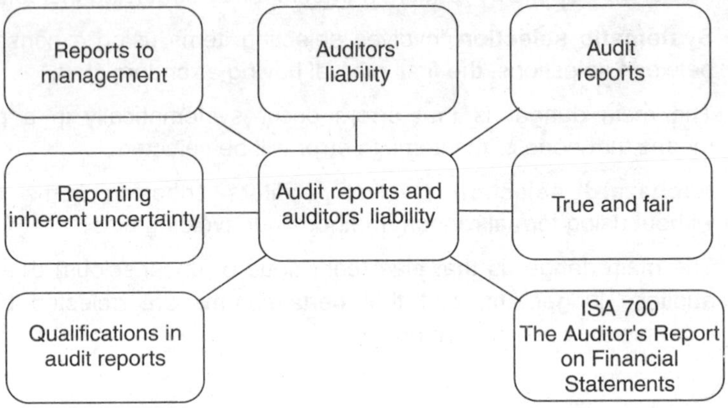

Introduction

The **audit report** is the means by which the external auditors express their opinion on the **truth and fairness** of a company's financial statements. This is for the benefit principally of the shareholders, but also for other users as the audit report is usually kept on public record, with the filed financial statements.

As we have seen, many of the contents of the auditor's report are prescribed by statute. They are also subject to professional requirements in the form of ISA 700 *The Auditor's report on financial statements.* This makes it extremely different from the private reports to management auditors produce which we will look at in more detail at the end of this chapter.

There are two key differences between the report to the shareholders and the report to management:

- Purpose
- Understandability

The **purpose** of the publicised audit report is, as you know, to report to the **shareholders** on whether the accounts show a **true and fair view.** The private reports are for the purposes of directors and management.

The second issue is that of **understandability**, how the purpose and conclusion of the public report is **communicated** to shareholders. Directors and management work in the business, the report submitted to them may well be more meaningful to them than the audit report is to more isolated shareholders. We discussed the expectations gap in Chapter 25.

BPP LEARNING MEDIA

Learning objectives

In this chapter you will learn about the following.

(a) Unqualified audit reports

(b) The meaning of the phrase 'true and fair'

(c) ISA 700 on the Auditor's Report on Financial Statements

(d) Qualifications in audit reports

(e) The liability of the auditor to those relying on the financial statements

(f) The auditors' report to management

1 AUDIT REPORTS

The audit report is the end product of the auditor's work, whether the audit took a week, in the case of a small company, or a number of months, in the case of a large conglomerate. The content and format of the audit report are set out in law, reflecting its importance.

1.1 Unqualified reports

An **unqualified** audit report communicates an assurance to the user, that an independent examination of the accounts has discovered no material problems and that the accounts show a '**true and fair view**'. We will discuss truth and fairness in the next section of this chapter.

An unqualified report also conveys certain implications. These are unstated because the auditors only report **by exception**. In other words, these assumptions will only be mentioned (by a **qualified** audit report) if they do not hold true. An unqualified report implies that (under s 237 Companies Act 1985):

(a) **Proper accounting records** have been kept and proper returns adequate for the audit received from branches not visited.

(b) The **accounts** agree with the **accounting records** and **returns.**

(c) **All information and explanations** have been **received** as the auditors think necessary and they have had access at all times to the company's books, accounts and vouchers.

(d) **Details** of **directors' emoluments** and **other benefits** have been correctly **disclosed** in the financial statements.

(e) Particulars of **loans** and **other transactions** in favour of **directors** and others have been correctly disclosed in the financial statements.

2 TRUE AND FAIR

The accounts of a limited company are required by s 226(2) of the Companies Act 1985 to show a **true and fair view** of the company's financial position as at the balance sheet date and of its profit or loss for the year ending on that date. The auditors are required to state in their report whether, in their opinion, the accounts satisfy that requirement.

Most commentators give definitions of truth and fairness along the following lines.

Definitions

> **True:** Information is factual and conforms with reality, not false. In addition the information conforms with required standards and law. The accounts have been correctly extracted from the books and records.
>
> **Fair:** Information is free from discrimination and bias and in compliance with expected standards and rules. The accounts should reflect the commercial substance of the company's underlying transactions.

3 ISA 700 THE AUDITOR'S REPORT ON FINANCIAL STATEMENTS

3.1 Main provisions of ISA 700

Auditors' reports on financial statements should contain a clear expression of opinion, based on review and assessment of the conclusions drawn from evidence obtained in the course of the audit.

The auditors' report should be placed before the financial statements. The directors' responsibilities statement (explained later) should be placed before the auditors' report.

3.2 Basic elements of the auditors' report

> ISA 700 explains the contents of a basic auditors report as follows:

Basic elements of audit report	Explanation
Title	The title should indicate that the report is by an **independent** auditor to confirm all the relevant ethical standards have been met.
Addressee	The addressee will be determined by national law, but is likely to be the **shareholders** or **board of directors**.
Introductory paragraph	This should identify the entity being audited, state that the financial statements have been audited, identify the financial statements being audited (for example, profit and loss account, balance sheet, cash flow statement and the period they cover), specify the date and period covered by the financial statements. The auditor may be able to refer to specific page numbers if the financial statements are contained in a larger report.

Basic elements of audit report	Explanation
Statement of management's responsibility	The report must contain a statement that management is responsible for the presentation of the financial statements. This responsibility includes designing, implementing and maintaining internal controls, selecting appropriate accounting policies and making reasonable accounting estimates.
Statement of auditor's responsibility	The report must state that the auditor is responsible for expressing an opinion on the financial statements. The auditor should distinguish his duties from the relevant responsibilities of those charged with governance by referring to the summary of the responsibilities of those charged with governance contained elsewhere in the published information. If this information has not been published elsewhere, the auditor should include it in the report.
Scope paragraph	The scope paragraph should explain that the auditor adhered to international standards on auditing and ethical requirements and that he planned and performed the audit so as to obtain reasonable assurance that the financial statements are free from material misstatements. The report should describe the audit as including: (a) Examining, on a test basis, evidence to support the financial statement amounts and disclosures (b) Assessing the accounting policies used in the preparation of the financial statements (c) Assessing the significant estimates made by management in the preparation of the financial statements (d) Evaluating the overall financial statement presentation The scope paragraph should also include a statement by the auditor that the audit provides a reasonable basis for the opinion.

Basic elements of audit report	Explanation
Opinion paragraph	If the auditor concludes that the financial statements give a true and fair view, he should express an **unqualified** opinion. An unqualified opinion states that the financial statements give a true and fair view or present fairly, in all material respects, in accordance with the applicable financial reporting framework. It should clearly indicate the financial reporting framework used, and, if IFRSs are not used, the country of origin of the framework, such as UK accounting standards. In addition the auditor must state his opinion whether the directors' report is consistent with the financial statements.
Date of the report	The report must be dated. This date shows the completion date of the audit and should not be before management has approved the financial statements.
Auditor's address	The location where the auditor practises must be included. This is usually the city where the auditor has his office.
Auditor's signature	The report must contain the auditor's signature, whether this is the auditor's own name or the audit firm's name.

EXAMPLE

The following is an example of an unqualified audit report in the UK.

Example 1. Unqualified opinion: company incorporated in Great Britain

INDEPENDENT AUDITOR'S REPORT TO THE SHAREHOLDERS OF XYZ LIMITED

We have audited the financial statements of XYZ Limited for the year ended … which comprise [state the primary financial statements such as the profit and loss account, the balance sheet, the cash flow statement, the statement of total recognised gains and losses] and the related notes. These financial statements have been prepared under the accounting policies set out therein.

Respective responsibilities of directors and auditors

The directors' responsibilities for preparing the annual report and the financial statements in accordance with applicable law and United Kingdom Accounting Standards (UK Generally Accepted Accounting Practice) are set out in the Statement of Directors' Responsibilities.

Our responsibility is to audit the financial statements in accordance with relevant legal and regulatory requirements and International Standards on Auditing (UK and Ireland).

We report to you our opinion as to whether the financial statements give a true and fair view and are properly prepared in accordance with the Companies Act 1985. We report to you whether in our opinion the information given in the directors' report is consistent with the financial statements. [The information given in the directors' report includes that specific information presented in the Operating and Financial Review that is cross referred from the Business Section of the directors' report.]

In addition we report to you if, in our opinion, the company has not kept proper accounting records, if we have not received all the information and explanations we require for our audit, or if information specified by law regarding directors' remuneration and other transactions is not disclosed.

We read other information contained in the annual report, and consider whether it is consistent with the audited financial statements. This other information comprises only [the directors' report, the chairman's statement and the operating and financial review]. We consider the implications for our report if we become aware of any apparent misstatements or material inconsistencies with the financial statements. Our responsibilities do not extend to any other information.

Basis of audit opinion

We conducted our audit in accordance with International Standards on Auditing (UK and Ireland) issued by the Auditing Practices Board. An audit includes examination, on a test basis, of evidence relevant to the amounts and disclosures in the financial statements. It also includes an assessment of the significant estimates and judgments made by the directors in the preparation of the financial statements, and of whether the accounting policies are appropriate to the company's circumstances, consistently applied and adequately disclosed.

We planned and performed our audit so as to obtain all the information and explanations which we considered necessary in order to provide us with sufficient evidence to give reasonable assurance that the financial statements are free from material misstatement, whether caused by fraud or other irregularity or error. In forming our opinion we also evaluated the overall adequacy of the presentation of information in the financial statements.

Opinion

In our opinion the financial statements:

- give a true and fair view, in accordance with United Kingdom Generally Accepted Accounting Practice, of the state of the company's affairs as at ... and of its profit [loss] for the year then ended;
- have been properly prepared in accordance with the Companies Act 1985; and
- the information given in the directors' report is consistent with the financial statements.

Registered auditors *Address*
Date

The report should use a standard format as an aid to the reader, including headings for each section, for example 'Opinion'. The title and addressee and the introductory paragraph are fairly self explanatory. You may have noticed that the audit report does not refer to the company's cash flow statement in the opinion paragraph. This is discussed in the next section.

3.3 Statements of responsibility and basic opinion

(a) Auditors should distinguish between their responsibilities and those of the directors by including in their report:

  (i) A statement that the financial statements are the responsibility of the reporting entity's directors;

  (ii) A reference to a description of those responsibilities when set out elsewhere in the financial statements or accompanying information; and

  (iii) A statement that the auditors' responsibility is to express an opinion on the financial statements.

(b) Where the financial statements or accompanying information (for example the directors' report) do not include an adequate description of directors' relevant responsibilities the auditors' report should include a description of those responsibilities.

3.4 Explanation of auditors' opinion

Auditors should explain the basis of their opinion by including in their report:

(a) A statement as to their compliance or otherwise with Auditing Standards, together with the reasons for any departure therefrom;

(b) A statement that the audit process includes:

  (i) Examining, on a test basis, evidence relevant to the amounts and disclosures in the financial statements;

  (ii) Assessing the significant estimates and judgements made by the reporting entity's directors in preparing the financial statements;

  (iii) Considering whether the accounting policies are appropriate to the reporting entity's circumstances, consistently applied and adequately disclosed;

(c) A statement that they planned and performed the audit so as to obtain reasonable assurance that the financial statements are free from material misstatement, whether caused by fraud or other irregularity or error, and that they have evaluated the overall presentation of the financial statements. (ISA 700.16)

Other than in exceptional circumstances, a departure from an auditing standard is a limitation on the scope of work undertaken by the auditors.

3.5 Expression of opinion

An auditors' report should contain a clear expression of opinion on the financial statements and on any further matters required by statute or other requirements applicable to the particular engagement.

An unqualified opinion on financial statements is expressed when in the auditors' judgement they give a true and fair view and have been prepared in accordance with relevant accounting or other requirements. This judgement entails concluding whether *inter alia*:

(a) The financial statements have been prepared using **appropriate, consistently applied accounting policies.**

(b) The financial statements have been **prepared** in accordance with **relevant legislation, regulations** or **applicable accounting standards** (and that any departures are justified and adequately explained in the financial statements).

(c) There is **adequate disclosure** of all information relevant to the proper understanding of the financial statements.

3.6 Date and signature of the auditors' report

(a) Auditors should not express an opinion on financial statements until those statements and all other financial information contained in a report of which the audited financial statements form a part have been approved by the directors, and the auditors have considered all necessary available evidence.

(b) The date of an auditors' report on a reporting entity's financial statements is the date on which the auditors sign their report expressing an opinion on those statements.

If the date on which the auditors sign the report is later than that on which the directors approve the financial statements, then the auditors must check that the post balance sheet event review has been carried out up to the date they sign their report and that the directors would also have approved the financial statements on that date.

3.7 Forming an opinion on financial statements

The principal matters which auditors consider in forming an opinion may be expressed in three questions.

(a) Have they **completed all procedures necessary** to meet auditing standards and to obtain all the information and explanations necessary for their audit?

(b) Have the financial statements been **prepared in accordance** with the **applicable accounting requirements**?

(c) Do the financial statements, as prepared by the directors, give **a true and fair view**?

Activity 1 **(15 minutes)**

The following is a series of extracts from an unqualified audit report which has been signed by the auditors of Little Panda Limited.

AUDITORS' REPORT TO THE SHAREHOLDERS OF LITTLE PANDA LIMITED

We have audited *the financial statements on pages .... to ....* which have been prepared under the historical cost convention.

We have conducted our audit *in accordance with Auditing Standards* issued by the Auditing Practices Board. An audit includes examination on a test basis of evidence relevant to the amounts and disclosures in the financial statements.

In our opinion the financial statements give a true and fair view of the state of the company's affairs as at 31 December 20X7 and of its profit for the year then ended and have been properly prepared in accordance with the Companies Act 1985.

Required

Explain the purpose and meaning of the following phrases taken from the above extracts of an unqualified audit report.

(a) '... the financial statements on pages .... to ....'
(b) '... in accordance with Auditing Standards.'
(c) 'In our opinion ...'

4 MODIFICATIONS IN AUDIT REPORTS

4.1 Modifications to the auditor's report

ISA 700 goes on to deal with situations where the auditor cannot issue an unmodified report. There are two general types of modified report:

(a) **Matters that do not affect the auditor's opinion: emphasis of matter**

(b) **Matters that do affect the auditor's opinion**

- Qualified opinion
- Disclaimer of opinion
- Adverse opinion

4.2 Matters that do not affect the auditor's opinion

In certain circumstances, an auditor's report may be modified by adding an **emphasis of matter** to highlight a matter affecting the financial statements which is included in a note to the financial statements that more extensively discusses the matter. The addition of such an emphasis of matter paragraph **does not affect** the auditor's opinion. The auditor may also modify the auditor's report by using an emphasis of matter paragraph(s) to report matters other than those affecting the financial statements.

The paragraph would preferably be included after the opinion paragraph and would ordinarily refer to the fact that the auditor's opinion is not qualified in this respect.

The ISA distinguishes between **going concern matters** and other matters, saying 'the auditor should modify the auditor's report by adding a paragraph to highlight a material matter regarding a going concern problem. The auditor should consider modifying the auditor's report by adding a paragraph if there is a **significant uncertainty** (other than a going concern problem), the resolution of which is dependent upon future events and which may affect the financial statements.'

An **uncertainty** is a matter whose outcome depends on future actions or events not under the direct control of the entity but that may affect the financial statements.

The following is an example of an emphasis of matter paragraph.

Unqualified opinion with emphasis of matter describing a fundamental uncertainty

Significant uncertainty (insert just after opinion paragraph)

In forming our opinion, we have considered the adequacy of the disclosures made in the financial statements concerning the possible outcome to litigation against B Limited, a subsidiary undertaking of the company, for an alleged breach of environmental regulations. The future settlement of this litigation could result in additional liabilities and the closure of B Limited's business, whose net assets included in the consolidated balance sheet total £... and whose profit before tax for the year is £... . Details of the circumstances relating to this uncertainty are described in note .... . Our opinion is not qualified in this respect.

This type of paragraph will usually be sufficient to meet the auditor's reporting responsibilities. In extreme cases, however, which involve multiple uncertainties that are significant to the financial statements, a **disclaimer of opinion** may be required instead (see below).

The auditor may also modify the report by using an emphasis of matter paragraph for matters which do **not** affect the financial statements. This might be the case if amendment is necessary to other information in documents containing audited financial statements and the entity refuses to make the amendment. An emphasis of matter paragraph could also be used for **additional statutory reporting responsibilities**.

4.3 Matters that do affect the auditor's opinion

An auditor may not be able to express an unqualified opinion when either of the following circumstances exist and, in the auditor's judgement, the effect of the matter is or may be **material** to the financial statements:

(a) There is a **limitation on the scope** of the auditor's work.

(b) There is a **disagreement** with management regarding the acceptability of the accounting policies selected, the method of their application or the adequacy of financial statement disclosures.

There are different types and degrees of modified opinion.

(a) A limitation on scope may lead to a **qualified opinion** or a **disclaimer of opinion**.

(b) A disagreement may lead to a **qualified opinion** or an **adverse opinion**.

The following table summarises the different types of qualified opinion, and we will look at the detail of each of these in turn.

Nature of circumstances	*Material but not pervasive*	*Pervasive*
Disagreement	Except for ... (auditors disclaim an opinion on a particular aspect of the accounts which is not considered pervasive)	Disclaimer of opinion (auditors state they are unable to form an opinion on truth and fairness)
Limitation in scope	Except for ... (auditors express an adverse opinion on a particular aspect of the accounts which is not considered pervasive)	Adverse opinion (auditors state that the accounts do not give a true and fair view)

The ISA describes these different modified opinions and the circumstances leading to them as follows. 'A **qualified opinion** should be expressed when the auditor concludes that an unqualified opinion cannot be expressed but that the effect of any disagreement with management, or limitation on scope is not so material and pervasive as to require an adverse opinion or a disclaimer of opinion. A qualified opinion should be expressed as being 'except for the effects of the matter to which the qualification relates.'

A **disclaimer of opinion** should be expressed when the possible effect of a limitation on scope is so material and pervasive that the auditor has not been able to obtain sufficient, appropriate audit evidence and accordingly is unable to express an opinion on the financial statements.

An **adverse opinion** should be expressed when the effect of a disagreement is so material and pervasive to the financial statements that the auditor concludes that a qualification of the report is not adequate to disclose the misleading or incomplete nature of the financial statements'.

The concept of materiality was discussed earlier and you can now see its fundamental importance in auditing. ISA 700 says 'whenever the auditor expresses an opinion that is other than unqualified, a clear description of all the substantive reasons should be included in the report and, unless impracticable, a quantification of the possible effect(s) on the financial statements'.

This would usually be set out in a **separate paragraph** preceding the opinion or disclaimer of opinion and may include a reference to a more extensive discussion (if any) in a note to the financial statements.

Limitation on scope

There are two circumstances identified by the standard where there might be a limitation on scope.

Firstly, a limitation on the scope of the auditor's work may sometimes be **imposed by the entity** (for example, when the terms of the engagement specify that the auditor will not carry out an audit procedure that the auditor believes is necessary).

However, when the limitation in the terms of a proposed engagement is such that the auditor believes the need to express a disclaimer of opinion exists, the auditor would usually not accept such a limited audit engagement, unless required by statute. Also, a statutory auditor would not accept such an audit engagement when the limitation infringes on the auditor's statutory duties.

Secondly, a scope limitation may be **imposed by circumstances** (for example, when the timing of the auditor's appointment is such that the auditor is unable to observe the counting of physical stock). It may also arise when, in the opinion of the auditor, the entity's accounting records are inadequate or when the auditor is unable to carry out an audit procedure believed to be desirable. In these circumstances, the auditor would attempt to carry out reasonable alternative procedures to obtain sufficient, appropriate audit evidence to support an unqualified opinion.

'Where there is a limitation on the scope of the auditor's work that requires expression of a qualified opinion or a disclaimer of opinion, the auditor's report should describe the limitation and indicate the possible adjustments to the financial statements that might have been determined to be necessary had the limitation not existed'.

The following examples are reports given under a limitation of scope.

Qualified opinion: limitation on the auditors' work

(Basis of opinion: extract)

Except for the financial effects of such adjustments, if any, as might have been determined to be necessary had we been able to satisfy ourselves as to physical stock quantities, in our opinion the financial statements:

- Give a true and fair view, in accordance with United Kingdom Generally Accepted Accounting Practice, of the state of the company's affairs as at 31 December 20X1 and of its profit [loss] for the year then ended; and
- Have been properly prepared in accordance with the Companies Act 1985.

In respect solely of the limitation on our work relating to stocks:

- We have not obtained all the information and explanations that we considered necessary for the purpose of our audit; and
- We were unable to determine whether proper accounting records had been maintained.

In our opinion the information given in the Directors' Report is consistent with the financial statements.

Disclaimer of opinion

(Basis of opinion: extract)

.... or error. However, the evidence available to us was limited because we were unable to observe the counting of physical stock having a carrying amount of £X and send confirmation letters to trade debtors having a carrying amount of £Y due to limitations placed on the scope of our work by the directors of the company. As a result of this we have been unable to obtain sufficient appropriate audit evidence concerning both stock and trade debtors. Because of the significance of these items, we have been unable to form a view on the financial statements.

In forming our opinion we also evaluated the overall adequacy of the presentation of information in the financial statements.

5 AUDITORS' LIABILITY

The main part of this section deals with **auditor liability** for professional negligence. This is a subject of great concern to auditors. Press reports of actions against auditors for large financial damages have become more common over the last few years. Audit firms can take out professional indemnity insurance to protect their assets, but this has its drawbacks, since arguably it provides a ready source of compensation which therefore makes auditors easy targets.

You may have covered the basics of contract and tort, including professional negligence, back in Mandatory Unit 5, Common Law I.

5.1 Contract

Auditors face potential liability to clients under the **law of contract**. A client who brings an action under contract law does so to enforce upon auditors responsibility for loss which has occurred through the failure of auditors to carry out their duties imposed by the contract with the client. In this chapter we shall discuss what these duties are, what a client has to prove in order to bring a successful action under the law of contract and whether auditors have any defences.

5.2 Tort

Auditors may also be liable under the **law of tort**. We cannot discuss the law of tort in detail but its effect may be to impose upon auditors a duty of care over and above what is imposed by statute or contract. In theory clients may sue in tort, but in practice the law of contract will most likely offer them better remedies. The law of tort is more likely to be a remedy for third parties. In this chapter we shall see how far auditor liability stretches, emphasising in particular the importance of the **Caparo case** which restricted the scope of auditor liability in this area.

One reason why auditors may face court actions is because of misunderstandings over the role of auditors – known as the expectation gap, which was defined back in Chapter 25.

5.3 Statute

The Companies Act 2006 introduces two new additional concepts to auditor liability.

Reckless auditing

The Act includes a new criminal offence, punishable by an unlimited fine, for 'knowingly or recklessly' to cause an audit report to include 'any matter that is misleading, false, deceptive in a material particular, or cause a report to omit a statement that is required under certain sections of the Act' – s. 507 CA2006. The offence can be committed by a partner, director, employee or agent of the audit firm if that person would be eligible for appointment as auditor of the company. In other words, the offence is not just related to the partners of the firm, but to any member of staff who has a practicing certificate.

The Government's view is that 'recklessness' has a very high hurdle and would only catch an auditor who is 'aware that an action or failure to act carried risks, that they personally knew that the risks were not reasonable ones to take, and that, despite knowing that, they went ahead. The real point is that this is a long way above negligence; one cannot be reckless inadvertently'. In other words, 'recklessly' is a subjective test because a risk taken must be unreasonable in the mind of the person taking it.

The offence has yet to be tested in court. However, professional bodies continue to argue that 'honest mistakes' should not be punishable.

Audit liability

Sections 534–538 of the Act allow members to pass an ordinary resolution to limit the liability of their auditors for negligence, default, breach of duty or breach of trust occurring during the course of an audit, by means of a limitation of liability agreement. Key points of this agreement are:

(a) Liability can only be limited where to do so would be 'fair and reasonable' in regard to all circumstances. In other words, the agreement could be set aside by the court where the auditor appeared to be contracting out of liability too much, or where a high standard of work was expected and the auditor failed to provide this

(b) Shareholder approval can be obtained either before or after the company enters into the agreement with the auditor

(c) The agreement must be disclosed in the directors' report

(d) The agreement must be renewed annually

(e) The members can terminate the agreement by ordinary resolution at any time

The actual terms of the agreement therefore have to be decided between the auditor and the client. However, the Act does not contain automatic proportional liability, which appeared to be the objective of the audit profession.

6 LIABILITY UNDER CONTRACT LAW

When auditors accept appointment, they enter into a contract which imposes certain obligations upon them. These obligations arise from the terms of the contract.

Both **express** and **implied** terms of contracts impact upon auditors. Express terms are those stated explicitly in the contract.

6.1 Express terms

The express terms of the audit contract cannot over-ride the Companies Act by restricting company auditors' statutory duties or imposing restrictions upon auditors' statutory rights which are designed to assist them in discharging those duties.

Express terms will, however, be significant if auditors and client agree that auditor responsibilities should be extended beyond those envisaged by the Companies Act. Additionally, if auditors are involved in a non-statutory audit, the express terms will only be those contained in any specific contract that may exist with the client.

In these circumstances auditors are likely to be judged on the content of any report which they have issued, and so they should ensure that their report clearly states the effect of any limitations that there have been upon the extent and scope of their work. The auditors must take special care to ensure that their report does not in any way imply that they have in fact done more work than that required by the terms of the contract.

6.2 Implied terms

'Implied terms' are those which the parties to a contract may have left unstated because they consider them too obvious to express, but which, nevertheless, the law will impart into a contract.

The 'implied terms' which the law will impart into a contract of the type with which we are currently concerned are as follows:

(a) The auditors have a duty to exercise **reasonable care.**

(b) The auditors have a duty to carry out the work required with **reasonable expediency.**

(c) The auditors have a right to **reasonable remuneration.**

6.3 The auditors' duty of care

The auditors' duty of care arose under the Supply of Goods Act 1982; a higher degree of care arises in work of a specialised nature or where negligence is likely to cause substantial loss.

Auditors should use generally accepted auditing techniques. In addition, if auditors' suspicions are aroused (they are put upon enquiry) they must conduct further investigations until the suspicions are confirmed or put to rest.

When the auditors are exercising judgement they must act both honestly and carefully. Obviously, if auditors are to be 'careful' in forming an opinion, they must give due consideration to all relevant matters. Provided they do this and can be seen to have done so, then their opinion should be above criticism.

However if the opinion reached by the auditors is one that no reasonably competent auditor would have been likely to reach then they would still possibly be held negligent. This is because however carefully the auditors may appear to have approached their work, it clearly could not have been careful enough, if it enabled them to reach a conclusion which would be generally regarded as unacceptable.

6.4 Actions for negligence against auditors

Definition

> **Negligence** is some act or omission which occurs because the person concerned has failed to exercise the degree of professional care and skill, appropriate to the case, which is expected of accountants or auditors.

If a client is to bring a successful action against an auditor then the client, as the claimant, must satisfy the court in relation to three matters, all of which must be established.

(a) **Duty of care**

There existed a duty of care enforceable at law.

(b) **Negligence**

In a situation where a duty of care existed, the auditors were negligent in the performance of that duty, judged by the accepted professional standards of the day.

(c) **Damages**

The client has suffered some monetary loss as a direct consequence of the negligence on the part of the auditors.

6.5 Excluding or restricting liability to a client

An agreement with a client designed to exclude or restrict an accountant's liability may not always be effective in law. S 310 Companies Act 1985 makes void (save in exceptional circumstances) any provision in a company's articles or any contractual arrangement purporting to **exempt the auditors from** or to **indemnify** them against, any **liability** for negligence, default, breach of duty or breach of trust. In addition the Unfair Contract Terms Act 1977 introduced extensive restrictions upon the enforceability of exclusions of liability for negligence and breaches of contract.

As noted in paragraph 5.3 above, this liability is changing with the implementation of the Companies Act 2006.

7 LIABILITY TO THIRD PARTIES IN TORT

An accountant may be liable for negligence not only in contract, but also in tort if a person to whom he owed a **duty of care** has suffered **loss** as a result of the accountant's negligence. The key question in the law of tort is to whom does an auditor owe a duty of care.

7.1 To whom does the auditor owe a duty of care?

An accountant will almost always owe a duty of care to his own client. However that duty is likely to be co-existent with his contractual duty. In practice, the possibility of liability in tort will be important mainly in the context of claims by third parties.

Certain relatively recent decisions of the courts appeared to expand the classes of case in which a person professing some special skill (as an accountant does) may be liable for negligence to someone other than his own client: *Hedley Byrne & Co Ltd v Heller & Partners 1963* and *Anns v Merton London Borough Council 1978.*

7.2 The Caparo case

However in 1990 the law was authoritatively stated in the *Caparo* case.

> *Caparo Industries plc v Dickman & Others 1990*
> *The facts:* In 1984 Caparo Industries purchased 100,000 Fidelity shares in the open market. On June 12 1984, the date on which the accounts (audited by Touche Ross) were published, they purchased a further 50,000 shares. Relying on

information in the accounts, further shares were acquired. On September 4, Caparo made a bid for the remainder and by October had acquired control of Fidelity. Caparo alleged that the accounts on which they had relied were misleading in that an apparent pre-tax profit of some £1.3 million should in fact have been shown as a loss of over £400,000. The plaintiffs argued that Touche owed a duty of care to investors and potential investors.

Decision: (by the House of Lords)

(a) The auditors of a public company's accounts owed **no duty of care** to members of the public at large who relied upon the accounts in deciding to buy shares in the company.

(b) As a purchaser of further shares, while relying upon the auditors' report, a **shareholder stood** in the **same position** as any other investing member of the public to whom the auditors owed no duty.

(c) The purpose of the audit was simply that of fulfilling the statutory requirements of the Companies Act 1985.

(d) There was nothing in the statutory duties of company auditors to suggest that they were intended to protect the interests of investors in the market. In particular, there was no reason why any special relationship should be held to arise simply from the fact that the affairs of the company rendered it susceptible to a takeover bid.

In its report *The Financial Aspects of Corporate Governance*, the Cadbury Committee gave an opinion on the legal situation as reflected in the *Caparo* ruling. It felt that *Caparo* **did not lessen** auditors' duty to use skill and care because auditors are still fully liable in negligence to the companies they audit and their shareholders collectively.

Thus the decision in *Caparo v Dickman* has considerably narrowed the auditors' **potential liability** to third parties. The judgement would appear to imply that users such as creditors, potential investors or others, will not be able to sue the auditors for negligence by virtue of their placing reliance on audited annual accounts.

8 REPORTS TO MANAGEMENT

Auditors should report any weaknesses discovered in the system of internal control to the management of the company. This report usually takes the form of a **management letter**, but other types of report are acceptable. ISA 260 *Communication of audit matters with those charged with governance* covers this topic.

8.1 Reasons for a report to management

The main purposes of reports to directors or management are for auditors to communicate various points that have come to their attention during the audit. ISA 260 provides a list of matters that the auditor can report on including:

(a) Material weaknesses in internal control identified during the audit

(b) The auditors' views about the qualitative aspects of the entity's accounting practices and financial reporting

Note that such a report to management is *not* a substitute for a qualified audit report, when such a qualification is required. Inconsistencies between reports to management and the auditors' report should be avoided.

8.2 Material weaknesses in the accounting and internal control systems

When material weaknesses in the accounting and internal control systems are identified during the audit, auditors should report them in writing to the directors, the audit committee or an appropriate level of management on a timely basis.

A **material weakness** is one which may result in a **material misstatement** in the financial statements. If it is corrected by management, it need not be reported, but the discovery and correction should be documented.

To be effective, the report should be made **as soon as possible** after **completion** of the **audit procedures**. A written report is usual, but some matters may be raised orally with a file note to record the auditors' observation and the directors' response.

Where no report is felt to be necessary, the auditors should inform the directors that no material weaknesses have been found.

8.3 Interim letters

Where the audit work is performed on more than one visit, the auditors will normally report to management after the interim audit work has been completed as well as after the final visit.

8.4 Final letters

The final management letter can cover the following issues.

(a) Additional matters under the same headings as the interim letter, if sent.

(b) Details of inefficiencies or delays in the agreed timetable for preparation of the accounts or of working schedules which delayed the completion of the audit and may have resulted in increased costs.

(c) Any significant differences between the accounts and any management accounts or budgets which not only caused audit problems but also detract from the value of management information.

(d) Any results of the auditors' analytical procedures of which management may not be aware and may be of benefit to them.

8.5 Other matters regarding reports to directors or management

If the auditors choose not to send a formal letter or report but consider it preferable to discuss any weaknesses with management, the discussion should be **minuted** or otherwise recorded in writing. Management should be provided with a copy of the note.

The auditors should explain in their report to management that it **only** includes those matters which came to their attention as a result of the audit procedures, and that it should not be regarded as a comprehensive statement of all weaknesses that exist or all improvements that might be made.

The auditors should request a **reply** to all the points raised, indicating what action management intends to take as a result of the comments made in the report.

If **previous points** have **not** been **dealt with effectively** and they are still considered significant, the auditors should enquire why action has not been taken.

The report may contain matters of varying levels of significance and thus make it difficult for senior management to identify points of significance. The auditors can deal with this by giving the report a **'tiered' structure** so that major points are dealt with by the directors or the audit committee and minor points are considered by less senior personnel.

Other points to note about the management letter are as follows.

(a) The recommendations should take the form of **suggestions** backed up by **reason and logic.**

(b) The letter should be in **formal terms** unless the client requests otherwise.

(c) **Weaknesses** that **management** are aware of but **choose not to do anything about** should be **mentioned** to protect the auditors.

(d) If management or staff have **agreed to changes,** this should be mentioned in a letter.

8.6 Third parties interested in reports to directors or management

Any report made to directors or management should be regarded as a confidential communication. The auditors should therefore not normally reveal the contents of the report to any third party without the prior written consent of the directors or management of the company.

In practice, the auditors have little control over what happens to the report once it has been despatched. Occasionally management may provide third parties with copies of the report, for example their bankers or certain regulatory authorities.

Thus care should be taken to protect the auditors' position from exposure to liability in negligence to any third parties who may seek to rely on the report. Accordingly, the auditors should state clearly in their report that it has been prepared for the private use of the client.

8.7 Specimen management letter

A specimen letter is provided below which demonstrates how the principles described in the previous paragraphs are put into practice.

NOTES

EXAMPLE

SPECIMEN MANAGEMENT LETTER

ABC & Co
Certified Accountants
29 High Street
London, N10 4KB

The Board of Directors,
Manufacturing Co Limited,
15 South Street
London, S20 1CX

1 April 200X

Members of the board,

Financial statements for the year ended 31 May 200X

In accordance with our normal practice we set out in this letter certain matters which arose as a result of our review of the accounting systems and procedures operated by your company during our recent interim audit.

We would point out that the matters dealt with in this letter came to our notice during the conduct of our normal audit procedures which are designed primarily for the purpose of expressing our opinion on the financial statements of your company. In consequence our work did not encompass a detailed review of all aspects of the system and cannot be relied on necessarily to disclose defalcations or other irregularities or to include all possible improvements in internal control.

1 *Purchases: ordering procedures*

Present system

During the course of our work we discovered that it was the practice of the stores to order certain goods from X Ltd orally without preparing either a purchase requisition or purchase order.

Implications

There is therefore the possibility of liabilities being set up for unauthorised items and at a non-competitive price.

Recommendations

We recommend that the buying department should be responsible for such orders and, if they are placed orally, an official order should be raised as confirmation.

2 *Purchase ledger reconciliation*

Present system

Although your procedures require that the purchase ledger is reconciled against the control account on the nominal ledger at the end of every month, this was not done in December or January.

Implications

The balance on the purchase ledger was short by some £2,120 of the nominal ledger control account at 31 January 200X for which no explanation could be offered. This implies a serious breakdown in the purchase invoice and/or cash payment batching and posting procedures.

Recommendations

It is important in future that this reconciliation is performed regularly by a responsible official independent of the day to day purchase ledger, cashier and nominal ledger functions.

3 *Sales ledger: credit control*

Present system

As at 28 February 200X debtors account for approximately 12 weeks' sales, although your standard credit terms are cash within 30 days of statement, equivalent to an average of about 40 days (6 weeks) of sales.

Implications

This has resulted in increased overdraft usage and difficulty in settling some key suppliers accounts on time.

Recommendations

We recommend that a more structured system of debt collection be considered using standard letters and that statements should be sent out a week earlier if possible.

4 *Preparation of payroll and maintenance of personnel records*

Present system

Under your present system, just two members of staff are entirely and equally responsible for the maintenance of personnel records and preparation of the payroll. Furthermore, the only independent check of any nature on the payroll is that the chief accountant confirms that the amount of the wages cheque presented to him for signature agrees with the total of the net wages column in the payroll. This latter check does not involve any consideration of the reasonableness of the amount of the total net wages cheque or the monies being shown as due to individual employees.

Implications

It is a serious weakness of your present system, that so much responsibility is vested in the hands of just two people. This situation is made worse by the fact that there is no clearly defined division of duties as between the two of them. In our opinion, it would be far too easy for fraud to take place in this area (eg by inserting the names of 'dummy workmen' into the personnel records and hence on to the payroll) and/or for clerical errors to go undetected.

Recommendations

(i) Some person other than the two wages clerks be made responsible for maintaining the personnel records and for periodically (but on a surprise basis) checking them against the details on the payroll;

(ii) The two wages clerks be allocated specific duties in relation to the preparation of the payroll, with each clerk independently reviewing the work of the other;

(iii) When the payroll is presented in support of the cheque for signature to the chief accountant, that he should be responsible for assessing the reasonableness of the overall charge for wages that week.

Our comments have been discussed with your finance director and the chief accountant and these matters will be considered by us again during future audits. We look forward to receiving your comments on the points made. Should you require any further information or explanations do not hesitate to contact us.

This letter has been produced for the sole use of your company. It must not be disclosed to a third party, or quoted or referred to, without our written consent. No responsibility is assumed by us to any other person.

We should like to take this opportunity of thanking your staff for their co-operation and assistance during the course of our audit.

Yours faithfully

ABC & Co

Activity 2 **(15 minutes)**

During the audit of AJ (Paper) Ltd you have ascertained the following weaknesses within the systems of internal control.

(a) The ordering, recording and payment for purchases of materials are made by the administration department manager.

(b) All production department workers are paid on an hourly basis as per the hours on their time records. These records are completed by each worker on a weekly basis and are not checked by the supervisor prior to being submitted to the payroll department.

Tasks

Based on the above information

(i) Describe the weakness
(ii) Explain the implications of the weakness
(iii) Give recommendations to address the weakness

Chapter roundup

- An unqualified audit report demonstrates to the user that an independent examination of the accounts has discovered no material problems and that the accounts show a true and fair view.
- True and fair means that the accounts are factually materially correct, comply with relevant standards and the law and are free from bias.
- The standard unqualified audit report is set out in ISA 700.
- Wherever possible a qualified audit report should provide a full explanation of the reasons for the qualification and a quantification of its effect on the financial statements.
- Qualifications can arise due to limitations on scope or disagreements.
- The auditor may be liable for professional negligence in both contract and tort. The key case is Caparo Industries v Dickman and Others, 1990.
- Auditors should report any weaknesses that they discover in the system of internal control to the management of the company.

Quick quiz

1 What is implied by an unqualified audit report?

2 What are the two categories of circumstance giving rise to a qualification?

3 What is an auditor saying in a disclaimer of opinion?

4 What was the decision in the Caparo Case?

NOTES

Answers to quick quiz

1 Proper accounting records have been kept
The accounts agree with the underlying records and returns
All information and explanations have been received
Directors' emoluments, benefits and loans have been correctly disclosed (see para 1.1)

2 Limitation in scope of work, leading to uncertainty, and disagreement. (para 4.1)

3 That he is unable to form an opinion on the truth and fairness of the financial statements. (para 4.1)

4 That the auditors of a public company's accounts owe no duty of care to the public at large who rely upon the accounts in deciding to buy shares in the company. (para 7.2)

Answers to activities

1 (a) '...the financial statements on pages ... to ...'

Purpose

The purpose of this phrase is to make it clear to the reader of an audit report the part of a company's annual report upon which the auditors are reporting their opinion.

Meaning

An annual report may include documents such as a chairman's report, employee report, five year summary and other voluntary information. However, under the Companies Act, only the profit and loss account, balance sheet and associated notes are required to be audited in true and fair terms. Thus the page references (for instance, 8 to 20) cover only the profit and loss account, balance sheet, notes to the accounts, cash flow statement and statement of total recognised gains and losses. The directors' report, although examined and reported on as to whether it contains inconsistencies, is not included in these page references.

(b) '...in accordance with Auditing Standards...'

Purpose

This phrase is included in order to confirm to the reader that best practice, as laid down in Auditing Standards, has been adopted by the auditors in both carrying out their audit and in drafting their audit opinion. This means that the reader can be assured that the audit has been properly conducted, and that should he or she wish to discover what such standards are, or what certain key phrases mean, he or she can have recourse to Auditing Standards to explain such matters.

Meaning

Auditing Standards are those auditing standards prepared by the Auditing Practices Board.

These prescribe the principles and practices to be followed by auditors in the planning, designing and carrying out various aspects of their audit

BPP LEARNING MEDIA

NOTES

work, the content of audit reports, both qualified and unqualified and so on. Members are expected to follow all of these standards.

(c) 'In our opinion ...'

Purpose

Under the Companies Act, auditors are required to report on every balance sheet, profit and loss account or group accounts laid before members. In reporting, they are required to state their opinion on those accounts. Thus, the purpose of this phrase is to comply with the statutory requirement to report an opinion.

Meaning

An audit report is an expression of opinion by suitably qualified auditors as to whether the financial statements give a true and fair view, and have been properly prepared in accordance with the Companies Act. It is not a certificate; rather it is a statement of whether or not, in the professional judgement of the auditors, the financial statements give a true and fair view.

2 (a) **Segregation of duties in administration department**

Weakness

Segregation of duties in the administration department is **inadequate**, as the administration manager is responsible for all the tasks involved in purchasing goods.

Implication

Unauthorised purchases may be made and posted to the purchase ledger.

Recommendation

Different members of staff should perform the tasks of ordering, recording and payment.

(b) **Wages of production staff**

Weakness

Timesheets completed by production department workers are **submitted** to the payroll department **without being checked**.

Implication

Staff in the production department could **complete** their **timesheets incorrectly** and hence be **paid** the **wrong amounts**.

Recommendation

The **production department supervisor** should **check** all **timesheets** before they are submitted to the payroll department. The company should also consider introducing a **computerised clock in system**.

PART D

TAXATION (FINANCE ACT 2007)

Chapter 30 :

THE TAX PRACTITIONER AND THE UK TAX ENVIRONMENT

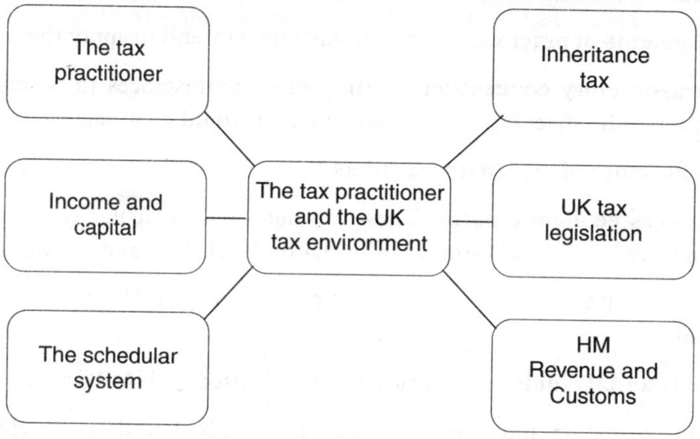

Introduction

Taxation is a fact of life, which will affect everyone in many different ways. The purpose of taxation is to enable central government to raise funds which then effectively pay for the running of the country, for example, education, roads and the health service.

Taxation is largely administered by the HM Revenue and Customs on behalf of the government.

Your objectives

In this chapter you will learn about the following.

(a) The main sources of UK tax legislation

(b) The key reference sources for UK tax legislation

(c) The organisation of HM Revenue and Customs and its terms of reference including the appeals system

(d) The appeals process – special and general commissioners

(e) The classification of income and the aggregation of income which is then subject to income tax

(f) The difference between income and capital profits/losses

NOTES

1 UK TAX LEGISLATION

1.1 The role of government and HM Revenue & Customs (HMRC)

Central government raises revenue through a wide range of taxes. Tax law is made by **statute** (ie by Acts of Parliament). This comprises not only **Acts of Parliament** but also regulations laid down by **Statutory Instruments.** Statute is interpreted and amplified by **case law.**

HM Revenue and Customs also issue:

(a) **Statements of practice,** setting out how they intend to apply the law

(b) **Extra-statutory concessions,** setting out circumstances in which they will not apply the strict letter of the law where it would be unfair

(c) A wide range of **explanatory leaflets**

(d) **Business economic notes.** These are notes on particular types of business, which are used as background information by HMRC and are also published

(e) The **Tax Bulletin**. This is a newsletter giving HMRC's view on specific points

(f) The **Internal Guidance,** a series of manuals used by HMRC staff

A great deal of information and HMRC publications can be found on the HM Revenue and Customs' Internet site (www.hmrc.gov.uk).

1.2 The main taxes

The main taxes, their incidence and their sources, are set out in the table below.

Tax	Suffered by	Source
Income tax	**Individuals** **Partnerships**	Capital Allowances Act 2001 (CAA 2001); Income Tax (Earnings and Pensions) Act 2003 (ITEPA 2003); Income Tax (Trading and Other Income) Act 2005 (ITTOIA 2005); Income Tax Act 2007 (ITA 2007)
Corporation tax	**Companies**	Income and Corporation Taxes Act 1988 (ICTA 1988) and subsequent Finance Acts, CAA 2001 as above
Capital gains tax	**Individuals** **Partnerships** **Companies** (which pay tax on capital gains in the form of corporation tax)	Taxation of Chargeable Gains Act 1992 (TCGA 1992) and subsequent Finance Acts

The taxes set out in the table are the main ones with which the Edexcel guidelines expect you to be familiar.

However, the guidelines also mention one further tax of which you should be aware: inheritance tax (IHT). This will be discussed in brief at the end of this chapter.

NOTES

1.3 Finance Acts

Finance Acts are passed each year, incorporating proposals set out in the **Budget**. They make changes which apply mainly to the tax year ahead. This book includes the provisions of the Finance Act 2007.

Definition

The **tax year**, or fiscal year, or year of assessment, runs from 6 April to 5 April the following year. For example, the tax year 2007/08 runs from 6 April 2007 to 5 April 2008.

2 THE ORGANISATION OF HM REVENUE & CUSTOMS

2.1 The framework

The **Treasury** formally imposes and collects taxation. The management of the Treasury is the responsibility of the Chancellor of the Exchequer. **The administrative function for the collection of tax is undertaken by Her Majesty's Revenue and Customs (HMRC).** Previously there were two separate bodies called the Inland Revenue (responsible for direct taxes such as income tax and corporation tax) and HM Customs and Excise (responsible for indirect taxes such as VAT). Rules on these administrative matters are contained in the **Taxes Management Act 1970 (TMA 1970).**

2.2 Administration and collection of income tax

HMRC consists of the commissioners for Her Majesty's Revenue and Customs and staff known **as Officers of Revenue and Customs.**

The UK has historically been divided into **tax districts.** These are being merged into larger **areas,** with the separate offices in each area being responsible for different aspects of HMRC's work. For example, one office may be designated to deal with taxpayer's queries, another to deal with the PAYE procedures for joiners and leavers, whilst end of year PAYE returns may be dealt with by a third office. Some offices also act as **enquiry offices,** where taxpayers can visit the office and see a member of HMRC staff in person without an appointment.

Each area is headed by an area director. HMRC staff were historically described as '**Inspectors**' and '**Collectors**'. The legislation now refers to an '**Officer of the Revenue and Customs**' when setting out HMRC's powers. They are responsible for supervising the self-assessment system and agreeing tax liabilities. Collectors (or **receivable management officers**) are local officers who are responsible for following up amounts of unpaid tax referred to them by the **HMRC Accounts Office.**

Taxpayer service offices do routine checking, computation *and* collection work, while **Taxpayer district offices** investigate selected accounts, deal with corporation tax and enforce the payment of tax when it is not paid willingly. **Taxpayer assistance offices** handle enquiries and arrange specialist help for taxpayers.

2.3 Appeals

The **Generaı Commissioners** (not to be confused with the Commissioners for HMRC) are (currently) appointed by the Lord Chancellor to hear **appeals** against HMRC decisions. They are part-time and unpaid. They are appointed for a local area (a **division**). They appoint a clerk who is often a lawyer or accountant and who is paid for his services.

The **Special Commissioners** are also appointed by the Lord Chancellor. They are full-time paid professionals. They generally hear the more complex appeals.

3 THE CLASSIFICATION OF INCOME

Some income is received in full, with no tax deducted in advance. An example of such income is gilt interest (interest paid on government securities) which is normally paid gross.

Other income is received after deduction of tax. This is income taxed at source. The taxable income for a tax year (6 April in one year to 5 April in the next) is the **gross** amount (that is, adding back any tax deducted at source). We will look at taxed income in the context of the personal tax computation in the next chapter.

Dividends on UK shares are received net of a 10% tax credit. The taxable income for a tax year is the gross dividend (that is, the dividends received multiplied by 100/90). We will look at dividends in the next chapter.

3.1 Classification of income

All income received must be classified according to the nature of the income. This is because different computational rules apply to different types of income. The main types of income are:

(a) Income from employment and pensions
(b) Profits of trades, professions and vocations
(c) Income from property letting
(d) Savings and investment income, including interest and dividends
(e) Miscellaneous income

4 INCOME AND CAPITAL PROFITS/LOSSES

As a general rule, income tax is charged on income profit which might be expected to recur (such as weekly wages or profits from running a business) whereas capital gains tax is charged on one-off capital profits (for example from selling a painting owned for 20 years).

5 THE ROLE OF THE TAX PRACTITIONER

Many taxpayers arrange for their accountants to prepare and submit their tax returns. The taxpayer is still the person responsible for submitting the return and for paying whatever tax becomes due; the accountant is only acting as the taxpayer's agent.

The role of the tax practitioner in dealing with the HMRC on behalf of the client is dealt with fully in Chapter 34, *Tax documentation and payment of tax*.

NOTES

6 INHERITANCE TAX

Inheritance tax (IHT) is primarily a tax on wealth left by an individual on death. It also applies to gifts made by individuals in the seven years prior to their death, and to some other large lifetime transfers of wealth.

IHT is different from the other taxes which you deal with in this Unit (such as income tax, corporation tax and capital gains tax) in that it is not concerned with the profit or income made by an individual, but with the amount of wealth **given away** by that person. The amount which is taxed is the amount transferred out of their estate, whether on death or in the period beforehand.

6.1 Rate of tax

The first £300,000 of transfers is tax free, although technically it is described as being the 'nil band'. However, it is not possible to evade IHT by making a number of separate transfers of just under £300,000 each, as transfers made are regarded on a cumulative basis over a seven year period.

Transfers above the £300,000 threshold are then taxed at 40%, known as the full rate.

These rates apply to lifetime transfers made in the seven years before death, that are taxed on death and on the value of an estate being taxed on death. This is death tax and calculated at the time of death. Lifetime tax can sometimes apply to large lifetime transfers of wealth and is calculated at the time of the gift, at half the death rate (currently 20%).

6.2 Exemptions

There are various exemptions available to eliminate or reduce the chargeable (taxable) amount of a lifetime transfer or property passing on a person's death.

These are:

(a) Outright gifts to individuals totalling £250 or less per donee in any one tax year (so that the donor can give £250 tax-free each year to each of as many donees as he wants)

(b) There is an overall annual exemption of £3,000 per tax year. This exemption, if unused, can only be carried forward for one year. This is to prevent someone making a lifetime transfer of £30,000 and then applying ten years' worth of unused annual exemption to the amount.

(c) Any transfers made between husband and wife, as long as the transferee (the recipient) is domiciled in the UK at the time of the transfer. This means that a spouse can leave their estate to their spouse free of IHT. However, the value of the estate would then be taxed on the death of the surviving spouse, when the estate passes to their children or others.

(d) Gifts to UK charities

(e) Gifts to UK political parties

(f) Gifts for national purposes (eg to museums, art galleries and the National Trust)

The first two of these exemptions apply only to lifetime transfers, not to property passing on death.

6.3 Valuation of assets

The value of any property for IHT is the value which it might reasonably be expected to fetch on the open market at the time of the transfer.

There are certain complex rules for the valuation of assets such as shares and securities, interests in family businesses and interests in agricultural property.

6.4 Administration of IHT

IHT is administered by HMRC Inheritance Tax. The personal representatives of the deceased (usually the executors) have to submit an account to HMRC showing the value of the estate on death and the amount of any chargeable lifetime transfers in the preceding seven years. This must be done within the 12 months following the month of death.

HMRC will then issue a notice of determination to the effect that IHT is payable.

The tax on the death estate is paid by the personal representatives, with the burden generally falling on the residuary legatee. This is the person named in the will as receiving the remainder of the estate after all specific gifts have been distributed.

Any tax due on lifetime transfers within the seven years before death, is suffered by the recipient.

Chapter roundup

- HM Revenue and Customs (HMRC) administers taxes.
- General and Special Commissioners hear appeals.
- Income is taxed classified according to the nature of the income.
- Income profits are receipts which recur regularly. Capital profits are one-off receipts.

Quick quiz

1. What are the main UK taxes?
2. What tax do companies pay?
3. What are HMRC staff known as?
4. Under which type of income would you tax the profits from the trade of a self employed greengrocer?
5. How much is the IHT annual exemption?

Answers to quick quiz

1 Income tax, capital gains tax and corporation tax. (see para 1.2)

2 Corporation Tax (para 1.2)

3 'Officers of Revenue and Customs' (para 2.2)

4 Profits of trades, professions and vocations (para 3.1)

5 £3,000 per tax year, plus £3,000 carried forward from the previous year if unused (para 6.2)

Chapter 31 :
THE PERSONAL TAX COMPUTATION

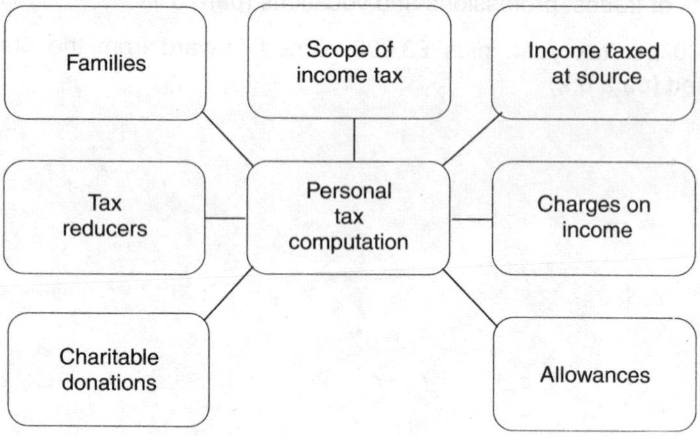

Introduction

Personal tax is a topic which will inevitably affect every reader of this book, and the subject matter of this chapter should be of practical as well as academic interest.

It is important that you understand the basic elements of the personal tax computation and when they are applicable.

The whole of this Unit is based on the Finance Act 2007. You should be aware that although many of the figures used for allowances will change in each successive Finance Act, most of the principles will remain the same.

Your objectives

In this chapter you will learn about the following.

(a) The scope of income tax: chargeable persons, chargeable income

(b) The key elements of a personal income tax computation - total income (savings/non-savings/dividend), net income, taxable income, computation of income tax liability

(c) The key stages in the transition from computation of income tax liability to income tax payable

(d) The different categories of charges

(e) Personal allowances and the circumstances in which they can be claimed

(f) How to prepare income tax computations

NOTES

1 THE SCOPE OF INCOME TAX

As a general rule, income tax is charged on receipts which might be expected to recur (such as weekly wages or profits from running a business). **An individual's income from all sources is brought together in a personal tax computation for the tax year.**

Definition

> The **tax year**, or **fiscal year**, or **year of assessment** runs from 6 April to 5 April. For example, the tax year 2007/08 runs from 6 April 2007 to 5 April 2008.

Three columns are needed in the computation. Here is an example. All items are explained later in this Course Book.

EXAMPLE

RICHARD: INCOME TAX COMPUTATION 2007/08

	Non-savings income	*Savings income*	*Dividend income*	*Total*
	£	£	£	£
Income from employment	43,000			
Building society interest		1,000		
National savings & investments account interest		360		
UK dividends			1,000	
Total income	43,000	1,360	1,000	
Less interest paid	(2,000)			
Net income	41,000	1,360	1,000	43,360
Less personal allowance	(5,225)			
Taxable income	35,775	1,360	1,000	38,135

	£	£
Income tax on non savings income		
£2,230 × 10%		223
£32,370 × 22%		7,121
£1,175 × 40%		470
Tax on savings income		
£1,360 × 40%		544
Tax on dividend income		
£1,000 × 32.5%		325
		8,683
Less tax reducer		
Investment under the EIS £10,000 × 20%		(2,000)
Tax liability		6,683
Less tax suffered		
PAYE tax on salary (say)	5,650	
Tax on building society interest	200	
Tax credit on dividend income	100	
		(5,950)
Tax payable		733

Definitions

Total income is all income subject to income tax. Each of the amounts which make up total income is called a **component**. **Net income** is total income less deductible interest and trade losses. The **tax liability** is the amount charged on the individual's income. **Tax payable** is the balance of the liability still to be settled in cash.

Income tax is charged on '**taxable income**'. Non-savings income is dealt with first, then savings income and then dividend income.

1.2 Tax rates

For non-savings income, the first £2,230 is taxed at the starting rate (10%), the next £32,370 is taxed at the basic rate (22%) and the rest at the higher rate (40%).

Savings (excl. dividend) income is taxed as the next slice of income after non-savings income has been taxed. Any savings (excl. dividend) income falling within the starting rate band is taxed at the starting rate (10%). **Any savings (excl. dividend) income that falls within the basic rate band is taxed at 20% (not 22%)** whilst any such income in excess of the basic rate threshold of £34,600 (£2,230 + 32,370) is taxed at 40%.

Any dividend income falling within the starting or basic rate bands is taxed at 10%. Dividend income in excess of the basic rate threshold is taxed at 32.5%.

Any tax already suffered and the tax credit on dividend income comes off the tax liability. However, the tax credit on dividend income cannot be repaid.

Activity 1 **(5 minutes)**

An individual has taxable income (all non-savings income) of £50,000 for 2007/08. What is the total income tax?

The remainder of this chapter gives more details of the income tax computation.

2 VARIOUS TYPES OF INCOME

2.1 Classification of income

All income received must be classified according to the nature of the income. This is because different computational rules apply to different types of income. The main types of income are:

- Income from employment, pensions and some social security benefits
- Profits of trades, professions and vocations
- Profits of property businesses
- Savings and investment income, including interest and dividends
- Miscellaneous income

NOTES

2.2 Savings income

2.2.1 What is savings income?

Savings income comprises the following.

(a) **Interest** (includes interest from banks, building societies, gilts and debentures and under the accrued income scheme)

2.2.2 Savings income received gross

The following savings income is received gross.

(a) **Interest on National Savings & Investments accounts** (eg. Investment account, Easy Access Savings account)

(b) Interest paid to individuals by listed UK companies on **debentures and loan stock**

(c) **Gilt interest**

2.2.3 Savings income received net of 20% tax

The following savings income is received net of 20% tax. **This is called income taxed at source.**

(a) Bank and building society interest paid to individuals (but not National Savings & Investments account interest)

(b) Interest paid to individuals by unlisted UK companies on debentures and loan stocks

The amount received is grossed up by multiplying by 100/80 and is included gross in the income tax computation. The tax deducted at source is deducted in computing tax payable and may be repaid.

Although bank and building society interest paid to individuals is generally paid net of 20% tax, if a recipient is not liable to tax, he can recover the tax suffered, or he can certify in advance that he is a non-taxpayer and receive the interest gross.

2.3 Dividends on UK shares

Dividends on UK shares are received net of a 10% tax credit. This means a dividend of £90 has a £10 tax credit, giving gross income of £100 to include in the income tax computation. The tax credit can be deducted in computing tax payable but it cannot be repaid.

Higher rate taxpayers pay tax at 32½% on their gross dividends and can deduct the 10% tax credit. This is the same as taxing the net dividend at 25%. For example, a higher rate taxpayer receiving a net dividend of £9,000 will pay tax of £2,250, which is £3,250 (£10,000 @ 32½%) less £1,000 (£10,000 @ 10%). This is the same as taking 25% × £9,000.

Stock dividends

Sometimes a company will offer shares in lieu of a cash dividend. A shareholder who takes the shares receives a stock dividend. The amount of the stock dividend is:

(a) The cash alternative, if that equals the market value of the shares offered plus or minus 15%;

(b) The market value of the shares offered, if that differs from the cash alternative by more than 15% or if there is no cash alternative.

The shareholder is treated as receiving a gross dividend of the stock dividend × 100/90, with a tax credit of 10% of the gross dividend.

2.4 Exempt income

Some income is exempt from income tax. Several of these exemptions are mentioned at places in this Course Book where the types of income are described in detail, but you should note the following types of exempt income now.

(a) Scholarships (exempt as income of the scholar. If paid by a parent's employer, a scholarship may be taxable income of the parent)

(b) Betting and gaming winnings, including premium bond prizes

(c) Interest or terminal bonus on National Savings Certificates

(d) Many social security benefits, although the jobseeker's allowance, the state pension and certain incapacity benefits are taxable

(e) Gifts

(f) Damages and payments for personal injury. The exemption applies to both lump sum and periodical payments, including payments made via trusts and payments made by buying annuities. Payments under annuities are made gross (unlike most annuities)

(g) Payments under insurance policies to compensate for loss of income on illness or disability (permanent health insurance) or while out of work (eg policies to pay interest on mortgages), so long as the person benefiting paid the premiums and did not get tax relief for them

(h) The amount by which a pension awarded on a retirement due to a disability caused at work, by a work related illness or by war wounds exceeds the pension that would have been payable if the retirement had been on ordinary ill health grounds. This exemption only applies to pensions paid under non-approved pension schemes.

(i) Interest on amounts repaid to borrowers under the income contingent student loans scheme

(j) Income on investments made though individual savings accounts (ISAs).

NOTES

Activity 2 **(10 minutes)**

An individual has the following income in 2007/08.

	£
Building society interest received	6,400
Dividends received	7,875
Premium bond prize	5,000

His personal allowance is £5,225. What is his taxable income?

3 CHARGES ON INCOME

Charges on income are deducted in computing taxable income.

Definition

A **charge on income** is a payment by the taxpayer which income tax law allows as a deduction.

Examples of charges on income are:

- Eligible interest
- Patent royalties (non-trading)
- Copyright royalties (non-trading)

3.1 Categories of charges on income

Charges on income paid in money fall into two categories: those from which basic rate (22%) income tax is first deducted by the payer (charges paid net) and those which are paid gross (without any tax deduction). Always deduct the gross figure in the payer's tax computation.

Patent royalties are an example of a charge on income which is paid net. Eligible interest and copyright royalties are paid gross.

In the personal tax computation of someone who **receives** a charge, for example the owner of a patent who gets royalties from someone who exploits the patent you should:

(a) Include the **gross** amount under non-savings income. If the charge is paid gross, the gross amount is the amount received. If it is paid net, the gross amount is the amount received × 100/78.

(b) If the charge was received net, then under the heading 'less tax suffered' (between tax liability and tax payable) include the tax deducted. This is the gross amount × 22%.

3.2 Eligible interest

Interest on a loan is a charge when the loan is used for one of the following qualifying purposes.

BPP LEARNING MEDIA

(a) The purchase of an interest in a partnership, or contribution to the partnership of capital or a loan. The borrower must be a partner (other than a limited partner), and relief ceases when he ceases to be one.

(b) The purchase of ordinary shares in a close company (other than a close investment holding company) or the loan of money to such a company for use in its business, provided that when the interest is paid, the individual either has (with any associates) a material (more than 5%) interest in the close company, or holds (ignoring associates) some ordinary share capital and works full time as a manager or director of the company. A close company is (broadly) a company controlled by its shareholder-directors or by five or fewer shareholders.

(c) Investment in a co-operative. This provision applies to investment in shares or through loans to the co-operative. The borrower must work for the greater part of his time in the co-operative.

(d) The purchase of shares in an employee-controlled company. The company must be an unquoted trading company resident in the UK with at least 50% of the voting shares held by employees.

(e) The purchase by a partner of plant or machinery used in the business. Interest is allowed only until three years from the end of the tax year in which the loan was taken out. If the plant is used partly for private purposes, then the allowable interest is proportionately reduced.

(f) The purchase by an employee of plant or machinery used by him in the performance of his duties. The interest is allowable only until three years from the end of the tax year in which the loan was taken out.

(g) The replacement of other loans qualifying under (a) to (f) above.

Interest on a loan within (a) to (d) above continues to be allowable if a partnership is succeeded by a new partnership or is incorporated into a co-operative or an employee controlled company, or if shares in a company of one of these kinds are exchanged for shares in a company of another of these kinds, provided that interest on a new loan (to make the loan to or buy the shares in the new entity) would have qualified.

Interest is never allowed if it is payable under a scheme or arrangement of which the expected sole or main benefit was tax relief on the interest. Interest on an overdraft or on a credit card debt does not qualify. Relief under (a) to (d) above is reduced or withdrawn if capital is withdrawn from the business.

3.3 Business traders

A taxpayer paying interest, patent royalties or copyright royalties wholly and exclusively for business purposes should deduct such items in the computation of his taxable profit, instead of as a charge. The interest need not fall into any of the categories outlined above, and it may be on an overdraft or a credit card debt.

If interest is allowable as a deduction when calculating taxable profits, the amount payable (on an accruals basis) is deducted.

3.4 Charges in personal tax computations

The gross amount of any charge is deducted from the taxpayer's income to arrive at Net Income. Deduct charges from non-savings income, then from savings (excl dividend) income and lastly from dividend income.

If a charge has been paid net, the basic rate income tax deducted (22% of the gross charge) is added to any tax liability. The taxpayer obtained tax relief because the charge reduced his income: he cannot keep the basic rate tax as well, but must pay it to the HMRC.

If charges paid net exceed total income (ignoring charges paid net) minus allowances deductible from total income, the payer of the charge must pay HMRC the tax withheld when the excess charge was paid. In other words, HMRC ensure that you do not get tax relief for charges if you are not a payer of tax.

EXAMPLE

Three taxpayers have the following Trading profits and allowances for 2007/08. Taxpayers A and B pay a non-trade royalty of £176 (net). Taxpayer C pays a non-trade royalty of £1,248 (net).

	A	*B*	*C*
	£	£	£
Trading Profits	6,000	3,000	42,195
Less: charge on income (×100/78)	(226)	(226)	(1,600)
	5,774	2,774	40,595
Less: personal allowance	(5,225)	(5,225)	(5,225)
Taxable income	549	-	35,370
Income tax			
10% on £549/-/£2,230	55	-	223
22% on -/-/£32,370			7,121
40% on -/-/770	—	—	308
	55	-	7,652
Add: 22% tax retained on charge	50	50	352
Tax payable	105	50	8,004

---

4 ALLOWANCES DEDUCTED FROM NET INCOME

Once taxable income from all sources has been aggregated and any charges on income deducted, the remainder is the taxpayer's net income. Two allowances, the personal allowance and the blind person's allowance, are deducted from Net Income. Like charges, they come off non savings income first, then off savings (excl. dividend) income and lastly off dividend income. The amounts given in the following paragraphs are for 2007/08.

Other allowances are not deducted from Net Income, but reduce tax instead. These allowances are explained below.

4.1 PA: personal allowance

Once taxable income from all sources has been aggregated and any deductible interest deducted, the remainder is the taxpayer's net income. The personal allowance is deducted from net income. Like deductible interest, it is deducted from non savings income first, then from savings income and lastly from dividend income. The amounts given in the following paragraphs are for 2007/08.

All persons (including children) are entitled to the personal allowance of £5,225.

A person aged 65 or over (at any time in the tax year) gets an age allowance of £7,550 instead of the ordinary PA of £5,225.

Where net income exceeds £20,900, cut the age allowance by £1 for every £2 of income over £20,900 until it comes down to £5,225.

EXAMPLE

Jonah is 69 and single. In 2007/08 he has pension income totalling £18,800 plus bank interest received of £4,000. What is Jonah's taxable income?

	Non savings	*Savings*	*Total*
2007/08	£	£	£
Pension income	18,800		
Interest 4,000 × 100/80		5,000	
Net income	18,800	5,000	23,800
Less PAA (W1)	(6,100)		
Taxable income	12,700	5,000	17,700

W1

PAA 65+	7,550
Less income restriction (23,800 – 20,900) × ½	(1,450)
	6,100

PAA of £6,100 exceeds basic allowance of £5,225.

Individuals aged 75 or over (at any time in the tax year) get a slightly more generous age allowance of £7,690. In all respects, the higher age allowance works in the same way as the basic age allowance, with the same income limit of £20,900.

Someone who dies in the tax year in which they would have had their 65th or 75th birthday receives the age allowance (for 65 year olds or 75 year olds) for that year.

4.2 BPA: blind person's allowance

A taxpayer who is registered with a local authority as a blind person gets an allowance of £1,730. The allowance is also given for the year before registration, if the taxpayer had obtained the proof of blindness needed for registration before the end of that earlier year.

> **Activity 3** **(15 minutes)**
>
> Susan has an annual salary of £37,000. She has a loan of £7,000 at 10% interest to buy shares in her employee-controlled company, and another loan of £5,000 at 12% interest to buy double glazing for her house. She receives building society interest of £2,000 a year. What is her taxable income for 2007/08?

5 GIFT AID

5.1 Gift aid donations

Definition

> One-off and regular charitable gifts of money qualify for tax relief under the **gift aid scheme** provided the donor gives the charity a gift aid declaration.

Gift aid declarations can be made in writing, electronically through the internet or orally over the phone. A declaration can cover a one-off gift or any number of gifts made after a specified date (which may be in the past).

The gift must not be repayable, and must not confer any more than a minimal benefit on the donor. Gift aid may be used for entrance fees (for example to National Trust properties or historic houses) provided the right of admission applies for at least one year or the visitor pays at least 10% more than the normal admission charge.

5.2 Tax relief for gift aid donations

A gift aid donation is treated as though it is paid net of basic rate tax (22%). Additional tax relief for higher rate taxpayers is given in the personal tax computation by increasing the donor's basic rate band by the gross amount of the gift. To arrive at the gross amount of the gift you must multiply the amount paid by 100/78.

No additional relief is due for basic rate taxpayers. Extending the basic rate band is then irrelevant as taxable income is below the basic rate threshold.

EXAMPLE

James earns a salary of £60,530 but has no other income. In 2007/08 he paid £7,800 (net) under the gift aid scheme.

Compute James' income tax liability for 2007/08.

		Non-savings income
		£
Salary/Net income		60,530
Less: personal allowance		(5,225)
Taxable income		55,305
Income tax	£	£
Starting rate band	2,230 × 10%	223
Basic rate band	32,370 × 22%	7,121
Basic rate band (extended)	10,000 × 22%	2,200
Higher rate band	10,705 × 40%	4,282
	55,305	13,826

The basic rate band is extended by the gross amount of the gift (£7,800 × 100/78)

Activity 4 **(10 minutes)**

James earns a salary of £58,000 but has no other income. In 2007/08 he paid £7,800 (net) under the gift aid scheme.

Compute James' income tax liability for 2007/08.

6 FAMILIES

6.1 Spouses and civil partners

Spouses and civil partners are taxed as two separate people. Each spouse/civil partner is entitled to a personal allowance or an age related personal allowance depending on his or her own age and income.

6.2 Joint property

When spouses/civil partners jointly own income-generating property, it is assumed that they are entitled to equal shares of the income. This does not apply to income from shares held in close companies (see later in this Text for an explanation of close companies).

If the spouses/civil partners are not entitled to equal shares in the income-generating property (other than shares in close companies), **they may make a joint declaration to HMRC, specifying the proportion to which each is entitled.** These proportions are used to tax each of them separately, in respect of income arising on or after the date of the declaration. For capital gains tax purposes it is always this underlying beneficial ownership that is taken into account.

6.3 Example: income tax planning for spouses/civil partners

Mr Buckle is a higher rate taxpayer who owns a rental property producing £20,000 of property income on which he pays tax at 40%, giving him a tax liability of £8,000. His spouse has no income.

If he transfers only 5% of the asset to his wife, they will be treated as jointly owning the property and will each be taxed on 50% of the income. Mr Buckle's tax liability will be reduced to £4,000. His wife's liability is only £783, giving an overall tax saving of £3,217.

6.4 Minor children

Income which is directly transferred by a parent to his minor child, or is derived from capital so transferred, remains income of the parent for tax purposes. This applies only to parents, however, and tax saving is therefore possible by other relatives. Even where a parent is involved, the child's income is not treated as the parent's if it does not exceed £100 (gross) a year. **The legislation does not apply to income from a Child Trust Fund (CTF).** CTFs are dealt with later in this Course Book.

7 THE LAYOUT OF PERSONAL TAX COMPUTATIONS

7.1 Steps in the income tax computation

Step 1 The first step in preparing a personal tax computation is to set up three columns
One column for non-savings income, one for savings income and one for dividend income. Add up income from different sources. The sum of these is known as 'total income'.

Step 2 Deal with non-savings income first
Income of up to £2,230 is taxed at 10%. Next any income in the basic rate band is taxed at 22%, and finally income above the basic rate threshold is taxed at 40%.

Step 3 Now deal with savings income
If any of the starting or basic rate bands remain after taxing non savings income, they can be used here. Savings income is taxed at 10% in the starting rate band. If savings income falls within the basic rate band it is taxed at 20% (not 22%). Once income is above the higher rate threshold, it is taxed at 40%.

Step 4 Lastly, tax dividend income
If dividend income falls within the starting or basic rate bands, it is taxed at 10% (never 20% or 22%). If, however, the dividend income exceeds the basic rate threshold of £34,600, it is taxable at 32.5%.

Step 5 Add the amounts of tax together. The resulting figure is the income tax liability.

Step 6 Next, deduct the tax credit on dividends. Although deductible this tax credit cannot be repaid if it exceeds the tax liability calculated so far.

Step 7 Finally deduct the tax deducted at source from savings income and any PAYE. These amounts can be repaid to the extent that they exceed the income tax liability.

NOTES

EXAMPLES: Personal tax computations

1 Kathy has a salary of £10,000 and receives dividends of £4,500.

	Non-savings income	*Dividend income*	*Total*
	£	£	£
Earnings	10,000		
Dividends £4,500 × 100/90		5,000	
Net income	10,000	5,000	15,000
Less personal allowance	(5,225)		
Taxable income	4,775	5,000	9,775

	£
Income tax	
Non savings income	
£2,230 × 10%	223
£2,545 × 22%	560
Dividend income	
£5,000 × 10%	500
Tax liability	1,283
Less tax credit on dividend	(500)
Tax payable	783

Some of the tax payable has probably already been paid on the salary under PAYE.

The dividend income falls within the basic rate band so it is taxed at 10% (*not* 22%).

NOTES

2 Jules has a salary of £20,000, business profits of £30,000, net dividends of £6,750 and building society interest of £3,000 net. He is entitled to relief on interest paid of £2,000.

	Non-savings income	*Savings income*	*Dividend income*	*Total*
	£	£	£	£
Business profits	30,000			
Employment income	20,000			
Dividends £6,750 × 100/90			7,500	
Building society interest £3,000 × 100/80	-	3,750	-	
Total income	50,000	3,750	7,500	
Less interest paid	(2,000)			
Net income	48,000	3,750	7,500	59,250
Less personal allowance	(5,225)			
Taxable income	42,775	3,750	7,500	54,025

	£
Income tax	
Non savings income	
£2,230 × 10%	223
£32,370 × 22%	7,121
£8,175 × 40%	3,270
Savings income	
£3,750 × 40%	1,500
Dividend income	
£7,500 × 32.5%	2,437
Tax liability	14,551
Less tax credit on dividend income	(750)
Less tax suffered on building society interest	(750)
Tax payable	13,051

Savings income and dividend income fall above the basic rate threshold so they are taxed at 40% and 32.5% respectively.

3 Jim does not work. He receives net bank interest of £38,000. He is entitled to relief on interest paid of £2,000.

	Savings income	*Total*
	£	£
Bank interest × 100/80/Total income	47,500	
Less interest paid	(2,000)	
Net income	45,500	45,500
Less personal allowance	(5,225)	
Taxable income	40,275	40,275

	£
Savings income	
£2,230 × 10%	223
£32,370 × 20%	6,474
£5,675 × 40%	2,270
Tax liability	8,967
Less tax suffered	(9,500)
Tax repayable	(533)

Savings income within the basic rate band is taxed at 20% (*not* 22%).

BPP LEARNING MEDIA

Chapter roundup

- The fiscal year is the year that runs from 6 April in one year to 5 April in the next.
- In a personal income tax computation, we bring together income from all sources, splitting the sources into non-savings, savings (excl dividend) and dividend income.
- We deduct charges and then the personal allowance in computing net income.
- Finally, we work out income tax on the taxable income, and take account of tax retained on charges and tax already suffered. We extend the basic rate band by the gross amount of any gift aid donation.
- Husbands, wives and children are all separate taxpayers. There are special rules to prevent parents from exploiting a child's personal allowance.

Quick quiz

1 At what rates is income tax on non-savings income charged?

2 What types of income are taxed at source?

3 How is UK dividend income taxed?

4 What charges on income are paid net?

5 What loan interest is allowable as a charge?

6 What is the amount of personal age allowance available to a 70-year old?

7 How is income from property jointly owned by spouses taxed?

NOTES

Answers to quick quiz

1 10% on first £2,230 of income. 22% on next £32,370 of income. 40% on all excess. (see para 1.2)

2 Interest paid to individuals by banks, building societies, and interest on company loan stocks or debentures. (para 2.3)

3 As the top slice of taxable income and always at 10% tax unless it falls into the higher tax band when 32.5% tax is due. (para 2.3)

4 Patent royalties. (para 3.1)

5 Loans to

- purchase an interest in a partnership
- purchase ordinary shares in a close company
- invest in a co-operative
- purchase shares in an employee controlled company
- purchase plant and machinery (para 3.2)

6 £7,550 (para 4.1)

7 The income is split equally between the spouses unless actual ownership is not 50:50 and a declaration as such is made to HMRC. (para 7.2.)

Answers to activities

1

	£
£2,230 × 10%	223
£32,370 × 22%	7,121
£15,400 × 40%	6,160
£50,000	13,504

Note. Taxable income is the amount after deducting personal allowance(s).

2

	Savings (excl dividend) £	*Dividend* £	*Total* £
Building society interest £6,400 × 100/80	8,000		
Dividends £7,875 × 100/90		8,750	
Premium bond prize: exempt			
Net Income	8,000	8,750	16,750
Less personal allowance	(5,225)		
Taxable income	2,775	8,750	11,525

BPP LEARNING MEDIA

NOTES

3

	Non-savings	Savings (excl dividend)	Total
	£	£	£
Salary	37,000		
Building society interest £2,000 × 100/80		2,500	
	37,000	2,500	
Less charge £7,000 × 10%	(700)		
Net Income	36,300	2,500	38,800
Less personal allowance	(5,225)		
Taxable income	31,075	2,500	33,575

Note. Susan's Net income is £38,800, so even if she is aged 65 or more she will not get any age allowance. The loan to purchase double glazing is not a qualifying loan.

4

	Non-savings
	£
Salary	58,000
Less personal allowance	(5,225)
Taxable income	52,775

Income tax	£	£
Starting rate band	2,230 × 10%	223
Basic rate band	32,370 × 22%	7,121
Basic rate band (extended)	10,000 × 22%	2,200
Higher rate band	8175 × 40%	3,270
	52,775	12,814

Note. £7,800 × 100/78 = £10,000 extension to basic rate tax band re the gift aid payment.

Chapter 32 :
TAXATION OF EMPLOYMENT

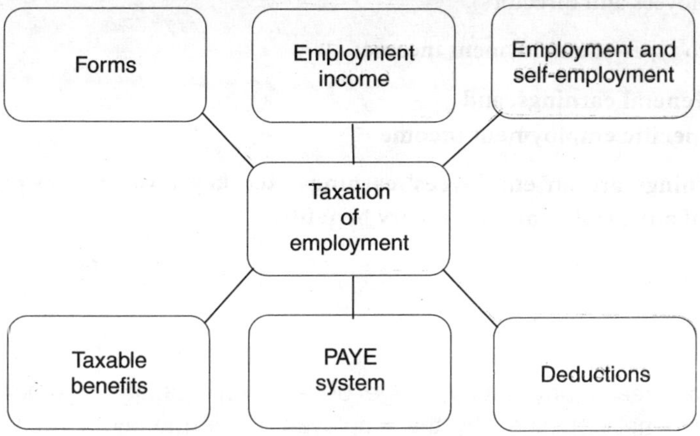

Introduction

The system for the taxation of employment is quite straightforward but includes a large amount of detail, which can at first sight make the system seem complicated. The main thrust of the law here is to ensure that employees pay a fair amount of tax; they cannot be paid in non-monetary ways, for example, and thereby avoid paying tax.

Your objectives

In this chapter you will learn about the following.

(a) Assessable employment income

(b) The difference between employment and self-employment

(c) The basis of assessment (directors and others)

(d) The principal categories of allowable deductions and their scope

(e) The employer's responsibility to collect tax from its employees and how the PAYE system works (including key documents and the net pay scheme)

(f) The information required on the P11D and the P9D

(g) Benefits assessable on all employees and how to compute their value

(h) Benefits assessable only on certain employees and how to compute their value

BPP LEARNING MEDIA

1 EMPLOYMENT INCOME

1.1 Outline of the charge

Employment income includes income arising from an employment under a contract of service (see below) and the income of office holders, such as directors. The term 'employee' is used in this Course Book to mean anyone who receives employment income (ie both employees and directors).

There are two types of employment income:

- **General earnings**, and
- **Specific employment income.**

General earnings are an employees' earnings (see key term below) plus the 'cash equivalent' of any taxable non-monetary benefits.

Definition

'Earnings' means any salary, wage or fee, any gratuity or other profit or incidental benefit obtained by the employee if it is money or money's worth (something of direct monetary value or convertible into direct monetary value) or anything else which constitutes an emolument of the employment.

'Specific employment income' includes payments on termination of employment and share related income.

The residence and domicile status of an employee determines whether earnings are taxable. If an employee is resident, ordinarily resident and domiciled in the UK, **taxable earnings from an employment in a tax year are the general earnings received in that tax year.**

1.2 When are earnings received?

General earnings consisting of money are treated as received at the earlier of:

- **The time when payment is made**
- **The time when a person becomes entitled to payment of the earnings**

If the employee is a director of a company, earnings from the company are received on the earliest of:

- The earlier of the two alternatives given in the general rule (above)
- The time when the amount is credited in the company's accounting records
- The end of the company's period of account (if the amount was determined by then)
- The time the amount is determined (if after the end of the company's period of account).

Taxable benefits are generally treated as received when they are provided to the employee.

NOTES

The receipts basis does not apply to pension income or taxable social security benefits. These sources of income are taxed on the amount accruing in the tax year, whether or not it is received in that year.

Activity 1 **(10 minutes)**

John is a director of X Corp Ltd. His earnings for 2007/08 are:

Salary	£60,000
Taxable benefits	£5,000

For the year ended 31 December 2007 the Board of Directors decide to pay John a bonus of £40,000. This is decided on 1 March 2008 at a board meeting and credited in the company accounts seven days later.

However John only received the bonus in his April pay on 30 April 2008.

What is John's taxable income from employment for 2007/08?

1.3 Net taxable earnings

Total taxable earnings less total allowable deductions (see below) **are net taxable earnings of a tax year. Deductions cannot usually create a loss: they can only reduce the net taxable earnings to nil.**

1.4 Person liable for tax on employment income

The person liable to tax on employment income is generally the **person to whose employment the earnings relate**. However, if the tax relates to general earnings received after the death of the person to whose employment the earnings relate, the person's personal representatives are liable for the tax. The tax is a liability of the estate.

1.5 Employment and self-employment

The distinction between employment (receipts taxable as earnings) and self-employment (receipts taxable as trading income) is a fine one. Employment involves a contract of service, whereas self-employment involves a contract for services. Taxpayers tend to prefer self-employment, because the rules on deductions for expenses are more generous.

Factors which may be of importance include:

- The degree of control exercised over the person doing the work
- Whether he must accept further work
- Whether the other party must provide further work
- Whether he provides his own equipment
- Whether he hires his own helpers
- What degree of financial risk he takes
- What degree of responsibility for investment and management he has
- Whether he can profit from sound management
- Whether he can work when he chooses
- The wording used in any agreement between the parties.

BPP LEARNING MEDIA

Relevant cases include:

(a) *Edwards v Clinch 1981*

A civil engineer acted occasionally as an inspector on temporary *ad hoc* appointments.

Held: there was no ongoing office which could be vacated by one person and held by another so the fees received were from self-employment not employment.

(b) *Hall v Lorimer 1994*

A vision mixer was engaged under a series of short-term contracts.

Held: the vision mixer was self-employed, not because of any one detail of the case but because the overall picture was one of self-employment.

(c) *Carmichael and Anor v National Power plc 1999*

Individuals engaged as visitor guides on a casual 'as required' basis were not employees. An exchange of correspondence between the company and the individuals was not a contract of employment as there was no provision as to the frequency of work and there was flexibility to accept work or turn it down as it arose. Sickness, holiday and pension arrangements did not apply and neither did grievance and disciplinary procedures.

A worker's status also affects national insurance. The self-employed generally pay less than employees.

2 TAXABLE BENEFITS

2.1 Introduction

The Income Tax (Earnings and Pensions) Act 2003 (ITEPA 2003) provides comprehensive legislation covering the taxation of benefits. **The legislation generally applies to all employees. However, only certain parts of it apply to 'excluded employees'.**

(a) **An excluded employee is an employee in lower paid employment who is either not a director of a company or is a director but has no material interest in the company** ('material' means control of more than 5% of the ordinary share capital) and either:

(i) **He is a full-time working director**, or

(ii) **The company is non-profit-making or is established for charitable purposes only.**

(b) **The term 'director' refers to any person who acts as a director or any person in accordance with whose instructions the directors are accustomed to act** (other than a professional advisor).

(c) **Lower paid employment is one where earnings for the tax year are less than £8,500.** To decide whether this applies, add together the **total earnings and benefits that would be taxable if the employee were *not* an excluded employee.**

(d) A number of **specific deductions** must be taken into account to determine lower paid employment. These include **contributions to authorised pension schemes and payroll giving**. However, general deductions from employment income (see later in this chapter) are not taken into account.

(e) Where a car is provided but the employee could have chosen a cash alternative, then the higher of the cash alternative and the car benefit should be used in the computation of earnings to determine whether or not the employee is an excluded employee.

Activity 2 **(10 minutes)**

Tim earns £6,500 per annum working full time as a sales representative at Chap Co Ltd. The company provides the following staff benefits to Tim:

Private health insurance	£300
Company car	£1,500
Expense allowance	£2,000

Tim used £1,900 of the expense allowance on business mileage petrol and on entertaining clients.

Is Tim an excluded employee?

2.2 General business expenses

If business expenses on such items as travel or hotel stays, are reimbursed by an employer, the reimbursed amount is a taxable benefit for employees other than excluded employees. To avoid being taxed on this amount, **an employee must then make a claim to deduct it as an expense** under the rules set out below. **In practice,** however, **many such expense payments are not reported to HMRC and can be ignored because it is agreed in advance that a claim to deduct them would be possible (a P11D dispensation**).

When an individual has to spend one or more nights away from home, his employer may reimburse expenses on items incidental to his absence (for example meals and private telephone calls). **Such incidental expenses are exempt** if:

(a) The expenses of travelling to each place where the individual stays overnight, throughout the trip, are incurred necessarily in the performance of the duties of the employment (or would have been, if there had been any expenses).

(b) The total (for the whole trip) of incidental expenses not deductible under the usual rules is no more than £5 for each night spent wholly in the UK and £10 for each other night. If this limit is exceeded, all of the expenses are taxable, not just the excess. The expenses include any VAT.

This incidental expenses exemption applies to expenses reimbursed, and to benefits obtained using credit tokens and non-cash vouchers.

BPP LEARNING MEDIA

2.3 Vouchers

If any employee (including an excluded employee):

(a) Receives cash vouchers (vouchers exchangeable for cash)

(b) Uses a credit token (such as a credit card) to obtain money, goods or services, or

(c) Receives exchangeable vouchers (such as book tokens), also called non-cash vouchers

he is taxed on the cost of providing the benefit, less any amount made good.

However, the first 15p per working day of meal vouchers (eg luncheon vouchers) is not taxed. In addition, the first £55 per week of child care vouchers is exempt (see below).

2.4 Accommodation

The taxable value of accommodation provided to an employee (including an excluded employee) is the rent that would have been payable if the premises had been let at an amount equal to their annual value (taken to be their **rateable value). If the premises are rented** rather than owned by the employer, then **the taxable benefit is the higher of the rent actually paid and the annual value.** If property does not have a rateable value HMRC estimate a value.

If a property cost the employer more than £75,000, an additional amount is chargeable:

Formula to learn

(Cost of providing the accommodation – £75,000) × the official rate of interest at the start of the tax year.

Thus with an official rate of 6.25%, the total benefit for accommodation costing £90,000 and with an annual value of £2,000 would be £2,000 + £(90,000 – 75,000) × 6.25% = £2,937.

The 'cost of providing' the living accommodation is the aggregate of the cost of purchase and the cost of any improvements made before the start of the tax year for which the benefit is being computed. It is therefore not possible to avoid the charge by buying an inexpensive property requiring substantial repairs and improving it.

If a property was acquired more than six years before first being provided to the employee, the market value when first provided plus the cost of subsequent improvements is used as the cost of providing the accommodation. However, unless the actual cost plus improvements to the start of the tax year in question exceeds £75,000, the additional charge cannot be imposed, however high the market value. In addition, the additional charge can only be imposed if the employer owns (rather than rents) the property concerned.

NOTES

There is no taxable benefit in respect of job-related accommodation. Accommodation is job-related if:

(a) Residence in the accommodation **is necessary for the proper performance of the employee's duties** (as with a caretaker), or

(b) The accommodation is provided **for the better performance of the employee's duties** and the employment is of a kind in which it is **customary for accommodation to be provided** (as with a policeman), or

(c) The **accommodation is provided as part of arrangements in force because of a special threat to the employee's security.**

Directors can only claim exemptions (a) or (b) if:

(i) They have no **material interest** ('material' means over 5%) in the company, and

(ii) Either they are **full-time working directors** or the company is **non-profit making or is a charity.**

Any contribution paid by the employee is deducted from the annual value of the property and then from the additional benefit.

If the employee is given a cash alternative to living accommodation, the benefits code still applies in priority to treating the cash alternative as earnings. If the cash alternative is greater than the taxable benefit, the excess is treated as earnings.

2.5 Expenses connected with living accommodation

In addition to the benefit of living accommodation itself, **employees, other than excluded employees, are taxed on related expenses paid by the employer,** such as:

(a) **Heating, lighting or cleaning the premises**
(b) **Repairing, maintaining or decorating the premises**
(c) **The provision of furniture (the annual value is 20% of the cost)**

Unless the accommodation qualifies as 'job related' (as defined above) **the full cost of ancillary services** (excluding structural repairs) **is taxable. If the accommodation is 'job related'**, however, **taxable ancillary services are restricted to a maximum of 10% of the employee's 'net earnings'.**

For this purpose, net earnings are all earnings from the employment (excluding the ancillary benefits (a)–(c) above) less any allowable expenses, statutory mileage allowances, contributions to registered occupational pension schemes (but not personal pension plans), and capital allowances.

If there are ancillary benefits other than those falling within (a)–(c) above (such as a telephone) they are taxable in full.

Council tax and water or sewage charges paid by the employer are taxable in full as a benefit unless the accommodation is 'job-related'.

Activity 3 **(10 minutes)**

Mr Quinton has a gross salary in 2007/08 of £28,850. He normally lives and works in London, but he is required to live in a company house in Scotland, which costs £70,000 three years ago, so that he can carry out a two year review of his company's operations in Scotland. The annual value of the house is £650. In 2007/08 the company pays an electricity bill of £550, a gas bill of £400, a gardener's bill of £750 and redecoration costs of £1,800. Mr Quinton makes a monthly contribution of £50 for his accommodation. He also pays £1,450 occupational pension contributions.

Calculate Mr Quinton's taxable employment income for 2007/08.

2.6 Cars

A car provided by reason of the employment to an employee or member of his family or household for private use gives rise to a taxable benefit. This does not apply to excluded employees. **'Private use' includes home to work travel.**

(a) A tax charge arises whether the car is provided by the employer or by some other person. The benefit is computed as shown below, even if the car is taken as an alternative to another benefit of a different value.

(b) The starting point for calculating a car benefit is the list price of the car (plus accessories). **The percentage of the list price that is taxable depends on the car's CO_2 emissions.**

(c) The price of the car is the sum of the following items.

(i) The list price of the car for a single retail sale at the time of first registration, including charges for delivery and standard accessories. The manufacturer's, importer's or distributor's list price must be used, even if the retailer offered a discount. A notional list price is estimated if no list price was published.

(ii) The price (including fitting) of all optional accessories provided when the car was first provided to the employee, excluding mobile telephones and equipment needed by a disabled employee. The extra cost of adapting or manufacturing a car to run on road fuel gases is not included.

(iii) The price (including fitting) of all optional accessories fitted later and costing at least £100 each, excluding mobile telephones and equipment needed by a disabled employee. Such accessories affect the taxable benefit from and including the tax year in which they are fitted. However, accessories which are merely replacing existing accessories and are not superior to the ones replaced are ignored. Replacement accessories which *are* superior are taken into account, but the cost of the old accessory is then ignored.

(d) There is a special rule for classic cars. If the car is at least 15 years old (from the time of first registration) at the end of the tax year, and its market value at the end of the year (or, if earlier, when it ceased to be available to the employee) is over £15,000 and greater than the price found under (c), that market value is used instead of the price. The market value takes account of all accessories (except mobile telephones and equipment needed by a disabled employee).

(e) Capital contributions are payments by the employee in respect of the price of the car or accessories. In any tax year, we take account of capital contributions made in that year and previous years (for the same car). The maximum deductible capital contributions is £5,000; contributions beyond that total are ignored.

(f) If the price or value found under (c) or (d) exceeds £80,000, then £80,000 is used instead of the price or value. This £80,000 is after capital contributions (see (e) above) have been taken into account.

(g) For cars that emit **CO_2 of 140g/km (2007/08) or less, the taxable benefit is 15% of the car's list price. This percentage increases by 1% for every 5g/km (rounded down to the nearest multiple of 5) by which CO_2 emissions exceed 140g/km up to a maximum of 35%.**

(h) Diesel cars have a supplement of 3% of the car's list price added to the taxable benefit. However, the benefit is discounted for cars that are particularly environmentally friendly. The maximum percentage, however, remains 35% of the list price.

(i) **The benefit is reduced on a time basis where a car is first made available or ceases to be made available during the tax year** or is incapable of being used for a continuous period of not less than 30 days (for example because it is being repaired).

(j) **The benefit is reduced by any payment the user must make for the private use of the car** (as distinct from a capital contribution to the cost of the car). Payments for insuring the car do not count *(IRC v Quigley 1995)*. The benefit cannot become negative to create a deduction from the employee's income.

(k) Pool cars are exempt. A car is a pool car if **all** the following conditions are satisfied.

   (i) It is used by more than one employee and is not ordinarily used by any one of them to the exclusion of the others

   (ii) Any private use is merely incidental to business use

   (iii) It is not normally kept overnight at or near the residence of an employee

There are many ancillary benefits associated with the provision of cars, such as insurance, repairs, vehicle licences and a parking space at or near work. No extra taxable benefit arises as a result of these, with the exception of the cost of providing a driver.

2.7 Fuel for cars

Where fuel is provided there is a further benefit in addition to the car benefit.

No taxable benefit arises where either

(a) **All the fuel provided was made available only for business travel**, or

(b) **The employee is required to make good, and has made good, the whole of the cost of any fuel provided for his private use.**

Unlike most benefits, a reimbursement of only part of the cost of the fuel available for private use does not reduce the benefit.

The taxable benefit is a percentage of a base figure. The base figure for 2007/08 is £14,400. The percentage is the same percentage as is used to calculate the car benefit (see above).

The fuel benefit is reduced in the same way as the car benefit **if the car is not available for 30 days or more.**

The fuel benefit is also reduced if private fuel is not available for part of a tax year. However, if private fuel later becomes available in the same tax year, the reduction is not made. If, for example, fuel is provided from 6 April 2007 to 30 June 2007, then the fuel benefit for 2007/08 will be restricted to just three months. This is because the provision of fuel has permanently ceased. However, if fuel is provided from 6 April 2007 to 30 June 2007, and then again from 1 September 2007 to 5 April 2008, then the fuel benefit will not be reduced since the cessation was only temporary.

Activity 4 **(5 minutes)**

An employee was provided with a new car costing £15,000. The car emits 191g/km of CO_2. During 2007/08 the employer spent £900 on insurance, repairs and a vehicle license. The firm paid for all petrol, costing £1,500, without reimbursement. The employee paid the firm £270 for the private use of the car.

Calculate the taxable benefit.

2.8 Vans and heavier commercial vehicles

If a van (of normal maximum laden weight up to 3,500 kg) **is made available for an employee's private use, there is an annual scale charge of £3,000.** The scale charge covers ancillary benefits such as insurance and servicing. Paragraphs 2.6 (i) and (j) above apply to vans as they do to cars.

There is, however, **no taxable benefit where an employee takes a van home** (ie uses the van for home to work travel) but is not allowed any other private use.

If the employer provides **fuel for unrestricted private use**, an additional **fuel charge of £500** applies.

If a commercial vehicle of normal maximum laden weight over 3,500 kg is made available for an employee's private use, but the employee's use of the vehicle is not wholly or mainly private, no taxable benefit arises except in respect of the provision of a driver.

NOTES

2.9 Statutory mileage allowances

A single authorised mileage allowance for business journeys in an employee's own vehicle applies to all cars and vans. There is no income tax on payments up to this allowance and employers do not have to report mileage allowances up to this amount. The allowance for 2007/08 is 40p per mile on the first 10,000 miles in the tax year with each additional mile over 10,000 miles at 25p per mile. The authorised mileage allowance for employees using their own motor cycle is 24p per mile. For employees using their own pedal cycle it is 20p per mile.

If employers pay less than the statutory allowance, employees can claim tax relief up to that level.

The statutory allowance does not prevent employers from paying higher rates, but any excess will be subject to income tax. There is a similar (but slightly different) system for NICs, covered below.

Employers can make income tax and NIC free payments of up to 5p per mile for each fellow employee making the same business trip who is carried as a passenger. If the employer does not pay the employee for carrying business passengers, the employee cannot claim any tax relief.

EXAMPLE

Sophie uses her own car for business travel. During 2007/08, Sophie drove 15,400 miles in the performance of her duties. Sophie's employer paid her 35p a mile. How is the mileage allowance received by Sophie treated for tax purposes?

	£
Mileage allowance received (15,400 × 35p)	5,390
Less tax free [(10,000 × 40p) + (5,400 × 25p)]	(5,350)
Taxable benefit	40

£5,350 is tax free and the excess amount received of £40 is a taxable benefit.

2.10 Beneficial loans

2.10.1 Introduction

Employment related loans to employees (other than excluded employees) and their relatives give rise to a benefit equal to:

(a) **Any amounts written off** (unless the employee has died), and

(b) **The excess of the interest based on an official rate prescribed by the Treasury, over any interest actually charged ('taxable cheap loan')**. Interest payable during the tax year but paid after the end of the tax year is taken into account, but if the benefit is determined before such interest is paid a claim must be made to take it into account.

The following loans are normally not treated as taxable cheap loans for calculation of the interest benefits (but not for the purposes of the charge on loans written off).

NOTES

(a) A loan on normal commercial terms made in the ordinary course of the employer's money-lending business.

(b) A loan made by an individual in the ordinary course of the lender's domestic, family or personal arrangements.

2.10.2 Calculating the interest benefit

There are two alternative methods of calculating the taxable benefit. The simpler **'average' method** automatically applies unless the taxpayer or HMRC elect for the alternative **'strict' method**. (HMRC normally only make the election where it appears that the 'average' method is being deliberately exploited.) In both methods, the benefit is the interest at the official rate minus the interest payable.

The 'average' method averages the balances at the beginning and end of the tax year (or the dates on which the loan was made and discharged if it was not in existence throughout the tax year) and applies the official rate of interest to this average. If the loan was not in existence throughout the tax year only the number of complete tax months (from the 6th of the month) for which it existed are taken into account.

The 'strict' method is to compute interest at the official rate on the actual amount outstanding on a daily basis.

EXAMPLE

At 6 April 2007 a taxable cheap loan of £30,000 was outstanding to an employee earning £12,000 a year, who repaid £20,000 on 7 December 2007. The remaining balance of £10,000 was outstanding at 5 April 2008. Interest paid during the year was £250. What was the benefit under both methods for 2007/08, assuming that the official rate of interest was 6.25%?

Average method

	£
$6.25\% \times \frac{30{,}000 + 10{,}000}{2}$	1,250
Less interest paid	(250)
Benefit	1,000

Alternative method (strict method)

	£
£30,000 × $\frac{245}{365}$ (6 April – 6 December) × 6.25%	1,259
£10,000 × $\frac{120}{365}$ (7 December – 5 April) × 6.25%	205
	1,464
Less interest paid	(250)
Benefit	1,214

HMRC might opt for the alternative method.

BPP LEARNING MEDIA

NOTES

2.10.3 The *de minimis* test

The benefit is not taxable if:

(a) The total of all taxable cheap loans to the employee did not exceed £5,000 at any time in the tax year, or

(b) The loan is not a qualifying loan and the total of all non-qualifying loans to the employee did not exceed £5,000 at any time in the tax year.

A qualifying loan is one on which all or part of any interest paid would qualify as a charge on income.

When the £5,000 threshold is exceeded, a benefit arises on interest on the whole loan, not just on the excess of the loan over £5,000.

When a loan is written off and a benefit arises, there is no £5,000 threshold: writing off a loan of £1 gives rise to a £1 benefit.

2.10.4 Qualifying loans

If the whole of the interest payable on a qualifying loan is eligible for tax relief as deductible interest, then no taxable benefit arises. If the interest is only partly eligible for tax relief, then the employee is treated as receiving earnings because the actual rate of interest is below the official rate. He is also treated as paying interest equal to those earnings. This **deemed interest paid may qualify as a business expense or as deductible interest in addition to any interest actually paid.**

Activity 5 **(10 minutes)**

Anna, who is single, has an annual salary of £30,000, and two loans from her employer.

(a) A season ticket loan of £2,300 at no interest

(b) A loan, 90% of which was used to buy shares in her employee-controlled company, of £54,000 at 3% interest

The official rate of interest is to be taken at 6.25%.

What is Anna's tax liability for 2007/08?

2.11 Other assets made available for private use

When assets are made available to employees or members of their family or household, the taxable benefit is the higher of 20% of the market value when first provided as a benefit to any employee, or on the rent paid by the employer if higher. The 20% charge is time-apportioned when the asset is provided for only part of the year. The charge after any time apportionment is reduced by any contribution made by the employee.

Certain assets, such as bicycles provided for journeys to work, are exempt. These are described later in this chapter.

BPP LEARNING MEDIA

If an asset made available is subsequently acquired by the employee, the taxable benefit on the acquisition is the *greater* of:

- **The current market value minus the price paid by the employee.**
- **The market value when first provided minus any amounts already taxed (ignoring contributions by the employee) minus the price paid by the employee.**

This rule prevents tax free benefits arising on rapidly depreciating items through the employee purchasing them at their low second-hand value.

There is an exception to this rule for bicycles which have previously been provided as exempt benefits. The taxable benefit on acquisition is restricted to current market value, minus the price paid by the employee.

EXAMPLE

A suit costing £400 is purchased by an employer for use by an employee on 6 April 2006. On 6 April 2007 the suit is purchased by the employee for £30, its market value then being £50.

The benefit in 2006/07 is £400 × 20%		£80
The benefit in 2007/08 is £290, being the **greater** of:		
		£
(a)	Market value at acquisition by employee	50
	Less price paid	(30)
		20
(b)	Original market value	400
	Less taxed in respect of use	(80)
		320
	Less price paid	(30)
		290

EXAMPLE

Rupert is provided with a new bicycle by his employer on 6 April 2007. The bicycle is available for private use as well as commuting to work. It cost the employer £1,500 when new. On 6 October 2007 the employer transfers ownership of the bicycle to Rupert when it is worth £800. Rupert does not pay anything for the bicycle.

What is the total taxable benefit on Rupert for 2007/08 in respect of the bicycle?

Use benefit	Exempt
Transfer benefit (use MV at acquisition by employee only)	
MV at transfer	£800

NOTES

2.12 Scholarships

If scholarships are given to members of an employee's family, the **employee is taxable on the cost** unless the scholarship fund's or scheme's payments by reason of people's employments are not more than 25% of its total payments.

2.13 Residual charge

We have seen above how certain specific benefits are taxed. **A 'residual charge' is made on the taxable value of other benefits. In general, the taxable value of a benefit is the cost of the benefit less any part of that cost made good by the employee to the persons providing the benefit.**

The residual charge applies to any benefit provided for an employee or a member of his family or household, by reason of the employment. There is an exception where the employer is an individual and the provision of the benefit is made in the normal course of the employer's domestic, family or personal relationships.

This rule does not apply to taxable benefits provided to excluded employees. **These employees are taxed only on the second hand value of any benefit that could be converted into money.**

3 EXEMPT BENEFITS

Various benefits are exempt from tax. These include:

(a) **Entertainment provided to employees by genuine third parties** (eg seats at sporting/cultural events), even if it is provided by giving the employee a voucher.

(b) **Gifts of goods** (or vouchers exchangeable for goods) from third parties (ie not provided by the employer or a person connected to the employer) if the total cost (incl. VAT) of all gifts by the same donor to the same employee in the tax year is £250 or less. If the £250 limit is exceeded, the full amount is taxable, not just the excess.

(c) **Non-cash awards for long service** if the period of service was at least twenty years, no similar award was made to the employee in the past ten years and the cost is not more than £50 per year of service.

(d) **Awards under staff suggestion schemes if:**

(i) There is a formal scheme, open to all employees on equal terms.

(ii) The suggestion is outside the scope of the employee's normal duties.

(iii) Either the award is not more than £25, or the award is only made after a decision is taken to implement the suggestion.

(iv) Awards over £25 reflect the financial importance of the suggestion to the business, and either do not exceed 50% of the expected net financial benefit during the first year of implementation or do not exceed 10% of the expected net financial benefit over a period of up to five years.

(v) Awards of over £25 are shared on a reasonable basis between two or more employees putting forward the same suggestion.

If an award exceeds £5,000, the excess is always taxable.

BPP LEARNING MEDIA

(e) **The first £8,000 of removal expenses if:**

 (i) The employee does not already live within a reasonable daily travelling distance of his new place of employment, but will do so after moving.

 (ii) The expenses are incurred or the benefits provided by the end of the tax year following the tax year of the start of employment at the new location.

(f) The cost of running a **workplace nursery or play scheme (without limit). Otherwise up to £55 a week of childcare is tax free** if the employer contracts with an approved childcare or provides childcare vouchers to pay an approved childcare. The childcare must be available to all employees and the childcare must either be registered or approved home-childcare.

(g) **Sporting or recreational facilities available to employees generally and not to the general public,** unless they are provided on domestic premises, or they consist in an interest in or the use of any mechanically propelled vehicle or any overnight accommodation. Vouchers only exchangeable for such facilities are also exempt, but membership fees for sports clubs are taxable.

(h) **Assets or services used in performing the duties of employment** provided any private use of the item concerned is insignificant. This exempts, for example, the benefit arising on the private use of employer-provided tools.

(i) **Welfare counselling** and similar minor benefits if the benefit concerned is available to employees generally.

(j) **Bicycles or cycling safety equipment provided to enable employees to get to and from work or to travel between one workplace and another.** The equipment must be available to the employer's employees generally. Also, it must be used mainly for the aforementioned journeys.

(k) **Workplace parking**

(l) **Up to £7,000 a year paid to an employee who is on a full-time course lasting at least a year,** with average full-time attendance of at least 20 weeks a year. If the £7,000 limit is exceeded, the whole amount is taxable.

(m) **Work related training and related costs. This includes the costs of** training material and assets either made during training or incorporated into something so made.

(n) **Air miles or car fuel coupons** obtained as a result of business expenditure but used for private purposes.

(o) **The cost of work buses and minibuses or subsidies to public bus services.**

A work bus must have a seating capacity of 12 or more and a works minibus a seating capacity of nine or more but not more than 12 and be available generally to employees of the employer concerned. The bus or minibus must mainly be used by employees for journeys to and from work and for journeys between workplaces.

(p) Transport/overnight costs where public transport is disrupted by industrial action, late night taxis and travel costs incurred where car sharing arrangements unavoidably breakdown.

(q) The private use of one **mobile phone**. Top-up vouchers for exempt mobile phones are also tax free. If more than one mobile phone is provided to an employee for private use only the second or subsequent phone is a taxable benefit.

(r) **Employer provided uniforms** which employees must wear as part of their duties.

(s) The cost of **staff parties** which are open to staff generally provided that the **cost per staff member per year (including VAT) is £150 or less**. The £150 limit may be split between several parties. If exceeded, the full amount is taxable, not just the excess over £150.

(t) **Private medical insurance premiums paid to cover treatment when the employee is outside the UK in the performance of his duties.** Other medical insurance premiums are taxable as is the cost of medical diagnosis and treatment except for routine check ups. Eye tests and glasses for employees using VDUs are exempt.

(u) **The first 15p per day of meal vouchers (eg luncheon vouchers).**

(v) Cheap loans **that do not exceed £5,000** at any time in the tax year (see above).

(w) **Job-related accommodation** (see above).

(x) **Employer contributions towards additional household costs incurred by an employee who works wholly or partly at home.** Payments up to £2 pw (£104 pa) may be made without supporting evidence. Payments in excess of that amount require supporting evidence that the payment is wholly in respect of additional household expenses.

(y) **Meals or refreshments for cyclists** provided as part of official 'cycle to work' days.

Where a voucher is provided for a benefit which is exempt from income tax the provision of the voucher itself is also exempt.

4 ALLOWABLE DEDUCTIONS

4.1 General principles

Certain expenditure is specifically deductible in computing net taxable earnings:

(a) **Contributions** (within certain limits) **to registered occupational pension schemes** (see earlier in this Course Book).

(b) **Subscriptions to professional bodies** on the list of bodies issued by HMRC (which includes most UK professional bodies), if relevant to the duties of the employment

(c) Payments for certain **liabilities relating to the employment** and for insurance against them (see below)

(d) **Payments to charity made under the payroll deduction scheme** operated by an employer

(e) **Mileage allowance** relief (see above)

Otherwise, allowable deductions are notoriously hard to obtain. They are limited to:

(a) Qualifying travel expenses (see below)

(b) Other expenses the employee is obliged to incur and pay as holder of the employment which are incurred wholly, exclusively and necessarily in the performance of the duties of the employment

(c) Capital allowances on plant and machinery (other than cars or other vehicles) necessarily provided for use in the performance of those duties.

4.2 Liabilities and insurance

If a director or employee incurs a liability related to his employment or pays for insurance against such a liability, the cost is a deductible expense. If the employer pays such amounts, there is no taxable benefit.

A liability relating to employment is one which is imposed in respect of the employee's acts or omissions as employee. Thus, for example, liability for negligence would be covered. Related costs, for example the costs of legal proceedings, are included.

For insurance premiums to qualify, the insurance policy must:

(a) Cover only liabilities relating to employment, vicarious liability in respect of liabilities of another person's employment, related costs and payments to the employee's own employees in respect of their employment liabilities relating to employment and related costs.

(b) It must not last for more than two years (although it may be renewed for up to two years at a time), and the insured person must not be not required to renew it.

4.3 Travel expenses

Tax relief is not available for an employee's normal commuting costs. This means relief is not available for any costs an employee incurs in getting from home to his normal place of work. However **employees are entitled to relief for travel expenses which basically are the full costs that they are obliged to incur and pay as holder of the employment in travelling in the performance of their duties or travelling to or from a place which they have to attend in the performance of their duties (other than a permanent workplace).**

EXAMPLE: TRAVEL IN THE PERFORMANCE OF DUTIES

Judi is an accountant. She often travels to meetings at the firm's offices in the North of England returning to her office in Leeds after the meetings. Relief is available for the full cost of these journeys as the travel is undertaken in the performance of her duties.

> **Activity 6** **(10 minutes)**
>
> Zoe lives in Wycombe and normally works in Chiswick. Occasionally she visits a client in Wimbledon and travels direct from home. Distances are shown in the diagram below:
>
> 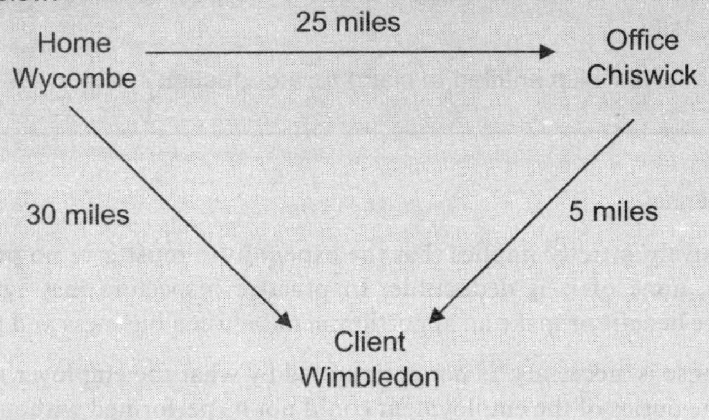
>
>
> What tax relief if available for Zoe's travel costs?

To prevent manipulation of the basic rule normal commuting will not become a business journey just because the employee stops en-route to perform a business task (eg make a 'phone call'). Nor will relief be available if the journey is essentially the same as the employee's normal journey to work.

EXAMPLE: NORMAL COMMUTING

Judi is based at her office in Leeds City Centre. One day she is required to attend a 9.00 am meeting with a client whose premises are around the corner from her Leeds office. Judi travels from home directly to the meeting. As the journey is substantially the same as her ordinary journey to work relief is not available.

Site based employees (eg construction workers, management consultants etc) who do not have a permanent workplace, are entitled to relief for the costs of all journeys made from home to wherever they are working. This is because these employees do not have an ordinary commuting journey or any normal commuting costs. However there is a caveat that the employee does not spend more than 24 months of continuous work at any one site.

Tax relief is available for travel, accommodation and subsistence expenses incurred by an employee who is working at a temporary workplace on a secondment expected to last up to 24 months. If a secondment is initially expected not to exceed 24 months, but it is extended, relief ceases to be due from the date the employee becomes aware of the change. When looking at how long a secondment is expected to last, HMRC will consider not only the terms of the written contract but also any verbal agreement by the employer and other factors such as whether the employee buys a house etc.

Activity 7 **(10 minutes)**

Philip works for Vastbank at its Newcastle City Centre branch. Philip is sent to work full-time at another branch in Morpeth for twenty months at the end of which he will return to the Newcastle branch. Morpeth is about twenty miles north of Newcastle.

What travel costs is Philip entitled to claim as a deduction?

4.4 Other expenses

The word 'exclusively' strictly implies that the expenditure must give no private benefit at all. If it does, none of it is deductible. In practice inspectors may ignore a small element of private benefit or make an apportionment between business and private use.

Whether an expense is 'necessary' is not determined by what the employer requires. The test is whether the duties of the employment could not be performed without the outlay.

(a) *Sanderson v Durbridge 1955*

The cost of evening meals taken when attending late meetings was not deductible because it was not incurred in the performance of the duties.

(b) *Blackwell v Mills 1945*

As a condition of his employment, an employee was required to attend evening classes. The cost of his textbooks and travel was not deductible because it was not incurred in the performance of the duties.

(c) *Lupton v Potts 1969*

Examination fees incurred by a solicitor's articled clerk were not deductible because they were incurred neither wholly nor exclusively in the performance of the duties, but in furthering the clerk's ambition to become a solicitor.

(d) *Brown v Bullock 1961*

The expense of joining a club that was virtually a requisite of an employment was not deductible because it would have been possible to carry on the employment without the club membership, so the expense was not necessary.

(e) *Elwood v Utitz 1965*

A managing director's subscriptions to two residential London clubs were claimed by him as an expense on the grounds that they were cheaper than hotels.

The expenditure was deductible as it was necessary in that it would be impossible for the employee to carry out his London duties without being provided with first class accommodation. The residential facilities (which were cheaper than hotel accommodation) were given to club members only.

(f) *Lucas v Cattell 1972*

The cost of business telephone calls on a private telephone is deductible, but no part of the line or telephone rental charges is deductible.

(g) *Fitzpatrick v IRC 1994; Smith v Abbott 1994*

Journalists cannot claim a deduction for the cost of buying newspapers which they read to keep themselves informed, since they are merely preparing themselves to perform their duties.

The cost of clothes for work is not deductible, except that for certain trades requiring protective clothing there are annual deductions on a set scale.

An employee required to work at home may be able to claim a deduction for an appropriate proportion of his or her expenditure on lighting, heating and (if a room is used exclusively for work purposes) **the council tax.** Employers can pay up to £2 per week without the need for supporting evidence of the costs incurred by the employee (see above). Payments above the £2 limit require evidence of the employee's actual costs.

5 PERSONAL SERVICE COMPANIES

5.1 Application and outline of computation

We looked at the distinction between employment and self-employment earlier in this chapter. Taxpayers normally prefer to avoid being classified as employees. Consequently, there are anti-avoidance rules which prevent workers avoiding tax and National Insurance contributions by offering their services through an intermediary, such as a personal service company. **These provisions are commonly known as the IR35 provisions.**

Broadly, the IR35 provisions provide that:

(a) If an individual ('the worker') performs, or has an obligation to perform, services for 'a client', and

(b) The performance of those services is referable to arrangements involving a third party (eg the personal service company), rather than referable to a contract between the client and the worker, and

(c) If the services were to be performed by the worker under a contract between himself and the client, he would be regarded as employed by the client

then **a salary payment may be deemed to have been made to the worker at the end of the tax year.** This deemed payment is subject to PAYE and NICs.

The following steps should be followed to compute the amount of the deemed payment.

Step 1 Take 95% of all payments and benefits received in respect of the relevant engagements by the third party.

Step 2 **Add amounts received in respect of the relevant engagements by the worker otherwise than from the third party,** if they are not chargeable as employment income, but would have been so chargeable if the worker had been employed by the client.

Step 3 **Deduct expenses met by the third party** if those expenses would have been deductible had they been paid out of the taxable earnings of the employment by the worker. This also includes expenses paid by the worker and reimbursed by the third party. Mileage allowances up to the statutory amounts are also deductible where a vehicle is provided by the third party.

Step 4 **Deduct capital allowances on expenditure incurred by the third party** if the worker would have been able to deduct them had he incurred the expenditure and had he been employed by the client.

Step 5 **Deduct any 'registered' pension contributions and employer's NICs paid by the third party** in respect of the worker.

Step 6 **Deduct amounts received by the worker from the third party** that are chargeable as employment income but were not deducted under Step 3.

Step 7 Find the amount that together with employer's NIC (see below) on it, is equal to the amount resulting from Step 6 above. This means that you should multiply the amount in Step 6 by 12.8/112.8 and deduct this amount from the amount in Step 6.

Step 8 The result is the amount of the deemed employment income.

5.2 Effect on company

The deemed employment income is an allowable trading expense for the personal service company and is treated as made on the last day of the tax year.

The personal service company should consider having an accounting date of 5 April, or shortly thereafter.

For example, if accounts are prepared to 5 April the deemed employment income for 2007/08 is deductible in the company in the year to 5 April 2008, whereas with a 31 March year end the deemed payment would be deductible in the year to 31 March 2009.

EXAMPLE

Alison offers technical writing services through a company. During 2007/08 the company received income of £40,000 in respect of relevant engagements performed by Alison. The company paid Alison a salary of £20,000 plus employer's NIC of £1,891. The company also pays £3,000 into an occupational pension scheme in respect of Alison. Alison incurred travelling expenses of £400 in respect of the relevant engagements.

The deemed employment income taxed on Alison is

	£
Income (£40,000 × 95%)	38,000
Less: travel	(400)
pension	(3,000)
salary	(20,000)
employer's NIC on actual salary	(1,891)
	12,709
Less: employer's NIC on deemed payment	
$\frac{12.8}{112.8} \times$ £12,709	(1,442)
Deemed employment income	11,267

---

6 THE PAYE SYSTEM

6.1 Introduction

6.1.1 Cash payments

The objective of the PAYE system is to deduct the correct amount of tax over the year. Its scope is very wide. It applies to most cash payments, other than reimbursed business expenses, and to certain non cash payments.

In addition to wages and salaries, PAYE applies to round sum expense allowances and payments instead of benefits. It also applies to any readily convertible asset.

A readily convertible asset is any asset which can effectively be exchanged for cash. The amount subject to PAYE is the amount that would be taxed as employment income. This is usually the cost to the employer of providing the asset.

Tips paid direct to an employee are normally outside the PAYE system (although still assessable as employment income). An exception may apply in the catering trades where tips are often pooled. Here the PAYE position depends on whether a 'tronc', administered other than by the employer, exists.

It is the employer's duty to deduct income tax from the pay of his employees, whether or not he has been directed to do so by HMRC. **If he fails to do this he** (or sometimes the employee) **must pay over the tax which he should have deducted and the employer may be subject to penalties.** Interest will also run from 14 days after the end of the tax year concerned on any underpaid PAYE. Officers of HMRC can inspect employer's records in order to satisfy themselves that the correct amounts of tax are being deducted and paid over to HMRC.

6.1.2 Benefits

PAYE is not normally operated on benefits; instead the employee's PAYE code is restricted (see below).

However, PAYE must be applied to remuneration in the form of a taxable non-cash voucher if at the time it is provided:

(a) the voucher is capable of being exchanged for readily convertible assets; or
(b) the voucher can itself be sold, realised or traded.

PAYE must normally be operated on cash vouchers and on each occasion when a director/employee uses a credit-token (eg a credit card) to obtain money or goods which are readily convertible assets. However, a cash voucher or credit token which is used to defray expenses is not subject to PAYE.

6.2 How PAYE works

6.2.1 Operation of PAYE

To operate PAYE the employer needs:

(a) deductions working sheets
(b) codes for employees that reflect the tax allowances to which the employees are entitled
(c) tax tables.

The employer works out the amount of PAYE tax to deduct on any particular pay day by using the employee's code number (see below) in conjunction with the PAYE tables. The tables are designed so that tax is normally worked out on a cumulative

basis. This means that with each payment of earnings the running total of tax paid is compared with tax due on total earnings to that date. The difference between the tax due and the tax paid is the tax to be deducted on that particular payday.

National insurance tables are used to work out the national insurance due on any payday.

6.2.2 Records

The employer must keep records of each employee's pay and tax at each pay day. The records must also contain details of National Insurance. The employer has a choice of three ways of recording and returning these figures:

- He may use the official deductions working sheet (P11)
- He may incorporate the figures in his own pay records using a substitute document
- He may retain the figures on a computer.

These records will be used to make a return at the end of the tax year.

6.3 Payment under the PAYE system

Under PAYE income tax and national insurance is normally paid over to HMRC monthly, 14 days after the end of each tax month.

If an employer's average monthly payments under the PAYE system are less than £1,500, the employer may choose to pay quarterly, within 14 days of the end of each tax quarter. Tax quarters end on 5 July, 5 October, 5 January and 5 April. Payments can continue to be made quarterly during a tax year even if the monthly average reaches or exceeds £1,500, but a new estimate must be made and a new decision taken to pay quarterly at the start of each tax year. Average monthly payments are the average net monthly payments due to HMRC for income tax and NICs.

6.4 PAYE codes

An employee is normally entitled to various allowances. Under the PAYE system an amount reflecting the effect of a proportion of these allowances is set against his pay each pay day. To determine the amount to set against his pay the allowances are expressed in the form of a code which is used in conjunction with the Pay Adjustment Table (Table A).

An employee's code may be any one of the following.

L	tax code with basic personal allowance
P	tax code with age 65–74 age allowance
Y	tax code with age 75+ age allowance

The codes BR, DO and OT are generally used where there is a second source of income and all allowances have been used in a tax code which is applied to the main source of income.

Generally, a tax code number is arrived at by deleting the last digit in the sum representing the employee's tax free allowances. Every individual is entitled to a personal tax free allowance of £5,225. The code number for an individual who is entitled to this but no other allowance is 522L.

NOTES

The code number may also reflect other items. For example, **it will be restricted to reflect benefits, small amounts of untaxed income** and **unpaid tax on income from earlier years.** If an amount of tax is in point, it is necessary to gross up the tax in the code using the taxpayer's estimated marginal rate of income tax.

EXAMPLE

Adrian is a 40-year old single man (suffix letter L) who earns £15,000 pa. He has benefits of £560 and his unpaid tax for 2005/06 was £57.50. Adrian is entitled to a tax free personal allowance of £5,225 in 2007/08.

Adrian pays income tax at the marginal rate of 22%.

What is Adrian's PAYE code for 2007/08?

	£
Personal allowance	5,225
Benefits	(560)
Unpaid tax £57.50 × 100/22	(261)
Available allowances	4,404

Adrian's PAYE code is 440L

Codes are determined and amended by HMRC. They are normally notified to the employer on a code list. The employer must act on the code notified to him until amended instructions are received from HMRC, even if the employee has appealed against the code.

By using the code number in conjunction with the tax tables, an employee is generally given $1/52^{nd}$ or $1/12^{th}$ of his tax free allowances against each week's/month's pay. However because of the cumulative nature of PAYE, if an employee is first paid in, say, September, that month he will receive six months' allowances against his gross pay. In cases where the employee's previous PAYE history is not known, this could lead to under-deduction of tax. To avoid this, codes for the employees concerned have to be operated on a 'week 1/month1' basis, so that only $1/52^{nd}$ or $1/12^{th}$ of the employee's allowances are available each week/month.

6.5 PAYE forms

At the end of each tax year, the employer must provide each employee with a form P60. This shows total taxable earnings for the year, tax deducted, code number, NI number and the employer's name and address. **The P60 must be provided by 31 May following the year of assessment.**

Following the end of each tax year, the employer must send HMRC:

(a) **By 19 May:**

- (i) **End of year Returns P14** (showing the same details as the P60)
- (ii) **Form P35** (summary of total tax and NI deducted from all employees)

BPP LEARNING MEDIA

(b) **by 6 July:**

   (i) **Forms P11D** (benefits etc for directors and employees paid £8,500+ pa)
   (ii) **Forms P11D(b)** (return of Class 1A NICs (see later in this Course Book))
   (iii) **Forms P9D** (benefits etc for other employees)

A copy of the form P11D (or P9D) must also be provided to the employee by 6 July. The details shown on the P11D include the full cash equivalent of all benefits, so that the employee may enter the details on his self-assessment tax return. Specific reference numbers for the entries on the P11D are given to assist with the preparation of the employee's self assessment tax return.

When an employee leaves, a form P45 (particulars of Employee Leaving) must be prepared. This form shows the employee's code and details of his income and tax paid to date and is a four part form. One part is sent to HMRC, and three parts handed to the employee. One of the parts (part 1A) is the employee's personal copy.

If the employee takes up a new employment, he must hand the other two parts of the form P45 to the new employer. The new employer will fill in details of the new employment and send one part to HMRC, retaining the other. The details on the form are used by the new employer to calculate the PAYE due on the next payday. If the employee dies a P45 should be completed, and the whole form sent to HMRC.

If an employee joins with a form P45, the new employer can operate PAYE. If there is no P45 the employer still needs to operate PAYE. **The employee is required to complete a form P46.**

If he declares that the employment is his first job since the start of the tax year and he has not received a taxable state benefit, or that it is now his only job but he previously had another job or received a taxable state benefit, the emergency code (522L for 2007/08) applies, on a cumulative basis or week 1/month 1 basis respectively. If the employee declares that he has another job or receives a pension the employer must use code BR.

The P46 is sent to HMRC, unless the pay is below the PAYE and NIC thresholds, and the emergency code applies. In this case no PAYE is deductible until the pay exceeds the threshold.

6.6 Penalties

A form P35 is due on 19 May after the end of the tax year. In practice, a seven-day extension to the due date of 19 May is allowed.

Where a form P35 is late, a penalty of £100 per month per 50 employees may be imposed. This penalty cannot be mitigated. **This penalty ceases 12 months after the due date and a further penalty of up to 100% of the tax (and NIC) for the year which remains unpaid** at 19 April may be imposed. This penalty can be mitigated. HMRC automatically reduce the penalty by concession to the greater of £100 and the total PAYE/NIC which should be reported on the return.

Where a person has fraudulently or negligently submitted an incorrect form P35 the penalty is 100% of the tax (and NIC) attributable to the error. This penalty can be mitigated.

6.7 PAYE settlement agreements

PAYE settlement agreements (PSAs) are arrangements under which employers can make single payments to settle their employees' income tax liabilities on expense payments and benefits which are minor, irregular or where it would be impractical to operate PAYE.

7 P11D DISPENSATIONS

As we have seen, expense payments to P11D employees should be reported to HMRC. They form part of the employee's employment income and a claim must be made to deduct the expenses in computing net employment income.

To avoid this cumbersome procedure **the employer and HMRC can agree for a dispensation to apply to avoid the need to report expenses covered by the dispensation, and the employee then need not make a formal claim for a deduction.**

Dispensations can only apply to genuine business expenses. Some employers only reimburse business expenses, so that a dispensation may be agreed to cover all payments. Other employers may agree to cover a particular category of expenses, such as travel expenses.

A dispensation cannot be given for mileage allowances paid to employees using their own cars for business journeys as these payments are governed by a statutory exemption (see earlier in this Course Book).

Chapter roundup

- Most employees are taxed on benefits under the benefits code. 'Excluded employees' (lower paid/non-directors) are only subject to part of the provisions of the code.
- The benefit in respect of accommodation is its annual value. There is an additional benefit if the property cost over £75,000.
- Employees who have a company car are taxed on a % of the car's list price which depends on the level of the car's CO_2 emissions. The same % multiplied by £14,400 determines the benefit where private fuel is also provided.
- Cheap loans are charged to tax on the difference between the official rate of interest and any interest paid by the employee.
- 20% of the value of assets made available for private use is taxable.
- There is a residual charge for other benefits, usually equal to the cost to the employer of the benefits.
- There are a number of exempt benefits including removal expenses, childcare, meal vouchers and workplace parking.
- Most tax in respect of employment income is deducted under the PAYE system. The objective of the PAYE system is to collect the correct amount of tax over the year. An employee's PAYE code is designed to ensure that allowances etc are given evenly over the year.
- Employers must complete forms P60, P14, P35, P9D, P11D and P45 as appropriate. A P45 is needed when an employee leaves. Forms P9D and P11D record details of benefits. Forms P60, P14 and P35 are year end returns.

Quick quiz

1 What is employment income?

2 What are the conditions for expenses other than travel expenses to be deductible?

3 Give an example of a PAYE code.

4 What accommodation does not give rise to a taxable benefit?

5 How are assets made available for private use (other than vehicles, accommodation and computers) taxed?

Answers to quick quiz

1 Employment income is income and taxable benefits arising from an employment under a contract of service. (see para 1.1)

2 To be incurred wholly, exclusively and necessarily in the performance of duties. (para 4.1)

3 461L for example. (para 6.4)

4 Job-related accommodation. (para 2.4)

5 20% × Market value when first provided. (para 2.11)

Answers to activities

1

Salary	£60,000
Taxable benefits	5,000
Bonus (1.3.07)	40,000
Taxable employment Income	105,000

The salary and benefits were paid/made available during 2007/08 and hence taxed in 2007/08. The bonus was paid/made available on 30 April 2008 (2008/09) *but* was determined after the company's year end (31.12.07) by the board meeting on 1 March 2008 (2007/08) – hence taxed in 2007/08.

2 No. Although Tim's taxable income is less than £8,500 this is only after his expense claim. The figure to consider and compare to £8,500 is the £10,300 as shown below.

	£
Salary	6,500
Benefits: health insurance	300
car	1,500
expense allowance	2,000
Earnings to consider if Tim is lower paid	10,300
Less: claim for expenses paid out	(1,900)
Taxable income	8,400

3

	£	£
Salary		28,850
Less occupational pension scheme contributions		(1,450)
Net earnings		27,400
Accommodation benefits		
Annual value: exempt (job related)		
Ancillary services		
Electricity	550	
Gas	400	
Gardener	750	
Redecorations	1,800	
	3,500	
Restricted to 10% of £27,400	2,740	
Less employee's contribution	(600)	
		2,140
Employment income		29,540

NOTES

4 Round CO_2 emissions figure down to the nearest 5, ie 190 g/km.

Amount by which CO_2 emissions exceed the baseline:

(190 – 140) = 50 g/km
Divide by 5 = 10

Taxable percentage = 15% + 10% = 25%

	£
Car benefit £15,000 × 25%	3,750
Fuel benefit £14,400 × 25%	3,600
	7,350
Less contribution towards use of car	(270)
	7,080

If the contribution of £270 had been towards the petrol the benefit would have been £7,350.

5

	£
Salary	30,000
Season ticket loan not over £5,000	0
Loan to buy shares £54,000 × (6.25 – 3 = 3.25%)	1,755
Earnings	31,755
Less deductible interest paid (£54,000 × 6.25%× 90%)	(3,038)
	28,717
Less personal allowance	(5,225)
Taxable income	23,492
Income tax	
£2,230 × 10%	223
£21,262 × 22%	4,678
Tax liability	4,901

6 Zoe is not entitled to tax relief for the costs incurred in travelling between Wycombe and Chiswick since these are normal commuting costs. However, relief is available for all costs that Zoe incurs when she travels from Wycombe to Wimbledon to visit her client.

7 Although Philip is spending all of his time at the Morpeth branch it will not be treated as his normal work place because his period of attendance will be less than 24 months. Thus Philip can claim relief in full for the costs of travel from his home to the Morpeth branch.

Chapter 33 :

INCOME FROM INVESTMENTS AND PROPERTY

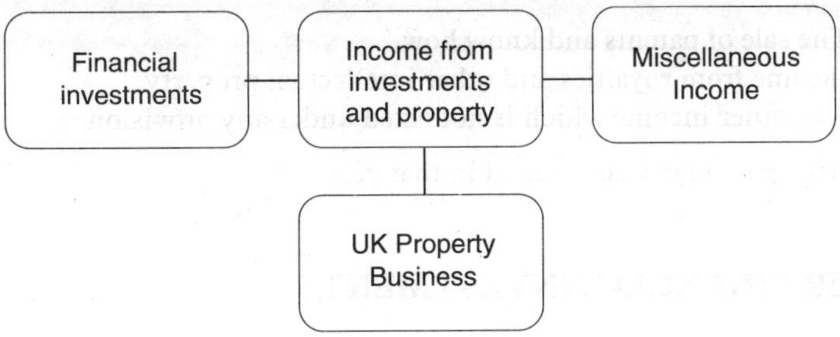

Introduction

The main sources of income from investments are savings. The main source of income from property is rental income which is taxable under Schedule A. 'Property' is usually taken to mean houses or flats, but Schedule A also encompasses rent a room relief, when tax is not payable on a small amount of rent received from letting out a single room.

Your objectives

In this chapter you will learn about the following.

(a) Investments taxed at source

(b) Tax free investments

(c) Miscellaneous income

(d) Income assessable from a UK Property Business and the basis of assessment (including losses)

(e) Deductions obtainable for capital allowances, wear and tear, repairs and renewals

(f) The effect of private use on the deductibility of expenses

(g) The way the rules are adapted for furnished holiday lettings

(h) Rent-a-room relief

1 MISCELLANEOUS INCOME

Definition

Miscellaneous Income deals with any income not falling into any other category.

Examples are income or profits from:

- The sale of patents and know how
- Income from royalties and other intellectual property
- Any other income which is not taxed under any provision

The income arising in a tax year is taxed in that year.

2 OTHER FINANCIAL INVESTMENTS

2.1 Savings income

2.1.1 What is savings income?

Savings income is interest. Interest is paid on bank and building society accounts, on Government securities, such as Treasury Stock, and on company debentures and loan stock.

Interest may be paid net of 20% tax or it may be paid gross.

2.1.2 Savings income received net of 20% tax

The following savings income is received net of 20% tax. **This is called income taxed at source.**

(a) Bank and building society interest paid to individuals (but not National Savings & Investments bank account interest)

(b) Interest paid to individuals by unlisted UK companies on debentures and loan stocks

The amount received is grossed up by multiplying by 100/80 and is included gross in the income tax computation. The tax deducted at source is deducted in computing tax payable and may be repaid.

In examinations you may be given either the net or the gross amount of such income: read the question carefully. If you are given the net amount (the amount received or credited), you should gross up the figure at the rate of 20%. For example, net building society interest of £160 is equivalent to gross income of £160 × 100/80 = £200 on which tax of £40 (20% of £200) has been suffered.

NOTES

2.1.3 Savings income received gross

Some savings income is received gross, ie without tax having been deducted. Examples are:

(a) National Savings & Investments bank account Interest
(b) Interest on government securities (these are also called 'gilts')
(c) Interest from quoted company debentures and loan stock.

2.2 Dividend income

Dividends on UK shares are received net of a 10% tax credit. This means a dividend of £90 has a £10 tax credit, giving gross income of £100 to include in the income tax computation. The tax credit can be deducted in computing tax payable but it cannot be repaid.

This treatment applies to dividends received from open ended investment companies (OEICs) and to dividend distributions from unit trusts.

2.3 Tax exempt income

2.3.1 Types of tax exempt investments

Income from certain investments is exempt from income tax.

2.3.2 Individual savings accounts

An individual savings account (ISA) is a special tax exempt way of saving. Each year an individual can invest either:

(a) Up to £7,000 in a maxi ISA, or

(b) Up to £3,000 in a mini cash ISA and/or up to £4,000 in a stocks and shares ISA.

Funds invested in a maxi ISA are used to buy stock market investments, such as shares in quoted companies or OEICs, units in unit trusts, fixed interest investments, or insurance policies.

Dividend income and interest received from ISAs is exempt from income tax, whether it is paid out to the investor or retained and reinvested within the ISA.

2.3.3 Savings certificates

Savings certificates are issued by National Savings and Investments (NS&I). They may be fixed rate certificates or index linked, and are for fixed terms of between two and five years. On maturity the profit is tax exempt. This profit is often called interest.

2.3.4 Premium bonds

Prizes received from premium bonds are exempt from tax.

NOTES

Activity 1 **(10 minutes)**

A single taxpayer's only income in 2007/08 is bank deposit interest of £9,600 net. What tax repayment is due?

3 UK PROPERTY BUSINESS

3.1 Profits of a UK property business

Income from land and buildings in the UK, including caravans and houseboats which are not moved, is taxed as non-savings income.

(a) **A taxpayer (or a partnership) with UK rental income is treated as running a business, his 'UK property business'. All the rents and expenses for all properties are pooled, to give a single profit or loss. Profits and losses are computed in the same way as trading profits are computed for tax purposes,** on an accruals basis.

Expenses will often include rent payable where a landlord is himself renting the land which he in turn lets to others. For individuals, interest on loans to buy or improve properties is treated as an expense (on an accruals basis). The rules on post-cessation receipts and expenses apply to UK property businesses in the same way that they apply to trades (see later in this Course Book).

Relief is available for irrecoverable rent as an impaired debt.

(b) **Capital allowances are given on plant and machinery used in the UK property business and on industrial buildings, in the same way as they are given for a trading business** with an accounting date of 5 April. Capital allowances are not normally available on plant or machinery used in a dwelling. As someone who lets property furnished cannot claim capital allowances on the furniture he can choose instead between the **renewals** basis and the **10% wear and tear allowance.**

(i) Under the **renewals** basis, there is no deduction for the cost of the first furniture provided, but the cost of replacement furniture is treated as a revenue expense. However, the part of the cost attributable to improvement, as opposed to simple replacement, is not deductible.

(ii) Under the **10% wear and tear** basis, the actual cost of furniture is ignored. Instead, an annual deduction is given of 10% of rents. The rents are first reduced by amounts which are paid by the landlord but are normally a tenant's burden. These amounts include any **water rates** and **council tax** paid by the landlord.

If plant and machinery is used partly in a dwelling house and partly for other purposes a just and reasonable apportionment of the expenditure can be made.

NOTES

3.2 Losses of UK property business

A loss from a UK property business is carried forward to set against the first future profits from the UK property business. **It may be carried forward until the UK property business ends, but it must be used as soon as possible.**

Activity 2 **(20 minutes)**

Pete over the last few years has purchased several properties in Manchester as 'buy to let' investments.

5 Whitby Ave is let out furnished at £500 per month. A tenant moved in on 1 March 2007 but left unexpectedly on 1 May 2008 having paid rent only up to 31 December 2007. The tenant left no forwarding address.

17 Bolton Rd has been let furnished to the same tenant for a number of years at £800 per month.

A recent purchase, 27 Turner Close has been let unfurnished since 1 August 2007 at £750 per month having been empty while Pete redecorated it after its purchase March 2007.

Pete's expenses during 2007/08 are:

	No 5	*No 17*	*No27*
	£	£	£
Insurance	250	200	200
Letting agency fees	-	-	100
Repairs	300	40	-
Redecoration	-	-	500

No 27 was in a fit state to let when Pete bought it but he wanted to redecorate the property as he felt this would allow him to achieve a better rental income.

Water rates and council tax are paid by the tenants. Pete made a UK property business loss in 2006/07 of £300.

What is Pete's taxable property income for 2007/08?

3.3 Premiums on leases

When a premium or similar consideration is received on the grant (that is, by a landlord to a tenant) **of a short lease (50 years or less), part of the premium is treated as rent received in the year of grant**. A lease is considered to end on the date when it is most likely to terminate.

The premium taxed as rental income is the whole premium, less 2% of the premium for each complete year of the lease, except the first year using the following formula:

Premium	P
Less: 2% × (n–1) × P	(a)
Taxable as income	X

BPP LEARNING MEDIA

This rule does not apply on the **assignment** of a lease (ie one tenant selling his entire interest in the property to another).

3.4 Premiums paid by traders

Where a trader pays a premium for a lease he may deduct an amount from his taxable trading profits in each year of the lease. The amount deductible is the figure treated as rent received by the landlord divided by the number of years of the lease. For example, suppose that B, a trader, pays A a premium of £30,000 for a ten year lease. A is treated as receiving £30,000 – (£30,000 × (10 – 1) × 2%) = £24,600. B can therefore deduct £24,600/10 = £2,460 in each of the ten years. He starts with the accounts year in which the lease starts and apportions the relief to the nearest month.

3.5 Premiums for granting subleases

A tenant may decide to sublet property and to charge a premium on the grant of a lease to the subtenant. This premium is treated as rent received in the normal way (because this is a grant and not an assignment, the original tenant retaining an interest in the property). **Where the tenant originally paid a premium for his own head lease, this deemed rent is reduced by:**

$$\text{Rent part of premium for head lease} \times \frac{\text{duration of sub-lease}}{\text{duration of head lease}}$$

If the relief exceeds the part of the premium for the sub-lease treated as rent (including cases where there is a sub-lease with no premium), the balance of the relief is treated as rent payable by the head tenant, spread evenly over the period of the sub-lease. This rent payable is an expense, reducing the overall profit from the UK property business.

Activity 3 **(10 minutes)**

C granted a lease to D on 1 March 1997 for a period of 40 years. D paid a premium of £16,000. On 1 June 2007 D granted a sublease to E for a period of ten years. E paid a premium of £30,000. Calculate the amount treated as rent out of the premium received by D.

3.6 Real Estate Investment Trusts (REITs)

Property companies may operate as **Real Estate Investment Trusts** (REITs).

REITs can elect for their property income (and gains) to be exempt from corporation tax and must withhold basic rate (22%) tax from distributions paid to shareholders (who cannot own more than 10% of a REIT's shares) out of these profits. These distributions are taxed as property income, not as dividends.

Distributions by REITs out of other income (ie not property income or gains) are taxed as dividends in the normal way.

4 FURNISHED HOLIDAY LETTINGS

There are special rules for furnished holiday lettings. The letting is treated as if it were a trade. This means that, although the income is taxed as income from a UK property business, the provisions which apply to actual trades also apply to furnished holiday lettings, as follows.

(a) Relief for losses is available as if they were trading losses, including the facility to set losses against other income. The usual UK property business loss reliefs do not apply.

(b) Capital allowances are available on furniture: the renewals basis and the 10% wear and tear basis do not apply if capital allowances are claimed.

(c) The income qualifies as relevant UK earnings for pension relief (see earlier in this Course Book).

(d) Capital gains tax rollover relief, business asset taper relief and relief for gifts of business assets are available (see later in this Course Book).

Note, however, that the basis period rules for trades do not apply, and the profits or losses must be computed for tax years.

The letting must be of furnished accommodation made on a **commercial basis with a view to the realisation of profit**. The property must also satisfy the following three conditions.

(a) **The availability condition** – during the **relevant period**, the accommodation is available for **commercial let** as **holiday accommodation** to the **public** generally, for **at least 140 days**.

(b) **The letting condition** – during the **relevant period**, the accommodation is **commercially let** as holiday accommodation to members of the public **for at least 70 days**. If the **landlord has more than one FHL**, at least one of which satisfies the 40 day rule ('qualifying holiday accommodation') and at least one of which does not, ('the underused accommodation') , he may elect to **average the occupation of the qualifying holiday accommodation and any or all of the underused accommodation**. If the average of occupation is at least 70 days, the under-used accommodation will be treated as qualifying holiday accommodation.

(c) The pattern of occupation condition – during the relevant period, not more that 155 days fall during periods of longer-term occupation. Longer-term occupation is defined as a continuous period of more than 31 days during which the accommodation is in the same occupation unless there are abnormal circumstances.

If someone has furnished holiday lettings and other lettings, **draw up two profit and loss accounts as if they had two separate UK property businesses.** This is so that the profits and losses treated as trade profits and losses can be identified.

5 RENT A ROOM RELIEF

If an individual lets a room or rooms, furnished, in his or her main residence as living accommodation, a special exemption may apply.

The limit on the exemption is gross rents (before any expenses or capital allowances) of £4,250 a year. This limit is halved if any other person (including the first person's spouse/civil partner) also received income from renting accommodation in the property while the property was the first person's main residence.

If gross rents (plus balancing charges arising because of capital allowances in earlier years) **are not more than the limit, the rents** (and balancing charges) **are wholly exempt from income tax** and expenses and capital allowances are ignored. However, the taxpayer may claim to ignore the exemption, for example to generate a loss by taking into account both rent and expenses.

If gross rents exceed the limit, the taxpayer will be taxed in the ordinary way, ignoring the rent a room scheme, unless he elects for the 'alternative basis'. If he so elects, he will be taxable on gross receipts plus balancing charges less £4,250 (or £2,125 if the limit is halved), with no deductions for expenses or capital allowances.

An election to ignore the exemption or an election for the alternative basis must be made by the 31 January which is 22 months from the end of the tax year concerned.

An election to ignore the exemption applies only for the tax year for which it is made, but an election for the alternative basis remains in force until it is withdrawn or until a year in which gross rents do not exceed the limit.

Activity 4 **(10 minutes)**

Sylvia owns a house near the sea in Norfolk. She has a spare bedroom and during 2007/08 this was let to a chef working at a nearby restaurant for £85 per week which includes the cost of heating, lighting etc.

Sylvia estimates that each year her lodger costs her an extra:

£50 on gas
£25 on electricity
£50 on insurance

How much property income must Sylvia pay tax on?

NOTES

Chapter roundup

- Miscellaneous income is taxed in the year of receipt.
- There are several tax exemptions for investment income.
- Income from a UK property is computed for tax years on an accruals basis.
- Special rules apply to income from furnished holiday lettings.
- Rents received from letting a room in the taxpayer's home may be tax free under the rent-a-room scheme.
- Part of a premium received on grant of a short lease is as rent.
- Traders can receive relief for premium payments over the life of the lease.

Quick quiz

1 What income falls within the category Miscellaneous Income?

2 What is the tax treatment of Individual Savings Accounts?

3 When may interest be paid to individuals gross?

4 Describe the renewals basis.

5 What are the advantages of furnished holiday letting income over other UK property business income?

6 How much income per annum is tax free under the rent a room scheme?

Answers to quick quiz

1 Income not falling under any other category. (see para 1)

2 ISAs produce tax free income. (para 2.3.2)

3 NS&I bank account interest, gilt interest and interest from quoted company debentures and loan stock may all by paid gross. (para 2.1.3)

4 Under the renewals basis there is no deduction for the cost of the first furniture provided but the cost of replacement furniture is treated as a revenue expense. (para 3.1)

5 (i) Relief for losses are available as if they were trading losses
(ii) Capital allowances are available on furniture
(iii) Capital gains tax reliefs are available (para 4)

6 £4,250. (para 5)

NOTES

Answers to activities

1

	£
Net Income (bank deposit interest) £9,600 × 100/80	12,000
Less personal allowance	(5,225)
Taxable income	6,775
	£
Income tax on savings (excl dividend) income	
£2,230 × 10%	223
£4,545 × 20% (savings income)	909
Tax suffered £12,000 × 20%	(2,400)
Repayment due	(1,268)

2

	No 5	*No 17*	*No 27*
2007/08	£	£	£
Accrued income			
12 × £500	6,000		
12 × £800		9,600	
8 × £750			6,000
Less:			
Insurance	(250)	(250)	(200)
Letting agency			(100)
Impairment (irrecoverable rent)			
3 × £500	(1,500)		
Repairs	(300)	(40)	
Redecoration (note)			(500)
Wear and tear allowance			
£(6,000 – 1,500) × 10%	(450)		
£9,600 × 10%		(960)	
Property Income	3,500	8,350	5,200
Total property income			17,050
Less: loss b/fwd			(300)
Taxable property income for 2007/08			16,750

Note. The redecoration is allowable as the property was already in a usable state. If the redecoration had been needed to put the property into a fit state to be rented, it would not be allowable.

3

	£
Premium received by D	30,000
Less £30,000 × 2% × (10 – 1)	(5,400)
	24,600
Less allowance for premium paid	
(16,000 – (£16,000 × 39 × 2%)) × 10/40	(880)
Premium treated as rent	23,720

4 Sylvia has a choice:

(1) Total rental income of £85 × 52 = £4,420 exceeds £4,250 limit so taxable income is £170 (ie £4,420 – 4,250) ie rent a room relief claim.

(2) Alternatively she can be taxed on her actual profit:

	£
Rental income	4,420
Less expenses (50 + 25 +50)	(125)
	4,295

Sylvia should be advised to claim rent a room relief.

Chapter 34 :
TAX DOCUMENTATION AND PAYMENT OF TAX

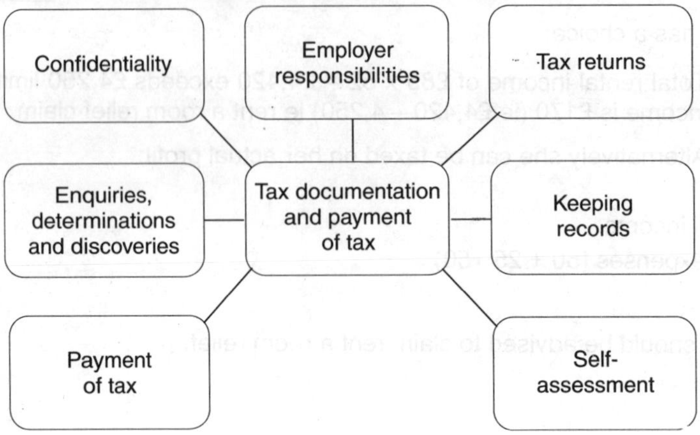

Introduction

The tax practitioner will often effectively 'run' the client's tax affairs on their behalf. This involves keeping the necessary records, filing the appropriate returns (on time) and dealing with the HMRC should there be any disputes. In doing this, the tax practitioner is expected to observe client confidentiality and professionalism at all times.

Your objectives

In this chapter you will learn about the following.

(a) Notification of liability to income tax and CGT

(b) Tax returns and keeping records

(c) Self assessment and claims

(d) Payment of income tax and capital gains tax

(e) Enquiries, determinations and discovery assessments

(f) Client confidentiality

NOTES

1 NOTIFICATION OF LIABILITY TO INCOME TAX AND CGT

Individuals who have not received a notice to file a return, or who have a new source of income or gains in the tax year, are required to give notice of chargeability to HMRC within six months from the end of the year ie by 5 October 2008 for 2007/08.

A person who has no chargeable gains and who is not liable to higher rate tax does not have to give notice of chargeability if all his income:

(a) Is taken into account under PAYE
(b) Is from a source of income not subject to tax under a self-assessment
(c) Has had (or is treated as having had) income tax deducted at source, or
(d) Is a UK dividend.

The maximum mitigable penalty where notice of chargeability is not given is 100% of the tax assessed which is not paid on or before 31 January following the tax year.

2 TAX RETURNS AND KEEPING RECORDS

2.1 Tax returns

The tax return comprises a Tax Form, together with supplementary pages for particular sources of income. Taxpayers are sent a Tax Form and a number of supplementary pages depending on their known sources of income, together with a Tax Return Guide and various notes relating to the supplementary pages. Taxpayers with new sources of income may have to ask the orderline for further supplementary pages. Taxpayers with simple tax returns may be asked to complete a short four page tax return.

If a return for the previous year was filed electronically the taxpayer may be sent a notice to file a return, rather than the official HMRC form.

Partnerships must file a separate return which includes 'a partnership statement' showing the firm's profits, losses, proceeds from the sale of assets, tax suffered, tax credits, charges on income and the division of all these amounts between partners.

A partnership return must include a declaration of the name, residence and tax reference of each partner, as well as the usual declaration that the return is correct and complete to the best of the signatory's knowledge.

Each partner must then include his share of partnership profits on his personal tax return.

2.2 Time limit for submission of tax returns

Definition

The latest **filing date for a personal tax return** for a tax year (Year 1) is:

- 31 October in the next tax year (Year 2), for a non-electronic return (eg a paper return).
- 31 January in Year 2, for an electronic return (eg made via the internet).

This rule applies where Year 1 is the tax year 2007/08 and for subsequent years.

There are **two exceptions to this general rule.**

The **first exception applies if the notice to file a tax return is issued by HMRC to the taxpayer after 31 July in Year 2, but on or before 31 October in Year 2.** In this case, the **latest filing date is:**

- **The end of three months following the notice, for a non-electronic return.**
- **31 January in Year 2, for an electronic return.**

The second exception applies **if the notice to file the tax return is issued to the taxpayer after 31 October in Year 2.** In this case, **the latest filing date is the end of three months following the notice.**

EXAMPLE

Advise the following clients of the latest filing date for her personal tax return for 2007/08 if the return is:

(a) Non-electronic; or
(b) Electronic.

Norma	Notice to file tax return issued by HMRC on 6 April 2008
Melanie	Notice to file tax return issued by HMRC on 10 August 2008
Olga	Notice to file tax return issued by HMRC on 12 December 2008

	Non-electronic	*Electronic*
Norma	31 October 2008	31 January 2009
Melanie	9 November 2008	31 January 2009
Olga	11 March 2009	11 March 2009

A partnership return may be filed as a non-electronic return or an electronic return. **The general rule and the exceptions to the general rule for personal returns apply also to partnership returns.**

2.3 PENALTIES FOR LATE FILING

2.3.1 Individual returns

The maximum penalties for delivering a tax return after the filing due date are:

(a)	**Return up to six months late:**	**£100**
(b)	**Return more than six months but not more than 12 months late:**	**£200**
(c)	**Return more than 12 months late:**	**£200 + 100% of the tax liability**

In addition, the General or Special Commissioners can direct that a maximum penalty of £60 per day be imposed where failure to deliver a tax return continues after notice of the direction has been given to the taxpayer. In this case the additional £100 penalty, imposed under (b) if the return is more than six months late, is not charged.

The fixed penalties of £100/£200 can be set aside by the Commissioners if they are satisfied that the taxpayer had a reasonable excuse for not delivering the return. If the tax liability shown on the return is less than the fixed penalties, the fixed penalty is reduced to the amount of the tax liability. The tax geared penalty is mitigable by HMRC or the Commissioners.

2.3.2 Partnership returns

The maximum penalties for late delivery of a partnership tax return are as shown above, save that there is no tax-geared penalty if the return is more than 12 months late. The penalties apply separately to each partner.

2.3.3 Reasonable excuse

A taxpayer only has a reasonable excuse for a late filing if a default occurred because of a factor outside his control. This might be non-receipt of the return by the taxpayer, an industrial dispute in the post office after the return was posted, serious illness of the taxpayer or a close relative, or destruction of records through fire and flood. Illness etc is only accepted as a reasonable excuse if the taxpayer was taking positive steps to complete the return, and if the return is filed as soon as possible after the illness etc.

2.4 Standard accounting information

'Three line' accounts (ie income less expenses equals profit) only need be included on the tax return of businesses with a turnover (or gross rents from property) of less than £15,000 pa. This is not as helpful as it might appear, as underlying records must still be kept for tax purposes (disallowable items etc) when producing three line accounts.

Large businesses with a turnover of at least £5 million which have used figures rounded to the nearest £1,000 in producing their published accounts can compute their profits to the nearest £1,000 for tax purposes.

The tax return requires trading results to be presented in a standard format. Although there is no requirement to submit accounts with the return, accounts may be filed. If accounts accompany the return, HMRC's power to raise a discovery assessment (see below) is restricted.

2.5 Keeping of records

All taxpayers must keep and retain all records required to enable them to make and deliver a correct tax return.

Records must be retained until the later of:

(a) (i) **Five years after the 31 January following the tax year where the taxpayer is in business** (as a sole trader or partner or letting property), or

(ii) **One year after the 31 January following the tax year, or**

(b) Provided notice to deliver a return is given before the date in (a):

(i) **The time after which enquiries by HMRC into the return can no longer be commenced**, or

(ii) **The date any such enquiries have been completed.**

Where a person receives a notice to deliver a tax return after the normal record keeping period has expired, he must keep all records in his possession at that time until no enquiries can be raised in respect of the return or until such enquiries have been completed.

The maximum (mitigable) penalty for each failure to keep and retain records is £3,000 per tax year/accounting period.

The duty to preserve records can generally be satisfied by retaining copies of original documents except that the originals of documents which show domestic or foreign tax deducted or creditable (eg dividend certificates) must be kept.

Record keeping failures are taken into account in considering the mitigation of other penalties. Where the record keeping failure is taken into account in this way, a penalty will normally only be sought in serious and exceptional cases where, for example, records have been destroyed deliberately to obstruct an enquiry or there has been a history of serious record keeping failures.

3 SELF-ASSESSMENT AND CLAIMS

3.1 Self-assessment

Definition

> A **self-assessment** is a calculation of the amount of taxable income and gains after deducting reliefs and allowances, a calculation of income tax and CGT payable after taking into account tax deducted at source and tax credits on dividends.

If the taxpayer is filing a **non-electronic return (other than a Short Tax Return), he may make the tax calculation on his return or ask HMRC to do so on his behalf.**

If the taxpayer wishes HMRC to make the calculation for Year 1, a non-electronic return must be filed:

- **On or before 31 October in Year 2 or,**
- **If the notice to file the tax return is issued after 31 August in Year 2, within two months of the notice.**

A Short Tax Return filed non-electronically must be filed by these dates.

If the taxpayer is filing an **electronic return, the calculation of tax liability is made automatically when the return is made online.**

3.2 Amending the self-assessment

The taxpayer may amend his return (including the tax calculation) for Year 1 within 12 months after the filing date. For this purpose the filing date means:

- **31 January of Year 2**; or
- **Where the notice to file a return was issued after 31 October in Year 2, the last day of the three-month period starting with the issue.**

A return may be amended by the taxpayer at a time when an enquiry is in progress into the return. The amendment does not restrict the scope of an enquiry into the return but may be taken into account in that enquiry. If the amendment made during an enquiry is the amount of tax payable, the amendment does not take effect while the enquiry is in progress.

A return may be amended by HMRC to correct any obvious error or omission in the return (such as errors of principle and arithmetical mistakes). The correction must be usually be made within nine months after the day on which the return was actually filed. The taxpayer can object to the correction but must do so within 30 days of receiving notice of it.

Similar rules apply to the amendment and correction of partnership returns.

3.3 Claims

3.3.1 Making claims

All claims and elections which can be made in a tax return must be made in this manner if a return has been issued. A claim for any relief, allowance or repayment of tax must be quantified at the time it is made. These rules do not apply to claims involving two or more years.

Certain claims have a time limit that is longer than the time limit for filing or amending a tax return. A claim may therefore be made after the time limit for amending the tax return has expired. Claims not made on the tax return are referred to as **'stand alone' claims.**

Claims made on a tax return are subject to the administrative rules governing returns, for the making of corrections, enquiries and so on.

3.3.2 Claims involving more than one year

Self-assessment is intended to avoid the need to reopen earlier years, so relief should be given for the year of the claim. This rule can best be explained by considering a claim to carry back a trade loss to an earlier year of assessment:

(a) The claim for relief is treated as made in relation to the year in which the loss was actually incurred;

(b) The amount of any tax repayment due is calculated in terms of tax of the earlier year to which the loss is being carried back; and

(c) Any tax repayment etc is treated as relating to the later year in which the loss was actually incurred. A repayment supplement may accrue from the later year.

3.3.3 Time limits

In general the time limit for making a claim is five years from 31 January following the tax year. Where different time limits apply these have been mentioned throughout this Course Book.

3.3.4 Error or mistake claims

An error or mistake claim may be made for errors in a return or partnership statement where tax would otherwise be overcharged. The claim may not be made where the tax liability was computed in accordance with practice prevailing at the time the return or statement was made.

An error or mistake claim may not be made in respect of a claim. If a taxpayer makes an error or mistake in a claim, he may make a supplementary claim within the time limits allowed for the original claim.

The taxpayer may appeal to the Special Commissioners against any refusal of an error or mistake claim.

4 PAYMENT OF INCOME TAX AND CAPITAL GAINS TAX

4.1 Payments on account and final payment

4.1.1 Introduction

The self-assessment system may result in the taxpayer making three payments of income tax and Class 4 NICs.

Date	Payment
31 January in the tax year	First payment on account
31 July after the tax year	Second payment on account
31 January after the tax year	Final payment to settle the remaining liability

HMRC issue payslips/demand notes in a credit card type 'Statement of Account' format, but there is no statutory obligation for it to do so and **the onus is on the taxpayer to pay the correct amount of tax on the due date.**

4.1.2 Payments on account

Definition

Payments on account are usually required where the income tax and Class NICs due in the previous year exceeded the amount of income tax deducted at source; this excess is known as **'the relevant amount'**. Income tax deducted at source includes tax suffered, PAYE deductions and tax credits on dividends.

The payments on account are each equal to 50% of the relevant amount for the previous year.

Payments on account of CGT are never required.

NOTES

Activity 1 **(15 minutes)**

Sue is a self-employed writer who paid tax for 2007/08 as follows.

		£
Total amount of income tax charged		9,200
This included:	Tax deducted on savings income	3,200
She also paid:	Class 4 NIC	1,900
	Class 2 NIC	114
	Capital gains tax	4,800

How much are the payments on account for 2008/09?

Payments on account are not required if the relevant amount falls below a *de minimis* limit of £500. Also, payments on account are not required from taxpayers who paid 80% or more of their tax liability for the previous year through PAYE or other deduction at source arrangements.

If the previous year's liability increases following an amendment to a self-assessment, or the raising of a discovery assessment, an adjustment is made to the payments on account due.

4.1.3 Reducing payments on account

Payments on account are normally fixed by reference to the previous year's tax liability but if a taxpayer expects his liability to be lower than this **he may claim to reduce his payments on account to:**

(a) **A stated amount**, or
(b) **Nil.**

The claim must state the reason why he believes his tax liability will be lower, or nil.

If the taxpayer's eventual liability is higher than he estimated he will have reduced the payments on account too far. Although the payments on account will not be adjusted, the taxpayer will suffer an interest charge on late payment.

A penalty of the difference between the reduced payment on account and the correct payment on account may be levied if the reduction was claimed fraudulently or negligently.

4.1.4 Balancing payment

The balance of any income tax and Class 4 NICs together with all CGT due for a year, is normally payable on or before the 31 January following the year.

Activity 2 **(10 minutes)**

Giles made payments on account for 2007/08 of £6,500 each on 31 January 2008 and 31 July 2008, based on his 2006/07 liability. He then calculates his total income tax and Class 4 NIC liability for 2007/08 at £18,000 of which £2,750 was deducted at source. In addition he calculated that his CGT liability for disposals in 2007/08 is £5,120.

BPP LEARNING MEDIA

NOTES

Required

What is the final payment due for 2007/08?

In one case the due date for the final payment is later than 31 January following the end of the year. **If a taxpayer has notified chargeability by 5 October but the notice to file a tax return is not issued before 31 October, then the due date for the payment is three months after the issue of the notice.**

Tax charged in an amended self-assessment is usually payable on the later of:

(a) The normal due date, generally 31 January following the end of the tax year, and

(b) The day following 30 days after the making of the revised self-assessment.

Tax charged on a discovery assessment (see below) is due thirty days after the issue of the assessment.

4.2 Surcharges

Definition

Surcharges are normally imposed in respect of amounts paid late:

Paid	*Surcharge*
(a) Within 28 days of due date:	none
(b) More than 28 days but not more than six months after the due date:	5%
(c) More than six months after the due date	10%

Surcharges apply to:

(a) Balancing payments of income tax and Class 4 NICs and any CGT under self-assessment or a determination

(b) Tax due on the amendment of a self-assessment

(c) Tax due on a discovery assessment

The surcharge rules do not apply to late payments on account.

No surcharge will be applied where the late paid tax liability has attracted a tax-geared penalty on the failure to notify chargeability to tax, or the failure to submit a return, or on the making of an incorrect return (including a partnership return).

4.3 Interest on late paid tax

Interest is chargeable on late payment of both payments on account and balancing payments. In both cases interest runs from the due date until the day before the actual date of payment.

NOTES

Interest is charged from 31 January following the tax year (or the normal due date for the balancing payment, in the rare event that this is later), even if this is before the due date for payment on:

(a) Tax payable following an amendment to a self-assessment
(b) Tax payable in a discovery assessment, and
(c) Tax postponed under an appeal which becomes payable

Since a determination (see below) is treated as if it were a self-assessment, interest runs from 31 January following the tax year.

If a taxpayer claims to reduce his payments on account and there is still a final payment to be made, interest is normally charged on the payments on account as if each of those payments had been the lower of:

(a) The reduced amount, plus 50% of the final income tax liability; and
(b) The amount which would have been payable had no claim for reduction been made

Activity 3 **(20 minutes)**

Herbert's payments on account for 2007/08 based on his income tax liability for 2006/07 were £4,500 each. However when he submitted his 2006/07 income tax return in January 2007 he made a claim to reduce the payments on account for 2007/08 for £3,500 each. The first payment on account was made on 29 January 2008, and the second on 12 August 2008.

Herbert filed his 2007/08 tax return in December 2008. The returned showed that his tax liabilities for 2007/08 (before deducting payments on account) were income tax and Class 4 NIC: £10,000, capital gains tax: £2,500. Herbert paid the balance of tax due of £5,500 on 19 February 2009.

For what periods and in respect of what amounts will Herbert be charged interest?

Where interest has been charged on late payments on account but the final balancing settlement for the year produces a repayment, all or part of the original interest is repaid.

4.4 Repayment of tax and repayment supplement

Tax is repaid when claimed unless a greater payment of tax is due in the following 30 days, in which case it is set-off against that payment.

Interest is paid on overpayments of:

(a) Payments on account,

(b) Final payments of income tax and Class 4 NICs and CGT, including tax deducted at source or tax credits on dividends, and

(c) Penalties and surcharges.

Repayment supplement runs from the original date of payment (even if this was prior to the due date), until the day before the date the repayment is made. Income tax deducted at source and tax credits are treated as if they were paid on the 31 January following the tax year concerned.

Repayment supplement paid to individuals is tax free.

5 ENQUIRIES, DETERMINATIONS AND DISCOVERY ASSESSMENTS

5.1 Enquiries into returns

5.1.1 Opening an enquiry

An officer of HMRC has a limited period within which to commence enquiries into a return or amendment. For an enquiry into a return for 2007/08 or a subsequent year the officer must give written notice of his intention by:

(a) **The first anniversary of the actual filing date (if the return was delivered on or before the due filing date)**, or

(b) **If the return is filed after the due filing date, the quarter day following the first anniversary of the actual filing date. The quarter days are 31 January, 30 April, 31 July and 31 October.**

If the taxpayer amended the return after the due filing date, the enquiry 'window' extends to the quarter day following the first anniversary of the date the amendment was filed. Where the enquiry was not raised within the limit which would have applied had no amendment been filed, the enquiry is restricted to matters contained in the amendment.

The officer does not have to have, or give, any reason for raising an enquiry. In particular the taxpayer will not be advised whether he has been selected at random for an audit. Enquiries may be full enquiries, or may be limited to 'aspect' enquiries.

5.1.2 During the enquiry

In the course of his enquiries **the officer may require the taxpayer to produce documents, accounts or any other information required. The taxpayer can appeal to the Commissioners.**

During the course of his enquiries an officer may amend a self-assessment if it appears that insufficient tax has been charged and an immediate amendment is necessary to prevent a loss to the Crown. This might apply if, for example, there is a possibility that the taxpayer will emigrate.

If a return is under enquiry HMRC may postpone any repayment due as shown in the return until the enquiry is complete. HMRC have discretion to make a provisional repayment but there is no facility to appeal if the repayment is withheld.

At any time during the course of an enquiry, the taxpayer may apply to the Commissioners to require the officer to notify the taxpayer within a specified period that the enquiries are complete, unless the officer can demonstrate that he has reasonable grounds for continuing the enquiry.

If both sides agree, disputes concerning a point of law can be resolved through litigation without having to wait until the whole enquiry is complete.

5.1.3 Closing an enquiry

An officer must issue a notice that the enquiries are complete, state his conclusions and amend the self-assessment, partnership statement or claim accordingly.

If the taxpayer is not satisfied with the officer's amendment he may, within 30 days, appeal to the Commissioners.

Once an enquiry is complete the officer cannot make further enquiries. HMRC may, in limited circumstances, raise a discovery assessment if they believe that there has been a loss of tax (see below).

5.2 Determinations

HMRC may only raise enquiries if a return has been submitted.

If notice has been served on a taxpayer to submit a return but the return is not submitted by the due filing date, an officer of HMRC may make a determination of the amounts liable to income tax and CGT tax and of the tax due. Such a determination must be made to the best of the officer's information and belief, and is then treated as if it were a self-assessment. This enables the officer to seek payment of tax, including payments on account for the following year and to charge interest.

The determination must be made within the period ending five years after 31 January following the tax year. It may be superseded by a self-assessment made within the same period or, if later, within 12 months of the date of the determination.

5.3 Discovery assessments

If an officer of HMRC discovers that profits have been omitted from assessment, that any assessment has become insufficient, or that any relief given is, or has become excessive, an assessment may be raised to recover the tax lost.

If the tax lost results from an error in the taxpayer's return but the return was made in accordance with prevailing practice at the time, no discovery assessment may be made.

A discovery assessment may only be raised where a return has been made if:

(a) There has been **fraudulent or negligent conduct** by the taxpayer or his agent, or

(b) At the time that enquiries into the return were completed, or could no longer be made, the officer **did not have information** to make him aware of the loss of tax.

Information is treated as available to an officer if it is contained in the taxpayer's return or claim for the year or either of the two preceding years, or it has been provided as a result of an enquiry covering those years, or it has been specifically provided.

These rules do not prevent HMRC from raising assessments in cases of genuine discoveries, but prevent assessments from being raised due to HMRC's failure to make timely use of information or to a change of opinion on information made available.

5.4 Appeals and postponement of payment of tax

A taxpayer may appeal against an amendment to a self-assessment or partnership statement, or an amendment to or disallowance of a claim, following an enquiry, or against an assessment which is not a self-assessment, such as a discovery assessment.

The appeal must normally be made within 30 days of the amendment or self-assessment.

The notice of appeal must state the **grounds** of appeal. These may be stated in general terms. At the hearing the Commissioners may allow the appellant to put forward grounds not stated in his notice if they are satisfied that his omission was not wilful or unreasonable.

In some cases it may be possible to agree the point at issue by negotiation with HMRC, in which case the appeal may be settled by agreement. If the appeal cannot be agreed, it will be heard by the General or Special Commissioners.

An appeal does not relieve the taxpayer of liability to pay tax on the normal due date unless he obtains a 'determination' of the Commissioners or agreement of the Inspector that payment of all or some of the tax may be postponed pending determination of the appeal. The amount not postponed is due 30 days after the determination or agreement is issued, if that is later than the normal due date.

If any part of the postponed tax becomes due a notice of the amount payable is issued and the amount is payable 30 days after the issue of the notice. Interest, however, is still payable from the normal due date.

NOTES

Chapter roundup

- Direct taxes are administered by Her Majesty's Revenue and Customs (HMRC).
- Individuals who do not received a tax return or who have a new source of income or gains must notify their chargeability to income tax or CGT.
- Tax returns must usually be filed by 31 October (non-electronic) or 31 January (electronic) following the end of the tax year.
- If a return is filed non-electronically the taxpayer can ask HMRC to compute the tax due. Electronic returns have tax calculated automatically.
- Two payments on account and a final balancing payment of income tax and Class 4 NICs are due. All capital gains tax is due on 31 January following the end of the tax year.
- HMRC can enquire into tax returns but strict procedural rules govern enquiries.

Quick quiz

1 By when must a taxpayer who has a new source of income give notice of his chargeability to capital gains tax due in 2007/08?

2 By when must a taxpayer file a non-electronic tax return for 2007/08?

3 What are the normal payment dates for income tax?

4 What surcharges are due in respect of income tax payments on account that are paid two months late?

NOTES

Answers to quick quiz

1 Within six months of the end of the year, ie by 5 October 2008. (see para 1)

2 By 31 October 2008 or, if the return is issued after 31 July 2008, by the end of 3 months following the issue of the notice to file the return. (para 2.2)

3 Two payments on account of income tax are due on 31 January in the tax year and on the 31 July following. A final balancing payment is due on 31 January following the tax year. (para 4.1)

4 None. Surcharges do not apply to late payment of payment on account. (para 4.2)

Answers to activities

1

		£
Income tax:		
Total income tax charged for 2007/08		9,200
Less tax deducted for 2007/08		(3,200)
		6,000
Class 4 NIC		1,900
'Relevant amount'		7,900
Payments on account for 2008/09:		
31 January 2008	£7,900 × ½	3,950
31 July 2008	As before	3,950

There is no requirement to make payments on account of capital gains tax nor Class 2 NIC.

2 Income tax and Class 4 NIC: £18,000 – £2,750 – £6,500 – £6,500 = £2,250. CGT = £5,120.

Final payment due on 31 January 2009 for 2007/2008 £2,250 + £5,120 = £7,370

3 Herbert made an excessive claim to reduce his payments on account, and will therefore be charged interest on the reduction. The payments on account should have been £4,500 each based on the original 2006/07 liability (not £5,000 each based on the 2007/08 liability). Interest will be charged as follows:

(a) First payment on account

(i) On £3,500 – nil – paid on time

(ii) On £1,000 from due date of 31 January 2008 to day before payment, 18 February 2009

(b) Second payment on account

(i) On £3,500 from due date of 31 July 2008 to day before payment, 11 August 2008

(ii) On £1,000 from due date of 31 July 2008 to day before payment, 18 February 2009

(c) Balancing payment

(i) On £3,500 from due date of 31 January 2009 to day before payment, 18 February 2009

Chapter 35 :
THE TAXATION OF BUSINESSES

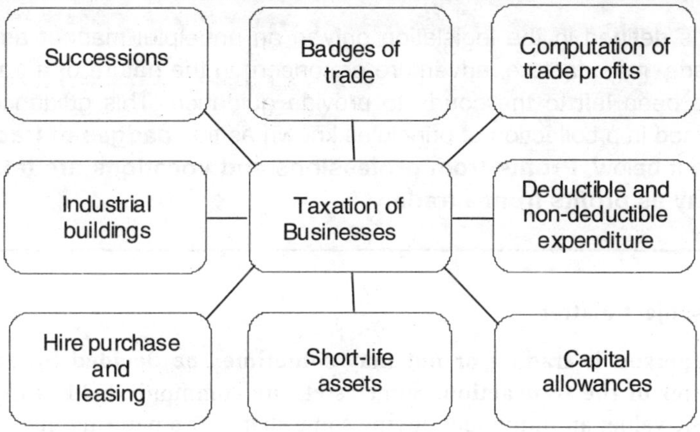

Introduction

We are now moving away from the taxation of the individual, most notably taxation of the employee, to the taxation of businesses. It is important to be able to establish exactly what constitutes 'a business'. One important feature of business taxation is the use of capital allowances, which may be treated as trading expenditure and thus reduce taxable profits.

Your objectives

In this chapter you will learn about the following.

(a) The nature of a trade with reference to the 'Badges of Trade'
(b) The principles of deductible and non-deductible expenditure
(c) How to prepare adjusted profit computations (including capital allowances)
(d) The principles relating to capital allowances on plant and machinery including the definition of plant, private use assets, short-life assets, hire purchase and leasing
(e) The eligibility to claim capital allowances on cars and assets acquired by hire purchase or lease
(f) How to prepare capital allowance computations (plant and machinery)
(g) The principles relating to capital allowances on industrial buildings as they relate to general industrial buildings and hotels
(h) Non-industrial use and notional allowances
(i) How to prepare basic capital allowance computations (industrial buildings) including acquisitions and disposals

1 THE BADGES OF TRADE

1.1 Introduction

Before a tax charge can be imposed it is necessary to establish the existence of a trade.

Definition

A trade is defined in the legislation only in an unhelpful manner as including every trade, manufacture, adventure or concern in the nature of a trade. It has therefore been left to the courts to provide guidance. This guidance is often summarised in a collection of principles known as the **'badges of trade'**. These are set out below. **Profits from professions and vocations are taxed in the same way as profits from a trade.**

1.2 The subject matter

Whether a person is trading or not may sometimes be decided by examining the subject matter of the transaction. Some assets are commonly held as investments for their intrinsic value: an individual buying some shares or a painting may do so in order to enjoy the income from the shares or to enjoy the work of art. A subsequent disposal may produce a gain of a capital nature rather than a trading profit. But **where the subject matter of a transaction is such as would not be held as an investment** (for example 34,000,000 yards of aircraft linen (*Martin v Lowry 1927*) or 1,000,000 rolls of toilet paper (*Rutledge v CIR 1929*)), **it is presumed that any profit on resale is a trading profit.**

1.3 The frequency of transactions

Transactions which may, in isolation, be of a capital nature will be interpreted as trading transactions where their **frequency indicates the carrying on of a trade.** It was decided that whereas normally the purchase of a mill-owning company and the subsequent stripping of its assets might be a capital transaction, where the taxpayer was embarking on the same exercise for the fourth time he must be carrying on a trade (*Pickford v Quirke 1927*).

1.4 The length of ownership

The courts may infer adventures in the nature of trade where items purchased are sold soon afterwards.

1.5 Supplementary work and marketing

When work is done to make an asset more marketable, or steps are taken to find purchasers, the courts will be more ready to ascribe a trading motive. When a group of accountants bought, blended and recasked a quantity of brandy they were held to be taxable on a trading profit when the brandy was later sold (*Cape Brandy Syndicate v CIR 1921*).

NOTES

1.6 A profit motive

The absence of a profit motive will not necessarily preclude a tax charge as trading income, but its presence is a strong indication that a person is trading. The purchase and resale of £20,000 worth of silver bullion by the comedian Norman Wisdom, as a hedge against devaluation, was held to be a trading transaction *(Wisdom v Chamberlain 1969)*.

1.7 The way in which the asset sold was acquired

If goods are acquired deliberately, trading may be indicated. If goods are acquired unintentionally, for example by gift or inheritance, their later sale is unlikely to be trading.

1.8 The taxpayer's intentions

Where a transaction is clearly trading on objective criteria, **the taxpayer's intentions are irrelevant**. If, however, a transaction has (objectively) a dual purpose, the taxpayer's intentions may be taken into account. An example of a transaction with a dual purpose is the acquisition of a site partly as premises from which to conduct another trade, and partly with a view to the possible development and resale of the site.

This test is not one of the traditional badges of trade, but it may be just as important.

2 THE COMPUTATION OF TRADE PROFITS

2.1 The adjustment of profits

The net profit before taxation shown in the accounts is the starting point in computing the taxable trade profits. Many adjustments may be required to calculate the taxable amount.

Here is an illustrative adjustment.

		£	£
Net profit per accounts			140,000
Add:	expenditure charged in the accounts which is not deductible for tax purposes	50,000	
	income taxable as trade profits which has not been included accounts in the	30,000	
			80,000
			220,000
Less:	profits included in the accounts but which are not taxable as trade profits	40,000	
	expenditure which is deductible for tax purposes but has not been charged in the accounts	20,000	
			(60,000)
Trade profits as adjusted for tax purposes			160,000

You may refer to deductible and non-deductible expenditure as allowable and disallowable expenditure respectively. The two sets of terms are interchangeable.

BPP LEARNING MEDIA

2.2 Accounting policies

The fundamental concept is that the profits of the business must be calculated in accordance with generally accepted accounting practice (GAAP). These profits are subject to any adjustment specifically required for income tax purposes.

2.3 Capital allowances

Under the Capital Allowances Act 2001 (CAA 2001) **capital allowances are treated as trade expenses and balancing charges are treated as trade receipts** (see later in this Course Book).

2.4 Non-deductible expenditure

Certain expenses are specifically disallowed by the legislation. These are covered in Paragraphs 2.4.1–2.4.10. If however a deduction is specifically permitted this overrides the disallowance.

2.4.1 Capital expenditure

Income tax is a tax solely on income so capital expenditure is not deductible. This denies a deduction for depreciation or amortisation (although there are special rules for companies in relation to intangible assets – see later in this text). **The most contentious items of expenditure will often be repairs** (revenue expenditure) **and improvements** (capital expenditure).

(a) The cost of restoration of an asset by, for instance, replacing a subsidiary part of the asset is revenue expenditure. Expenditure on a new factory chimney replacement was allowable since the chimney was a subsidiary part of the factory (*Samuel Jones & Co (Devondale) Ltd v CIR 1951*). However, in another case a football club demolished a spectators' stand and replaced it with a modern equivalent. This was held not to be repair, since repair is the restoration by renewal or replacement of subsidiary parts of a larger entity, and the stand formed a distinct and **separate** part of the club (*Brown v Burnley Football and Athletic Co Ltd 1980*).

(b) The cost of initial repairs to improve an asset recently acquired to make it fit to earn profits is disallowable capital expenditure. In *Law Shipping Co Ltd v CIR 1923* the taxpayer failed to obtain relief for expenditure on making a newly bought ship seaworthy prior to using it.

(c) The cost of initial repairs to remedy normal wear and tear of recently acquired assets is allowable. *Odeon Associated Theatres Ltd v Jones 1971* can be contrasted with the *Law Shipping* judgement. Odeon were allowed to charge expenditure incurred on improving the state of recently acquired cinemas.

Other examples to note include:

(a) A one-off payment made by a hotel owner to terminate an agreement for the management of a hotel was held to be revenue rather than capital expenditure in *Croydon Hotel & Leisure Co v Bowen 1996.* The payment did not affect the whole structure of the taxpayer's business; it merely enabled it to be run more efficiently.

(b) A one-off payment to remove a threat to the taxpayer's business was also held to be revenue rather than capital expenditure in *Lawson v Johnson Matthey plc 1992*.

(c) An initial payment for a franchise (as opposed to regular fees) is capital and not deductible.

2.4.2 Expenditure not wholly and exclusively for the purposes of the trade

Expenditure is not deductible if it is not for trade purposes (the remoteness test), or if it reflects more than one purpose (the duality test). The private proportion of payments for motoring expenses, rent, heat and light and telephone expenses of a proprietor is not deductible. If an exact apportionment is possible relief is given on the business element. Where the payments are to or on behalf of employees, the full amounts are deductible but the employees are taxed under the benefits code (see earlier in this Course Book).

The remoteness test is illustrated by the following cases.

(a) *Strong & Co of Romsey Ltd v Woodifield 1906*

A customer injured by a falling chimney when sleeping in an inn owned by a brewery claimed compensation from the company. The compensation was not deductible: 'the loss sustained by the appellant was not really incidental to their trade as innkeepers and fell upon them in their character not of innkeepers but of householders'.

(b) *Bamford v ATA Advertising Ltd 1972*

A director misappropriated £15,000. The loss was not allowable: 'the loss is not, as in the case of a dishonest shop assistant, an incident of the company's trading activities. It arises altogether outside such activities'.

(c) Expenditure which is wholly and exclusively to benefit the trades of several companies (for example in a group) but is not wholly and exclusively to benefit the trade of one specific company is not deductible *(Vodafone Cellular Ltd and others v Shaw 1995)*.

(d) *McKnight (HMIT) v Sheppard (1999)* concerned expenses incurred by a stockbroker in defending allegations of infringements of Stock Exchange regulations. It was found that the expenditure was incurred to prevent the destruction of the taxpayer's business and that as the expenditure was incurred for business purposes it was deductible. It was also found that although the expenditure had the effect of preserving the taxpayer's reputation, that was not its purpose, so there was no duality of purpose.

The **duality test** is illustrated by the following cases.

(a) *Caillebotte v Quinn 1975*

A self-employed carpenter spent an average of 40p per day when obliged to buy lunch away from home but just 10p when he lunched at home. He claimed the excess 30p. It was decided that the payment had a dual purpose and was not deductible: a taxpayer 'must eat to live not eat to work'.

(b) *Mallalieu v Drummond 1983*

Expenditure by a lady barrister on black clothing to be worn in court (and on its cleaning and repair) was not deductible. The expenditure was for the dual purpose of enabling the barrister to be warmly and properly clad as well as meeting her professional requirements.

(c) *McLaren v Mumford 1996*

A publican traded from a public house which had residential accommodation above it. He was obliged to live at the public house but he also had another house which he visited regularly. It was held that the private element of the expenditure incurred at the public house on electricity, rent, gas, etc was not incurred for the purpose of earning profits, but for serving the non-business purpose of satisfying the publican's ordinary human needs. The expenditure, therefore had a dual purpose and was disallowed.

However, the cost of overnight accommodation when on a business trip may be deductible and reasonable expenditure on an evening meal and breakfast in conjunction with such accommodation is then also deductible.

2.4.3 Impaired trade receivables (bad debts)

Under FRS 26 *Financial Instruments*: *Measurement*, a review of all trade receivables should be carried out to assess their fair value at the balance sheet date, and any impairment debts written off. The tax treatment follows the accounting treatment so no adjustment is required for tax purposes.

Loans to employees written off are not deductible unless the business is that of making loans, or it can be shown that the writing-off of the loan was earnings paid out for the benefit of the trade.

2.4.4 Unpaid remuneration

If earnings for employees are charged in the accounts but are not paid within nine months of the end of the period of account, the cost is only deductible for the period of account in which the earnings are paid. When a tax computation is made within the nine month period, it is initially assumed that unpaid earnings will not be paid within that period. The computation is adjusted if they are so paid.

Earnings are treated as paid at the same time as they are treated as received for employment income purposes.

2.4.5 Entertaining and gifts

The general rule is that expenditure on entertaining and gifts is non-deductible. This applies to amounts reimbursed to employees for specific entertaining expenses and gifts, and to round sum allowances which are exclusively for meeting such expenses.

There are specific exceptions to the general rule.

(a) **Entertaining for and gifts to employees are normally deductible** although where gifts are made, or the entertainment is excessive, a charge to tax may arise on the employee under the benefits legislation.

(b) **Gifts to customers not costing more than £50 per donee per year are allowed if they carry a conspicuous advertisement for the business and are not food, drink, tobacco or vouchers exchangeable for goods.**

(c) Gifts to charities may also be allowed although many will fall foul of the 'wholly and exclusively' rule above. If a gift aid declaration is made in respect of a gift, tax relief will be given under the gift aid scheme, not as a trading expense.

2.4.6 Lease charges for expensive cars

Although leasing costs will normally be an allowable expense, there is a restriction for costs relating to expensive cars. **If the retail price of the car when new exceeds £12,000 the deductible part of any leasing charge is reduced by multiplying it by the fraction (£12,000 + RP)/2RP, where RP is the retail price of the car.**

Thus for a car with a retail price of £20,000 and an annual leasing charge of £5,000 the allowable deduction is £5,000 × [(12,000 + 20,000)/2 × 20,000] = £4,000, so £1,000 of the charge is added back.

This restriction does not apply to low emission cars, ie those with carbon dioxide emissions not exceeding 120 g/km and electrically propelled cars.

2.4.7 Interest payments

Interest which is allowed as deductible interest (see earlier in this Text) is not also allowed as a trading expense.

2.4.8 National insurance contributions

No deduction is allowed for any national insurance contributions **except for employer's contributions.** For the purpose of your exam, these are Class 1 secondary contributions and Class 1A contributions (Class 1B contributions are not examinable). National insurance contributions for self employed individuals are dealt with later in this chapter.

2.4.9 Penalties and interest on tax

Penalties and interest on late paid tax are not allowed as a trading expense. Tax includes income tax, capital gains tax, VAT and stamp duty land tax.

2.4.10 Crime related payments

A payment is not deductible if making it constitutes an offence by the payer. This covers protection money paid to terrorists, bribes and similar payments made overseas which would be criminal payments if they were made in the UK. Statute also prevents any deduction for payments made in response to blackmail or extortion.

2.5 Deductible expenditure

Most expenses will be deductible under the general rule that expenses incurred wholly and exclusively for the purpose of the trade are not disallowed. Some expenses which might otherwise be disallowed under the 'wholly or exclusively' rule, or under one or other of the specific rules discussed above are, however, specifically allowed by the legislation. These are covered in Paragraphs 2.5.1–2.5.12.

2.5.1 Pre-trading expenditure

Expenditure incurred before the commencement of trade is deductible, if it is incurred within seven years of the start of trade and it is of a type that would have been deductible had the trade already started. **It is treated as a trading expense incurred on the first day of trading.**

2.5.2 Incidental costs of obtaining finance

Incidental costs of obtaining loan finance, or of attempting to obtain or redeeming it, are deductible other than a discount on issue or a premium on redemption (which are really alternatives to paying interest). This deduction for incidental costs does not apply to companies because they obtain a deduction for the costs of borrowing in a different way. We will look at companies later in this Course Book.

2.5.3 Short leases

A trader may deduct an annual sum in respect of the amount liable to income tax on a lease premium which he paid to his landlord (see earlier in this Course Book). Normally, the amortisation of the lease will have been deducted in the accounts (and must be added back as capital expenditure).

2.5.4 Renewals

Where a tool is replaced or altered then the cost of the renewal or alteration may be deducted as an expense in certain instances. These are that:

(a) A deduction would only be prohibited because the expenditure is capital expenditure, and

(b) No deduction can be given under any other provisions, such as under the capital allowances legislation.

2.5.5 Restrictive covenants

When an employee leaves his employment he may accept a limitation on his future activities in return for a payment. **Provided the employee is taxed on the payment as employment income** (see earlier in this Course Book) **the payment is a deductible trading expense.**

2.5.6 Secondments

The **costs of seconding employees to charities or educational establishments are deductible.**

2.5.7 Contributions to agent's expenses

Many employers run payroll giving schemes for their employees. **Any payments made to the agent who administers the scheme towards running expenses are deductible.**

NOTES

2.5.8 Counselling and retraining expenses

Expenditure on providing counselling and retraining for leaving employees is allowable.

2.5.9 Redundancy

Redundancy payments made when a trade ends are deductible on the earlier of the day of payment and the last day of trading. If the trade does not end, they can be deducted as soon as they are provided for, so long as the redundancy was decided on within the period of account, the provision is accurately calculated and the payments are made within nine months of the end of the period of account. **The deduction extends to additional payments of up to three times the amount of the redundancy pay on cessation of trade.**

2.5.10 Personal security expenses

If there is a particular security threat to the trader because of the nature of the trade, **expenditure on his personal security is allowable.**

2.5.11 Contributions to local enterprise organisations/urban regeneration companies

This allows a deduction for donations made to a local enterprise agency, a training and enterprise council, a Scottish local enterprise company, a business link organisation or an urban regeneration company. If any benefit is received by the trade from the donation, this must be deducted from the allowable amount.

2.5.12 Patents, trade marks and copyrights

The costs of **registering patents and trade marks** are deductible for trades only (not professions or vocations). Copyright arises automatically and so does not have to be registered. **Patent royalties and copyright royalties paid in connection with a trade are deductible as trading expenses.**

2.6 Trading income

There are also statutory rules governing whether certain receipts are taxable or not. These are discussed in 2.6.1 to 2.6.5.

2.6.1 Capital receipts

As may be expected, capital receipts are not included in trading income. They may, of course, be taken into account in the capital allowances computation, or as a capital gain.

However, compensation received in one lump sum for the loss of income is likely to be treated as income (*Donald Fisher (Ealing) Ltd v Spencer 1989*).

In some trades, (eg petrol stations and public houses), a wholesaler may pay a lump sum to a retailer in return for the retailer only supplying that wholesaler's products for several years (an **exclusivity agreement**). If the payment must be used for a specific capital purpose, it is a capital receipt. If that is not the case, it is an income receipt. If the sum is repayable to the wholesaler but the requirement to repay is waived in tranches over the

BPP LEARNING MEDIA

term of the agreement, each tranche is a separate income receipt when the requirement is waived.

2.6.2 Debts released

If the trader incurs a deductible expense but does not settle the amount due to the supplier, then if the creditor releases the debt other than under a statutory arrangement, the amount released must be brought into account as trading income.

2.6.3 Takeover of trade

If a trader takes over a trade from a previous owner, then if he receives any amounts from that trade which related to a period before the takeover they must be brought into account unless the previous owner has already done so.

2.6.4 Insurance receipts

Insurance receipts which are revenue in nature, such as for loss of profits, are trading receipts. Otherwise the receipt must be brought in as trading income if, and to the extent that, any deduction has been claimed for the expense that the receipt is intended to cover.

2.6.5 Gifts of trading stock to educational establishments or schools

When a business makes a gift of equipment manufactured, sold or used in the course of its trade to an educational establishment or for a charitable purpose, nothing need be brought into account as a trading receipt or (if capital allowances had been obtained on the asset) as disposal proceeds, so full relief is obtained for the cost.

2.7 Excluded income

2.7.1 Income taxed in another way

Although the accounts may include other income, such as interest, such income is not trading income. It will instead be taxed under the specific rules for that type of income, such as the rules for savings income.

Certain types of income are specifically exempt from tax, and should be excluded from trade profits.

2.8 Application of general rules

These general rules can be applied to particular types of expenditure and income that you are likely to come across.

2.8.1 Appropriations

Salary or interest on capital paid to a proprietor are not deductible.

2.8.2 Subscriptions and donations

The general 'wholly and exclusively' rule determines the deductibility of expenses. Subscriptions and donations are not deductible unless the expenditure is for the benefit of the trade.

The following are the main types of subscriptions and donations you may meet and their correct treatments.

(a) **Trade subscriptions** (such as to a professional or trade association) are generally deductible.

(b) **Charitable donations** are deductible only if they are small and to local charities. Tax relief may be available for donations under the gift aid scheme. In the latter case they are not a deductible trading expense.

(c) **Political subscriptions** and donations are generally not deductible.

(d) Where a donation represents the most effective commercial way of **disposing of stock** (for example, where it would not be commercially effective to sell surplus perishable food), the donation can be treated as for the benefit of the trade and the disposal proceeds taken as £Nil. In other cases, the amount credited to the accounts in respect of a donation of stock should be its market value.

2.8.3 Legal and professional charges

Legal and professional charges relating to capital or non-trading items are not deductible. These include charges incurred in acquiring new capital assets or legal rights, issuing shares, drawing up partnership agreements and litigating disputes over the terms of a partnership agreement.

Charges are deductible if they relate directly to trading. Deductible items include:

(a) Legal and professional charges incurred defending the taxpayer's title to fixed assets

(b) Charges connected with an action for breach of contract

(c) Expenses of the **renewal** (not the original grant) of a lease for less than 50 years

(d) Charges for trade debt collection

(e) Normal charges for preparing accounts/assisting with the self-assessment of tax liabilities

Accountancy expenses arising out of an enquiry into the accounts information in a particular year's return are not allowed where the enquiry reveals discrepancies and additional liabilities for the year of enquiry, or any earlier year, which arise as a result of negligent or fraudulent conduct.

Where, however, the enquiry results in no addition to profits, or an adjustment to the profits for the year of enquiry only and that assessment does not arise as a result of negligent or fraudulent conduct, the additional accountancy expenses are allowable.

2.8.4 Goods for own use

The usual example is when a proprietor takes goods for his own use. In such circumstances the normal selling price of the goods is added to the accounting profit. In other words, the proprietor is treated for tax purposes as having made a sale to himself (*Sharkey v Wernher 1955*). This rule does not apply to supplies of services, which are treated as sold for the amount (if any) actually paid (but the cost of services to the trader or his household is not deductible).

2.8.5 Other items

Here is a list of various other items that you may meet.

Item	Treatment	Comment
Educational courses for staff	Allow	
Educational courses for proprietor	Allow	If to update existing knowledge or skills, not if to acquire new knowledge or skills
Removal expenses (to new business premises)	Allow	Only if not an expansionary move
Travelling expenses to the trader's place of business	Disallow	*Ricketts v Colquhoun 1925*: unless an itinerant trader (*Horton v Young 1971*)
Compensation for loss of office and ex gratia payments	Allow	If for benefit of trade: *Mitchell v B W Noble Ltd 1927*
Pension contributions (to schemes for employees and company directors)	Allow	Special contributions may be spread over the year of payment and future years
Parking fines	Allow	For employees using their employer's cars on business.
	Disallow	For proprietors/directors
Damages paid	Allow	If not too remote from trade: *Strong and Co v Woodifield 1906*
Preparation and restoration of waste disposal sites	Allow	Spread preparation expenditure over period of use of site. Pre-trading expenditure is treated as incurred on the first day of trading. Allow restoration expenditure in period of expenditure
Dividends on trade investments	Deduct	Taxed as savings income
Rental income from letting part of premises	Deduct	Taxed as income of a UK property business unless it is the letting of surplus business accommodation.

In the assessment you could be given a profit and loss account and asked to calculate 'taxable trade profits'. You must look at every expense in the accounts to decide if it is (or isn't) 'tax deductible'. This means that you must become familiar with the many expenses you may see and the correct tax treatment. Look at the above paragraphs again noting what expenses are (and are not) allowable for tax purposes. Similarly you must decide whether income included in the accounts should be included in the taxable trade profits, or whether it should be excluded.

NOTES

Activity 1 **(15 minutes)**

Here is the profit and loss account of S Pring, a trader

	£	£
Gross operating profit	30,000	
Taxed interest received	860	
		30,860
Wages and salaries	7,000	
Rent and rates	2,000	
Depreciation	1,500	
Impairment of trade receivables	150	
Entertainment expenses	750	
Patent royalties	1,200	
Bank interest	300	
Legal expenses on acquisition of new factory	250	
		(13,150)
Net profit		17,710

(a) Salaries include £500 paid to Mrs Pring who works full-time in the business.

(b) No staff were entertained.

(c) Taxed interest and patent royalties are shown gross.

Compute the taxable trade profits.

2.9 The cessation of trades

2.9.1 Post cessation receipts and expenses

Post-cessation receipts (including any releases of debts incurred by the trader) **are chargeable to income tax as miscellaneous income.**

If they are received in the tax year of cessation or the next six tax years, the trader can elect that they be treated as received on the day of cessation. The time limit for electing is the 31 January which is 22 months after the end of the tax year of receipt.

Certain post cessation expenses paid within seven years of discontinuance may be relieved against other income. The expenses must relate to costs of remedying defective work or goods, or legal expenses of or insurance against defective work claims. Relief is also available for trade receivable that subsequently prove to be impaired.

2.9.2 Valuing trading stock on cessation

When a trade ceases, the closing stock must be valued. The higher the value, the higher the profit for the final period of trading.

BPP LEARNING MEDIA

If the stock is sold to a UK trader who will deduct its cost in computing his taxable profits, it is valued under the following rules.

(a) If the seller and the buyer are unconnected, take the actual price.

(b) If the seller and the buyer are connected (see below), take what would have been the price in an arm's length sale.

(c) However, if the seller and the buyer are connected, the arm's length price exceeds both the original cost of the stock and the actual transfer price, and both the seller and the buyer make an election, then take the greater of the original cost of the stock and the transfer price. The time limit for election for unincorporated business is the 31 January which is 22 months after the end of the tax year of cessation (for companies, it is two years after the end of the accounting period of cessation).

In all cases covered above, the value used for the seller's computation of profit is also used as the buyer's cost.

Definition

An individual is **connected** (connected person) with his spouse (or civil partner), with the relatives (brothers, sisters, ancestors and lineal descendants) of himself and his spouse (or civil partner), and with the spouses (or civil partners) of those relatives. In-laws and step family are included; uncles, aunts, nephews, nieces and cousins are not. He is also connected with his business partners (except in relation to *bona fide* commercial arrangements for the disposal of partnership assets), and with their spouses (or civil partners) and relatives (see diagram below).

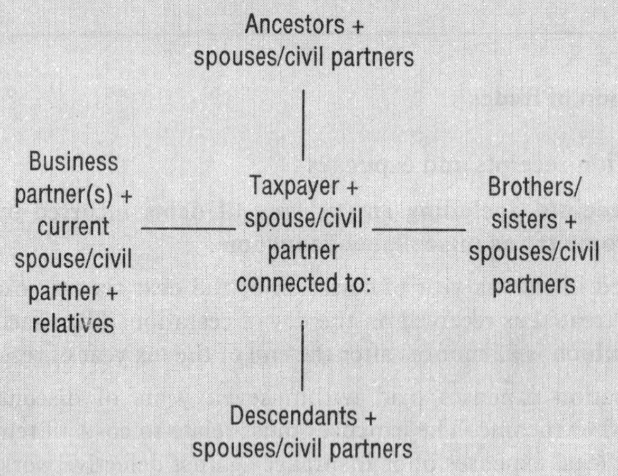

If the stock is not transferred to a UK trader who will be able to deduct its cost in computing his profits, then it is valued at its open market value as at the cessation of trade.

3 CAPITAL ALLOWANCES IN GENERAL

Capital expenditure cannot be deducted in computing taxable trade profits, but it *may* attract capital allowances. Capital allowances are treated as a trading expense and are deducted in arriving at taxable trade profits. Balancing charges, effectively negative allowances, are added in arriving at those profits.

Capital expenditure on plant and machinery qualifies for capital allowances. Expenditure on industrial buildings may also qualify for allowances.

Both unincorporated businesses and companies are entitled to capital allowances. For completeness, in this chapter we will look at the rules for companies alongside those for unincorporated businesses. We will look at companies in more detail later in this Course Book.

For unincorporated businesses, capital allowances are calculated for periods of account. These are simply the periods for which the trader chooses to make up accounts. For companies, capital allowances are calculated for accounting periods (see later in this Course Book).

For capital allowances purposes, expenditure is generally deemed to be incurred when the obligation to pay becomes unconditional. This will often be the date of a contract, but if for example payment is due a month after delivery of a machine, it would be the date of delivery. However, amounts due more than four months after the obligation becomes unconditional are deemed to be incurred when they fall due.

4 PLANT AND MACHINERY – QUALIFYING EXPENDITURE

4.1 Introduction

Capital expenditure on plant and machinery qualifies for capital allowances if the plant or machinery is used for a qualifying activity, such as a trade. 'Plant' is not defined by the legislation, although some specific exclusions and inclusions are given. The word 'machinery' may be taken to have its normal everyday meaning.

4.2 The statutory exclusions

4.2.1 Buildings

Expenditure on a building and on any asset which is incorporated in a building or is of a kind normally incorporated into buildings does not qualify as expenditure on plant, but see below for exceptions.

In addition to complete buildings, **the following assets count as 'buildings', and are therefore not plant.**

- Walls, floors, ceilings, doors, gates, shutters, windows and stairs
- Mains services, and systems, of water, electricity and gas
- Waste disposal, sewerage and drainage systems
- Shafts or other structures for lifts etc

NOTES

4.2.2 Structures

Expenditure on structures and on works involving the alteration of land **does not qualify as expenditure on plant,** but see below for exceptions.

A 'structure' is a fixed structure of any kind, other than a building.

4.2.3 Exceptions

Over the years a large body of case law has been built up under which plant and machinery allowances have been given on certain types of expenditure which might be thought to be expenditure on a building or structure. Statute therefore gives a list of various assets which *may* still be plant. These are:

- Any machinery not within any other item in this list
- Electrical (including lighting), cold water, gas and sewerage systems:
  - Provided mainly to meet the particular requirements of the trade, or
  - Provided mainly to serve particular machinery or plant used for the purposes of the trade
- Space or water heating systems and powered systems of ventilation
- Manufacturing and display equipment
- Cookers, washing machines, refrigeration or cooling equipment, sanitary ware, furniture and furnishings
- Lifts etc
- Sound insulation provided mainly to meet the particular requirements of the trade
- Computer, telecommunication and surveillance systems
- Sprinkler equipment, fire alarm and burglar alarm systems
- Strong rooms in bank or building society premises, safes
- Partition walls, where movable and intended to be moved
- Decorative assets provided for the enjoyment of the public in the hotel, restaurant or similar trades, advertising hoardings
- Glasshouses which have, as an integral part of their structure, devices which control the plant growing environment automatically
- Swimming pools (including diving boards, slides) and structures for rides at amusement parks
- Caravans provided mainly for holiday lettings
- Movable buildings intended to be moved in the course of the trade
- Expenditure on altering land for the purpose only of installing machinery or plant
- Dry docks and jetties
- Pipelines, and also underground ducts or tunnels with a primary purpose of carrying utility conduits

- Silos provided for temporary storage and storage tanks, slurry pits and silage clamps
- Fish tanks, fish ponds and fixed zoo cages
- A railway or tramway

Items falling within the above list of exclusions will only qualify as plant if they fall within the meaning of plant as established by case law. This is discussed below.

4.2.4 Land

Land or an interest in land does not qualify as plant and machinery. For this purpose 'land' excludes buildings, structures and assets which are installed or fixed to land in such a way as to become part of the land for general legal purposes.

4.3 The statutory inclusions

Certain expenditure is specifically deemed to be expenditure on plant and machinery.

The following are deemed to be on plant and machinery.

(a) Expenditure incurred by a trader in complying with fire regulations for a building which he occupies

(b) Expenditure by a trader on thermal insulation of an industrial building

(c) Expenditure by a trader in meeting statutory safety requirements for sports ground

(d) Expenditure (by an individual or a partnership, not by a company) on *security assets* provided to meet a special threat to an individual's security that arises wholly or mainly due to the particular trade concerned. Cars, ships, aircraft and dwellings are specifically excluded from the definition of a security asset

On disposal, the sale proceeds for the above are deemed to be zero, so no balancing charge (see below) can arise.

Capital expenditure on computer software (both programs and data) **qualifies as expenditure on plant and machinery**:

(a) Regardless of whether the software is supplied in a tangible form (such as a disk) or transmitted electronically, and

(b) Regardless of whether the purchaser acquires the software or only a licence to use it.

Disposal proceeds are brought into account in the normal way, except that if the fee for the grant of a licence is taxed as income of the licensor, no disposal proceeds are taken into account in computing the licensee's capital allowances.

Where someone has incurred expenditure qualifying for capital allowances on computer software (or the right to use software), and receives a capital sum in exchange for allowing someone else to use the software, that sum is brought into account as disposal proceeds. However, the cumulative total of disposal proceeds is not allowed to exceed the original cost of the software, and any proceeds above this limit are ignored for capital allowances purposes (although they may lead to chargeable gains).

If software is expected to have a useful economic life of less than two years, its cost may be treated as revenue expenditure.

For companies the rules for computer software are overridden by the rules for intangible fixed assets unless the company elects otherwise.

4.4 Case law

The original case law **definition of plant** (applied in this case to a horse) is **'whatever apparatus is used by a businessman for carrying on his business: not his stock in trade which he buys or makes for sale; but all goods and chattels, fixed or movable, live or dead, which he keeps for permanent employment in the business'** *(Yarmouth v France 1887)*.

Subsequent cases have refined the original definition and have largely been concerned with the **distinction between plant actively used in the business (qualifying) and the setting in which the business is carried on (non-qualifying). This is the 'functional' test**. Some of the decisions have now been enacted as part of statute law, but they are still relevant as examples of the principles involved.

The whole cost of excavating and installing a swimming pool was allowed to the owners of a caravan park. *CIR v Barclay Curle & Co 1969* was followed: the pool performed **the function** of giving 'buoyancy and enjoyment' to the persons using the pool *(Cooke v Beach Station Caravans Ltd 1974)* (actual item now covered by statute).

A barrister succeeded in his claim for his law library: 'Plant includes a man's tools of his trade. It extends to what he uses day by day in the course of his profession. It is not confined to physical things like the dentist's chair or the architect's table' *(Munby v Furlong 1977)*.

Office partitioning was allowed. Because it was movable it was not regarded as part of the setting in which the business was carried on *(Jarrold v John Good and Sons Ltd 1963)* (actual item now covered by statute).

A ship used as a floating restaurant was regarded as a 'structure in which the business was carried on rather than apparatus employed ... ' (Buckley LJ). No capital allowances could be obtained *(Benson v Yard Arm Club 1978)*. The same decision was made in relation to a football club's spectator stand. The stand performed no function in the actual carrying out of the club's trade *(Brown v Burnley Football and Athletic Co Ltd 1980)*.

At a motorway service station, false ceilings contained conduits, ducts and lighting apparatus. **They did not qualify because they did not perform a function in the business. They were merely part of the setting in which the business was conducted** *(Hampton v Fortes Autogrill Ltd 1979)*.

Light fittings, decor and murals can be plant. A company carried on business as hoteliers and operators of licensed premises. The function of the items was the creation of an atmosphere conducive to the comfort and well being of its customers *(CIR v Scottish and Newcastle Breweries Ltd 1982)* (decorative assets used in hotels etc, now covered by statute).

On the other hand, it has been held that when an attractive floor is provided in a restaurant, the fact that the floor performs the function of making the restaurant attractive to customers is not enough to make it plant. It functions as premises, and the cost therefore does not qualify for capital allowances (*Wimpy International Ltd v Warland 1988*).

General lighting in a department store is not plant, as it is merely setting. Special display lighting, however, can be plant (*Cole Brothers Ltd v Phillips 1982*).

Free-standing decorative screens installed in the windows of a branch of a building society qualified as plant. Their function was not to act a part of the setting in which the society's business was carried on; it was to attract local custom, and accordingly the screens formed part of the apparatus with which the society carried on its business (*Leeds Permanent Building Society v Proctor 1982*).

In *Bradley v London Electricity plc 1996* an electricity substation was held not to be plant because it functioned as premises in which London Electricity carried on a trading activity rather than apparatus with which the activity was carried out.

5 ALLOWANCES ON PLANT AND MACHINERY

5.1 Pooling expenditure

Most expenditure on plant and machinery is put into a pool of expenditure on which capital allowances may be claimed. An addition increases the pool whilst a disposal decreases it.

Exceptionally the following items are not pooled.

(a) Cars costing more than £12,000
(b) Assets with private use by the proprietor
(c) Short life assets where an election has been made.

Each of these items is dealt with in further detail below.

5.2 Writing-down allowances

Definition

A **writing-down allowance (WDA)** is given on pooled expenditure **at the rate of 25% a year** (on a reducing balance basis). The WDA is calculated on the written-down value (WDV) of pooled plant, after adding the current period's additions and taking out the current period's disposals.

When plant is sold, proceeds (**limited to a maximum of the original cost**) are taken out of the pool. Provided that the trade is still being carried on, the pool balance remaining is written down in the future by WDAs, even if there are no assets left.

EXAMPLE: CAPITAL ALLOWANCES

Elizabeth has a balance of unrelieved expenditure on her general pool of plant and machinery of £16,000 on 1.4.07. In the year to 31.3.08 she bought a car for £8,000 and she disposed of plant which originally cost £4,000 for £6,000.

Calculate the capital allowances available for the year.

	£
Pool value b/f	16,000
Addition	8,000
Less: Disposal (limited to cost)	(4,000)
	20,000
WDA @ 25%	(5,000)
TWDV c/f	15,000

WDAs are 25% × months/12:

(a) For unincorporated businesses where the period of account is longer or shorter than 12 months

(b) For companies where the accounting period is shorter than 12 months (a company's accounting period for tax purposes is never longer than 12 months), or where the trade concerned started in the accounting period and was therefore carried on for fewer than 12 months. Remember that we will be studying companies in detail later in this Course Book.

Expenditure on plant and machinery by a person about to begin a trade is treated as incurred on the first day of trading. Assets previously owned by a trader and then brought into the trade (at the start of trading or later) are treated as bought for their market values at the times when they are brought in.

Allowances are claimed in the tax return.

Note that from a tax planning point of view any business can claim less than the full allowances. Adjusting capital allowances may be advantageous, if, for example, a trader wants to avoid making such a large loss claim as to lose the benefit of the personal allowance (see earlier in this Course Book). Higher capital allowances will then be available in later years because the WDV carried forward will be higher.

5.3 First-year allowances

5.3.1 Spending by medium-sized enterprises

Expenditure incurred on plant and machinery (other than leased assets, cars, sea going ships, railway assets or long life assets) by **medium-sized enterprises qualifies for a first-year allowance (FYA) of 40%.**

Definition

> A **medium-sized enterprise** is an individual, partnership or company that either satisfies at least two of the following conditions in the chargeable period/financial year in which the expenditure is incurred.
>
> (a) Turnover not more than £22.8 million
> (b) Assets not more than £11.4 million
> (c) Not more than 250 employees.
>
> or which was medium-sized in the previous year. A company must not be a member of a large group when the expenditure is incurred.

5.3.2 Spending by small sized enterprises

Expenditure incurred on plant and machinery by small-sized enterprises **qualifies for a FYA** in the same way as for medium-sized enterprises, but a higher rate of FYA may be available. The rates are:

Before 6 April 2004 (1 April 2004 for companies)	40%
6 April 2004 to 5 April 2005 (1 April 2004 to 31 March 2005 for companies)	50%
6 April 2005 to 5 April 2006 (1 April 2005 to 31 March 2006 for companies)	40%
6 April 2006 to 5 April 2008 (1 April 2006 to 31 March 2008 for companies)	50%
6 April 2009 (1 April 2009 onwards for companies)	40%

Definition

> A **small enterprise** is an individual, partnership or company, which satisfies at least two of the following conditions in the chargeable period/financial year in which the expenditure is incurred:
>
> (a) Turnover not more than £5.6 million
> (b) Assets not more than £2.8 million
> (c) Not more than 50 employees
>
> or which was small in the previous year. If a company is a member of a group, the group must also be small when the expenditure is incurred.

5.3.3 100% FYAs

A car registered between 17 April 2002 and 31 March 2008 qualifies for 100% FYAs for all businesses if it either:

- **Emits not more than 120 gm/km CO_2; or**
- **It is electrically propelled**

In addition, the special rules for expensive cars (see below), which restrict the availability of capital allowances and the deductibility of lease rental payments, do not apply to low emission cars.

A 100% FYA is available to all businesses in respect of expenditure incurred on plant to refuel vehicles with compressed natural gas or hydrogen, between 17 April 2002 and 31 March 2008.

Equipment acquired for leasing does not normally qualify for the 100% FYA. Exceptionally, leased low emission and electric cars and natural gas/hydrogen refuelling equipment do qualify for FYAs.

5.3.4 Calculation

For FYA purposes, the provisions which treat capital expenditure incurred prior to the commencement of trading as incurred on the first day of trading do not apply except insofar as they require the FYAs to be given in the first period of account (or accounting period for companies).

First-year allowances are given in the place of writing-down allowances. For subsequent years a WDA is given on the balance of expenditure at the normal rate. You should therefore transfer the balance of the expenditure to the pool at the end of the first period.

FYAs are given for incurring expenditure. It is irrelevant whether the basis period of expenditure is 12 months or not. FYAs are not scaled up or down by reference to the length of the period.

Activity 2 **(20 minutes)**

Walton starts a trade on 1 March 2005, and has the following results (before capital allowances).

Period of account	*Profits*
	£
1.3.05–31.7.05	42,500
1.8.05–31.7.06	36,800
1.8.06–31.7.07	32,000

Plant (none of which is eligible for 100% FYAs) is bought as follows.

Date	*Cost*
	£
1.5.05	13,000
1.6.05	9,500
1.5.06	4,000
1.6.07	1,600

On 1 May 2006, plant which cost £7,00 is cold for £4,000.

Walton's business is a small enterprise for FYA purposes.

Show the taxable trade profits arising in the above periods of account.

NOTES

5.4 The disposal value of assets

The most common disposal value at which assets are entered in a capital allowances computation is the sale proceeds. But there are a number of less common situations.

Where the asset is sold at below market value (or is given away) the market value is used instead of the actual sale proceeds. This general rule has two exceptions. The actual proceeds of sale are used:

(a) Where the buyer will be able to claim capital allowances on the expenditure

(b) Where an employee acquires an asset from his employer at undervalue (or as a gift) and so faces a charge under the employment income benefit rules

If the asset is demolished, destroyed or otherwise lost, the disposal value is taken to be the actual sale proceeds from any resulting scrap, plus any insurance or other compensation monies.

With all these rules, there is an overriding rule that the capital allowances **disposal value cannot exceed the original cost.**

When a building is sold, the vendor and purchaser can make a joint election to determine how the sale proceeds are apportioned between the building and its fixtures. There are anti-avoidance provisions that ensure capital allowances given overall on a fixture do not exceed the original cost of the fixture.

5.5 Balancing charges and allowances

Balancing charges occur when the disposal value deducted exceeds the balance remaining in the pool. The charge equals the excess and is effectively a negative capital allowance, increasing profits. Most commonly this happens when the trade ceases and the remaining assets are sold. It may also occur, however, whilst the trade is still in progress.

Balancing allowances on the capital allowance pool of expenditure arise only when the trade ceases. The balancing allowance is equal to the remaining unrelieved expenditure after deducting the disposal value of all the assets. Balancing allowances also arise on items which are not pooled (see below) whenever those items are disposed of.

5.6 Assets which are not pooled

A separate record of allowances and WDV must be kept for each asset which is not pooled. When it is sold a balancing allowance or charge arises.

5.6.1 Motor cars

Cars costing more than £12,000 are not pooled. The maximum WDA is £3,000 a year. The limit is £3,000 × months/12:

(a) For short or long periods of account of unincorporated businesses
(b) For short accounting periods of companies (see later in this Course Book)

FYAs are not available on cars (except for certain low emission or electric cars – see above).

5.6.2 Private use assets

An asset (eg a car) which is used partly for private purposes by a sole trader or a partner is not pooled. Make all calculations on the full cost but claim only the business use proportion of the allowances. An asset with some private use by an employee (not a proprietor) suffers no such restriction. The employee may be taxed under the benefits code so the business receives capital allowances on the full cost of the asset.

Activity 3 **(10 minutes)**

A trader started trading on 1 July 2005, making up accounts to 31 December each year. On 1 August 2004 he bought a car for £15,500. The private use proportion is 10%. The car was sold in July 2007 for £4,000. What are the capital allowances.

5.6.3 Other assets

Short life assets are not pooled and long life assets are also kept in a separate pool (see below).

5.7 The cessation of a trade

When a business ceases to trade no FYAs or WDAs are given in the final period of account (unincorporated businesses) or accounting period (companies – see later in this Text). Each asset is deemed to be disposed of on the date the trade ceased (usually at the then market value). Additions in the relevant period are brought in and then the disposal proceeds (limited to cost) are deducted from the balance of qualifying expenditure. If the proceeds exceed the balance then a balancing charge arises. If the balance of qualifying expenditure exceeds the proceeds then a balancing allowance is given.

Activity 4 **(20 minutes)**

Bradley has been trading for many years, preparing accounts to 31 December. He ceases trading on 31 August 2007. The written down value of the general pool at 1 January 2006 was £25,260 and the written down value of the expensive motor car (40% private use by Bradley) was £21,225. Bradley's business is a small sized enterprise for FYA purposes.

Bradley made the following purchases and sales of plant and machinery in the last 20 months to 31 August 2007:

		£
7 June 2006	Bought machinery	1,620
12 May 2007	Bought machinery	1,740
31 August 2007	Sold all pool items (all less than original cost)	25,295
31 August 2007	Sold car	16,500

What is balancing adjustment is required on cessation?

6 SHORT-LIFE ASSETS

A trader can elect that specific items of plant be kept separately from the general pool. The election is irrevocable. For an unincorporated business, the time limit for electing is the 31 January which is 22 months after the end of the tax year in which the period of account of the expenditure ends. (For a company, it is two years after the end of the accounting period of the expenditure.) **Any asset subject to this election is known as a 'short-life asset', and the election is known as a 'de-pooling election'.**

Definition

Provided that the asset is disposed of within four years of the end of the period of account or accounting period of which it was bought, it is a **short life asset** and a balancing charge or allowance is made on it disposal.

The receipt of a capital sum in return for the right to use computer software does not count as a disposal for this purpose. If the asset is not disposed of in the correct time period, its tax written down value is added to the general pool at the end of that time. The election should be made for assets likely to be sold within four years for less than their tax written down values. It should not be made for assets likely to be sold within four years for more than their tax written down values. (These are, of course, only general guidelines based on the assumption that a trader will want to obtain allowances as quickly as possible. There may be other considerations, such as a desire to even out annual taxable profits.)

BPP LEARNING MEDIA

EXAMPLE

Caithlin bought an asset on 1 May 2003 for £12,000 and elected for de-pooling. Her accounting year end is 30 April. Calculate the capital allowances due if:

(a) The asset is scrapped for £300 in August 2007.

(b) The asset is scrapped for £200 in August 2008.

(a)

	£
Year to 30.4.04	
Cost	12,000
WDA 25%	(3,000)
	9,000
Year to 30.4.05	
WDA 25%	(2,250)
	6,750
Year to 30.4.06	
WDA 25%	(1,688)
	5,062
Year to 30.4.07	
WDA 25%	(1,266)
	3,796
Year to 30.4.08	
Disposal proceeds	(300)
Balancing allowance	3,496

(b) If the asset is still in use at 30 April 2008, a WDA of 25% × £3,796 = £949 would be claimable in the year to 30 April 2008. The tax written-down value of £3,796 – £949 = £2,847 would be added to the general pool at the beginning of the next period of account. The disposal proceeds of £200 would be deducted from the general pool in that period's capital allowances computation and no balancing allowance would arise.

Short-life asset treatment cannot be claimed for:

- Motor cars
- Plant used partly for non-trade purposes
- Plant brought into use for the trade following non-business use
- Plant received by way of gift
- Plant in respect of which a subsidy is received
- Long-life assets

Where a short-life asset is disposed of within the four-year period to a connected person.

(a) The original owner receives a balancing allowance calculated as normal and the new owner receives WDAs on the cost to him, but

(b) **If both parties so elect, the asset is treated as being sold for its tax written down value at the start of the chargeable period in which the transfer takes place, so there is no balancing charge or allowance for the vendor.**

In both situations, the acquiring party will continue to 'de-pool' the asset up to the same date as the original owner would have done.

NOTES

7 LONG-LIFE ASSETS

Definition

> **Long-life assets** are assets with an expected working life of 25 years or more.

The writing-down allowance available on such assets is 6% per annum on a reducing balance basis. Expenditure on such assets must be kept in a pool that is separate from the general pool.

The following are not **treated as long-life assets** (and therefore (with the exception of expensive cars: see above) still qualify for writing-down allowances of 25% per annum):

(a) **Plant and machinery in dwelling houses, retail shops, showrooms, hotels and offices**

(b) **Motor cars**

(c) **Ships and railways assets** bought before 1 January 2011

(d) **Second-hand machinery in respect of which the vendor obtained allowances at 25%**

The **long-life asset rules do not apply to companies whose total expenditure on long life assets in a chargeable period is £100,000,** or less. If the expenditure exceeds £100,000, the whole of the expenditure qualifies for allowances at 6% per annum only. For this purpose all expenditure incurred under a contract is treated as incurred in the first chargeable period to which that contract relates.

Individuals and partnerships spending less than £100,000 a year are also excluded from the long life asset rules provided the individual, or at least half the partners, works full time in the business.

The £100,000 limit is reduced or increased proportionately in the case of a chargeable period of less or more than 12 months. In the case of groups of companies, the limit must be divided between the number of associated companies in the group (see later in this Text).

The £100,000 exclusion is not available in respect of leased assets, second-hand assets where the vendor was only able to claim allowances of 6%, or assets in which the trader has only bought a share.

8 HIRE PURCHASE AND LEASING

8.1 Assets on hire purchase or long-term leases

Any asset (including a car) bought on hire purchase (HP) is treated as if purchased outright for the cash price. Therefore:

(a) The buyer normally obtains **capital allowances on the cash price** when the agreement begins.

(b) He may write off the **finance charge as a trade expense** over the term of the HP contract.

Long-term leases, (those with a term of five or more years), are treated in the same way as HP transactions.

BPP LEARNING MEDIA

8.2 Assets on long-term leases

Under a long-term lease, the lessee merely hires the asset over a period. The hire charge can normally be deducted in computing trade profits. If an expensive car (one costing over £12,000) is leased, the maximum allowable deduction from trading profits for lease rentals is limited as described earlier in this text.

A long-term lessor of plant normally obtains the benefit of capital allowances although there are anti-avoidance provisions which deny or restrict capital allowances on certain finance leases. Leasing is thus an activity which attracts tax allowances and which can be used to defer tax liabilities where the capital allowances given exceed the rental income. For individuals, any losses arising from leasing are available for offset against other income only if the individual devotes substantially all of his time to the conduct of a leasing business.

9 SUCCESSIONS

Balancing adjustments arise on the cessation of a business. No writing-down allowances are given, but the final proceeds (limited to cost) on sales of plant are compared with the tax WDV to calculate balancing allowances or charges.

Balancing charges may be avoided where the trade passes from one connected person to another. If a succession occurs both parties must elect if the avoidance of the balancing adjustments is required. **An election will result in the plant being transferred at its tax written-down value for capital allowances purposes.** The predecessor can write-down the plant for the period prior to cessation and the successor can write it down from the date of commencement. The election must be made within two years of the date of the succession.

If no election is made on a transfer of business to a connected person, assets are deemed to be sold at their market values.

As we saw earlier, an individual is connected with his spouse, his, or his spouse's brothers, sisters, ancestors and lineal descendants, with their spouses, with business partners and their spouses and relatives, and with a company he controls. 'Spouses' includes civil partners.

Where a person succeeds to a business under a will or on intestacy, then even if he was not connected with the deceased he may elect to take over the assets at the lower of their market value and their tax written-down value.

For both connected persons transfers and transfers on death, where the elections are made, the limit on proceeds to be brought into account on a later sale of an asset is the original cost of the asset, not the deemed transfer price.

NOTES

10 INDUSTRIAL BUILDINGS – TYPES

10.1 Introduction

A special type of capital allowance (an **industrial buildings allowance** or IBA) is available in respect of **expenditure on industrial buildings**. It is being phased out over the next few years and will be abolished from 2011/12.

The allowance is available to:

- Traders
- Landlords who let qualifying buildings to traders.

Traders can choose whether to segregate expenditure on long life assets in buildings and claim plant and machinery allowances (see above) or whether to claim industrial buildings allowances on the expenditure. Since industrial buildings allowance is being phased out it would be better to claim plant and machinery allowances in such a case.

Definition

Industrial buildings include:

(a) All factories and ancillary premises used in:

  (i) A manufacturing business
  (ii) A trade in which goods and materials are subject to any process
  (iii) A trade in which goods or raw materials are stored

(b) Staff welfare buildings (such as workplace nurseries and canteens, but not directors' restaurants) where the trade is qualifying

(c) Sport pavilions in any trade

(d) Buildings in use for a transport undertaking, agricultural contracting, mining or fishing

(e) Roads operated under highway concessions. The operation of such roads is treated as a trade for capital allowances purposes. The operator is treated as occupying the roads.

The key term in (a) (ii) above is 'the subjection of goods to any process'.

- The unpacking, repacking and relabelling of goods in a wholesale cash and carry supermarket did not amount to a 'process' but was a mere preliminary to sale (*Bestway Holdings Ltd v Luff 1998*).
- The mechanical processing of cheques and other banking documents was a process but pieces of paper carrying information were not 'goods' and thus the building housing the machinery did not qualify (*Girobank plc v Clarke 1998*).

Estate roads on industrial estates qualify, provided that the estate buildings are used wholly or mainly for a qualifying purpose.

Dwelling houses, retail shops, showrooms and offices are not industrial buildings (although see below for exception.)

BPP LEARNING MEDIA

Drawing offices (ie those used for technical product and manufacturing planning) which serve an industrial building are regarded as industrial buildings themselves (*CIR v Lambhill Ironworks Ltd 1950*).

Warehouses used for storage often cause problems in practice. A warehouse used for storage which is merely a transitory and necessary incident of the conduct of the business is not an industrial building. Storage is only a qualifying purpose if it is an end in itself.

Any building is an industrial building if it is constructed for the welfare of employees of a trader whose trade is a qualifying one (that is, the premises in which the trade is carried on are industrial buildings). Sports pavilions provided for the welfare of employees qualify as industrial buildings. In this case, it does not matter whether the taxpayer is carrying on a trade in a qualifying building or not. Thus a retailer's sports pavilion would qualify for IBAs.

10.2 Hotels

Allowances on hotels are given as though they were industrial buildings.

Definition

For a building to qualify as a **'hotel'** for industrial buildings allowance purposes:

(a) It much have at least ten letting bedrooms

(b) It must have letting bedrooms as the whole or main part of the sleeping accommodation

(c) It must offer ancillary services including at least:

- (i) Breakfast
- (ii) Evening meals
- (iii) The cleaning of rooms
- (iv) The making of beds

(d) It must be open for at least four months during the April to October season.

10.3 Eligible expenditure

Capital allowances are computed on the amount of eligible expenditure incurred on qualifying buildings. The eligible expenditure is:

- The original cost of a building if built by the trader, or
- The purchase price if the building was acquired from a person trading as a builder.

If the building was acquired other than from a person trading as a builder, the eligible expenditure is the lower of the purchase price and the original cost incurred by the person incurring the construction expenditure.

If a building is sold more than once before being brought into use, the last buyer before the building is brought into use obtains the allowances. If, in such cases, the building

NOTES

was first sold by someone trading as a builder, the eligible expenditure is the lower of the price paid by the first buyer and the price paid by the last buyer.

In all cases where a building is sold before use and artificial arrangements have increased the purchase price, it is reduced to what it would have been without those arrangements.

Where part of a building qualifies as an industrial building and part does not, the whole cost qualifies for IBAs, provided that the cost of the non-qualifying part is not more than 25% of the total expenditure. If the non-qualifying part of the building does cost more than 25% of the total, its cost must be excluded from the capital allowances computation.

Difficulties arise where non-qualifying buildings (particularly offices and administration blocks) are joined to manufacturing areas. In *Abbott Laboratories Ltd v Carmody 1968* a covered walkway linking manufacturing and administrative areas was not regarded as creating a single building. The administrative area was treated as a separate, non-qualifying building.

The cost of land is disallowed but expenditure incurred in preparing land for building does qualify. The cost of items which would not be included in a normal commercial lease (such as rental guarantees) also does not qualify.

Professional fees, for example architects' fees, incurred in connection with the construction of an industrial building qualify. The cost of repairs to industrial buildings also qualifies, provided that the expenditure is not deductible as a trading expense.

11 ALLOWANCES ON INDUSTRIAL BUILDINGS

11.1 Writing-down allowances

A writing-down allowance (WDA) is given to the person holding the 'relevant interest'. Broadly, the relevant interest is the interest of the first acquirer of the industrial building and may be a freehold or leasehold interest.

Where a long lease (more than 50 years) has been granted on an industrial building, the grant may be treated as a sale so that allowances may be claimed by the lessee rather than the lessor. A claim must be made by the lessor and lessee jointly, within two years of the start of the lease. The election allows allowances to be claimed on industrial buildings where the lessor is not subject to tax (as with local authorities).

The WDA is given for a period provided that the industrial building was in use as such on the last day of the period concerned.

If the building was not in use as an industrial building at the end of the relevant period it may have been:

- **Unused** for any purpose, or
- **Used for a non-industrial purpose.**

The distinction is important in ascertaining whether WDAs are due to the taxpayer. **If any disuse is temporary and previously the building had been in industrial use, WDAs may be claimed in exactly the same way as if the building were in industrial use.** The legislation does not define 'temporary' but in practice, any subsequent qualifying use of the building will usually enable the period of disuse to be regarded as temporary.

BPP LEARNING MEDIA

Non-industrial use has different consequences. If this occurs a notional WDA is deducted from the balance of unrelieved expenditure but no WDA may be claimed by the taxpayer.

The WDA is 4% of the eligible expenditure incurred by the taxpayer.

The allowance is calculated on a straight line basis (in contrast to WDAs on plant and machinery which are calculated on the reducing balance), starting when the building is brought into use.

The WDA is 4% × months/12 if the period concerned is not 12 months long.

Buildings always have a **separate computation for each building.** They are never pooled.

11.2 Sales of industrial buildings

11.2.1 First users – position on sale

Until 21 March 2007, the disposal of an industrial building gave rise to a balancing adjustment (ie a balancing change or a balancing allowance).

In preparation for the eventual abolition of industrial buildings allowance, **no balancing adjustments apply for disposals from 21 March 2007 onwards.**

11.2.2 Second-hand users

The buyer obtains annual straight line WDAs in relation to the remainder of the building's tax life (25 years after it is first used). This life is calculated to the nearest month. The allowances are granted on the residue before sale which is computed thus.

	£
Cost	X
Less allowances previously given	(X)
Residue before sale (ie WDV)	X

11.2.3 Example

Lipatti Ltd bought an industrial building for £180,000 on 1 November 2000 and brought it into use immediately. It sold the building on 1 November 2007 for £150,000 to Kapell plc who brought the building into industrial use immediately. Both companies make up accounts to 31 March each year. The IBA available to Kapell plc for the year ending 31 March 2008 is calculated as follows:

	£
Cost 1.11.00	180,000
Y/e 31.3.01 to y/e 31.3.07	
WDA £180,000 × 4% = £7,200 × 7	(50,400)
Residue before sale	129,600

Tax life of the building ends on 1.11.00 + 25 years = 31.10.25

The date of Kapell plc's purchase is 1.11.07

The unexpired life is therefore 18 years

Kapell plc's WDA for y/e 31 March 2008 is therefore

£129,600 / 18	7,200

You will see that the WDA for Kapell plc is the same as for Lipatti Ltd. This is because there is a whole number of years of the tax life remaining at the date of sale. Note also that no WDA was given to Lipatti Ltd in the year the building was sold.

Activity 5 **(15 minutes)**

Frankie started to trade in 2002 preparing account to 31 December and bought an industrial building for £100,000 (excluding land) on 1 October 2003. He bought it into use as a factory immediately. On 1 September 2007 he sells it for £120,000 to Holly, whose accounting date is 30 September and who brought the building into industrial use immediately. Show the IBA available to Holly for the year ended 31 September 2007.

11.2.4 Second-hand users – Sales after non-industrial use

If at the end of a period, an industrial building was in non-industrial use, then the owner will not have been able to claim WDAs, but the building will have been written down by notional WDAs.

Therefore, the second hand user will take over the same residue of cost whether or not the building has been in industrial use throughout the first user's ownership or not.

Chapter roundup

- The badges of trade can be used to decide whether or not a trade exists. If one does exist, the accounts profits need to be adjusted in order to establish the taxable profits.
- Expenditure which is not incurred wholly and exclusively for trade purposes is disallowable.
- Capital allowances are available on plant and machinery and industrial buildings
- Statutory rules generally exclude specified items from treatment as plant, rather than include specified items as plant.
- There are several cases on the definition of plant. To help you to absorb them, try to see the function/setting theme running through them
- With capital allowances computations, the main thing is to get the layout right. Having done that, you will find that the figures tend to drop into place.
- Most expenditure on plant and machinery qualifies for a WDA at 25% every 12 months.
- First-year allowances (FYA) may be available for certain expenditure. FYAs are never pro-rated in short or long periods of account.
- Private use of assets by sole traders and partners restricts capital allowances.
- Short-life asset elections can bring forward the allowances due on an asset.
- Capital allowances are available on assets acquired by hire purchase or lease.
- Balancing adjustments are calculated when a business ceases. If the business is transferred to a connected person, the written down value can be transferred instead.
- Industrial buildings allowances on most factories.
- An allowance, normally at the rate of 4% per annum, is given if a building is in industrial use on the last day of the period of account concerned. If the building is non-industrial use a notional allowance may be given.

NOTES

Quick quiz

1 List the six traditional badges of trade.

2 What pre-trading expenditure is deductible?

3 In which period of account are earnings paid 12 months after the end of the period for which they are charged deductible?

4 What is the maximum allowable amount of redundancy pay on the cessation of a trade?

5 For what periods are capital allowance for unincorporated businesses calculated?

6 Are writing-down allowances pro-rated in a six-month period of account?

7 Are first year allowances pro-rated in a six-month period of account?

8 When may balancing allowances arise?

9 Within what period must an asset be disposed of if it is to be treated as a short-life asset?

10 List four types of building which do not qualify for industrial building allowance.

11 When are drawing offices industrial buildings?

12 What are the conditions for a hotel to qualify for allowances?

13 When must a 'notional allowance' be deducted from the qualifying cost of an industrial building?

14 Marcus acquires a second-hand industrial building during his accounting period ending 31 December 2007. The residue before sale is £160,000 and the unexpired tax life is 20 years. What WDA is Marcus entitled to for y/e 31.12.07?

NOTES

Answers to quick quiz

1 The subject matter
The frequency of transactions
The length of ownership
Supplementary work and marketing
A profit motive
The way in which goods were acquired (see para 1)

2 Pre-trading expenditure is deductible if it is incurred within seven years of the start of the trade and is of a type that would have been deductible if the trade had already started. (para 2.5.1)

3 In the period in which they are paid. (para 2.4.4)

4 3 × statutory amount. (para 2.5.9)

5 Periods of account. (para 3)

6 Yes. In a six month period, writing down allowance are pro-rated by multiplying by 6/12. (para 5.3)

7 No. First year allowances are given in full in a short period of account. (para 5.4.4)

8 Balancing allowances may arise in respect of pooled expenditure only when the trade ceases. Balancing allowances may arise on non-pooled items whenever those items are disposed of. (para 5.6)

9 Within four years of the end of the period of account (or accounting period) in which it was bought. (para 6)

10 Dwelling houses, retail shops, showrooms and offices. (para 10.1)

11 Drawing offices are industrial buildings if they serve an industrial building. (para 10.1)

12 (a) It must have ten letting bedrooms.

(b) It must have letting bedrooms as the whole or main part of the sleeping accommodation.

(c) It must offer ancillary services including at least

(i) Breakfast
(ii) Evening meals
(iii) The cleaning of rooms
(iv) The making of beds

(d) It must be open for at least four months during the April to October letting season. (para 10.2)

13 A notional allowance will be given if a building was in non-industrial use at the end of the period of account (accounting period) concerned. (para 11.1)

14 £160,000 / 20 = £8,000. (para 11.2.2)

Answers to activities

1

	£	£
Profit per accounts		17,710
Add: Depreciation	1,500	
Entertainment expenses	750	
Legal expenses	250	
		2,500
		20,210
Less interest received (to tax as savings income)		(860)
Taxable trade profits		19,350

2 The capital allowances are as follows.

	£	Pool £	Allowances £
FYA			
1.3.05 – 31.7.05			
Additions (1.5.05 and 1.6.05)	22,500		
FYA 40%	(9,000)		9,000
		13,500	
1.8.05 – 31.7.06			
Disposals (1.5.06)		(4,000)	
		9,500	
WDA 25%		(2,375)	2,375
		7,125	
Addition (1.5.06)	4,000		
FYA 50%	(2,000)		2,000
		2,000	4,375
c/f		9,125	
b/f		9,125	
1.8.06 – 31.7.07			
WDA 25%		(2,281)	2,281
		6,844	
Addition (1.6.07)	1,600		
FYA 50%	(800)		800
		800	
TWDV c/f		7,644	
			3,081

Note. First year allowances are not pro-rated in a short period of account.

The profits of the first three periods of account are as follows.

Period of account	*Working*	*Profits* £
1.3.05–31.7.05	£(42,500 – 9,000)	33,500
1.8.05–31.7.06	£(36,800 – 4,375)	32,425
1.8.06–31.7.07	£(32,000 – 3,081)	28,919

NOTES

3

	Car	Allowances 90%
1.7.04 – 31.12.04	£	£
Purchase price	15,500	
WDA 25% × 6/12 of £15,500 = £1,938		
Limited to £3,000 × 6/12 = £1,500	(1,500)	1,350
	14,000	
1.1.05 – 31.12.05		
WDA 25% of £14,000 = £3,500, limited to £3,000	(3,000)	2,700
	11,000	
1.1.06 – 31.12.06		
WDA 25% of £11,000	(2,750)	2,475
	8,250	
1.1.07 – 31.12.07		
Proceeds	(4,000)	
Balancing allowance	4,250	3,825

4

	FYAs	General pool	Car (60%)	Allowances
	£	£	£	£
1.1.06 – 31.12.06				
WDV b/f		25,260	21,225	
WDA @ 25%		(6,315)		6,315
WDA @ £3,000 (restricted)			(3,000) × 60%	1,800
Addition 7.6.06	1,620			
FYA @ 50%	(810)			810
		810		
WDV c/f		19,755	18,225	
Total allowances				8,925
1.1.07 – 31.8.07				
Addition 12.5.07		1,740		
Disposals		(25,295)	(16,500)	
No WDA in year of cessation		(3,800)	1,725	
Balancing charge		3,800		(3,800)
Balancing allowance			(1,725)	1,035
Total balancing charge (taxable as profits)				(2,765)

5

	£
Cost 1.1.03	100,000
Y/e 31.12.03 to y/e 31.12.06 WDA 4 × 4 %	(16,000)
Residue before sale	84,000

The tax life of the building ends on 1.1.03 + 25 years = 30.9.2028
The date of Holly's purchase is 1.9.07
The unexpired life is therefore 21 years 1 month.

Y/e 30.9.07 WDA £84,000/21.0833333	£3,984

BPP LEARNING MEDIA

Chapter 36 :

TRADE PROFITS – BASIS PERIODS AND LOSSES

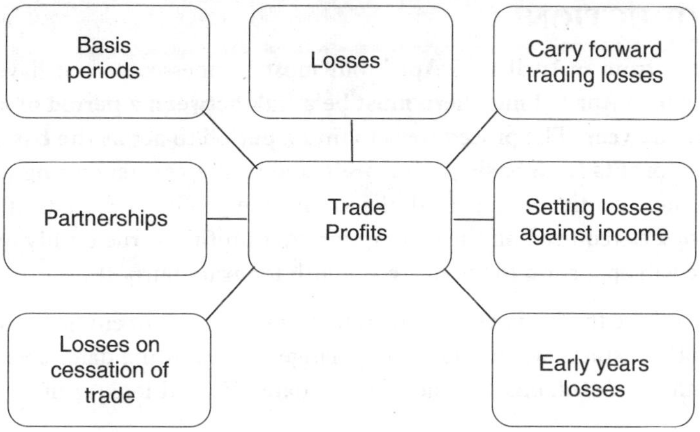

Introduction

Businesses are able to make use of favourable tax provisions in their starting and closing years, and also if they are making losses on an ongoing basis. The impact of losses may be carried both forward and back to subsequent and previous accounting periods, thus smoothing over the tax liability.

This chapter also introduces the tax implications of a group of people trading together as a partnership.

Accounting for partnerships is covered in Unit 10 of the HNC/HND qualification.

Your objectives

In this chapter you will learn about the following.

(a) The basis of assessment for a continuing business

(b) The principles which apply on commencement and cessation

(c) How to compute taxable trade profits in a tax year.

(d) How to calculate overlap relief and its subsequent use

(e) The loss reliefs available to a sole trader who is neither commencing nor ceasing a business

(f) The alternative loss reliefs in an income tax computation

(g) The loss reliefs available on commencement and the implications

(h) The loss reliefs available on cessation

(i) The way in which the rules for sole traders are adapted to deal with partnerships

(j) The capital allowances for a partnership (include assets owned individually by partners)

(k) The position when there is a change in profit-sharing arrangements

(l) Outline the position of new partners, ongoing partners, retiring partners

(m) Trade Profit assessments for individual partners

(n) Basic adjustments for notional profits/losses

1 INTRODUCTION

A tax year runs from 6 April to 5 April, but most businesses do not have periods of account ending on 5 April. **Thus there must be a link between a period of account of a business and a tax year.** The procedure is to **find a period to act as the basis period for a tax year. The profits for a basis period are taxed in the corresponding tax year.** If a basis period is not identical to a period of account, the profits of periods of account are time-apportioned as required on the assumption that profits accrue evenly over a period of account. We will apportion to the nearest month for exam purposes.

We will now look at the basis period rules that apply in the opening, continuing and closing years of a business when there is no change of accounting date. Special rules are needed when the trader changes his accounting date. We will look at these rules in the next section.

The first tax year is the year during which the trade commences. For example, if a trade commences on 1 June 2007 the first tax year is 2007/08.

1.2 The first tax year

The **basis period for the first tax year runs from the date the trade starts to the next 5 April** (or to the date of cessation if the trade does not last until the end of the tax year).

So continuing the above example a trader commencing in business on 1 June 2007 will be taxed on profits arising from 1 June 2007 to 5 April 2008 in 2007/08, their first tax year.

1.3 The second tax year

(a) **If the accounting date falling in the second tax year is at least 12 months after the start of trading, the basis period is the 12 months to that accounting date.**

(b) **If the accounting date falling in the second tax year is less than 12 months after the start of trading, the basis period is the first 12 months of trading.**

(c) **If there is no accounting date falling in the second tax year,** because the first period of account is a very long one which does not end until a date in the third tax year, **the basis period for the second tax year is the year itself (from 6 April to 5 April).**

NOTES

The following flowchart may help you determine the basis period for the second tax year.

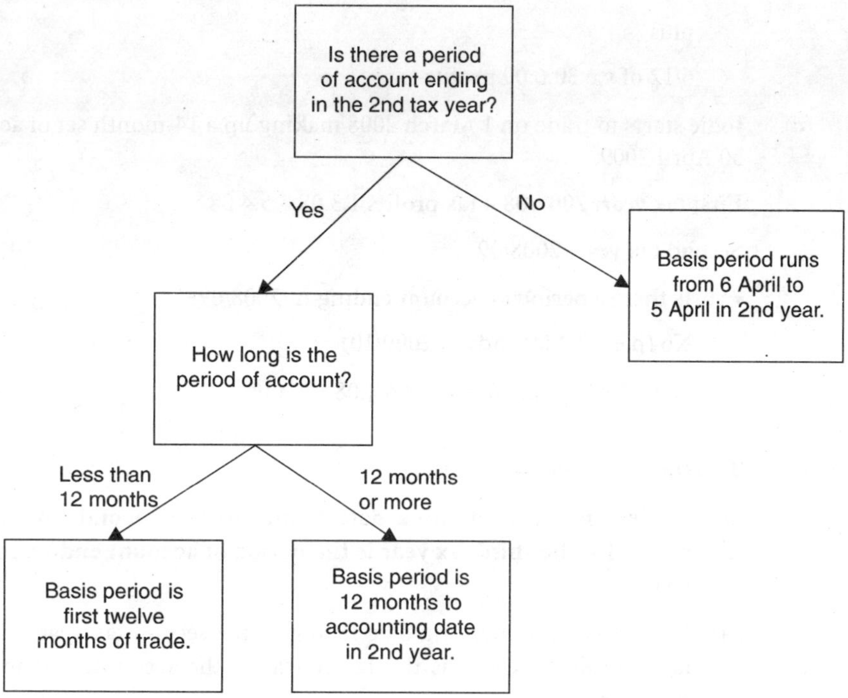

1.4 Examples: the first and second tax year

(a) John starts to trade on 1 January 2008 making up accounts to 31 December 2008.

First tax year: 2007/08 – tax profits 1.1.08 – 5.4.08

Second tax year: 2008/09

- Is there a period of account ending in 2008/09?

  Yes – Y.E. 31.12.08 ends 31.12.08.

- How long is the period of account?

  12 months or more ie 12 months (exactly) to 31.12.08.

- So in 2008/09 tax profits of 12 months to 31.12.08.

(b) Janet starts to trade on 1 January 2008 making up accounts as follows:

6 months to 30 June 2008
12 months to 30 June 2009.

First tax year: 2007/08 – tax profits 1.1.08 – 5.4.08

Second tax year: 2008/09.

- Is there a period of account ending in 2008/09?

  Yes – p.e. 30.6.08 ends 30.6.08

- How long is the period of account?

  Less than 12 months ie 6 months long.

- So in 2008/09 tax profits of first 12 months of trade ie 1.1.08 – 31.12.08, ie

  p.e. 30.6.08 profits

  plus

  6/12 of y.e 30.6.09 profits

(c) Jodie starts to trade on 1 March 2008 making up a 14-month set of accounts to 30 April 2009.

First tax year: 2007/08 – tax profits 1.3.08 – 5.4.08

Second tax year: 2008/09

- Is there a period of account ending in 2008/09?

  No (p.e. 30.4.09 ends in 2009/10)

- So in 2008/09 tax profits of 6.4.08 – 5.4.09.

1.5 The third tax year

(a) **If there is an accounting date falling in the second tax year, the basis period for the third tax year is the period of account ending in the third tax year.**

(b) If there is no accounting date falling in the second tax year, the basis period for the third tax year is the 12 months to the accounting date falling in the third tax year.

1.6 Later tax years

For later tax years, except the year in which the trade ceases, **the basis period is the period of account ending in the tax year.** This is known as the **current year basis of assessment.**

1.7 The final year

(a) If a trade starts and ceases in the same tax year, the basis period for that year is the whole lifespan of the trade.

(b) If the final year is the second year, the basis period runs from 6 April at the start of the second year to the date of cessation. This rule overrides the rules that normally apply for the second year.

(c) If the final year is the third year or a later year, **the basis period runs from the end of the basis period for the previous year to the date of cessation.** This rule overrides the rules that normally apply in the third and later years.

1.8 Overlap profits

Definition

Profits which have been taxed more than once are called **overlap profits**.

NOTES

When a business starts, some profits may be taxed twice because the basis period for the second year includes some or all of the period of trading in the first year or because the basis period for the third year overlaps with that for the second year.

Overlap profits may be deducted on a change of accounting date (see below). Any overlap profits unrelieved when the trade ceases are deducted from the final year's taxable profits. **Any deduction of overlap profits may create or increase a loss. The usual loss reliefs (covered later in this Course Book) are then available.**

1.9 Example: accounting date in second year at least 12 months

Jenny trades from 1 July 2002 to 31 December 2007, with the following results.

Period	*Profit*
	£
1.7.02–31.8.03	7,000
1.9.03–31.8.04	12,000
1.9.04–31.8.05	15,000
1.9.05–31.8.06	21,000
1.9.06–31.8.07	18,000
1.9.07–31.12.08	5,600
	78,600

The profits to be taxed in each tax year from 2002/03 to 2007/08, and the total of these taxable profits are calculated as follows.

Year	*Basis period*	*Working*	*Taxable profit*
			£
2002/03	1.7.02–5.4.03	£7,000 × 9/14	4,500
2003/04	1.9.02–31.8.03	£7,000 × 12/14	6,000
2004/05	1.9.03–31.8.04		12,000
2005/06	1.9.04–31.8.05		15,000
2006/07	1.9.05–31.8.06		21,000
2007/08	1.9.06–31.12.07	£(18,000 + 5,600 – 3,500)	20,100
			78,600

The overlap profits are those in the period 1 September 2002 to 5 April 2003, a period of seven months. They are £7,000 × 7/14 = £3,500. Overlap profits are either relieved on a change of accounting date (see below) or are deducted from the final year's taxable profit when the business ceases. In this case the overlap profits are deducted when the business ceases. Over the life of the business, the total taxable profits equal the total actual profits.

BPP LEARNING MEDIA

NOTES

Activity 1 **(20 minutes)**

Peter trades from 1 September 2002 to 30 June 2007, with the following results.

Period	*Profit*
	£
1.9.02–30.4.03	8,000
1.5.03–30.4.04	15,000
1.5.04–30.4.05	9,000
1.5.05–30.4.06	10,500
1.5.06–30.4.07	16,000
1.5.07–30.6.07	950
	59,450

Show the profits to be taxed in each year from 2002/03 to 2007/08, the total of these taxable profits and the overlap profits.

EXAMPLE: NO ACCOUNTING DATE IN THE SECOND YEAR

Thelma starts to trade on 1 March 2006. Her first accounts, covering the 16 months to 30 June 2007, show a profit of £36,000. The taxable profits for the first three tax years and the overlap profits are as follows.

Year	*Basis period*	*Working*	*Taxable profits*
			£
2005/06	1.3.06 – 5.4.06	£36,000 × 1/16	2,250
2006/07	6.4.06 – 5.4.07	£36,000 × 12/16	27,000
2007/08	1.7.06 – 30.6.07	£36,000 × 12/16	27,000

The overlap profits are the profits from 1 July 2006 to 5 April 2007: £36,000 × 9/16 = £20,250.

1.10 The choice of an accounting date

A new trader should consider which accounting date would be best. There are **three factors to consider** from the point of view of taxation.

(a) **If profits are expected to rise, a date early in the tax year** (such as 30 April) will delay the time when rising accounts profits feed through into rising taxable profits, whereas a date late in the tax year (such as 31 March) will accelerate the taxation of rising profits. This is because with an accounting date of 30 April, the taxable profits for each tax year are mainly the profits earned in the previous tax year. With an accounting date of 31 March the taxable profits are almost entirely profits earned in the current year.

(b) If the accounting date in the second tax year is less than 12 months after the start of trading, the taxable profits for that year will be the profits earned in the first 12 months. If the accounting date is at least 12 months from the start of trading, they will be the profits earned in the 12 months to that date. **Different profits may thus be taxed twice (the overlap profits)**, and if profits are fluctuating this can make a considerable difference to the taxable profits in the first few years. **It may be many years before relief for the overlap profits is obtained.**

(c) **The choice of an accounting date affects the profits shown in each set of accounts**, and this may affect the taxable profits.

2 LOSSES – AN OVERVIEW

2.1 Trade losses in general

This chapter considers how losses are calculated and how a loss-suffering taxpayer can use a loss to reduce his tax liability. Most of the chapter concerns the trade losses in respect of trades, professions and vocations.

The rules in this chapter apply only to individuals, trading alone or in partnership. Loss reliefs for companies are completely different and are covered later in this Text.

When computing taxable trade profits, profits may turn out to be negative, that is a loss has been made in the basis period. **A loss is computed in exactly the same way as a profit**, making the same adjustments to the accounts profit or loss.

If there is a loss in a basis period, the taxable trade profits for the tax year based on that basis period are nil.

2.2 The computation of the loss

The trade loss for a tax year is the trade loss in the basis period for that tax year. However, **if basis periods overlap then a loss in the overlap period is a trade loss for the earlier tax year only.**

EXAMPLE: COMPUTING THE TRADING LOSS

Here is an example of a trader who starts to trade on 1 July 2007 and makes losses in opening years.

Period of account	*Loss*
	£
1.7.07 – 31.12.07	9,000
1.1.08 – 31.12.08	24,000

Tax year	*Basis period*	*Working*	*Trade loss for the tax year*
			£
2007/08	1.7.07 – 5.4.08	£9,000 + (£24,000 × 3/12)	15,000
2008/09	1.1.08 – 31.12.08	£24,000 – (£24,000 × 3/12)	18,000

EXAMPLE: LOSSES AND PROFITS

The same rule against using losses twice applies when losses are netted off against profits in the same basis period. Here is an example, again with a commencement on 1 July 2007 but with a different accounting date.

Period of account	*(Loss)/profit*
	£
1.7.07 – 30.4.08	(10,000)
1.5.08 – 30.4.09	24,000

Tax year	*Basis period*	*Working*	*Trade (Loss)/Profit*
			£
2007/08	1.7.07 – 5.4.08	£(10,000) × 9/10	(9,000)
2008/09	1.7.07 – 30.6.08	£(10,000) × 1/10 + £24,000 × 2/12	3,000

3 CARRY FORWARD TRADE LOSS RELIEF

A trade loss not relieved in any other way must be **carried forward to set against the first available trade profits of the same trade** in the calculation of net trading income. Losses may be carried forward for any number of years.

EXAMPLE: CARRYING FORWARD LOSSES

B has the following results.

Year ending	£
31 December 2005	(6,000)
31 December 2006	5,000
31 December 2007	11,000

B's net trading income, assuming that he claims carry forward loss relief, are:

	2005/06		*2006/07*		*2007/08*
	£		£		£
Trade profits	0		5,000		11,000
Less carry forward loss relief	(0)	(i)	(5,000)	(ii)	(1,000)
Profits	0		0		10,000

Loss memorandum		£
Trading loss, y/e 31.12.05		6,000
Less: claim in y/e 31.12.06	(i)	(5,000)
claim in y/e 31.12.07 (bal of loss)	(ii)	(1,000)
		0

4 TRADE LOSS RELIEF AGAINST GENERAL INCOME

Where a loss relief claim is made, trade losses can be set against general income and then gains in the current and/or prior year.

4.1 Introduction

Instead of carrying a trade loss forward against future trade profits, it may be relieved against general income.

4.2 Relieving the loss

Relief is against the income of the tax year in which the loss arose. In addition or instead, relief may be claimed **against the income of the preceding year.**

If there are losses in two successive years, and relief is claimed against the first year's income both for the first year's loss and for the second year's loss, relief is given for the first year's loss before the second year's loss.

A claim for a loss must be made by the 31 January which is 22 months after the end of the tax year of the loss: so by 31 January 2010 for a loss in 2007/08.

The taxpayer cannot choose the amount of loss to relieve: so the loss may have to be set against income part of which would have been covered by the personal allowance. However, the taxpayer can choose whether to claim full relief in the current year and then relief in the preceding year for any remaining loss, or the other way round.

Set the loss against non-savings income, then against savings income and finally against dividend income.

Relief is available by carry forward for any loss not relieved against general income.

Activity 2 **(10 minutes)**

Janet has a loss in her period of account ending 31 December 2007 of £25,000. Her other income is £18,000 rental income a year, and she wishes to claim loss relief for the year of loss and then the preceding year. Her trading income in the previous year was £nil. Show her taxable income for each year, and comment on the effectiveness of the loss relief. Assume that tax rates and allowances for 2007/08 have always applied.

4.3 Capital allowances

The trader may adjust the size of the total loss relief claim by not claiming all the capital allowances he is entitled to: a reduced claim will increase the balance carried forward to the next year's capital allowances computation. This may be a useful **tax planning point where the effective rate of relief for capital allowances in future periods will be greater than the rate of tax relief for the loss relief.**

4.4 Trading losses relieved against capital gains

Where relief is claimed against general income of a given year, the taxpayer may include **a further claim to set the loss against his chargeable gains for the year** less any allowable capital losses for the same year or for previous years. This amount of net gains is computed ignoring taper relief and the annual exempt amount (see later in this Course Book).

The trading loss is first set against general income of the year of the claim, and only any excess of loss is set against capital gains. The taxpayer cannot specify the amount to be set against capital gains, so the annual exempt amount may be wasted. We include an activity here for completeness. You will study chargeable gains later in this Course Book and we suggest that you come back to this activity at that point.

Activity 3 **(20 minutes)**

Sybil had the following results for 2007/08.

	£
Loss available for loss relief against general income	27,000
Income	19,500
Capital gains less current year capital losses	10,000
Annual exemption for capital gains tax purposes	9,200
Capital losses brought forward	4,000

Assume no taper relief is due.

Show how the loss would be relieved against income and gains.

4.5 Restrictions on trade loss relief against general income

Relief cannot be claimed against general income unless a business is conducted on a commercial basis with a view to the realisation of profits; this condition applies to all types of business.

4.6 The choice between loss reliefs

When a trader has a choice between loss reliefs, he should aim to obtain relief both quickly and at the highest possible tax rate. However, do consider that losses relieved against income which would otherwise be covered by the personal allowance are wasted.

Another consideration is that a trading loss cannot be set against the capital gains of a year unless relief is first claimed against general income of the same year. It may be worth making the claim against income and wasting the personal allowance in order to avoid a CGT liability.

EXAMPLE

Felicity's trading results are as follows.

Year ended 30 September	*Trading profit/(loss)*
	£
2005	1,900
2006	(21,000)
2007	13,000

Her other income (all non-savings income) is as follows.

	£
2005/06	2,200
2006/07	26,500
2007/08	15,000

Show the most efficient use of Felicity's trading loss. Assume that the personal allowance has been £5,225 throughout.

Relief could be claimed against general income for 2005/06 and/or 2006/07, with any unused loss being carried forward. Relief in 2005/06 would be against general income of £(1,900 + 2,200) = £4,100, all of which would be covered by the personal allowance anyway, so this claim should not be made. A loss relief claim against general income should be made for 2006/07 as this saves tax more quickly than a carry forward loss relief claim in 2007/08 would. The final results will be as follows.

	2005/06	*2006/07*	*2007/08*
	£	£	£
Trading income	1,900	0	13,000
Less carry forward loss relief	(0)	(0)	(0)
	1,900	0	13,000
Other income	2,200	26,500	15,000
	4,100	26,500	28,000
Less loss relief against general income	(0)	(21,000)	(0)
Net income	4,100	5,500	28,000
Less personal allowance	(5,225)	(5,225)	(5,225)
Taxable income	0	275	22,775

5 EARLY TRADE LOSSES RELIEF

Early trade losses relief is available for trading losses incurred in the first four tax years of a trade.

Relief is obtained by **setting the allowable loss against general income in the three years preceding the year of loss,** applying the loss to the earliest year first. Thus a loss arising in 2007/08 may be set off against income in 2004/05, 2005/06 and 2006/07 in that order.

A claim for early trade losses relief applies to all three years automatically, provided that the loss is large enough. The taxpayer cannot choose to relieve the loss against just one or two of the years, or to relieve only part of the loss. However, the taxpayer could reduce the size of the loss by not claiming the full capital allowances available to him. This will result in higher capital allowances in future years.

Do not double count a loss. If basis periods overlap, a loss in the overlap period is treated as a loss for the earlier tax year only.

Claims for the relief must be made by the 31 January which is 22 months after the end of the tax year in which the loss is incurred.

The 'commercial basis' test is stricter for this loss relief. The trade must be carried on in such a way that profits could reasonably have been expected to be realised in the period of the loss or within a reasonable time thereafter.

EXAMPLE

Mr A is employed as a dustman until 1 January 2006. On that date he starts up his own business as a scrap metal merchant, making up his accounts to 30 June each year. His earnings as a dustman are:

	£
2002/03	5,000
2003/04	6,000
2004/05	7,000
2005/06 (nine months)	6,000

NOTES

His trading results as a scrap metal merchant are:

	Profit/(Loss)
	£
Six months to 30 June 2006	(3,000)
Year to 30 June 2007	(1,500)
Year to 30 June 2008	(1,200)

Assuming that loss relief is claimed as early as possible, show the final taxable income before personal allowances for each of the years 2002/03 to 2008/09 inclusive.

Since reliefs are to be claimed as early as possible, early trade losses relief is applied. The losses available for relief are as follows.

	£	£	*Years against which relief is available*
2005/06 (basis period 1.1.06 – 5.4.06)			
3 months to 5.4.06 £(3,000) × 3/6		(1,500)	2002/03 to 2004/05
2006/07 (basis period 1.1.06 – 31.12.06)			
6 months to 30.6.06 (omit 1.1.06 – 5.4.06: overlap) £(3,000) × 3/6	(1,500)		
6 months to 31.12.06 £(1,500) × 6/12	(750)		
		(2,250)	2003/04 to 2005/06
2007/08 (basis period 1.7.06 – 30.6.07)			
12 months to 30.6.07 (omit 1.7.06 – 31.12.06: overlap) £(1,500) × 6/12		(750)	2004/05 to 2006/07
2008/09 (basis period 1.7.07 – 30.6.08)			
12 months to 30.6.08		(1,200)	2005/06 to 2007/08

The net income is as follows.

	£	£
2002/03		
Original	5,000	
Less 2005/06 loss	(1,500)	
		3,500
2003/04		
Original	6,000	
Less 2006/07 loss	(2,250)	
		3,750
2004/05		
Original	7,000	
Less 2007/08 loss	(750)	
		6,250
2005/06		
Original	6,000	
Less 2008/09 loss	(1,200)	
		4,800

The taxable trade profits for 2005/06 to 2008/09 are zero. There were losses in the basis periods.

NOTES

6 TERMINAL TRADE LOSS RELIEF

Loss relief against general income will often be insufficient on its own to deal with a loss incurred in the last months of trading. For this reason there is a special relief, **terminal trade loss relief, which allows a loss on cessation to be carried back for relief against taxable trading profits in previous years.**

6.1 Computing the terminal loss

A terminal loss is **the loss of the last 12 months of trading.**

It is built up as follows.

	£
(a) The actual trade loss for the tax year of cessation (calculated from 6 April to the date of cessation)	X
(b) The actual trade loss for the period from 12 months before cessation until the end of the penultimate tax year	X
Total terminal loss	X

If either (a) or (b) above yields a profit rather than a loss, the profit is treated as zero.

Any unrelieved overlap profits are included within (a) above.

If any loss cannot be included in the terminal loss (eg because it is matched with a profit) it can be relieved instead by the loss relief against general income.

6.2 Relieving the terminal loss

Relief is given in the tax year of cessation and the three preceding years, later years first.

EXAMPLE

Set out below are the results of a business up to its cessation on 30 September 2007.

	Profit/(loss)
	£
Year to 31 December 2004	2,000
Year to 31 December 2005	400
Year to 31 December 2006	300
Nine months to 30 September 2007	(1,950)

Overlap profits on commencement were £450. These were all unrelieved on cessation.

Show the available terminal loss relief, and suggest an alternative claim if the trader had had other non-savings income of £10,000 in each of 2006/07 and 2007/08. Assume that 2007/08 tax rates and allowances apply to all years.

The terminal loss comes in the last 12 months, the period 1 October 2006 to 30 September 2007. This period is split as follows.

2006/07 Six months to 5 April 2007

2007/08 Six months to 30 September 2007

BPP LEARNING MEDIA

The terminal loss is made up as follows.

		£	£
Unrelieved trading losses			
2007/08			
6 months to 30.9.07	£(1,950) × 6/9		(1,300)
Overlap relief			(450)
2006/07			
3 months to 31.12.06	£300 × 3/12	75	
3 months to 5.4.07	£(1,950) × 3/9	(650)	
			(575)
			(2,325)

Taxable trade profits will be as follows.

Year	*Basis period*	*Profits*	*Terminal loss relief*	*Final taxable profits*
		£	£	£
2004/05	Y/e 31.12.04	2,000	1,625	375
2005/06	Y/e 31.12.05	400	400	0
2006/07	Y/e 31.12.06	300	300	0
2007/08	1.1.07–30.9.07	0	0	0
			2,325	

If the trader had had £10,000 of other income in 2006/07 and 2007/08, we could consider loss relief claims against general income for these two years, using the loss of £(1,950 + 450) = £2,400 for 2007/08.

The final results would be as follows (we could alternatively claim loss relief in 2006/07).

	2004/05	*2005/06*	*2006/07*	*2007/08*
	£	£	£	£
Trade profits	2,000	400	300	0
Other income	0	0	10,000	10,000
	2,000	400	10,300	10,000
Less loss relief against general income	0	0	0	(2,400)
Net income	2,000	400	10,300	7,600

Another option would be to make a loss relief claim against general income for the balance of the loss not relieved as a terminal loss. £(2,400 – 2,325) = £75 in either 2006/07 or 2007/08.

However, as there is only taxable income in 2006/07 and 2007/08 the full claim against general income is more tax efficient.

7 PARTNERSHIPS

7.1 Introduction

A partnership is treated like a sole trader when computing its profits. Partners' salaries and interest on capital are not deductible expenses and must be added back in computing profits, because they are a form of drawings.

Once the partnership's profits for a period of account have been computed, they are shared between the partners according to the profit sharing arrangements for that period of account.

7.2 The tax positions of individual partners

Each partner is taxed like a sole trader who runs a business which:

(a) Starts when he joins the partnership

(b) Finishes when he leaves the partnership

(c) Has the same periods of account as the partnership (except that a partner who joins or leaves during a period will have a period which starts or ends part way through the partnership's period)

(d) Makes profits or losses equal to the partner's share of the partnership's profits or losses

7.3 Changes in profit sharing ratios

The profits for a period of account are allocated between the partners according to the profit sharing agreement. If the salaries, interest on capital and profit sharing ratio change during the period of account the profits are time apportioned to the periods before and after the change and allocated accordingly. The constituent elements are then added together to give each partner's share of profits for the period of account.

7.4 Changes in membership

When a trade continues but partners join or leave (including cases when a sole trader takes in partners or a partnership breaks up leaving only one partner as a sole trader), **the special rules for basis periods in opening and closing years do not apply to the people who were carrying on the trade both before and after the change. They carry on using the period of account ending in each tax year as the basis period for the tax year ie the current year basis. The commencement rules only affect joiners, and the cessation rules only affect leavers.**

However, when no one same individual carries on the trade both before and after the change, as when a partnership transfers its trade to a completely new owner or set of owners, the cessation rules apply to the old owners and the commencement rules apply to the new owners.

7.5 Loss reliefs

Partners are entitled to the same loss reliefs as sole traders. A partner is entitled to early trade losses relief for losses in the four tax years starting with the year in which he is treated as starting to trade and he is entitled to terminal loss relief when he is treated as ceasing to trade. This is so even if the partnership trades for many years before the partner joins or after he leaves. Loss relief under against general income and carry forward loss relief is also available to partners. Different partners may claim loss reliefs in different ways.

When a partnership business is transferred to a company, each partner can carry forward his share of any unrelieved losses against income from the company.

There is a restriction for loss relief for a partner who does not spend a significant amount of time (less than 10 hours a week) in running the trade of the partnership. Such a partner can only use loss relief against general income or against capital gains and early trade losses relief **up to an amount equal to the amount that he contributes to the partnership** and there is an overall cap on relief of £25,000. These rules apply in any of the first four years in which the partner carries on a trade.

EXAMPLE: LOSS RELIEF RESTRICTION

Laura, Mark and Norman form a partnership and each contribute £10,000. Laura and Mark run the trade full time. Norman is employed elsewhere and plays little part in running the trade. Profits and losses are to be shared 45:35:20 to L:M:N. The partnership makes a loss of £60,000 of which £12,000 is allocated to Norman.

Norman may only use £10,000 of loss against general income (plus against capital gains) or early trade loss relief. £2,000 is carried forward, for example to be relieved against future profits.

7.6 Assets owned individually

Where the partners own assets (such as their cars) individually, a capital allowances computation must be prepared for each partner in respect of the assets he owns (not forgetting any adjustment for private use). The capital allowances must go into the partnership's tax computation.

WORKED EXAMPLE: A PARTNERSHIP

Alice and Bertrand start a partnership on 1 July 2004, making up accounts to 31 December each year. On 1 May 2006, Charles joins the partnership. On 1 November 2007, Charles leaves. On 1 January 2008, Deborah joins. The profit sharing arrangements are as follows.

	Alice	*Bertrand*	*Charles*	*Deborah*
1.7.04–31.1.05				
Salaries (per annum)	£3,000	£4,500		
Balance	3/5	2/5		
1.2.05–30.4.06				
Salaries (per annum)	£3,000	£6,000		
Balance	4/5	1/5		
1.5.06–31.10.07				
Salaries (per annum)	£2,400	£3,600	£1,800	
Balance	2/5	2/5	1/5	
1.11.07–31.12.07				
Salaries (per annum)	£1,500	£2,700		
Balance	3/5	2/5		
1.1.08 onwards				
Salaries (per annum)	£1,500	£2,700		£600
Balance	3/5	1/5		1/5

Profits and losses as adjusted for tax purposes are as follows.

Period	*Profit(loss)*
	£
1.7.04–31.12.04	22,000
1.1.05–31.12.05	51,000
1.1.06–31.12.06	39,000
1.1.07–31.12.07	15,000
1.1.08–31.12.08	(18,000)

Show the taxable trade profits for each partner for 2004/05 to 2007/08, and outline the loss reliefs available to the partners in respect of the loss in the year ending 31 December 2008. All the partners work full time in the partnership. Assume that the partnership will continue to trade with the same partners until 2019.

NOTES

ANSWER

We must first share the trade profits and losses for the periods of account between the partners, remembering to adjust the salaries for periods of less than a year.

	Total	*Alice*	*Bertrand*	*Charles*	*Deborah*
	£	£	£	£	£
1.7.04–31.12.04					
Salaries	3,750	1,500	2,250		
Balance	18,250	10,950	7,300		
Total (P/e 31.12.04)	22,000	12,450	9,550		
1.1.05–31.12.05					
January					
Salaries	625	250	375		
Balance	3,625	2,175	1,450		
Total	4,250	2,425	1,825		
February to December					
Salaries	8,250	2,750	5,500		
Balance	38,500	30,800	7,700		
Total	46,750	33,550	13,200		
Total for y/e 31.12.05	51,000	35,975	15,025		
1.1.06–31.12.06					
January to April					
Salaries	3,000	1,000	2,000		
Balance	10,000	8,000	2,000		
Total	13,000	9,000	4,000		
May to December					
Salaries	5,200	1,600	2,400	1,200	
Balance	20,800	8,320	8,320	4,160	
Total	26,000	9,920	10,720	5,360	
Total for y/e 31.12.06	39,000	18,920	14,720	5,360	
1.1.07–31.12.07					
January to October					
Salaries	6,500	2,000	3,000	1,500	
Balance	6,000	2,400	2,400	1,200	
Total	12,500	4,400	5,400	2,700	
November and December					
Salaries	700	250	450		
Balance	1,800	1,080	720		
Total	2,500	1,330	1,170		
Total for y/e 31.12.07	15,000	5,730	6,570	2,700	
1.1.08–31.12.08					
Salaries	4,800	1,500	2,700		600
Balance	(22,800)	(13,680)	(4,560)		(4,560)
Total loss for y/e 31.12.08	(18,000)	(12,180)	(1,860)		(3,960)

The next stage is to work out the basis periods and hence the taxable trade profits for the partners. All of them are treated as making up accounts to 31 December, but Alice and Bertrand are treated as starting to trade on 1 July 2004, Charles as trading only from 1 May 2006 to 31 October 2007 and Deborah as starting to trade on 1 January 2008. Applying the usual rules gives the following basis periods and taxable profits.

BPP LEARNING MEDIA

Alice

Year	*Basis period*	*Working*	*Taxable profits*
			£
2004/05	1.7.04–5.4.05	£12,450 + (£35,975 × 3/12)	21,444
2005/06	1.1.05–31.12.05		35,975
2006/07	1.1.06–31.12.06		18,920
2007/08	1.1.07–31.12.07		5,730

Note that for 2004/05 we take Alice's total for the year ended 2005 and apportion that, because the partnership's period of account runs from 1 January to 31 December 2005. Alice's profits for 2004/05 are *not* £12,450 + £2,425 + (£33,550 × 2/11) = £20,975.

Alice will have overlap profits for the period 1 January to 5 April 2005 (£35,975 × 3/12 = £8,994) to deduct when she ceases to trade.

Bertrand

Year	*Basis period*	*Working*	*Taxable profits*
			£
2004/05	1.7.04–5.4.05	£9,550 + (£15,025 × 3/12)	13,306
2005/06	1.1.05–31.12.05		15,025
2006/07	1.1.06–31.12.06		14,720
2007/08	1.1.07–31.12.07		6,570

Bertrand's overlap profits are £15,025 × 3/12 = £3,756.

Charles

Year	*Basis period*	*Working*	*Taxable profits*
			£
2006/07	1.5.06–5.4.07	£5,360 + (£2,700 × 3/10)	6,170
2007/08	6.4.07–31.10.07	£2,700 × 7/10	1,890

Because Charles ceased to trade in his second tax year of trading, his basis period for the second year starts on 6 April and he has no overlap profits.

Deborah

Year	*Basis period*	*Working*	*Taxable profits*
			£
2007/08	1.1.08–5.4.08	A loss arises	0

Finally, we must look at the loss reliefs available to Alice, Bertrand and Deborah. Charles is not entitled to any loss relief, because he left the firm before any loss arose.

Alice and Bertrand

For 2008/09, Alice has a loss of £12,180 and Bertrand has a loss of £1,860. They may claim loss relief against general income or carry forward loss relief.

Deborah

Deborah's losses are as follows, remembering that a loss which falls in the basis periods for two tax years is only taken into account in the earlier year.

Year	*Basis period*	*Working*	*Loss*
			£
2007/08	1.1.08–5.4.08	£3,960 × 3/12	990
2008/09	1.1.08–31.12.08	£3,960 – £990 (used in 2007/08)	2,970

NOTES

Deborah may claim relief for these losses against general income, under early trade losses relief or by carry forward loss relief.

7.7 Partnership investment income

A partnership may have non-trading income, such as interest on the partnership's bank deposit account or dividends on shares, or non-trading losses. **Such items are kept separate from trading income, but they** (and any associated tax credits) **are shared between the partners in a similar way to trading income.** That is, the following steps are applied.

Step 1 Find out which period of account the income arose in

Step 2 Share the income between the partners using the profit sharing arrangements for that period. If partners have already been given their salaries and interest on capital in sharing out trading income, do not give them those items again in sharing out non-trading income

Step 3 For income not taxed at source attribute each partner's share of the income to tax years using the same basis periods as are used to attribute his share of trading profits to tax years. When working out the basis periods for untaxed income (which excludes income taxed at source and dividends) or for non-trading losses, we always have a commencement when the partner joins the partnership and a cessation when he leaves, even if he carried on the trade as a sole trader before joining or after leaving. If the relief for overlap untaxed income on leaving the firm exceeds the partner's share of untaxed income for the tax year of leaving, the excess is deducted from his total income for that year

Step 4 For income taxed at source assume that income accrued evenly over the accounting period and time apportion on an actual basis into tax years (6 April to 5 April)

8 LIMITED LIABILITY PARTNERSHIPS

It is possible to form a limited liability partnership. The difference between a limited liability partnership (LLP) and a normal partnership is that **in a LLP the liability of the partners is limited to the capital they contributed.**

The partners of a LLP are taxed on virtually the same basis as the partners of a normal partnership (see above). However, the amount of loss relief that a partner can claim against general income or by early years trade loss relief when the claim is against non-partnership income is restricted to the capital he contributed and is subject to an overall cap of £25,000. This rule is not restricted to the first four years of trading and the rules apply to all partners whether or not involved in the running of the trade.

BPP LEARNING MEDIA

Chapter roundup

- Basis periods are used to link periods of account to tax years.
- In opening and closing years, special rules are applied so that a new trader can start to be taxed quickly, and a retiring trader need not be taxed long after his retirement.
- On a change of accounting date, special rules apply for fixing basis periods.
- Trade losses may be relieved against future profits of the same trade, against general income and against capital gains.
- A trade loss carried forward must be set against the first available trade profits of the same trade.
- Where a loss relief claim is made, trade losses can be set against general income and then gains in the current and/or prior year.
- It is important for a trader to choose the right loss relief, so as to save tax at the highest possible rate and so as to obtain relief reasonably quickly.
- If a business is transferred to a company, a loss of unincorporated business can be set against income received from the company.
- In opening years, a special relief involving the carry back of losses against general income is available. Losses arising in the first four tax years of a trade may be set against general income in the three years preceding the loss making year, taking the earliest year first.
- On the cessation of a trade, a loss arising in the last 12 months of trading may be set against trade profits of the tax year of cessation and the previous three years, taking the last year first.
- Capital losses arising on certain unquoted shares can be set against general income of the year of the loss and then against general income of the preceding year.
- A partnership is simply treated as a source of profits and losses for trades being carried on by the individual partners. Divide profits or losses between the partners according to the profit sharing ratio in the period of account concerned. If any of the partners are entitled to a salary or interest on capital, apportion this first, not forgetting to pro-rate in periods of less than 12 months.
- The commencement and cessation rules apply to partners individually when they join or leave.
- Limited liability partnerships are taxed on virtually the same basis as normal partnerships but loss relief is restricted for all partners.

Quick quiz

1 What is the basis period for the tax year in which a trade commenced?

2 On what two occasions may overlap profits potentially be relieved?

3 Against what income may trade losses carried forward be set off?

4 When a loss is to be relieved against total income, how are losses linked to particular tax years?

5 Against which years' total income may a loss be relieved against general income for a continuing business which has traded for many years?

6 For which losses is early years trade loss relief available?

7 In which years may relief for a terminal loss be given?

8 How are partnership trading profits divided between the individual partners?

9 What loss reliefs are partners entitled to?

10 Janet and John are partners sharing profits 60:40. For the years ended 30 June 2007 and 2008 the partnership made profits of £100,000 and £150,000 respectively. What are John's taxable trading profits in 2007/08?

11 Pete and Doug have been joint partners for many years. On 1 January Dave joins the partnership and it is agreed to share profits 40:40:20. For the year ended 30 June 2007 profits are £100,000.

What is Doug's share of these profits?

Answers to quick quiz

1 Date of commencement to 5 April in that year. (see para 1.2)

2 On a change of accounting date where a basis period resulting from the change exceeds 12 months or on the cessation of a business. (para 1.8)

3 Against trade profits from the same trade. (para 3)

4 The loss for a tax year is the loss in the basis period for that year. However, if basis periods overlap, a loss in the overlap period is a loss of the earlier tax year only. (para 4)

5 The year in which the loss arose and/or the preceding year. (para 4)

6 Losses incurred in the first four tax years of a trade. (para 5)

7 In the year of cessation and then in the three preceding years, later years first. (para 6)

8 Profits are divided in accordance with the profit sharing ratio that existed during the period of account in which the profits arose. (para 7.1)

9 Partners are entitled to the same loss reliefs as sole traders. These are loss relief against general income, early years trade loss relief, carry forward loss relief, terminal loss relief, and loss relief on transfer of a trade to a company. (para 7.5)

10 £40,000
2007/08: ye 30 June 2007
£100,000 × 40% = £40,000. (para 7.5)

11 £45,000

	Pete	Doug	Dave
	£	£	£
Y/e 30 June 2007			
1.7.06 – 31.12.06			
6m × £100,000			
£50,000 50:50	25,000	25,000	
1.1.07 – 30.6.07			
6m × £100,000			
£50,000 40:40:20	20,000	20,000	10,000
	45,000	45,000	10,000

(para 7.8)

Answers to activities

1

Year	Basis period	Working	Taxable profits
			£
2002/03	1.9.02–5.4.03	£8,000 × 7/8	7,000
2003/04	1.9.02–31.8.03	£8,000 + (£15,000 × 4/12)	13,000
2004/05	1.5.03–30.4.04		15,000
2005/06	1.5.04–30.4.05		9,000
2006/07	1.5.05–30.4.06		10,500
2007/08	1.5.06–30.6.07	£(16,000 + 950 – 12,000)	4,950
			59,450

The overlap profits are the profits from 1 September 2002 to 5 April 2003 (taxed in 2002/03 and in 2003/04) and those from 1 May 2003 to 31 August 2003 (taxed in 2003/04 and 2004/05).

	£
1.9.02–5.4.03 £8,000 × 7/8	7,000
1.5.03–31.8.03 £15,000 × 4/12	5,000
Total overlap profits	12,000

2 The loss-making period ends in 2007/08, so the year of the loss is 2007/08.

	2006/07	2007/08
	£	£
Income	18,000	18,000
Less loss relief against general income	(7,000)	(18,000)
Net income	11,000	0
Less personal allowance	(5,225)	(5,225)
Taxable income	5,775	0

In 2007/08, £5,225 of the loss has been wasted because that amount of income would have been covered by the personal allowance. If Janet claims loss relief against general income, there is nothing she can do about this waste of loss relief or the personal allowance.

NOTES

3

	£
Income	19,500
Less loss relief against general income	(19,500)
Net income	0
Capital gains	10,000
Less loss relief: lower of £(27,000 – 19,500) = £7,500 (note 1) and £(10,000 – 4,000) = £6,000 (note 2)	(6,000)
	4,000
Less annual exemption (restricted)	(4,000)
	0

Note 1 This equals the loss left after the loss relief against general income claim

Note 2 This equals the gains left after losses b/fwd but ignoring taper relief and the annual exemption.

A trading loss of £(7,500 – 6,000) = £1,500 is carried forward. Sibyl's personal allowance and £(9,200 – 4,000) = £5,200 of her capital gains tax annual exemption are wasted. Her capital losses brought forward of £4,000 are carried forward to 2008/09. Although we deducted this £4,000 in working out how much trading loss we were allowed to use in the claim, we do not actually use any of the £4,000 unless there are gains remaining in excess of the annual exemption.

Chapter 37 :
CORPORATION TAX

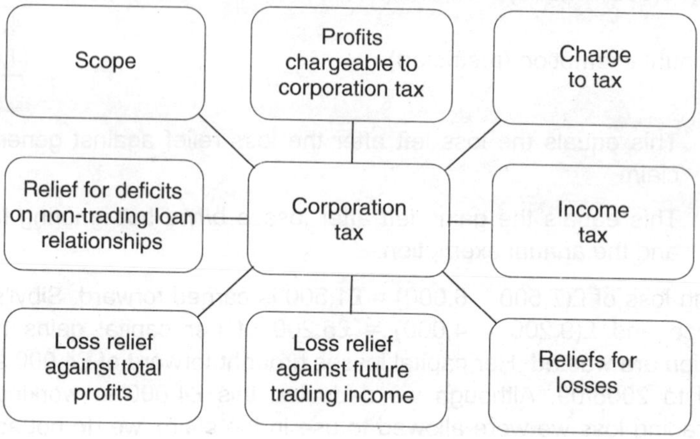

Introduction

Corporation tax is the tax on profits paid by public or private limited companies. Many of the principles you see here will be already familiar from your studies of personal and business taxation.

You may want to refresh your memory as to the specific features of limited companies and how they draw up their accounts, and you will find this in Chapter 18 of this Course Book.

Your objectives

In this chapter you will learn about the following.

(a) The scope of corporation tax; chargeable entities; chargeable income

(b) Chargeable accounting periods for corporation tax

(c) How to compute profits chargeable to corporation tax for the chargeable accounting period

(d) The financial year(s) relevant to a chargeable accounting period

(e) The rate(s) of corporation tax which apply

(f) How to compute the corporation tax liability

(g) How to compute the corporation tax liability for periods longer or shorter than 12 months

(h) Set off of income tax against corporation tax liability

(i) The loss reliefs available

(j) How to compute corporation tax repayable following a loss relief claim

1 THE SCOPE OF CORPORATION TAX

1.1 Companies

Companies must pay corporation tax on their **profits chargeable to corporation tax** for each **accounting period**. We look at the meaning of these terms below.

Definition

> A **'company'** is any corporate body (limited or unlimited) or unincorporated association, eg sports club.

1.2 Accounting periods

Corporation tax is chargeable in respect of accounting periods. It is important to understand the difference between an accounting period and a period of account.

Definition

> A **period of account** is any period for which a company prepares accounts; usually this will be 12 months in length but it may be longer or shorter than this.

Definition

> An **accounting period** is the period for which corporation tax is charged and cannot exceed 12 months. Special rules determine when an accounting period starts and ends.

An accounting period starts when a company starts to trade, or otherwise becomes liable to corporation tax, or immediately after the previous accounting period finishes. An accounting period finishes on the earliest of:

- 12 months after its start
- The end of the company's period of account
- The commencement of the company's winding-up
- The company's ceasing to be resident in the UK
- The company's ceasing to be liable to corporation tax

If a company has a period of account exceeding 12 months (a long period), it is split into two accounting periods: the first 12 months and the remainder. For example, if a company prepares accounts for the sixteen months to 30 April 2007, the two accounting periods for which the company will pay corporation tax will be the 12 months to 31 December 2006 and the four months to 30 April 2007.

1.3 Financial year

The rates of corporation tax are fixed for financial years.

Definition

A financial year runs from 1 April to the following 31 March and is identified by the calendar year in which it begins. For example, the year ended 31 March 2008 is the Financial year 2007 (FY 2007). This should not be confused with a tax year, which runs from 6 April to the following 5 April.

2 PROFITS CHARGEABLE TO CORPORATION TAX

2.1 Proforma computation

A company may have both income and gains. As a general rule income arises from receipts which are expected to recur regularly (such as the profits from a trade) whereas chargeable gains arise on the sale of capital assets which have been owned for several years (such as the sale of a factory used in the trade).

A company pays corporation tax on its profits chargeable to corporation tax (PCTCT). A company may receive income from various sources. All income received must be classified according to the nature of the income as different computational rules apply to different types of income. The main types of income for a company are:

- Profits of a trade
- Profits of a property business
- Investment income
- Miscellaneous income

For unincorporated businesses and all other income tax purposes (see earlier in this Text) these classes of income have replaced the old classification system under which the different types of income were known as **Schedules,** some of which were divided into **Cases**. These old rules still apply for corporation tax purposes, for example trading profits are strictly known as Schedule D Case I profits and the profits of a property business are called Schedule A profits. However, the plain English terminology above will also be used for corporation tax purposes in your exam and therefore only this new terminology is used in this Course Book.

A company's profits chargeable to corporation tax are arrived at by aggregating its various sources of income and its chargeable gains and then deducting gift aid donations. Here is a *pro forma* computation. All items are explained later in this chapter.

NOTES

	£
Trading profits	X
Investment income	X
Foreign income	X
Miscellaneous income	X
Property business profits	X
Chargeable gains	X
Total profits	X
Less gift aid donations	(X)
Profits chargeable to corporation tax (PCTCT) for an accounting period	X

Dividends received from UK resident companies are not included in the profits chargeable to corporation tax.

3 TRADING INCOME

3.1 Adjustment of profits

The trading income of companies is derived from the net profit figure in the accounts, just as for individuals, adjusted as follows.

	£	£
Net profit per accounts		X
Add expenditure not allowed for taxation purposes		X
		X
Less: income not taxable as trading income	X	
expenditure not charged in the accounts but allowable for the purposes of taxation	X	
capital allowances	X	
		(X)
Trading income		X

The adjustment of profits computation for companies broadly follows that for computing business profits subject to income tax. There are, however, some minor differences. There is no disallowance for 'private use' for companies; instead the director or employee will be taxed on the benefit received.

Gift aid donations are added back in the calculation of adjusted profit. They are treated instead as a deduction from total profits.

Investment income including rents is deducted from net profit in arriving at trading income but brought in again further down in the computation (see below).

3.2 Pre-trading expenditure

Pre-trading expenditure incurred by the company within the seven years before trade commences is treated as an allowable expense incurred on the first day of trading provided it would have been allowable had the company been trading when the expense was actually incurred.

BPP LEARNING MEDIA

3.3 Capital allowances

The calculation of capital allowances follows income tax principles.

For companies, however, there is never any reduction of allowances to take account of any private use of an asset. The director or employee suffers a taxable benefit instead. As shown above capital allowances must be deducted in arriving at taxable trading income.

A company's accounting period can never exceed 12 months. If the period of account is longer than 12 months it is **divided into two**; one for the first 12 months and one for the balance. **The capital allowances computation must be carried out for each period separately.**

4 PROPERTY BUSINESS INCOME

Rental income is deducted in arriving at trading income but brought in again further down in the computation as property business income.

The calculation of property business income follows income tax principles.

The income tax rules for property businesses were set out earlier in this Course Book. In summary all UK rental activities are treated as a single source of income calculated in the same way as trading income.

However there are certain differences for companies:

(a) **Property business losses** are:

  (i) **First set off against non-property business income and gains of the company for the current period**; and any excess is

  (ii) **Carried forward for set off against future income** (of all descriptions).

(b) **Interest paid by a company on a loan to buy or improve property is not a property business expense. The loan relationship rules apply** instead (see below).

5 LOAN RELATIONSHIPS (INTEREST INCOME)

5.1 General principle

If a company borrows or lends money, including issuing or investing in debentures or buying gilts, it has a loan relationship. This can be a creditor relationship (where the company lends or invests money) **or a debtor relationship** (where the company borrows money or issues securities).

5.2 Treatment of trading loan relationships

If the company is a party to a **loan relationship for trade purposes, any debits – ie interest paid or other debt costs – charged through its accounts are allowed as a trading expense** and are therefore deductible in computing trading income.

Similarly **if any credits – ie interest income or other debt returns – arise on a trading loan these are treated as a trading receipt and are taxable as trading income.** This is not likely to arise unless the trade is one of money lending.

NOTES

5.3 Treatment of non-trading loan relationships

If a loan relationship is not one to which the company is a party for trade purposes any debits or credits must be pooled. A net credit on the pool is chargeable as interest income.

Interest charged on underpaid tax is allowable and interest received on overpaid tax is assessable under the rules for non-trading loan relationships.

5.4 Accounting methods

Debits and credits must be brought into account using the UK generally accepted accounting practice (GAAP) or using the International Accounting Standards (IAS). This will usually be the accruals basis.

5.5 Incidental costs of loan finance

Under the loan relationship rules expenses ('debits') are allowed if incurred directly:

(a) to bring a loan relationship into existence

(b) entering into or giving effect to any related transactions

(c) making payment under a loan relationship or related transactions or

(d) taking steps to ensure the receipt of payments under the loan relationship or related transaction.

A related transaction means 'any disposal or acquisition (in whole or in part) of rights or liabilities under the relationship, including any arising from a security issue in relation to the money debt in question'.

The above categories of incidental costs are also allowable even if the company does not enter into the loan relationship (ie abortive costs). Costs directly incurred in varying the terms of a loan relationship are also allowed.

5.6 Other matters

It is not only the interest costs of borrowing that are allowable or taxable. The capital costs are treated similarly. Thus if a company issues a loan at a discount and repays it eventually at par, the capital cost is usually allowed on redemption (if the accruals basis is adopted).

6 MISCELLANEOUS INCOME

Patent royalties received which do not relate to the trade are taxed as miscellaneous income. Patent royalties which relate to the trade are included in trading income normally on an accruals basis.

7 CHARGEABLE GAINS

7.1 Introduction

Companies do not pay capital gains tax. Instead their chargeable gains are included in the profits chargeable to corporation tax. A company's capital gains or allowable losses are computed in a similar way to individuals but with a few major differences.

(a) Indexation allowance continues after 6 April 1998

(b) Taper relief does not apply

(c) No annual exemption is available

(d) The FA 1985 pool for shares does not stop at 5 April 1998 and different matching rules for shares apply if the shareholder is a company.

8 GIFT AID DONATIONS

Gift aid donations are deductible in computing PCTCT.

Almost all donations of money to charity can be made under the **gift aid scheme** whether they are one off donations or are regular donations. **Gift aid donations are paid gross.**

Donations to local charities which are incurred wholly and exclusively for the purposes of a trade are deducted in the calculation of the tax adjusted trading profits.

9 LONG PERIODS OF ACCOUNT

As we saw above, if a company has a long period of account exceeding 12 months, it is split into two accounting periods: the first 12 months and the remainder.

Where the period of account differs from the corporation tax accounting periods, profits are **allocated to the relevant periods** as follows.

(a) **Trading income** before capital allowances is apportioned on a **time basis.**

(b) **Capital allowances** and balancing charges are **calculated for each accounting period.**

(c) **Other income is allocated to the period to which it relates** (eg rents to the period when accrued). Miscellaneous income, however, is apportioned on a time basis.

(d) **Chargeable gains and losses** are allocated to the **period in which they are realised.**

(e) **Gift aid donations** are deducted in the accounting **period in which they are paid.**

Activity 1 **(10 minutes)**

Xenon Ltd makes up an 18-month set of accounts to 30 September 2008 with the following results.

	£
Trading profits	180,000
Property income	
18 months @ £500 accruing per month	9,000
Capital gain (1 August 2008 disposal)	250,000
Less: Gift aid donation (paid 31 March 2008)	(50,000)
	389,000

What are the profits chargeable to corporation tax for each of the accounting periods based on the above accounts?

10 CHARGE TO CORPORATION TAX

10.1 'Profits'

Although we tax PCTCT another figure needs to be calculated ('profits') to determine the rate of corporation tax to use to tax PCTCT.

'Profits' means profits chargeable to corporation tax plus the grossed-up amount of dividends received from UK companies other than those in the same group. The grossed-up amount of UK dividends is the dividend received multiplied by 100/90. This is because dividends are treated as paid net of a 10% tax credit (see earlier in this text). You may see the grossed up amount of dividend received referred to as **franked investment income (FII)**.

Do not include overseas dividends in the computation of 'profits'. These will have been included as foreign income when calculating PCTCT (see later in this Course Book).

10.2 The full rate

The rates of corporation tax are fixed for financial years. The full rate of corporation tax is 30% for FY 2007, and applies to companies with 'profits' of £1,500,000 or more, having remained unchanged since FY 1999. A company with PCTCT of, say, £2 million, will pay £600,000 corporation tax.

10.3 The small companies' rate (SCR)

The SCR of corporation tax of 20% for FY 2007 (FY 2006 and FY 2005 19%) applies to the profits chargeable to corporation tax of UK resident companies whose 'profits' are not more than £300,000.

NOTES

Activity 2 **(5 minutes)**

B Ltd had the following results for the year ended 31 March 2008

	£
Trading profits	42,000
Dividend received 1 May 2007	9,000

10.4 Marginal relief

Small companies' marginal relief applies where the 'profits' of an accounting period of a UK resident company are over £300,000 but under £1,500,000.

We first calculate the corporation tax at the full rate and then deduct:

(M – P) × I/P × marginal relief fraction

where M = upper limit (currently £1,500,000)
P = 'profits' (see above)
I = PCTCT

The marginal relief fraction is 1/40 for FY 2007 (FY 2006 and FY 2005 11/400).

This information is given in the rates and allowances section of the exam paper.

EXAMPLE

Lenox Ltd has the following results for the year ended 31 March 2008.

	£
PCTCT	296,000
Dividend received 1 December 2007	12,600

Calculate the corporation tax liability.

	£
PCTCT	296,000
Dividend plus tax credit £12,600 × 100/90	14,000
'Profits'	310,000

'Profits' are above £300,000 but below £1,500,000, so marginal relief applies.

	£
Corporation tax on PCTCT £296,000 × 30%	88,800
Less small companies' marginal relief	
£(1,500,000 – 310,000) × 296,000/310,000 × 1/40	(28,406)
	60,394

In exam questions you often need to be aware that there is a marginal rate of 32.5 % which applies to any PCTCT that lies in between the small companies' limits.

BPP LEARNING MEDIA

This is calculated as follows.

	£			£
Upper limit	1,500,000	@	30%	450,000
Lower limit	(300,000)	@	20%	(60,000)
Difference	1,200,000			390,000

$$\frac{390{,}000}{1{,}200{,}000} = 32.5\%$$

Effectively the band of profits (here £1,200,000) falling between the upper and lower limits are taxed at a rate of 32.5%

10.5 Example: effective marginal rate of tax

A Ltd has PCTCT of £350,000 for the year ended 31 March 2008. Its corporation tax liability is:

	£
£350,000 × 30%	105,000
Less small companies' marginal relief	
£(1,500,000 – 350,000) × $^{1}/_{40}$	(28,750)
	76,250

This is the same as calculating tax at 20% × £300,000 + 32.5% × £50,000 = £60,000 + £16,250 = £76,250.

Consequently tax is charged at an effective rate of 32.5% on PCTCT that exceeds the small companies' lower limit.

Note that although there is an effective corporation tax charge of 32.5%, this rate of tax is never used in actually calculating corporation tax. The rate is just an effective marginal rate that you must be aware of. It will be particularly important when considering loss relief and group relief (see later in this Course Book).

The marginal rate of corporation tax for FY 2006 and FY 2005 was 32.75%.

10.6 Accounting period in more than one financial year

An accounting period **may fall within more than one financial year. If the rates and limits for corporation tax are the same in both financial years, tax can be computed for the accounting period as if it fell within one financial year.**

However, **if the rates and/or limits for corporation tax are different in the financial years, PCTCT and 'profits' are time apportioned between the financial years.** This will be the case where a company is a small company (or marginal relief company) with an accounting period partly in FY 2006 and partly in FY 2007. **It is also necessary to adjust the upper and lower limits.**

NOTES

EXAMPLE

Wentworth Ltd makes up its accounts to 31 December each year.

For the year to 31 December 2007, it has PCTCT of £174,000. It receives a dividend of £5,400 on 1 December 2007.

The corporation tax payable by Wentworth Ltd is calculated as follows.

	£
PCTCT	174,000
Dividend plus tax credit £5,400 × 100/90	6,000
'Profits'	180,000

	FY 2006 *3 months* *to 31.3.07*	*FY 2007* *9 months* *to 31.12.07*
	£	£
PCTCT (3:9)	43,500	130,500
'Profits' (3:9)	45,000	135,000
Lower limit:		
£300,000 × 3/12	75,000	
£300,000 × 9/12		225,000
Small companies' rate applies in both FYs:		
FY 2006 £43,500 × 19%	8,265	
FY 2007 £130,500 × 20%		26,100
Total corporation tax payable		
£(8,265 + 26,100)		£34,365

Activity 3 **(20 minutes)**

Elliot Ltd has the following results for the year to 30 September 2007.

	£
PCTCT	360,000
Dividend received 15 July 2007	8,100

Calculate the corporation tax payable to Elliot Ltd.

10.7 Short accounting periods

The upper and lower limits which are used to be determine tax rates are pro-rated on a time basis if an accounting period lasts for less than 12 months.

EXAMPLE

Ink Ltd prepared accounts for the six months to 31 March 2008. Profits chargeable to corporation tax for the period were £200,000. No dividends were received. Calculate the corporation tax payable for the period.

Upper limit £1,500,000 × 6/12 = £750,000

Lower limit £300,000 × 6/12 = £150,000

As 'profits' fall between the limits small companies' marginal relief applies.

	£
Corporation tax (FY 07)	
£200,000 × 30%	60,000
Less: small companies' marginal relief	
1/40 × (£750,000 – £200,000)	(13,750)
Corporation tax	46,250

10.8 Long periods of account

Remember that an accounting period cannot be more than 12 months long. If the period of account exceeds 12 months it must be split into two accounting periods, the first of 12 months and the second of the balance.

EXAMPLE

Xenon Ltd in the previous chapter made up an 18-month set of accounts to 30 September 2008.

The 18 month period of account is divided into:

Year ending 31 March 2008
6 months to 30 September 2008

Results were allocated:

	Y/e 31.3.08	*6m to 30.9.08*
	£	£
Trading profits 12:6	120,000	60,000
Property income	6,000	3,000
Capital gain (1.8.08)		250,000
Less: Gift aid donation (31.3.08)	(50,000)	
PCTCT	76,000	313,000

NOTES

Assuming Xenon Ltd received FII of £27,000 on 31 August 2008 calculate the corporation tax payable for each accounting period. Assume the rates of corporation tax for FY 2007 apply in FY 2008.

	Y/e 31.3.08	*6m to 30.9.08*
	£	£
PCTCT	76,000	313,000
FII	0	27,000
Profits	76,000	340,000
Small companies lower limit	300,000	150,000
Small companies upper limit	1,500,000	750,000
	Small company	*Marginal relief*
CT payable		
£76,000 × 20%	15,200	
£313,000 × 30%		93,900
Less marginal relief £(750,000 – 340,000) × 313,000/340,000 × 1/40		(9,436)
		84,464
Total corporation tax payable £(15,200 + 84,464)		99,664

11 TRADING LOSSES

In summary, the following reliefs are available for trading losses incurred by a company.

(a) Set-off against current profits
(b) Carry back against earlier profits
(c) Carry forward against future trading profits

Reliefs (a) and (b) must be claimed, and are given in the order shown. Relief (c) is given automatically for any loss for which the other reliefs are not claimed.

12 CARRY FORWARD TRADE LOSS RELIEF

A company must set off a trading loss against income from the same trade in future accounting periods (unless it has been otherwise relieved see below). **Relief is against the first available profits.**

NOTES

EXAMPLE

A Ltd has the following results for the three years to 31 March 2008.

	Year ended		
	31.3.06	*31.3.07*	*31.3.08*
	£	£	£
Trading profit/(loss)	(8,550)	3,000	6,000
Property income	0	1,000	1,000
Gift aid donation	300	1,400	1,700

Calculate the profits chargeable to corporation tax for all three years showing any losses available to carry forward at 1 April 2008.

	Year ended		
	31.3.06	*31.3.07*	*31.3.08*
	£	£	£
Trading profits	0	3,000	6,000
Less: carry forward loss relief		(3,000)	(5,550)
	0	0	450
Property income	0	1,000	1,000
Less: Gift aid donation	0	(1,000)	(1,450)
PCTCT	0	0	0
Unrelieved gift aid donation	300	400	250

Note that the trading loss carried forward is set only against the trading profit in future years. It cannot be set against the property income.

The gift aid donations that become unrelieved remain unrelieved as they cannot be carried forward.

Loss memorandum

	£
Loss for y/e 31.3.06	8,550
Less used y/e 31.3.07	(3,000)
Loss carried forward at 1.4.07	5,550
Less used y/e 31.3.08	(5,550)
Loss carried forward at 1.4.08	0

13 TRADE LOSS RELIEF AGAINST TOTAL PROFITS

13.1 Current year relief

A company may claim to set a trading loss incurred in an accounting period against total profits before deducting gift aid donations of the same accounting period.

13.2 Carry back relief

Such a loss may then be carried back and set against total profits before deducting gift aid donations of an accounting period falling wholly or partly within the 12 months of the start of the period in which the loss was incurred.

If a period falls partly outside the 12 months, loss relief is limited to the proportion of the period's profits (before gift aid donations) equal to the proportion of the period which falls within the 12 months.

Any possible loss relief claim for the period of the loss must be made before any excess loss can be carried back to a previous period.

Any carry-back is to more recent periods before earlier periods. Relief for earlier losses is given before relief for later losses.

13.3 Claims

A claim for relief against current or prior period profits must be made within two years of the end of the accounting period in which the loss arose. Any claim must be for the *whole* loss (to the extent that profits are available to relieve it). The loss can however be reduced by not claiming full capital allowances, so that higher capital allowances are given (on higher tax written down values) in future years.

Activity 4 **(20 minutes)**

Helix Ltd has the following results.

		Year ended	
	30.9.05	*30.9.06*	*30.9.07*
	£	£	£
Trading profit/(loss)	10,500	10,000	(35,000)
Bank interest	500	500	500
Chargeable gains	0	0	4,000
Gift Aid donation	250	250	250

Show the PCTCT for all the years affected assuming that loss relief against total profits is claimed.

Any loss remaining unrelieved after any loss relief claims against total profits is carried forward to set against future profits of the same trade.

NOTES

Activity 5 **(20 minutes)**

Patagonia Ltd has the following results for the four accounting periods to 31 July 2007.

	Y/e	*3 months*	*Y/e*	*Y/e*
	30.4.05	*31.7.05*	*31.7.06*	*31.7.07*
	£	£	£	£
Trading profit (loss)	20,000	15,000	(50,000)	35,000
Building society interest	1,000	400	1,800	1,000
Chargeable gains (loss)	(400)	-	1,900	2,000
Gift aid donations	600	500	-	600

Show the profits chargeable to corporation tax for all year affected. Assume loss relief is claimed against total profits where possible

13.4 Terminal trade loss relief

For trading losses incurred in the 12 months up to the cessation of trade the carry back period is extended from 12 months to three years, later years first.

EXAMPLE

Brazil Ltd had the following results for the accounting periods up to the cessation of trade on 30 September 2007.

	Y/e	*Y/e*	*Y/e*	*Y/e*
	30.9.04	*30.9.05*	*30.9.06*	*30.9.07*
	£	£	£	£
Trading profits	60,000	40,000	15,000	(180,000)
Gains	-	10,000	-	6,000
Rental income	12,000	12,000	12,000	12,000

You are required to show how the losses are relieved assuming the maximum use is made of loss relief against total profits.

	Y/e	*Y/e*	*Y/e*	*Y/e*
	30.9.04	*30.9.05*	*30.9.06*	*30.9.07*
	£	£	£	£
Trading profits	60,000	40,000	15,000	-
Rental income	12,000	12,000	12,000	12,000
Gains	-	10,000	-	6,000
	72,000	62,000	27,000	18,000
Less current period loss relief Y/e 30.9.07				(18,000)
				-
Less carry back loss relief	(72,000)	(62,000)	(27,000)	
PCTCT	-	-	-	-

BPP LEARNING MEDIA

Loss memorandum

	£
Loss in Y/e 30.9.07	180,000
Less used Y/e 30.9.07	(18,000)
Loss of Y/e 30.9.07 available for 36 months carry back	162,000
Less used Y/e 30.9.06	(27,000)
	135,000
Less used Y/e 30.9.05	(62,000)
	73,000
Less used Y/e 30.9.04	(72,000)
Loss remaining unrelieved	1,000

Chapter roundup

- Companies pay corporation tax on their profits chargeable to corporation tax(PCTCT).
- An accounting period cannot exceed 12 months in length so long period of account must be split into two accounting periods. The first accounting period is always 12 months in length.
- Tax rates are set for financial years.
- A company is UK resident if it is incorporated in the UK or if it is incorporated abroad and its central management and control are exercised in the UK.
- PCTCT comprises the company's income and chargeable gains, less gift aid donations. It does not include dividends received from other UK resident companies.
- Income includes trading income, property income, income from non-trading loan relationships (interest) and miscellaneous income.
- The adjustment of profits computation for companies broadly follows that for computing business profits subject to income tax. There are, however, some minor differences.
- Chargeable gains for companies are computed in broadly the same way as for individuals.
- Gift aid donations are paid gross by a company and deducted when computing PCTCT.
- A company pays corporation tax on its profits chargeable to corporation tax (PCTCT).
- 'Profits' is PCTCT plus franked investment income (FII).
- Companies may be taxed at the small companies' rate (SCR) or obtain marginal relief, depending on their 'profits'.

NOTES

Chapter roundup continued

- The marginal rate of corporation tax between the small companies' limits is 32.5%. The marginal tax rate is an effective rate; is it never actually used in working out corporation tax.
- The upper and lower limits which are used to determine tax rates are pro-rated on a time basis if an accounting period last for less than 12 months.
- The upper and lower limits which are used to determine tax rates are divided by the total number of associated companies. Broadly, associated companies are worldwide trading companies under common control.
- Trading losses may be relieved against current total profits, against total profits of earlier periods or against future trading income.
- Trading losses carried forward can only be set against future trading profits arising from the same trade.
- Loss relief against total profits is given before gift aid donations. Gift aid donations remain unrelieved.
- Loss relief against total profits may be given against current period profits and against profits of the previous 12 months.

  A claim for current period loss relief can be made without claim for carryback. However, if a loss is to be carried back a claim for current period relief must have been made first.
- Trading losses in the last 12 months of trading can be carried back and set against profits of the previous 36 months.

Quick quiz

1. When does an accounting period end?
2. What is the difference between a period of account and an accounting period?
3. Should interest paid on a trading loan be adjusted in the trading income computations?
4. How are trading profits (before capital allowances) of a long period of account divided between accounting periods?
5. Which companies are entitled to the small companies' rate of corporation tax?
6. What is the marginal relief formula?
7. Against what profits may trading losses carried forward be set?
8. To what extent may losses be carried back?

NOTES

Answers to quick quiz

1. An accounting period ends on the earliest of:

   (a) 12 months after its start
   (b) The end of the company's period of account
   (c) The commencement of the company's winding up
   (d) The company ceasing to be resident in the UK
   (e) The company ceasing to be liable to corporation tax (see para 1.2)

2. A period of account is the period for which a company prepares accounts. An accounting period is the period for which corporation tax is charged. If a company prepares annual accounts the two will coincide. (para 1.2)

3. Interest paid on a trading loan should not be adjusted in the trading income computation as it is an allowable expense, computed on the accruals basis. (para 5)

4. Trading income (before capital allowances) is apportioned on a time basis. (para 9)

5. Which companies are entitled to the small companies' rate of corporation tax? (para 10.3)

6. What is the marginal relief formula? (para 10.4)

7. Profits from the same trade. (para 12)

8. A loss may be carried back and set against total profits (before deducting gift aid donations) of the prior 12 months. A loss arising on the final 12 months of trading can be carried back to set against profits arising in the previous 36 months. The loss carried back is the trading loss left unrelieved after a claim against total profits (before deducting gift aid donations) of the loss making AP has been made. (paras 13.2 and 13.4)

NOTES

Answers to activities

1 The 18-month period of account is divided into:

Year ending 31 March 2008

Six months to 30 September 2008

Results are allocated:

	Y/e 31.3.08	*6m to 30.9.08*
	£	£
Trading profits 12:6	120,000	60,000
Property income		
12 × £500	6,000	
6 × £500		3,000
Capital gain (1.8.08)		250,000
Less: Gift aid donation (31.3.08)	(50,000)	
PCTCT (profits chargeable to corporation tax)	76,000	313,000

2

	£
Trading profits	42,000
Dividend plus tax credit £9,000 × 100/90	10,000
'Profits' (less than £300,000 limit)	52,000
Corporation tax payable	
£42,000 × 20%	£8,400

BPP LEARNING MEDIA

3

		£
PCTCT		360,000
Add: FII £8,100 × 100/90		9,000
'Profits'		369,000

	FY 2006 6 months to 31.3.07	FY 2007 6 months 30.9.07
	£	£
PCTCT (6:6)	180,000	180,000
'Profits' (6:6)	184,500	184,500
Lower limit: £300,000 × 6/12	150,000	150,000
Upper limit: £1,500,000 × 6/12	750,000	750,000

Marginal relief applies in both FYs

FY 2006		
£180,000 × 30%	54,000	
Less: marginal relief £(750,000 – 184,500) × $\frac{180,000}{184,500}$ × 11/400	(15,172)	
	38,828	
FY 2007		
£180,000 × 30%		54,000
Less: marginal relief £(750,000 – 184,500) × $\frac{180,000}{184,500}$ × 1/40		(13,793)
		40,207
Total corporation tax payable £(38,828 + 40,207)		£79,035

NOTES

4 The loss of the year to 30 September 2007 is relieved against current year profits and against profits of the previous 12 months.

	Year ended 30.9.05	30.9.06	30.9.07
	£	£	£
Trading profit	10,500	10,000	0
Investment income	500	500	500
Chargeable gains	0	0	4,000
	11,000	10,500	4,500
Less current period loss relief	0	0	(4,500)
	11,000	10,500	0
Less carry back loss relief	0	(10,500)	0
	11,000	0	0
Less gift aid donation	(250)	0	0
PCTCT	10,750	0	0
Unrelieved gift aid donation		250	250

Loss memorandum		£
Loss incurred in y/e 30.9.07		35,000
Less used:	y/e 30.9.07	(4,500)
	y/e 30.9.08	(10,500)
Loss available to carry forward		20,000

5

	Y/e 30.4.05	3 months to 31.7.05	Y/e 31.7.06	Y/e 31.7.07
	£	£	£	£
Trading profit	20,000	15,000	-	35,000
Less carry forward loss relief	-	-	-	(15,550)
	20,000	15,000	-	19,450
Interest income	1,000	400	1,800	1,000
Chargeable gains	-	-	1,500	2,000
£(1,900 – 400)	-	-	1,500	2,000
	21,000	15,400	3,300	22,450
Less current period loss relief			(3,300)	
	21,000	15,400	-	22,450
Less carry back loss relief	(15,750)	(15,400)		
	5,250	-	-	22,450
Less gift aid donations	(600)			(600)
PCTCT	4,650	-	-	21,850
Unrelieved gift aid donations	-	500	-	-

Loss memorandum		£
Loss incurred in Y/e 31.7.06		50,000
Less used y/e 31.7.06		(3,300)
		46,700
Less used 3 months to 31.7.05	15,400	
Y/e 30.4.05		
9/12 × £21,000 (before gift aid donations)	15,750	(31,150)
		15,550
Less: Loss carried forward used y/e 31.7.07		(15,550)
C/f		Nil

BPP LEARNING MEDIA

NOTES

Notes

1 The loss can be carried back to set against profits of the previous **12 months**. This means profits in the y/e 30.4.05 must be time apportioned by multiplying by 9/12.

2 Losses remaining after the loss relief claims against total profits are carried forward to set against **future trading profits**.

Chapter 38 :
SELF-ASSESSMENT AND PAYMENT OF TAX

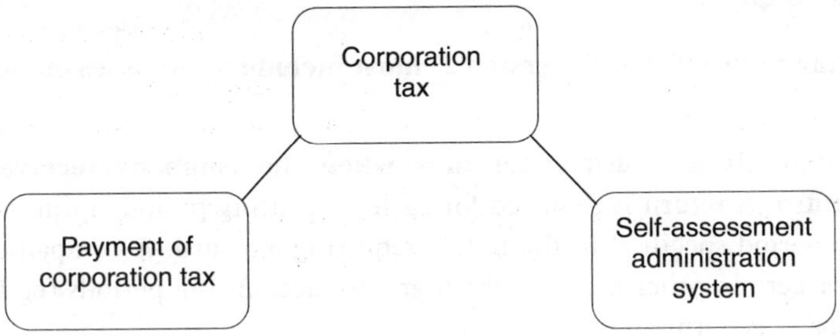

Introduction

This chapter covers two relatively small areas of corporation tax. The self-assessment system and the payments system, apply to all companies, regardless of status.

Your objectives

In this chapter you will learn about the following.

(a) The self-assessment administration system

(b) Payment of corporation tax

1 THE SELF-ASSESSMENT SYSTEM

1.1 Notification to HMRC

A company must notify HMRC of the beginning of its first accounting period (ie usually when it starts to trade) and the beginning of any subsequent period that does not immediately follow the end of a previous accounting period. The notice must be in the prescribed form and submitted within three months of the relevant date.

1.2 Returns

A company's tax return (CT 600 Version 2) must include a self-assessment of any tax payable.

An obligation to file a return arises only when the company receives a notice requiring a return. A return is required for each accounting period ending during or at the end of the period specified in the notice requiring a return. A company also has to file a return for certain other periods which are not accounting periods (eg for a period when the company is dormant).

A company that does not receive a notice requiring a return must, if it is chargeable to tax, **notify HMRC within 12 months of the end of the accounting period.** Failure to do so results in a maximum penalty equal to the tax unpaid 12 months after the end of the accounting period. Tax for this purpose includes corporation tax and notional tax on loans to participators of close companies (see later in this Course Book).

A notice to file a return may also require other information, accounts and reports. For a UK resident company the requirement to deliver accounts normally extends only to the accounts required under the Companies Act.

A return is due on or before the filing date. This is the later of:

(a) **12 months after the end of the period to which the return relates**

(b) **If the relevant period of account is not more than 18 months long, 12 months from the end of the period of account**

(c) **If relevant the period of account is more than 18 months long, 30 months from the start of the period of account**, and

(d) **Three months from the date on which the notice requiring the return was made.**

The relevant period of account is that in which the accounting period to which the return relates ends.

Activity 1 **(10 minutes)**

A Ltd prepares accounts for the 18 months to 30 June 2007. A notice requiring a return for the period ended 30 June 2007 was issued to A Ltd on 1 September 2007. State the periods for which A Ltd must file a tax return and the filing dates.

There is a £100 penalty for a failure to submit a return on time, rising to £200 if the delay exceeds three months. These penalties become £500 and £1,000 respectively when a return was late (or never submitted) for each of the preceding two accounting periods.

An additional tax geared penalty is applied if a return is more than six months late. The penalty is 10% of the tax unpaid six months after the return was due if the total delay is up to 12 months, and 20% of that tax if the return is over 12 months late.

There is a tax geared penalty for a fraudulent or negligent return and for failing to correct an innocent error without unreasonable delay. The maximum penalty is equal to the tax that would have been lost had the return been accepted as correct. HMRC can mitigate this penalty. If a company is liable to more than one tax geared penalty, the total penalty is limited to the maximum single penalty that could be charged.

A company may amend a return within 12 months of the filing date. HMRC may amend a return to correct obvious errors within nine months of the day the return was filed, or if the correction is to an amended return, within nine months of the filing of an amendment. The company may amend its return so as to reject the correction. If the time limit for amendments has expired, the company may reject the correction by giving notice within three months.

1.3 Records

Companies must keep records until the latest of:

(a) Six years from the end of the accounting period
(b) The date any enquiries are completed
(c) The date after which enquiries may not be commenced.

All business records and accounts, including contracts and receipts, must be kept.

If a return is demanded more than six years after the end of the accounting period, any records which the company still has must be kept until the later of the end of any enquiry and the expiry of the right to start an enquiry.

Failure to keep records can lead to a penalty of up to £3,000 for each accounting period affected. However, this penalty does not apply when the only records which have not been kept are ones which could only have been needed for the purposes of claims, elections or notices not included in the return.

HMRC do not generally insist on original records being kept but original records of the following must be preserved.

(a) Qualifying distributions (eg dividends) and tax credits

(b) Gross and net payments and tax deducted for payments made net of tax

(c) Certificates of payments made to sub-contractors net of tax

(d) Details of foreign tax paid, although HMRC will accept photocopies of foreign tax assessments when calculating underlying tax (see later in this Course Book) on dividends from abroad

1.4 Enquiries

A return or an amendment need not be accepted at face value by HMRC. **They may enquire into it, provided that they first give written notice that they are going to enquire**. The notice must be given by a year after the later of:

(a) The filing date

(b) The 31 January, 30 April, 31 July or 31 October next following the actual date of delivery of the return or amendment.

Only one enquiry may be made in respect of any one return or amendment.

If a notice of an enquiry has been given, HMRC may demand that the company produce documents for inspection and copying. However, documents relating to an appeal need not be produced and the company may appeal against a notice requiring documents to be produced.

If HMRC demand documents, but the company does not produce them, there is a penalty of £50. There is also a daily penalty, which applies for each day from the day after the imposition of the £50 penalty until the documents are produced. The daily penalty may be imposed by HMRC, in which case it is £30. If, however, HMRC ask the Commissioners to impose the penalty, it is £150.

HMRC may amend a self-assessment at any time during an enquiry if they believe there might otherwise be a loss of tax. The company may appeal against such an amendment within 30 days. The company may itself make amendments during an enquiry under the normal rules for amendments. No effect will be given to such amendments during the enquiry but they may be taken into account in the enquiry.

An enquiry ends when HMRC give notice that it has been completed and notify what they believe to be the correct amount of tax payable. Before that time, the company may ask the Commissioners to order HMRC to notify the completion of its enquiry by a specified date. Such a direction will be given unless HMRC can demonstrate that they have reasonable grounds for continuing the enquiry.

The company has 30 days from the end of an enquiry to amend its self assessment in accordance with HMRC's conclusions. If HMRC are not satisfied with the company's amendments, they have a further 30 days to amend the self-assessment. The company then has another 30 days in which it may appeal against HMRC's amendments.

1.5 Determinations and discovery assessments

If a return is not delivered by the filing date, HMRC may **issue a determination of the tax payable** within the five years from the filing date. This is **treated as a self-assessment** and there is no appeal against it. However, it is automatically replaced by any self assessment made by the company by the later of five years from the filing date and 12 months from the determination.

If HMRC believe that not enough tax has been assessed for an accounting period they can make a discovery assessment to collect the extra tax. However, when a tax return has been delivered this power is limited as outlined below.

No discovery assessment can be made on account of an error or mistake as to the basis on which the tax liability ought to be computed, if the basis generally prevailing at the time when the return was made was applied.

A discovery assessment can only be made if either:

(a) The loss of tax is due to fraudulent or negligent conduct by the company or by someone acting on its behalf or

(b) HMRC could not reasonably be expected to have been aware of the loss of tax, given the information so far supplied to them, when their right to start an enquiry expired or when they notified the company that an enquiry had finished. The information supplied must be sufficiently detailed to draw HMRC's attention to contentious matters such as the use of a valuation or estimate.

The time limit for raising a discovery assessment is six years from the end of the accounting period but this is extended to 21 years if there has been fraudulent or negligent conduct. The company may appeal against a discovery assessment within 30 days of issue.

1.6 Claims

Wherever possible claims must be made on a tax return or on an amendment to it and must be quantified at the time the return is made.

If a company believes that it has paid excessive tax because of an error in a return, an error or mistake claim may be made within six years from the end of the accounting period. An appeal against a decision on such a claim must be made within 30 days. An error or mistake claim may not be made if the return was made in accordance with a generally accepted practice which prevailed at the time.

Other claims must be made by six years after the end of the accounting period, unless a different time limit is specified. These time limits are mentioned, where relevant, throughout this text.

If an error or mistake is made in a claim, a supplementary claim may be made within the time limit for the original claim.

If HMRC amend a self-assessment or issue a discovery assessment then the company has a further period to make, vary or withdraw a claim (unless the claim is irrevocable) even if this is outside the normal time limit. The period is one year from the end of the accounting period in which the amendment or assessment was made, or one year from the end of the accounting period in which the enquiry was closed if the amendment is the result of an enquiry. The relief is limited where there has been fraudulent or negligent conduct by the company or its agent.

2 PAYMENT OF CORPORATION TAX AND INTEREST

2.1 Due dates

Corporation tax is due for payment by small and medium sized companies **nine months after the end of the accounting period**.

Large companies, however, must pay their corporation tax in instalments. **Broadly, a large company is any company that pays corporation tax at the full rate** (profits exceed £1,500,000 in a 12-month period where there are no associated companies).

Instalments are due on the 14th day of the month, starting in the seventh month. Provided that the accounting period is 12 months long subsequent instalments are due in the tenth month during the accounting period and in the first and fourth months after the end of the accounting period.

If an accounting period is less than 12 months long subsequent instalments are due at three monthly intervals but with the final payment being due in the fourth month of the next accounting period.

EXAMPLE: QUARTERLY INSTALMENTS

X Ltd is a large company with a 31 December accounting year end. Instalments of corporation tax will be due to be paid by X Ltd on:

- 14 July and 14 October in the accounting period
- 14 January and 14 April after the accounting period ends

So for the year ended 31 December 2007 instalment payments are due on 14 July 2007, 14 October 2007, 14 January 2008 and 14 April 2008.

Instalments are based on the estimated corporation tax liability for the current period (not the previous period). It will be extremely important for companies to forecast their tax liabilities accurately. Large companies whose directors are poor at estimating may find their company's incurring significant interest charges. The amount of each instalment is computed by:

(a) Working out $3 \times CT/n$ where CT is the amount of the estimated corporation tax liability payable in instalments for the period and n is the number of months in the period

(b) Allocating the smaller of that amount and the total estimated corporation tax liability to the first instalment

(c) Repeating the process for later instalments until the amount allocated is equal to the corporation tax liability. This gives four equal instalments for 12-month accounting periods and also caters for periods which end earlier than expected.

The company is therefore required to estimate its corporation tax liability before the end of the accounting period, and must revise its estimate each quarter.

Activity 2 **(10 minutes)**

A large company has a CT liability of £880,000 for the eight month period to 30 September 2007. Accounts had previously always been prepared to 31 January. Show when the CT liability is due for payment.

A company is not required to pay instalments in the first year that it is 'large', unless its profits exceed £10 million. The £10 million limit is reduced proportionately if there are associated companies. For this purpose only, a company will be regarded as an associated company where it was an associated company at the **start** of an accounting period. (This differs from the normal approach where being an associated company for any part of the AP affects the CT thresholds of both companies for the whole of the AP.)

Any company whose liability does not exceed £10,000 need not pay by instalments.

Interest runs from the due date on over/underpaid instalments. The position is looked at cumulatively after the due date for each instalment. HMRC calculate the interest position after the company submits its corporation tax return.

Chapter roundup

- A company must notify HMRC within three months of starting to trade.
- CT 600 returns must usually be filled within 12 months of the end of the accounting period.
- HMRC can enquire into returns.
- Large companies pay their corporation tax in four quarterly instalments. Other companies pay their tax nine months after the end of an accounting period.

Quick quiz

1 Youngs Ltd makes up a 12-month set of accounts to 31 December 2007. When must the company file its CT return based on these accounts?

2 What are the fixed penalties for failure to deliver a corporation tax return on time?

3 When must HMRC give notice that they are going to start an enquiry if a return was filed on time?

4 Which companies must pay quarterly instalments of their corporation tax liability?

5 State the due dates for the payment of quarterly instalments of corporation tax for a 12-month accounting period.

6 Freeman Ltd changes its accounting date and makes up accounts for the eight months to 31 December 2007. The company is large and is due to pay tax by instalments. Outline when the tax is due.

7 In question 6 if the CT liability is £1,000,000 for the eight-month period what amount is due at each date?

Answers to quick quiz

1 By 31 December 2008. (see para 1.2)

2 There is a £100 penalty for failure to submit a return on time rising to £200 if the delay exceeds three months. These penalties increased to £500 and £1,000 respectively when a return was late for each of the preceding two accounting periods. (para 1.2)

3 Notice must be given by one year after the filing date. (para 1.4)

4 'Large' companies ie: companies that pay corporation tax at the full rate. (para 2.1)

5 14th day of:

(a) 7th month in AP
(b) 10th month in AP
(c) 1st month after AP ends
(d) 4th month after AP ends (para 2.1)

6 Due dates are:

14 November 2007
14 February 2008
14 April 2008 (para 2.1)

7 £375,000, £375,000 and finally £250,000. (para 2.1)

Answers to activities

1 The company must file a return for the two accounting periods ending in the period specified in the notice requiring a return. The first accounting period is the 12 months to 31 December 2006 and the second is the six months to 30 June 2007. The filing date is 12 months after the end of the relevant period of account, 30 June 2008.

2 £880,000 must be paid in instalments.

The amount of each instalment is $3 \times \frac{£880,000}{8} = £330,000$

The due dates are:

	£
14 August 2007	330,000
14 November 2007	330,000
14 January 2008	220,000 (balance)

Chapter 39 : CAPITAL GAINS TAX

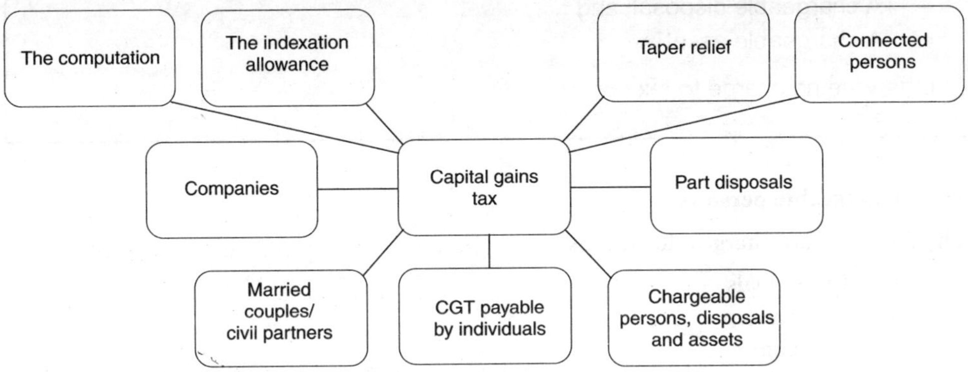

Introduction

Individuals, companies and partnerships are all liable to capital gains tax, which is effectively a tax on the profits made by virtue of selling an asset. There are many exemptions, however; for example, CGT is not payable on the sale of one's only or major home. As with other taxes there are reliefs for losses. This chapter gives you an overview of the basic principles of capital gains tax.

Your objectives

In this chapter you will learn about the following.

(a) Chargeable persons, chargeable disposals and chargeable assets

(b) The key elements of a personal capital gains tax computation

(c) The allocation of the tax bands between income tax (savings and non-savings income) and capital gains tax

(d) The relief for losses

(e) Taper relief for individuals

(f) The circumstances when market value is the transfer value

(g) How to compute the indexation allowance and taper relief

(h) The basis of 'no gain no loss' transfers

(i) Computations of gains and losses

(j) How to compute the gain on an asset only part disposed of

NOTES

1 CHARGEABLE PERSONS, DISPOSALS AND ASSETS

Definition

For a **chargeable gain** to arise there must be:

- A chargeable person; and
- A chargeable disposal; and
- A chargeable asset

otherwise no charge to tax occurs.

1.1 Chargeable persons

The following are chargeable persons.

- Individuals
- Partnership
- Companies

1.2 Chargeable disposals

The following are chargeable disposals.

- Sales of assets or parts of assets
- Gifts of assets or parts of assets
- The loss or destruction of assets

A chargeable disposal occurs on the date of the contract (where there is one, whether written or oral), or the date of a conditional contract becoming unconditional. This may differ from the date of transfer of the asset. However, when a capital sum is received for example on the loss or destruction of an asset, the disposal takes place on the day the sum is received.

Where a disposal involves an acquisition by someone else, the date of acquisition for that person is the same as the date of disposal.

Transfers of assets on death are exempt disposals.

1.3 Chargeable assets

All forms of property, wherever in the world they are situated, are chargeable assets unless they are specifically designated as exempt.

1.4 Exempt assets

The following are exempt assets.

- **Motor vehicles** suitable for private use
- **National Savings and Investments certificates** and **premium bonds**
- Foreign currency for private use
- Decorations for bravery where awarded, not purchased
- Damages for personal or professional injury
- **Gilt-edged securities (treasury stock)**

NOTES

- **Qualifying corporate bonds (QCBs)**
- **Certain chattels**
- Debts (except debts on a security)
- Investments held in individual savings accounts

If an asset is an exempt asset any gain is not taxable and any loss is not allowable.

2 THE ANNUAL EXEMPTION

There is an annual exemption for each tax year. For each individual for 2007/08 it is £9,200. The annual exemption is deducted from the chargeable gains for the year after the deductions of losses and other reliefs.

Thus if Susie has chargeable gains for 2007/08 of £15,000 her taxable gains are £15,000 – £9,200 = £5,800.

Companies are not entitled to the annual exemption.

3 CAPITAL LOSSES

3.1 Calculation of losses

Losses are, in general, calculated in the same way as gains.

The indexation allowance (see next chapter) **cannot create or increase an allowable loss.** If there is a gain before the indexation allowance, the allowance can reduce that gain to zero, but no further. If there is a loss before the indexation allowance, there is no indexation allowance. (A gain remaining after the indexation allowance is called an **indexed gain.**)

3.2 Allowable losses of the same year

Allowable capital losses arising in a tax year are deducted from indexed gains arising in the same tax year.

Any loss which cannot be set off is carried forward to set against future indexed gains. Losses must be used as soon as possible (see below).

Losses are offset against gains before taper relief (see below).

3.3 Allowable losses brought forward

Allowable losses brought forward are only set off to reduce current year gains less current year allowable losses to the annual exempt amount. No set-off is made if net chargeable gains for the current year do not exceed the annual exempt amount.

Losses are offset against gains before taper relief (see below).

BPP LEARNING MEDIA

NOTES

EXAMPLES

(a) George has gains for 2007/08 of £10,000 and allowable losses of £6,000. As the losses are *current year losses* they must be fully relieved against the £10,000 of gains to produce net gains before taper relief of £4,000, despite the fact that net gains are below the annual exemption.

(b) Bob has gains of £13,100 for 2007/08 and allowable losses brought forward of £6,000. Bob restricts his loss relief to £3,900 so as to leave net gains before taper relief of £(13,100 – 3,900) = £9,200, which will be exactly covered by his annual exemption for 2007/08. The remaining £2,100 of losses will be carried forward to 2008/09.

(c) Tom has gains of £5,000 for 2007/08 and losses brought forward from 2006/07 of £4,000. He will leapfrog 2007/08 and carry forward all of his losses to 2008/09. His gains of £5,000 are covered by his annual exemption for 2007/08.

3.4 Capital losses for companies

Companies are not eligible for taper relief and do not have an annual exemption. Losses of the current accounting period must be deducted from the gains of the current accounting period. Excess losses are carried forward and deducted from net gains in future accounting periods (see later in this Course Book).

4 TAPER RELIEF

4.1 Rates of relief

Taper relief may be available to reduce gains realised after 5 April 1998 by individuals. Taper relief does not apply to companies.

Taper relief reduces the percentage of the gain chargeable according to how many complete years the asset has been held since acquisition or 6 April 1998 if later. Taper relief is more generous for business assets than for non-business assets.

The percentages of gains which remain chargeable after taper relief are set out below.

Number of complete years after 5.4.98 for which asset held	*Gain on business assets % of gain chargeable*	*Gain on non business assets % of gain chargeable*
0	100	100
1	50	100
2	25	100
3	25	95
4	25	90
5	25	85
6	25	80
7	25	75
8	25	70
9	25	65
10	25	60

Non-business assets acquired before 17 March 1998 qualify for an additional one year (a 'bonus year') of taper relief. For disposals of non-business assets during 2007/08, taper relief will be based on ten complete years of ownership where the asset was owned prior to 17 March 1998. Only 60% of the gain will be chargeable.

EXAMPLE

Peter buys a non-business asset on 1 January 1998 and sells it on 1 July 2007. For taper relief purposes Peter is treated as if he had held the asset for ten complete years (nine complete years after 5 April 1998 plus one additional year).

If the asset had been a business asset, Peter holds the asset for nine years only but in any case has maximum taper relief after two years ownership.

4.2 Application of taper relief

Taper relief is applied to net gains after the deduction of current year and brought forward losses to give chargeable gains for the year.

The annual exemption is then deducted from the chargeable gains to give the taxable gains.

Definitions

Chargeable gain: The capital gain after deducting the indexation allowance and taper relief, but before deducting the annual exemption.

Taxable gain: The chargeable gain less the annual exemption.

EXAMPLE

Ruby sold a business asset in July 2007 which she had purchased in January 2006. She realised a gain (before taper relief) of £18,400. She also sold a painting in 2007/08 realising an allowable loss of £6,000. She has a capital loss brought forward from 2006/07 of £10,000.

Losses are dealt with **before** taper relief. However losses brought forward are only deducted from net current gains to the extent that the gains exceed the CGT annual exemption:

	£
Gain	18,400
Loss	(6,000)
Current net gains	12,400
Less brought forward loss	(3,200)
Net gains before taper relief	9,200
Chargeable gains (after taper relief) (1 year ownership) £9,200 × 50%	4,600
Less annual exemption	(9,200)
Taxable gains	Nil

Note that the benefit of the taper relief is effectively wasted since the brought forward loss reduces the gain down to the annual exemption amount but taper is then applied to that amount reducing it further.

The loss carried forward is £6,800 (£10,000 – £3,200).

Allocate losses to gains in the way that produces the lowest tax charge. **Losses should therefore be deducted from the gains attracting the lowest rate of taper** (ie where the highest percentage of the gain remains chargeable).

EXAMPLE

Alastair made the following capital losses and gains in 2007/08:

	£
Loss	10,000
Gains (before taper relief)	
Asset A (non-business asset)	25,000
Asset B (business asset)	18,000

Asset A was purchased in December 1997 and sold in January 2008. Taper relief reduces the gain to 60% of the original gain (10 years including additional year; non-business asset). Asset B was purchased on 5 November 2004 and sold on 17 December 2007. Taper relief reduces the gain to 25% of the original gain (3 years; business asset).

NOTES

The best use of the loss is to offset it against the gain on the non-business asset, as shown.

	£	£
Gain – Asset A	25,000	
Less loss	(10,000)	
Net gain before taper relief	15,000	
Gain after taper relief (£15,000 × 60%)		9,000
Gain – Asset B	18,000	
Gain after taper relief £18,000 × 25%		4,500
Chargeable gains		13,500
Less annual exemption		(9,200)
Taxable gains		4,300

4.3 Business assets

A business asset is:

(a) An asset **used for the purposes of a trade** carried on by any individual or partnership (whether or not the owner of the asset is involved in carrying on the trade concerned) or by a qualifying company.

(b) An asset **held for the purposes of any office or employment** held by the individual owner with a person carrying on a trade.

(c) **Shares in a qualifying company** held by an individual.

A **trading company** (or holding company of a trading group) is a qualifying company if:

(a) It is **not listed** on a recognised stock exchange nor a 51% subsidiary of a listed company (companies listed on the Alternative Investment Market (AIM) are unlisted for this purpose), or

(b) The individual shareholder is an **officer or employee** of the company, or

(c) The individual holds at least **5% of the voting rights** in the company.

A **non-trading company** (or holding company of a non-trading group) is also a qualifying company if:

(a) The individual is an **officer or employee** of the company, and

(b) The individual did not have a **material interest** in the company or in any other company which at that time had control of the company.

A **material interest** is defined as possession or the ability to control more than 10% of the issued shares or voting in the company, or an entitlement to more than 10% of the income or the assets of the company available for distribution. It is necessary to look at the combined rights of the individual and of any person connected with him.

A taxpayer is broadly **connected** with his own or his spouse's/civil partner's close relatives and their spouses/civil partners and with his business partners (and their spouses/civil partners). A company is connected with the persons controlling them and with other companies under the same control.

4.4 Miscellaneous points

There are certain special situations which will affect the operation of taper relief and will be covered later in this Course Book.

(a) Where there has been a transfer of assets between spouses or civil partners (a no loss/no gain transfer) the taper on a subsequent disposal will be based on the combined period of holding by the spouses or civil partners

(b) Where gains have been relieved under a provision which reduces the cost of the asset in the hands of a new owner (such as gift relief) the taper will operate by reference to the holding period of the new owner.

5 CGT PAYABLE BY INDIVIDUALS

Taxable gains are chargeable to capital gains tax as if the gains were an extra slice of savings income for the year of assessment concerned. This means that CGT may be due at 10%, 20% or 40%.

The rate bands are used first to cover income and then gains. If a gift aid payment and/or personal pension contribution is made, the basic rate can be extended, as for income tax calculations (see earlier).

Activity 1 **(15 minutes)**

In 2007/08, Carol, a single woman, has the following income, gains and losses.

	£
Salary	37,540
Chargeable gain (not eligible for taper relief)	27,100
Allowable capital losses	7,700

Calculate the CGT payable

6 COMPUTING A GAIN OR LOSS

6.1 Basic calculation

An indexed gain (or an allowable loss) is generally calculated as follows.

	£
Disposal consideration	45,000
Less incidental costs of disposal	(400)
Net proceeds	44,600
Less allowable costs	(21,000)
Unindexed gain	23,600
Less indexation allowance (if available)	(8,800)
Indexed gain	14,800

For individuals, taper relief may then apply (see earlier in this Course Book).

NOTES

Usually the disposal consideration is the proceeds of sale of the asset, but a disposal is deemed to take place at market value where the disposal is:

- **Not a bargain at arm's length**
- Made for a **consideration which cannot be valued**
- By way of a **gift**.

Special valuation rules apply for shares (see later in this Course Book).

Incidental costs of disposal may include:

- Valuation fees
- Estate agency fees
- Advertising costs
- Legal costs

These costs should be deducted separately from any other allowable costs (because they do not qualify for any indexation allowance if it is available on that disposal).

Allowable costs include:

- The original cost of acquisition
- Incidental costs of acquisition
- Capital expenditure incurred in enhancing the asset

Incidental costs of acquisition may include the types of cost listed above as incidental costs of disposal, but acquisition costs do qualify for indexation allowance (from the month of acquisition) if it is available on the disposal.

Enhancement expenditure is capital expenditure which enhances the value of the asset and is reflected in the state or nature of the asset at the time of disposal, or expenditure incurred in establishing, preserving or defending title to, or a right over, the asset. Excluded from this category are:

- Costs of repairs and maintenance
- Costs of insurance
- Any expenditure deductible from trading profits
- Any expenditure met by public funds (for example, council grants)

Enhancement expenditure may qualify for indexation allowance from the month in which it becomes due and payable. Taper relief, however, will apply to the whole gain from April 1998 or the date of acquisition, if later, regardless of the date of the enhancement expenditure.

Activity 2 **(10 minutes)**

Joanne bought a piece of land as an investment on 1 October 2005 for £20,000. The legal costs of purchase were £250.

Joanne sold the land on 12 December 207 for £35,000. She incurred estate agency fees of £700 and legal costs of £500 on the sale.

Calculate Joanne's gain on sale.

BPP LEARNING MEDIA

7 THE INDEXATION ALLOWANCE

The purpose of having an indexation allowance is to remove the inflationary element of a gain from taxation. It is calculated by reference to the movement in the Retail Prices Index (RPI).

Individuals are entitled to an indexation allowance from the date of acquisition of an asset until April 1998. From April 1998 the indexation allowance has been replaced by taper relief.

The indexation factor is multiplied by the cost of the asset to calculate the indexation allowance. If the RPI has fallen, the indexation allowance is zero: it is not negative.

Activity 3 **(20 minutes)**

Tracey acquired an asset on 15 February 1983 at a cost of £5,000. Enhancement expenditure of £2,000 was incurred on 10 April 1984. The asset is sold for £25,500 on 20 December 2007/ Incident costs of sale are £500. The indexation factor from February 1983 to April 1998 is 0.949 and from April 1984 to April 1998 to 0.835. The indexation factor from February 1983 to December 2007 is 1.532 and from April 1984 to December 2007 is 1.370.

Calculate the indexed arising.

The indexation allowance cannot create or increase an allowable loss. If there is a gain before the indexation allowance, the allowance can reduce that gain to zero, but no further. If there is a loss before the indexation allowance, there is no indexation allowance.

8 TRANSFERS BETWEEN SPOUSES/CIVIL PARTNERS

Spouses and civil partners are taxed as separate individuals. Each has his own annual exemption, and losses of one spouse or civil partner cannot be set against gains of the other spouse or civil partner.

Disposals between spouses or civil partners living together give rise to no gain no loss, whatever actual price (if any) was charged by the transferor. This means that there is no chargeable gain or allowable loss, and the transferee takes over the transferor's indexed cost.

For taper relief purposes disposals by the transferee will be based on the combined period of ownership. For assets other than shares, business use by the transferor will be treated as business use by the transferee. Shares will only be treated as business assets whilst the company is a qualifying company for the transferee.

9 PART DISPOSALS

The disposal of part of a chargeable asset is a chargeable event. The chargeable gain (or allowable loss) is computed by deducting a fraction of the original cost of the whole asset from the disposal value. The balance of the cost is carried forward until the eventual disposal of the asset.

The fraction is:

$$\text{Cost} \times \frac{A}{A+B} = \frac{\text{value of the part disposed of}}{\text{value of the part disposed of} + \text{market value of the remainder}}$$

In this fraction, A is the proceeds *before* deducting incidental costs of disposal.

The part disposal fraction should not be applied indiscriminately. Any expenditure incurred wholly in respect of a particular part of an asset should be treated as an allowable deduction in full for that part and not apportioned. An example of this is incidental selling expenses, which are wholly attributable to the part disposed of.

EXAMPLE

Mr Heal owns a painting which originally cost him £27,000 in March 1984 and had an indexed cost at April 1998 of £50,166. He sold a quarter interest in the painting in July 2007 for £18,000. The market value of the three-quarter share remaining is estimated to be £36,000. What is the chargeable gain after taper relief?

The amount of the indexed cost attributable to the part sold is

$$\frac{18{,}000}{18{,}000+36{,}000} \times £50{,}166 = £16{,}722$$

	£
Proceeds	18,000
Less indexed cost (see above)	(16,722)
Gain before taper relief	1,278

Gain after taper relief (6.4.98 – 5.4.07 = 9 years plus additional year = 10 years)

60% × £1,278 = £767

---

10 COMPANIES

Companies do not pay capital gains tax. Instead their chargeable gains are included in the profits chargeable to corporation tax. A company's capital gains or allowable losses are computed in a similar way to individuals but with a few major differences:

- Indexation allowance continues after 6 April 1998
- Taper relief does not apply
- No annual exemption is available
- The FA 1985 pool for shares does not stop at 5 April 1998 and different matching rules for shared apply if the shareholder is a company.

Companies are entitled to indexation allowance from the date of acquisition until the date of disposal of an asset.

For example, if J Ltd bought a painting on 2 January 1987 and sold it on 19 November 2007 the indexation allowance is available from January 1987 until November 2007, not just until April 1998.

The indexation factor is:

$$\frac{\text{RPI for month of disposal} - \text{RPI for month of acquisition}}{\text{RPI for month of acquisition}}$$

The calculation is expressed as a decimal and is rounded to three decimal places.

An asset is acquired by a company on 15 February 1983 (RPI = 83.0) at a cost of £5,000. Enhancement expenditure of £2,000 is incurred on 10 April 1984 (RPI = 88.6). The asset is sold for £25,000 on 20 December 2007 (RPI = 210.1). Incidental costs of sale are £500. Calculate the chargeable gain arising.

The indexation allowance is available until December 2007 and is computed as follows.

	£
$\frac{210.1 - 83.0}{83.0} = 1.531 \times £5,000$	7,655
$\frac{210.1 - 88.6}{88.6} = 1.371 \times £2,000$	2,742
	10,397

The computation of the chargeable gain is as follows.

	£
Proceeds	25,500
Less incidental costs of sale	(500)
Net proceeds	25,000
Less allowable costs	(7,000)
Unindexed gain	18,000
Less indexation allowance (see above)	(10,397)
Chargeable gain	7,603

Chapter roundup

- A gain is chargeable if there is a chargeable disposal of a chargeable asset by a chargeable person.
- Capital gains are chargeable on individuals and companies.
- CGT applies primarily to persons resident or ordinarily resident in the UK.
- An individual is entitled to an annual exemption for each tax year.
- Losses are set off against gains of the same year (or accounting period) and any excess carried forward. Losses of individuals are set off before taper relief. For individuals, brought forward losses are only set off to reduce net gains down to the amount of the annual exemption.
- Individuals are also entitled to taper relief, depending on the length of ownership of the asset. There is more generous taper relief for business assets than non-business assets.
- Individuals pay CGT on gains arising in a tax year at 10%, 20% or 40%.
- An indexed gain is computed by taking the proceeds and deducting both the cost and the indexation allowance. Incidental costs of acquisition and disposal may be deducted together with any enhancement expenditure reflected in the state and nature of the asset at the date of disposal.
- The indexation allowance gives relief to the inflationary element of a gain but, for individuals, is only available up to April 1998.
- Disposals between spouses or members of a civil partnership are made on a no gain no loss basis and do not give rise to a chargeable gain or allowable loss.
- On a part of disposal, the cost must be apportioned between the part disposed or and the part retained.

Quick quiz

1 Give some examples of chargeable disposals.

2 To what extent must allowable losses be set against chargeable gains?

3 Mike owned a business asset for two and a half years. His gain on sale is £20,000. What is his gain after taper relief?

4 At what rate or rates do individuals pay CGT?

5 What is enhancement expenditure?

6 10 acres of land are sold for £15,000 out of 25 acres. Original cost in 1999 was £9,000. Costs of sales are £2,000. Rest of land valued at £30,000. What is the total amount deductible from proceeds?

Answers to quick quiz

1 The following are chargeable disposals.

- Sales of assets or parts of assets
- Gifts of assets or parts of assets
- Receipts of capital sums following the loss or destruction of an asset (see para 1.2)

2 Current year losses must be set off against gains in full, even if this reduces net gains below the annual exemption. Losses brought forward are set off to bring down untapered gains to the level of the annual exemption. (para 3)

3 Two complete years' ownership

25% × £20,000 = £5,000 (para 4)

4 10% (gains within starting rate band), 20% (gains within basic rate band) or 40%. (para 5)

5 Enhancement expenditure is capital expenditure enhancing the value of the asset and reflected in the state/nature of the asset at disposal, or expenditure incurred in establishing, preserving or defending title to asset. (para 6.1)

6 $\frac{15,000}{15,000 + 30,000} \times$ £9,000 = £3,000 + £2,000 (costs of disposal) = £5,000 (para 9)

Answers to activities

1 (a) Carol's taxable income is as follows.

	£
Salary	37,540
Less personal allowance	(5,225)
Taxable income	32,315

(b) The gains to be taxed are as follows.

	£
Gains	27,100
Less losses	(7,700)
	19,400
Less annual exemption	(9,200)
Taxable gains	10,200

(c) The tax bands are allocated as follows.

	Total	*Income*	*Gains*
Starting rate	2,230	2,230	0
Basic rate	32,370	30,085	2,285
Higher rate	7,915	0	7,915
		32,315	10,200

(d) The CGT payable is as follows.

	£
£2,285 × 20%	457
£7,915 × 40%	3,166
Total CGT payable	3,623

NOTES

2

	£
Proceeds of sale	35,000
Less costs of disposal £(700 + 500)	(1,200)
	33,800
Less costs of acquisition £(20,000 + 250)	(20,250)
Gain	13,550

3 The indexation allowance is available until April 1998 and is computed as follows.

	£
0.949 × £5,000	4,745
0.835 × £2,000	1,670
	6,415

The computation of the indexed gain is as follows.

	£
Proceeds	25,500
Less incidental costs of sale	(500)
Net proceeds	25,000
Less allowable costs £(5,000 + 2,000)	(7,000)
Unindexed gain	18,000
Less indexation allowance (see above)	(6,415)
Indexed gain	11,585

TAX RATES AND ALLOWANCES

TAX RATES AND ALLOWANCES (FINANCE ACT 2007)

A INCOME TAX

1 *Rates*

	2006/07		*2007/08*	
	£	%	£	%
Starting rate	1–2,150	10	1–2,230	10
Basic rate	2,151–33,300	22	2,231–34,600	22
Higher rate	33,301 and above	40	34,601 and above	40

Savings (excl. Dividend) income is taxed at 20% if it falls in the basic rate band. Dividend income in both the starting rate and the basic rate bands is taxed at 10%. Dividend income within the higher rate band is taxed at 32.5%.

2 *Personal allowance*

	2006/07	*2007/08*
	£	£
Personal allowance	5,035	5,225

3 *Cars – taxable percentage 2007/08*

The taxable percentage is 15% for petrol engined cars with a baseline CO_2 emissions figure of 140g/km or less.

4 *Car fuel charge – 2007/08*

Set figure £14,400

5 *Authorised mileage rates (AMR) 2007/08 rates*

The rates for the maximum tax free mileage allowances for 2007/08 are as follows:

*Car mileage rates**

First 10,000 miles	40p per mile
Over 10,000 miles	25p per mile

Bicycles	*Motor cycles*
20p per mile	24p per mile
Passenger payments	5p per mile

* For NIC purposes, a rate of 40p applies irrespective of mileage.

6 *Capital allowances*

	%
Plant and machinery	
Writing-down allowance*	25
First year allowance	50
Small sized business first year allowance (acquisitions 6.4.06 – 5.4.08)	50
First year allowance (energy/water saving equipment, low emission car)	100
Industrial buildings allowance	
Writing-down allowance:	4

* 6% reducing balance for certain long-life assets.

B CORPORATION TAX

1 *Rates*

Financial year	*2006*	*2007*
Small companies rate	19%	20%
Full rate	30%	30%
	£	£
Lower limit	300,000	300,000
Upper limit	1,500,000	1,500,000
Taper relief fraction		
Small companies rate	11/400	1/40

2 *Marginal relief*

(M – P) × I/P × Marginal relief fraction

C RATES OF INTEREST

Official rate of interest: 5% (assumed)

Rate of interest on unpaid tax: 6.5% (assumed)

Rate of interest on overpaid tax: 2.5% (assumed)

D CAPITAL GAINS TAX

1 *Annual exemption (individuals)*

	£
2006/07	8,800
2007/08	9,200

2 *Taper relief: Disposals after 6 April 2002*

Complete years after 5.4.98 for which asset held	*Gains on business assets*	*Gains on non business assets*
1	50	100
2	25	100
3	25	95
4	25	90
5	25	85
6	25	80
7	25	75
8	25	70
9	25	65
10 and over	25	60

APPENDIX

Edexcel Guidelines for the HND/HNC Qualification in Business

This book is designed to be of value to anyone who is studying Finance, whether as a subject in its own right or as a module forming part of any business-related degree or diploma.

However, it provides complete coverage of the topics listed in the Edexcel Guidelines for specialist Units 9 to 12. We include the Edexcel Guidelines here for your reference, mapped to the topics covered in this book.

EDEXCEL GUIDELINES FOR UNIT 9 MANAGEMENT ACCOUNTING

Description of the Unit

In this Unit learners will consider cost information both current and future. Cost data will be collected, compiled and analysed, and will be processed into information of use to management. The unit goes on to deal with budgetary planning and control, preparing forecasts and budgets and then comparing them to actual results. Learners will consider different costing and budgetary systems and will discuss the cause of resulting variances.

Summary of learning outcomes

To achieve this unit a learner must:

1 Collect and analyse **cost information** within a business

2 Propose methods to **reduce costs and enhance value** within a business

3 Prepare **forecasts and budgets** for a business

4 Monitor **performance against budgets** within a business

Content

		Chapter coverage
1	**Cost information**	
	Types of costs and classification: materials, labour, overheads, direct and indirect, fixed, variable and semi-variable	1
	Costing methods: job costing, batch costing, process costing, contract costing, service costing	6, 7
	Cost measurement: absorption and marginal costing, traditional overhead absorption and activity-based costing, stock valuation methods (FIFO, LIFO, AVCO, standard costing)	2, 3, 4
	Costing as basis for pricing and stock valuation: cost plus pricing, market pricing, target costing	5
	Data collection and analysis: sampling methods and purpose, presentation of data eg tabular, diagrammatical, graphical, index numbers	See note below
2	**Reduce costs and enhance value**	
	Cost reports: preparation, comparison with other data, explanation of implications	10
	Performance indicators: monitor and assess to identify potential improvements	10
	Quality and value: definitions and interactions, added value, total quality management	5, 10

		Chapter coverage
3	**Forecasts and budgets**	
	The budgeting process: purpose, benefits, links with organisational objectives/strategy, the budget manual, budgets as planning, co-ordinating, motivation and control devices	8
	Budget preparation: limiting or key factors, master, subsidiary and functional budgets, cash budgets, the preparation of sales budgets, debtors' budgets, creditors' budgets, production cost, raw materials and finished goods budgets	8
	Budgeting methods: incremental, zero-based, fixed and flexible	8
	Behavioural consequences of budgets: padding the budget, spending to budget, creative budgets	8
4	**Performance against budgets**	
	Variances: types, analysis, calculation, possible causes, corrective action	9
	Reporting: operating statement, reconciliation of budgeted and actual results	9
	Responsibility centres: relevance to budgeting, identification of responsibility for variances	10

Note. The topics listed under the heading Data collection and analysis in Section 1, Cost Information, are also covered in Mandatory Unit 6, Business Decision Making. You should refer back to your work for that unit to revise these areas.

Outcomes and assessment criteria

The learning outcomes and the criteria used to assess them are shown in the table below.

Outcomes	Assessment criteria To achieve each outcome a learner must demonstrate the ability to:
1 Collect and analyse **cost information** within a business	• identify and classify different types of cost • explain the need for, and operation of, different costing methods • calculate costs using appropriate techniques • collect, analyse and present data using appropriate techniques
2 Propose methods to **reduce costs and enhance value** within a business	• prepare and analyse cost reports • calculate and evaluate indicators of productivity, efficiency and effectiveness • explain the principles of quality and value, and identify potential improvements
3 Prepare **forecasts and budgets** for a business	• explain the nature and purpose of the budgeting process • select appropriate budgeting methods for the organisation and its needs • prepare budgets according to the chosen budgeting method • prepare a cash budget
4 Monitor **performance against budgets** within a business	• calculate variances, identify possible causes and recommend corrective action • prepare an operating statement reconciling budgeted and actual results • report findings to management in accordance with identified responsibility centres

EDEXCEL GUIDELINES FOR UNIT 10 FINANCIAL REPORTING

Description of the Unit

In this Unit learners will discover how to prepare financial statements for different types of business taking into account the relevant legal and regulatory provisions. Included will be the basic principles of group accounts. Learners will also develop tools for the interpretation of financial statements.

Summary of learning outcomes

To achieve this unit a learner must:

1 Explain the **legal and regulatory framework** for financial reporting

2 Prepare **financial statements** from complete or incomplete records

3 Present financial reports in accepted **formats for publication**

4 **Interpret financial statements**

Content

		Chapter coverage
1	**Regulatory framework**	
	User groups: owners, management, employees, suppliers, customers lenders, government, potential investors, different needs from financial statements	11
	User needs: profitability, liquidity, gearing, cash flow, job security, ASB's statement of principles, IASB's framework for the presentation of financial statements	11
	Legislation: Companies Act 1985 and 1989, Partnership Act 1890, European directives	
	Other regulations: Statements of Standard Accounting Practice (SSAPs) and Financial Reporting Standards (FRSs), the Accounting Standards Board (ASB), International Accounting Standards (IASs)	11
2	**Financial statements**	
	Statements: trial balance, assets, liabilities, income, expenses, capital, profit and loss accounts, balance sheet, cash-flow statement, notes to the accounts, statement of recognised gains and losses	12, 20
	Types of business: sole trader, partnership, limited company (public and private), manufacturing/service/retail, group of companies	18, 21
	Preparation: from trial balance with adjustments eg stock, prepayments, accruals, bad debts, depreciation, from incomplete records, basic consolidation of accounts	15, 16, 17, 18

		Chapter coverage
3	**Formats for publication**	
	Types of business: different formats for organisations described in Outcome 2 above; annual report	18, 21
	Formats: requirements of law and generally accepted accounting practice	18, 21
4	**Interpret financial statements**	
	Ratios: calculate ratios to reflect profitability, liquidity, efficiency, gearing, investment; comparison of these ratios both externally (other companies, industry standards) and internally (previous periods), interpretation of results	22
	Reporting: present findings in a format appropriate to users, weaknesses and limitations of analysis	22

Outcomes and assessment criteria

The learning outcomes and the criteria used to assess them are shown in the table below.

Outcomes	Assessment criteria To achieve each outcome a learner must demonstrate the ability to:
1 Explain the **legal and regulatory framework** for financial reporting	• describe the different users of financial statements and their needs • explain the legal and regulatory influences on financial statements • assess the implications for users • describe how different policies are dealt with by accounting and reporting standards
2 Prepare **financial statements** from complete or incomplete records	• prepare financial statements for a variety of businesses from a trial balance, making appropriate adjustments • prepare financial statements from incomplete records • prepare a consolidated balance sheet and profit and loss account for a simple group of companies
3 Present financial reports in accepted **formats for publication**	• explain how the information needs of different user groups vary • prepare financial statements in a form suitable for publication by a sole trader, partnership and limited company
4 **Interpret financial statements**	• Calculate accounting ratios to assess the performance and position of a business • prepare a report incorporating and interpreting accounting ratios, including suitable comparisons

EDEXCEL GUIDELINES FOR UNIT 11 FINANCIAL SYSTEMS AND AUDITING

Description of the Unit

This Unit examines the accounting and management control systems of a business. Learners will analyse these systems and evaluate their effectiveness, particularly in terms of controls and safeguards against error and fraud. The purpose and conduct of an audit will be covered, together with the process of audit reporting.

Summary of learning outcomes

To achieve this unit a learner must:

1 Evaluate the effectiveness of **accounting systems** within a business

2 Analyse the **management control systems** of a business

3 Contribute to the **planning and conduct of an audit assignment**

4 Prepare **audit reports**

Content

		Chapter coverage
1	**Accounting systems**	
	Accounting records: books of prime entry (daybooks), accounts and ledgers (sales, purchases, nominal/general), trial balance, final accounts	13, 14 (Unit 10)
	Fundamental accounting concepts: accruals, prudence, consistency, going concern, materiality, business entity	19, (Unit 10) 26
	Accounting systems: Manual and computerised, effect of business size and structure	23
2	**Management control systems**	
	Business risk: types eg operational, financial, compliance; identification of risk and responsibility for risk management, influences on corporate governance (eg Cadbury Code)	24
	Control: control systems and procedures within the business eg segregation of duties, authorisation	24
	Fraud: types, implications, detection	24
3	**Planning and conduct of an audit assignment**	
	Regulatory environment: legal duties and status of auditors, liability of auditors, auditing standards and guidelines	25, 29
	Role of the auditor: internal and external audit and the relationship between the two, responsibilities of management as opposed to auditors	25
	Audit planning: scope, materiality, risk	26

		Chapter coverage
	Audit testing: systems based (compliance) and substantive testing, sampling methods eg random, stratified, systematic; confidence intervals	27, 28
	Records: audit files and working papers, checklists and programmes, flowcharts and questionnaires	27
4	**Auditing reports**	
	Statutory reports: purpose, content (opinion of auditor), qualified and unqualified, types of qualification	29
	Management letters: purpose and content	29

Outcomes and assessment criteria

The learning outcomes and the criteria used to assess them are shown in the table below.

Outcomes	Assessment criteria To achieve each outcome a learner must demonstrate the ability to:
1 Evaluate the effectiveness of **accounting systems** within a business	• explain the purpose and use of the different accounting records • explain the importance and meaning of the fundamental accounting concepts • assess the factors which influence the nature and structure of accounting systems
2 Analyse the **management control systems** of a business	• identify the different components of business risk • describe and evaluate the control systems in place in a business • assess the risk of fraud within a business, and suggest methods of detection of fraud
3 Contribute to the **planning and conduct of an audit assignment**	• define and explain the duties, status and liability of the auditor • describe the relationship between internal and external audit • plan an audit with reference to scope, materiality and risk • identify and use appropriate audit tests • record the audit process in an appropriate manner
4 Prepare **audit reports**	• explain the purpose and content of a statutory audit report • explain and illustrate different types of qualification within an audit report • draft suitable management letters in relation to a statutory audit

EDEXCEL GUIDELINES FOR UNIT 12 TAXATION

Description of the Unit

This Unit considers the taxation of both individuals and limited companies. Learners will calculate taxable income and tax payable, allowing for different sources of income, relevant allowable expenditure and applicable tax-free allowances. Income tax, corporation tax and capital gains tax are all covered.

Summary of learning outcomes

To achieve this unit a learner must:

1 Explain the duties and responsibilities of the **tax practitioner and the UK tax environment**

2 Calculate **personal tax liabilities** for individuals and partnerships

3 Calculate **corporation tax liabilities** for companies

4 Calculate **capital gains tax** payable for individuals and businesses.

BPP LEARNING MEDIA NOTE:

The tax unit in this book is based on the provisions of Finance Act 2007.

		Chapter coverage
1	**Tax practitioner and the UK tax environment**	
	UK tax environment: purpose and types of taxation (income tax, corporation tax, capital gains tax, inheritance tax), different methods of collection, tax legislation	30
	Tax practitioner: dealing with HM Revenue and Customs advising clients, calculating liabilities, respecting confidentiality, seeking advice when needed	30
2	**Personal tax liabilities**	
	Sources of income: income from employment including taxable benefits in kind; from self-employment eg sole trader or partnership; from investment/savings	31, 32, 33
	Tax computations: relevant and allowable expenses, charges on income, payments to charities, tax free allowances, tax rates and payment dates	31
	Tax of the self-employed: bases of assessment, adjustment of profits and losses eg disallowed expenditure, tax losses, capital expenditure and allowances	35, 36, 38
	Documentation: tax returns, P60, P45, P11D	32, 34

NOTES

		Chapter coverage
3	**Corporation tax liabilities**	
	Bases of assessment: scope of corporation tax, accounting periods and chargeable profits, due dates	37
	Computation: adjusted profits, treatment of losses, corporation tax rates, capital expenditure and allowances, treatment of income tax deductions	37
4	**Capital gains tax payable**	
	Incidence and administration of CGT: chargeable persons/assets/ disposals, basis of assessment, payment dates	39
	Computation: layout of computation, allowable expenditure indexation allowance and taper relief, dealing with losses, allowances, rates	39

BPP LEARNING MEDIA

Outcomes and assessment criteria

The learning outcomes and the criteria used to assess them are shown in the table below.

Outcomes	Assessment criteria To achieve each outcome a learner must demonstrate the ability to:
1 Explain the duties and responsibilities of the **tax practitioner and the UK tax environment**	• describe the UK tax environment • explain the role and responsibilities of the tax practitioner • explain the nature and purpose of taxation
2 Calculate **personal tax liabilities** for individuals and partnerships	• identify relevant income, expenses and allowances • calculate taxable amounts and tax payable, for employed and self-employed individuals, and advise on payment dates • complete relevant documentation and returns
3 Calculate **corporation tax liabilities** for companies	• calculate chargeable profits and losses for a limited company, together with available allowances • calculate the tax liability of a limited company and advise on payment dates • explain how income tax deductions are to be dealt with
4 Calculate the **capital gains tax payable** for individuals and companies	• identify chargeable assets and disposals for an individual or company • calculate the capital gains and losses for an individual and a company, together with relevant allowances • calculate the tax payable in respect of capital gains

INDEX

NOTES

BPP LEARNING MEDIA

NOTES